McGraw-Hill Series in Education

HAROLD BENJAMIN, *Consulting Editor*

Social Studies in the Secondary School

Selected Titles from

McGraw-Hill Series in Education

HAROLD BENJAMIN, *Consulting Editor*

ALLEN · The Federal Government and Education
BEAUMONT AND MACOMBER · Psychological Factors in Education
BENT AND KRONENBERG · Principles of Secondary Education
BOGUE · The Community College
BROOM, DUNCAN, EMIG, AND STEUBER · Effective Reading Instruction
BRUBACHER · A History of the Problems of Education
BRUBACHER · Modern Philosophies of Education
BUTLER AND WREN · The Teaching of Secondary Mathematics
BUTTERWORTH AND DAWSON · The Modern Rural School
BUTTS · A Cultural History of Education
COOK AND COOK · A Sociological Approach to Education
CROW AND CROW · Mental Hygiene
CROXTON · Science in the Elementary School
DAVIS · Educational Psychology
DAVIS AND NORRIS · Guidance Handbook for Teachers
DE BOER, KAULFERS, AND MILLER · Teaching Secondary English
DE YOUNG · Introduction to American Public Education
FEDDER · Guiding Homeroom and Club Activities
FERNALD · Remedial Techniques in Basic School Subjects
FOREST · Early Years at School
GOOD · Dictionary of Education
HAGMAN · The Administration of American Public Schools
HAMMONDS · Teaching Agriculture
HECK · The Education of Exceptional Children
HOPPOCK · Group Guidance
KAULFERS · Modern Languages for Modern Schools
KAULFERS, KEFAUVER, AND ROBERTS · Foreign Languages and Cultures in American Education
MCCULLOUGH, STRANG, AND TRAXLER · Problems in the Improvement of Reading

McKown · Activities in the Elementary School
McKown · Home Room Guidance
McKown and Roberts · Audio-Visual Aids to Instruction
McNerney · Educational Supervision
Mays · Principles and Practices of Vocational Education
Micheels and Karnes · Measuring Educational Achievement
Mort · Principles of School Administration
Mort and Reusser · Public School Finance
Mort and Vincent · Modern Educational Practice
Mursell · Developmental Teaching
Mursell · Successful Teaching
Myers · Principles and Techniques of Vocational Guidance
Pittenger · Local Public School Administration
Remmlein · School Law
Samford and Cottle · Social Studies in the Secondary School
Sanford, Hand, and Spalding · The Schools and National Security
Schorling · Student Teaching
Schorling and Wingo · Elementary-school Student Teaching
Sears · The Nature of the Administrative Process
Smith, Standley, and Hughes · Junior High School Education
Sorenson · Psychology in Education
Thorpe · Psychological Foundations of Personality
Thut and Gerberich · Foundations of Method for Secondary Schools
Tidyman and Butterfield · Teaching the Language Arts
Warters · High-school Personnel Work Today
Wells · Elementary Science Education
Wells · Secondary Science Education
Wilson, Stone, and Dalrymple · Teaching the New Arithmetic
Winslow · Art in Elementary Education
Winslow · The Integrated School Art Program

SOCIAL STUDIES IN THE SECONDARY SCHOOL

Clarence D. Samford
Professor of Education
Southern Illinois University

Eugene Cottle
Assistant Professor of Social Studies Education
The University of Wyoming

FIRST EDITION

New York Toronto London
McGRAW-HILL BOOK COMPANY, INC.
1952

SOCIAL STUDIES IN THE SECONDARY SCHOOL

Library of Congress Catalog Card Number: 51-12642

PREFACE

Social Studies in the Secondary School is designed to be helpful to the student teacher specializing in this area. In addition, the topics have been selected in such manner as to be valuable to the large number of social studies teachers now in the field who are eagerly striving to maintain a commendable program of in-service growth. A third group that can profitably consider the topics herewith presented is the supervisory staff. Superintendents, principals, department heads, social studies supervisors, in fact all who are charged with responsibility for improving instruction in this area, should find useful helps and suggestions.

The present publication is entirely new, not a revision of a previous work. This is especially desirable from the viewpoint of the authors since they feel that many publications have been lacking in practicability. Too much philosophy and history of procedures have often been included causing neglect of material that would help a teacher in his efforts to do a better job in the classroom.

Every effort has been exerted to take into account current trends in educational thinking. Changes resulting from the period following the Second World War have been enumerated. Those interested in topics dealing with general education, core curriculum, and education for life adjustment will find help.

Special attention is called to the fact that the present publication stresses the teaching of social studies in grades 13 and 14. Those who teach or have ambitions to work in school systems organized on the 6–6–4 basis, in junior colleges, or in community colleges will find this emphasis helpful. Rather than organizing this content as a separate chapter the authors have divided it among various other sections; this plan was followed on the assumption that most often successful teachers of these upper grades gain their initial teaching experience in lower secondary grades.

Supervisors will naturally expect to study all the topics. Groups engaged in special study, workshop activities, etc., will do well to make appropriate selection. The content is easily adapted to the work of a regular quarter or semester depending upon the number of suggested activities pursued.

Grateful appreciation is extended to publishers, organizations, and individuals who have been so generous in their willingness to grant permission to quote certain materials and to our colleagues who have been helpful during the preparation of the manuscript, particularly Dr. L. R. Kilzer for his advice and suggestions. Tribute is extended to both graduate and undergraduate students who have taken work with both authors and in so doing offered inspiration and valuable suggestions. Each of the authors is deeply grateful to his wife for encouragement and help without which the work could not have been completed.

CLARENCE D. SAMFORD
EUGENE COTTLE

CARBONDALE, ILL.
LARAMIE, WYO.
January, 1952

CONTENTS

Chapter 1

GETTING THE OBJECTIVES CLEARLY IN MIND

Preview. There must be a general philosophy to support the objectives of any activity. The objectives for education in general determine in part the objectives for the social studies. Specific objectives for the social studies at the secondary level include the goals toward which teachers are moving in this group of studies as a whole and in the individual subjects specifically.

Reasons for Having Objectives. In any phase of human endeavor it is necessary to have a purpose. The absence of this vital point forbodes failure. Teaching in the social studies field is no exception. One is quite safe in saying that no teacher in this area can lay claims to successful work over a given period of time unless he has been constantly guided by well-conceived objectives. There might, conceivably, be occasional days of good work in classes without this careful planning; but the absence of articulation with work within the given social study, with other subjects in the same field, and with other areas of the secondary-school program would be regrettably pronounced.

External Factors That Operate to Determine Objectives. In determining social studies objectives one has to be cognizant of the objectives of the nation in which the teaching is to take place. Assuming that the present interest centers upon the United States of America, it seems reasonable that the idea of democratic government, the processes necessary to attain it, and the resulting way of life that follows are pertinent points. Closely allied to an interest in the objectives of the nation should be an examination of the general objectives for its entire educational program. For instance, over a period of many years, all became quite familiar with the cardinal objectives of education as stated by the Commission on Reorganization of Secondary Education. Democracy as a way of life was stressed for our total society and for each individual member. In order that the person could fit properly into this picture the Commission concluded that the main objectives of education were health, command of fundamental processes, worthy home membership, vocation, citizenship, worthy use of leisure time, and ethical character.[1] More recently the Educational Policies Commission [2] has made pointed statements related to the objectives for general education. Following statements dealing with peculiarities of the present social order, recommendations were made that

> Schools should be dedicated to the proposition that every youth in the United States—regardless of sex, economic status, geographic location, or race—should experience a broad and balanced education which will: (1) equip him to enter an occupation suited to his abilities and offering reasonable opportunity for personal growth and social usefulness; (2) prepare him to assume the full responsibilities of American citizenship; (3) give him a fair chance to exercise his right to the pursuit of happiness; (4) stimulate intellectual curiosity, engender satisfaction in intellectual achievement, and cultivate the ability to think rationally; and (5) help him to develop an appreciation of the ethical values which should undergird all life in a democratic society.

Another quotation because of its stress on social values has immediate application. In the publication, *Planning for American Youth,*[3] is a discussion of programs for "Farmville" and "American City." The four assumptions upon which it is based are as follows:

1. Education should be planned for all youth, so that economic, geographical, social, occupational, and racial limitations may have full understanding and consideration.
2. Education should *be free,* provided as a service of the State to its citizens.
3. Education must be suited to the personal and *social needs* of the people it serves.
4. Education should be *continuous;* it should go on after *youth leave the school.*

[1] *Cardinal Principles of Secondary Education,* Washington, D.C.: U.S. Office of Education, *Bulletin* No. 35, 1918, pp. 5–10.

[2] *Education for All American Youth,* Washington, D.C.: Educational Policies Commission, National Education Association, 1944, p. 21.

[3] *Planning for American Youth, An Educational Program for Youth of Secondary-school Age,* Washington, D.C.: National Association of Secondary-school Principals, 1944, p. 4.

Pupils should have a part in stating what these phrases really mean and suggesting how the whole idea is related to education in general and to the social studies in particular. The reader is asked to imagine a group of pupils in a particular school at the beginning of the year ready to spend one period per day in a social studies class. When asked about a philosophy of education, what they expect to gain from being in school, and where the social studies fit into the pattern they will at first hesitate to attempt answers. However, by skillful guidance the discussion can well become animated. Even within the first hour a workable definition of democracy can be established. Pupils can quickly see the need for education and enlightenment if it is to succeed. The place of the individual who is socially efficient becomes apparent. Pupils given to deeper analyses will readily start gaining traits of those who actually contribute to the true democratic pattern. In the end it will be seen that all these points are well within the range of objectives of the social studies.

The teacher can be better prepared for this opening day as well as for the work of the year as a whole if he surveys the literature and thinking that has taken place in educational circles related to objectives.

Objectives in Relation to the Social Studies as a Whole. Let us now return to the classroom mentioned above. We take for granted that the teacher is well-informed on the subject of philosophy and objectives. The task of assisting the pupils to arrive at conclusions which are real to them becomes mandatory. A secretary can assist by taking down all suggestions offered. Depending upon the area, age, grade, etc., the following objectives are among those that have been offered for the field as a whole:

1. To contribute as much as possible to the generally accepted goals of education in our country.

2. To furnish adequate background for certain areas of subject matter other than social studies.

3. To develop attitudes that will foster a desire on the part of our younger citizens to attain civic efficiency.

4. To demonstrate as fully as possible the values derived from cooperative living and to show the evils that result individually and collectively when other methods are attempted.

5. To set forth a group of words and terms, the mastery of which would assure that the individual pupil is a cultured person in so far as this area is concerned.

6. To help the individual function efficiently in situations demanding judgment based upon social studies information.

7. To develop an awareness of individual and social rights, duties, and obligations.

8. To develop a proper conception of the broader patriotism as opposed to a narrower view of the same.

9. To develop critical thinking which will analyze properly sources of information, type of reasoning employed, and propaganda devices.

10. To create a respect for the truth and logical means of arriving at sound conclusions.

11. To emphasize the place of industry and reliability in the conduct of individuals.

12. To stress the idea that the liberty of the individual must end where that of others begins.

13. To give an insight into the conditions of all groups of mankind in our own and in foreign countries.

14. To develop such mental faculties as imagination, reasoning, and memory as related to the social studies area.

15. To see at least superficially the place of arts and sciences in mankind's development.

16. To afford help in the learning of certain other school subjects in which a social studies background is involved.

17. To develop habits of reading and interests that will contribute something vital to use of leisure time.

18. To contribute to the all-round development of a rich personality.

19. To make commendable growth in the classroom dealing with matters of knowledge, desirable traits of character, and democratic procedures.

It is not to be assumed that the pupils will phrase the above statements as given. However, it would be surprising to find a class that did not furnish the ideas. Refinement of statements can be a function of a committee selected for that purpose or of a teacher working with such a committee.

It seems quite appropriate at this point to take into consideration the relatively recent work of the Educational Policies Commission. While the results were intended to apply to the entire educational program, it is indisputable that practically every statement has a social studies implication. Hence the entire list should be most carefully considered in relation to the function of the complete social studies area in the secondary school. The goals are grouped under four headings and are as follows:

THE OBJECTIVES OF SELF-REALIZATION [4]

The Inquiring Mind. The educated person has an appetite for learning.
Speech. The educated person can speak the mother tongue clearly.
Reading. The educated person reads the mother tongue efficiently.
Writing. The educated person writes the mother tongue effectively.
Number. The educated person solves his problems of counting and calculating.
Sight and Hearing. The educated person is skilled in listening and observing.
Health Knowledge. The educated person understands the basic facts concerning health and disease.
Health Habits. The educated person protects his own health and that of his dependents.
Public Health. The educated person works to improve the health of the community.
Recreation. The educated person is participant and spectator in many sports and other pastimes.
Intellectual Interests. The educated person has mental resources for the use of leisure.
Esthetic Interests. The educated person appreciates beauty.
Character. The educated person gives responsible direction to his own life.

THE OBJECTIVES OF HUMAN RELATIONSHIP [5]

Respect for Humanity. The educated person puts human relationships first.
Friendships. The educated person enjoys a rich, sincere, and varied social life.
Cooperation. The educated person can work and play with others.
Courtesy. The educated person observes the amenities of social behavior.
Appreciation of the Home. The educated person appreciates the family as a social institution.
Conservation of the Home. The educated person conserves family ideals.
Homemaking. The educated person is skilled in homemaking.
Democracy in the Home. The educated person maintains democratic family relationships.

[4] "The Purposes of Education in American Democracy," in *Policies for Education in American Democracy*, Washington, D.C.: Educational Policies Commission, National Education Association, 1946, p. 192. Quoted by permission of the publisher.

[5] *Ibid.*, p. 212.

The Objectives of Economic Efficiency [6]

Work. The educated producer knows the satisfaction of good workmanship.

Occupational Information. The educated producer understands the requirements and opportunities for various jobs.

Occupational Choice. The educated producer has selected his occupation.

Occupational Efficiency. The educated producer succeeds in his chosen vocation.

Occupational Adjustment. The educated producer maintains and improves his efficiency.

Occupational Appreciation. The educated producer appreciates the social value of his work.

Personal Economics. The educated consumer plans the economics of his own life.

Consumer Judgment. The educated consumer develops standards for guiding his expenditures.

Efficiency in Buying. The educated consumer is an informed and skillful buyer.

Consumer Protection. The educated consumer takes appropriate measures to safeguard his interests.

The Objectives of Civic Responsibility [7]

Social Justice. The educated citizen is sensitive to the disparities of human circumstance.

Social Activity. The educated citizen acts to correct unsatisfactory conditions.

Social Understanding. The educated citizen seeks to understand social structures and social processes.

Critical Judgment. The educated citizen has defenses against propaganda.

Tolerance. The educated citizen respects honest differences of opinion.

Conservation. The educated citizen has a regard for the nation's resources.

Social Applications of Science. The educated citizen measures scientific advance by its contribution to the general welfare.

World Citizenship. The educated citizen is a cooperating member of the world community.

[6] *Ibid.*, p. 226.

[7] *Ibid.*, p. 240.

dition of rapport. Appreciation for groups outside the classroom is constantly mentioned with positive suggestions for translating principles into action.

In the development of individuals who possess economic efficiency, many social studies departments offer courses specifically designed to this end. Economics, Problems in American Democracy, and Occupations are examples. In some cases vocational guidance is associated with the social studies. Even previous to the statement of the list of objectives by the Educational Policies Commission consumer economics was stressed at the expense of philosophical theories of economics.

The question of whether the objectives of civic responsibility equal or excel in importance those of human relationships in the social studies field is debatable. One of the basic reasons for tax-supported education throughout our nation's history has been the desire to produce citizens who would have intelligence and ideals that would make for an effective democracy. Accordingly, social studies teachers do find it possible and take occasion in any and all of their classes to develop pupils who sense social problems, who seek to gain factual information about them, and who, in turn, attempt to exercise sober judgment in extending solutions. Naturally, pupils trained in this fashion will be interested in social justice, social activity, social understanding, etc.

Justice would not be done to this phase of the consideration of objectives without stressing the teacher's responsibility to demonstrate them as functioning in one's personal life. Just as good practices of mental hygiene are "caught" by the pupils from a teacher who is emotionally well-adjusted, so are good procedures of living in situations involving a social studies setting. If the teacher is a person who has attained in a large measure the objectives listed under these four headings it can be assumed with safety that the pupils will move noticeably in the same direction.

In the consideration of objectives for different types of communities the teacher must be aware of the constant and the variable factors. In respect to the former, there are many well-defined objectives that should be attained in any school by reason of the fact that it is situated in the United States of America. Regardless of whether the teaching is done in one of our fifteen largest cities or in the most isolated rural community, such topics as good citizenship, tolerance,

Law Observance. The educated citizen respects the law.
Economic Literacy. The educated citizen is economically literat
Political Citizenship. The educated citizen accepts his civic dutie
Devotion to Democracy. The educated citizen acts upon an unswer loyalty to democratic ideals.

By the very nature of this list it becomes increasingly appa that it fits in exceedingly well with what forward-looking teacher the social studies are attempting to do in regular classes.

For instance, no conscientious social studies teacher would happy if the pupils did not advance in the area of self-realizat The field is so broad that any pupil possessing an inquiring mind find here a sense of satisfaction. Basic skills involving speech, re ing, writing, and numbers are brought into use very frequently fact the most successful social studies teacher has adeptness in th functions, demonstrates the same, and insists upon pupil devel ment in them. Sight and hearing are made use of more as teach skills are improved. Individual pupil investigations make use of th skills. Entire classes taking field trips bring their experiences t climax through the media of sight and hearing. Health knowled health habits, public health, and recreation are definitely recogni as modern social problems; they are regularly studied in plan courses or as a part of contemporary affairs in connection with ot social studies. Not only are they studied, but they afford deep sincere areas of interest on the part of the pupils concerned. In lectual interests are closely related to the inquiring mind which been mentioned above. Aesthetic interests come to have meanin pupils as they read about places having unusual appeal in this c nection or about people who have held this human attribute in h esteem. Comparing the aesthetic interests of people of our own nat with those of specific foreign groups usually proves challenging

Under the heading of the objectives of human relationships have the social studies at their best. This section comes very close being a replica of the objectives advanced for the entire field of so studies. Not only do social studies teachers teach that individu should get along well in all phases of group life; they also make th classrooms laboratories in demonstrating excellent group relati ships. Opinions of others are respected. All are given a just and p portionate share of time for presentation of results of directed w and participation in discussion. The teacher cultivates a general c open-mindedness, cooperation with other nations, patriotism, economic efficiency, civic responsibility, and many others must be stressed. Certain other points of emphasis, however, should vary with local conditions.

Let us take the case of the social studies in a high school in a large American city. Certain problems become far more real than mere words on a printed page. Recreation presents a problem that has to be met and solved by hard work and clear thinking. Young people are definitely involved. It follows naturally that they like to gather information, reach conclusions, and make recommendations. In such communities public libraries become a necessity and a possibility. Fire and police protection are points of vital concern. Conflicting interests of labor and capital may be very pronounced. Crime is sometimes on a rampage. Race relations are frequently strained. Making a living in the immediate future often appears to be directly related to opportunities for gaining vocational knowledge. It behooves the teacher working in the midst of these problems to recognize their presence and to isolate for emphasis the objectives that are related to them. This may have to be done to the apparent neglect of others that have claims to being worth while.

At the other extreme, the high school may be located in a sparsely settled rural community. Food, clothing, and shelter are often not very pressing problems. Economic survival usually seems fairly certain. However, it would be quite erroneous to suggest that the rural scene has no pressing problems. A survey may show that in the place where a specific teacher works the health record of the pupils is not up to the nation's average. Media for gathering news by reading, listening, and observations may be entirely inadequate. Marketing of surplus products may be fraught with difficulties because of transportation problems. Communication and electrification facilities may need to be developed. Just as mentioned above in connection with an urban environment and its problems, the youth of rural areas become interested in their own needs and perplexities. Not only does the teacher do the correct thing pedagogically in seizing upon interest; he also renders a valuable service through the proper emphasis on objectives peculiar in value to local conditions.

Objectives Related to American History. In teaching special areas of social studies pupils and teacher must determine respective objectives. American history represents the most widely taught field. Of course it must be thought of in its broadest aspects as including not only the usual political, social, and economic but also the cultural, literary, and scientific phases. At any grade level a class can be stimulated to thinking and planning by being asked, "What would you like to learn from the work in this subject this year?" Maybe the teacher can preface the discussion advantageously by giving as an example the objective, "To learn how our nation's present is related to its past." More time than is usually taken should be given to getting pupils to think seriously on the purposes of the particular course. The following are among those that are likely to be accepted by pupils in American history, the choice depending upon age and grade level:

1. To gain a general chronological idea of the story of our country from the earliest times as an aid to understanding the present.

2. To learn a great deal about the biographies of a restricted list of the men and women who have contributed to our nation's present greatness. (Examples: outstanding presidents, leading inventors, and a few pioneers in social reforms.)

3. To learn fully about a restricted list of important events that serve as a foundation for current ideas and institutions. (Examples: the struggle for independence, the War Between the States, and early settlements in the West.)

4. To learn the use of aids necessary to effective study. Special reference is made to encyclopedias, atlases, world almanac, globe, simple source materials, parallel textbooks, etc.

5. To gain unbounded enthusiasm for the ideals of democracy as a form of government.

6. To become acquainted with the methods by which community resources may be used in the study of history.

7. To learn the story of our nation's history so accurately and completely that those who take the course will thenceforth never be accused of not knowing the facts of our country's past.

8. To appreciate the manner in which our nation has developed through the stages of dependency, isolation, imperialism, and cooperation in international affairs.

9. To gain an understanding of and appreciation for the American way of life as opposed to other beliefs and practices.

10. To gain a generous amount of information that is often overlooked about leaders in social, political, and economic affairs.

11. To stress especially the history of our nation since the middle of the nineteenth century. (The typical pupil has made a much more ex-

tensive study of the nation's early history in the lower grades than he has of more recent developments.)

12. To sense fully the possibilities that our country has, through the United Nations, of assuming the leadership in activities leading to world peace.

13. To gain information as to how our nation's social pattern is changing due to advancements in science and inventions. (Particular emphasis should be given to the concept of the age of flight.)

14. To become more appreciative of the nation's history by giving some time to a detailed study of a particular state. (This usually results in a working knowledge of the history and government of the state in which the school is located.)

15. To gain a conception of our nation's history in terms of carefully selected topics as well as a knowledge of general chronology. (Examples: tariff, political parties, education, etc.)

16. To develop attitudes that are harmonious with notions of preserving the best in American institutions.

Objectives Related to World History and International Relations. As indicated in Chapter 15, World History as a one-year course has generally taken the place of the two years of work that was formerly offered under such titles as Ancient and Medieval History and Modern History. With this change in mind it becomes imperative to determine the objectives for this relatively new course. The process by which pupils and teacher arrive at objectives in World History and International Relations courses is the same as that used in any other social study. Pupils must be stimulated to think and in turn become willing to express their ideas as to what they want to learn. These desires, supplemented by teacher experience, will culminate in reasonable objectives. The following are typical of those likely to be suggested:

1. To learn the causes and possible solutions of the principal conflicts existing throughout the world today.

2. To give adequate consideration to such phrases as "one world or none," "education for survival," etc.

3. To study various efforts that have been made to live cooperatively, with special emphasis on the League of Nations and the UN.

4. To develop an awareness of the likenesses and differences that exist among various groups throughout the world.

5. To gain a suitable background for the study of the history of one's own country.

6. To get an accurate picture of man's progress from a state of savagery to that of a complex civilization.

7. To appreciate the particular epochs of historical development. (We might cite as example the Dark Ages, the Renaissance, and the Commercial Revolution.)

8. To evaluate the methods used by man in the past as he attempted to solve national and international problems.

9. To derive a background for the study of school subjects other than social studies, particularly literature, art, and music.

10. To gain a special mastery of information relative to those movements, events, and personalities that have most profoundly altered our present status.

11. To cultivate the power of seeing relationships in a large setting commonly discussed under the heading of cause and effect.

12. To develop the concept of a changing world, constantly in need of new means of carrying on.

13. To gain a knowledge of current methods by which various countries of the world are governed.

14. To become acquainted with the effect of cultural background upon political traditions and methods of procedures throughout the world.

15. To observe world regions that are attempting to follow specific philosophies of government and trying to influence others to do likewise.

16. To see the effects of prejudice, ill will, and misunderstanding in international problems.

17. To increase knowledge of and interest in current events having a world setting.

18. To show the necessity for world cooperation and the impossibility of isolationism.

19. To make a worthy contribution to the efforts of all laudable social and political organizations that are attempting to foster peace, happiness, and prosperity.

20. To bring into full view the facts about smaller nations and minority groups that have previously been too little studied and too much disregarded.

21. To show the relationship of material achievement to cultural environment.

Objectives Related to Problems in Democracy. Problems in American Democracy is taught with a great deal of variation from one part of the country to another and even from one school to another. Maybe the recency of the adoption of this name for the course is a partial explanation. Furthermore, textbook writers have not standardized the course to the extent that they have many of the others in social studies. Even so, it seems safe to say that in most instances the problems treated can be classified under three headings, namely, social, economic, and political. In following this pattern much attention is given to content that was formerly included in Sociology, Economics, and American Government. Some teach this course giving emphasis to the American historical backgrounds involved. At the other extreme there are instances where in the course of the same name a group of modern problems is selected for investigation and discussion with contemporary emphasis only. There is probably no other secondary-school social study that brings forth more pupil interest in respect to objectives. Pupils at the time this course is taken are usually more mature than those in the majority of courses in this area. Furthermore, young people today are more aware than those of previous generations that our nation must demonstrate its superiority when compared with other countries having contrasting systems of government. Of course the imminence of induction into the armed services adds to this spirit of seriousness of youth.

What do students reply when asked as a group what they would like to accomplish in a course designed to study our social, political, and economic order? The following are among the potential objectives:

1. To gain skill in identifying the most important social, economic, and political problems that exist today within the framework of American democracy.
2. To study the proposals that have been advanced in an effort to solve these problems; to offer suggestions coming from the class related to the same issues.
3. To develop traits of critical thinking, sound judgment, and correct evaluations.
4. To learn well the customary vocabulary used in newspapers and magazines dealing with social, economic, and political problems.
5. To develop habits of reading good newspapers, magazines, and publications that deal with topics included in the course; likewise, to develop a habit of listening to good radio programs that are pertinent.
6. To develop an understanding of case-study work, habits of observing the functioning of local community institutions, and an interest in the mechanics of government in action.
7. To develop an appreciation for social-civic-political institutions that exist in America today.

8. To create attitudes of respect for obedience to law and preservation of order.

9. To stress the principles upon which an enduring and progressively developing society exists.

10. To develop a willingness to make full utilization of American institutions.

11. To secure training in the study of the records of leaders in the current American scene with special emphasis on those who hold and seek office.

12. To develop skill in leading and participating in public discussions related to American democracy.

13. To make a special study of propaganda techniques; to develop a willingness to be a propagandist for American democracy.

14. To develop a desire on the part of each pupil to select a useful vocation, to prepare adequately for it, to render meritorious service, and to become economically self-sufficient.

Objectives Related to Community Civics and Occupational Choices. The majority of secondary schools have taken the position that pupils will gain a clearer picture of the entire social order if they see intimately man's activity in the local setting. Accordingly the course in Community Civics is sometimes offered for a semester, to be followed with special attention to choices available for life work. In other instances a still different proportion of time allotment is practiced. The following objectives are typical of those that teacher and class may reach through group discussion:

1. To gain a detailed knowledge of how local institutions operate; to see how they could be improved; to learn how youth may contribute to local civic affairs.

2. To learn how to participate in and to gain maximum value from the social studies field trip.

3. To arouse a desire for group and individual improvement.

4. To stimulate a willingness on the part of youth to prepare to do that which they might do well rather than to do something they would prefer to do but for which they have less aptitude.

5. To encourage a wide investigation of the various means by which mankind earns a living and to study the preparation required for various occupations.

6. To develop a knowledge of how personal interviews are arranged, executed, and used to advantage.

7. To gain a comprehensive idea of the meaning of social efficiency.

The pattern of organization of the social studies program will naturally vary from school to school. Some systems will devote a year or a semester to areas that others include merely as units in their own established courses. Examples of such areas are the Pacific and the Orient, Latin-American history, history of specific nations, the age of flight, current events, salesmanship, vocations, orientation courses, social psychology, personal and social problems, and state history.

Regardless of the names given to courses, the organization pattern, and the methods of teaching, there are several sound principles involved in arriving at a statement of objectives. One relates to the need of a sound definition of education. The thought of development, adaptation, and adjustment should prevail. The older concept of merely preserving a heritage of a dim and distant past coupled with a mastery of basic facts must be discarded. Likewise, education must embrace the concept that youth are living here and now and not merely preparing for a role to be played in an abstract future.

After having satisfactorily defined education, the social studies teacher must formulate a philosophy of education. It should express a profound faith in youth, a zeal for democratic processes, and a belief in the high potentialities of the classroom as a laboratory in the development of social efficiency. The role of the teacher should be that of guide, counselor, and friend. In such manner social studies can indeed become social.

Finally the phrasing of objectives becomes a group obligation. The teacher can legitimately have a preconceived list but must not impose it upon his pupils. If such a list is normally arrived at by the teacher, the pupils are most likely to advance comparable ideas. Arriving at them in group discussion is a privilege and a learning act which must not be denied. Full meaning can surround an objective only when it is fully identified as belonging to the group. A final advantage of pupil-arrived-at objectives is that the alert and motivated secondary-school pupils will advance laudable goals that an individual teacher cannot phrase working alone.

Objectives, Grades Thirteen and Fourteen. As pointed out above, no program attains full stature that is not based on a sound philosophy followed by a concise statement of objectives. This is true to as great a degree in courses in social studies in grades 13 and 14 as elsewhere. One of the first principles upon which the course should be built is a belief that a functional knowledge of various fields should be attained rather than a narrow specialization in any one or a few of them. Closely related to this idea is another, namely, that the most usable content for citizenship in a democracy should be gleaned from various social studies areas and carefully placed under well-organized and appealing units of study. Such a slogan as "social studies beyond the classroom" should be seized upon, accepted, and practiced. The community should serve as a laboratory for observation, investigation, and even experimentation. Critical thinking, detailed analysis, and free expression should characterize all such classrooms.

The objectives posed for social studies in other secondary grades should be reexamined frequently as the study proceeds in grades 13 and 14. This should be done for the purpose of deciding which ones have already been most nearly attained and of determining which ones merit additional and special emphasis. The process of arriving at final statements of objectives should remain the same here, namely, that the teacher approach with an initial conception of the course to present to the students for consideration. Their personal reactions should be urged. The teacher should have no adverse feelings if his original planning gets a great deal of revision. In fact, he should feel gratified that such indications of interest are manifested. The usual procedure should prevail of asking pertinent questions: "What do you think is important for investigation in the present social order?" "What do you really want to accomplish as a result of a year's work in social studies?" "Which topics logically come early?" Etc.

The following points with comments are among those likely to be brought out in the type of discussion outlined above:

1. To increase the factual information possessed by the student. The right to hold and express opinions is a privilege extended only to those who possess knowledge.

2. To bring to an adult level of attainment such traits as loyalty, tolerance, cooperation, leadership, etc. These manifest themselves in a different form from that which they take at lower grade levels.

3. To bring about an understanding of the present social order—one that shows how it has developed out of the past, its present complexities, and whither it is tending.

4. To show the interrelationship of all the social sciences. Just as general education stresses the elimination of subject names and compartmentalization, so should the work at this level continue.

5. To point out the role of our own nation in world affairs. It is quite essential that citizens learn a broad and international point of view as opposed to a concept of narrow nationalism.

6. To ever increase and strengthen faith in democracy as a form of government and in the institutions which promote it. Along with this goes the necessity of discussing the means of preserving democracy.

7. To develop critical thinking in things social, political, and economic. Too many are willing to accept the point of view of a leader, party, or institution.

8. To create the practice of careful analysis of newspapers, periodicals, and radio broadcasts. Such points as who the author is, for whom he is speaking or writing, and what point of view he is trying to create should become important considerations.

9. To show the necessity of actively participating in community, state, and national affairs rather than passively observing others carry on such functions. It is such neglect as failure to vote, hesitancy to volunteer for unpaid service, and unwillingness to seek and hold office that causes disintegration of democratic processes.

10. To show that the good in our present social order did not come as a national heritage like the soil, forest, and products of the mines. Sacrificial giving of time, talents, and means must be extolled as virtues.

The objectives suggested above are strictly in line with Knowlton's [8] statement, "An understanding of the contemporary world is a major objective, if not the principal objective sought in social studies at the junior college level."

Summary. An effort has been made in this chapter to indicate the value of objectives regardless of the scale on which they are applied. The fact that the objectives of society as a whole and of education in general influence objectives in social studies has been pointed out. No statements have been made as to the source of the objectives of society. Reference has been made to the role of groups within the National Education Association in setting objectives for education. A list of objectives for social studies as a whole has been given; this was followed with a list of specific objectives for each of several social studies.

Recognition was given to the fact that some schools teach social studies other than those for which objectives were listed. The rela-

[8] D. C. Knowlton, "Map Project for the Junior College," *Junior College Journal,* XVII (October, 1946), p. 54.

tionship of accomplishment to the manner in which objectives are established and pursued was stressed for social studies in all secondary-school grade levels.

Questions on the Text

1. Why is it important that the social studies teacher have a carefully defined set of objectives in mind before starting a year of work?
2. What is the relationship of the objectives of the society in which the teaching is done to the objectives of the social studies being taught?
3. In what way can the objectives of education for the nation and for particular states influence the objectives of social studies?
4. How do the social studies rank compared with other high-school subjects in respect to offering media for attaining the objectives of education quoted from "The Purposes of Education in American Democracy"?
5. After examining a list of objectives for the social studies as a whole, do you feel that this one area is attempting to accomplish all the objectives of the entire educational program?
6. What points do you notice in the objectives for world history that indicate that it should precede the study of American history in the upper high-school grades?
7. What points do you observe in the objectives for Problems in Democracy that justify the usual practice of offering this course in the last year of high school?
8. In what year of high school do you think that Community Civics and Occupations should be offered?
9. Mention several objectives that teachers of social studies in grades 13 and 14 should strive to attain.

Suggested Activities

1. Choose any one of the subjects for which a list of objectives has been given. Revise the list by making it more comprehensive and representative of your own thinking as to what should really be included.
2. Have a personal interview with a teacher whom you regard as very successful in the social studies. Ask for a statement of objectives for the social studies as a whole and for one social study in particular.
3. Select one of the social studies for which no list of objectives was given and develop a list for it.
4. Do you feel that the objectives for American history should be different in the lower grades from those in the upper secondary level? Make extensive comments to justify your conclusions.

5. Do you feel that there are enough worthy objectives to justify a semester or a full year course in each of the following: the Pacific and the Orient, Latin-American history, the age of flight, vocations, orientation, social psychology, and state history? For those to which the answer is "yes," make a list of objectives.

6. Interview high-school pupils who are taking one or more social studies. Try to determine what the objectives are that they have set up for themselves. Compare these with traditional teacher objectives.

7. Write to one or more city school systems or state departments of education or both. Ask for statements of objectives for the social studies areas in which you are most interested.

8. Read an article in a current education periodical dealing with objectives in this area. Make a summary in which you give special emphasis to current trends.

9. Narrow the list of objectives for social studies in grades 13 and 14 to the three that you consider to be most important. Defend your selection.

Selected References

ALBERTY, HAROLD, *Reorganizing the High-School Curriculum,* New York: The Macmillan Company, 1948.

ANDERSON, HOWARD R., "The Social Studies, Patriotism, and Teaching Democracy," *Social Education,* V (January, 1941), pp. 9–14.

———, "Education for What?" *Social Education,* VII (October, 1943), pp. 257–258.

ATKINSON, RALPH N. D., "Teach to Meet the Changes in Home Life," *Social Studies,* XXXVI (March, 1945), pp. 100–101.

BANVARD, ADELE F., "Some Objectives in Modern European History," *Social Studies,* XXXII (March, 1941), pp. 109–111.

BARDOLPH, RICHARD, "The Social Sciences and the Citizen," *Social Education,* X (November, 1946), pp. 295–300.

BARNES, SHERMAN B., "Present-minded or Past-minded History," *Social Studies,* XXXII (December, 1941), pp. 340–343.

———, "Democracy and the Social Studies," *Social Studies,* XXXIV (April, 1943), pp. 147–153.

BARTLETT, RUHL J., "The Social Studies and Democracy," *Social Education,* VII (April, 1943), pp. 161–164.

BERGER, M., "Objectives of the Social Studies in Vocational Schools," *Industrial Arts and Vocational Education,* XXXIV (March, 1945), p. 122.

BLATCHFORD, E., "Laying the Foundations of National Unity with History and Geography," *School Arts,* XLVI (March, 1947), p. 248.

BOODISH, H., "Why Social Studies for Vocational Students?" *Social Studies,* XXXV (May, 1944), pp. 213–214.

BREINAN, ALEXANDER, "Mental Hygiene in Social-studies Teaching," *Social Education,* X (December, 1946), pp. 355–357.

BRICKMAN, BENJAMIN, "The Relation between Indoctrination and the Teaching of Democracy," *Social Studies,* XXXV (October, 1944), pp. 248–252.

BRUNNER, E. D., "Role of the Social Sciences in the American Scene," *Teachers College Record,* XLVII (April, 1946), pp. 416–429.

BURKHART, J. A., "The Teaching of History Never Had a Greater Challenge," *Social Studies,* XXXV (December, 1944), pp. 339–340.

Cardinal Principles of Secondary Education, Washington, D.C.: U.S. Office of Education, *Bulletin* No. 35, 1918.

CASNER, MABEL, "Getting Democracy into the Social-studies Classroom," *Social Education,* VI (January, 1942), pp. 23–26.

COHEN, BARNET, "Pupil Democracy in Action," *Social Education,* V (December, 1941), pp. 586–589.

COLE, HOUSTON, "Objectives in High School Social Studies," *Social Studies,* XXXI (December, 1940), pp. 356–363.

CONNER, J. D., "Recommendations of the California State Curriculum Commission for a Framework for the Social Studies," *California Journal of Elementary Education,* XIV (November, 1945), pp. 87–95.

COOK, LLOYD ALLEN, "Educating for Community Action and Unity," *Social Education,* VI (November, 1942), pp. 304–308.

CORYELL, VANSANT, "New Objectives for the Social Studies," *Social Studies,* XXXIV (May, 1943), pp. 195–201.

CRAF, JOHN R., and MAURICE P. MOFFATT, "Teaching Democracy through Personalities," *Social Studies,* XXXV (May, 1944), pp. 211–213.

CRARY, RYLAND W., "The Moral and Ethical Responsibility of the Social Studies," *Social Education,* VII (March, 1943), pp. 105–106.

DARLING, EDWARD, "Twelve-year-olds Can Think Critically," *Social Education,* IX (February, 1945), pp. 65–66.

DAVIS, WILLIAM R., "Making History Practical," *Social Studies,* XXXIV (March, 1943), pp. 99–103.

DE KIEWIET, C. W., "The Practical Uses of History," *Social Education,* VIII (December, 1944), pp. 348–350.

DONDINEAU, ARTHUR, "Education and Democratic Citizenship," *Social Studies,* XXXI (October, 1940), pp. 243–247.

Education for All American Youth, Washington, D.C.: Educational Policies Commission, National Education Association, 1944.

FAHERTY, W. B., "A Neglected Objective in the Teaching of History," *Social Studies,* XXXIII (January, 1942), pp. 27–28.

———, "A Renaissance Pedagogical Device," *Social Studies,* XXXIII (May, 1942), pp. 213–214.

FAISSLER, MARGARETA, "An Experiment in the Study of Democracy," *Social Studies,* XXXIII (December, 1942), pp. 343–354.

FERRARO, EUGENE T., "Lessons of History," *Social Studies,* XXXIII (January, 1942), pp. 3–5.

FISHER, WILLIAM, "Teaching History for Attitudes," *Social Studies,* XXXVI (April, 1945), pp. 156–157.

FLINKER, I., "Promoting Social Understanding in Social Studies Classes," *School Review,* LIV (October, 1946), pp. 476–479.

FOLSOM, J. K., "Aims and Structure of the Social Sciences," *Education,* LXVI (April, 1946), pp. 521–528.

GRAHAM, H., "Proper Function of Social Studies," *Catholic Education Review,* XLIV (November, 1946), pp. 541–544.

HAEFNER, JOHN H., "The Historical Approach to Controversial Issues," *Social Education,* VI (October, 1942), pp. 267–269.

HEINTZ, E., "Objectives in the Social Studies," *Progressive Education,* XXV (November, 1947), pp. 270–271.

HORROCKS, JOHN E., "An Experiment in American History," *Social Studies,* XXXIV (April, 1943), pp. 154–161.

———, "Democracy Demands Debate," *Social Studies,* XXXIV (December, 1943), pp. 350–352.

HUGHES, R. O., "In Defense of Social Studies," *School and Society,* LXI (June 23, 1945), pp. 415–416.

HYSLOP, BEATRICE F., "World Cooperation and the High-school Student," *Social Studies,* XXXII (November, 1941), pp. 302–303.

KERRISON, I. L., and R. O. HUGHES, "A Positive Philosophy for the Social Studies: Two Interpretations," *Social Education,* VIII (February, 1944), pp. 79–81.

KING, A. Y., "School Interprets Democracy through the Social Studies Program," *National Association of Secondary-school Principals Bulletin,* XXV (October, 1941), pp. 16–22.

KNOWLTON, D. C., "Map Project for the Junior College," *Junior College Journal,* XVII (October, 1946), p. 54.

LONG, HAROLD M., "The Dynamics of Democracy," *Social Education,* V (November, 1941), pp. 485–487.

MCNUTT, PAUL V., "Education of Youth in a Democracy," *Social Education,* VI (January, 1942), pp. 11–14.

MEYER, FRANK, "The School, a Laboratory for Democratic Living," *Social Studies,* XXXII (February, 1941), pp. 51–52.

———, "The City: A Social Studies Class," *Social Studies,* XXXII (October, 1941), pp. 260–261.

———, "Golden Texts from the American Scriptures," *Social Studies,* XXXVI (February, 1945), pp. 75–77.

———, "Let's Educate for Politics," *Social Studies,* XXXVI (November, 1945), pp. 289–291.

MICHENER, J. A., "Democratic Education," *Social Education,* V (April, 1941), pp. 247–249.

MORSE, R. EUGENE, "On Being a Citizen," *Social Studies,* XXXVI (February, 1945), pp. 66–69.

NOSOFSKY, WILLIAM, "The Law against Discrimination and the Social Studies," *Social Education,* IX (December, 1945), pp. 364–365.

OLSEN, EDWARD G., "Social Lag and Civic Education," *Social Education,* V (October, 1941), pp. 419–423.

PETERS, CHARLES C., "Teaching History and the Social Studies for Citizenship Training," *Social Studies,* XXXIX (February, 1948), pp. 53–58.

Planning for American Youth, An Educational Program for Youth of Secondary-school Age, Washington, D.C.: National Association of Secondary-school Principals, 1944.

PLATT, DAVID, and AARON LIPTON, "A Living Experiment in Democracy," *Social Education,* XIII (January, 1949), pp. 22–24.

PRICE, ETHEL E., "Democratic Living: A School Experience," *Social Education,* IX (February, 1945), pp. 60–62.

"The Purposes of Education in American Democracy," in *Policies for Education in American Democracy,* Washington, D.C.: Educational Policies Commission, National Education Association, 1946.

REIFF, HENRY, "Freedom of Speech—Some Newly Needed Safeguards," *Social Education,* V (October, 1941), pp. 435–437.

SCHMIDT, BERNARDINE G., "Developing Competency in America's Retarded Adolescents: Part I, Competence in Learning," *Social Education,* VI (March, 1942), pp. 119–122; "Developing Competency in America's Retarded Adolescents: Part II, Political and Social Competence," *Social Education,* VI (April, 1942), pp. 168–171.

SCHMITT, ADELAIDE, "Putting Objectives to Work," *Social Education,* V (March, 1941), pp. 202–203.

SCHWARZ, JOHN, "Needed: A Philosophy of Social Study," *Social Education,* V (January, 1941), pp. 7–8.

SCOTT, A. J., "Education for Citizenship," *National Association of Secondary-school Principals Bulletin,* XXVIII (April, 1944), pp. 53–65.

SCRIVEN, E. PEARLE, "Making Pupils Like History," *Social Studies,* XXXV (January, 1944), pp. 10–12.

SFORZA, CARLO, "Democracy Is Stronger—If Only We Knew It," *Social Education,* V (May, 1941), pp. 325–327.

SLICK, SEWELL E., "Scholastic Pauperism," *Social Studies,* XXXVI (April, 1945), pp. 146–147.

SMITH, P. C., "Practical, Functional Social Studies Program," *Secondary Education,* XII (November, 1945), pp. 9–11.

TAYLOR, EDGAR A., Jr., "Education for Better Intercultural Relations," *Social Education,* VII (January, 1943), pp. 22–24.

TERMAN, E. L., "Building for Democracy through School Forums," *Social Studies,* XXXI (March, 1940), pp. 109–111.

THAYER, V. T., "How the Teacher of the Social Studies Can Foster and Defend Democracy," *Harvard Educational Review,* XI (October, 1941), pp. 459–472.

THURSFIELD, RICHARD E., "Developing the Ability to Think Reasonably," *The Study and Teaching of American History,* Washington, D.C.: The National Council for the Social Studies, *Seventeenth Yearbook,* 1946, pp. 77–93.

TUTTLE, HAROLD SAXE, "Keep Democracy in Perspective!" *Social Studies,* XXXIV (November, 1943), pp. 291–294.

VAN LOAN, W. L., and MILDRED WILLIAMS, "Education for Racial Equality," *Social Studies,* XXXIV (November, 1943), pp. 308–311.

VAN TIL, WILLIAM, "Developing Desirable Attitudes," *The Study and Teaching of American History,* Washington, D.C.: The National Council for the Social Studies, *Seventeenth Yearbook,* 1946, pp. 64–76.

WALLICK, R. G., "Social Studies for Use," *Pennsylvania School Journal,* XC (April, 1947), pp. 271–273.

WILLIAMS, ESTHER, "Facts and Democratic Values Reduce Racial Prejudices," *Social Education,* X (April, 1946), pp. 154–156.

WILSON, HOWARD E., "From Thought to Action," *Social Education,* V (October, 1941), pp. 407–411.

Chapter 2

THOSE WHO TEACH SOCIAL STUDIES

Preview. The problem of selecting a profession is one of paramount importance to anyone. The prospective social studies teacher is no exception. Criteria that teacher-training institutions apply in selecting and recommending candidates for admission should be known. The number of semester hours required in various areas and in specific subjects should likewise be investigated. Early contemplation can aptly include thoughts about securing the first position, how to attain teaching success, and the steps necessary in order to attain professional advancement.

Do You Want to Be a Social Studies Teacher? Many of the factors that determine success or failure in teaching the social studies have to do with the individual's selection of his life work and the criteria applied by the teacher-training institution for admission. In respect to the first point the person who thinks that he would like to teach social studies to high-school pupils should study carefully the nature of the preparation required, the duties involved, and the rewards to be reasonably expected. If after having made such study the individual feels that teaching social studies is the work preferred to all others, then efforts to prepare adequately should follow. Taking well-known personal-inventory and vocational-preference tests is a helpful beginning. For instance, the individual's reactions on such items as those offered by John F. Showalter [1] are quite revealing. All items are answered by "strongly agree," "agree," "undecided," "disagree," or "strongly disagree." Typical of statements are the following:

Schools prepare young people for life as it really is.

The schools cannot do much to promote international good will.

People having no children should not be taxed for the support of public schools.

[1] John F. Showalter, "A Scale for Measuring Attitudes with Respect to Public Education and to Teaching as a Profession," unpublished manuscript.

Personal discussion of the matter with teachers who have attained success in the field always opens some pertinent avenues of thought. In short, the choice of a profession encounters the same considerations here that it does in other fields.

Does the Teacher-education Institution Want You to Be a Social Studies Teacher? Administrators of teacher-training institutions would give a great deal to know precisely how to select and admit candidates who would beyond doubt make successful teachers. Those of us who are primarily interested in social studies have the same concern as applied to this area. While the evidence is not conclusive we feel reasonably assured that some criteria have predictive value. Success in an academic way in high school is usually considered very important. For instance, if one has a rank placing him in the upper one-half of his class he should feel more disposed than otherwise to take up teaching. This gives some assurance of being able to master the subject matter required and of having a reasonable amount of information in related fields. It is vitally important for the social studies teacher to possess a breadth of information for illustrative purposes as well as for teaching fundamental content.

A partial picture of a person's fitness for teaching or any other work can be gained from the score made on a reputable test of mental ability. Accordingly, such a test should be administered with strict adherence to procedures. There could be established a score below which no one contemplating teaching social studies should go. On the other hand, a score could not be high enough to ensure teaching success per se. A high score would, however, indicate the possibility of more easily attaining all requisite traits.

Most institutions desire that the prospective teacher show a high degree of physical fitness. The duties of the teacher may not require the muscular development associated with manual labor; nevertheless, they do require sound conditions of health. The qualities that make control of others possible—the possession of what speech teachers call *presence*—are based largely upon physical well-being. Likewise, many of the other qualities to be mentioned below are closely related to the same. Maybe the evidence of physical fitness based upon competent medical examination should be part of the criteria.

The results of a personal interview with a faculty committee should be taken into consideration. Unfortunately, this is not a task the committee can conduct with full assurance of reaching the objective desired. It is relatively easy to administer intelligence and achievement tests; the physician can readily determine physical condition. But the desire of those conducting a personal interview to determine social studies teaching aptitude involves something more subtle. Those in charge should have at hand numerous specific and general questions that will engage the candidate in discussion of a type that will reveal teaching interest. With proper preparation for the interview and reasonable time devoted to it, the opinions of such a committee should be given weight by both the institution and the candidate.

The institution should require certain minimum standards of speech, and in this the individual should show proficiency at the outset. This does not mean that upon entrance to college the individual must be a fluent public speaker. It does mean that there should be no organic physical conditions which seriously impede clear speech and which cannot be corrected. The reasons for good speech practices on the part of the teacher are obvious. There should be a close relationship throughout the college career between the departments of speech and teacher training.

Reputation for and actual possession of good moral character are important for all prospective teachers and for social studies teachers in particular. This becomes quite evident when the objectives for social studies are examined (see Chapter 1). The individual knows his personal character better than others can possibly evaluate it. Even so, testimonials from representative people should be required by and submitted to the teacher-training institution before enrollment.

While it is impossible for the young person contemplating social studies teaching or a life profession actually to evaluate his teaching skill, he can ask himself certain searching questions. These need not be mere chance ones. For instance, Smith's [2] list of common attributes as reported to the American Historical Association's Commission on the Social Studies is excellent. If one feels that he can answer favorably in respect to them, his security in the selection of this particular profession is increased. They are as follows: reverence for truth, intel-

[2] Edward Payson Smith, "A Study of Personal Qualities Essential in the Superior Teacher of Social Studies," in W. C. Bagley and Thomas Alexander, *The Teacher of the Social Studies*, Part XIV, Report of the Commission on the Social Studies, New York: Charles Scribner's Sons, 1937, p. 251.

ligent optimism, social altruism, sympathy, impartiality, interpretive mind, progressiveness, curiosity, culture, imagination, dramatic instinct, selective mind, balance, vigorous personality, tactfulness, ability to inspire confidence, and loyalty to ideals.

Pursuit of the Curriculum. Once the profession of teaching social studies has been decided upon and opportunity for preparation secured, the question of choice of subjects to pursue becomes important. In many cases a large percentage of the courses are required; other times a generous amount of election is left to the student. The following areas of study are among those that should be found in the work completed by graduation: social sciences, content and courses from other subjects that are related to social sciences, basic courses in education and student teaching, English, and prescribed courses deemed by the institution where the work is taken to contribute to the culture of the individual. Wolfe [3] stresses the necessity of broad training by stating that "the wise administrator seeking a teacher of social science in his school will not look for a highly trained economist, political scientist, or sociologist. . . . He will look for an educated man or woman." It will be found that there is little uniformity in these matters. However, it sometimes occurs that an entire state will attempt to organize a comparable program in its own institutions; the case of West Virginia can be cited as an example.[4] The reason is that there is so little evidence available to prove that certain course combinations produce graduates who will succeed while others do not. Ordinarily one expects to take enough hours in a field of specialization to constitute a major and enough hours in a second and possibly in a third also to constitute a minor or minors. It is presumed that most of the future teaching will be done in the major and possibly some additional work in the minors. Many institutions offer a major in what they call *social science.* Under these circumstances a specified number of hours are usually required in American history, history of civilization, political science, economics, sociology, and geography, with the possibility that local requirements call for courses in state history and government. Most schools ask the candidates in this field to major in one subject only, such as history, eco-

[3] A. B. Wolfe, "Teacher Training in the Social Sciences," *School and Society,* LVI (Oct. 10, 1942), pp. 325–329.

[4] Charles E. Prall, "Social Studies for the Prospective Teacher," *Social Education,* X (October, 1946), pp. 261–264.

nomics, political science, etc. One or more minors might be earned in others of the social sciences; on the other hand an entirely different field might be selected. English, foreign language, science, or any of the subjects taught in secondary schools could conceivably be selected. One might make a generalized statement with some degree of safety and say that twenty-four semester hours of work are required on the average for a major and eighteen semester hours for a minor.

Students specializing in social sciences should consider carefully the teaching schedule they are most likely to encounter in schools where the anticipated teaching will take place. In regions having large enrollments in secondary schools it is possible to secure positions calling for teaching in no more than one or two specific subjects. In smaller secondary schools one is often called upon to teach most of the social studies courses; there may even be a demand that one teach in an unrelated minor. As indicated above, the size of the school dictates some things along this line. In other instances there has been too little attention to scheduling the specific teacher's classes in relation to his preparation.

In Maul's [5] study of teacher supply and demand in the United States, eighteen states, Alaska, the District of Columbia, and Hawaii are taken into consideration. For the year studied, 1,091 teachers were being sought to teach social sciences only. The remaining demands for social science teachers carried with them requirements to teach the following subjects, the number of requests being indicated: agriculture, 11; art, 8; commerce, 44; English, 245; foreign languages, 30; home economics, 8; industrial arts, 5; journalism, 9; library science, 12; mathematics, 77; music, 27; physical education (men), 184; physical education (women), 48; general science, 72; biology, 37; physics, 6; chemistry, 6; speech, 21; and other, 12.

The states included in the report were Alabama, Arizona, Connecticut, Illinois, Kansas, Maryland, Minnesota, Missouri, Nebraska, Nevada, New Hampshire, New Mexico, North Carolina, Ohio, South Dakota, Utah, Virginia, and Wisconsin, as well as Alaska, the District of Columbia, and Hawaii.

These figures lead to a number of inferences. First, the geograph-

[5] Ray C. Maul, "Teacher Supply and Demand in the United States," *Report of the 1950 National Teacher Supply and Demand Study*, Washington, D.C.: National Education Association, 1950.

ical areas used are rather representative and show well the tendency for the nation as a whole. Second, the same table [6] used as a basis for the data given also indicates that the available supply of social science teachers for the year considered was 4,418 whereas the demand was only 1,953. This shows the need for well-trained people and for a training that includes at least one good strong minor in a second teaching field. Third, the data show that only slightly more than half of those demanded were desired for social science teaching only. Fourth, the order in which demand for additional subjects was called for is as follows: English, physical education (men), mathematics, general science, physical education (women), commerce, biology, foreign languages, music, speech, library science, agriculture, journalism, art, home economics, and chemistry. Fifth, one is caused to wonder whether or not many demands actually called for even more than two teaching fields; also, whether or not most of the teaching positions in social science required the candidates to teach several subjects of the group (history, problems of democracy, political science, international relations, etc.).

In any instance we may safely conclude that not only is it expected that social science teachers have a broad general education but that they also be able to teach fully within the field and in at least one minor area.

As intimated above, the administrative groups in teacher-training institutions have worked diligently to distribute properly the hours that prospective social studies teachers should take in various areas. The description that follows is offered as being somewhat typical of current practice and not as that which is necessarily best. Hours are quoted on a semester basis, and it is assumed that approximately 120 are required for graduation. It is also assumed that specialization is in just one of the social sciences.

English composition, 6
One social studies major, 24
Related social studies, 16
One selected minor, 18
Education, including introduction to teaching, history of education, and special methods, 12
Psychology (introductory and educational), 6
Directed observation, participation, and student teaching, 7

[6] *Ibid.*

Science surveys, 9
Art or music, 3
Health and physical education, 7
Free electives, 12

One can safely assume that certain guiding principles have operated in arriving at the curriculum approved by any given institution. It is generally felt that all teachers should be able to speak and write the English language effectively, that in addition to being prepared to teach a particular subject a broad background of general cultural information should be possessed, that a knowledge of learning processes and techniques be readily available, and that the first teaching experiences should be carefully supervised. Furthermore, since individuals have their own varying personal interests it seems advisable to offer some opportunities for free election of courses.

In order to alter the above curriculum to accommodate individuals who wish to major in the social sciences as a group rather than in a specific one, the hours allotted to the one major and those to the related social sciences are sometimes combined and redistributed. The largest division usually goes to American history on the assumption that more teaching assignments will be made in this subject. In this case the number of hours might be eight. Since European history constitutes an appropriate background for world history the allocation could aptly be six hours. Courses in sociology, economics, and political science are helpful in teaching high-school subjects by the same name or courses bearing other names such as Problems in Democracy, Modern Problems, etc. Consequently the allocations might aptly be three hours each. Many states feel that teachers of social studies should know state and local history quite thoroughly. At least three hours could well be given over to this area. In order to produce a balanced training, a knowledge of geography would be generally helpful. The four remaining hours are often earned in this area.

In addition to the fact that there are at least the two points of view described above in respect to the training of social studies teachers, there is a relatively recent publication that may alter both. Reference is made to a study dealing with general education in the social studies.[7] As recommendations become effective calling for an inte-

[7] Albert William Levi, *General Education in the Social Studies,* Washington, D.C.: American Council on Education, 1948, Part IV.

grated course for all college students in the first two years, they will be heeded in the field of teacher training. The topics listed have a strong appeal and are as follows: (1) "The Conflicts of Our World," (2) "The Organization of Social Living," (3) "The Historical Development of Modern Society," and (4) "The Institutions and Problems of the Modern World." It is advocated that this material be of an integrated nature and that it should not be taught by so-called "experts" in any one of the social sciences.

The guiding principles are the same regardless of the type of major pursued. The pattern of requirements in other parts of the curriculum remains constant. The subjects required other than those related to majors and minors are related closely to institutional history and philosophy. If certain subjects were required years ago they usually continue to be required. In other words, it is much easier to add a requirement than it is to drop one. In committee meetings where the matter of required subjects is discussed it is usually revealed that all heads of departments feel very sincerely that their own subjects would contribute a vital and required part of the background needed by a social studies teacher. This situation should be resolved by permitting an investigating committee to frequently reexamine the objectives of secondary education and of the social studies in particular. When it is found that the social order is undergoing changes, there might aptly follow changes in the list of subjects required for graduation. While it is difficult to make general statements about subjects other than social sciences required of those majoring in this area, there does seem to be a central tendency to have the candidates take the education courses and student teaching mentioned above, from one to two years of English, a year of science, and regular institutional requirements in health and physical education.

Some critics of the present-day curricula for the preparation of social studies teachers have felt that too little planning has characterized the offerings. Baldwin,[8] after examining the 1940–1941 catalogues of forty state universities and one hundred teachers colleges, concluded that "these institutions take for granted that specialized preparation of teachers for the social studies is as necessary as is such preparation of teachers for any other subject matter area."

There is another agency that helps determine the curriculum to be

[8] J. W. Baldwin, "Specialized Professional Preparation of Social Studies Teachers," *School and Society*, LV (Jan. 10, 1942), pp. 53–55.

pursued by prospective teachers in their respective fields, namely, state legislatures. Their requirements are imposed not only directly upon tax-supported teacher-training institutions but indirectly upon other institutions and include a specific number of hours each for education, student teaching, major and minor subjects; in addition to these they often deal specifically with courses required in political science, state history, and health education. (Sometimes a teacher who has met the requirements for certification in one state and has taught several years moves to another state, where it is not uncommon for him to have to meet additional requirements immediately or within a specified probationary period.) State laws often require the teaching of particular social studies subjects in secondary schools. Most common among these are American history and government, state history and government, and problems in democracy. This sort of legislation somewhat predetermines institutional requirements in respect to curricula.

How to Secure and Hold a Teaching Position. After taking the work required for becoming a social studies teacher it becomes imperative to secure a position that harmonizes with such preparation. Locating teaching vacancies comes to our attention first. Most teacher-training institutions maintain a placement bureau. The candidate should approach that office early in the senior year, secure its regular forms, and fill them out fully and accurately. There is far more likelihood of putting down too little information than there is of including too much. Those whom he wishes to give as references should be consulted and their permission secured in advance. The required number of recent application photos should be provided. There are many instances when one's record will be inspected in his absence. It should represent him well.

There are many other possible ways of hearing of vacancies. State departments of education and state teachers' associations often maintain placement services at little or no cost. Brief attention should be given the commercial teachers' agency. It too collects data, finds vacancies, and notifies candidates. The difference is that since it exists because of potential profits there is a substantial charge for services rendered. The authors know of cases where the fee has been as low as 3 per cent and others as high as 10 per cent. Naturally one should give more attention to the cost-free media. However, if a position can be found through an agency that operates in accordance with ethical principles and an equally good placement cannot be found elsewhere, it is logical to be willing to pay the fee.

The prospective teacher should not apply for a position unless there is a known vacancy. It is legitimate to write a brief letter of simple inquiry to find out whether any openings are in view. Frequently one's friends know of potential vacancies or are willing to make inquiry. An occasional item in a newspaper gives information revealing vacancies. The head of the high school from which one graduated is often eager to suggest leads for finding the first teaching job. The above are among the methods most frequently employed in securing positions; certainly they do not represent all possibilities.

After one has located a vacancy the task of making a good application follows. First, one should go in person if possible. Second, a telephone conversation is next best; it should be used if the cost does not seem prohibitive. Finally, the written application is most common. It can lead to securing the position and should be used in addition to the methods mentioned above. A few simple suggestions regarding the written application follow. Use a good quality of business stationery. Type or write neatly, using blue or black ink. Make an initial statement telling from where notice of the vacancy came. Include an early statement telling the manner in which you believe that you can be of special service to the particular school. Include on carefully prepared sheets an outline of your training, personal data, references, and transcript of credits. Make the letter friendly and courteous in tone. Offer to go for a personal interview at the convenience of the employer. The letter should be perfect in respect to grammar, spelling, and form. If you are not certain of these items, enlist the help of an expert to read the materials before they are sent. All applications should include a photo.

During the process of considering the opening determine whether you would actually like to work in the particular school. Social studies teachers should have strong feelings about the philosophy of education, definition of education, and objectives. In fact the candidate for a teaching position has just as much right to ask the employer a question on these points as does the latter to ask his customary questions. In the last analysis the underlying purposes of the school's educational program should conform well with the democratic practices of the nation. The community as a background for the school's environment should be examined. Communities are like individuals, some desirable and others undesirable. Of course the perfect community has not been found; on the other hand, it should merit the description of being social-minded. In addition to teaching respect for the beliefs of others, general tolerance, etc., the teacher has the right to demand to work in a community where he as a citizen may practice those virtues. Important questions concern salary schedule, housing facilities, retirement system, sick-leave policy, and general professional spirit existing among staff members.

After having secured the position, it becomes important to carry on in such manner as to be able to keep it. Job retention needs to be a matter of study. It involves adaptation to the school and community, the exercise of good judgment in matters of conduct, and the execution of a personal program of in-service growth. Most of these points are social in nature, while others apply more generally to the profession as a whole. The following list was compiled by one of the authors [9] and is pertinent in this connection:

1. Remember that cooperation is absolutely a prerequisite for success in teaching. This applies to one's relationships with superintendent, principal, subject-matter supervisor, fellow teachers, building custodian, students, and patrons.

2. Be prompt in attending to all routine matters required by the school. Reports asked for by a certain day or time of day are needed by the office at the time called for.

3. Follow without deviation the rules set forth by the school in such matters as time of reporting for work, helping maintain the general rules of student conduct on school premises, and attending local, state, and national teachers' meetings.

4. Plan to handle well all problems of discipline and irregularities that arise in connection with your own work. Call upon the principal for help only on rare occasions. Administrators need to use their time for the constructive work of the school as a whole and should not be asked to give excessive time to helping with the problems of individual teachers.

5. Attempt to make your class work so interesting and inspiring that almost all students will willingly do a quality of work that will entitle them to a passing grade in the subject. An unusually large number of failures is an indication that the teaching is poor rather than superior. An excessive number of failures causes a corresponding number of awk-

[9] Clarence D. Samford, "Final Conference of Supervising Critic and Student Teachers," *Educational Administration and Supervision,* XXVIII (November, 1942), pp. 624–629.

ward situations in which child, parent, teacher, and administrator become unpleasantly involved.

6. Know each student in your class as soon as possible so well that you can talk intelligently to his parents about his scholastic background, special talents, shortcomings, and apparent achievement.

7. Plan to do something to help with the extracurricular program of the school. Likewise, be willing to give as much time to the community's program of projects as is consistent with effective teaching.

8. Assist the cause of public education by helping to interpret correctly for the individuals and groups with whom you come in contact the philosophy and purposes underlying the school program where you are employed.

9. Maintain steady professional growth by reading recent books and magazine articles in the field being taught, joining national and state organizations related to education as a whole and to your own subject in particular, and pursuing additional training that will lead to more advanced degrees.

10. Add to your general culture by adopting a program of comprehensive reading and extensive travel.

11. Always have a plan for your professional advancement whereby you attempt to reach specific goals as often as each five years extending over a period of at least three such intervals.

In presenting the qualifications that the history teacher in the public schools should possess, Black [10] insists that there should be high ratings under three divisions: teacher qualifications, classroom techniques, and teacher-administrator problems.

It behooves one who desires to be a successful teacher of social studies to make frequent and critical self-analyses. The securing and use of some widely used teacher-rating scales is highly recommended. Not only is it good practice for the teacher to make personal use of them, but it is also helpful to ask the pupils to express their judgment by filling them out near the end of the year. Naturally pupils will be more honest in their ratings if they are not asked to affix their names to the scales used. If one does not have access to commercially published rating sheets, it is possible to prepare and mimeograph one that will suffice for the purpose. Such points as the following can be included and placed well toward the left: knowledge of subject matter, treatment of pupils, ability to explain and make the work inter-

[10] Wilfred Black, "The Teacher of History in Public Schools," *Social Studies,* XLI (April, 1950), pp. 155–159.

esting, grading, voice, dress, sense of humor, special knowledge of contemporary affairs, and interest in community welfare and government. To the right could be placed columns headed *Excellent, Fair,* and *Low.* Helpful suggestions for improving a particular social studies course can come through a discussion of the year's work in which free participation is encouraged.

There are obviously many things that do not stand forth as absolute prerequisites for success in teaching the social studies. Some successful teachers have received their training in almost any type of higher institution of learning that could be named. Effective work is being done somewhere by social studies teachers of all age groups represented in the profession. Possibly no positive correlation could be found to exist between physical attributes and success in teaching in these areas. On the other hand, it can be said that those teachers who exerted their best efforts during their period of training, who are willing to set up for themselves the best of tested guiding principles in teaching, and who have a sincere conviction that the knowledge pupils gain in the classroom is going to help in the solution of present-day problems are most likely to succeed.

How Does a Social Studies Teacher Get Along in School and Community? After the position has been secured the problem arises of the most wholesome procedure to follow to maintain it. If a beginning teacher fails to make a satisfactory adjustment and finds it expedient to drop out of the profession, a considerable loss is involved. The teacher has spent much time and money on work that has less value in relation to other professions; in addition there is a loss that is related to the individual's self-confidence. Furthermore, the institution in which the training was done spent a great deal that is represented in per capita cost during the period of instruction. Fortunately it is possible to predetermine many causes of initial teaching failures. Probably in most instances when a teacher has been branded as a failure the administrator would say that it was due to inability to handle the children; in other words, discipline. This factor is very intimately related to the possession of the desirable traits discussed above. It does not in any manner consist of a list of "do's and don'ts." The social studies classrooms that have the best teacher-pupil relationships are those in which very little is said about discipline. In the end the successful teacher handles well almost every situation that presents itself in the classroom and does not send pupils to the office or call for help from the principal.

Administrators are quite concerned about cooperation with the entire school program. If administrators are efficient they have a positive philosophy about the goals of education in general and in the local community in particular. They expect social studies teachers along with the others to help in the attainment of these goals. If one is not in accord with these concepts, one's teaching should be in the setting of a different community. An additional word about cooperation seems essential. No administrator finds it easy to reemploy a staff member who habitually fails to get along well with the other teachers. Pupils sense the situation quickly and use it as fuel for flames that are not wholesome. Since social studies include the goal of teaching cooperation, it must be demonstrated in the teacher's practices.

Many other points could be mentioned that have caused social studies teachers to fail at the outset. Most of them have applied only to a few isolated instances. Among them are the following: indulgence in questionable leisure-time activities, spending too much time out of the community, expressing opinions injudiciously on controversial issues, improper personal relationships with pupils outside of school, and failure to make reasonable professional growth. From the foregoing discussion, it will be observed that practically all the causes of failure in teaching during the beginning periods are definitely within the control of the teacher; this should be encouraging. With proper personal attention, foresight, and good judgment, success is within the grasp of almost all who earnestly seek it.

In-service Growth. Another aspect of the topic under discussion is what might be called the in-service growth of the social studies teacher. According to Cordier [11] the expression, "in-service growth," generally refers to such matters as reading of professional literature, research, experimentation, advanced summer-school study, and travel. Regardless of how excellent the initial preparation for teaching may have been, it will not suffice in itself to enable the teacher to continue rendering superior performance throughout the years. The first help to be suggested has to do with the teacher's reading

[11] R. W. Cordier, "A Continuous Program for In-service Professional Growth," *Social Education,* V (December, 1941), p. 595.

program. A successful social studies teacher must read widely and should thoroughly enjoy doing so. The range of material should include current books and periodicals designed for the professional advancement of teachers as a whole, those written for the special benefit of social studies teachers, and a generous amount of material written for the lay public. If one is at a loss to know what selection to make, a considerable amount of help can be had by starting with *The Journal of the National Education Association, School and Society, The School Review,* and the official publication of the state education association. All these can be read profitably, and the book reviews that they carry should not be neglected. Judicious selection of some of the books for more detailed reading can be made.

Most teachers start working in the social studies without having read many classic works in the area, because of lack of time in college days. These should be given attention as rapidly as possible. In addition, there are few fields in which new publications appear with greater rapidity than in social studies. Many of them are reviewed at some length in the monthly issues of *Social Education* and *Social Studies.* As mentioned in the preceding paragraph, personal judgment can be exercised in determining which publications, and how many, to pursue to final and complete reading. Not only can the two periodicals mentioned be used for reviews of current books; they are also helpful for those who find pleasure in reading shorter articles dealing with objectives in social studies, practical methods and devices to be used in teaching, current changes in curricula, results of controlled experiments, etc. In addition, brief reports of news in social studies teaching groups and activities, where to secure free and inexpensive materials, latest helps available in audio and visual education, and current classroom teaching materials are found in most issues. Supplementing the reading of the periodicals mentioned above, the social studies teacher should reread certain standard reference works dealing with the entire professional approach. For instance the various volumes that appeared a few years ago as the *Report of the Commission on the Social Studies* are very apt references to have in the school library or as a part of the teacher's personal collection.

Undoubtedly the same organization, or some other one that commands national respect, will relatively soon publish results of surveys, give formal reports, and make pertinent recommendations. These are as inevitable as social change. If and when their true worth is demonstrated they should supplement or replace the above-mentioned works. Age of volumes alone is not a final criterion on which to judge their worth. For instance, it is reasonable to predict that Henry Johnson's *Teaching of History in Elementary and Secondary Schools* will be read by social studies teachers for a full generation to come.

Additional stimuli to growth and professional advancement on the part of the social studies teacher lie in being a member of professional organizations, attending general and sectional teachers' meetings, reading prepared papers on professional subjects, attending carefully selected conferences, and joining groups seeking increased knowledge through educational travel.

Much careful thought should be given by the social studies teacher to this last point. As Olson [12] pointed out, "The value of travel to 'broaden the mind' has always been recognized, but in practice much of the value is destroyed if 'travel' is identified merely with transporting oneself through physical space in the pursuit of a classical culture." Conferences with experienced teachers will yield helpful suggestions. Consultations with commercial concerns which deal with conducted travel tours are often more valuable.

Teachers of Social Studies, Grades 13 and 14. One of the most natural questions to consider in relation to social studies in grades 13 and 14 is who should do the teaching. Personal qualities take high rank in the determination of this point. Pleasing appearance, good sportsmanship, enthusiasm for living an abundant life, belief in the potentialities of youth, honesty, tolerance, fair play, and good judgment would probably be among the qualities readily observable in successful teachers in this area. In addition, it could be stated that all the desirable qualities that should be possessed by teachers of social studies, grades 10 through 12, should likewise be part of the equipment of teachers in these higher levels. Requirements for physical fitness and skill in speech abilities are exacting. General cultural background is probably judged with more severity by upper-grade students than by pupils in lower grades. If a teacher shows pronounced limitations outside of the teaching field, lack of range in general reading habits, limited travel experience, superficial knowledge of current affairs, etc., the feeling of respect on the part of those

[12] Edgar G. Olson, "Tours and Travel Courses for Social Studies Teachers," Washington, D.C.: The National Council for the Social Studies, *Tenth Yearbook,* 1937, p. 124.

being taught will be regrettably low. Fortunately, these are matters largely within the control of the teacher. In-service growth demands attention to all the points just mentioned. Specifically, it calls for continuous reading about and attention to changes that are normally taking place in the social order.

In planning the college of university training that a prospective social studies teacher of these grades should take, a generous amount of professional education should be included. Most of that proposed for the preparation of senior-high-school teachers belongs here. In addition, courses dealing specifically with either the junior college or these grades should be incorporated. Jarvie [13] feels that, in connection with training teachers for these grades, "A teacher of social studies needs a substantial background of the usual specific fields of history, economics, sociology, political science, and social psychology, but even more he needs applied anthropology and human ecology to enable him to observe and work with whole communities." Narrow specialization in any sense is out of order for these teachers. It is generally agreed that students should gain a broad general education in social studies in grades 13 and 14. Granting the validity of this reasoning it becomes readily apparent that those who teach them should be broadly trained. Koos,[14] in his study of forty-eight local public junior colleges, scattered over a rather extensive range geographically, concluded that "junior college teachers should be prepared to teach at least two related subjects, and probably in some areas, even more." Such findings give emphasis to the desirability of the prospective teacher's taking numerous survey courses and showing interest in general areas.

Teachers of grades 13 and 14 should much more closely resemble teachers of grades 10 through 12, inclusive, than they should teachers of more advanced levels. This is true for many reasons. In the first place, the trend is to have students in grades 13 and 14 who are far more heterogeneous than those found in higher grades. Just as the high-school program has grown in America, so has the enrollment in these grades increased. Second, physical and intellectual develop-

[13] L. L. Jarvie, "Proposals Respecting the Preparation of Teachers for New-type Colleges," American Association of Colleges for Teacher Education, *Twenty-sixth Yearbook*, 1947, pp. 196–209.

[14] L. V. Koos, "Junior College Teachers: Subjects Taught and Specialized Preparation," *Junior College Journal*, XVIII (December, 1947), p. 209.

ment of students of this age does not reach the maturity that is noticeable especially about two years later. Finally, these grades are more often organized within the administrative pattern of the lower grades mentioned than as a part of higher grades.

Summary. In this chapter an effort has been made to point out that the selection of secondary-school social studies teaching should not be entered into lightly. Personal preferences in the matter should be checked against reputable tests in the area of teaching. In addition, teacher-training institutions should apply criteria for admission covering the points of intelligence, high-school achievement, physical fitness, speech skill, and moral character. After the individual has been admitted to a training institution, a curriculum should be pursued that offers a major and minor field of specialization, a reasonable amount of written and spoken English, courses in education and student teaching, a science sequence, some training in personal and community health, limited participation in physical education, and the fine arts. Beginning with the first year of teaching experience an effort should be made to develop well the personal qualities associated with teaching success. Self-analysis and rating sheets are very helpful means to this end. In addition to rendering a desirable service in the classroom, it is quite essential to make satisfactory community adjustments. Entering the profession is to be regarded as only the first step. In-service growth should follow through professional and general reading, becoming an active member in appropriate state and national organizations, participation in movements for the improvement of teaching, and educational travel.

Questions on the Text

1. Should teacher-training institutions admit for preparation all who desire to become social studies teachers? Why?
2. Name several criteria upon which admission depends in those institutions where selective processes operate.
3. What are some of the areas of knowledge in which prospective social studies teachers should study in addition to work in the major subject or subjects?
4. What proportion of the total hours required for graduation is devoted to the major in the illustration given? to the minor?
5. If a major is granted in social science, what fields are usually included in the group? Which ones receive major emphasis?

6. What factors should determine whether or not a teacher-training institution should alter its curriculum for social science majors?

7. In what manner may state legislatures influence the curriculum pursued by social science majors?

8. What help can the college or university graduate expect in securing the first teaching position in social studies?

9. Name several personal qualities that pupils in social studies classes like in their teachers.

10. Does it seem that being successful is a matter that is within or beyond the control of the social studies teacher? Justify your answer.

11. Mention some of the points that a school administrator is greatly concerned about when measuring teaching success.

12. On what bases is a community likely to judge a social studies teacher as successful or unsuccessful?

13. Some social studies teachers do not show much greater teaching skill after several years of experience than they exhibited the first year. Why?

14. In what manner, if any, should the personal qualifications and training of a social studies teacher for grades 13 and 14 differ from those of an excellent teacher of the same subject at lower grade levels?

Suggested Activities

1. Examine the catalogues of representative teacher-training institutions. Tabulate data on the following points:

a. Requirements for admission

b. Requirements for a major or minor in a given social science and in social sciences

c. Requirements in education, psychology, and directed teaching for social studies majors

d. Requirements in fields other than social sciences

2. Set forth in some detail a list of points that you think should be answered in the affirmative by those who propose to become social studies teachers.

3. Make a list of questions that should all be answered "yes" if the social studies teacher is doing successful work.

4. Prepare an outline of activities which a teacher of social studies might pursue over a fifteen-year period following the earning of the first degree and which might lead to recognition for successful teaching and worthy professional service to the state and nation.

5. Have interviews with five or more recent high-school graduates. Ask them to make statements about qualities that they liked and disliked most in their social studies teachers. Summarize the answers obtained.

6. Read and make a report on a recent article found in an educational periodical dealing with a topic discussed in this chapter.

7. Outline in detail the college or university training that you would recommend for the social studies teacher of grades 13 and 14. Defend the allotment of semester hours that you have given to general education, professional courses, and subject matter in the area of specialization.

Selected References

Anderson, G. L., "Popular and Professional Misconceptions Concerning the Teaching Profession," *Educational Forum,* XIII (November, 1948), pp. 51–62.

Anderson, H. R., "Should Colleges Prepare Teachers Who Know What to Teach or How to Teach?" *Social Education,* XI (February, 1947), pp. 65–67.

Baldwin, J. W., "Specialized Professional Preparation of Social Studies Teachers," *School and Society,* LV (Jan. 10, 1942), pp. 53–55.

Black, Wilfred, "The Teacher of History in Public Schools," *Social Studies,* XLI (April, 1950), pp. 155–159.

Burke, V. J., "Equilibrium of Social Studies Teachers," *Social Studies,* XXXVIII (May, 1947), pp. 198–200.

Dodson, D. W., "Human Relations in Teacher Training," *Journal of Educational Sociology,* XXII (October, 1948), pp. 106–115.

Douglass, Harl R., and Hubert H. Mills, *Teaching in High School,* New York: The Ronald Press Company, 1948, Chaps. I and XXVII.

Cordier, R. W., "A Continuous Program for In-service Professional Growth," *Social Education,* V (December, 1941), p. 595.

Dodge, A. F., "Study of Personality Traits of Successful Teachers," *Occupations,* XXVII (November, 1948), pp. 107–112.

Froehlich, C. P., "In-service Training Programs That Succeed," *Clearing House,* XXIII (January, 1949), pp. 259–262.

Graham, H., "Proper Function of Social Studies," *Catholic Educational Review,* XLIV (November, 1946), pp. 541–544.

Irwin, L. B., "Good Teachers," *Social Studies,* XXXIX (November, 1948), pp. 324–327.

Jarvie, L. L., "Proposals Respecting the Preparation of Teachers for New-type Colleges," American Association of Colleges for Teacher Education, *Twenty-sixth Yearbook,* 1947, pp. 85–92.

King, Allen Y., "Pre-induction Training in the Social Studies," *Teachers College Record,* XLV (December, 1943), pp. 154–160.

Kingsbury, F. A., "Psychology in the Education of Social Science Teachers," *Social Education,* X (May, 1946), pp. 208–212.

KOOS, L. V., "Junior College Teachers: Subjects Taught and Specialized Preparation," *Junior College Journal,* XVIII (December, 1947), p. 209.

LEVI, ALBERT WILLIAM, *General Education in the Social Studies,* Washington, D.C.: American Council on Education, 1948.

MCGRATH, G. D., "Facts in Teacher Education," *School Executive,* LXVIII (June, 1949), pp. 25–26.

MAUL, RAY C., "Teacher Supply and Demand in the United States," *Report of the 1950 National Teacher Supply and Demand Study,* Washington, D.C.: National Education Association, 1950.

MOFFATT, MAURICE P., *Social Studies Instruction,* New York: Prentice-Hall, Inc., 1950, Chap. XVI.

OLSON, EDGAR G., "Tours and Travel Courses for Social Studies Teachers," Washington, D.C.: The National Council for the Social Studies, *Tenth Yearbook,* 1937.

PRALL, CHARLES E., "Social Studies for the Prospective Teacher," *Social Education,* X (October, 1946), pp. 261–264.

RICE, T. D., "How Can We Administer In-service Education Programs through Workshops?" *National Association of Secondary-school Principals Bulletin,* XXXIII (May, 1949), pp. 3–8.

RICHEY, R. W., and W. H. FOX, "How Do Teachers Compare with Other Community Members?" *Educational Research Bulletin,* XXVII (December, 1948), pp. 238–241.

RISK, THOMAS M., *Principles and Practices of Teaching in Secondary Schools,* New York: American Book Company, 1947, Chap. I.

RIVLIN, HARRY N., *Teaching Adolescents in Secondary Schools,* New York: Appleton-Century-Crofts, Inc., 1948, Chaps. IV and XVI.

SAMFORD, CLARENCE D., "Final Conference of Supervising Critic and Student Teachers," *Educational Administration and Supervision,* XXVIII (November, 1942), pp. 624–629.

SHOWALTER, JOHN F., "A Scale for Measuring Attitudes with Respect to Public Education and to Teaching as a Profession," unpublished manuscript.

SIBLEY, E., "Education of Social Science Teachers," *Journal of General Education,* III (January, 1949), pp. 113–120.

SMITH, EDWARD PAYSON, "A Study of Personal Qualities Essential in the Superior Teacher of Social Studies," in W. C. Bagley and Thomas Alexander, *The Teacher of the Social Studies,* Part XIV, Report of the Commission on the Social Studies, New York: Charles Scribner's Sons, 1937.

STODDARD, G. D., "Random Remarks on Teacher Education," *School and Society,* LXVIII (Dec. 18, 1948), pp. 417–419.

UMSTATTD, J. G., *Secondary School Teaching,* Boston: Ginn & Company, 1944, Chaps. I and XVII.

"Where to Go for Junior College Teacher Preparation," *Junior College Journal,* XVIII (April, 1948), pp. 444–445.

WOLCOTT, L. B., "Social Structure and Teacher Education," *Harvard Educational Review,* XV (October, 1945), pp. 258–269.

WOLFE, A. B., "Teacher Training in the Social Sciences," *School and Society,* LVI (Oct. 10, 1942), pp. 325–329.

Chapter 3

SOME PROBLEMS OF THE BEGINNING TEACHER

Preview. The beginning social studies teacher will probably encounter problems for which he may have had little specific preparation. His judgment and good sense must serve him here. Obviously there are some problems which are to be expected, and for these some discussion may be helpful. The list of problems suggested here is not exhaustive, nor may these all be found in the experience of every beginning teacher. From observation it seems that gaining a knowledge of pupils, helping pupils solve problems, supervising study, guiding discussion, planning work, selecting materials, and encouraging a classroom learning atmosphere are phases of teaching which may present significant problems to the beginning teacher of the social studies.

The Problem of Knowing the Pupils.[1] The successful teacher must be well acquainted with pupils in his classes. For the social studies teacher, learning to know the pupils is a problem of greater significance, perhaps, than for the teacher in any other subject area. Pupil personality, attitudes, and ideals enter the social studies class in a rather unique way in that the objectives of the social studies involve these pupil traits. Learning to know one's pupils cannot be a rapid process. A continual observation of pupil attitudes, habits, manners, and responses must become the teacher's practice, if successful social studies teaching is to result.

The environments from which pupils come will be impressive determinants in the types of reaction pupils make to the teacher, fel-

[1] For an expanded discussion of this topic see articles in *Fifteenth Yearbook* of the Claremont College Reading Conference, Claremont College Curriculum Laboratory, Claremont, Calif., 1950, and materials from the Mid-century White House Conference on Children and Youth. See *The Survey*, LXXXVII (January, 1951).

low pupils, discussions, and school life in general. Homes in which suspicion of society, antagonism toward neighbors, and a general atmosphere of insecurity are present cannot send children into schoolrooms free of these qualities. Children of minority racial groups present further background differences, including racial social traditions, religious factors, and possibly speech difficulties. The potential conflict within the individual as he adapts his family experience to his total environment may be so great as to affect his reaction to the present classroom. As Davis [2] points out, economic needs frequently cause families to evaluate living in terms of money values. Children from such homes have too often experienced the closing of doors against them in their sharing in pleasures of the entertainment world and enjoying an equality with their more fortunate contemporaries. Limited economic resources in a family restrict the activity of the family and thus narrow the experience of the child. Consequently, at the beginning of a teacher's directing of a class, much time and attention must be given to such activities as shall enable the teacher to observe pupils in their classroom situation, how they respond to other pupils, and how they react to topics of interest to their daily living. This teacher activity must be a continuing process.

It is only by attempting to understand his pupils that the teacher can know when specific abilities are being challenged, when certain pupils may be overcoming undesirable attitudes or outgrowing timidity in group discussion. When the teacher is aware of interests which certain pupils may have, he is better able to guide those pupils in whatever class activity may be at hand. A teacher's recognition of a pupil interest or hobby may so encourage the pupil that, inspired to increased appreciation of his hobby, he will not only develop interests to provide for his leisure-time activities, but he may find a life career. Participation by the teacher with pupils in the recognition and enjoyment of hobbies helps the pupil to see his school life as a part of his life not unlike life outside of school. The teacher may arrange to have classes observe a hobby day at stated times when each pupil brings his hobby to school and is given an opportunity to talk about it and share it with his classmates.

Experience in working with many pupils over a period of years will provide the teacher with various approaches to this problem of

[2] Allison Davis, "Socio-Economic Influences on Learning," *The Phi Delta Kappan*, XXXII (January, 1951), pp. 253–256.

learning to know each pupil. For the beginning teacher there are some simple techniques which may be used, some of which, no doubt, can be of value even to the experienced teacher. To obtain a considerable amount of the same type of information about each pupil quickly, the teacher may devise a questionnaire, such as the following, to be filled out by each pupil.

UNIVERSITY HIGH SCHOOL PERSONNEL SHEET

1. Name ____________
2. Age ________ Birth date ____________ State ________
3. Address ____________
4. Church membership ____________
5. Parents' name ____________
6. Father's occupation ____________
7. How many brothers? ________ Younger ________ Older ________
8. How many sisters? ________ Younger ________ Older ________
9. What hobbies do you have? ____________
____
10. What radio programs do you follow regularly? ____________
____
11. What newspapers come regularly to your home? ____________
____
12. What magazines do you read regularly? ____________
____
13. What musical instrument do you play? ____________
14. In what sports do you participate? ____________
____
15. Are you responsible for any particular job in your home? ________
Explain ____________
16. Do you ever earn spending money by work outside home? ________
Kind of work ____________
17. What school subject do you find least difficult? ____________
____

The information in such a questionnaire gives some facts about each pupil which can serve as a basis upon which the teacher may establish a more thorough knowledge of the child. The response in almost every such questionnaire will carry some item of information which will give much insight into the pupil's personality.

As the class is meeting in its first days, the teacher might ask for an autobiography by each pupil. This device is somewhat similar to the questionnaire but may reveal different items of information about each pupil, since it is more subjective. The teacher may suggest some few examples of items to include in a biography but not so many as to reduce the subjective quality. In writing their autobiographies the pupils will reveal indirectly many traits of ability and personality. It will be evident whether the pupil can organize materials, whether he can express himself clearly and in well-formed sentences. The type of content material emphasized in the biography will perhaps reveal his particular interest, or attitude toward life, and some background experiences. The following autobiographies are typical examples of a pupil's writing about himself at the beginning of the eighth grade:

My Life Story

I was the second child in my family, my sister being two years older. I was born in Cheyenne and during the younger years of my life lived on my grandparents' farm. When I was about four we left the farm and started traveling in the South. My father was a soldier and every time the army would give him orders to move to another town my mother would load baggage and children into the car and go with him. I never had a really permanent home until I moved back to my grandparents' farm when I was eight years old. We stayed there until I was in the fourth grade and then moved to Laramie. When I was ready for the fifth grade I entered the University Elementary School. We lived in several houses in Laramie until we finally found our dream house. It is a large one with plenty of room for our family of six. A sort of hobby has been developed by our family in the raising of registered cocker spaniels. The entire family is heartbroken whenever some pups must be sold but our house, big as it is, would be overrun with dogs otherwise.

My Autobiography

I was born March 15, 1936, at Denver, Colorado. When I was five years old I went to Astoria, Oregon. I did a lot of traveling from the age of five to ten years. I went to California, Idaho, and Wyoming where most of my traveling was located. I have lived in these Wyoming towns: Rock River, Green River, and Laramie. I started to school when I was five. I love to hunt and fish and I enjoy other sports. I killed my first antelope when I was seven. I have gone hunting with my dad many times. That is all I can think of for now.

My Autobiography

I was born near Loveland, Colorado, on a small farm December 12, 1936. I lived there until I was eight years old and went to Big Thompson School. Then we moved to Loveland because we thought Dad was going to the war. Here I went to Lincoln Grade School. Before the end of my first year of school here I was carrying the *Rocky Mountain News.* I carried it for about six months and then stopped carrying that and started carrying *The Denver Post.* I didn't carry that long until I started carrying *The Reporter Herald* which I carried for about two weeks and then a car hit me and broke my arm and leg, so I stopped carrying papers for a while.

I finished grade school and went to Loveland Junior High. Then Dad and Mom decided to move to Laramie so Dad resigned from his church in Loveland and the whole family worked on a ranch in North Park this summer and then he started to preach at his church in Laramie.

More casual investigations, perhaps, can also be helpful to the teacher in becoming acquainted with the pupils. The teacher may suggest a topic of current interest or ask a question involving a school problem. In the discussion which develops among the pupils it may be possible to observe attitudes, prejudices, habits of thinking, mannerisms, and other personal characteristics.

Helping Pupils Face Personal Problems. The social studies teacher cannot feel that the personal problems of pupils are outside his realm and wholly the responsibility of the guidance director. As has been pointed out above, it is essential that the social studies teacher become thoroughly acquainted with the individual pupils in order that maximum learning may result. If the school is to function constructively in the lives of pupils and not be merely a time-consuming legal requirement, the individual pupil must find there an answer to his needs. The area of the social studies seems to offer this opportunity to the pupil in that his problems are to a greater or less degree related to this area of the school program. As long as the child is entangled in a problem which he cannot solve, an anxiety, a fear, or a feeling of inferiority, he cannot live fully and happily or benefit from contacts with his fellow pupils. To help pupils solve their problems is as important a learning procedure as that implied in the statement setting up the goal of maximum learning, where some general problem of life is considered. Pupils worry about things which adults may have forgotten ever loomed large in the process of their growing up.

The pupil's world is a world of limited experience in contrast to that of most adults; although his sense of proportion may seem childishly out of focus, it does, nevertheless, control his reaction to life. Some children worry about personal physical traits which may seem unusual or different from other people's traits. A child may feel a great need for companionship and yet be unable somehow to attract friends; others may fear loss of status in a particular group. Home conditions, parental fears, or parent-and-child relationships often constitute serious maladjustment problems. Boy-and-girl relationships present problems that are many times of paramount importance and should be included in the social studies program. (See Chapter 4 on Curriculum.)

Much of the pupil's individual problem solving will grow out of his own personal experience in the group in which he moves through school. Obviously, the majority of personality problems cannot be made the topic of class discussion as a means of solution. Learning to work together with other people, to trust individuals, having confidence in the teacher are phases of the approach to personal problem solving. As pupils participate in class discussion and in small group discussion within the class, they apply to their own specific problems the ideas gained from these experiences. The ideas may be facts acquired from subject matter or from their observation of conduct and attitudes of other pupils. Helping pupils interpret their experience is the important guiding influence of the teacher.

Such help will come through the teacher's guiding the class through problem-solving activities until certain habits are fixed in the pupils' thinking. To define a problem, to list the causes, to be able to distinguish between the direct causes and contributing conditions, to see the problem from various points of view, and to suggest possible solutions for the problem are parts of such an activity. Through these efforts pupils learn to evaluate their own thinking and actions, a process which is essential in the expression of good judgment and fundamental to their personal happiness.

Helping Pupils Work Together. In the social studies the teacher has a great opportunity to develop individual skills in group relationships. In our democracy we emphasize the value of the individual and insist upon the right of the fullest possible achievement within the individual's ability, but at the same time we require the individual to submit to demands of the group and to consider the welfare and the rights of others as a condition of his own privilege. In the school, as we have recognized the importance of the individual pupil's interest, we have moved away from the teacher-controlled situation. The resulting teacher-pupil group has afforded the valuable opportunity of learning to work in groups, a practice essential to our American democracy. The class becomes a group having a sense of belonging together, by working on common problems, accepting one another, questioning one another, and helping one another understand when one pupil's experience may have been more meaningful for some than for others. Leadership is recognized wherever it is genuine, and the right of the individual within the group to express his opinion and to demonstrate his ability is maintained. Attempts to dominate may become evident as the group senses ability, and the would-be dictator is held in place by the consciousness of individual rights in the group as a whole. Thus we see that no small part of the responsibility of the social studies teacher is the establishment in the class of that group morale and ability which recognizes individual worth at the same time that it maintains the power and vitality of the group. In this experience children establish early the pattern of democracy in their personalities.

The Problem of Selecting Materials for Study. The preparation of the social studies teacher must of necessity be very broad, since the entire range of human activities comes within his teaching area. Because of this fact the social studies teacher must read widely, follow in-service training programs, travel, and seek in all ways to improve his preparation for teaching. Realizing that the courses which he must direct are limited by time and other factors, he must choose those topics which seem most essential for the realization of the objectives of the social studies course. These objectives (see Chapter 1) are concerned with values desired for the pupils. The result of the educative process is the enlarged life, a broader vision of personal development, an effective citizenship, and democratic ideals functioning in all human relationships. Thus a problem presents itself to the social studies teacher concerning the selection from the vast materials of this field of those portions which will contribute to the realization of these objectives.

It would seem that the practice by the teacher of those ideals and objectives involved in the democratic way of life would be a helpful method of establishing desirable habit patterns among the pupils.

The problem of selection of material for study, then, can be partially solved when the teacher is willing to share the planning of the course with the pupils. This has been the authors' experience, and Gould and Yoakam [3] point out that when pupils realize that their interests, their questions or suggestions, have been the basis for a class project, there will be far greater motivation toward the achievement of desired ends than when an assignment has been dictated by the teacher without any recognition of pupil reaction to a given topic.

This democratic procedure removes the problem of how to make a dictated assignment meaningful, challenging, inspirational, and individually aimed. The traditional type of assignment (see pp. 81–283) probably could not engage pupil initiative so extensively nor could it always provide experience which would establish functioning concepts. The plans which a class makes to attack a problem become an assignment, as they decide their procedure.

It may seem difficult for the beginning social studies teacher to permit the pupils to share in planning. He may feel impatient with their inability to distinguish between the significant factors, or themes, involved in a certain problem or topic. Because of his knowledge of the topic and his experience the teacher will many times be thinking ahead of the pupils; he may see an idea, a question, or a further step essential to the development of the unit while the pupils fail to realize this additional phase. Growth of pupil personality, knowledge, and understanding, from which increased appreciation and creative effort evolve, are possible only when pupils gain new concepts for themselves through personal experience. The teacher must participate in the group discussion only as a guide, not as a source of the answers. It is difficult for the teacher at times to refrain from dominating a discussion that seems to be futile in accomplishing the objectives which he recognizes as possible. It is a valued characteristic of our democratic way that we discuss problems at length before we reach decisions. As the group examines a problem, each member seeing it from his own unique point of view, not only do solutions appear, but pupils gain new insight through the experience. It is from such experiences that pupils learn to recognize their personal problems and to see what the various related parts of their own problems may be. When the group has defined its problem, the teacher

[3] George Gould and Gerald Allan Yoakam, *The Teacher and His Work*, New York: The Ronald Press Company, 1947, p. 121.

and pupils together may decide upon the methods by which the problem may be solved. Such an approach to the work of the course will enable the teacher to accomplish far more than the restricted activities set up in a teacher-dictated assignment of a job to do. The pupils will bring to the work their own contribution and influence. The teacher will guide the work by his understanding of the fundamental themes of American life and in keeping with those educational principles which enable him to direct pupil experience in well-planned units, thus aiding the pupils in their quest for understanding of the world.

The beginning social studies teacher might well ask for guidance as to how to invite pupils to share in planning their work. As Krug [4] points out, the aim here is not to allow pupils to dictate a course without reference to the more mature judgment of the teacher. Teacher-pupil planning is a cooperative experience. For those teachers who feel that they are obliged to follow an established course of study, there is just as great an opportunity to develop the course by the cooperation of the pupils as for those teachers who are not held to a specific topical outline. It is always helpful to arouse pupil interest in a topic by approaching that topic from the point of view of the present. This not only gives the experience of the pupil a chance to function by comparison, but it also aids the pupil in relating to his present experience what may be far removed in time or place. On the basis of his own knowledge what does he imagine about the new topic? Out of his imagination may come questions which serve as guides to the formulation of the problem to be studied. This will probably not result quickly. Time must be allowed to permit pupil response and teacher guidance to work together.

Pupils in an eighth-grade class became interested in a large map of Canada displayed in the room. There were various remarks about the map.

"Canada is big but has fewer states than the United States has."

"They don't call them states."

"There are lots of lakes so the people must fish."

"Canada has mountains in almost the same places our country has them."

"Do people live all over Canada?"

[4] Edward A. Krug, *Curriculum Planning*, New York, Harper & Brothers, 1950, pp. 200–201.

The teacher felt justified in encouraging further pupil expressions because of the importance of Canada to the United States and the various details of this international relationship which can be of significance to the present world. Further pupil observation of the map brought additional comparisons between the prairie provinces of Canada and such Western states of the United States as Wyoming, the Dakotas, and Nebraska. The teacher asked the class if they would like to study about Canada for several days, and the majority raised their hands and assented vocally. The teacher then inquired what the individual members would be interested in knowing about Canada. The following list of topics resulted after various pupils had contributed their ideas: the people and what they do for a living, Canadian defenses, government and the mounted police, national parks, wildlife, natural resources, schools, scientific development, and products. Various members of the class chose from this list topics which they would investigate and report to the class.

From this example it might appear that the pupils decided to study about Canada without any chance of the teacher's showing his interest in the decision. The map of Canada had been placed by the teacher in an obvious location in the room as part of his effort to maintain a classroom environment which might prompt learning through individual pupil observation. Thoughts in a pupil's mind suggested by contact with his environment frequently lead to worth-while pupil experience even though no class discussion of such items may have been developed. The unit was not teacher-dominated because pupil interest and questioning entered the planning of the work. The pupils saw their share in the study plan as their own ideas were listed on the blackboard. The realization that his own contribution was there inspired each pupil to an enthusiastic effort and a keen interest in what his classmates were doing in their own specific topics.

An interesting study of the principles for which Americans have been willing to involve themselves in war resulted from a group discussion of news events as the United Nations forces were suffering losses in Korea.

"Why should we be over in Korea, anyway?" was the line of thought most evident in the group. Sensing the pupils' outraged feelings, as they were experiencing a sense of defeat and not understanding the significance of the event, the teacher asked why the United States had ever participated in any war. There followed the pupil activity of listing the various wars in which the United States had been involved. Groups of pupils to investigate the causes of each war resulted from the selecting by individual pupils of a war to study. Within two days the groups began bringing their findings to the attention of the entire class. Emphasis in the study was given to the original problem of why the United States went to war in each instance. The class discussions based on the group reports resulted in pupils' realizing that conditions which had brought American participation in the Korean incident were typical of some conditions which had led to our being involved in earlier wars.

Thus we see that this democratic procedure of planning by pupils and teacher together serves various purposes. The objectives of the course become functioning guides in day-by-day pupil relationships, as individuals consider one another's interests and as pupils try to solve their problems. An increased motivation seems to occur as pupils invest their own ideas in a plan. The teacher can guide pupils to a broader experience as he observes the unique interests and abilities of each in the planning of the work.

The Problem of Making Daily Lesson Plans. The beginning social studies teacher realizes that he must know what is to be the procedure for the work of a class period. Unless a study guide is written out, it is possible for the work to bog down in a variety of activities which do not eventually come together to produce the desired outcomes of the study unit. The beginning teacher may have such questions as "How detailed shall a daily lesson plan be?" or "Do I always need to make a plan?" It seems obvious that the plan will grow largely from the developments within the class and must, therefore, possess an elasticity to permit further developments as the unit unfolds under pupil exploration.

With experience every teacher will devise a type of lesson plan most helpful to himself. The plan need not be lengthy or detailed; it should serve as a reminder to hold a class activity within the general line of development toward recognized objectives. No plan must ever be considered as too valuable, however, to be discarded if pupil interests bring more significant problems to the attention of the class. The objectives of the course, those values believed to be of paramount worth to young Americans, can be realized through experiences growing out of many types of problems and are not limited to fixed routines for all pupils. Most plans will include a statement of the over-all general objectives and also those specific objectives tentatively related to the immediate day's work. The activities in which the pupils are to engage may be listed, and what the teacher expects to do may also be noted. The following suggested plan for a day's class indicates one kind of teaching guide:

Daily Lesson Plan

Topic: "The Geography of Canada"

I. Background for topic—pupil questions and comments:
  A. Canada has some provinces that seem to resemble states in the United States.
  B. Would Hudson Bay be for Canada what the Great Lakes are for the United States? Do the Great Lakes belong to Canada?
  C. How far north do people live on farms in Canada? Where do Eskimos live?
  D. What is Canada's largest city? What makes it have the most people?

II. Objectives
  A. To understand the resemblance between Canadian and United States geographic divisions
  B. To understand the problem presented to Canadians by the Laurentian Shield
  C. To understand the significance of climate in the development of Canadian life
  D. To understand the advantages and disadvantages of Canadian waterways
  E. To understand Canadian regionalism resulting from population distribution

III. Specific objectives
  A. To develop skill in the locating of materials needed for problem solving
  B. To develop skill in the selecting and organizing of material from various sources
  C. To develop ability in recognizing related problems or topics not previously indicated
  D. To encourage pupils to share materials with one another
  E. To help Earl overcome extreme shyness by encouraging him to enter a conversation
  F. To aid any pupils who seem to encounter difficulties in the mechanics of research
  G. To encourage all pupil interests expressed in the topic

IV. Teacher activities

A. Before class assembles write on the blackboard the four questions and comments taken from yesterday's discussion which form the pupil guide for this portion of the unit on Canada

B. Open the period by inviting a quick summarizing statement of the general remarks made in yesterday's exploratory discussion about Canada

1. Get a statement from James, if he volunteers (needs recognition)
2. Invite further comments

C. Direct pupils' attention to the four questions and comments written on the board

1. Develop discussion as follows:
   a. What type of information do these four items seem to call for?
   b. What will we have to do in order to understand these questions and comments fully? (Response will probably be in terms of previous-unit exploratory periods:
   —Some will suggest investigating the file for material on Canada
   —Some will suggest textbooks, encyclopedias, and general reference books as sources of information
   —Some will suggest checking the file of *National Georgraphic Magazine* for articles about Canada
   —Some will probably indicate a wish to pursue a specific topic or to arrange a bulletin-board exhibit
   —Some will probably propose a group project of two or three working together on a specific topic
   —One or two—probably Earl and Martha—may make no suggestions)

D. Supervise the study period
(Remaining time will probably be thirty or thirty-five minutes, allowing time for putting materials away at close of period)

1. Begin period by encouraging pupils to carry out their suggestions as to location of materials
2. Observe groups and individuals in this process:
   a. Jerry continues to have difficulty in using an index efficiently; watch for evidence of improvement
   b. Marie frequently bogs down in other articles which divert her attention; observe her activity and inquire concerning success to keep her on the track
   c. Watch for John's decision as to his work plans—good judgment and his imagination may call for suggestions about more difficult tasks
   d. If any pupils are backward about entering the activity, sug-

gest some phase for them, allowing a choice; if these do not attract, invite help from the hesitant person either for a pupil or for the teacher in some activity related to the period

e. Allow a few minutes at close of work period for each person or group to make an appraisal of what has been accomplished and what is to be the next step

E. Close the period

1. Pupils to return all materials to proper locations
2. Furniture to be arranged in order
3. Scrap paper on floor to be disposed of properly
4. Pupils wishing to sign for materials to be used outside the room to follow established routine for this procedure
5. Teacher to make any office announcements which have been requested
6. Class to move from the room when all routine items have been cared for

The specific objectives listed in the plan for the day's work may not all be realized in this one day. Their presence in the plan, however, will be a reminder for the teacher as he guides the activities based on the material which will make these goals, and those of the unit, possible.

The teacher activities in this plan emphasize the teacher's awareness of individual pupil traits and problems. The supervised study period is indicated as a teacher activity because this period cannot accomplish its purpose without constant teacher participation in the activities of the individual pupils as they proceed with their study (see Chapter 13).

The beginning social studies teacher may find it extremely helpful to jot down brief, meaningful notes on certain items at the close of a class period or at the end of the day in order to plan more effectively for the succeeding day's work. These notes may be entered on the plan intended for the class or day just completed, pointing out unsatisfactory accomplishments, tangents of activity not expected when the plan was made, and recognition of individual pupil traits as shown in some class activity.

The teacher's philosophy of education, his understanding of the share of the social studies in the whole program of education, his teaching ability, and the extent of his content preparation will combine to help him answer the questions he may have about preparing daily lesson plans. It would seem that for efficient teaching and for the maximum welfare of his pupils the beginning teacher of the social studies should construct daily lesson plans. The plans should be a practical help, not a burden to be shouldered as a daily task in preparation for the next class.

The Problem of Making an Assignment from a Course of Study. That the making of an assignment based on a textbook is a problem of the beginning social studies teacher is evidenced by the fact that too often he forgets that his pupils are less mature than he is and that they frequently possess inadequate backgrounds with which to approach the new material which is being presented. To make an assignment involves far more than directing a class to read a certain section of material. In keeping with the objectives of the unit the teacher will call the pupils' attention to every significant detail of the material involved in the assignment. Usually an assignmnt will call for materials from several general texts and reference books; it may also include periodicals or newspapers. The pupil must be directed to these with care in order to be sure that he will find and make proper use of the items called for. The social studies teacher can seldom assume that every pupil knows a specific item, although the item may seem to be of an elementary nature. Details in most social studies assignments include such items as vocabulary, pictures, charts, graphs, maps, and cited references to related materials or facts. The teacher must investigate to determine whether each pupil can interpret the graphic material and can use such reference books as are called for.

The Problem of Supervised Study. In the social studies, perhaps more than in any other area of the curriculum, the problem of guiding pupils in efficient study practices is of much concern to the teacher. To make use of the materials from which come the solutions to most of the problems social studies classes are concerned with requires that pupils possess certain fundamental skills. The acquisition and use of these skills by the pupils become a major objective of the social studies teacher.

The social studies teacher must be informed as to the specific social studies skills, must understand the use of resources of the library, and must exercise judgment in guiding pupils toward the achievement of desirable study habits involving these skills, resources, and analyses of problems. Preplanning for the supervised study period will be evident in the assignment upon which the study period depends. For a more detailed discussion of supervised study in the social studies see Chapter 13.

The Problem of Guiding Discussion. Discussion holds an extensive place in social studies classes but does not exist solely for its own sake. It is the means by which many of the objectives of the social studies can be achieved. Pupils must be guided into efficient habits of discussion, recognizing the purpose involved and knowing when values have resulted. To guide the discussion period toward the accomplishment of the objectives of the unit requires considerable skill on the part of the teacher. There are some conditions which, if they are present, can offer difficulty. One or two pupils may desire to talk at length on any topics before the group, thus dominating the discussion. Timidity may cause some pupils to refrain from participating in the discussion. Inadequate information or prejudice may bring forth unsound argument leading to personal clashes. In preparation for the discussion of a topic, the social studies teacher must have investigated the various aspects of that topic in order to be informed upon the values to be derived from such a discussion. He must be able to present the topic in such a way that the pupils will approach it as a problem to be solved. If pupil comments are slow in response to the problem, a planned question from the teacher may serve as an opening to the problem. The teacher will remain in the background as much as possible, entering the discussion only when it seems that the line of thought departs from the development needed for the realization of the objectives. The authors' experience has been that when the teacher must enter the discussion, a question is the desirable device by which to redirect pupil thought. To guide pupils in critical analysis of a problem is a significant teacher activity and requires much preplanning and alertness.

The Problem of Controversial Issues. Discussion in the social studies class may not proceed far before a topic arises which brings out elements of controversy in the pupils' reactions. Such topics may result from pupil differences and from community attitudes. The social studies teacher must not avoid such topics, because this type of discussion affords an opportunity for guidance in the formation of desirable citizenship habits and practices. The citizen's recognition of such problems and his doing something intelligent about them is the life of our democracy. It involves the essential right to speak about problems significant to our people. Neither should the social studies teacher seek to inject a controversial topic into the class discussion unless the over-all situation seems to warrant such discussion. The social studies teacher should look upon this kind of topic as one to be dealt with when it develops naturally in the class activity. When a controversial topic arises, the teacher must maintain an objective point of view to allow freedom of discussion, reminding pupils when necessary of the essential right of freedom of discussion and expression of ideas. It becomes the duty of the teacher to guide pupils in analyzing the topic in order to distinguish the facts which relate to it. When prejudice or intolerance becomes evident, care must be exercised to help pupils discriminate between truth and emotional reaction and unsound reasoning. The teacher's knowledge of the individual pupil will be a significant factor in the handling of this difficult type of discussion. The teacher must use great tact and be guided by wise judgment in his direction of the discussion. It is essential that he have an adequate understanding of the issues involved in the topic. The following techniques for discussing controversial topics are taken from a list by Wilhelms [5] and seem to be practical aids for the teacher and the class:

1. Focus on the problem, not on the fight.
2. Hunt for common ground.
3. Define the issues.
4. Develop criteria or standards of reference.
5. Be realistic about the proposed alternatives.

Maintaining a Learning Atmosphere in the Classroom. Learning is the result for which we hope when pupils spend many hours each year in their classrooms. That there will be learning of some kind we do not doubt. The all-important factor for the social studies teacher is that the learning be worth while for the learner, that it increase his depth of personality, that it give him new tools for living, that he solve some of his own problems, and that he acquire an appreciation of some of the principles of our democratic way of life. The youth entering the social studies classroom must find there the challenging invitation to explore for himself some question which has attracted his interest. He must feel the assurance from his contact with the

[5] Fred T. Wilhelms, "Letter to a Teacher: On Handling Controversial Questions," *Progressive Education*, XXVI (October, 1948), pp. 8–12. Quoted by permission of the publisher.

teacher that a sympathetic interest will give him the freedom essential for such personal investigation. The physical arrangement of the social studies room should enable pupils to work alone and uninterrupted when they so desire. Furthermore, the youth should feel upon entering the social studies room that here is epitomized within the day's program the democratic way of life, for here are freedom of discussion and friendly disagreement, opportunity for achieving new understandings, the recognition by himself of his own worth and that of others, and the awareness of the group as a significant part of his life.

Such an atmosphere within the room is not the work of the teacher alone. It can be found only in those rooms where teacher and pupils have found a group-consciousness and hence maintain within their room the atmosphere which is an answer to their needs. The furniture and equipment of the room contribute significantly to this atmosphere, although they are not of first importance. The well-furnished social studies room must maintain the element of flexibility in its furniture arrangement. Today the room may be arranged for the meeting of a mock Security Council of the U.N., tomorrow its furniture may be placed in a circle for a group discussion, and upon another day it may be arranged for a panel to report to the group. At times it is not arranged by plan but is the result of normal groupings of pupil committees and individual pupils all busy on projects related to some problem which is being investigated. At all times there must be space for moving about and for ease of access to materials and equipment. Tables afford more adequate surface for much of the handwork pupils will do, although every pupil should have his own individual desk and chair. In the social studies room it seems that bulletin-board space is in greater demand than is blackboard space, so as to enable several classes to have their own display areas. Exhibits of relics and documents call for glass-doored cases. The departmental library should be in open shelves, where pupils may serve themselves. Maps need to be located where they may be viewed by the entire group at one time if necessary. There will undoubtedly be examples of pupil workmanship throughout the room. Displayed on bulletin boards and exhibit tables will be maps, graphs, charts, models, collections of relics, and pictures attesting to pupil interest and creative activity inspired by the work of the class. Large wall maps may be kept unrolled when they do not obstruct the view;

not only do they add to the appearance of the room, but they may serve as indirect learning opportunities. The social studies teacher should arrange for the placing in the room of several reproductions of recognized works of art significant to the social studies so that aesthetic attitudes may be cultivated. Pupils may find in creative art a means of interpreting some topic in the social studies. The resulting painting or drawing may become a semipermanent frieze or mural for that particular school year. Such handwork indicates the pupil interest and enthusiasm in the social studies activities. By sharing the management of the room with the pupils, the social studies teacher is able to maintain an attractive classroom to which pupils enjoy coming. In addition to these items which give character to the social studies classroom and are essential to its appearance, there are other problems of room management which the social studies teacher faces, such as the problem of lighting, of furniture selection and arrangement, of housing resource materials, and of planning a wise use of time in each class period. There may be other problems related to individual teaching situations, and one teacher may experience a problem where another finds none.

Summary. The beginning teacher of the social studies will encounter problems and difficulties which, as his experience grows, will gradually be eliminated. Understanding pupils in order to guide them in their learning activities will continue to be a responsibility as long as one teaches, but for the inexperienced teacher the problem may be of great importance. A failure to understand the pupil, being unwilling to devote time to what appears to be unrelated to the school task, may result in poor teaching. Various devices may be used to aid the teacher in gaining helpful information about individual pupils. With experience the teacher will determine methods which he finds most effective for his use. The important fact remains that the social studies teacher, in particular, must gain a fairly accurate knowledge of individual pupil traits and personality.

Careful planning by the social studies teacher is essential to effective teaching. In choosing topics for study, he must be guided by pupil interest and his own judgment based on valid educational principles expressive of American ideals. Supervising study, guiding discussion, and maintaining a democratic relationship among pupils are significant tasks for the social studies teacher. Closely related to the guiding of pupil activities is the important problem of aiding pupils in the solution of personal problems and in acquiring habits of critical thinking based on problem-solving techniques. In the social studies classroom the teacher and pupils will plan together the most desirable arrangement to bring about vital and worth-while learning experiences at all times and in answer to the needs of the group.

Questions on the Text

1. Why does the knowledge of individual pupil personality have a peculiar significance for a teacher of the social studies?
2. What advantage does a questionnaire have over an autobiography as a source of information about pupils?
3. What problems concerning the discussion period face the social studies teacher?
4. Why is problem solving an important technique for pupils to acquire?
5. Why should the social studies teacher have a thorough knowledge of topics which may be controversial?
6. Suggest ways by which the social studies teacher may encourage pupil participation in planning class activities.
7. Show how the personal problems of pupils are significant in social studies classes.
8. Why is teacher-pupil planning a desirable procedure in selecting subjects for study?
9. How may the individual be helped by learning to work in groups?
10. Why is supervised study of particular importance in the social studies?
11. What relationship exists between over-all unit objectives and the objectives found in a plan for a day's activity?
12. What ideas seem to be essential in an adequate lesson plan?
13. List the types of activity which may be classified as room management.
14. In what ways does room management contribute to successful teaching?
15. Suggest some problems of room management which may confront the social studies teacher in particular.

Suggested Activities

1. Draw a plan of a social studies classroom in detail as you would arrange it for maximum learning opportunity.
2. Suggest activities a social studies teacher might propose to challenge the brighter pupils.

3. Collect a file of free materials which might be used to illustrate a topic in one of the social studies.

4. Construct a lesson plan for a day's work in one of the social studies.

5. Plan and draw up a questionnaire which you believe would help you to understand a class of twelfth-grade pupils.

6. Select one of the social studies and list the principal topics you think should be covered in that area in a school year.

7. Investigate and report to the class means by which the slow learner in social studies may be guided to more successful achievement.

8. Prepare, as you would for teaching, a unit on a topic of your choosing and list devices you might use to encourage pupils to share in a teacher-pupil planning period.

9. Compile a list of possible controversial topics upon which a social studies teacher might need to be prepared.

10. Visit a social studies classroom to observe evidences of efficient management.

11. List the industries and institutions of your community which should be included in the laboratory experience of pupils in the social studies.

12. Construct a self-evaluation chart to be used by high-school pupils on such topics as personal manners, attitudes toward people, home relationships, or leisure-time use.

Selected References

BERGER, DONALD, "Handling Human Relations in Co-operative Learning," *Progressive Education,* XXVI (April, 1949), pp. 180–183.

BINING, ARTHUR C., and DAVID H. BINING, *Teaching the Social Studies in Secondary Schools,* New York: McGraw-Hill Book Company, Inc., 1941.

BOSSING, NELSON L., *Progressive Methods of Teaching in Secondary Schools,* Boston: Houghton Mifflin Company, 1935.

DAVIS, ALLISON, "Education and the Conservation of Human Resources," Washington, D.C., American Association of School Administrators, *Official Report,* 1949, pp. 74–83.

———, "Socio-economic Influences on Learning," *The Phi Delta Kappan,* XXXII (January, 1951), pp. 253–256.

———, "Ability and Survival," *The Survey,* LXXXVII (February, 1951), pp. 60–63.

ELLIOTT, LLOYD H., and SAMUEL E. DUNCAN, "Resource-use Education: A New Kind of School," *School and Society,* LXXII (July 29, 1950), pp. 71–73.

———, "Small High School Has Valuable Community Resources," *The Nation's Schools,* XLVI (October, 1950), pp. 47–48.

EVANS, HUBERT M., "The Social Nature of Problem Solving," *Progressive Education,* XXVI (April, 1949), pp. 161–165.

Fifteenth Yearbook, Claremont College Reading Conference, Claremont, Calif.: Claremont College Curriculum Laboratory, 1950.

Fostering Mental Health in Our Schools, Washington, D.C.: Association for Supervision and Curriculum Development, *Yearbook,* 1950.

Fourteenth Yearbook, Claremont College Reading Conference, Claremont, Calif.: Claremont College Curriculum Laboratory, 1949.

GOETTING, M. L., *Teaching in the Secondary School,* New York: Prentice-Hall, Inc., 1942.

GOULD, GEORGE, and GERALD ALLAN YOAKAM, *The Teacher and His Work,* New York: The Ronald Press Company, 1947.

JOHNSON, HENRY, *Teaching of History* (revised), New York: The Macmillan Company, 1940.

KING, NORRIS A., "Teachers Discover Their Community," *Educational Leadership,* VIII (December, 1950), pp. 176–180.

LEGGITT, DOROTHY, "The Adolescent in the Social Studies Classroom," *The Social Studies,* XL (October, 1949), pp. 253–256.

MAXWELL, C. R., and W. C. REUSSER, *Observation and Directed Training in Secondary Schools,* New York: Prentice-Hall, Inc., 1939.

MICHENER, JAMES A., "The Beginning Teacher," *In-service Growth of Social Studies Teachers,* Cambridge, Mass.: The National Council for the Social Studies, *Tenth Yearbook,* 1939.

ORTH, ALBERT A., "Planning the Social Studies Classroom," *American School Board Journal,* XCII (January, 1936), pp. 30–32.

RISK, THOMAS M., *Principles and Practices of Teaching in Secondary Schools,* New York: American Book Company, 1941.

SCHORLING, RALEIGH, *Student Teaching,* New York: McGraw-Hill Book Company, Inc., 1940.

SMITH, B. OTHANEL, "What Is a Social Problem?" *Progressive Education,* XXVI (April, 1949), pp. 165–168.

STANLEY, WILLIAM O., "What We Learn from Problem-Solving," *Progressive Education,* XXVI (April, 1949), pp. 173–179.

The Survey, LXXXVII (January, 1951), pp. 17–32.

THUT, I. N., and J. RAYMOND GERBERICH, *Foundations of Method for Secondary Schools,* New York, McGraw-Hill Book Company, Inc., 1949.

Toward Better Teaching, Washington, D.C.: Association for Supervision and Curriculum Development, *Yearbook,* 1949.

UMSTATTD, J. B., *Secondary School Teaching,* Boston: Ginn & Company, 1937.

WESLEY, EDGAR BRUCE, *Teaching the Social Studies in High Schools,* Boston: D. C. Heath and Company, 1950.

Chapter 4

THE SOCIAL STUDIES IN THE CURRICULUM

Preview. This chapter presents the contribution made by the social studies to the high-school curriculum as a means of providing experiences in democratic living to aid youth in solving their present and future problems. Present-day American life is surveyed briefly in order to point out those values which seem significant for all American citizens and which will be the focal points about which curriculum arrangements must be made. A discussion of trends evident in the organization of the curriculum with reference to the social studies reveals the importance of life-adjustment education as a development following the core curriculum and the general education program.

The Importance of the Social Studies in the Curriculum. The social studies in some form have been a significant part of the program of courses in American schools almost from the very beginning of public education in our country. It has been the accepted purpose of education to prepare youth for effective living. The social studies, dealing exclusively with man's problems, become essential in any program of education which aims to preserve known values and to achieve new heights of social relationships. To be sure, the names of courses have at times set boundaries to fields of learning which we may now regard as closely related in their contribution to solutions of social problems, but the goals of education have made the knowledge of this field essential, whether as separate courses or under the inclusive title of the social studies. In no other area of the school program is it possible to provide experiences which express and interpret life as effectively as in the social studies. That the trend in this field has been away from separate courses of definite subjects toward the general, inclusive area of the social studies is an indication of the effort of education to afford learning experiences of the greatest worth to the individual. No longer is it held to be all-important that the pupil master the material of a subject area, such as history, but rather that he find in history certain principles which, related to principles, ideas, or facts of sociology, of economics, or of political science, he may apply to a given problem as these together serve to guide him to a solution. Thus we see the curriculum pattern changing in response to the value placed on life in our society at the present as well as in the future. The problem of youth today is as significant as the problem of the adult in the future. Changes in the programs of schools are the reflection of the curriculum planner's understanding of society and society's problems, which are the guides in charting the social studies program.

American Life Today. As we observe the present American scene, we are aware of tensions, a sense of insecurity, a trend toward increased governmental control of individual life, and an evidence that the masses of our population do not have an understanding of the structure and condition of contemporary life. Within the past twenty-five years our country has changed rapidly, but under the stress of economic depression and war, citizens have not been able to stand aloof to view the scene and analyze the shifting pattern. The expansion of technical knowledge in the first quarter of the century has now, in mid-century, changed man's outlook on the world completely. Not only has it opened to him almost magical vistas of more abundant living, but it has also afforded him the terrorizing spectacle of the total destruction of civilization. The airplane, proved in the First World War, opened the door to the new age of One World, although it seems to have taken the atomic bomb to awaken the masses to this new condition of man; and as the great mass of humanity around the world stirs to adjust to life under the impact of this new conception, we find significant changes within our own country. The United States, once sitting comfortably and securely behind the natural barriers of two oceans, now thinks of its frontiers of defense as somewhere in central Europe and in the western Pacific Ocean. In addition to this change from isolationism we have seen our way of life challenged by a doctrine which is fundamentally opposed to the freedom of the individual. This conflict with our ideal, no longer a passive situation, has caused our people to think in terms of survival rather than the usual complacent indulgence of personal desires and ambitions. Technical knowledge, together with our ever-increasing population, has brought a new type of civilization to our country as contrasted with that at the turn of the century. Great metropolitan areas have developed as industry has expanded its need for workers. Family life has undergone changes, not only in the stability of the family, but in its service to its members. The family has become dependent upon many institutions and services. In contrast to life in the nineteenth century, we are now aware of the emphasis upon the specialized worker. This trend has influenced vocational training in many lines of work as it sets up specific requirements for meeting the economic, social, and physical service needs of our society.

Increased leisure time has enabled individuals to pursue many personal interests and avocational lines, to broaden their understanding of human nature by contact with other cultures through travel, and it has also created an influential factor in our society, that of commercial entertainment. As society spends time with motion pictures, radio, and television, it may find there entertainment only and unconsciously accept this experience as the standard by failing to use these media for educational advancement and personal enlightenment, for which they may be of outstanding worth in addition to the entertainment possibility.

Coupled with our growth in urban population has been the increasing mobility of our people, as vocational opportunity and the ease of movement made possible by the family automobile have invited them to change locations. The impact of war upon our society has been an additional influence in causing people to move from one place to another as defense work called for great numbers of workers.

Pressure groups, propaganda, advertising, and the false standards of a materialistic interpretation of living pull the individual in many directions, confuse and blind him to his own and society's needs and problems. Cynicism, distrust, and a hopelessness about the future seem to be increasing personal traits of our society. Racial discrimination and social-economic rivalry war against our proclaimed democracy.

Realizing the nature of our present society, the social studies teacher seeks for an adequate reply to the all-important question, "What shall the social studies contribute to our high school youth?" The youth who come from the homes of our land are individuals in the total complex social and economic pattern, and they reflect their families' reactions to the vast culture of which they are a part. How shall they best be armed to cope with this present culture and at the same time live to bring about a more democratic culture and consequently a more effective life for our society?

Values of the Social Studies to Be Provided in the Curriculum. In the light of the present cultural development of our country and in terms of an effective educational program, what are the values which need to be experienced by youth in order to equip them for more efficient living? This important question has been the problem facing all conscientious curriculum-planning groups. As we examine the results of investigation by some of the most outstanding groups concerned with the aim of education, we note a similarity in the values they have listed. The educational needs of youth as listed by the Educational Policies Commission in *Planning for American Youth* [1] are an expression of these values. It appears that in an interpretation of our present culture in terms of the recognized needs of youth, certain values seem to be outstanding and can serve as a guide in planning the curriculum. For the social studies these values appear to be world-mindedness, civic consciousness, economic intelligence, vocational understanding, and appreciation of family relationships. A brief examination of these values may suggest how each of them may serve as a guide in planning the social studies program, recognizing that such a program will vary from one community to another.

World-mindedness. This value may seem to involve an awareness of conditions far from the pupils' immediate experience, hence possessing a quality of unreality to them. The opposite is true. Successful living in our present requires that all citizens understand as much as possible of the problem of world relationships. This understanding, to be meaningful, must possess that element of human sympathy by which one individual may comprehend the cultural experience of another. Such an ability begins in every contact the individual has and is extended to those whom he may never have seen, entirely by his ability to imagine and visualize. As we recognize problems common to all people, we increase our ability to regard all people with more charitable attitudes. For our world today reduced to the conditions of a community neighborhood by man's scientific skill, we can hope for survival only through the cooperative spirit of understanding and by accepting all peoples as seekers for those elements of life satisfaction which we ourselves seek. The social studies, bet-

[1] *Planning for American Youth,* Washington, D.C.: National Association of Secondary-school Principals, Educational Policies Commission, 1944, p. 10.

ter than most areas of the curriculum, seem able to provide experiences that will enable youth to attain attitudes of world citizenship.

Civic consciousness. The privileges of the citizen in our democracy involve duties, obligations, and attitudes on the part of all our people. This value, civic consciousness, means more than the knowledge relating to voting and elections, significant as these are to our political well-being. We need to understand the structure of our local, state, and national government from the standpoint of why it is so planned and how it is an expression of the democratic principle. We need to know the relationship between all public institutions and society, to be able to evaluate their place in our society, and to understand how changes in institutional organization may develop in response to social needs. There must be an understanding on the part of all citizens that government and the institutions of our national life are significant only in terms of the individuals for whom they exist and through whom they function. This value has perhaps a more personal element as well. It involves a social sensitivity on the part of the individual which becomes a control to guide him in his community life. From it comes a pride in the well-kept appearance of his neighborhood, a consideration of his neighbor, a desire to serve in whatever way his ability may be of benefit to his community.

Economic intelligence. The knowledge of how to use money wisely seems to be of great importance today. On all sides we are confronted with advertisements of things essential to happiness. The vast wealth of our nation has made possible such a variety of material possessions that we may unconsciously estimate personal worth and the value of life itself in terms of material evidence. A sense of proportion in terms of economic values is an essential quality for all individuals. To know how to buy wisely, to be able to estimate worth through information on labels, to know how to budget income, are all significant elements in the consumer's effective direction of his living.

Vocational understanding. A helpful area of experience for all young people in the social studies is the exploration of many kinds of vocations. To become aware of the qualifications, responsibilities, problems, and opportunities in socially desirable occupations is a valuable background in helping youth decide on a choice of life work. Too often we find that someone has failed to choose a vocation in which he might have been eminently successful merely because he was unaware of that type of occupation at a time when he might have prepared for it. Furthermore, it is highly desirable that individuals know some of the types of activity and environmental conditions of many kinds of work in order to be more understanding of other people, to realize the necessity for the variety of occupations in modern society, and to respect those workers who serve in various capacities.

Appreciation of family relationships. Although many aspects of family life today are different from those of the American family of a half-century ago, youth must realize the fundamental importance of family relationships in our society. Here in this primary group the first lessons of democratic living are learned in the consideration of the welfare and interests of the entire group. Facing and sharing family problems develops responsibility, and participation in family projects such as outings, parties, or traditional family celebrations makes for a sense of security and belonging, essential to the mental health of the individual. It is desirable that leisure-time activities find some expression in the midst of the family in order for boys and girls to know that many personal interests can be developed within their immediate environment, that commercial entertainment of various types is not the sole outlet for leisure-time living. The satisfactions which result from the happy home life of a family are a means of easing tensions and preventing unhealthful attitudes. The economic life of the family may be a source for understanding of the place of work in the life of the individual, as the youth sees the need for gainful employment in socially desirable occupations. The importance of all work which serves society in constructive ways can be seen in the total work pattern of all the families in the community.

Trends in Social Studies Programs. The curriculum of the secondary school has undergone changes from time to time as teachers and planning groups have felt the need for more effective learning by pupils in the light of social needs. We have witnessed the change from the curriculum which was centered around subject matter to that one in which the immediate problems and interests of pupils became the controlling factors in curriculum planning. The change has not been rapid. Many factors enter the picture, and frequently when more effective plans have been attempted, the preparation for the new program has been inadequate; the entire school program may not have been involved; the type of community may not have been considered or its interests included. Teachers whose college preparation for teaching has held a subject-matter emphasis and specialization do not feel competent to launch out into untried areas. Too often their personal satisfaction in material mastered by pupils becomes the standard by which they evaluate their teaching.

As a result of the efforts to provide effective learning experiences for youth, we have seen a variety of procedures and organizations of the curriculum. There have been many variations of what appear to be some basic plans for organizing the social studies. There has also been disagreement in terminology, at times to such an extent that one cannot always accept a title as definitive of the program. The general types have been fusion courses, the broad-fields organization, correlation, and the core curriculum. The last named is sometimes spoken of as general education. Whatever the plan, each is an experiment moving away from the traditional subject fields in order to provide significant experiences for youth. The recognition by social studies teachers that valuable resources for the school program lie in the local community and in the questions raised by pupils is a significant factor in planning the social studies program.

The Subject-fields Organization. A brief description of the subject-fields organization will, perhaps, show by contrast some of the trends of more recent experiments in curriculum planning. The subject-fields plan, as the name implies, emphasizes separation of subject matter into channels of development or subjects. The mastery by the pupil of factual materials is the aim, and no attempt is made to use the subject matter in the solution of problems of pupil experience or of community interest. By the subject-matter approach to learning, the curriculum becomes a fixed routine and the school is set apart from the life of the community. Despite these disadvantages examples of this plan of organization can still be found in many secondary schools today.

The Core Curriculum. In the core curriculum the felt needs of youth become the guiding factor in planning the school program. This plan is not based on a particular body of subject matter but attempts to make use of any knowledge from all areas that might be pertinent to the problem being studied. Furthermore it is impossible for core programs in different schools to be similar, because the program must reflect the needs of youth in the specific school-community setting where the program is attempted. The core curriculum is an attempt to provide youth with an opportunity to experience activities in the school which will make their life in the community more meaningful to them and to establish patterns of approach to future life situations. Much planning is required of the teacher whose responsibility it becomes to guide pupil activities into educationally justifiable lines. It is desirable in the core program to plan for a given teacher to work with the same core class more than one year in order to be able to understand the individuals in the group more thoroughly. There have been many examples of successful core programs in the junior high schools of the nation, and some high schools have attempted this type of organization.

An excellent description of a typical core program is that found in the *Eighth Yearbook* of the John Dewey Society.[2] This description is summarized as follows:

1. It places value upon the individual and upon his group relationships as he develops.
2. The teacher of the course must be aware of the problems and traits of youth in relation to course planning.
3. It occupies a block of time in the school day sufficient for experiences necessary to realize the course objectives.
4. The course will not be a regrouping of existing courses but rather one in which life needs and interests of pupils select valuable materials from such areas of learning as may be concerned.
5. It emphasizes experience by pupils as an essential technique made possible by the increased time allotment.
6. The courses will serve as a considerable phase of the school guidance program, since the teacher will come to know pupil needs and interests more thoroughly.
7. The course calls for a close cooperation of all teachers and pupils concerned with planning a program in response to youth needs.

Planning the Core Program. It is obvious that a program based upon the present and future needs of youth must be under constant evaluation by teachers and pupils and will be to a considerable degree experimental. Such a program cannot be instituted easily. It requires much preparation and will grow over a period of years into a program which aims to provide meaningful experiences for youth. Much thoughtful planning and patient endeavor must be carried on by those concerned with it. If possible the teachers in a school should

[2] Hollis L. Caswell, ed., *The American High School,* John Dewey Society, *Eighth Yearbook,* New York: Harper & Brothers, 1946, pp. 118–119.

be given the privilege of choosing to work in the core program or not, as they prefer. There must be much investigation in methods and techniques of core-curriculum planning, and the interested teachers should be given opportunity to visit schools where core programs are in process in order to observe the procedure. Study groups within the school faculty are very helpful, as are also workshops where a curriculum specialist may be brought in to work with the teachers in planning the program. In all the planning one very essential element is the sharing with parents of the problem undertaken by the school. No core curriculum can be successful if it does not reflect the culture of the community of which the school is a part, but even more essential for the operation of the program is the need for understanding among parents of the purposes involved in the attempted curriculum. When parents understand the aims of the program, they will realize that in an easier way for pupils and in a more practical application of teaching, the basic values of our democratic way of life are here being made a living experience. The core program necessitates a revision in the arrangement of the daily schedule, as large blocks of time are required for the program. The teachers responsible for the core program should have time available within the school day for planning work, for conferences, and for study. In addition to this change in the school routine, there is an emphasis on many types of materials to provide learning opportunity. It is no longer possible to find the materials for learning in a lone textbook.

The Social Studies in the Core Curriculum. Although the program of the core curriculum moves away from a subject-defined plan, it is necessary to use the materials of subject areas in the solution of problems arising from the needs of pupils. Because the objectives of the social studies do to so great an extent parallel and even repeat the aims of education, it follows that this area will be a great contributor to the core program. Some schools have centered their core programs around problems which lie within the area of the social studies. It becomes the responsibility of those who plan the core program to enumerate the needs of youth and from this list to select those needs whose satisfactions can be drawn from the social studies area, choosing the elements which may afford most emphatically those ideas whose understanding will be a significant experience for youth. Thus the teacher in the core curriculum must be able to interpret the values of the social studies in keeping with the needs of pupils. The core teacher must be prepared in wide areas, or if teachers from specific subjects are to cooperate in the core program, each must be able to make use of his subject in terms of the broader need.

General Education. The general education curriculum seems to offer many advantages, as suggested by Quillen and Hanna: [3]

1. It cuts across subject-matter boundaries and draws upon material from all fields for the solution of problems.
2. It leaves the elective portion of the curriculum free to focus upon the special needs and interests of boys and girls.
3. It emphasizes the necessity for teachers to work cooperatively in planning the educational experiences of students.
4. It especially emphasizes the importance of student-teacher planning because it focuses upon the personal-social needs of pupils.
5. It provides for a larger block of time in which to consider problems.
6. It offers greater flexibility in organization, procedure, content, and materials.
7. It affords greater opportunity for more effective guidance because of the emphasis on the student and his needs and because of the longer period of time which general education teachers have with the students in their classes.
8. It emphasizes the development of the whole personality of the student and is as much concerned with the development of such characteristics as attitudes, interests, critical thinking, and social sensitivity as with the acquisition of skills and information.

The Social Studies in General Education. The program of general education is based on the theory that there exists a body of knowledge the command of which is an essential for all citizens. This general learning is fundamental for effective living in our democracy. The program of general education does not include vocational training or specializing in a given area. It is concerned with subject matter less as the end of the learning process than as a means toward an experience whose significance for the pupil will be in the background thus acquired as he is confronted with other problems. The experiences of pupils must not be in terms of preparation for adult life but must bring understanding of their present living, and by so doing, the individual will live more effectively and happily at the present

[3] I. James Quillen and Lavone A. Hanna, *Education for Social Competence,* Chicago: Scott, Foresman & Company, 1948, pp. 101–106. Quoted by permission of the publisher.

time, and, as the program continues consistent with his maturing, his adult years will be proportionately more satisfying. This program requires extensive acquaintance of the teacher with the pupil and with his specific needs and interests.

In many aspects the program of general education seems to resemble in its basic philosophy the program of the core curriculum. However, there may be one advantage of considerable significance in the general education plan in that under this program it is possible to proceed with less change of the school routine of each day, if that offers help in starting the program. Every course can become a course in general education. It is essential, first, that the administration and faculty agree on the purposes of education in this particular school and community. When the teacher is planning these objectives, sufficient time must be allowed to consider in detail the life of the community. Pupils, parents, and interested members of the community from business, industry, the professions, and various social agencies, such as youth organizations, churches, and libraries, should share in the planning. It seems that the essential values suggested above in this chapter as guides toward the objectives of the social studies today should be the focal point around which every planning group will center its thinking and decisions. It follows, then, that every teacher can interpret his courses in the light of these planned objectives. In the social studies each subject area may continue to be defined and yet be a course in the general education program, recognizing the experiences possible under the guise of this particular course which may satisfy the needs and interests of all youth in this school and community. The program may go further by removing subject boundaries and replacing history, civics, sociology, economics, American problems, and geography with the all-inclusive social studies, drawing from every included area whatever information may be pertinent to the solution of problems which confront pupils in their daily living.

Life-adjustment Education. In the process of curriculum development American education has moved far from the first effort, which saw education as a means toward college entrance and indirectly a vocational preparation in the limited plan of providing ministers for the church. Preparation for college and training to enter a vocation have become valuable services of our educational programs. However, as we have seen the tremendous growth of the American high school in which are enrolled more and more youth of secondary-school age, it has become apparent that all our worth-while planning and our attempt to make education meaningful has been a benefit for only a portion of all the youth who have experienced it. There are many boys and girls who will not or cannot go to college and who will not find in the high-school program a vocational interest of value to them. It is the purpose of life-adjustment education to follow the program of general education with such emphasis upon the needs of all youth that this total objective may be realized.

Undoubtedly in schools across the nation some such education has occurred in the past when there have been isolated instances of far-seeing teachers who have attempted to lead pupils into an understanding and appreciation of living in its limitless opportunity and challenge. With our present culture as involved and complicated as it has become, it is essential to the American way of life that all youth be given the opportunity to participate intelligently in our society. Only through such an educational provision can we hope to strengthen our democracy, to provide a resistance against the appeal of foreign ideologies to a portion of our citizens who might otherwise be unable to withstand the insidious approach. To aid the schools of all communities in starting life-adjustment programs, the Commission on Life Adjustment Education for Youth has proposed some guiding principles.[4] These are as follows:

1. The supreme test of life-adjustment education shall be in terms of individual development identified by accurate knowledge of each individual pupil's characteristics, his purposes, and those of society.
2. Secondary schools developing life-adjustment education seek to enroll, retain, and meet the needs of all normal adolescents who are not yet ready for next steps, such as full-time participation in safe and gainful occupations, or for further formal education.
3. Learning experiences required of all are selected and planned in terms of common recurring problems of living faced by all people rather than those of college-entrance requirements or other specialized needs of the relatively few.

[4] *Philosophy—Principles—Purposes,* Cheyenne, Wyo.: State Steering Committee, Wyoming Program of Life-adjustment Education, State Department of Education, *Bulletin* No. 1, pp. 8–9. Quoted by permission from State Department of Education, Cheyenne, Wyoming.

4. The emphasis is upon direct pupil-teacher planning, sharing, and participation in real-life experience while seeking solutions to individual, social, and civic problems.

5. Administrators in schools which stress life-adjustment education for every youth will organize and administer through the active participation of pupils, parents, and teachers, as well as of organized civic, lay, industrial, and business groups.

6. Records and data are used in counseling with pupils and parents, improving instruction, developing all desirable latent qualities of pupils' individual self-approval, placement, and as basic material for continuing curriculum evolution.

7. Life-adjustment-education programs are evaluated in terms of desirable changes in pupil behavior rather than in terms of the mastering of abstract concepts in logically organized subject-matter courses.

Social Studies Topics in an Education for Life Adjustment. As has been previously stated, the program of life-adjustment education must serve the needs of the youth involved and must reflect the life of the local community. These two controlling groups will apply to their own situation the meaning for them of the essential values of our culture which education must foster. Each school will proceed in its own manner to achieve a desirable program, using all available aids for effective application of its proposed methods and revising its program through experiment and reevaluation. Whether the planning group removes subject boundary lines in a complete revision of the school program, or simply accepts each social studies area as an opportunity for education for life adjustment, a thorough understanding of the following general topics from the various areas seems essential. Each school will adapt these as it sees its own needs; there may be additions in each area.

I. World History
   - *A.* Asiatic peoples and problems
   - *B.* Nationalism; the rise of France, Italy, Germany
   - *C.* The Industrial Revolution
   - *D.* Humanitarianism
   - *E.* Scientific advance
   - *F.* International cooperation
   - *G.* The air-age world

II. United States History
   - *A.* Modern American culture
   - *B.* Our evolving democracy

   C. Development of government
   D. Growth of "Big Business"
   E. Social reform
   F. Development of transportation
   G. International relations

III. Civics
   A. Local, state, and national government
   B. Community relationships
   C. Vocational guidance
   D. Conservation

IV. American Problems
   A. Health
   B. Labor and management
   C. Consumer education
   D. Family life
   E. Crime; juvenile delinquency
   F. Conservation
   G. Communication; propaganda
   H. Recreation
   I. Vocational guidance
   J. The U.N.

Curricular Aspects of Social Studies in Grades 13 and 14. Many city school systems are expanding their organization to include two more years of work. Likewise the trend is toward a growth in the number of community and junior colleges. In such cases the question of curricular content arises. The social studies area presents a most vital part of such content. All that has been said above regarding American life today, values of the social studies, trends in the program, and the social studies in current organization patterns remains pertinent. In brief, these upper two years offer a medium through which to do better that which was being attempted in less time.

General Education in the Social Studies, by Levi,[5] has gone more into detail on the matter of content than most works dealing with this subject. After stating the guiding principles involved, it is suggested that this two-year course in social studies be required of students and comprise the material embraced in the following outline:

[5] Albert William Levi, *General Education in the Social Studies,* Washington, D.C.: American Council on Education, 1948, Chap. IX and XI. Quoted by permission of the publisher.

General Outline

Part I: The Organization of Social Living
(Semester 1)

A. The individual in a world of social conflict
1. The individual in an industrial world
2. The problem of agrarian poverty
3. Poverty and underprivileged groups
4. The unemployed individual
5. The problem of delinquent youth
6. The individual and labor conflict
7. Black men in a white man's world

B. From the individual to the community
1. The social conditioning of the human person
2. The community setting of individual life; the structure and functioning of the American community
   a. The middle western community
   b. The southern town
   c. The Yankee city
   d. The tools and concepts of community life

C. From the community to the total society
1. The tools of social analysis
2. The factors of the social environment
3. The structure of the social environment
4. The variations of culture
5. Social dynamics: the nature of cultural change

Part II: The Historical Development of Modern Society
(Semester 2)

A. The structure of medieval society
1. The nature and decay of the feudal age

B. The beginnings of modern social change
1. The expansion of Europe
2. The rise of the Western state system

C. Technology and the acceleration of social change
1. The beginnings of the Industrial Revolution
2. The diffusion of technology and its culture

D. The formation and development of an American society
1. The American Revolution
2. The founding of the American government
3. The irresistible expansion of the United States
4. Nationalism and sectional controversy

5. Industrialization and the growth of big business
6. The development of an American foreign policy

E. American society in a changing world
1. The liberal movement in the Western world
2. The American empire: the growth of imperialism
3. The first World War
4. Groupings toward a consciousness of the need of world-order
5. Domestic trends in totalitarian states
6. Postwar developments in the democracies
7. The second World War
8. A new age of revolution?

Part III. The Institutions and Problems of the Modern World
(Semesters 3 and 4)

A. The social institutions and problems of the modern world
1. The problems of family life
2. The problem of housing
3. Recreation in the modern world
4. The problem of health
5. Education in the modern world
6. Religion in the modern world
7. The problem of delinquency and crime
8. The problem of group prejudice
9. The problem of population

B. The economic institutions and problems of the modern world
1. Toward an understanding of economic institutions and problems
2. The methods and problems of production in the modern world
3. How goods and services are exchanged in the modern world
4. The distribution of the national income
5. The worker in an industrial world
6. The farmer in an industrial world
7. The consumer in an industrial world
8. Business and government
9. Economics and international life

C. The political institutions and problems of the modern world
1. Democracy as a way of life
2. The organization of the American democratic idea
   a. The legislative process
   b. The courts and the administration of justice
   c. The executive and public administration
3. The democratic state and the citizen
   a. Democracy and the service state

   b. Taxation in the service state
   c. The democratic process
4. International democracy and the problem of war and peace
   a. The second World War
   b. Internal organization
   c. American foreign policy
5. The problems and prospects of political democracy
   a. The future of the democratic idea

The frame of reference underlying the three divisions of the course is that "the seemingly discrete fields of geography, history, psychology, sociology, ethnology, economics, and political science constitute one single 'science of society.'"[6]

Herskovits[7] describes well the two-year course divided into two parts. The first carries the name, The Bases of Social Life. Much of the content is found in a study of the great civilizations of antiquity as well as the medieval and Renaissance periods of European history. All this is directed toward a better understanding of the forces that have produced the modern world in which we live. The sophomore course is entitled Modern Society. How the present is related to the period of migration from the old is stressed. Social, economic, and political forces are taught in an integrated manner. Interwoven with these is an emphasis on the structure of today's industrial and technological society.

Knowlton[8] has described the two-year social science program at Cazenovia. In order to understand the contemporary world, three periods a week are given to the geographic, historical, governmental, and economic considerations involved. The second year places emphasis on the American cultural scene, starting intensive study on the period dated by the end of the War Between the States and ending with the present.

Stutz and Layman,[9] in describing the social studies portion of a basic college program, indicate that the materials should come from

[6] *Ibid.*, p. 237.

[7] Melville J. Herskovits, "The Social Science Units of Northwestern University Liberal Arts Program," *Journal of General Education*, I (April, 1947), pp. 216–233.

[8] Knowlton, D. C., "Map Project for the Junior College," *Junior College Journal*, XVII (October, 1946), pp. 53–60.

[9] F. H. Stutz and M. E. Layman, "Social Education in a Basic College Program," *Social Education*, X (November, 1946), pp. 305–306.

anthropology, economics, geography, history, philosophy, political science, and sociology. One of the courses, called Social Science, is divided into nine parts. Typical of these are "Relationship between Man and Government," "Organization for Production," and "The Maintenance of International Peace." The other course, History of Civilization, is divided into ten parts, with such titles as "The Roman World Order," "The Christian World of the Middle Ages," and "Ordeal of Our Times: the Second World War."

Elder [10] offers a description of work at Colgate that definitely places its emphasis upon current affairs. It is for freshmen, extends over a full year, and meets three times a week. Examples of topics are "The Indian and His Groups," "Structure, Function, and Change," and "Leadership and Authority in Groups." A very pertinent quotation follows: "There is no one engaged in teaching the course who does not believe that Colgate students who have gone through it will examine changing social situations more objectively than they might otherwise have done and will in later years as community leaders be more conscious of the needs to adapt social, economic, and political institutions to changing conditions."

Mendenhall [11] once expressed the idea that the work and abilities of an expert historian have an apt place in the survey course. The abilities to determine facts, weigh evidence, judge the complexities of civilization, and identify bias were specifically mentioned.

The Harvard Report [12] was probably as extensively read and exerted as much influence as any work of similar proportions in recent years in the field of general education. A plea was made for a required course for all students called Western Thought and Institutions. It was proposed that it would include a historical analysis of certain significant movements and changes in Western society together with the reading of substantial portions of certain of the classics of political, economic, and social thought which those changes have helped to produce.[13]

It will be seen from the foregoing discussion that most authorities

[10] R. E. Elder, "Problem Method in Freshman Social Science at Colgate University," *Teachers College Journal*, XIX (May, 1948), pp. 122–123.

[11] Thomas C. Mendenhall, "The Introductory College Course in Civilization," *American Historical Review*, XLIX (July, 1944), pp. 681–684.

[12] *General Education in a Free Society, Report of the Harvard Committee*, Cambridge, Mass.: Harvard University Press, 1945, Chap. V.

[13] *Ibid.*, p. 214.

take the point of view that general education in the social studies extends through and ends with the completion of the fourteenth year. In the end the individual who has taken the work should have had a superior type of life-adjustment experiences. Grades 13 and 14 of a typical public school system or a regular junior college ordinarily require this work. The modern social scene is a laboratory from which content is drawn. A fusion of all the social studies thus becomes easy because humanity itself is considered from all approaches as it relates to individual achievement.

Summary. It has been the purpose of this chapter to show the trend of curriculum organization from the traditional subject-fields plan to the last experimental attempt to provide meaningful life experiences through the social studies in the form of the life-adjustment-education program. Emphasis is given to the need for having the program planned by representatives of the community and the school. Individual pupil needs and interests are pointed out as of controlling importance when the life-adjustment program attempts to function. With the recognition of the possibility that clearly defined subject areas within the social studies, or the general area of social studies without the traditional subject boundaries, may be followed in the life-adjustment approach, the significant topics of the entire field as related to the essential values of our democratic way of life are indicated.

Questions on the Text

1. What is the theme of the social studies?
2. Of what significance are general social conditions to the high-school curriculum?
3. Compare the objectives of the social studies with the general objectives of education.
4. In what way is life-adjustment education a reinterpretation of general education?
5. In what way may life-adjustment education seem to resemble a core curriculum?
6. Suggest criteria to be used as a guide in planning a social studies program.
7. Describe the change in theories of education which has occurred in this century.

8. Why is a subject-fields curriculum unsatisfactory in answering the needs of youth?

9. List the characteristics of a core curriculum.

10. What advantages may be expected from a core curriculum?

11. Why does the social studies area invite core-curriculum organization?

12. Discuss the possible obstacles or disadvantages of the core curriculum.

13. How does the core curriculum make possible a more effective guidance program?

14. Give some practices in determining content of social studies courses in grades 13 and 14 that have fairly general acceptance.

15. Summarize some specific examples of courses offered at these levels.

Suggested Activities

1. Plan a program for the social studies using a core-type organization.

2. Visit a school where a core curriculum is in progress to investigate (*a*) teacher and pupil cooperation in planning; (*b*) units of study; (*c*) time allotments; (*d*) grades involved; (*e*) use of materials and equipment.

3. Investigate the core programs of three or more school systems to discover ways in which they are alike and ways in which they are unlike.

4. Construct a diagram showing grade placement and time allotment for a core curriculum for grades 7 through 14.

5. Make a list of disadvantages of the core-type program and match the items of the list with suggested remedies.

6. Plan a unit of work for a core-curriculum program at junior-high level.

7. Make a detailed plan to be followed by a high-school faculty in planning a core curriculum.

8. Visit a school where a life-adjustment program is being attempted. Investigate the procedures followed in social studies courses and discover what topics are being considered.

9. Evaluate the content of the courses given in this chapter, with suggested additions or deletions.

10. Collect materials on planning a life-adjustment program which would help a faculty in starting such a program.

11. Visit the social studies classes in either a junior college or grades 13 and 14 of a 6-4-4 organization in a public school. Compare and contrast the program being offered with the implications of the present chapter.

12. Select one or more of the references found at the close of this chapter

for reading and summarization. If preferred, use library guides to educational periodicals and find references of purely personal interest related to these topics.

Selected References

Alberty, Harold, *Reorganizing the High-school Curriculum,* New York: The Macmillan Company, 1947.

Aldrich, J. C., "Freshmen Deal with Realities," *Educational Leadership,* VI (November, 1948), pp. 88–91.

Alexander, William M., "Do New Courses of Study Help Social Studies Teachers?" *Social Education,* VI (November, 1942), pp. 315–317.

Bining, Arthur C., Walter H. Mohr, and Richard H. McFeely, *Organizing the Social Studies in Secondary Schools,* New York: McGraw-Hill Book Company, Inc., 1941.

Bostwick, Prudence, "A High-school Core Program," *Curriculum Journal,* IX (May, 1938), pp. 204–207.

Cartwright, William H., "Evolution of American History in the Curriculum," *The Study and Teaching of American History,* Washington, D.C.: The National Council for the Social Studies, *Seventeenth Yearbook,* 1946, pp. 17–34.

Cassels, John M., "The Rise of Consumer Education," *Education,* LX (January, 1940), pp. 268–272.

Caswell, Hollis L., ed., *The American High School,* John Dewey Society, *Eighth Yearbook,* New York: Harper & Brothers, 1946.

Cordier, Ralph W., "The Social Studies in Perspective," *Social Education,* IX (January, 1945), pp. 29–31.

Crary, Ryland W., "Challenging Areas in the Developing Social Studies Curriculum," *Teachers College Record,* XLVIII (December, 1946), pp. 140–147.

Dotson, G. E., "Terminal Education Program in the Junior College," *National Association of Secondary-school Principals Bulletin,* XXXII (March, 1948), pp. 125–133.

Douglass, Harl R., ed., *The High-school Curriculum,* New York: The Ronald Press Company, 1947.

———, *Education for Life Adjustment,* New York: The Ronald Press Company, 1950.

Education for All American Youth, Washington, D.C.: Educational Policies Commission, National Education Association and Association of School Administrators, 1940.

Education for International Understanding in American Schools, Washington, D.C.: Committee on International Relations, National Education Association, Association for Supervision and Curriculum Development, and The National Council for the Social Studies, 1948.

EDWARDS, NEWTON, "The Place of United States History in General Education," *Social Education,* VII (December, 1943), pp. 347–351.

ELDER, R. E., "Problem Method in Freshman Social Science at Colgate University," *Teachers College Journal,* XIX (May, 1948), pp. 122–123.

FAUNCE, ROLAND C., and NELSON L. BOSSING, *Developing the Core Curriculum,* New York: Prentice-Hall, Inc., 1951.

General Education in a Free Society, Report of the Harvard Committee, Cambridge, Mass.: Harvard University Press, 1945.

GRAVES, A. D., "The Core Curriculum and the Social Studies," *California Schools,* XV (September, 1944), pp. 215–221.

Group Planning in Education, Washington, D.C.: Department of Supervision and Curriculum Development, National Education Association, *1945 Yearbook.*

HAND, HAROLD C., "The Case for the Planned Curriculum," *Educational Administration and Supervision,* XXXIII (April, 1947), pp. 193–200.

HERSKOVITS, MELVILLE J., "The Social Science Units of the Northwestern University Liberal Arts Program," *Journal of General Education,* I (April, 1947), pp. 216–223.

HOCKETT, J. A., "The Nature and Function of Social Studies in Education," *Review of Educational Research,* XI (October, 1941), pp. 421–428.

HUNSUCKER, F., "Social Studies Curriculum Revision in Grades Seven and Eight," *Teachers College Journal* (March, 1947), pp. 104–108.

HUNT, ERLING M., "Interrelationships in the Curriculum," *The Study and Teaching of American History,* Washington, D.C.: The National Council for the Social Studies, *Seventeenth Yearbook,* 1946.

KELLEY, EARL C., *Education for What Is Real,* New York: Harper & Brothers, 1947.

KING, A. H., "From History to Social Studies in the Secondary School," *Education Digest,* XII (September, 1946), pp. 42–47.

KNOWLTON, D. C., "Map Project for the Junior College," *Junior College Journal,* XVII (October, 1946), pp. 53–60.

Learning the Ways of Democracy, Washington, D.C.: Educational Policies Commission, National Education Association and Association of School Administrators, 1940.

LEVI, ALBERT WILLIAM, *General Education in the Social Studies,* Washington, D.C.: American Council on Education, 1940, Chaps. IX and X.

———, "Social Beliefs of College Students," *Journal of Higher Education,* XV (March, 1944), pp. 127–134.

MACKENZIE, GORDON N., and HUBERT EVANS, "The Challenge of General Education for the Secondary School," *The Journal of General Education,* I (October, 1946), pp. 64–71.

MCCLOSKEY, GORDON, "Economics in the Functional Curriculum," *Economic Education,* Washington, D.C.: The National Council for the Social Studies, *Eleventh Yearbook,* 1940, pp. 92–100.

MENDENHALL, THOMAS C., "The Introductory College Course in Civilization," *American Historical Review,* XLIX (July, 1944), pp. 681–684.

MERIDETH, DOROTHY, "Secondary-school Social Studies in 1945," *Secondary Education,* IX (December, 1945), pp. 345–349.

———, "Changing Content of American History Courses," *The Study and Teaching of American History,* Washington, D.C.: The National Council for the Social Studies, *Seventeenth Yearbook,* 1946, pp. 35–57.

MIHANOVICH, CLEMENT S., "Sociology: Yesterday and Today," *Social Studies,* XXXI (October, 1940), pp. 251–252.

MUDD, DOROTHY A., *A Core Program Grows,* Bel Air, Md.: Board of Education of Harford County, 1949.

NICKELL, VERNON L., and HARL R. DOUGLAS, "How Can We Develop an Effective Program of Education for Life Adjustments?" *National Association of Secondary-school Principals Bulletin,* XXXIII (April, 1949), pp. 153–159.

PARHAM, L. C., "Needed Changes in the Social Studies," *National Association of Secondary-school Principals Bulletin,* XXX (March, 1946), pp. 131–133.

PERRIGO, LYNN I., "The Social Studies Tomorrow," *Social Education,* IX (November, 1945), pp. 313–314.

Philosophy—Principles—Purposes, Cheyenne, Wyo.: State Steering Committee, Wyoming Program of Life-adjustment Education, State Department of Education, *Bulletin* No. 1.

Planning for American Youth, Washington, D.C.: National Association of Secondary-school Principals, 1944.

QUILLEN, I. JAMES, "Current Trends in Social Studies," *California Journal of Secondary Education,* XIX (November, 1944), pp. 372–375.

——— and LAVONE A. HANNA, *Education for Social Competence,* Chicago: Scott, Foresman & Company, 1948.

REDFIELD, R., "Social Science in the Atomic Age," *Journal of General Education,* I (January, 1947), pp. 120–124.

REHAGE, K. J., "Social Studies in a Junior-high-school Program," *School Review,* LIII (October, 1945), pp. 471–477.

ROMINE, STEPHEN, "Improving the Secondary-school Curriculum," *Educational Administration and Supervision,* XXXIII (November, 1947), pp. 385–398.

SHANTZ, JOHN H., and ROBERT T. STICKLER, "How Can Consumer Education Improve Our Instructional Program?" *National Association of Secondary-school Principals Bulletin,* XXXIII (May, 1949), pp. 65–70.

SIBLEY, ELBRIDGE, "The Place of Social Science in General Education," *The Journal of General Education,* I (October, 1946), pp. 52–57.

SINGER, M. B., "Social Sciences Program in the College of the University of Chicago," *Journal of General Education,* II (April, 1948), pp. 251–258.

SMITH, GLADYS L., "Student Differences and the Core Program," *Adapting Instruction in the Social Studies to Individual Differences,* Washington, D.C.: The National Council for the Social Studies, *Fifteenth Yearbook,* 1944, pp. 45–54.

SMITH, JAMES L., "Economics in the Curriculum," *Social Studies,* XXXV (January, 1944), p. 33.

SMITH, VICTOR C., "A Practical Function Social Studies Program," *Secondary Education,* XII (November, 1945–January, 1946), pp. 9–11.

The Social Studies Curriculum, Washington, D.C.: Department of Superintendence, National Education Association, *Fourteenth Yearbook,* 1936.

SPEARS, HAROLD, *The Emerging High School Curriculum and Its Direction,* New York: American Book Company, 1948.

SPIESEKE, ALICE WINIFRED, "Current Trends in the Selection and Organization of Content," *The Study and Teaching of American History,* Washington, D.C.: National Council for the Social Studies, *Seventeenth Yearbook,* 1946, pp. 58–63.

STELTER, ROSE, "Building Courses to Meet Student Needs," *Social Education,* V (January, 1941), pp. 41–44.

STITZ, F. H., and M. E. LAYMAN, "Social Education in a Basic College Program," *Social Education,* X (November, 1946), pp. 305–306.

Suggestions for Starting a Program of Action, Cheyenne, Wyo.: State Steering Committee, Wyoming Program of Life-adjustment Education, State Department of Education, *Bulletin* No. 2.

TABA, HILDA, and WILLIAM VAN TIL, eds., "Curriculum Problems," *Democratic Human Relations,* Washington, D.C.: National Council for the Social Studies, *Sixteenth Yearbook,* 1945, pp. 21–62.

———, Commission on Curriculum Planning and Development, "The Imperative Needs of Youth of Secondary-school Age," *National Association of Secondary-school Principals Bulletin,* XXXI (March, 1947).

The Social Studies in General Education—A Report of the Committee on the Function of the Social Studies in General Education for the Commission on Secondary-school Curriculum, New York: Appleton-Century-Crofts, Inc., 1940.

The Social Studies in Secondary Education, Report of the Committee on Social Studies of the Commission on the Reorganization of Secondary

Education of the National Education Association, Washington, D.C.: U.S. Bureau of Education, *Bulletin* No. 28, 1916.

Toward Better Teaching, Washington, D.C.: Association for Supervision and Curriculum Development, National Education Association, 1949.

Toward a New Curriculum, Washington, D.C.: Department of Supervision and Curriculum Development, National Education Association, *1944 Yearbook,* 1944.

TRYON, ROLLA M., *The Social Sciences as School Subjects, Part XI, Report of the Commission on the Social Studies,* New York: Charles Scribner's Sons, 1935.

TYLER, RALPH, "How Can We Improve High-school Teaching?" *The School Review,* LVI (September, 1948), pp. 387–399.

VOLWILER, A. T., "American History in Schools and Colleges," *Social Studies,* XXXV (November, 1944), pp. 293–297.

WALKER, E. R., "General Education in the Social Sciences," *Southwestern Social-science Quarterly,* XXIX (June, 1948), pp. 15–26.

WESLEY, E. B., "National Objectives and the Social Studies Curriculum," *Scholastic,* XXXIX (Oct. 27, 1941), Part 1.

———, *American History in Schools and Colleges,* New York: The Macmillan Company, 1944.

———, *Teaching the Social Studies in High Schools,* Boston: D. C. Heath and Company, 1950.

WOLFE, ALICE R., "Social Science in a Junior-high-school Core Program," *Social Education,* V (April, 1941), pp. 280–282.

ZIMMERMAN, G. FRANK, and STEWART B. HAMBLEN, "Consumer Education and the Social Studies," *Social Education,* VI (April, 1942), pp. 157–159.

Chapter 5

TEXTBOOKS AND THE SOCIAL STUDIES

Preview. The inclusion of a chapter entitled Textbooks and the Social Studies does not at all imply that we should be using the textbook method of teaching. At least we should not have it in its traditional and bad form. Certainly, it should not be the plan sought for use; in fact, it is scarcely conceivable that it needs to be made a matter of resort. Rather, the chapter is presented with the thought that textbooks and other materials are essential in working with a class following any method. The selection and adoption of textbooks is a matter of prime concern in any secondary-school area. In the social studies the importance of the task assumes unusual proportions. First, the teachers of these subjects actually face a grave responsibility in shaping attitudes and formulating ideals on the part of tomorrow's adult citizens. Second, the professional group and lay public both entertain a feeling of being skilled in judging these books—a skill that is not claimed to any such degree in other fields. This chapter will attempt to present pertinent historical facts related to social studies textbook selection, criteria that might well be applied in an effort to select these books objectively and scientifically, and comments related to the textbook method of teaching.

Groups That Have Been Interested in Social Studies Textbooks. In attempting to treat a topic of this nature in a historical fashion it is not the intention of the authors to suggest approval or disapproval of present practices or past status of individuals, groups, or organizations. Rather, the desire is to point out relationships to the present topic, namely, textbook selection. In the social studies area we have regularly had a generous amount of suggestions coming from nonacademic sources. Lawmakers have felt that the objectives of education in a democracy are met to such a large extent in this area that they have taken a hand. Diversity of interest in various sections of our country has led to a more critical examination of our textbooks than has been customary in smaller and more compact areas. Patriotic organizations have been quite outspoken in their opinions as to what should not be included as content material. Groups representing racial and religious interests have examined our books to determine what favorable or unfavorable comments might be found. Various organizations representing conflicting economic interests have praised or condemned textbooks that were in use in the schools.

None charged with the responsibility for writing or selecting textbooks would fail to approve heartily of a friendly and constructive interest in the matter. Any criticism of such nature that might be offered should be accepted gratefully and weighed carefully. On the other hand, it would be too much to ask textbook writers to distort facts for the sole purpose of aggrandizing the place or the efforts of any one group in American history or in contemporary affairs. No doubt organizational or regional enthusiasm has blinded many sponsors of such efforts to the facts of what they were really promoting.

Legal requirements in the social studies have tended generally in the direction of requiring a study of our national history, state and local history, and the machinery of government. These requirements have frequently been enlarged upon following periods of national crises. (See Chapter 15 for a discussion of recent changes related to the teaching of social studies.) To the extent that sectionalism has had an influence, it too has sometimes taken legal expression in demanding that textbooks not be "partisan" in their manner of presentation. In the South the United Confederate Veterans in 1892 became very active in their efforts to get proper textbooks adopted.[1] They felt that some were definitely prejudiced against the South, that some made an honest failure to present facts correctly, and that others were wholly suitable for use in the schools. It was probably this group as much as any other that brought into popular usage the expression *The War Between the States.* Simultaneously, the Grand Army of the Republic was studying the chapters dealing with Southern history and usually condemned the efforts of Northern writers who presented the more recent epochs.

Something of a wave of hysteria swept over the country following the First World War, based on the fear that our textbooks had a pro-

[1] *Minutes of the Third Annual Meeting and Reunion of the Confederate Veterans—1892,* as quoted by Bessie Louise Pierce, *Public Opinion and the Teaching of History,* New York: Alfred A. Knopf, Inc., 1926, p. 146.

British emphasis. Apparently the chapters on the Revolutionary War received most review in this connection. Popular newspapers were very active in stressing this "propitiatory spirit toward England" that they felt was being fostered in school textbooks.[2] Many authors generally regarded as America's foremost scholars and writers were thoroughly censured.

In some manner each of the following patriotic organizations has shown an interest in points that should be emphasized in social studies textbooks: Sons of the American Revolution, Descendants of the Signers of the Declaration of Independence, The Veterans of Foreign Wars, and The American Legion. As one would naturally suspect, these groups desired that heroism of illustrious characters, development of national traditions, and superiority of the American way of life should be stressed. Specific textbooks, individual authors, and periodicals which failed to meet the standards expected were on occasion identified and appraised. O. K. Armstrong's article, "Treason in Textbooks," published in the *American Legion Magazine* (September, 1940) is illustrative.

The following are among the organizations that have been actively interested at some time in social studies textbooks from the standpoint of a racial interest: Steuben Society of America, Ancient Order of Hibernians, and National Association for the Advancement of Colored People. Many immigrant groups develop fraternal societies. Not among the least of their interests is the manner in which their national origins are discussed in school textbooks. Closely related in intensity of feeling is the interest that religious groups have in textbooks. The particular needs of some have been met by writing special textbooks for their use.

To the extent that there is a divergent point of view on the part of the leaders of labor and the leaders of capital, one would naturally expect each to be vitally interested in secondary-school textbooks. Probably the American Federation of Labor has been most active in this connection. As early as 1903 it was advocating that these textbooks be written with a purpose of presenting ideas of the dignity of manual labor, the importance to society of the role of labor, and the desirability of elevating the place of labor as an entire group. Later investigations showed that the organization was pleased with the tendency of authors to deal with the broader aspects of social devel-

[2] Pierce, *ibid.*, deals with this topic in detail.

opment and current problems rather than with formal organization of government, military events, and generalities. The examinations of textbooks to assure that the viewpoints of labor are properly handled have been made not by labor organizations alone but by scholars who have a deep-seated interest in the problems involved and a sincere desire to fathom the trends of the times.[3]

A charge of recent decades has been that "big business" has exercised too much influence on the writing of social studies textbooks and likewise upon teaching within the classes. Some have questioned the sincerity of the motives of corporations in furnishing illustrative materials, pamphlets, visual aids, etc. As a result of a government investigation by the Federal Trade Commission in 1928 to determine the methods used by holding companies to acquaint the public with facts relative to the public utility industry, it was found that the organizations thought that many texts in civics and economics showed a definite bias in favor of government ownership and misrepresentations of the utility industry. Probably no one author in human experience ever received more wholesale criticism for his textbook productions than did Harold Rugg. The volumes most critically examined were those six designed for junior-high-school textbooks in social studies. Business leaders felt that he belittled the grandeur of famous early Americans and that propaganda for a much-changed social order was constantly kept before the pupil reader.

The following quotation from one critic [4] shows clearly the nature of the attacks made upon these textbooks:

> There we have the technique of Rugg's system of indoctrination. First, in developing in the child an "attitude of expectancy, of change. . . ." Second, the student is given a distorted picture of conditions in America, together with shameful propaganda material pointing to utter failure as the result of the workings of our present system of private enterprise and the republican form of government. Third, the very beginnings of this nation and the founding of our present social and economic organization are brought into question, together with the motives of the founders.

[3] *Control of Social Studies Textbooks,* issued for the National Council for the Social Studies in cooperation with the Research Division of the National Education Association, May, 1941, gives a fuller discussion of the material described in the three preceding paragraphs.

[4] Alfred T. Falk, *The Rugg Technique of Indoctrination,* as quoted in *Control of Social Studies Textbooks,* p. 25.

American history is made a drab story of selfishness, greed, imperialist expansion, exploitation, and class antagonisms. Fourth, the coming era is placed within the students' vision. It is to be an era of Marxian Socialism embroidered with technocracy!

As one might expect, author Rugg did not pass these criticisms by passively. He wrote a book of 350 pages, entitled *That Men May Know,* in which he set forth his purpose in writing textbooks. Furthermore, many periodicals came to his defense, principally on the grounds of academic freedom.

The one organization representing the leaders of industry in America that became very active following the attack on the Rugg books is the National Association of Manufacturers. In 1940 it announced that it would shortly undertake an analysis of secondary-school textbooks. Educators were greatly aroused over motives, means to be employed, and results that would follow. The entire venture proved much less exciting than was expected at first. Ralph W. Robey, assistant professor of banking at Columbia University, was placed in charge of a committee to abstract the books. It was decided not to interpret various authors' points of view; rather, a statement of grade for which the book was intended, summary of table of contents, and pertinent quotations were given. The following abstract of Magruder's *American Government* is illustrative:

AUTHOR: Magruder, Frank Abbott

TITLE: *American Government*

PUBLISHER: Allyn and Bacon, New York, 1939, 710 pp.

EXPLANATION: This text on American government for high school use, is divided into ten units and forty chapters. The first unit deals with the development of government in general. Then the various phases of American government and politics are taken up in the following order: legislative powers, the executive department, administrative agencies, the judiciary and civil rights, political rights and practices, the states, local government, suffrage. The last unit deals with the betterment of society.

ABSTRACT: The following two quotations are illustrative of some of the discussion:

ON CONCENTRATION OF CAPITAL:

"One outcome of the conditions mentioned above is the concentration of capital, especially in large cities. Advanced nations have developed expensive factory machines which make large-scale production profitable. The maintenance of such factories requires large capital. Similarly the application of steam to boats and railroads, which bring raw material and food supplies to the concentration of capital. The development of banking systems has aided in bringing about the same world-wide monopolies. Such monopolies could control prices and the wages of the workmen. As a protection against this danger, Congress has established such administrative bodies as the Federal Trade Commission and the Securities and Exchange Commission." (p. 35)

From Scarcity to Overabundance:

"Our capitalistic system has given us more food than we can eat, more fabrics than we can wear, more buildings than we can fill, more railroads than we can supply with freight, more automobiles than our city streets can accommodate, more electricity than can be sold at present prices, and more of all commodities than people can buy. That competitive system which rewards those who reduce costs or improve quality naturally stimulates the invention of better and better processes and more efficient organization.

"Unless otherwise educated, the general run of people have an acquisitive nature. They will work longer hours and spend more sleepless nights to build individual homes and buy individual cars than they will if working for community houses and community cars." (p. 702)

Other Data: On the title page the author is listed as Professor of Political Science, Oregon State College, formerly instructor in Politics, Princeton University.

The teacher can quickly gain several impressions from reading the foregoing abstract. First, it shows the points in which an organization of the type sponsoring the work is interested. Authorship stands forth prominently. Who the author is, where he works, and his qualifications are considered pertinent. The interest in grade levels at which the book is to be used might imply questions as to the time and place for certain topics to be introduced. The quotations used could conceivably be an index to determine content about which such groups have most concern. Second, the teacher can and must use such materials as the above-mentioned abstract when he is thinking about the following professional topics: academic freedom, teaching of controversial topics, arranging for forum discussion, study of contemporary affairs, and pupil guidance.

The critical examination of textbooks seems to come with some regularity like panics and epidemics. We have reason to believe that others will come; just when and from what sources, we know not. In any event, authors and teachers should be cognizant of the potential approach.

It is quite possible that the attention given the abstracting of social studies textbooks by the National Association of Manufacturers surprised the organization both by its nature and by its extent. The following paragraphs from a letter to one of the authors under the date of Mar. 31, 1941 illustrate the point:

> Here is the real story: The abstracts represent an inherently constructive undertaking, which can be of service to teachers and school administrators as well as to the non-teaching public. The study was undertaken because many of our members were disturbed at the discussion which has been going on for years about the contents of the nation's textbooks and which has resulted, far too often, in name-calling instead of rational discussion of the issues actually involved.
>
> May I add, parenthetically, that from the outset we believed that the issue of "subversiveness" in textbooks was being immensely exaggerated. The only legitimate question may be whether or not the books deal with highly controversial issues in such a fashion that the student gets an adequate picture of the various points of view regarding them. By this, we do not infer that only books that completely ignore human imperfections and bias are suitable for school use. We do believe, however, that if a text seems heavily weighted on one side of a controversial issue, any citizen has a right to ask that the bias of the book be understood by the student and that the other side of the controversy be presented equally well.
>
> In approaching this subject we recognized many inherent dangers, and we ran the risk of injecting ourselves into the controversy only because we believed that unless some groups would take the initiative and treat the problem on a rational rather than an emotional basis, it would continue interminably and would serve only to create distrust and suspicion on all sides.

To emphasize that investigations and surveys of social studies textbooks are usually undertaken and conducted in good faith this example is cited. A few years ago one of the authors was shocked to read in a nationally circulated magazine an article that thoroughly condemned a number of well-known secondary-school textbooks in this field. In fact, the basic textbook that he was using in his classes in world history was listed as objectionable. He wrote the editor, and the following paragraph was included in the reply:

> I note your inquiry in reference to the inclusion of ________, in a list appended to the article by ________, published in the September number

of this magazine. May I say that through a thoroughly regrettable misunderstanding of the purpose of the list which the author obtained from what he considered an unimpeachable source (and was so accepted by us) this book was inadvertently listed. A letter expressing regret for the inadvertence has been sent to ——— publishers.

The same magazine willingly apologized to the editors of a well-known publication that is used in numerous high-school social studies classes as a basis of study of current events for inadvertently including their name.

It was pointed out at the beginning of this chapter that the textbook can and does go far in shaping attitudes on the part of the pupils who read them. This is probably true in the entire range of social concepts. Reference is now made to just one area as illustrative.

Orr [5] attempted to analyze the attitudes of adolescent boys and girls toward the peoples of other nations. Three hundred unselected pupils in high-school history classes were asked to fill in a simple questionnaire. After being asked to state their feelings toward the people of specified nations they were given a chance to indicate what they thought to be the reason for the feeling. These choices included family feeling, some teacher, some textbook, and some other reason. The conclusion reached, based upon this particular study, was that the textbook, next to the home, is the most important factor in international attitudes among adolescent children.

Crofts [6] has pointed out aptly the peculiar place of the historian in relation to textbooks. The following quotation is illustrative:

> To social scientists, especially historians, has gone the place of hazard and honor in the advancement of human thought. There were purges of "history books" even before books were printed. The emperor Shih Huang Ti (pronounced *Sher Wang Dee*), misliking the works of Confucius, ordered that every book in China be burned except those dealing with medicine and agriculture. Writing was done in those times on bamboo strips, which were difficult to conceal, requiring a mule load of bamboo for a chapter of text. But the scholars of China at the risk of their lives plastered the classics into their walls and, as a result of their persecution,

[5] Harriett Knight Orr, "History Textbooks and International Attitudes," *Social Studies*, XXXII (October, 1941), pp. 254–255.

[6] Alfred Crofts, "A Historian Looks at Textbooks," *Journeys Behind the News*, Vol. X, No. 20, The Social Science Foundation of the University of Denver in cooperation with The Rocky Mountain Radio Council, by permission.

they have remained Confucianist for twenty-one hundred years. Part of the popularity of the Bible derives from the centuries during which it was proscribed by secret police—when it was kept hidden beneath the floorboards and read with fear and reverence.

The court historians of China, men of high integrity, could consign the emperor himself to future honor or contempt. Every tyrant used threats—often attempting violence—to make them flatter his achievements. But after a contest that lasted for generations, the victory of the historians was complete; the only place in an oriental kingdom sacrosanct from the emperor himself, was the locked archive which held the day-by-day historical records of his reign; this could be opened once a year by an inspector who had to be illiterate, so that he would never betray the information they contained; and they were published only after the death of the emperor; fear of what might be charged against him in the record was the strongest check upon the power of the Son of Heaven.

Selection of Textbooks in the Social Studies. At the outset it is possible to be optimistic about textbook selection in that today the classroom teacher has an important rôle. Not many years ago administrators assumed too generously the function of selection. This practice had many obvious evils. Lack of knowledge of objectives, content, and modern teaching methods in all subjects heads the list. The effort to economize frequently appeared with undue emphasis. Personal relationships with firms and individuals not infrequently had a place. Naturally, the correct procedure that evolved was that of cooperative effort, in which the principal or department head secures written statements from the teachers setting forth the shortcomings of the book to be displaced and the expectations from a potential new selection. The preparation of a pertinent bibliography related to new materials in the field is in order. Samples of recent books should be secured by the administrator, kept in a central location, and made readily available to the staff. In order to arrive at an objective result a score sheet should be evolved and probably applied to as many as five leading books available. Maybe after the first evaluation has been made a reevaluation of the two or three books that rated highest should follow. The points given below are offered as general and suggestive. They could readily be placed to the left on a sheet of paper. The names of books being considered could be given one column each to the right. While there are twelve points, it is not at all suggested that they be given equal weight. The committee in charge can usually agree upon the values to be assigned.

1. *Authorship.* It is a matter of concern to select textbooks that have been written by authors who have a background of sound scholarship, experience in teaching pupils of the grade for which the book is intended, and knowledge of the basic laws of learning. In brief, one must have more than a casual interest when one asks, "Who wrote the book?"

2. *Style of writing.* The book should be read to determine whether the manner of expression is one that would appeal to children of the grade for which it is intended. By way of illustration it might be suggested that a student of college rank would willingly read a book for good content alone whereas a junior-high-school pupil could scarcely be expected to read willingly unless a certain type of reading appeal for younger readers was present.

3. *Vocabulary.* Most writers of textbooks sold by major companies now recognize the need to check vocabulary with standard word lists and see that the reading can be accomplished by the grade level involved. Often the author of social studies material will ask a reading expert to review the manuscript previous to publication. It is tremendously important to have the book score well on this and the preceding point. Many actual failures to learn social studies well are directly traceable to poor reading abilities and bad habits related to reading. Not only should the teacher read the textbook for examination of these points; a few of the pupils should be selected to read portions of the book and express their opinions.

4. *Selection of content.* No basic textbook can give more than a treatment of details that seem to be most important. Therefore, before examining one, the teacher should decide in advance what topics should receive fuller treatment in order to make the accomplishment of objectives easier. In history texts most teachers have rather definite notions about the manner in which political, social, and economic events should, they feel, be stressed; likewise, they have definite ideas as to the amount of space that should be devoted to particular epochs. The same type of analogy can be used in the consideration of other social studies textbooks. By the use of simple mathematics one can compute fractional parts allotted to various phases of subject matter in books under consideration.

In a very elementary fashion a student teacher recently examined the table of contents of the basic textbook that he was using in world history. He found that the following topics were treated, with the per cent of the entire book's content allotted to each as indicated: "Prehistoric Man," 3; "Oriental Peoples," 5; "Ancient Greece," 10; "Ancient Rome," 10; "Teutonic Peoples," 4; "Life of the Middle Ages," 3; "Nations of the Middle Ages," 7; "Reformation," 12; "Old Regime," 4; "French Revolution," 11; "Progress of Democracy," 17; "Two World Wars," 14.

This type of analysis can help one decide whether various topics have received the relative emphasis that they should have. It may even reveal a complete absence of treatment that should have been included.

5. *Unbiased presentation.* The book should be read carefully to determine whether the author is attempting to promote a personal point of view or to sponsor an idea that is basic in the platform of an organized group. The best authors recognize that their obligation is to present the truth and that academic freedom demands and permits them to write accordingly. After such a presentation has been made, pupil reading and study will naturally result in the forming of personal conclusions by individual members of the class.

6. *Accuracy.* Social studies teachers are quite well within their rights when they insist that statements made in textbooks be absolutely true. If the author is expressing an opinion of a group or his personal ideas, clear indications should be given. Many authors have eliminated errors be using their material in mimeographed form with actual classes prior to publication. Additional help is often secured by having teachers in the same field read the manuscript before it goes to the printer.

The Committee on Textbooks of the American Committee for Democracy and Intellectual Freedom[7] recognizes the preeminent position of accuracy. Its comments are as follows:

> The fundamental criterion to apply is whether a book tells the truth—the truth that Christ said "shall make you free." Telling the truth about history, economics, sociology, or political science is a difficult task. The facts are so numerous that only a small selection from among the multitude can be included in an elementary text. One obvious rule is that no facts

[7] *General Statement on Social Science Textbooks,* New York: Committee on Textbooks of the American Committee for Democracy and Intellectual Freedom, p. 2.

should be stated that cannot be supported by evidence. Another rule, less obvious but in our opinion sound, is that it is better to limit the range of problems treated in an elementary text to a number that can be dealt with rather fully than to attempt a coverage so wide that only the bare bones can be exhibited. The topics chosen should be broad in scope and of high significance. But this criterion must not be applied to bar the attempt to show even young students—most of whom will not go on for advanced study although they must later act as citizens—how complex and interdependent is the structure of society.

7. *Use of opportunity to capitalize on fundamental laws of learning.* It is known that pupils learn more readily when good overviews, topic sentences, summaries, and thought questions are included. Thus, in selecting a textbook the social studies teacher is concerned with more than just the facts included; they must be presented in a setting that stimulates learning in the most economical fashion.

8. *Maps, charts, pictures, graphs, and other visual aids.* Pupils differ individually in their abilities to learn through different media. More of them make greater accomplishments when a variety is used. In observing pupils examine a book for the first time it is quite general to find that they sincerely like an abundance of illustrative materials; this is especially true if the presentation is artistic and colorful. Pupils' reaction to the textbook selected certainly cannot well be ignored.

9. *Teaching aids.* Reference is made to such points as questions on the text, topics suitable for special reports, suggestions for individual and group projects, bibliographic aids, lists of reading for correlation with other subjects, etc. Many times the publishers furnish teacher manuals that contain elaborate suggestions. While no teacher can properly expect to secure a self-teaching course, it is quite helpful to have from the author teaching suggestions which can be altered to fit local situations.

Almost any well-written secondary-school social studies textbook will give emphasis to the unit idea. The chapter headings will provide a definite frame for the subject matter. Brief overviews will be given. A world and national setting for the units will be emphasized. Chronological, logical, or interests arrangement will be followed. Titles should be worded in simple and realistic terms that contribute to the understanding of modern problems. Skeleton outlines provided at either the beginning or the close of chapters are very helpful to most pupils.

10. *Recognition of modern trends.* This idea has at least two implications. The first deals with study and research relating to factual materials. A chapter written about ancient Egyptian history twenty years ago does not offer itself logically today as one suitable for reprinting in a current textbook. Too many facts have been learned recently through archaeological investigation and research. The same principle would apply in other social studies areas.

The next place that modern trends would be noted would be in the author's recognition of changes in the way of thinking on the part of the American people. For instance, woman suffrage is generally recognized by both law and contemporary thought as having a rightful place. Not only should one be concerned about modern trends related to subject matter; one should also be mindful of the most recently stated and accepted objectives for education as a whole and for the subject in which a textbook selection is being made. In brief, an alert author will write a book that will make the attainment of objectives relatively easy (see Chapter 1). Early Americans did not generally hold this point of view. A judgment that a teacher might sometimes render against an author's work is that a trend is regarded as a permanent change which may not actually become such.

11. *Physical aspects.* Pupils and teachers gain initial impressions by merely looking at the cover of the textbook. It is quite desirable that it shall be artistic and appealing rather than drab and commonplace. The size of the print used throughout the book and the quality and color of the paper should be such as to cause a minimum of eyestrain or fatigue. Economy dictates that a book should be well constructed so that it will be durable. Some books do not have to be rebound nearly as frequently as others. This point becomes quite important now that boards of education are buying books with the expectation that they will last over a period of years.

12. *Pupil reaction.* After all, a textbook that is selected is supposed to have a very strong appeal to the pupils who are to use it. What could be more logical than to give them a chance to express personal reactions? Not only is the potential selection expected to appeal strongly to the most gifted pupils; it is also mandatory that it

be interesting to the middle- and low-ability groups. It is suggested that six pupils be placed on a committee, two from each level mentioned or implied. This group should be given a few periods from regular social studies class time to examine the books under consideration. Each member may be asked to rank in order his preference and to write short and descriptive reasons for his choices.

Individual teachers will have additional ideas to consider when selecting textbooks. The ones given above are offered as basic in any more complete list that might be compiled. The following are offered without comment as possible additional criteria: stress on ideas and movements rather than personalities and events, adequacy of treatment of fundamental institutions, subordination of purely military implications, manner in which recommendations of professional organizations are met, scientific point of view maintained, emphasis upon the rise and growth of democracy, and attention to the cultural growth of society.

There are certain points related to textbook selection that might properly be considered under the heading of the word *ethics*. For instance, the only motive on the part of the committee should be that of attempting sincerely to secure the best book available. Little or no negotiation should take place between committee members and representatives of publishing companies. Books and materials should be selected exclusively on their own merits. It can be taken for granted that publishers of textbooks will be glad to cooperate in every way possible. This generosity should not be exploited. If samples are requested, this should be done only when there is definitely some chance that they will be adopted. One sample can ordinarily serve the needs of the entire committee. Certainly no individual should be the richer by so much as one personal copy of a book because of having served. All such books received should become school property and be clearly stamped as such. Many publishers even go so far in their efforts to be helpful that they furnish teaching aids with some regularity. These various favors should be reciprocated with cooperation on the part of social studies teachers in not making unreasonable demands of publishers.

One might conclude that after the above procedure is carried out there would be need for no additional cautions or suggestions. Such is not the case. A book may not bring the results in actual usage that are anticipated. Accordingly, if one or more committee members can confer with fellow teachers in other school systems who have used the book, potentially helpful suggestions can be secured. Furthermore, it is sometimes sound procedure to use the book for one semester on an experimental basis with one or more sections. If in actual practice satisfactory results follow, the adoption may be considered a reasonably safe one.

After the book has been selected, ordered, and received it is possible to spend a few minutes to good advantage by talking with a class about the manner of proper care. For instance, the group may take a book each, open a few pages starting alternately at the front and back, and press these few leaves down firmly. This will add many months of service to a book in contrast with one that has been opened first in the center. Attractive jackets may frequently be purchased at a local bookstore stressing a current theme. This is a matter of economy. The usual points of freedom from marking, mutilating, etc. are in order. These points are related to civic responsibility or personal economic efficiency, depending upon whether the books are furnished by the school or privately purchased.

The Textbook Method of Teaching. As mentioned above, the fact that attention has been given to the matter of textbook selection does not in itself give endorsement to the textbook method. It seems quite proper, however, to discuss points in favor of using the textbook, things to avoid, and means of making most effective use of the textbook.

One of the first teacher aids gained is that the body of knowledge and facts desired are available in a relatively brief space. The breadth of training and experience of the author ensures this point. Furthermore, the material is compactly organized according to some logical system. Both these items contribute to economy of the teacher's time, a factor of tremendous importance in the first year or two. The place of the textbook in the teaching process is most interesting; it is almost an institution. It has been highly praised and soundly condemned. It has been used to excellent effect and with poor results. In any event it is most likely that today the average and below-average teachers will be all too often called *textbook teachers.* Finally, the textbook is easy for the pupil to follow both in advance reading and in noting special assignments suggested at the end of units. Many pupils have consistently followed textbook methods and find it easy to do so.

Social studies teachers should endeavor to avoid certain pitfalls in connection with the use of the textbooks. Probably the error committed most frequently is that of confining the entire teaching program to one textbook. This procedure becomes very monotonous to the pupils. They appreciate going beyond what they have read. Some of them will feel that recitations based upon one assigned reading are almost wasted time. In the same connection, some teachers seem to expect the textbook to do the teaching for them. They tend to accept responsibility only for designating pages to be read and exercises performed. Such teaching is likely to cause both teacher and pupils to subscribe to the one author's point of view or even fail to recognize the existence of other schools of thought at all.

In a situation where library facilities are limited and the teacher's schedule is unduly crowded it may be necessary to rely a great deal on the textbook for help. Even so, there are fortunately many ways to make the method less subject to criticism than it otherwise might be. One of these has to do with making current applications. It would be impossible to conceive of many social studies lessons in which this could not be done advantageously. This will increase the general body of knowledge gained by the class and will add immeasurably to pupil interest. The use of parallel texts is very helpful in obviating the difficulties mentioned above. The presence of even just a few of these in the social studies classroom rather than in a central library makes them readily accessible and inviting for use. If they are not available through a library budget, it works out very nicely in some courses to have texts by different authors in the hands of individual pupils. In American history, for instance, one can assign topics such as colonial life, steps leading up to the formation of the constitution, and the reconstruction era and have them read in any one of several good textbooks. The class discussions that follow are very likely to show quality far superior to that in which all read the same book. Maybe we should proceed with mild caution at this stage. The point of view just advocated has not always met complete acceptance. For instance, Becker [8] set forth seven points that have been advanced in favor of the multiple-textbook plan in social studies classes. Among them are the ideas

[8] Harry A. Becker, "Multiple Texts Multiply Textbook Problems," *The Social Studies,* XXXII (November, 1941), pp. 294–296.

that such a plan is modern and progressive, that students obtain different points of view, and that critical abilities are developed. The important thing to note, however, is that his entire article refuted points that had more or less acceptance. Basic text users therefore have some comfort. The assigning of special reports is a helpful means of supplementing the discussion that might otherwise be too narrow because of the use of one basic text. Finally, the well-read teacher will be able regularly to add many facts to those brought out in a basic text, from reading done partly in the preparation for teaching and partly as a matter of in-service routine. Pupils will gain much from teacher contributions because they are usually presented effectively from a forensic standpoint. The suggestions made are not offered to condemn a method; they are set forth as a plea for enrichment of what might become a monotonous routine emanating from a restricted point of view.

Summary. In this chapter it has been pointed out that the selection of a textbook is a serious matter in any secondary-school area. In the social studies it is extremely important because of civic responsibilities involved and of public scrutiny that is ever present. The interest of various institutional groups has been stressed. In order to offer concrete help to social studies teachers a list of evaluation criteria was given. The points included were authorship; unbiased presentation; style of writing; vocabulary; selection of content; accuracy; use of opportunity to capitalize on fundamental laws of learning; inclusion of maps, charts, pictures, graphs, and other visual aids; teaching aids; recognition of modern trends; physical aspects; and pupil reaction. The textbook method of teaching was presented; its effectiveness was shown to be directly related to the skill of the teacher in charge. If the teacher is one who feels that the textbook is a self-teaching device, the results are foredoomed to failure. On the other hand, it is possible to utilize the textbook as an aid to organization and to achieve commendable classroom results.

Questions on the Text

1. Name several types of organizations existing or formerly prominent in American society that have taken an active interest in social studies textbooks. Give examples.
2. What types of law do we frequently find enacted by state legislatures

that have a bearing on the general subject of textbooks in social studies?

3. Show by examples that criticism of social studies textbooks is more often sporadic than continuous.

4. List several criteria that a social studies teacher might aptly apply if placed on a committee to select a textbook. Explain briefly the meaning of each.

5. What type of helps and services can a teacher expect to secure from publishing houses when confronted with the problem of textbook selection?

6. Describe ways and means by which the teacher who is limited to textbook methods of teaching can enrich the course.

Suggested Activities

1. Examine a textbook in one of the social studies with the idea of determining whether it treats topics in an unbiased manner. Summarize your conclusions, including a number of quotations to lend support to them.

2. Attempt to find an account in a recent newspaper or magazine of a controversy related to high-school textbooks in the social studies. Report your findings, stressing the issue involved.

3. Examine two textbooks in a given social study, one the oldest that you can find and the other the most recent that is available. Indicate the differences and similarities that you find.

4. Interview successful teachers of social studies to find out their opinions about criteria for selection of textbooks in this area.

5. Read an article from a recent educational periodical dealing with selection of social studies textbooks. Summarize the ideas advanced.

Selected References

Becker, Harry A., "Multiple Texts Multiply Textbook Problems," *Social Studies*, XXXII (November, 1941), pp. 294–296.

Black, Wilfred W., "The Tradition of Pioneer Hardships in American History Textbooks," *Social Studies*, XXXIV (February, 1943), pp. 54–57.

Curtis, Merle (chairman), *Control of Social Studies Textbooks*, Washington, D.C.: The National Council for the Social Studies, May, 1941.

Douglass, Harl R. and Hubert H. Mills, *Teaching in High School*, New York: The Ronald Press Company, 1948, Chap. XV.

Galloway, O. F., "Subversive Social-studies Textbooks; Reply to D. L. Geyer," *School and Society*, LXVII (June 5, 1948), p. 428.

General Statement on Social Science Textbooks, New York: Committee on Textbooks of the American Committee for Democracy and Intellectual Freedom, mimeographed.

GEYER, D. L., "Attack on Social-studies Textbooks," *School and Society,* LXVII (Mar. 6, 1948), pp. 187–188.

HEAPS, WILLARD A., "Supplementary Readings in American History Textbooks," *Social Studies,* XXXII (May, 1941), pp. 212–219.

HUNT, ERLING M., "The Manufacturers and the Textbooks," *Social Education,* V (February, 1941), pp. 87–90.

———, "Learning the Ways of Democracy," *Social Education,* V (March, 1941), pp. 165–166.

———, "Dr. Robey versus the N.A.M.?" *Social Education,* V (April, 1941), pp. 288–292.

JUDD, CHARLES H., "The Unique Origin of a Textbook," *School Review,* LII (February, 1944), pp. 80–83.

MCLENDON, J. C., "South in Social Studies Textbooks," *Social Education,* X (December, 1946), pp. 341–344.

NIETZ, JOHN A., and WAYNE E. MASON, "Early American Civil Government Textbooks: An Analysis of Their Content," *Social Education,* XIV (May, 1950), pp. 201–202.

ORR, HARRIET KNIGHT, "History Textbooks and International Attitudes," *Social Studies,* XXXII (October, 1941), pp. 254–255.

PIERCE, BESSIE LOUISE, *Public Opinion and the Teaching of History,* New York: Alfred A. Knopf, Inc., 1926.

SIMPSON, R. E. and H. M. MCPHERSON, "Summary of Actions of the State Board of Education and the State Curriculum Commission in Adopting *Building America,*" *California Schools,* XVIII (April, 1947), pp. 59–69.

Chapter 6

USING AUDIO-VISUAL MATERIALS

Preview. It is the purpose of this chapter to acquaint the social studies teacher with the need for the extensive use of audio-visual aids to learning in the social studies. The chapter emphasizes that the teacher should be informed on the types of aids, their use, and how to include these materials in the teacher-pupil planning of units of work. Values resulting from their use are repeatedly pointed out. A description of a typical class experience in the use of a film is included to suggest the kind of pupil reaction possible from a film.

Definition of Audio-Visual Aids. Any device which by sight or sound increases the individual's experience beyond that acquired through reading may be described as an audio-visual aid to learning. By providing an additional approach to understanding, the teacher increases the meaning of an event or of an idea for the pupil. Without the background of the total teaching situation, the audio-visual device is of little value. The teacher who searches for means to provide broad experiences for his pupils will use every method and device available. The devices are a means to an end and will at times contribute valuable aid to the learning situation. The teacher must be able to judge when a specific device may be used most effectively. Visual aids range from the simple illustration in a magazine, newspaper, or book to those which can be seen only by means of a mechanical contrivance. For example, an illustration in a textbook is a visual aid to the understanding of the related material of the textbook. So also are graphs, maps, and charts. The opaque projector is a mechanical device to make greater use of a simple type of visual aid. Films, filmstrips, and slides are visual aids which call for more elaborate equipment and a somewhat more detailed preparation for their use. Auditory aids are the radio and phonograph. The sound film may be classified as both visual and auditory, like television, although the use of the latter is restricted to those areas where telecasting has been made possible. The wire recorder is a helpful device, enabling a class to review a previous activity. The wire recorder is also a means of bringing to a class a transcription of a radio program not available otherwise.

Need for Audio-Visual Materials in Social Studies. The meaning which we derive from life about us is the total perception of our environment in so far as we are able to interpret it. Color and sound, in particular, emphasize many of our experiences. When the social studies program includes the use of the many present-day techniques of expression which our civilization offers, we broaden the pupil's conception of an idea, and we probably create a more vital experience for him. It is natural that the modern graphic representations of social facts in pictures, maps, charts, or graphs should be essential to the interpretation and understanding of our time. Not only do maps and graphs and the other visual or auditory devices of our age serve the social studies classroom as aids to learning, but they may also be described as sources of information which the pupil needs in daily living. Furthermore, it is the place of the social studies program to provide acquaintance with such media of expression in order for pupils to see the functioning within the school of such devices as he may encounter upon innumerable occasions outside the classroom. By the use of radio and recorded incidents, speeches, or music, the pupil is aided in developing a new approach to the understanding of an event. It is evident that these particular devices require different techniques to adapt them to classroom use. The use of such materials increases the pupil's ability to be alert to the flood of ideas to which he is continually being subjected and to respond intelligently to all such stimuli.

The Teacher and Audio-Visual Aids. As has been indicated earlier in this chapter, the audio-visual device is only an aid to provide a more complete experience. Its value as an aid depends to a great extent on the ability of the teacher to use it effectively. Thus as Glick [1] points out, the teacher is the significant influence in guiding learning activities. In the preparation of a possible unit of work

[1] Annette Glick, "The Use of Visual Aids in Teaching the Social Studies—Past and Present," *The Historical Approach to Methods of Teaching the Social Studies,* Washington, D.C.: The National Council for the Social Studies, *Fifth Yearbook,* 1935, pp. 125–126.

the teacher will consider all the possible angles of approach to the unit. When the stage of teacher-pupil planning has been reached, it will be necessary to investigate the availability of such materials as will contribute to an effective presentation of the unit, including illustrations on the bulletin board; pupil activities involving the construction of graphs, charts, or maps; the collection of objects for exhibits; and the more complicated materials, films, phonograph records, or possible radio programs. When decisions have been made concerning the types of audio-visual aids the class will expect to use, the next problem concerns the time of their use. Knowing when an individual pupil should be given an opportunity to construct a graph, sensing when the attention of the class should be directed to a specific picture on the bulletin board, or when a pupil's chart should be displayed by means of the opaque projector, or just when a certain record should be played for most valuable application to the unit are examples of timing the use of audio-visual aids.

Effective use of any teaching device requires that the teacher relate the resulting activity to the unit in order that the pupil may realize the additional contribution. If a pupil reads a given selection on the life of some character in history, the teacher intends the pupil to recognize the relationship of the reading to the unit. When audio-visual aids are used to increase pupil experience, whatever value they may offer must be recognized as an actuality by the pupil. Pupil reaction through discussion after experiencing the audio-visual aid is a common method of emphasis. It is through such discussion that the pupil expresses his feelings. This is a significant phase of pupil experience because there must be opportunity for expression of enjoyment of the beautiful, understanding of and sympathy for misfortune, and approval of commendable ideals or actions. The teacher must plan ways to encourage pupil expression of reactions in order to realize a more valuable experience from the audio-visual device.

Pictures as Teaching Aids. The emphasis in our modern world on communication of ideas through pictures is one of the distinguishing elements of our civilization. Their constant presence in our daily experience, however, does offer an aid to teaching. A picture enables the individual to realize elements of a situation which his more or less limited experience otherwise prevents. This is especially true as one reads about historic events. The reader does not live in the past, and consequently many details of an earlier culture are not included in his thinking. The picture brings to the attention such enriching elements as might otherwise be omitted. All teachers in social studies make use of pictures, but in all probability more use could be made. Pictures should be chosen for accuracy of subject matter, for legibility, and for size. One of the interesting hobbies of some social studies teachers is the keeping of a picture file. Pictures can be quickly mounted on a lightweight cardboard for ease of handling. Uniform cardboard size makes for ease in handling the file of pictures. As the picture file grows, the teacher will be able to have pictures available quickly for most units. When pictures are displayed on the bulletin board, it is desirable to have an explanatory note to accompany them. This helps the pupil relate the picture to his unit of study and may stimulate him to further thinking, particularly if the explanation carries a question about the picture. As the social studies teacher travels to places of interest, he may wisely collect postcard views of worth-while scenes. In the classroom such collections are valuable and may be shown to the class by means of the opaque projector, with appropriate comments. Small bulletin boards to stand upon a table may be quickly fashioned from heavy cardboard boxes by cutting down the sides to serve as braces. Such a device is helpful in relating a group of pictures to an exhibit of materials by using the pictures as a background. Pictures must be displayed in adequate light and must be available to all the pupils. Although considered primarily as supplementary material, they may occasionally be used by the teacher to introduce a new unit, if a sufficient variety of pictures is at hand to arouse interest in a proposed topic. In making assignments, the social studies teacher can enrich the pupil's experience by including pictures in the planning of the new work. Hartley [2] emphasizes the use of textbook illustrations, which are valuable aids and must be called to the attention of pupils. The teacher must not assume that its presence on a given page guarantees pupil use of a picture. Time spent investigating the content of an illustration is as meaningful as that devoted to other types of learning activity. When the teacher calls attention to a detail in a picture, pupils will usually discover further items previously

[2] William H. Hartley, "Audio-Visual Materials and Techniques," Washington, D.C.: The National Council for the Social Studies, *Seventeenth Yearbook*, 1946, pp. 306–310.

unobserved. The class and teacher together may select specific features in pictures which may be used to identify the picture and so increase the pupil's ability. For example, the class is aware of the statues of horses above the entrance to St. Mark's cathedral. They see that this cathedral has several domes, while the cathedral of Milan has no domes but is characterized by what appear to be many spires, which are actually statues rising above the main body of the building. Pictures can be used successfully as testing devices in the social studies. Test items using pictures calling for identification, comparison, general information, or appreciation are valuable. The social studies teacher will quickly perceive possible testing devices using pictures as a further means of evaluating pupil understanding.

Graphs as Teaching Aids. In the social studies graphs are helpful in explaining relationships and comparisons. The constant change which marks society can be easily demonstrated. The graph helps to show the growth and development of various elements of the culture as well as the decline of such elements. Whenever the opportunity for work with graphs appears, the teacher should provide for their use. If pupils do not recognize the opportunity for a graph, or are unfamiliar with the procedure of making a graph, they must be instructed. The teacher-pupil activity of working out a graph together may be an important phase of a planning period. Frequent use of graphs will establish pupil habits of sensitivity to the possibilities of their use and appreciation of them in daily living.

The use of graphs in textbooks will encourage pupils to apply graphic interpretations to materials they bring to discussion. Junior-high-school social studies texts seem to use more bar and picture graphs than line graphs. Line graphs seem to be found in wider use in the senior-high-school texts. A simple graph for pupils to make when they are not accustomed to the device is the bar graph. In this graph a vertical or horizontal bar represents each of the items being compared. A parallel measure will indicate quantity.

The line graph is more accurate than the bar type but is more difficult to construct. The line of this graph is the result of several points where numerical values of two factors intersect. When the points of intersection are established, a line is drawn connecting the points. This graph can carry two or more lines to show comparisons. Although it may be more difficult to construct, pupils should become skillful in its use as a tool as well as for accuracy in expression.

Circle and picture graphs seem to be enjoyed by pupils, although they possess somewhat less accuracy than the preceding types. The circle graph indicates portions of a total. The picture graph is made by a simple, filled-in picture representing a unit quantity. Multiples of the unit indicate variations.

In constructing graphs, pupils need to realize the necessity for accuracy, without which the graph fails to show what is intended. Neatness contributes to the appearance of the completed work, and a lack of neatness could in some instances reduce the accuracy of the graph. All graphs should be clearly labeled, and the elements which are being compared should be distinctly shown.

Graphs, like pictures, may be used as testing devices. Pupils can be asked to interpret a graph, to apply its evidence to a general problem, or to explain why the graph shows the conditions it may reveal in terms of historical fact.

Maps as Teaching Aids. Teachers of the social studies have probably made more use of maps over a longer period of time than they have of any other visual aid. Perhaps the map may have seemed to be a more integral part of the social studies than some other visual aids. An examination of textbooks in social studies will reveal that among the visual aids included, maps are usually second to pictures in number. One text revealed over fifty maps; another carried more than thirty. Despite this, maps are not always used properly, nor their full value realized, by pupils in the social studies. Maps vary in purpose and consequently require various skills of those who would make adequate use of the information shown. The establishment of these skills in pupils is a responsibility of the social studies teacher. The supervised study period with the preparatory planning and succeeding activity stages offers the opportunity for the teacher to conduct sufficient drill work with the class or to provide individualized instruction, depending on pupil need, to develop various map skills.

A map is a representation of the world or a portion of the world, and the best presentation of the idea of a map of any part of the world is by means of a globe. As the pupil examines a globe, he observes more accurately the relationship in size and distance of the various features of the earth. A map usually distorts the shape of some of the geographic elements, and this condition must be called to the pupil's attention together with the explanation. The meaning of latitude and longitude must be understood, and how these devices are used must become ready knowledge of the pupils. Parallels of latitude indicate degrees of distance north or south of the equator and are always parallel to the equator. Distances east or west are marked by meridians of longitude, which run from pole to pole with the prime meridian passing through Greenwich, England. The scale of miles is a further device to give the map more meaning, by indicating the distance on the map in proportion to the actual distance. Other features of a map or globe may be called to the pupil's attention as need may arise. Certainly the pupil must become aware of the cartographer's use of color and symbols to indicate surface features and significant details of the specific map in question. With the revision of world geographic relationships through air transportation, pupils need to develop mental images of the map of the United States in relation to other nations from the point of view of air travel. A polar-centered map of the world enables the pupil to observe this true world relationship by referring to the globe as he examines the map.

Map Information. Maps are sources of many kinds of information. Location is the most common fact revealed by maps, but there may be other equally important facts given at the same time. Physical features, political data, social knowledge, economic products, natural resources, and climatic facts are general types of information revealed on maps. For most adequate use of maps in the social studies, it is desirable that two or more maps be used simultaneously to illustrate relationships. For example, a map showing industrial areas used with one showing natural resources helps pupils to realize economic problems and processes resulting from the locations of the two phenomena under consideration. A relief map may be used to explain population distribution as well as such economic factors as the location of transportation lines.

Pupil Participation in Map Work. In addition to the use of the map as a tool in learning, it may sometimes seem desirable for pupils to construct maps. When the pupil engages in this activity, his purpose should be the justifiable one of an experience which carries meaning for him. By doing this particular bit of creative work, he will acquire an emphasis on some knowledge, or some information will become more significant. Pupils will become map-conscious to the degree that they are guided into study activities involving maps. When a pupil shows interest in constructing a map, he must be guided into meaningful and valuable activities relating to the map-construction process. Neatness, accuracy, and an evidence of knowledge applied to a specific problem must be found in the completed work. It is more desirable that a sense of relationship between geographic factors and man be shown by the map than that the map be merely an artistic product which has cost much time and labor, but which does not contribute to a pupil's knowledge. There may be times when it seems desirable for the entire social studies class to work on map construction. For example, a class in United States history may have discussed the Gadsden Purchase and, realizing that it was the last contiguous territory added to the United States, may have become interested in glancing over a map of the entire United States boundary. The question can so easily be raised, "How did the boundary of our country happen to follow the lines it does?" With such a problem calling for an investigation of the treaty settlements and purchases, the class may be launched on a map project to decide what sections of the national boundary were established by certain specific historic agreements. When such an occasion arises, the teacher and pupils should discuss the problem of map making from the point of view of the purpose of the map and the various techniques necessary for the pupils to produce an adequate map. Such items as a map legend, lettering, the title, its size in relation to other lettering, the scale of miles, color, and the signature are important.

Map Equipment for the Social Studies Classroom. The present output of map equipment for schools provides unusual opportunity to the teacher to equip the social studies classroom with valuable teaching aids at not too great a cost. It is the responsibility of the teacher to see to it that this essential equipment is a part of the laboratory facilities of the social studies classroom. The teacher must plan the room's map equipment in terms of needs and money available. To buy inexpensive maps is not necessarily a saving. Neither should the teacher make a heavy investment if funds are not adequate to cover all needs in proportion.

In selecting maps for the social studies room the teacher must consider various factors of room environment. In choosing the mounting for large maps the teacher must keep in mind the pupils' ease of viewing the maps. Some maps are mounted on a heavy pedestal-base stand, while some are supported by a metal tripod. The tripod seems to require more floor space and in a room of limited size is easily in the way of moving about the room. The wall-arm mounting, which swings from a hinged base fastened to the wall, allows two maps to be viewed readily by the swinging of the arm. This type serves best when space permits it to occupy a wall center removed from a corner. Roller maps have the advantage of being rolled up when not in use. In small rooms the roller type may be advantageous in this respect.

Accuracy of information and the amount and kind of information are significant items to consider in map selection. Some authors give more information on their maps than do others, although the teacher should examine the maps to see that information is easily read and that the map is not crowded in content.

The globe seems to be an essential for the social studies classroom. Here again room space may influence the teacher's choice of a globe. Sizes range from a small desk model to the large floor-stand type. A 16-inch globe seems to be a practical size, and a holder which allows the globe to be placed in any position is desirable.

The blackboard outline map is a helpful teaching device, as it permits pupils and teacher to demonstrate map details by drawing in such items as may relate to the unit under discussion. This map is printed on a glazed cloth so as to resemble a blackboard surface. Items drawn upon it in chalk are easily erased.

The social studies teacher will probably accumulate a variety of maps from many sources. It is desirable for a teacher to build a file of maps, arranging them by subject, mounting small sizes on light-weight cardboard and rolling large sizes for cupboard storage. In addition to these various ways in which the social studies teacher will plan the equipment of the room, the selection of textbooks will afford a further opportunity to bring map resources into the room. Present-day writers of social studies textbooks recognize the value of the map as a visual aid to understanding textbook material, and many textbooks supply the pupil with excellent maps.

Maps as Testing Devices. Maps can be helpful in evaluating pupil understanding. By the use of symbols on a map, pupils can respond to several kinds of problems: identification, replies to questions, showing relationship between regions and events. The following typical directions for a map test may suggest further testing devices.

On the map of the Southern states various symbols represent types of information. Capital letters indicate cities, Arabic numerals indicate geographic features, and Roman numerals indicate important military battles and campaigns. Respond to the questions, using the symbols for your replies on the blanks before the questions.

1. ________ What city is closely related to IV?
2. ________ The control of what river was a Federal objective?
3. ________ What natural barrier was a partial boundary between the North and South?
4. ________ In what campaign was Southern valor shown to a great degree?

In addition to testing for knowledge of facts, the map can be a device to allow pupils to demonstrate understanding. The pupil may be asked to sketch a map to explain certain ideas. For example, the request that a pupil draw a map to show why the early settlement of the Ohio region occurred as it did will cause the pupil to review the elements of this phase of the westward movement. He will probably show on the sketched map the trails which led to the Ohio country, the Ohio River, the Appalachian mountain barrier, the location of Marietta and Gallipolis, the site of the Battle of Fallen Timbers, and the treaty of Greenville.

Charts and Cartoons. A chart is an arrangement of information in pictorial or graphic form to aid in understanding an idea. It is a helpful device in the social studies, is used frequently in textbooks, and affords opportunity for creative pupil effort when included in the activities of a unit. Cartoons express significant ideas by means of a picture drawn to represent the event in such a way that the idea is portrayed. As a visual aid the cartoon is probably more effective with older pupils. An examination of social studies textbooks seems to show that more newspaper cartoons of the Thomas Nast type are used in senior-high-school textbooks than in those for the junior high school. Pupils usually enjoy cartoons, and to draw a good cartoon requires understanding of the topic and an ability to express ideas in terms of fairly wide knowledge.

Films, Filmstrips, and Lantern Slides. As has been pointed out earlier in the chapter, pictures are an effective means of supplementing information. When pupils are directed into situations which enable them to view pictures on a screen, there is an increase in interest and response. The moving picture, in particular, with its true-to-life presentation, affords such vicarious experience that pupils feel a personal knowledge of some topic not gained from other media. This same motivation seems to carry over to the filmstrip although possibly in reduced degree. As teachers of the social studies have become aware of the excellent additional experience that is afforded through films, the use of them has increased. This growing demand has brought about classroom-film production to such an extent that there now exist films for almost every unit in the social studies. Some films are produced specifically for school use; others suitable for schools are produced by business corporations as a form of advertising. The latter type should be previewed with care by the teacher before being shown to a class in order to avoid placing the school in the questionable position of favoring some particular manufacturer's product.

Using Films in Social Studies Classes. Most schools are now equipped to provide film service as an aid to teaching. It is possible that the school may own but one projector, which is used in a centrally located room. The desirable arrangement, of course, is for the social studies department to have its own projector in order to use a film at the most pertinent time and as often as needed. When each department must share the use of the projector, the time of use must be anticipated to prevent conflicts. When the film is used in a central room, the school often provides an operator, thus freeing the teacher from the responsibility of preparing and manipulating the machine.

All aids to learning require class preparation in order to be used successfully. Just as a teacher prepares pupils to use a map or a graph, he must prepare them to use a film. When a topic within a unit seems to indicate the use of a film specifically related to that area, the teacher must prepare the pupils with certain guiding activities for their viewing of the film. It is almost essential that the teacher should preview the film before presenting it to the class in order to select significant ideas to call to the pupils' attention. It seems desirable to show films a second time following a discussion of pupil impressions gained from the first showing. Films cannot be aids to learning if their presentation is not guided by discussion. In discussing the film, pupils evaluate their understanding of the film and have a better idea of what they need to watch for in the next showing. The teacher should plan questions which will emphasize the important theme of the film, thus enabling pupils to apply the ideas they have gained or to view the second showing with greater discrimination.

Film slides and lantern slides are valuable aids to learning. One useful pupil activity is the preparation of illustrated lectures on a topic of value to the unit, giving a floor talk to accompany the filmstrip or series of lantern slides. This same type of activity may be used with an opaque projector with even greater value to the pupil, as he must discover all the materials to be used in the projector and relate his talk to them. Filmstrips are less expensive than lantern slides, are more durable, and are more easily housed. It is important for the school to build up a film library to encourage the use of this valuable aid.

An Example of a Film Showing. The tenth grade world-history class had been studying Roman civilization and had spent some days in reading and discussing the period of Rome during the reign of Julius Caesar. To add further interest to the work already accomplished, the teacher prepared a three-day program based on the film, *Julius Caesar*. Circumstances prevented the teacher from previewing the film. Since the film consisted of two eleven-minute reels, about thirty minutes needed to be allowed for showing and rewinding. As the film was to be shown in a room separate from the social studies room, five minutes was allowed for the class to move to and from the projection room. The following directions and questions by the teacher were the preparation for viewing the film.

TEACHER. This film, *Julius Caesar*, which we are about to see, describes events in Rome immediately after Caesar's death. From your knowledge of that incident, what prominent Roman leaders will you expect to see in the picture?

JOHN. Brutus, probably, and maybe Cassius.

BILL. Pompey.

MARIE. No, Pompey was not in Rome then.

ARTHUR. Octavius might be there. He was Caesar's adopted son.

RUTH. Mark Antony might be seen because he made the funeral oration.

TEACHER. In addition to Roman leaders what other people may appear in the picture?

ANN. The Roman people were always in mobs on the streets; maybe they will be included.

CHARLES. Maybe some of Caesar's soldiers will be shown.

TEACHER. We are not sure what leaders and other people will appear, but your suggestions are logical. Let us watch to see how nearly we are correct in our imagining. Whoever is shown, let us try to find a word to characterize the leaders as they appear. If there is a mob scene at any time, what might be a character trait to look for in the mob?

ANN. Easily aroused to excitement.

TEACHER. What word do we need there stronger than *excitement*?

ESTHER. Violence.

TEACHER. In addition to these ideas we have suggested as possible to be seen in the movie, let us also watch for any evidence we may see of Roman customs or of Roman life from the general background of the scenes in the movie.

After this brief introduction the class moved to the projection room and viewed the picture. Aside from some distorted sound effects, the picture was easily followed. It consisted entirely of the scenes immediately after Caesar's assassination, when Brutus and Mark Antony appeared in turn before the Roman mob to make speeches concerning the death of Caesar. The final scene was the aroused fury of the mob as it fell under the sway of Mark Antony's clever oratory.

When the pupils returned to their room, very little time remained for the class period. Everyone seemed to have a reaction to the picture and wanted to be heard as he expressed his particular thought. The teacher called the class to attention and suggested that each person write down briefly (1) the scene from the picture that impressed him the most and (2) the word or phrase he thought best described Mark Antony. With the completion of this short activity the period closed.

When the class reconvened the following day, the discussion of the film was begun immediately. The teacher opened the discussion by recalling the activity at the close of the previous day's period. The following is typical of what occurred.

TEACHER. Yesterday each of you wrote a sentence indicating the scene you felt was most impressive. Let us hear some of these and tell why you were impressed.

MARIE. I liked the place where Mark Antony pretended to be overcome with grief. It was good acting to sway the mob.

JOHN. It was impressive when they carried Caesar's body into the scene. You felt a kind of mysterious awe as the people watched.

ESTHER. Well, who do you think that woman was who kept coming up toward Caesar's body? She was a good actress.

MAY. I think she was just supposed to be one of the mob, and she showed how they felt about Caesar.

BILL. When Brutus talked, you could certainly see how vain he was. When he bragged that he'd want somebody to murder him if he got too ambitious, you know he was just talking.

JOHN. It was a good thing he left before Mark Antony talked.

TEACHER. Why do you think so, John?

JOHN. Because when Brutus talked, the mob all felt it was good riddance that Caesar was dead, but Mark Antony made the mob regret Caesar's death and want revenge.

MARIE. Shows the fickleness of the mob.

ESTHER. Do you think that really was Caesar's will or just something Mark Antony made up?

ANN. He might have made it up because it's queer that he could get his hands on it so soon after Caesar's death.

JOHN. I'd like to know if Jane thinks Mark Antony was glad Caesar was dead. If he was, he was no better than Brutus.

CHARLES. Well, when Mark Antony got the mob started after Brutus to get revenge, he was doing it in order to gain power for himself. It's easy to see he was no better than Brutus.

ESTHER. I don't know whether Mark Antony was glad or not, but at least he was making the most of what seemed like a good opportunity for himself.

HELEN. Well, this doesn't have anything to do with all that, but did you see that man who must have been of the wealthier class give some money to that beggar? It seems to show that there were people in Rome who were charitable and who weren't selfish as we usually think of them.

JOHN AND OTHERS. No, I didn't see that. Where was it in the picture?

HELEN. I think it was before the people all heard about Caesar's murder.

TEACHER. Did you like Mark Antony's speech?

SEVERAL RESPONSES. Good speech. Clever. He knew how to guide the mob.

TEACHER. Do you think Mark Antony spoke truthfully of Caesar?

MARIE. He probably did speak truthfully of Caesar because we know Caesar had done much good, but Mark Antony was using Caesar's good works for Mark Antony's benefit. So if he was speaking truthfully, he could possibly not have been sincere, even so.

TEACHER. What did Mark Antony say which influenced the mob the most?
[Response to this question was undecided. The teacher wrote this question on the board.]

TEACHER. What did Brutus say that made the mob ignore Mark Antony and praise Brutus?
[Response to this question was undecided, and the question was written on the board with the previous one.]

TEACHER. Did you learn from the picture any particular Roman custom?

ARTHUR. They apparently were accustomed to make speeches in praise of their dead.

ANN. They believed it was a special honor apparently to burn the body as the mob did.

TEACHER. What particular word or words do you think Mark Antony used most effectively?

MAY. He used the word *ambitious.* He kept saying Caesar had been ambitious.

HELEN. Yes, but that was to mock Brutus. Mark Antony used the word *honorable* quite well because he made it sound sarcastic when he kept saying Brutus was an honorable man.
[Here the teacher wrote on the blackboard, "Watch for use of *honorable* by Mark Antony." The class was instructed to copy the items from the blackboard for further use.]

At the opening of the third day's period, the teacher asked the class to recall from the previous day the items about which they had not been sure in the discussion of the film. The pupils reviewed the three items copied from the blackboard, and then the class went to the projection room for a second showing of the picture.

Upon the return to the classroom there was again evident an eagerness to express new or revised impressions of the film. Several people spoke of seeing the wealthy Roman who gave money to the beggar and wondered how they had failed to see that event in the first showing. A pupil suggested that the class read Mark Antony's speech from the Shakespearean play, and that activity was planned for the following day. In response to the specific directions for further observation, the majority of the class had the scene in mind when Mark Antony spoke most effectively in arousing the mob. They did not recall the exact words, but someone spoke of his saying there could never be another like Caesar just as he finished reading Caesar's will to them. The class did agree that Brutus cleverly attacked Mark Antony as Brutus directed the mob to observe the approach of the funeral procession, remarking that Mark Antony, who would benefit by the death, accompanied the body and would address them. Several of the class spoke out, quoting, "And Brutus is an honorable man," giving considerable emphasis to the word *honorable.*

From this résumé of a typical class response to a film it is evident that the pupils are given an opportunity to feel more intimately the ideas, customs, institutions, and general culture of a period far removed from their own. From the pupil expression it is seen that they find elements of human nature in an earlier period which they understand as these are brought out in discussion in terms of their own experience. The film has lent reality to an otherwise distant past.

The Opaque Projector. This device seems almost indispensable in the social studies classroom. It enables the teacher or pupils to bring to the attention of the class some detail of material for close attention and observation. A map, a picture in a book, a graph, or a sample of pupil work placed in the projector is reflected and enlarged on the screen for the class to see. The preferable size of opaque projector is one which will accept materials up to 8½ by 11 inches.

The Blackboard. Although social studies classrooms usually have a blackboard as standard equipment, the most efficient use is not always made of it. Probably more wall space is given over to the blackboard than is needed when that same wall space is at a premium for bulletin boards. The blackboard should not be restricted to teacher use but should be available to pupils for demonstrations of ideas. The use of colored chalk makes possible various interesting interpretations and encourages pupil activity. For the teacher the blackboard is a tool for explanation and guidance; he must not hesitate to make quick sketches to illustrate points of information. The teacher's writing of a word on the blackboard following his use of it in discussion helps the class master the word, as the visual sense carries it to them in addition to their having heard it pronounced. In planning a unit of study with the pupils the teacher can make valuable use of the blackboard as steps in the plan are decided upon and listed with details of procedures or names of pupils responsible for their completion.

Radio in Social Studies Classes. The radio is a potential aid of much value in the social studies. It makes it possible for pupils to experience an event as it is occurring, and it stimulates pupil interest in current happenings. However, a great obstacle to the use of radio is the frequent lack of coordination of broadcast time with classroom time. In spite of this obvious difficulty, a radio receiving set should be included in the equipment of every social studies classroom. Probably less use is made of this aid by social studies teachers than of other supplementary devices. To use the radio extensively requires long-range planning of work based on program announcements supplied by the various networks. The teacher may be unable to include such a program when a fixed course of study is to be followed or when hours of broadcasts do not coincide with class hours. If a particularly worth-while program does not occur in school hours, the teacher can direct pupils to listen to the broadcast in their homes and follow this assignment with a discussion of the broadcast on the following day.

Some teachers have made worth-while use of the radio-broadcast type of class activity by planning with pupils to stage a broadcast using a dummy microphone. Pupils enjoy this procedure and are stimulated to contribute valuable activities to the class effort. Such a procedure is a kind of dramatization and encourages pupils to organize their thinking concerning a particular unit.

Recordings. The phonograph can make an important contribution to most social studies units. Recordings of speeches of outstanding world figures bring reality to the pupils. Increased use of recordings for presentation of dramatic incidents, speeches, plays, and music has resulted in the manufacture of many such records for school use. A record player which will operate at both 33⅓ and 78 revolutions per minute is desirable, thus enabling the class to have a wider range of selection of records. Recordings should be utilized as are all other supplementary aids with preparation for their use and with follow-up discussion. As the social studies teacher plans for additions to the library, he should include some records each year. A helpful list of sources of recordings is available to social studies teachers in the *Eighteenth Yearbook* of the National Council for the Social Studies.[3]

Television. In some schools television has been made possible as a teaching aid because of the availability of the telecasts. As this method of communication is yet to be further developed for gen-

[3] Alice Wood Manchester and Hazel L. Gibbony, "Recordings and Their Place in the Social Studies," Washington, D.C.: The National Council for the Social Studies, *Eighteenth Yearbook,* 1947, pp. 186–196.

eral use, educators should make known the tremendous value possible for schools from this device in order that suitable programs can be made available. By the telecast pupils can witness an event although removed from the actual scene by many miles. Cost, as well as obtaining suitable programs, has been one of the problems in the use of television. That some schools have used it successfully, however, is evidence that it can become a helpful teaching aid.

Summary. Audio-visual aids are essentials in the social studies. Teachers must be encouraged to make greater use of these aids in planning their work, not only as aids to learning but as sources of information which bring greater life and interest to the social studies. They are not, however, to be considered as a substitute for the necessary teacher influence in the classroom. All these aids require specific skills in their use both by the teacher and the pupils. From such supplementary devices pupils acquire new forms of expression and an ability to understand and evaluate many present-day types of communication. In this chapter the brief descriptions of various audio-visual aids and the discussions of the use of such aids as maps, graphs, cartoons, films, recordings, radio, and television has suggested the great potential value of this group of supplementary devices in the social studies.

Questions on the Text

1. How can visual aids be justified in the social studies?
2. Of what value are illustrations in textbooks?
3. *a.* Discuss the use of maps in the social studies.
   b. What is the advantage of the air-age map?
4. Discuss the use of graphs in the social studies.
5. How would you present graphs as a tool to a class?
6. To what uses do various types of graphs seem best adapted?
7. Suggest some methods a social studies teacher needs to employ in caring for pictures or other more or less permanent visual materials.
8. List the advantages to be expected from the use of films in the social studies.
9. What general plan should be followed in the use of a film in a social studies class?
10. *a.* Explain the advantage which may result from having a central projection room for the entire school.
    b. What disadvantages may result from having a central projection room?

11. *a.* Discuss the use of lantern slides and filmstrips in social studies classes.

b. What advantages are afforded by the filmstrip?

12. Why is an opaque projector of particular value in social studies?

13. How may the radio theme be used to advantage in social studies classes?

14. How may standard broadcasts be used in social studies classes?

15. Describe the use of recordings in social studies classes.

16. What practices are to be avoided in the use of all audio-visual aids?

Suggested Activities

1. Make a collection of types of maps useful in the social studies. Mount them in such a way as to afford explanation as to their purpose.

2. Construct a chart of information pertaining to a social studies topic to show the value of this type of visual aid.

3. Draw a cartoon. Explain the unique qualities of the cartoon as a visual device.

4. Examine the illustrations in several textbooks.

a. Set up a list of criteria for illustrations in textbooks.

b. Make a list, as in an assignment, of the qualities, elements, or conditions in the picture you would call to the pupils' attention.

5. Preview a film for use in social studies classes. Write up your evaluation of the film and suggest activities you would use in connection with it.

6. Visit a class where a film is to be shown. Report the entire procedure followed by the class in its use of the film.

7. To illustrate one of the valuable uses of the opaque projector, draw a large map from a small one by using the projector.

8. Construct a unit using recordings as part of the unit.

Selected References

Alilunas, Leo, "Blackboard Diagrams in Teaching American History," *Social Studies,* XXXIII (November, 1942), pp. 306–307.

Arnspiger, V. C., and G. H. Griffiths, "The Motion Picture in Economic Education," *Economic Education,* Washington, D.C.: The National Council for the Social Studies, *Eleventh Yearbook,* 1940, pp. 105–112.

Audio-visual Materials of Instruction, Chicago: The National Society for the Study of Education, *Forty-eighth Yearbook,* 1949.

Bettmann, O. L., "Towards a Visual History," *Social Studies,* XXXIII (December, 1942), pp. 358–361.

Bining, Arthur C., and David H. Bining, *Teaching the Social Studies in Secondary Schools,* New York: McGraw-Hill Book Company, Inc., 1941.

Cordier, R. W., "Pictures as Aids to Learning in the Social Studies," *Social Studies,* XXXIII (January, 1942), pp. 18–20.

Dale, Edgar, *Audio-visual Methods in Teaching,* New York, The Dryden Press, Inc., 1946.

Elliott, Godfrey M., "Documentary Films for Social Studies," *Social Studies,* XXXI (February, 1940), pp. 76–78.

Glick, Annette, "The Use of Visual Aids in Teaching the Social Studies—Past and Present," *The Historical Approach to Methods of Teaching the Social Studies,* Washington, D.C.: The National Council for the Social Studies, *Fifth Yearbook,* 1935, pp. 123–142.

Hartley, William H., ed., "The Use of Audio-visual Aids in Individualizing Instruction," *Adapting Instruction in the Social Studies to Individual Differences,* Washington, D.C.: The National Council for the Social Studies, *Fifteenth Yearbook,* 1944, pp. 100–111.

———, "Audio-visual Materials and Techniques," *The Study and Teaching of American History,* Washington, D.C.: The National Council for the Social Studies, *Seventeenth Yearbook,* 1946, pp. 305–316.

———, *Audio-visual Materials and Methods in the Social Studies,* Washington, D.C.: The National Council for the Social Studies, *Eighteenth Yearbook,* 1947.

———, *How to Use a Motion Picture,* How to Do It Series, No. 1, Washington, D.C.: National Council for the Social Studies, 1947.

Horn, Ernest, "Methods of Instruction in the Social Studies," Part XV, *Report of the Commission on the Social Studies, American Historical Association,* New York: Charles Scribner's Sons, 1937.

Jewitt, Robert E., "Visual and Other Aids," *Social Studies,* XXXII (November, 1941), pp. 321–323.

Johnson, Henry, *Teaching of History in Elementary and Secondary Schools with Applications to Allied Studies,* New York: The Macmillan Company, 1940.

Knowlton, D. C.,"Graphic Methods in the Social Studies," *Social Education,* II (March, 1938), pp. 181–186.

———, "The Factor of Selection in the Use of Visual Aids," *Educational Screen,* XIX (February, 1941), pp. 53–54.

March, Leland, "Pictures in Social Studies Teaching," *Social Education,* V (January, 1941), pp. 26–31.

McKown, Harry C., and Alvin B. Roberts, *Audio-Visual Aids to Instruction,* New York: McGraw-Hill Book Company, Inc., 1940.

Perry, H. A., "Using Audio-visual Aids in the Social Studies," *High School Journal,* XXIX (January, 1946), pp. 32–39.

RENNER, GEORGE, "The Map as an Educational Instrument," *Social Education,* IV (November, 1940), pp. 477–483.

SMITH, TIMOTHY E., "Class-made Visual Aids with Sound Effects," *Social Studies,* XXXIII (April, 1942), pp. 175–176.

THRALLS, ZOE A., "The Use of the Globe," *Social Education,* XI (April, 1947), pp. 165–166.

WESLEY, EDGAR B., *Teaching the Social Studies in High Schools,* Boston: D. C. Heath and Company, 1950.

Chapter 7

RESOURCE MATERIALS IN THE SOCIAL STUDIES

Preview. This chapter is divided into three sections, each devoted to a kind of resource which is valuable in social studies teaching. The first section deals with the social studies library, its significance and essential contents. The second section discusses the local community as a resource and how the social studies class may use this opportunity for experiencing many of the phenomena described in textbooks. The third section is concerned with current materials and the use of free and inexpensive publications which afford much valuable information for the social studies.

Using Library Resources

The Social Studies Library. Establishing and maintaining an adequate library are important responsibilities of the social studies teacher. Although the teacher may be restricted in his desires for library development, by careful planning he can add valuable materials to the library year by year at not too great an outlay of funds annually. When an administration becomes aware of a teacher's good judgment in the selection of library items, the teacher will probably be encouraged in his efforts. For the success of much of the teaching in the social studies it is necessary that a well-stocked library be obtained. The activities which pupils perform in a supervised study period give evidence of the need for a range of materials for successful study procedure. Some study skills which are essential to adequate preparation in the social studies are dependent on the type of material to be used. For example, skill in reading maps demands more map resources than those included in a textbook.

As we speak of the social studies library, we are indicating a separation between the high-school general library and the departmental library. If the high school does maintain a general library, there is no necessity for duplication of materials; but by close cooperation between the librarian and the social studies teacher a satisfactory arrangement can be devised. If there is a general high-school library, all library materials for the school should be centered there. This makes for efficiency in inventory, in repairing damaged books, and in distribution. With the general-library plan the social studies teacher may arrange to house certain materials in the social studies classroom, where they will be available for immediate use. The general librarian will see the economy of this arrangement and encourage it. By this plan the social studies room becomes a branch of the general library and the same rules for book loans to pupils will prevail. Reference books of particular value to the social studies will remain in the social studies room. Other materials from the general library will be returned when units involving their special area have been completed. At this time such materials as may seem valuable for the new unit of study can be withdrawn from the general library for temporary location in the social studies room.

Contents of the Social Studies Library. The extent of materials in the social studies library may be influenced by such factors as school size, available funds, teacher interest, and physical conditions of the school plant. An extensive library is not necessarily a well-equipped one. Out-of-date books and incomplete sets are frequently evidence of failure to consider the library as a significant part of the social studies department. Reference books should be considered the beginning investment in building the social studies library. The following suggestions are typical of essential reference works:

1. A world atlas such as *Rand McNally–Cosmopolitan World Atlas* or *Goode's School Atlas*
2. A historical atlas, such as Lord and Lord, or J. T. Adams in American history, and Robertson and Bartholomew for European history
3. *The World Almanac and Book of Facts*
4. An unabridged dictionary
5. A reputable encyclopedia

Some valuable sets of general-content materials are

1. *A History of American Life*, edited by Schlesinger and Fox
2. *Chronicles of America*
3. *The American Nation Series*
4. *The Dictionary of American Biography*

Investigation has shown that often the reference materials in the social studies library consist solely of an encyclopedia. Many schools do not have a historical atlas.

In addition to the references suggested, the social studies library is more adequate when source materials are included. For American history the source books edited by A. B. Hart are valuable additions to the library. A recent source book of American items is that edited by Commager and Nevins.[1] For the period of the War Between the States an excellent source book is *The Blue and the Gray*,[2] edited by Commager.

Some desirable single-volume reference works are *The American Citizen's Handbook*, edited by Joy Elmer Morgan; *Webster's Geographical Dictionary; Webster's Biographical Dictionary;* and *An Encyclopedia of World History*, compiled and edited by W. L. Langer.

The fields of nonfiction, fiction, and biography constitute extensive portions in the library. The teacher must be guided by his own continual investigation of books and by reference to such a guide as Hanna Logasa, *Historical Fiction and Other Reading References for Classes in Junior and Senior High School*, or to Otis W. Coan and Richard G. Lillard, *America in Fiction*.

State and local history constitute a valuable area for library interest. Pupils can sometimes be led into increased appreciation of history by contact with written accounts of events and institutions within their neighboring environment. Frequently such material may be in pamphlet form. Encouragement of interest in local history can build up this portion of the library when citizens of the community are contacted. A history club under the writer's direction at one time carried out an interesting project of compiling brief accounts of events, biographies, and descriptions of local institutions. Each pupil carried on the research which resulted in a paper. These papers were placed in pupil-made bindings and became a part of the social studies library. A somewhat similar project has been carried on under the writer's supervision at the University of Wyoming, where high-school pupils have gathered local historical data

[1] Henry Steele Commager and Allan Nevins, eds., *The Heritage of America*, Boston: Little, Brown & Company, 1947.

[2] Henry Steele Commager, ed., *The Blue and the Gray, The Story of the Civil War as Told by Participants*, Indianapolis: Bobbs-Merrill Company, 1950.

for articles to be published in a magazine composed solely of such materials and printed through the cooperation of the university archives department.

The social studies library must be permitted to draw periodicals and newspapers from the general high-school library. If there is no general library, then the social studies classroom library should include such periodicals as *Time, Newsweek, National Geographic Magazine, Current History,* and *U.S. News and World Report.*

Using Community Resources

The Community as a Resource. For the social studies the local community affords a kind of source material which surpasses almost all other materials in value for the pupil. In considering the community as a resource for the social studies, teachers are not only seeking to recognize the school as a functional part of the community but they are finding within it those materials necessary for social understandings. Seen in their actual relationship within the community, all the elements of community life become more vital and meaningful for the pupil than when these same elements are discussed from a textbook without actual experience. More and more social studies courses are utilizing the life of the local community in providing ways in which to achieve objectives which pupils recognize as significant.

There are many activities in which pupils may engage which can establish new social understandings and attitudes resulting from pupil participation in such community projects as may be open to youth. Nearly all communities carry on such welfare programs as the annual Community Chest drive. Pupils in social studies classes may become more aware of the responsibilities of citizenship in their community through a unit of work centering around this annual community project. Pupils may share in such a project in various ways, such as distributing literature and announcements, taking turns by groups at community chest headquarters as messengers, and managing some office administrative tasks assigned by the citizens' committee in charge.

In some communities the recreational facilities for youth are inadequate but need not continue so. A social studies class, aware of its local problem, can publicize the situation by a house-to-house canvass, by a committee's visit to the city council to present the problem and to urge the community administration to consider some means to provide for the recreational needs of the community, by writing a series of newspaper articles explaining the situation, or by selecting committees to appear before church groups and service organizations to arouse public interest in the problem.

During a national campaign to inform the public on the dangers of cancer, a social studies class, in cooperation with the school health classes, planned and carried out a community project in which each pupil interviewed people on the streets and in their homes asking such questions as the following:

1. Do you know about how many deaths occur annually from cancer?
2. Do you know what some possible symptoms of cancer are?
3. Do you know what should be done by each person to help prevent cancer deaths?

Such projects as those mentioned above, in addition to acquainting pupils with their community more intimately, provide experience in meeting and talking with business and professional members of the community and with housewives. From such personal contacts pupils gain new attitudes and understandings; they become aware of points of view other than those of their own family or social group. When community and school work together, pupils see no separation of the school from the life of the community and their participation in community enterprises is a natural activity.

The Citizenship Education Project conducted by Teachers College, Columbia University, is giving outstanding leadership in the trend toward school-community participation in local projects. This program attempts to vitalize the fundamentals of citizenship by providing opportunities for pupils to experience many of the community processes about which pupils have up to this time usually had only a reading knowledge.

Planning the Use of Community Resources. Before the community can be used by the social studies class, the teacher must have made some careful study of the community and must be aware of its chief characteristics, its history, its chief institutions, its basic economic structure, its organization, and many other details. A part of the training of a social studies teacher should involve such practice experiences as will give him a background for this important phase of his teaching career. Too often the teacher in training has been removed from the specific examples of social living by a curriculum which has stressed theory and has given too little attention to the life of the community as a means of preparation for teaching. The teacher must see the community in all its processes in order to guide pupils intelligently. In learning to know the community, the teacher will be one with the pupils, especially when he is new in the town. Much of his spare time should be given over to a concentrated effort to become acquainted with local institutions and to achieve a knowledge of the community in general. Following the local news items and editorials, belonging to service organizations, and sharing activity in community campaigns are helpful in learning to know the community.

Suggestions for Community Study. The social studies teacher may wonder how to begin using within the classroom the resources of the local scene. It is obvious that the teacher must lead and guide the pupils in becoming aware of community problems or activities worthy of consideration. Perhaps one approach for the teacher may be the planning for himself of what experiences might seem desirable for the pupils. When the teacher is a newcomer to the community he may need to give much time and thought to becoming acquainted with the area. Some of the possible points of consideration for the teacher may be

1. What are the characteristics of the local population?
2. What environmental factors dominate the economic scene?
3. Is the community mindful of the recreational needs of its citizens?
4. How is the community related to other nearby centers of population?
5. What is the employment situation in the community?
6. What transportation and communication facilities exist in the community?
7. From observation do any conditions appear which might be improved for the general welfare of the community?

From this list of suggestions the teacher will be led to think of others perhaps more pertinent to his own situation.

The daily discussion of news events is a fruitful source of projects for community activities by pupils. When it is observed that local news items are followed by a newspaper editorial comment, the project nearly always has an established significance. For example, a city is considering the addition of a fluorination process to its water purification, and the local newspaper will carry news items concerning the proposal. The resulting discussion in the community will lead to editorial comment in the newspaper concerning the desirability of such a process. From the discussion in the social studies class of this community problem a class has the opportunity to investigate the process, to interview citizens for opinions concerning the proposal, and to aid in any campaign of education of the public for what may be a worth-while community development. Similarly, an editorial in the newspaper about the dangers of rabies, urging citizens to have dogs inoculated against disease, is an opportunity for the social studies pupils to carry on a campaign of public education in cooperation with the city health department. Pupil discussion of such topics under the teacher's guidance presents a valuable background for actual contact with and observance of a local institution or process.

The Field Trip. Pupil observance of community activities is carried on in the form of field trips. The entire class may go on a trip, a committee from the class may go, or an individual pupil may investigate a given community activity and report his findings to the class. The field trip is a valuable device in teaching, but its worth depends upon the teacher's careful planning and organization (see Chapter 10).

The Individual Citizen Resources. Within every community there are individuals whose lifework or experience can be of great interest and value to pupils in the social studies. Members of the professions may visit a class to tell of some of their professional responsibilities, aims, and activities as guidance in vocational planning. Representatives of community organizations or institutions, such as a police officer, a sanitation engineer, a member of the fire department, or an official from a welfare agency, can bring valuable information into the classroom. A visit from an elderly person who is able to describe earlier times in the community is frequently a very instructive experience for pupils, as the past is brought to them by someone who remembers it. As with the field trip, a visit from an individual requires preparation by the class. The visit should be planned in relation to the unit of study, and pupil questions need to be planned in anticipation of the visit. A discussion of points of information gained and pupil reaction to the visit must follow, to hold the valuable experience for the class.

The Community Survey. Another approach to the study of the community is the survey. This activity can be so extensive that it may well involve other areas of the school program in addition to the social studies. As with all other uses of community resources, the survey calls for detailed planning by the teacher and by the teacher and pupils together. Unless such planning is done, so that organization is maintained in the survey, the result can well be a jumbled mass of material. Usually the class is helped if a specific problem or group of questions is the guiding theme of the survey. Pupils must plan what items each will investigate and what details of information will be sought for each. Since several pupils must work together on some types of community activities, it will be necessary for results to be brought together in well-organized form and written clearly for the benefit of the class. This phase of a survey presents a need for English skills. Pupils need to plan methods of interviewing persons concerned with the survey. As a device for studying the local community and becoming aware of local problems, as well as appreciating desirable programs of civic effort, the survey seems to be a worth-while device. It requires careful planning and constant revision of details as it proceeds, and it probably should be attempted only by upper-grade classes.

A Summary of a Survey. The class in Problems of Democracy was working on the general problem of what jobs are open to high-school graduates in the local community. This phase of the larger problem of choosing a life work developed some time after the class had discussed and investigated general phases of the larger problem and were somewhat prepared for the situation of applying recently acquired ideas about jobs to their own situation. Several questions were raised, such as

"How can we learn about work that we can do?"

"Do we have any skills that fit us for any work?"

"What can a high-school graduate expect from local employment as to permanence and salary?"

After some discussion as to procedure it was decided to list the types of jobs which would require no prior specialized training. The following seemed to be the obvious job opportunities: store clerk, waitress, dishwasher, mechanic's assistant, ticket seller, janitor, clerical worker, truck driver, laborer, salesman, dairy-route salesman, and receptionist.

By a series of interviews with employers and employees in the various types of work, members of the class would gather facts concerning the job possibilities from the standpoint of the questions indicated above. From this collected material it would be evident which jobs offered the most permanence and the best wage-and-hour schedule; how much training time was needed at the beginning of various types of employment; what different jobs might require concerning uniforms, health examination, union membership, etc.; the privileges resulting from employment, such as social security, health insurance, sick leave, or seniority rights; and in what lines opportunities seemed most frequent.

Using Current Materials

Free and Inexpensive Publications. One of the characteristics of our industrial age which may at times seem to be a wasteful consumption of materials is the abundance of published material in advertising. Much of this material is attractively designed and while it may emphasize a product or a process, it very often will include helpful information upon a general topic which relates to a unit of work in the social studies. Since these materials are usually intended primarily to advertise, the teacher will face the problem of careful selection in order not to appear to be encouraging the use of some product. Most commercial advertisers realize the educational value of these publications, which may be recognized as contributing a helpful service to the public. For example, the history of some business development can be of much value in a general description. The particular product whose manufacturer is publishing the pamphlet may be representative of several which are of similar nature and typical of the business development which is the significant element in some study unit.

A teacher is soon able to build up a very considerable file of pamphlet publications together with charts, maps, and posters. By careful observation of announcements concerning such materials, the teacher can maintain a file in an up-to-date and extensive condition. *Social Education, The Social Studies,* and the *NEA Journal* carry regular department listings of such materials. The Division of Surveys and Field Service, George Peabody College for Teachers, publishes information on *Free and Inexpensive Learning Materials.* In the public library the social studies teacher may find the *Educator's Index of Free Materials,* edited by John Guy Fowlkes. Government departments publish much information on many subjects, thus providing a valuable source of materials. At nominal annual rates the school can subscribe to various pamphlet services, such as the Foreign Affairs and the Public Affairs pamphlets. Steamship lines, railroad companies, air lines, and foreign governments are sources of valuable poster and map materials as well as pamphlets relating to their specific interests.

Some Advantages in Using Free and Inexpensive Materials. As school curricula have exhibited a growing trend toward general education, social studies teachers have recognized the great supply of helpful material available in free and inexpensive form as one of the chief sources of information to be used by their classes in studying the problems so closely related to everyday living as emphasized in this program. Thus it seems that this material does lend itself well to such use.

The slow reader may also find a benefit in some of these materials, although they may not be written with him in mind. The pamphlets seldom carry lengthy discussions, and they usually include simple explanations of the technical phases of their contents. Such writing enables the slow reader to achieve an understanding of what he reads, and thus the material becomes a source of satisfaction to him. The pamphlets frequently include illustrations and graphic representations which add to their attractiveness.

The use of these materials may encourage in the pupils the habit of using more than one source to arrive at conclusions. The pupil enjoys the variety of these publications, and as he makes use of several different kinds in the process of gathering information about a topic, he experiences pleasure in the exploration and a challenge in organizing his findings.

These materials may also serve as supplementary sources in units of study which are based upon a textbook. In this use they may aid the teacher in providing material for some particular pupil interest.

Materials from Periodicals and Newspapers. Magazine and newspaper articles are of great value in building up the file of information on some topic. When pupils are encouraged to read periodicals and newspapers with an eye toward the building up of resource files on various topics, their reading becomes a more worth-while experience as they examine the contents of an article with a given topic in mind. The periodical may frequently be one that carries in each issue a certain department, which affords opportunity for the pupil to gather a sequence of articles and data upon a topic or series of topics. By becoming well-acquainted with some given periodicals or newspapers, the pupil forms reading habits involving taste and appreciation which are of permanent value to him. As indicated earlier in this chapter, certain periodicals seem to be of particular interest and value to the social studies. It is frequently possible to build discussion periods around a particular magazine. The need for pupil understanding of current topics calls for such use of periodicals. Consistent use of periodicals whose value in social studies is recognized encourages pupils not only to read these particular publications but to evaluate other materials which they will read.

Using the Newspaper. The daily newspaper is an important element in our culture and affords great opportunity for the social studies teacher to guide pupils in their reading habits concerning current happenings. The radio news broadcast reaches many people, but it is of necessity brief in time and does not allow freedom of selection and range in contacting the news as does the newspaper. Teachers are in error when they assume that because the newspaper is so common an element in our civilization, pupils are acquainted with all the make-up of a paper. One of the most interesting, as well as valuable, units in the social studies can be one based on getting acquainted with newspapers.

A beginning on such a study can be made by having the class examine copies of large-city daily newspapers. Local newspaper agencies are usually cooperative in giving day-old papers to the school for such study purposes. It is a valuable experience for pupils to become acquainted with the names of such papers as *The New York Times, The Christian Science Monitor, The Cleveland Plain-Dealer, The Detroit Free Press, The Times-Picayune, The Cincinnati Times Star, The Chicago Tribune, The Denver Post,* and *The St. Louis Post-Dispatch.* As these papers are examined, pupils will discover many differences in form and in the style of publication. Recognition of these differences will raise questions which can lead to a valuable investigation of the newspaper.

The departments of a newspaper must be recognized and evaluated in terms of the type of news contained within that portion of the paper. The news section, editorial page, society section, sports-events pages, financial-news section, vital statistics, classified-advertising section, and comics or amusement section are the usual divisions of the large-city daily paper. Pupils need to understand the purpose of headlines and how to evaluate them. Becoming acquainted with the style of writing in a particular newspaper is a worth-while experience. Pupils realize by their own experience how news may affect the reader, as they compare news write-ups in different papers. Probably one of the most significant values for the pupil to develop from the study of the newspaper is an appreciation of editorial writing. Just as the class may set up criteria to evaluate a news article, so may they also decide on the characteristics of a good editorial. Learning to know the style of writing and the philosophy of a columnist increases pupil ability in using the newspaper. When such a study project is undertaken, the teacher will find it developing in various ways after the first stages of becoming acquainted with newspaper organization. This study sets the stage for valuable pupil experiences and growth as various tangent topics arise from pupil interest and reaction. It should be included in the year plans of all social studies teachers.

Building Resource Units. The trend toward general education courses has caused the social studies teacher more and more to depend upon a variety of materials and new classroom activities in which the textbook with its prearranged material is no longer adequate. The total plan and listed materials together with many explanations of topics for a given unit of work may be described as a resource unit. It is the full explanation for the teacher of all the probable lines of development which might occur in a large problem area or general over-all topic. When a class studies a unit involving some particular area, the teacher has at hand the guiding subject-matter materials and possible plan in his resource unit. Each year additions to the resource unit from new practices, activities, and materials will enrich it as a resource. As some phases seem to be no longer practical or efficient, these may be withdrawn from the resource-unit file. With the resource unit as a guide the teacher can share the planning of the pupils' unit with them, pointing toward desirable objectives suggested by the resource unit and giving suggestions to aid the pupils in the careful and judicious planning of their unit; for the resource unit gives cautions and characterizes as inefficient or less helpful certain procedures and activities recorded from past experience with this general topic.

Some commercially prepared resource units may be available for the social studies teacher, but all such aids must be used in a way most beneficial to the specific class situation. Resource units prepared by the National Council for the Social Studies will be found valuable and suggestive of the procedures of experienced teachers. With experience the social studies teacher will probably find that his own planning and collection of materials is of greatest value to him, although he will be on the watch for new approaches and materials at all times. It will probably be through the building of several resource units that the social studies teacher will lose the dread of trying new curricular procedures where no previously planned outline of work exists. Too often the general education program has been delayed by lack of materials and experience in planning the essential resource unit by the teacher.

Summary. In this chapter attention has been called to the significant resources which are of value to social studies teaching. In the section dealing with the library the responsibility of the teacher in selecting books for the social studies division of the school library is emphasized. Some essential items of a social studies library are listed, and suggestions for guiding pupils in the acquisition of library skills are made. The second section of the chapter explains the worth-while contribution the community can make to the social studies class both as a resource and as a stimulus for better citizenship ideals. The use of the field trip and the techniques involved and the bringing of outside speakers to a class are discussed as ways to have community contacts. The third section discusses the desirability of using published materials such as magazines and the free and inexpensive publications of various organizations. In all three sections the authors have emphasized the responsibility of the teacher in planning and selecting wisely as he makes use of these resources, all of which are supplementary to greater or less degree.

Questions on the Text

1. Why is a library essential in the social studies?
2. What is the responsibility of the social studies teacher concerning the library?
3. Explain the relation between the library and study skills.
4. What is meant by community resources?
5. How can community resources be related to social studies classes?
6. What is the teacher's responsibility concerning the resources of the community and their use in a social studies class?
7. Discuss the particular advantages of each method of making community contacts.
8. What are the techniques involved in a well-planned field trip?
9. How does the use of community resources contribute to a realization of the objectives of education?
10. *a.* What is meant by free and inexpensive materials?
    b. List the types of such materials.
    c. Which type is most reliable?
11. Why is material in pamphlet form frequently of particular value in social studies?
12. What precaution must the teacher observe in using free materials in his class?
13. Discuss the values found in using periodicals in the social studies.
14. *a.* How does the social studies teacher acquire a supply of free and inexpensive materials?
    b. What administrative problem does the teacher face concerning this material?
15. What is a resource unit and how is it to be used in the social studies class?
16. Describe the procedure of conducting a community survey. What problem may be encountered?

Suggested Activities

1. Imagine yourself conducting a class which is studying a given unit. Consult reading guides and select the books to list for pupils to read in relation to the unit.
2. As a social studies teacher you are to plan a library for your room.
   a. What items would you list as a minimum social studies library?
   b. Make a list which would provide any materials you feel would be valuable for a social studies class.

3. List the business enterprises and community activities to which you might conduct a class on an observation trip.

4. Arrange with a social studies teacher in a school near you to accompany him and a class on a field trip. Write up your observation of the techniques employed in conducting the trip.

5. Collect a file of pictures, posters, charts, pamphlets, and clippings on a unit topic. Construct a file case of cardboard to house such material as may be outsize.

6. Demonstrate by use of a chart or in some other manner the results of a teacher's evaluation of some free materials.

7. Construct a resource unit which you think might be useful to a social studies teacher.

Selected References

ALDRICH, JULIAN C., "The Teacher Explores the Community," *Utilization of Community Resources in the Social Studies,* Washington, D.C.: The National Council for the Social Studies, *Ninth Yearbook,* 1938, pp. 15–28.

BAUGH, KATHERYNE, "Teaching the Use of the Library," *Social Studies,* XXXV (January, 1944), pp. 15–16.

COLE, NORWOOD M., "Free Materials for the Social Studies Teacher," *The Social Studies,* XL (January, 1949), pp. 9–17.

ELLIOTT, LLOYD H., and SAMUEL E. DUNCAN, "Resource-use Education: A New Kind of School," *School and Society,* LXXII (July 29, 1950), pp. 71–73.

———, "Small High School Has Valuable Community Resources," *The Nation's Schools,* XLVI (October, 1950), pp. 47–48.

FARR, HENRY L., "Collecting and Using Current Materials," *Social Education,* IV (March, 1940), pp. 174–176.

GLUCK, HAROLD, "A Social Studies Library," *Social Education,* II (February, 1938), pp. 94–98.

GOODWIN, A. N., "Community Resources and the Social Studies," *Social Education,* IV (October, 1940), pp. 414–416.

HIGHLAND, HAROLD JOSEPH, "Federal Publications for American History Courses," *Social Studies,* XXXIII (October, 1942), pp. 261–262.

IRWIN, LEONARD B., "Pamphlet Material for Social Studies Courses," *Social Studies,* XXXII (November, 1941), pp. 320–321.

JOHNSON, WILLIAM H., "The Use of Community Resources in Education," *Social Studies,* XXXI (April, 1940), pp. 147–154.

LENROW, ELBERT, *Reader's Guide to Prose Fiction,* New York: Appleton-Century-Crofts, Inc., 1940.

The Library in General Education, Chicago: National Society for the Study of Education, *Forty-second Yearbook,* Part II, 1943.

McCloskey, Gordon, "The Use of Community Resources," *Adapting Instruction in the Social Studies to Individual Differences,* Washington, D.C.: The National Council for the Social Studies, *Fifteenth Yearbook,* 1944, pp. 112–130.

Memler, Henrietta, and Wayne Alvord, "Study Your Town," *Social Education,* X (November, 1946), pp. 311–313.

Moffatt, Maurice P., *Social Studies Instruction,* New York, Prentice-Hall, Inc., 1950.

Quillen, I. James, and Lavone A. Hanna, *Education for Social Competence,* New York: Scott, Foresman & Company, 1948.

Silverman, Albert, "Historical Fiction in Secondary-school Social Studies," *Social Education,* VIII (April, 1944), pp. 163–164.

Stewart, Nathaniel, "Government Documents Come of Age," *Social Studies,* XXX (March, 1939), pp. 125–128.

Taba, Hilda, and William Van Til, eds., "Community Utilization," *Democratic Human Relations,* Washington, D.C.: The National Council for the Social Studies, *Sixteenth Yearbook,* 1945, pp. 192–228.

Wesley, E. B., *Teaching Social Studies in High Schools,* Boston: D. C. Heath and Company, 1950.

West, Ruth, ed., *Utilization of Community Resources in the Social Studies,* Washington, D.C.: The National Council for the Social Studies, *Ninth Yearbook,* 1938.

Chapter 8

CURRENT EVENTS IN THE SOCIAL STUDIES

Preview. Social studies teachers have an obligation to teach current events, one that cannot be overlooked. Once the task has been undertaken there are certain desirable outcomes. A great deal of information has become available through surveys, experimentation, and investigation. One should regularly be alert for summaries of such. The social studies teacher must ascertain the best methods of presenting current events. This knowledge can come through ingenuity and professional reading. It is very helpful to compile a list of firms that cater to teachers working in this field. The list should represent publications prepared specifically for pupils of secondary-school age and those ordinarily read by adults that seem more or less appropriate.

Current-events Teaching Becomes a Must. Events related to two world-war periods and the years following their terminations caused leaders in educational fields to feel that youth need more training in the examination and interpretation of present-day happenings than they have been receiving. This training has been designated as instruction in contemporary affairs or current events. Some years ago Kimball [1] defined the field as that concerned with all those happenings, both domestic and international, social, political, or economic, a knowledge and understanding of which is necessary as a basis for a citizenship of loyalty and service. The eras of depression, the New Deal, and the Second World War and its aftermath have accelerated the movement. The undesirable features associated with these periods have caused many to feel that secondary-school social studies teachers have placed too great an emphasis upon the past and theories dealing with abstractions with a consequent neglect of the present, the essential, and the practical. In other words,

[1] Reginald S. Kimball, *Current Events Instruction*, Boston: Houghton Mifflin Company, 1929, p. 12.

many desire to prevent the recurrence of international and national maladjustments by giving the oncoming generation a thorough grounding in and a deep appreciation of the place of current events.

The quotation which follows [2] emphasizes strongly the ideas just set forth:

> While the history of former times is essential to a proper understanding of the present, such study is not in itself enough to equip today's citizens with the knowledge and attitudes which they must possess in order to have a sympathetic understanding of the complex and constantly changing world, the future of which they will help to shape. Contemporary events must be studied directly—not only for the sake of acquiring immediately useful information, but also as a means of developing a lively and intelligent interest in world affairs. Such information and such interest in world affairs are essential for young people if they are to fulfill their duties as citizens of their country and of the world.
>
> For these reasons, this Conference recommends a place for the study of current history in the curriculum, particularly in secondary schools.

Desirable Outcomes. If one is to follow the thought of present-day leaders in methodology as it pertains to social studies it seems fitting to examine their ideas as to desirable outcomes. The following are offered as typical:

1. Appreciation of democracy as a way of life. When one knows intimately the problems that are being faced by various governments and the methods that they are using to solve them, a deeper sympathy for our own type of government results. Furthermore, it follows that the many privileges which citizens of our country have come to be better understood and more fully appreciated.

2. Understanding the relationship of our country, together with its present aspirations and future plans, to other nations. A realization that we no longer live in isolation is soon developed. Such study shows clearly that a mature consideration of even domestic problems is intimately related to policies and plans of other countries.

3. Development of powers of observation of the practical manner in which social, economic, and political institutions function. Such an expression as the Community Chest has a deeper meaning when studied as a part of current events. A report dealing with a recent day's activity on the stock exchange brings a wealth of valuable and meaningful information to a

[2] *Proceedings,* World Conference of the Teaching Profession, Aug. 17–30, 1946, Endicott, N.Y.

class. An analysis of a typical week's activity in a national, state, or local office likewise proves interesting and informative.

4. Gaining attitudes of tolerance, open-mindedness, and freedom from prejudice. Current-events study stands for gaining truthful information—facts. Truth produces freedom of thought which often displaces preconceived notions.

5. Preparation of youth for the assumption of responsibilities that come to adult citizens. Intelligent voting is a very important duty that can be made a basis of careful study in secondary schools. Issues, platforms, and biographies of prospective candidates prove very interesting to pupils of this age. It is reasonable to assume that they will carry this enthusiasm over into later life.

6. Broadening the general culture of those who study current events. Many times people are judged favorably or unfavorably on the basis of their acquaintance with recent happenings that have significance; likewise some people expect those with whom they come in contact to know leading personalities in various fields. Furthermore, people who gain intellectual esteem are expected to hold definite opinions substantiated with good evidence.

7. Development of the powers of discrimination in the selection of current reading materials, radio newscasts, and newsreels. Some of the magazines read in connection with a high-school class in current events can be read regularly and with profit by the students throughout their lives. Not infrequently contemporary commentators are discussed and evaluated—an exercise that contributes immeasurably to listening habits. Not a great deal can be done about attitudes toward newsreels beyond the creation of puplic opinion.

8. Promotion of an appreciation for achievement in the many fields of laudable human endeavor. Current news becomes available in more fields than is usually suspected. The boy who thought sports alone important hears about science and art. The girl who previously had an interest only in movies comes to hear about education and religion. Famous writers, adventurers, and philanthropists are eventually given recognition in current-events discussion.

In discussing this same phase of the teaching of current events a pamphlet recently published by The Junior Town Meeting League [3] gave the following objectives:

1. To help pupils to identify important problems and issues, to see how these affect their lives, and to sense what they can do about them

[3] *Discussion and Current Affairs,* Columbus, O.: The Junior Town Meeting League, 1947, pp. 8–9.

2. To help pupils recognize and respect democratic values in reacting to processes, problems, and issues

3. To encourage pupils to develop habits of and a continued interest in reading, listening, inquiring, and observing as ways of keeping informed about current affairs

4. To help pupils acquire the greatest possible proficiency in the skills needed for obtaining and using social information

5. To help pupils acquire proficiency in locating, organizing, and evaluating information on important issues and in evaluating and analyzing the judgments of others on these issues

6. To encourage pupils to "put themselves in the shoes" of other people in evaluating their way of life and their position on problems and issues

7. To help pupils to develop facility in the democratic discussion of issues, orally and in writing

8. To help pupils to see the importance of revising judgments in the light of new evidence

9. To afford pupils a variety of opportunities for appropriate action to implement conclusions reached on important issues

In its *Report on the Teaching of Current Affairs* The National Council for the Social Studies [4] suggested that the following goals are possible of attainment in teaching current affairs:

I. To develop a concern for the immediate and long-range welfare of people in our own nation and in other countries.

II. To help pupils acquire and integrate information from many sources needed for an understanding of contemporary problems.

III. To develop competence in those skills which are necessary for clear and objective thinking: reading; listening; observing; discussing; obtaining, evaluating and organizing information; and reaching conclusions.

Points of Caution. While it is true that most individuals who have taken occasion to make any reference to teaching current events have favored the procedure, there are some points of caution. For instance, it would be most unwise to develop on the part of high-school pupils merely a desire to know the news. This implies that relationships are not clearly seen and understood; also that historical backgrounds are inadequately presented. The laudable objectives of tolerance, discrimination, and gaining the other person's point of view are lost.

[4] *Report on the Teaching of Current Affairs,* Washington, D.C.: The National Council for the Social Studies, May, 1948, p. 7.

In some classes there are evidences of loss of continuity. A topic or even a brief item is presented; another having little or no relationship to the former follows. This continues for an entire period, usually to be followed by another such hour a day or week later. Naturally, the way to obviate this difficulty is to have a topical organization for the reports or briefer presentations as the case may be. Thus a period of discussion can take on the finesse that characterizes a good discussion procedure in any other social study.

Some teachers have been unable to judge even reasonably well the relative importance of a present-day happening. Pupils have gained the impression that a passing event would eventually take up a great deal of space in history books. Possibly they have thought that individuals of mediocre caliber were almost ready to take places ranking along with Washington and Lincoln. Care on the part of the teacher and evaluation techniques executed by the group will prove helpful.

Some contend that since human nature does not change noticeably through the centuries, children could be introduced to the social problems of one epoch about as advantageously as to those of another or of the present. The study of earlier periods would offer an advantage in that a period of time in the distant past can be readily analyzed. On the other hand, it would not be satisfactory to those who contend that more history is learned when it is taught backward.

In certain instances teachers feel that sources of information should be carefully analyzed and classwork should be highly organized and systematized. Then they fall only a little short of the conclusion that there is not enough time for effective presentation of current events. They usually compromise by accepting summaries prepared for popular usage.

One of the most important points of caution has to do with the potential tendency of the parents to feel that current controversial topics are being wrongly presented. This could be especially true in communities where arguments between diverse groups were currently at great tension on questions that might be political, economic, religious, racial, social, etc., in nature. The heat that often surrounds such questions does not mean that teachers should omit them from discussion. It only means that the teacher shall direct pupils in seeking accurate information, in their discussion, and in their effort to render community service. Naturally, caution does need to be taken that the teacher shall not reach a personal point of view and ask the pupils to accept it uncritically. In fact, if the group or individuals within the class should reach conclusions different from those held by the teacher, that could be quite all right.

Surveys Dealing with the Teaching of Current Events. In January, 1934, The National Council for the Social Studies appointed a committee for investigation of the subject of teaching current events, consisting of Margaret A. Koch, Prudence Trimble, Julian C. Aldrich, John R. Davey, George C. Mosley, R. H. Mowbray, D. E. Temple, and Roy H. Price, chairman. After starting a list of general laudable aims for the teaching of the social studies, the committee [5] decided that ". . . we must equip pupils with desirable attitudes toward the present world of affairs and a desire to participate in the constructive solution of public problems." It was further decided that if the study of past civilization is centered chiefly around political history or if the emphasis is placed upon the memorization of certain events and places, it can hardly be assumed that children will be equipped for effective participation in citizenship. In addition, the committee stated vigorously that desirable objectives cannot be obtained in traditional courses or in the more favored unit or topical plan unless material in such courses is definitely related to present-day situations. It was further taken for granted that students must be purposefully led to use current materials, to gather factual materials pertaining thereto, and to evaluate the same.

The purposes of the committee were to (1) survey the field of current-events teaching throughout the United States to discover the extent to which magazines and newspapers are being used in connection with social science teaching; (2) discover the types of magazine and kinds of material within magazines which teachers of social studies consider most valuable; (3) discover the methods of using magazines which have been found most effective in social studies classes.

A questionnaire consisting of three parts relating to the purposes outlined above was prepared. Printing cost and mailing expenses

[5] Roy A. Price, chairman, "The Use of Periodical Literature in the Social Studies Classroom—A Report of a Preliminary Investigation by a Committee of the National Council for the Social Studies," *Social Studies*, XXVII (April, 1936), p. 223.

were defrayed by Scholastic Magazines. One thousand copies were distributed to teachers throughout the United States in accordance with geographical and population elements. Two hundred forty-four replies were received from forty-three states and the District of Columbia. Some of the findings of the committee which seem most significant are

1. Forty-three per cent of the teachers stated that they were too busy meeting information requirements to teach current events.
2. In the schools teaching current events, subscription costs for periodical material were borne by the pupils in 50 per cent of the cases, by the school and pupils in 30 per cent, and by the school alone in 20 per cent.
3. The objectives checked most frequently were training pupils to read and think about current problems and helping them to establish connections between subject matter and present-day situations.
4. The average practice in respect to method seemed to be to let the students bring to class clippings about things that seemed to interest them and to lead a discussion bearing upon the clippings.
5. The majority of the teachers reporting seemed to follow a practice of devoting about 20 per cent of the class time to reading and discussing current events.

In 1928, Hazel M. Woodruff and C. C. Crawford [6] made a survey of the teaching of current events in the high schools of California. They branded current events as a new subject, expressed little or no personal opinion as to whether or not current events should be taught or reaction to the results of the survey, but rather, reported a picture of what they found. They surveyed such topics as how time was found for current-events instruction, how materials of instruction were selected, methods of presentation used, how this new phase was integrated with other phases of the teaching program, and how difficulties growing out of partisan issues were avoided. The report of the survey gives a composite picture of methodology in the setting mentioned.

In a national current-events test sponsored by the American Education Press in January, 1937, 500,000 students participated, representing 199 cities of 10,000 or more population.[7] Of the cities tak-

[6] Hazel M. Woodruff and C. C. Crawford, "Methods of Teaching Current Events in High School," *Historical Outlook*, XIX (December, 1928), pp. 385–390.

[7] *National Current Events Survey*, Columbus, O.: American Education Press, 1937, pp. 1–10.

ing part, 169 sent in individual score sheets on which was given detailed procedure of current-events instruction in the schools responding. Some of the most interesting results of the tabulations secured are as follows:

1. In grades 7 through 12, 44.6 per cent of the teachers devoted one period per week to the teaching of current events; 11.6 per cent gave a few minutes each day to such instruction; 36.2 per cent taught current events incidentally; and 7.6 per cent did not teach current events at all.

2. A weekly paper prepared for class use was used by 43 per cent of the teachers; 46.4 per cent of the teachers asked their classes to bring in newspaper clippings; 10.6 per cent of the teachers reported that they used no materials.

3. In 72.5 per cent of the cases, current events were taught by social science teachers; English teachers presented them in 6.2 per cent of the classes; teachers of still other subjects presented them in 8 per cent of the classes; home-room teachers presented them in 4.6 per cent of the classes; and they were not presented at all in 8.7 per cent of the classes.

4. There were 3,652 out of 3,787 teachers (96 per cent) who reported that the test was helpful and that they would like it every year. The sponsoring company took this to mean that teachers wanted to stimulate greater interest in current events.

5. From the results as a whole, the sponsors concluded that best results are obtained on current events when the answer is "yes" to each of the three following questions: (1) Do you assign one definite period a week to current-events instruction? (2) Do you have the instruction given by teachers in the social science department? (3) Do you use as a text a weekly paper especially prepared for class use? [8]

It has been argued freely that current-events instruction is quite popular with parents, administrators, and students. Teachers have in many instances come to believe that it is good judgment to teach current events if they wish to be rated as superior teachers. The American Education Press [9] uses a point in keeping with this line of thought when it makes the plea, "Use current events as a means of interesting parents in school work. It is one subject that every parent will be interested in following because parents feel that they know something about this subject."

In presenting sidelights on the survey—following the 1937 test—

[8] *Ibid.*, p. 6.
[9] *Ibid.*, p. 9.

the same organization stated that one superintendent reported that his board members were so interested that they asked for the privilege of taking the test. It was also stated that a newspaper in one city reprinted the entire test in order that its readers might check their own knowledge of current events.

The editors of *Time* prepare and present to classes requesting them semester examinations covering the subject of current events. The reactions to this program have sometimes caused them to reprint in the magazine the entire test for their general reading clientele. They have offered also the tests gratis to organizations requesting copies, regardless of whether the general nature of the organization was related to classroom teaching.

Teachers have responded not only because the parents and the administrators have approved the teaching of current events but also because the teachers themselves have found the teaching of current events enjoyable. Certain qualities in this connection which appeal to the teachers are a challenge to the enterprise and initiative, flexibility, timeliness, and adaptability. Probably the fact that current-events teaching offers a change from the regular routine appeals to many teachers favorably.

In attempting to evaluate the manner in which students have received instruction in current events, many teachers have resorted to questionnaires and testimonials. The prevailing trend is for children to report that time spent in this manner, in their opinion, is enjoyable and profitable. The use of this plan has usually been on the basis of giving the children no advance notice of the desired survey and having them turn in papers not identified as to authorship.

During a recent school year one of the authors carried out a controlled experiment dealing with the teaching of current events. Pupils enrolled in the tenth grade modern-history classes at Athens, Ohio, were used as subjects. The purpose of the experiment was to find satisfactory answers to the following questions:

1. Do high-school students make greater achievement in modern European history classes when current events are taught as a part of the course? *

* In this and subsequent statements the expressions *teaching* and *study* of current events shall mean that the students read a weekly current-events maga-

2. Do they show a significant gain, if any, in the field of social information as a result of such study?

3. Do they gain in their ability to reason in life situations involving social science background as a result of the study of current events?

4. Do children who study current events make greater gains in reading comprehension and rate of silent reading than children who do not make this study?

5. Do children who study current events read more periodicals, listen to more radio newscasts, and observe more newsreels than do children who do not make this type of study?

6. Do children who study current events during the course of a year change their attitudes on international questions from conservative to liberal or vice versa to a greater degree than children who do not study current events?

The pupils in these classes during the first academic year constituted the experimental group and those in the classes during the second academic year made up the control group. The one variable factor was that the experimental group made a thorough study of current events in connection with their history course; the control group did not make any study of current events.

Some of the results of the experiment were

1. The experimental group made higher means scores on six tests that were used to show standards of achievement.

2. The experimental group showed a tendency to read more periodicals, listen to more newscasts, and see more newsreels than did the control group.

3. The experimental group showed a tendency to become slightly more liberal in the realm of international attitudes.

4. The experiment offered proof that the teacher has time to teach current events, with the result that pupils will not suffer loss in subject-matter achievement.

5. The experimental group enjoyed the time spent in the study of current events.

A pertinent reference related to studies and surveys is entitled *Report on the Teaching of Current Affairs.* It was prepared by a committee of The National Council for the Social Studies for the

---

zine, were encouraged to supplement the articles of the magazine with additional current-events information, and engaged in thirty or more minutes of discussion weekly dealing with current events.

National Education Association at the request of the World Organization of the Teaching Profession. It was given due consideration in July, 1948. The contents included the preface, introduction, basic purposes for studying current affairs, guiding principles for the teaching of current affairs, and examples of current-affairs teaching selected from schools in the United States. The last-mentioned section constitutes more than one-half of the report.

A formidable study dealing with the teaching and classroom use of current events appeared under the title of *Report on the Activities of the California Council on Improvement of Instruction,* January, 1946–June, 1947. In Part I, after setting forth the general need for study in this area, the purpose is clearly stated as follows:

> The teacher needs to know what materials are available, how each has been used effectively, what results have been achieved with them, and for what purposes they appear to be most promising. It was to provide information on these points that the study to be described on the following pages was carried on, and it is the purpose of this summary to present some of the information derived from it.

Frank B. Lindsay, assistant superintendent of public instruction and chief of the Division of Secondary Education of the California State Department of Education, arranged the study. Fifteen high schools participated. Cooperation of Time, Inc. was secured. Copies of *Time, Life,* and *Fortune,* the *March of Time* Forum Edition films, and *March of Time* radio recordings were made available. The publishers also bore the expenses of certain supervisory and conference activities. They had no voice, however, in the direction of the program. Attention was given to various current materials that can be utilized in English, science, and social studies. Experiments with various techniques for incorporating such materials in the work of the classroom were executed. Comprehensive descriptions under these headings appear in the full report. In Part V, which deals with evaluation, summaries of values to the student, citizenship values, values to the community, values to the teacher, and values to the profession are given. Among those that were reported in relation to the student are the following: [10]

[10] Reginald Bell and Lucien Kinney, *Report on the Activities of the California Council on Improvement of Instruction,* Stanford University, Calif.: School of Education, Stanford University, p. 117.

Increased interest in the subject.
Increased use of the library—especially the *Reader's Guide.*
Increased skill in preparing and presenting reports.
Increased skill in preparing and presenting cooperative projects.
Increased class attendance.
Increased ability in handling of new and unfamiliar adult materials.
Increased number of pertinent questions asked.
Increased number of magazines and newspapers voluntarily used.
Increased interest in national and international problems.
Increased integration of pupils' learning in various fields.

Prevailing Techniques in the Presentation of Current Events. The techniques that are employed in the teaching of current events are probably more diverse than those used in the teaching of social studies generally. This may be accounted for, in the first place, by the fact that the emphasis upon current-events instruction is of relatively recent origin; and in the second place, by the fact that very little research and experimentation dealing with current-events instruction have been completed.

The most common practice is to teach current events in connection with, or as a part of, courses in history, government, economics, and sociology. Occasionally the teaching is done in English classes. In other instances current-events instruction has been placed in the regular curriculum to be studied during a semester. In some places current-events instruction has been an incidental function of a home-room organization.

When current-events instruction is offered in connection with regular social studies courses as mentioned above, the most general practice has been to set aside one period per week for a special discussion of current events. Two other popular methods are (1) the teaching of current events incidentally as specific teaching situations might seem to justify; and (2) the giving systematically of a few minutes each day to this phase of the work.

Techniques of getting current events before the classes in the various patterns mentioned are quite diverse, too. Some are mentioned and defined below with an attempt to give priority to those described most frequently.

Committee method. This plan is one that is based upon the assigning of topics to certain class members who are obliged to report their findings to the entire class on a certain day. For instance, one committee might report on foreign news. Such topics as trade and commerce, international cooperation or the lack of it, activities of heads of governments and lawmaking bodies, and items that might have an effect upon our own country are usually included. A second committee might be assigned national news. Their report would ordinarily include such topics as Presidential activities, doings of Congress, recent decisions of the Supreme Court, and problems that are demanding immediate solution. A final committee could quite properly be assigned to report on state and local news. Items similar in nature to those reported on under the heading of national news are appropriate for the state. Local items can well cover not only governmental activities but also institutional functions. In this latter instance the classroom can indeed serve as a laboratory of community interest.

Collect clippings. The entire class is asked to read newspapers, magazines, periodicals, etc., and collect clippings which tell about significant current events. On given dates, the children bring them to class and summarize orally or read their clippings. The clippings collected may be those that have interested the student or that deal with topics assigned by the teacher. It is quite essential to urge a class to use considerable discrimination. There is a tendency for pupils to select clippings because they seem to be sensational in nature. It must constantly be urged that social values are sought rather than entertainment. Furthermore, many pupils will bring clippings without having previously read them in their entirety. An attractive headline is not sufficient reason for selection. Moreover, if clippings are not brought regularly on a certain day of the week there is a disposition to forget to bring them. In spite of all the necessary cautions, the method has many possibilities for good.

Notebook method. Usually each pupil is asked to compile a notebook to be handed in at a certain time. Clippings may be included as gathered from the sources mentioned in the above paragraph. A brief written interpretation of the clipping is frequently required. Occasionally a composite notebook is made which represents the work of the entire class. A good plan for organization of such material is to use the three divisions mentioned under Committee Method above. There is an excellent opportunity to correlate the work with that of the art department when the matter of the physical makeup of the notebook is approached.

Historical method. In history classes a definite effort is sometimes made to determine a list of current events which deal directly with topics being studied in the textbook. By emphasizing these particular items of news it is hoped to make more meaningful a study of the past by reference to the present. The same general technique can be applied to other social studies. For instance, the teacher of a class in American history making a study of the westward movement might ask the pupils to make a study of current events having their setting in the part of our country then being studied. A class in world history engaged in the study of the history of England would study the contemporary affairs of that country. If in a class in problems of American democracy a study of race relations was in progress, the procedure would be to attempt to find news items related to this topic.

Report on assigned topics. The teacher alone, or with suggestions from the class, may select topics as subjects for reports to be given at opportune times. The following are examples from those that have been successfully used: regular meeting of the United Nations, Republican and Democratic national nominating conventions, progress toward the settlement of a nationwide strike, weekly summary of congressional activity, and periodic sports review. This method offers the possibility of assigning reports to pupils who have a personal interest in the topic pursued. In addition there is abundant opportunity to develop skill in the presentation of an oral report.

Bulletin board. Individuals or committees are asked to bring newspaper clippings or pictures that are related to important events. Pupils logically bear the responsibility of displaying them artistically on a portion of the bulletin board reserved for this purpose. Cautions to observe have to do with relative importance of the items, frequency of change of materials, and balance in subject matter. Many pupils have been observed to spend time profitably looking at the bulletin board at the beginning of an hour, after they have finished other work during a supervised study period, and when leaving the room.

Dramatization. Events in the news are selected and presented in the manner of a stage production. The opening session of a legislative body, the procedure of a nominating convention, and conversations of a diplomatic gathering lend themselves well to this procedure. Very often individuals who have committee assignments will present their work as a mock radio broadcast.

Forum method. A topic selected from the news of the day and one that lends itself to discussion based upon differences of opinion is the basis of a forum discussion. The class elects a chairman, and a panel of speakers is selected. The latter present phases of factual information and opposing points of view. For a specified time the members of the panel discuss the topic among themselves. The chairman strives to see that no one member monopolizes the time, that members speak in turn after being recognized, and that the remarks offered deal directly with the question. When reasonable time has thus been expended, members of the audience are given opportunity to extend supplementary information or to ask specific questions of various members of the panel or both. Naturally the period ends without all those present being in agreement; however, it is quite certain that the entire group leaves better informed. In one school a teacher who taught four classes in the same social study had the same topic discussed in this manner in each of his classes on the same day. Each group elected two speakers whom they judged to have done best, and this group made up a new panel which discussed the same topic as a school-assembly program. It was interesting to note that phases of information were introduced that were omitted in all the classes originally, that each class was proud of its representatives, and that a commendable proportion of the student body took part in the discussion. In another instance a topic that had been used in a social studies class became the basis of a community program at the school building in the evening. One high school built its commencement program around this type of discussion, with selected seniors being the participants. It is probable that, as Torrens [11] has remarked, "The children like these open forums better than closed panel discussions or committee work because they like action."

After a pupil has participated in a panel exercise he should practice self-examination to determine whether he made a maximum con-

[11] Hazel L. Torrens, "Current Events in the Ninth Grade," *Social Education*, X (October, 1946), p. 256.

tribution. The following student check list for self-appraisal [12] is quoted as a pertinent instrument in this connection:

What part did I play in this group discussion?

1. Was I an active participant?
2. Was I an enthusiastic participant?
3. Was I an active listener to the contributions of others?
4. Did I dominate the group?
5. Did I stray from the point under discussion?
6. Was I timid about expressing my point of view?

Was I well prepared to participate in the group discussion?

1. Did I select facts pertinent to the problem?
2. Did I select and organize my facts in such a way as to make an interesting presentation to the group?
3. Did I support my point of view with adequate relevant facts?
4. Did I find questions unanswered in my mind because of insufficient data?
5. Did I use reliable sources of information for the facts I needed?

What was my attitude during the group discussion?

1. Was I opinionated?
2. Was I willing to respect the point of view held by other group members?
3. Was I willing to weigh the varying points of view presented before arriving at a final decision?
4. Was I concerned if the discussion became emotional?
5. Was I eager to hear what other members of the group were thinking?
6. Was I too willing to compromise on issues I regarded as important?
7. Was I, in general, opposed to compromise to the extent that I delayed or prevented the group from reaching a conclusion?

Did I benefit from participating in this group discussion?

1. Did I do clear thinking, or did I merely "rearrange my prejudices"?
2. Will the skills I acquired in the group discussion help me to think clearly and intelligently in new situations?

Cartoon method. Classes often make a study of cartoons that depict important news items. They are usually asked to look for them on the editorial and front pages of daily papers. Upon being brought to class they are displayed and explanations are given. Profitable

[12] *Learning through Group Discussion,* Columbus, O.: The Junior Town Meeting League, 1949, p. 30.

discussion of the correctness of the cartoonist's point of view usually takes place. Often questions of fact are raised by those who desire information. A subtle suggestion from the teacher to those who would like to try drawing a cartoon of their own based on current events usually meets with a generous response.

Debate method. Topics in the news which represent divergent opinion and reaction are selected. Students choose the viewpoints with which they sympathize and challenge other members of the class to debate. Attention is given simultaneously to learning regular rules of parliamentary procedure.

Topical method. The above discussion has intimated and been based upon the assumption that current events will emphasize the news as it develops. Obviously there is little possibility of knowing at the beginning of a year what trend the discussion will take. Regardless of the methods of presentation used, some teachers prefer to compile a list of general topics and have them studied intensively. They may be repeated annually or less frequently. A reasonable amount of recent historical background is included. Each can be thought of as constituting a brief unit of work. For example, the topic of housing might be used. After an overview has been presented to show the importance of the subject and to arouse interest in it, the following questions could well be included among those to be studied:

1. Has the nation been well housed throughout its history?
2. What factors produce housing shortages?
3. What is the relationship of science and invention to housing?
4. What types of law now in existence prevent the unrestricted building of houses?
5. In what manner has the Federal Government demonstrated an interest in this subject?
6. From what private and business sources may financial help be secured for building houses?
7. Is it cheaper to own a house or to rent one?
8. Is the housing problem more or less acute in our local community than elsewhere?
9. What portion of family income at various levels should be spent on shelter?
10. Where can those desiring to build receive helpful suggestions for planning, designing, etc.?

Sources of information are numerous in relation to a topic of this type. A good library is most helpful. Local contractors and architects often have good suggestions in pamphlet form. Appropriate agencies and departments of the Federal Government have materials for distribution at a nominal fee. Pupils properly encouraged bring materials from diverse miscellaneous sources.

Other topics that can be used at least as advantageously as the one just described are "Labor Organizations in the United States," "Our Relations with Latin America," "Presidential Candidates," "Means by Which We Secure the News," "Factors Tending toward War or Peace," "Recent Developments in Science," "Improvement of Health," "Life in a Selected Country," "Population Trends," etc.

In one instance where current events constituted a semester's course the following topics were used: [13]

"Should Our High School Have Some Form of Student Government?"

"What Are the Causes and Possible Solution of the Problem of Juvenile Delinquency?"

"How Can Relations between Negro and White Americans Be Solved?"

"How Can Russia and the United States Get Along in the Postwar World?"

"Should Compulsory Peacetime Military Training be Adopted?"

"Should the Voting Age Be Reduced to Eighteen?"

"How Can We Best Help the Returning Service Man to Readjust to Civilian Life?"

"How Can the Problem of the Postwar Air Age be Solved?"

The above lists of topics may appear at first to duplicate those presented in a course in Problems of American Democracy. This is not necessarily true, in that the range of selection is much broader. The entire world can be drawn upon for consideration. Furthermore, the list is in no manner restricted to ideas bearing directly upon democracy. Some teachers combine the selection-of-topic plan with that of having a frequent brief running account of news items.

Common Sources of Current-events Materials. The social studies teacher is frequently at a loss to know where to turn for suitable published materials. The following suggestions are offered on the basis of information recently received from some of the publishers in this field:

[13] Katherine Baugh, "A Semester Course in Current Problems," *Social Studies*, XXXVII (May, 1946), pp. 216–222.

American Educational Press, 400 South Front St., Columbus, O., publishes weekly *Current Events, Every Week,* and *Our Times,* with different grade levels recommended for each. Teaching helps are made available regularly, for example, *Education Today, Notebook Bulletin.* Testing programs and surveys are provided. Publications such as *Teaching Current Events* and *Discussion and Current Affairs* appear irregularly. Supplementing the use of the periodicals mentioned above, the Junior Town Meeting League is sponsored. Appropriate pamphlets are furnished local chapters to stimulate their organization procedures and the effectiveness of meetings.

Civic Education Service, 1733 K St. N.W., Washington, D.C., publishes *The Civic Leader,* sent to teachers and containing professional helps of varied types. *The Young Citizen, The Junior Review, Weekly News Review,* and *The American Observer* are published for classroom use.

Newsweek, 152 W. 42d St., New York 18, receives orders for subscriptions for classroom use. Tests, extended treatments of current problems, suggestions for club discussions, weekly study guides, "Map-of-the-Month," etc., are furnished to teachers.

The Ohio Scholarship Tests, State Department of Education, Columbus, O., regularly publishes two tests annually on contemporary affairs. One is available in April and the other in December. In addition, current-events responses are tabulated and evaluated as a part of periodic social studies surveys.

The Reader's Digest, 353 Fourth Ave., New York 10, under the auspices of its Educational Department offers its publication and services to schools. Among these is a *Teaching Guide.* Suggestions are classified under English, social studies, and reading.

Scholastic Magazines, 7 East 12th St., New York 3, publishes a group of weekly magazines among which the following are included: *Junior Scholastic, World Week, Senior Scholastic,* and *Practical English. Scholastic Teacher* is furnished in an effort to assist with classroom teaching problems.

Time, Time and Life Building, Rockefeller Center, New York 20, supplies this magazine. Tests, wall maps, suggestions for classroom use of *Time, Fortnightly Discussion Guide of Current Affairs,* etc., are furnished as aids for classroom use.

In addition to securing a set of magazines aggregating one per pupil it is desirable to have other materials and resources available. Among the magazines that are often made available for classroom use are *Life, Fortune, Current History, National Geographic, United States News, Survey Graphic, Atlantic,* magazine sections of *New York Times* and *Christian Science Monitor, Vital Speeches, Current*

Biography, Harper's, New Republic, Journal of Pan-American Union, and *American Mercury.* Local daily newspapers can be used quite advantageously.

Pamphlets constitute a source of help that should not be overlooked. *Building America, Headline Series, Problems in America, Public Affairs,* and *Wake Up America* are well-known. Many commercial and industrial concerns furnish pamphlets upon request. (For further discussion related to resources of various types see Chapter VII.)

Evaluation. In the realm of current events as in any other phase of instruction, careful evaluation must follow the teaching procedures. Was the time expended used to best advantage? Were the objectives attained? Did the pupils undergo changes of attitudes, habits, etc., that commended the entire proceedings? A publication cited above [14] presents evaluation under three headings as follows:

Evaluation of classroom work in terms of the pupil should be evidenced by:

1. Results of tests of information and understanding.
2. Results of tests of skill in the use of materials, such as maps, charts, statistical graphs.
3. Ability to evaluate materials critically—orally and in writing—as read, heard, or observed, and to analyze and understand the nature of propaganda.
4. A noticeable increase of interest in current affairs through listening to worth-while radio programs, reading, joining discussion groups, and leadership in discussion groups.
5. A positive influence on attitudes and on behavior in a variety of natural situations inside and outside of school. This includes such attitudes as: willingness to reserve judgment, respect for opposing points of view in the discussion or consideration of current affairs.

Evaluation of instruction in current affairs in terms of its influence on the school as a whole can be evidenced by:

1. Inclusion in the activities of the general student organization of the school of problems in the field of current affairs.
2. Membership and leadership in school social studies forums, clubs, discussion groups.
3. Issuance of school publications containing matters dealing with current affairs at the school, local, state, national, and international levels.

[14] *Discussion and Current Affairs,* pp. 17–18.

Evaluation of results of instruction in current affairs in terms of their influence in the community can be evidenced by:

1. Student participation in suitable community projects.
2. Student attendance at or participation in community forums or programs growing out of a current affairs situation, such as a Council for Better Community Relations, established interfaith meetings, etc.
3. Student participation in community social-service work growing out of current affairs.
4. Student participation in the activities of the school which influence the cultural development of the community, such as presenting to parents worth-while radio plays, films, and valuable information dealing with vital phases of the contemporary scene.
5. Leadership of students in bringing major problems to the attention of the community through school forums and school and student publications that are carried to the homes by the students.

Summary. In this chapter an effort has been made to indicate that the teaching of current events is a serious obligation for social studies teachers. If the job is well done, future catastrophes of national and international character may even be averted.

There are numerous desirable outcomes that may follow when current events are well taught. Among them are the following: appreciation of democracy as a way of life; understanding the relationship of our country to other nations; development of the powers of observation of the manner in which institutions function; gaining attitudes of tolerance; preparation of youth for the assumption of responsibilities that come to adult citizens; broadening of culture; development of the powers of discrimination in the selection of current reading materials, radio newscasts, and newsreels; and promotion of an appreciation for achievement in the many fields of laudable human endeavor.

Even though the teaching of current events is generally accepted by secondary-school social studies teachers there are cautions to observe. Pupils should not wish merely to know the news as an end in itself. Some pattern of study and discussion should be established that will ensure continuity. Discretion should be exercised by the teacher in an effort to determine which events of the day are merely interesting items and which ones are likely to have enduring significance.

Various experiments and surveys that have been executed should be known and studied by social studies teachers. These have frequently been sponsored by publishers of commercially prepared materials for instructional purposes, by The National Council for the Social Studies, and by individual classroom teachers.

Methods of teaching current events are as numerous as those applied to other phases of social studies teaching. Among those most commonly found in practice are the following: committee method, collecting clippings, notebook method, historical method, reports on assigned topics, bulletin-board work, dramatization, forum discussion, cartoon method, debate procedures, and topical method.

It is most convenient to know where materials of instruction and other resources can be found. A listing of such sources has been made a part of the chapter.

Questions on the Text

1. What is the relationship of epochs of national and international chaos to the emphasis on the teaching of current events?
2. Define current events.
3. Give eight desirable outcomes that should result from a well-planned and properly executed program of instruction in current events.
4. Mention some cautions that will need to be kept in mind by the teacher of current events.
5. Mention two or more surveys or studies dealing with current-events instruction. Give the name of the sponsor, purpose, and results secured.
6. Methods of presentation were grouped under ten headings. Name five or more of them and describe each procedure briefly.
7. Give the names and addresses of several publishing companies that furnish classroom materials related to current events.

Suggested Activities

1. Write a brief statement of your opinion as to whether or not current events are given enough emphasis in secondary-school social studies classes.
2. Make your own list of objectives for teaching current events. (If you use ideas found in the chapter rephrase them in your own words. Try to include some that are not found here.)
3. Examine some of the magazines and periodicals that are used in classes studying current events. Evaluate them in respect to their suitability for the grade level, news emphasized, and fair presentation.
4. Make a list of programs that will appear over the radio and/or television during the next few weeks that you think could be used to advantage in teaching current events.

5. Secure a list of coming attractions from the local movie houses. Indicate how any of them could be used in relation to the study of current events.

6. Some social studies teachers spend a few minutes daily discussing current events. Criticize this procedure.

7. Visit a class at a time that current events are being discussed. Evaluate your observation.

8. Make a general outline to show how you would handle current events in a specified social studies class during an entire semester.

9. Make some comments about the possible use of current events as a means of solving the problem of individual differences.

10. Give arguments for and against scheduling a class in current events to meet five days per week during an entire semester.

Selected References

Baugh, Katheryne E., "A Semester Course in Current Problems," *Social Studies,* XXXVII (May, 1946), pp. 216–222.

Bell, Reginald, and Lucien Kinney, *Report on the Activities of the California Council on Improvement of Instruction,* Stanford University: School of Education, Stanford University, June, 1947.

Brown, Ralph Adams, "The Town Meeting: Agency for Cooperation," *Social Studies,* XXXII (December, 1941), pp. 353–354.

Clogston, Evan B., "Using the Newspaper in Social Studies Instruction," *Social Education,* V (February, 1941), pp. 115–117.

Craf, John R., and M. P. Moffatt, "Current Events," *Social Studies,* XXXI (May, 1940), pp. 219–220.

Dewey, H. E., "Youth Speaks Out on Americanism," *Social Studies,* XXXII (April, 1941), pp. 151–153.

De Yonker, Marjorie, "The American Press, a Mirror of the Times," *Social Studies,* XXXVII (January, 1946), pp. 31–33.

Dresden, Katharine W., "The Newspaper in the Classroom," *Social Education,* V (December, 1941), pp. 581–583.

———, "Current Materials in the Classroom," *Social Education,* XIV (January, 1950), pp. 21–23.

Discussion and Current Affairs, Columbus, Ohio: The Junior Town Meeting League, 1947.

Friedman, Kapple C., "Practice in Formulating Public Opinion," *Social Studies,* XXXVII (May, 1946), pp. 198–199.

Gemmecke, R. H., "Current Events for Civic Competence," *Social Education,* VII (February, 1943), pp. 76–77.

HEATHCOTE, CHARLES WILLIAM, "Teaching Current History," *Social Studies*, XXXVI (December, 1945), pp. 357–359.

HOSKINS, LUELLA, "Student Opinion on the Air," *Social Education*, V (May, 1941), pp. 348–350.

KIMBALL, REGINALD S., *Current Events Instruction*, Boston: Houghton Mifflin Company, 1929.

KINNEY, LUCIEN, and KATHARINE DRESDEN, *Better Learning through Current Materials*, Stanford University, Calif.: Stanford University Press, 1949.

KRUGER, F. K., "The Teaching of Current Events in Our Public Schools," *Social Studies*, XXXII (March, 1941), pp. 101–105.

Learning through Group Discussion, Columbus, Ohio: The Junior Town Meeting League, 1949.

LONG, MADELINE S., "The Junior Town Meeting Comes to Minneapolis," *Social Education*, XII (April, 1948), pp. 169–171.

Make Youth Discussion-conscious, Columbus, Ohio: The Junior Town Meeting League, 1948.

MEYER, FRANK, "Current Events in the Junior High Schools of Michigan," *Social Studies*, XXXI (December, 1940), pp. 363–365.

MICHAELIS, JOHN U., "Current Instructional Problems in Secondary-school Social Studies," *Social Education*, X (November, 1946), pp. 307–310.

MOFFATT, MAURICE P., *Social Studies Instruction*, New York: Prentice-Hall, Inc., 1950, Chap. X.

———, "Parliamentary Current Events," *Social Education*, V (March, 1941), pp. 194–195.

PORTER, LOUISE, "Contemporary Political Thought and Its Implications for Social Studies Teachers," *Social Studies*, XXXI (April, 1940), pp. 154–158.

Proceedings, World Conference of the Teaching Profession, Aug. 17–30, 1946, Endicott, N.Y.

Report on the Teaching of Current Affairs, Washington, D.C.: The National Council for the Social Studies, May, 1948. (Mimeographed.)

Teaching Current Events, Columbus, Ohio: American Education Press, 1948.

TORRENS, HAZEL L., "Current Events in the Ninth Grade," *Social Education*, X (October, 1946), pp. 255–256.

WESLEY, EDGAR BRUCE, *Guide to the Study of World Affairs*, Minneapolis: The Minneapolis Star, 1947.

WESLEY, FAY MEDFORD, "Criteria for Selecting Current World Events," *Social Education*, XIII (February, 1949), pp. 76–78.

WOODRUFF, HAZEL M., and C. C. CRAWFORD, "Methods of Teaching Current Events in High School," *Historical Outlook*, XIX (December, 1928), pp. 385–390.

Chapter 9

SOCIAL STUDIES AND OTHER SECONDARY-SCHOOL SUBJECTS

Preview. The present trend in the teaching of social studies is to give less emphasis to the names of individual subjects as such. Some have designated such efforts as *fusion,* others as *integration,* and still others as *correlation.* The last-mentioned procedure will be illustrated amply with special reference to combining work in two fields, history and English.

Fusion. As intimated above, the present chapter deals with classroom practices where the individual and traditional subject is not stressed. Some years ago an effort to attain this end was approached through what was called *fusion.* In brief, this means to take the content of various social studies and merge it into one course of fewer courses than previously existed. The move presupposes a close relationship of content in nature and purpose. This movement gained emphasis for a time owing to at least two reasons. First, there was a consciousness that subjects have long been stressed to the neglect of the pupil and his efforts to adjust to life situations. Second, there has always been a tendency to add secondary-school subjects rather than to drop them. The number proposed in social studies became rather large. Thus fusion was a matter of expediency.

If one attempted to fuse content or find a book that had done this, some examples would show frequently in the pattern. History and geography can and are often taught simultaneously by the teacher during the same class hour and certainly during the time spent on a unit. Many of the cause-and-effect relationships of history are readily explained by geographical facts. Historical movements have been stimulated or deterred by geographical phenomena. Any event has location as well as time. Facts associated with this location are easily taught at the psychological moment.

Not only is history related to geography as pointed out above, it is definitely associated with economics. At one time certain courses were offered bearing such names as Economic History of the United States. With little effort we recall that in the history of our own country we studied panics, depressions, recovery, and prosperity. Our nation's history has always been closely related to problems of production, consumption, distribution, exchange, and taxation. It is not especially difficult to see that a resourceful teacher could fuse varying amounts of economics with the teaching of history or history and geography.

Government is so closely related to the study of history that the manner in which it is taught in various schools is indeed interesting. For instance, some teachers present topics in American government at appropriate places in connection with the study of history. A detailed examination of the Federal Constitution usually follows the historical study of the meeting of the Constitutional Convention; a study of state government naturally follows the period in history after which most of the states had been admitted to the union; and a study of municipal government logically follows the decades which stress the growth of large cities.

Little imagination and observation are needed to show the interrelationship of sociology, occupations, problems in democracy, Latin American history, etc., to such a program. In fact, it is readily observable that master teachers in any one of the regular social studies know and use the vital elements from the others in the study of any unit. They may or may not call the procedure fusion. In any event it is, although the degree involved may vary.

Those who have taught in departments stressing fusion or who have proceeded along this path in individual classes claim that the approach has the following advantages:

1. There is a marked economy of time. Pupils can gain a working knowledge of all the social studies by taking fewer units of work than would otherwise be possible.

2. Content that is most useful is selected and taught. That which has nothing more than cultural value is often deleted.

3. Noncollege-preparatory pupils gain a great deal from such a program. The fact that they drop out of school before graduation or at least do not enter higher institutions of learning makes it imperative that functional social studies information be mastered as early as possible.

4. Social studies content becomes more meaningful. Pupils are given immediate help in adjusting to environment.
5. Subjective impressions lead to the conclusion that pupils enjoy work more when it is presented in this manner rather than by traditional methods.

Those who oppose the method are likely to speak in such terms as "fusion becomes confusion." [1] The disadvantages usually suggested include the following:

1. Basic information is often overlooked. The complete vocabulary, concepts, and understandings necessary in any one of the social studies are never mastered.
2. Few or no good textbooks are available. Probably it is not possible to write such books. (The Rugg series was an effort in this direction.)
3. A great deal of information may be learned in the total pattern, but little competence is gained in any one area.
4. Teachers are not broadly enough prepared to handle such a program. Most of them have taken training that represented narrow specialization.
5. Those pupils taking college-preparatory courses enter higher institutions of learning poorly prepared.

This discussion of fused courses in the social studies is not presented as representing a trend of the times. In fact, the results of efforts in this direction have been somewhat disappointing. However, there is a belief on the part of many that resourceful individuals may yet make a contribution along these lines.

Integration. Integration will not be dealt with at great length except to the extent that it has relationship to fusion as described above and correlation which follows. Possibly *integration* is not so good a word in social studies education circles as it is in the field of mathematics. On the other hand Good,[2] in his definition of integration, gives it as synonymous with fusion, which is described as follows: "Course of study, integrated: A course of study in which pupil activity is centered in themes or areas of training and which draws on the content of the various school subjects as mutually associated in some genuine life relation." Maybe the perfectly integrated individual is yet to be found; however, we continue to strive in this direc-

[1] Edgar C. Bye, "Fusion or Confusion?" *Historical Outlook,* XXIV (May, 1933), pp. 264–267.

[2] Carter V. Good, ed., *Dictionary of Education,* New York: McGraw-Hill Book Company, Inc., 1945, p. 109.

tion. If we could observe a cross section of a school building with various teachers engaged in their routine classroom activities, some startling implications would probably emerge. Some of these teachers sit passively at their desks, ensconced in the seemingly impregnable fortresses of their special departments; other teachers are actively engaged with hammer, ax, crowbar, and saw, tearing down the walls which separate their departments from those of their neighbors. From the destruction of barriers less tangible, but often more formidable, there grows integration.

All learning, in order to be valuable to the individual pupil, must be integrated. If this unifying of learning is not assisted by the teacher, it will ultimately take place in a less efficient and less complete manner through the mental processes of the pupil, assuming that he is capable of seeing relationships in his learning and of strengthening them when he discovers them. Categorical learning is retained only as it is applied to allied fields of interest and endeavor. It is, indeed, a challenge to teachers to facilitate this integration, to assist in the discovering of relationships in learning, and to develop an independence on the part of the pupil in making his own integrative bonds in learning.

Correlation. There is a great deal that can be said with assurance about correlation. In this area we are not exploring a new field. For many years the elementary curricula have shown steps in this direction. More recently the secondary schools have made an effort to break down the boundary lines between subjects in conformity with Good's [3] definition of correlation: "(1) A course of study in which textual references or specific suggestions are made for relating materials in one subject field with pertinent materials in other subject fields. (2) A course of study that outlines a program to interrelate the instruction of two or more subject areas relative to specific topics and that lists under the respective subject-area headings the activities, knowledges, skills or appreciations that each subject area can or should contribute to the understanding of the topic in question." Probably more positive steps have been taken in some of the Southern states than elsewhere; this has been especially noticeable in those states that have reorganized curricula. The State of Virginia may be regarded as a pioneer in this activity. It laid out a program that had three points of emphasis. One analyzed our

[3] *Ibid.*

life and culture in terms of social functions; one was a description of objectives in terms of skills and attitudes; the third was a statement of levels of maturity as centers of interest.

Mississippi, Georgia, Arkansas, Texas, and California have made similar efforts to determine the scope and sequence of the curriculum.

The Eight-year Study[4] did much to define the limits of the curriculum in terms of pupil needs rather than in terms of adult concepts of them.

In addition, it should not be overlooked that many individual teachers throughout the nation have made ventures of their own in the direction of correlation. Of course, these have been most effective when carried out under the direction of teachers from both participating departments, supplemented by helps and encouragement from the school principal.

In this brief consideration of efforts, some attention should be given to objections that have been raised.

The administrators will find it difficult to make daily schedules for pupils in such manner that they are in the proper sections to benefit from the efforts proposed. The teacher of one of the two subjects is often definitely untrained in the second subject or lacks confidence in his ability to make a contribution to the venture. In some situations the idea is looked upon as a fad or fancy that will start with much fanfare and disappear before any worth-while results have been attained. Some have genuine fear that one of the subjects will be greatly forwarded at the expense or to the neglect of the other. Then, too, it is much easier to carry on as the teaching was done last year than it is to attempt innovations. Textbooks are more readily available for individual-subject emphasis. Parents and pupils are not, in general, acquainted with the aims of a program of correlation. It is not at all our purpose to describe a program that is a great departure from commonly accepted procedure; rather, we wish to show through one example that it is possible to have the teachers of history and English cooperate in the teaching program in a way that will be helpful to the students.

For the reasons stated above, we feel obligated to state the aims involved. The first one herewith presented is that it seems advisable

[4] This study is reported fully in *Thirty Schools Tell Their Story,* New York: Harper & Brothers, 1943.

to think always of the whole pupil rather than of his specific relationship to one area of subject matter. By pooling efforts in these two subjects, which lend themselves to this procedure, the goal of dealing with the pupil as a unified personality is more likely to be reached. Next, we too often find that pupils seem to feel that a particular subject has usefulness only in the classroom where it is taught; that is, if the work is of such quality that a passing grade is earned, there is no need to think about it beyond the setting involved. By making reference to the same materials in two or more classrooms, the pupil is led to see that a broader usefulness is involved. Furthermore, duplication of effort is avoided. If it is found that certain skills and information areas are being well taught in one class, it becomes unnecessary to teach this same work in a second class. Often the teachers of the two subjects desire that the same skills and information materials be learned; in such cases it is obvious that joint efforts in the same direction will attain better results than uncorrelated procedures. Finally, if there are certain goals of learning that are desirable, it is reasonable to assume that a dual approach to the attaining of them will prove helpful in the same way that a reasonable amount of drill helps in the formation of a habit.

For purposes of illustration, the material that is herewith presented will be confined to the traditional subjects of history and English.

Expectations of the History and English Teachers. One of the approaches that should be made in connection with this topic is to state some of the points that each teacher would like the other to stress in his class. Of course, the purpose is to get better results in the subject taught by the teacher who states the points. The following suggestions are those made by the history teacher as quasi requests of the English teacher:

1. Improve the speed and comprehension of students' reading. This applies especially to silent reading; however, there are numerous occasions when the children are asked to read orally. In such cases, it is highly desirable that they be able to pronounce readily the words that are included in the vocabulary range of their grade.

2. Improve the legibility of their written work. Too often even those pupils in the upper years of secondary work are careless or are unable to produce work that is easily read.

3. Improve the accuracy of spelling as applied to words commonly

used. (The history teacher will take care of teaching the spelling of special vocabulary as applied to the subject itself.)

4. Improve the quality of punctuation used by the students. Too frequently they fail to include subjects, verbs, and periods with declarative sentences.

5. Teach the pupils paragraph structure so that they will turn in written work and give oral reports in history that show topic sentences, logical development of thought, and good summary statements.

6. Stress the importance of producing written reports that represent the pupil's own thinking rather than a reproduction of the material found in a single encyclopedia or reference book. Best results can probably be attained by getting the pupils to use more than one reference for each report or topic approached.

7. As a result of a conference with different teachers involved in teaching a particular grade, reach a general agreement on techniques of placing name, date, subject of the paper, etc., on written materials.

8. Encourage the student to select as subjects for oral and written compositions topics that have been initiated in connection with the study of historical materials or contemporary affairs.

9. In regular classroom discussion it would be very helpful if the pupils would enunciate more distinctly and talk much more loudly than they usually do. The English teacher can be very helpful by stressing this point at the time oral reports are being given.

10. It is desired that the grammar used by the pupils be technically correct. Naturally, this is a point that requires patience and continuous efforts.

11. Giving the students an acquaintance with considerable historical fiction and with poetry having historical background is highly desirable. It is all the more beneficial if presented at about the same time that the subject under consideration is being studied in history. Good history and literature texts provide suggestions for correlated reading.

It would scarcely be equitable for the history teacher to set forth an elaborate list of expectations of the English teacher without being able to see of his own accord some specific services that he can give in return. The following are some points of common practice on the part of one author of the present article:

1. To correct immediately every grammatical error and mispronounced word that occurs in the history class.

2. To commend highly those students who regularly use correct rules of grammar, neatness, and legibility when preparing written work.

3. To make available to the English teacher periodically written work

done by the students so that he may check it to see how well the techniques taught in his class carry over to the other classes. Of course, the pupils will not know which sets of papers will be used for this purpose.

4. To make a report to the English teacher each time a pupil gives an oral report before the history class. (This will be done by means of a check sheet described below.)

5. To teach efficiently and completely the history of any particular period which will help the pupils to understand the literature being studied in the English class. Even if it is necessary to digress from the regular routine, a concentrated approach can be carried out in specific instances.

Without prejudice to the means of correlation suggested above, the following activities are given as examples of work that was recently done in certain history classes, representing opportunities for the use of skills learned in both subjects.

1. Imaginary letters that individuals of various historical periods might have written were prepared and read.
2. Crossword puzzles which used almost entirely the vocabulary of a period of history were prepared and presented to the class to solve.
3. Imaginary orations that statesmen of different periods might have delivered were prepared and presented to the groups.
4. Cartoons that showed class struggle were drawn and were made more effective by the addition of dialogue and titles.
5. Imaginary newspaper accounts, as modern reporters might have written vital historical events, were prepared, together with headlines, and placed on the bulletin board.
6. Songs that might have been sung by different historical groups in the throes of violent emotion were written.
7. Individual pupils imagined themselves to have been secretaries of different lawmaking bodies during the French Revolution; they wrote reports on various sessions.
8. Committees of pupils prepared topical outlines of units of work studied.
9. Current news and the events of an epoch of history were presented dramatically as newscasts over an improvised microphone.
10. A small group of students prepared and conducted a drill on a unit of work that had recently been completed.
11. Another group of pupils in the same class found a topic suitable for debate from the period of history being studied. They formed opposing teams, selected a chairman and timekeeper, provided judges, and presented the debate after preparation.

Technique of Correlation of History–English Oral Report. Reference has been made above to the fact that when a pupil makes a report in history, a check sheet setting forth reactions to the quality of the performance will be sent to the English teacher. The one given below was used effectively in the above-mentioned classes. There is no claim for perfection in respect to the items included; there is a claim that its use gave some criteria for oral expression covering qualities in which most of us would like to see pupils improve. Also, it is contended that the pupils seemed to take a greater interest in oral reports after the inauguration of the use of the sheet.

The manner in which the sheet was used is as follows: When the oral report was assigned, the pupil was given the sheet and asked to fill in the blanks calling for topic, references used, length of time spent in preparation, and pupil's name. On the day that the report was given, the pupil placed the sheet on the history teacher's desk before the giving of the report. Immediately following the class period the history teacher placed check marks in the spaces that represented, in his judgment, the quality of the report, made a record of the same in his class book, and then placed the sheet in the English teacher's mailbox. That teacher then inspected it, made a record of it in his class book, used the data in an effort to help the pupil improve his performance on similar work at later dates, and then returned the sheet to the pupil for his consideration as a help in steps for improvement.

SOCIAL STUDIES–ENGLISH ORAL REPORT CHECK SHEET

Topic:
References Used:
Length of Time Spent in Preparation of Report:

	I	II	III	IV	V
Organization of Material					
Independence of Notes					
Correctness of English					
Assimilation of Material					
Poise					
Voice					
Summarization and Conclusion					
Grade Assigned the Report					

Teacher Comment:

____
Student's Name

Suggested Use of Literature as a Basis of Discussion in the History Class. Literature having a historical setting can be used to great advantage in history class. If the entire group is familiar with the selection, it is indeed helpful; if not, one pupil can be of considerable assistance by presenting a special report on the novel, poem, or play. After one is assured that the class is acquainted with the selection, the following questions and suggestions are typical of those that are likely to result in profitable discussion:

1. Why did the author choose the particular period of history for use in this connection?
2. To the extent that facts of history are presented, would you say that they are accurate?
3. Do you feel that the characters used are typical of those of the period portrayed?
4. Did the selection make the period of history more easily understood?
5. Give an example of a scene that you think is an excellent reproduction of the situations that occurred as the incident was studied in our history class.
6. Give an example from the selection that you think is included more to give pleasure to the reader than to present accurately an event or a period of history.
7. Read portions of the selection and follow this with class discussion.
8. Suggest that dramatization of certain portions be made a joint project of the history and English classes.
9. When practicable to do so, use portions of the selection as a basis of forum discussion.
10. How has a character from one period of history been used to stimulate a course of action in a later period?

Aristotle suggests in his *Theory of Poetry and Fine Arts* that a poetic (literary) presentation of a historical event is truer than a historical interpretation. The implication of that statement is that a literary presentation gives the personal side of an incident, while the historical is likely to be merely cold, unimpassioned, factual detail. A study of the personal side of war, for instance, pays dividends by aiding in the development of a point of view toward the social and personal heritage which is the legacy of war.

The following list of poems is representative of the poetic reaction to wars in various countries and times. To save space, titles of books are keyed in according to the plan specified below.

AAL—*Adventures in American Literature,* H. C. Schweikert, R. B. Inglis, and John Gehlman, eds., New York: Harcourt, Brace and Company, Inc., 1930; H. C. Schweiker, R. B. Inglis, John Gehlman, and N. Foerster, eds., New York: Harcourt, Brace and Company, Inc., 1936; R. B. Inglis, John Gehlman, M. R. Bowman, and N. Foerster, eds., New York: Harcourt, Brace and Company, Inc., 1941.

AA—*Adventures in Appreciation,* H. C. Schweikert, H. A. Miller, and Luella B. Cook, eds., New York: Harcourt, Brace and Company, Inc., 1936.

ACL—*Anthology of Children's Literature,* Edna Johnson and Carrie Scott, eds., Boston: Houghton Mifflin Company, 1935.

AAWP—*An Anthology of World Poetry,* Mark Van Doren, ed., New York: Albert & Charles Boni, Inc., 1928.

ELAW—*Explorations in Literature, American Writers,* Edwin L. Miller, ed., Philadelphia: J. B. Lippincott Company, 1933; Edwin L. Miller, Ella K. Truesdale, and F. H. Whitmer, eds., Philadelphia: J. B. Lippincott Company, 1938.

LL, III—*Literature and Life, Book III,* Edwin Greenlaw and Dudley Miles, eds., Chicago: Scott, Foresman & Company, 1929; Dudley Miles, Robert C. Pooley, and Edwin Greenlaw, eds., Chicago: Scott, Foresman & Company, 1936.

LL, IV—*Literature and Life, Book IV, English Literature,* Dudley Miles, R. C. Pooley, and Edwin Greenlaw, eds., Chicago: Scott, Foresman & Company, 1935.

LLA—*Literature and Life in America,* Dudley Miles and Robert C. Pooley, eds., Chicago: Scott, Foresman & Company, 1943.

LHAL—*Literature, Heritage of American Literature,* E. A. Cross, G. A. Benscoter, Wm. A. Meacham, eds., New York: The Macmillan Company, 1944.

LHBL—*Literature, Heritage of British Literature,* E. A. Cross and Helen Daringer, eds., New York: The Macmillan Company, 1945.

LA—*The Literature of America,* A. H. Quinn, A. C. Baugh, and W. D. Howe, eds., New York: Charles Scribner's Sons, 1929.

LUL—*Literature, Understanding Literature,* E. A. Cross, Dorothy Dakin, and Helen J. Hanlon, eds., New York: The Macmillan Company, 1944.

MAP—*Modern American Poetry,* Louis Untermeyer, ed., New York: Harcourt, Brace and Company, Inc., 1921; New York: Harcourt, Brace and Company, Inc., 1936.

NV—*New Voices,* Marguerite Wilkinson, ed., New York: The Macmillan Company, 1924.

OLL—*Our Land and Its Literature,* Orton Lowe, ed., New York: Harper & Brothers, 1936.

SEL—*Selections from English Literature,* L. W. Payne and Nina Hall, eds., Chicago: Rand, McNally & Company, Inc., 1928.

TSWYC—*This Singing World for Younger Children,* Louis Untermeyer, ed., New York: Harcourt, Brace and Company, Inc., 1926.

TSW—*This Singing World,* Louis Untermeyer, ed., New York: Harcourt, Brace and Company, Inc., 1923.

WL—*World Literature,* Ruth Mary Weeks, Rollo L. Lyman, and H. C. Hill, eds., New York: Charles Scribner's Sons, 1938.

"A. E. F.," Carl Sandburg, MAP (1921), 204, (1936), 242; OLL, 273.

"After Blenheim," Robert Southey, ACL, 769–770.

"The Arsenal at Springfield," H. W. Longfellow, AAL (1930), 546–547, (1936), 474–476, (1941), 306–307; ELAW (1933), 314–315.

"As Toilsome I Wandered through Virginia's Woods," Walt Whitman, LL, III (1929), 513, (1936), 301, (1943), 301.

"The Battlefield," Wm. C. Bryant, AAL (1930), 533–534, (1936), 434–436, (1941), 295; LL, III (1929), 206–207, (1936) 100, (1943), 100; LA, 266–267.

"Beat! Beat! Drums!" Walt Whitman, AAL (1930), 657, (1936), 553–554, (1941), 344–345; LL, III (1929), 512–513, (1936), 300–301, (1943), 300–301.

"Bigelow Papers" (excerpt), James R. Lowell, ELAW (1933), 482–483, (1938), 254–255; LA, 385.

"The Bivouac of the Dead," Theodore O'Hara, LL, III (1929), 428, (1936), 273–274, (1943), 273–274.

"Breakfast," Wilfrid W. Gibson, NV, 255.

"Buttons," Carl Sandburg, AAL (1930), 736–737, (1936), 636–637, (1941), 388.

"The Charge of the Light Brigade," Alfred Tennyson, ACL, 769; LHBL, 368; SEL, 392; TSWYC, 200–202.

"Come Up from the Fields, Father," Walt Whitman, AA, 792–793; LUL, 319–320; MAP (1936), 68–69.

"Comrades," Richard Hovey, MAP (1936), 129; OLL, 247–268.

"The Cornucopia of Red and Green Comfits," Amy Lowell, NV, 265–268.

"Dawn," Richard Aldington, NV, 254.

"The Dead," Rupert Brooke, LL, IV, 760–761; NV, 253–254.

"Dirge for a Soldier," G. H. Boker, LA, 754; OLL, 227.

"Does It Matter?" Siegfried Sassoon, LL, IV, 762.

"Down Fifth Avenue," J. C. Underwood, NV, 263–265.

"Draw the Sword, O Republic," Edgar Lee Masters, NV, 262–263.

"Drummer Hodge," Thomas Hardy, AAWP, 1167.

"Drum Taps" (excerpt), Walt Whitman, ELAW (1933), 517–518; LA, 803–805.

"Dunkirk," Robert Nathan, LLA, 693–696; LUL, 23–27.
"The Father," Wilfrid W. Gibson, NV, 255.
"Fighting South of the Castle," Anon., AAWP, 10–11.
"Grass," Carl Sandburg, AAL (1930), 737, (1936), 637, (1941), 388; AAWP, 1260; LHAL, 379; MAP (1921), 205, (1936), 239.
"Gunga Din," Rudyard Kipling, LL, IV, 598–600; LUL, 342–344.
"If We Must Die," Claude McKay, MAP (1936), 482.
"I Have a Rendezvous with Death," Alan Seeger, AAL (1930), 763, (1936), 669, (1941), 711; ELAW (1933), 665, (1938), 594–595; LA, 1343; LHAL, 398; NV, 261–262.
"Incident of the French Camp," Robert Browning, ACL, 778; LHBL, 372; LL, IV, 570–571; TSWYC, 329–330; TSW, 409–410.
"In Flanders Fields," John McCrae, ACL, 806; LHBL, 399.
"The Iron Music," F. M. Hueffer, NV, 260.
"It's a Queer Time," Robert Graves, LL, IV, 761–762.
"Killed at the Ford," H. W. Longfellow, LL, III (1929), 346.
"The Kiss," Siegfried Sassoon, NV, 256.
"The Man Named Legion," Sara H. Hay, LLA, 705.
"Marco Bozzaris," Fitz-Greene Halleck, ELAW (1933), 128–130, (1938), 56–57; LA, 258–259; LL, III (1936), 103–105; LLA, 103–105.
"Memorial Day," Theodosia Garrison, LA, 1319–1320.
"The Messages," Wilfrid W. Gibson, NV, 254–255.
"The Murder of Lidice," Edna St. Vincent Millay, LLA, 699–704.
"Nearer," Robert Nichols, NV, 259.
"Ode in Memory of the American Volunteers Fallen for France," Alan Seeger, LA, 1342–1343.
"Ojibwa War Songs," H. H. Schoolcraft, AAWP, 1214–1215.
"The Old House in Flanders," F. M. Hueffer, NV, 260–261.
"On a Soldier Fallen in the Philippines," Wm. V. Moody, MAP (1921), 105–107, (1936), 137.
"On the Late Massacre in Piedmont," John Milton, AAWP (1928), 1069.
"Out of the Trenches: The Barn, Twilight," Robert Nicholas, NV, 258–259.
"The Revenge," Alfred Tennyson, AA, 755–759; LUL, 375–378; WL, 227–230.
"Rouge Bouquet," Joyce Kilmer, LA, 1344; NV, 269–271.
"Scots Wha Hae wi' Wallace Bled," Robert Burns, LL, IV, 374–375; SEL, 233–234.
"The Scythians," Alexander Blok, AAWP, 1017–1019.
"A Soldier," Robert Frost, LA, 1309.
"The Soldier," Rupert Brooke, ACL, 806; LHBL, 309; LL, IV, 760.
"Soldier, Rest," Walter Scott, AAWP, 1126–1127; LHBL, 315; WL, 805–806.

"Soldiers Dead," James R. Lowell, ELAW (1933), 486.
"Spring Sows Her Seeds," Mary C. Davies, NV, 268–269.
"They Went Forth to Battle, but They Always Fell," Shaemas O'Sheel, MAP (1921), 344-345.
"To Love-in-War-Time," Theodosia Garrison, LA, 1319.
"To Lucasta, on Going to the Wars," Richard Lovelace, AAWP, 1070–1071; LHBL, 624; LL, IV, 182–183.
"Tomorrow," John Masefield, AA, 847–848; SEL, 633–634.
"War and Peace," Franklin P. Adams, MAP (1921), 238.
"The War-song of Dinaw Vawr," T. L. Peacock, AAWP, 1131–1132.
"The White Cliffs of Dover" (excerpt), Alice Duer Miller, LLA, 697–699.
"Who Knows Where," Detlev von Liliencros, AAWP, 904.

The Aristotelian theory of the truth of a literary presentation is put into practice in the current biographies which contain all the color and trappings of fiction. Many contemporary biographies read like novels, but the addition of vivid background details gives vigor and reality to a life story, and the material is no less true because of these artistic inclusions.

The readability of Emil Ludwig's biographies gives evidence of the effectiveness of this type of biography. In contrast to the lengthy biographies of this type, one finds very short but extremely well-written biographies of the kind interspersed throughout the text of John Dos Passos' trilogy, *U.S.A.* (*Forty-second Parallel; 1919; The Big Money*), and though the text of the novels is not recommended as high-school fare, the extracted biographies of Henry Ford ("Tin Lizzie"), Woodrow Wilson ("Meester Veelson"), William Jennings Bryan ("The Boy Orator of the Platte"), Thorsten Veblen, and others make concise reading for pupils who want current evaluation of makers of history.

Such characters lend themselves most effectively to prose treatment, but men of greater historical stature, whose lives have something of epic quality, lend themselves to poetic treatment. Both history and English teachers should make available to their pupils the literary interpretations of the men who have brought our country out of the chaos of its beginnings.

The following list of poems dealing with Abraham Lincoln is only one unit of an extensive bibliography of poetry available to both the English and history departments.

"Abraham Lincoln," William C. Bryant, LA, 269–270.

"Abraham Lincoln," R. H. Stoddard, ACL, 805.

"Abraham Lincoln Walks at Midnight," Vachel Lindsay, AAL (1936), 644–645, (1941), 394–396; ELAW (1938), 575–576; LA, 1333–1334; LHAL, 376–377; MAP (1921), 232–234, (1936), 265; OLL, 277–278.

"A Farmer Remembers Lincoln," Witter Bynner, LHAL, 393; MAP (1921), 245–246.

"Anne Rutledge," Edgar Lee Masters, AAL (1930), 709, (1936), 629, (1941), 384; ELAW (1938), 572; LHAL, 366–367; LL, III (1929), 657, (1936), 673, (1943), 677; MAP (1921), 123, (1936), 165; NV, 374.

"Lincoln," John G. Fletcher, ACL, 805–806; MAP (1921), 323–327, (1936), 360–361.

"Lincoln," Nancy Byrd Turner, LUL, 154.

"The Lincoln Child," James Oppenheim, MAP (1921), 252–257, (1936), 283–285.

"Lincoln, the Man of the People," Edwin Markham, AAL (1936), 600–601, (1941), 370; ELAW (1933), 685–686, (1938), 565–566; LA, 1294; MAP (1921), 51–53, (1936), 110–111; NV, 105–106.

"The Master," Edwin A. Robinson, AAL (1930), 705–707, (1936), 606–608; LA, 1282–1283; LL, III (1929), 644; MAP (1921), 114–117, (1936), 146–147; OLL, 251–253; WL, 859–861.

"Nancy Hanks, 1784–1818," Stephen V. Benét and Rosemary C. Benét, LHAL, 391.

"Nancy Hanks, Mother of Abraham Lincoln," Vachel Lindsay, MAP (1936), 266.

"O Captain! My Captain!," Walt Whitman, ELAW (1933), 505, (1938), 395–396; LA, 811–812; LHAL, 454–455; MAP (1936), 74; TSWYC, 302–303; TSW, 360–361.

"Ode at Harvard Commemoration" (excerpt), J. R. Lowell, ELAW (1933), 492–493, (1938), 260–261; LA, 411–416.

"Ode on the Centenary of Abraham Lincoln," Percy MacKaye, LA, 1309–1314.

"Wanted—A Man (Sept. 8, 1862)," Edmund C. Stedman, LA, 754–755.

"When Lilacs Last in the Dooryard Bloomed," Walt Whitman, AAWP, 1237–1246; ELAW (1938), 396–397; LA, 807–811; LHAL, 455–457; MAP (1936), 69–74; OLL, 219–220.

For efficiency, materials must be easily accessible to teachers in all courses participating in the correlation project.

Reference has been made to the bibliography of poetry from which the preceding lists of poems were taken. Further information concerning the format of this file may offer suggestions to English teachers for developing a similar time-saving device, which will be helpful to teachers of other courses as well. This example is not set up as a perfect model, but a sample card is shown below to reveal the various possibilities for filing and the type of information needed.

Separate cards are made for each poem or short story. The initial letter of the author's name is in the upper left-hand corner; below this is his nationality, followed by his birth and death dates. Centered at the top is the title, followed by the author's name. The upper right-hand corner shows the subject. Beneath the title are listed the books in which the poem or story may be found, together with page numbers. The books in this list were selected because they are books which are likely to be found in any high-school library. At the bottom of the card is the first line of the poem, followed by an indication of the length and type of poetic form.

L	"Abraham Lincoln Walks at Midnight"	Lincoln
American	Lindsay, Vachel	
1879–1931	pp. 575–576, *Expl. in Lit., Am. Writers* (1938)	
	pp. 232–234, *Mod. Am. Poetry* (1921); (1936) 265	
	pp. 849–850, *Beacon Lts. of Lit.*, I	
	pp. 1333–1334, *Lit. of America* (1929)	
	pp. 376–377, *Lit., Heritage of Am. Lit.* (1944)	
	pp. 277–278, *Our Land and Its Lit.*	
	pp. 398–399, *My Poetry Book*	
	pp. 644–645, *Adv. in Am. Lit.*, Rev. Ed. (1936); (1941) 394–396	
"It is portentous, and a thing of state"		8 four-line stanzas

The time spent in organizing such a bibliography finds its compensation in time saved when time is at a premium. There is gratification on the part of both pupil and teacher when they know exactly where to look for the item they need.

Example of Correlation between World History and English. One of the most interesting and revealing facets of the life of a race is shown in its religious concepts. Out of a study of this phase of a people's life there arises a greater appreciation for the universal and basic religiosity of man, and out of that there comes greater understanding and tolerance.

Two classes cooperated in an attempt to enrich the background for the pupils in world history who were studying the classical periods of Greece and Rome. English reading was assigned from books of myth. Although numerous books of myths were available for supplementary materials, each pupil was provided with Herzberg's *Myths and Their Meaning* (Boston: Allyn & Bacon, 1943). Oral reports were given on stories for which general reading had not been assigned. Pictures such as "Aurora," by Boni; "The Story of the Argonauts"; "Atalanta's Race"; "The Parting of Hector and Andromache"; and "Circe and the Friends of Ulysses" were shown to the class for discussion in connection with the myths. Discussions were conducted in which pupils attempted to analyze the characteristics of a race that could evolve such a mythical tradition.

Not the least interesting and beneficial part of the classical study was the word study which developed from the reading of the myths. The following lists of words were given to the students for the dictionary and myth-text study. The first contains common words which are based on names of Greek and Roman gods and goddesses. The pupils' task was to discover the relationship between the dictionary definition of the word and its mythological significance.

Following this study, an analysis was made of characteristic names of Greeks and Romans. The Greek names were found to stimulate emulation, prowess, and glorious ideals. The Roman names, on the other hand, were found to be occupational, satirical, or merely an indication of the order of birth. This led to a curiosity on the part of the pupils concerning the meaning of their own names, an anticipated result considering the egocentric interest of younger adolescents.

A more thorough and inclusive unit on this study follows:

Words of Greek Derivation Pertaining to Greek Mythology

Achilles' tendon—Achilles
aeolian (harp or lyre)—Aeolus, god of winds
Aesculapian art (medicine)—Aesculapius (Latin, Aesculapius)
Amazonian, Amazon River—Amazons
amorous—Amor, god of love, son of Light and Day
atlas—Atlas, supporter of the heavens
aurora borealis (northern lights)—Aurora
calliope (circus parade instrument)—Calliope, one of the Muses
Cancer (sign of the zodiac)—Cancer (*see* Herculean)
chaos, chaotic—Chaos
chimera—Chimera

chronology, chronological—Chronos
echo—Echo
Elysian (heavenly)—Elysian fields; cf. Champs Elysées in Paris.
erotic—Eros, god of love
ether—Aither, light
geography—Gaea, or Ge, mother Earth; *graphe,* writing
geology—*logos,* a study
geometry—*metron,* a measure
halcyon—Halcyone
harpy—the Harpies, monsters, half woman, half bird; cf. "Old Ironsides":
"The harpies of the shore shall pluck
The eagle of the sea."
Herculean (task)—Hercules; cf. twelve labors
Hesperian (western)—Hesperia
hyacinth—Hyacinthus
hydrogen, hydrochloric, hydroplane, etc.—Hydro
hygiene—Hygeia, daughter of Aesculapius, goddess of health
hymeneal—Hymen, god of marriage
hypnotic—Hypnos, god of sleep
iris—Iris, goddess of the rainbow
Lethean—Lethe, river of forgetfulness
morphine—Morpheus, god of dreams
museum, music, amuse, amusement, etc.—the Muses
myrmidon (a subordinate)—Myrmidons
nectar—food for the gods
nemesis—Nemesis, god of retributive justice
Olympian—Olympus, home of the gods
panic—Pan
phaeton—Phaeton, son of Apollo
psyche (the mind or soul)—Psyche; cf. Poe's "Ulalume"
psychology, psychic—Psyche
python—Python
sibylline (prophetic)—Sibyl
stentorian—Stentor, loud-voiced herald in the *Iliad*
tantalize—Tantalus
terpsichorean—Terpsichore, Muse of dance and choral song
Thanatopsis (cf. Bryant's poem of that name)—Thanatos, death
Titanic—Titans, gigantic children of Gaea and Uranus

Words of Latin Derivation Pertaining to Roman Mythology

cereal—Ceres, goddess of grain
fame—Fama, goddess of fame
faun, fauna—Faunus, rural divinity, god of woods and plants
floral—Flora, goddess of flowers
fortune—Fortuna, goddess of plenty
janitor, January—Janus, god of present, past, and future; god of doors and gates
jovial—Jove
martial, March—Mars, god of war
mercury—Mercury, carrier of tidings, representing swiftness
mortal—Mors, god of death
nocturnal—Nox, night
pomology—Pomona, goddess of the fruit of trees
Saturday—Saturn, god of seed sowing
somnambulist, somnambulism—Somnus, god of sleep
sylvan—Silvanus, god of woods
terminal—Terminus, god of boundaries
terrestrial—*terra,* land
vestal—Vesta, goddess of hearth and fire
victory—Victoria, from *vincere, victum,* to vanquish
volcano, vulcanize—Vulcan, god of fire

MONTHS OF THE YEAR

January—Janus, two-headed god of portals and of the past, present, and future
February—from Februa, feast of purification, Feb. 15
March—Mars, god of war
April—Aprilis
May—Maia, goddess of the plains: Maia, majesty
June—Junius, name of a Roman gens; or Juno, wife of Jupiter
July—Julius (Caesar)
August—Augustus (Caesar)
September—*septem,* seven
October—*octo,* eight
November—*novem,* nine
December—*decem,* ten

Note and explain the discrepancy in the names of the last four months of the year.

Mythological Terms in Advertisements

Look for mythological references in advertisements and determine their significance. You will find many more than those listed below.

Ajax tires
Aetna Fire Insurance Company
Ambrosia skin tonic
Atlas cement
Phoenix hosiery
Pluto water
Mercury rubber heels
The *American Mercury*, a periodical
Vulcan springs

Classical Terms in Book Titles

Stuart Chase: The *Nemesis* of American Business; The *Tragedy* of Waste
Christopher Morley: *Parnassus* on Wheels
Victor Heiser: An American Doctor's *Odyssey*
Henry Ford: My *Philosophy* of Industry
Benjamin Franklin: *Autobiography*
Booth Tarkington: The *Plutocrat*
James Truslow Adams: The *Epic* of America
Richard Harding Davis: The Bar *Sinister*
Frank Norris: The *Octopus*
William Allen White: The *Martial* Adventures of Henry and Me
George M. Martin: The Right *Promethean* Fire
E. Barrington: *Glorious Apollo* (Byron)
G. B. Shaw: *Androcles* and the Lion; *Pygmalion*

How strange it seems that parents thrust names upon a child with no thought of the significance of those names and no consideration of the possibility that the child may not deserve that name in the future. This situation is an outgrowth of the fact that we have become as indifferent to the meaning of the names of people as we have become to the meanings of the days of the week and the names of the months.

Have you ever thought what your own name might mean?

Numerous sources have furnished the names in use at the present time. *The ancient Greeks, who gave us the most original literature of all Europe, from which all other countries have borrowed so freely, revealed in their names the glory and idealism which is so evident in their history and literature.* Let us consider the meaning of some of those Greek names which are familiar to you as a result of your reading and study or because of their present use. As you study these names, note their significance and consider the possible character of the individuals to whom these names were given.

Alexander—"protector of men" (*alexo,* to ward or keep off; *andros,* man)

Andromache—"man fighter" (*andros,* a man; *mache,* a fighter)

Aristophanes—"the best light-bringer" (*aristos,* the best; *phanein,* to bring to light)

Callicles—"beauty-famous" (*kalos,* beauty; *clio,* from *kleos,* glory, fame)

Cleopatra—"glory lineage" (*kleos,* glory; *patria,* lineage)

Cleophanes—"glory light" (see above)

Demosthenes—"people's strength" (*demos,* the people; *sthenos,* strength)

Eunice—"abundant victory" (*eu,* well, happy, good, abundant; *nike,* victory). [You are probably familiar with the famous statue, the "Nike of Samothrace."]

Euphemia—"good omen; to speak well" (*eu,* well; *phemia,* to speak). Our word *euphemism,* which means a pleasant term for an unpleasant person or situation, is based on this same root. To say "to pass away" instead of "to die" or "to prevaricate" instead of "to lie" is *euphemism.*

Hippocrates—"the strength of a horse" (*crates,* strength; *hippos,* horse). Cf. the word *hippopotamus,* from *potamus,* river, and *hippos,* horse.

Leander—"lion man" (*leo,* lion; *andros,* man)

Lycurgus—"wolf driver" (*lukos,* a wolf; *urgo,* to drive)

Nikophanes—"light-giving victory" (*nike,* victory; *phanes,* giving or bringing light)

Phillipos—"horse lover" (*philo,* lover; *hippos,* horse)

Protagoras—"first in assembly" (*protos,* first; *agora,* the public square or market place in a Greek town, answering to the Roman forum)

Sophocles—"wisdom-famous" (*sophos,* wise; *kleos,* glory, fame)

Theodoros—"God's gift" (*theos,* god; *doron,* a gift)

Theophile—"lover of God" (*theos,* god; *philo,* lover)

Timothy—"one who honors God" (*timao,* to honor; *theos,* god)

What familiar Christian names come to your mind as possible derivatives of these names?

Latin names or names familiar to you from your study of Roman history are interesting in their descriptive quality. The Romans lacked the idealism of the Greeks, and one finds the elements of satire in many of their names, which have the semblance of nicknames. Witness the name Longus, for instance, which doubtless carried the same jovial derision as the name "High-pockets" which schoolboys are accustomed to give to one of their fellows who is taller than the rest of his schoolmates. Only recently there was a newspaper reference to an attempted comeback by the mountainous

Italian prize fighter, Primo Carnera, who has been popularly referred to as the "ambling Alp." It is evident that the Roman did not always receive his entire name at birth, but that part of his name was often conferred as a result of occupation, physical characteristics, accomplishment, or order of birth.

We find, then, the following grouping of familiar names from Roman history:

Occupational names

Agricola—farmer

Cicero—(Latin *cicer*, a chick-pea). In "Cicero," *Plutarch's Lives*,[5] we find this comment on the name: ". . . who first of that house was surnamed Cicero seems to have been a person worthy to be remembered; since those who succeeded him not only did not reject but were fond of that name, though vulgarly made a matter of reproach. For the Latins called a vetch *cicer*, and a nick or dent at the tip of his nose, which resembled the opening in a vetch, gave him the surname of *Cicero*."

Fabius—"bean grower" (Latin *faba*, bean)

Piso—"pea grower" (Latin *pisum*, pea)

Satirical names

Claudius—"lame" (Latin *claudus*, lame)

Crassus—"fatty" (Latin *crassus*, thick, dense)

Julius—"downy-bearded" (Latin *Iulus*, from Greek *ioulos*, first-growth beard)

Longus—"tall"

Macer—"skinny" (Latin *macer*, lean)

Sulla—"splotchy." In "Sulla," *Plutarch's Lives*,[6] one reads, "His general personal appearance may be known by his statues; only his blue eyes, of themselves extremely keen and glaring, were rendered all the more forbidding and terrible by the complexion of his face, in which white was mixed with rough splotches of fiery red. Hence it is said, he was surnamed Sylla, and in allusion to it one of the scurrilous jesters at Athens made the verse upon him—'Sylla is a mulberry sprinkled o'er with meal.' "

[5] Plutarchus, *Plutarch's Lives* (The Dryden Plutarch), revised by Arthur Hugh Clough, Everyman's Library, New York: E. P. Dutton & Co., Inc., 1910, Vol. III, p. 186. *The Universal Dictionary of the English Language* suggests, for the derivation of the name, ". . . as Pliny asserts, because the first of the name successfully cultivated vetches."

[6] *Ibid.*, p. 141.

Names based on accomplishment

Achiacus

Africanus

Macedonicus—See "Caius Marius," *Plutarch's Lives:* "We are altogether ignorant of any third name of Caius Marius; as also of Quintus Sertorius, that possessed himself of Spain; or of Lucius Mummius that destroyed Corinth, though this last was surnamed Achiacus from his conquests, as Scipio was called Africanus, and Mettullas, Macedonicus."

Names based on order of birth

Primus (Primo)
Secundus
Tertius
Quartus
Quintus
Sextus
Septimus
Octavus
Nonus
Decimus

Find the meanings and derivations of some of the following words based upon the name study made.

Greek

Alexander
1. Alexander
2. alexipharmic
   a. pharmacist
   b. pharmacy

Aristophanes
1. aristocracy
2. aristocrat
3. aristocratic

Callicles
1. calligrapher
2. calligraphic
3. calligraphist
4. calligraphy
5. calliope

Demosthenes
1. democracy
2. democrat
3. democratic

Eunice
1. euphemism
2. euphony
3. euphonic
4. euphonious

Herodotus
1. hero
2. heroic
3. heroine
4. heroism

Hippocrates
1. hippodrome
2. hippogriff
3. hippopotamus

Leander
1. leonine
2. leopard

Lycurgus
1. lycanthrope
2. lyceum

Sophocles
1. sophism
2. sophist
3. sophister
4. sophisticate
5. sophistry
6. sophomore

Theodoros
Theophile
Timotheos
1. theologian
2. theological
3. theologium
4. theology
5. theophilanthropy

Latin

Agricola
1. agricultural
2. agriculture
3. agriculturist

Celeres
1. celerity

Claudius
1. claudication

Crassus
1. crash (fabric)
2. crass
3. crassamentum

Fabius
1. fabaceous

Porcius
1. porcine
2. porcupine

Summary. One of the means by which master social studies teachers have enriched their work is through fusion. Some such teachers attempted to solve a great deal of the mechanics involved by proposing to eliminate various individual social studies and to have only one course remaining, to be taught under the name of *Social studies.* Naturally it would extend over several semesters and be designated by Roman numerals I, II, III, etc. Other excellent teachers simply bring pertinent illustrative materials from one social study into the discussion periods of another social study.

Integration has failed to bring tangible results into social studies teaching. The term itself is in some respects a misnomer as related to the status of the pupil to whom it is applied. The fine balance and exact proportions of knowledge together with the synthesis and conclusions expected are probably unattainable.

Much progress has been made in attempts at correlation. Here, widely separated fields such as history and English are considered. There is an honest effort to make the information gained in each subject useful in the other. Relationships between the two subjects are emphasized. Work initiated in either may be concluded in the other. For example, the content of an oral report may be historical in nature while the mechanics of presentation may be a problem of English; or the setting of a particular novel may be a period studied in history while the style of writing is wholly related to English.

There is no claim that this presentation represents all the possible media for breaking down the divisions of traditional subjects. Neither is it contended that all teachers should use exactly these techniques.

There will naturally be local situations that call for deletion and the use of supplementary procedures. These statements do not imply that the general procedure lacks possiblities or that there is no obligation to explore the area. It would be felt that an important caution had been omitted if warning were not given that it is easier to start upon a worthy undertaking than it is to pursue it to a successful conclusion; therefore it is to be hoped that initial and natural obstacles do not prevent those in charge of these subjects from actually reaching their goals.[7]

Questions on the Text

1. What does the term *fusion* mean as applied to social studies teaching? Give examples.
2. How do good teachers of the social studies fuse the different areas in conducting recitation and discussion in any one class?
3. Give the advantages and disadvantages most often claimed for fusion as a method of teaching.
4. Define *correlation* in relation to teaching social studies. Give examples.
5. Why have many schools been slow to adopt this method of teaching?
6. Mention some reasonable helps that a social studies teacher could expect from the English teacher under such a program.
7. What are some activities that could well occur in a social studies class that would probably be accepted by the English teacher as helpful?
8. Make some specific statements as to how the oral report can become a basis of correlation between social studies and English.
9. What aspects of classical literature ordinarily lend themselves to correlation with history? Comment on poetry and biography in the same connection.
10. Give examples of correlation procedures between world history and English.

Suggested Activities

1. Present in some detail the manner in which you would carry out correlation activities between one social study and another traditional high-school subject not described in this chapter.

[7] A considerable part of the material contained in this chapter is also found in a *School Service Bureau Bulletin,* College of Education, University of Wyoming, Laramie. Ernestine Ernst Seiter and Clarence D. Samford are the authors. The title is, "Correlation Projects in English and Social Studies." The reference is Volume IV, No. 5, January, 1946.

2. Give a general description of the training you feel a social studies teacher should receive in order to successfully fuse, integrate, or correlate subject matter.

3. Examine curriculum outlines and syllabi from various school systems for evidences of the type of teaching mentioned in this chapter.

4. Interview high-school pupils for descriptions of correlation procedures. Record their reactions to this type of work.

5. Read one or more references related to procedures that tend to break down traditional subject-matter boundary lines and report on the references.

Selected References

Addison, Gertrude, "English in an Integrated Program," *English Journal*, Part II, XXX (February, 1941), pp. 6–8.

Aldrich, Julian C., "How Can the Teacher Help Meet the Needs of Youth?" *Scholastic, Teachers' Section*, XXXVIII (Nov. 11, 1940), pp. 1–2T.

———, "Correlating Instruction in English and Social Studies," *Scholastic, Teachers' Section*, XXXIX (Oct. 13, 1941), pp. 1–4T.

Bennett, R., "Integrated Program in Secondary Education," *High School Journal*, XXXI (January, 1948), pp. 22–26.

Broening, Angela, "Conducting Experience in English," National Council of Teachers of English, *English Monograph* No. 8, New York: Appleton-Century-Crofts, Inc., 1939.

Burdette, F. L., "Integration of the Social Studies," *Educational Forum*, VIII (March, 1944), pp. 339–347.

Burge, A., "English Classes Use Social-studies Reading," *Clearing House*, XXII (October, 1947), pp. 105–107.

Bye, Edgar C., "Fusion or Confusion?" *Historical Outlook*, XXIV (May, 1933), pp. 264–267.

Byres, L. W., "Unit in History and English," *Social Studies*, XXXIII (February, 1942), pp. 52–58.

Chiara, C., "Integrated Programs," *Social Studies*, XXXIII (March, 1942), pp. 103–106.

Committee on Social Studies in General Education, *Social Studies in General Education*, New York: Appleton-Century-Crofts, Inc., 1940.

Committee on the Function of English in General Education, *Languages in General Education*, New York: Appleton-Century-Crofts, Inc., 1940.

Cooke, Paul, "Social Education and the Teaching of Reading," *Social Education*, VIII (May, 1944), pp. 210–212.

DAVIS, HAZEL, "Science Contributes to the Social Studies," *Social Education,* VIII (October, 1944), p. 268.

GILES, H. H., "English in the Eight-year Study," *English Journal,* XXX (February, 1941), pp. 114–122.

GRENOBLE, E. M., "Correlating English Literature and the Social Studies," *Education for Victory,* II (Apr. 3, 1944), pp. 28–29.

HANSOME, IONE, "Literature and Social Purpose," *Social Studies,* XXXVII (October, 1946), pp. 245–250.

HORN, GUNNAR, *American History in Fiction,* Washington, D.C.: National Education Association.

HUNT, E. M., "The Relation of American History to Other Social Studies," *Study and Teaching of American History,* Washington, D.C.: The National Council for the Social Studies, *Seventeenth Yearbook,* 1946, pp. 173–208.

KRIDER, LAVONNE, "Poetry in the Teaching of History," *Social Studies,* XXXII (April, 1941), pp. 173–175.

KRONENBERG, HENRY, "Separate Subjects. Integration and Problems," *Social Education,* II (February, 1938), pp. 108–116.

LEONARD, J. PAUL, "Social Studies in the Virginia Curriculum," *Social Education,* I (May, 1937), pp. 340–343.

LEWIS, RUTH R., "Remedial Reading in the History Classroom," *Social Studies,* XXXVI (November, 1945), pp. 309–310.

LOTTICK, KENNETH C., "Literature and American History," *Social Education,* XIII (March, 1949), pp. 117–119.

MANHEIM, E., "Correlated Program in a Junior High School," *High Points,* XXIX (March, 1947), pp. 53–56.

MCFEELY, R. H., "Planning to Meet Individual Differences: for the Slow Learner," *Adapting Instruction in the Social Studies to Individual Differences,* Washington, D.C.: The National Council for the Social Studies, *Fifteenth Yearbook,* 1944, pp. 63–71.

MONRAD, MARGARET, "Relation of the Industrial Arts to the Social Studies in Elementary and Secondary Schools," *Social Studies,* XXXVI (October, 1945), pp. 248–255.

NEILL, J. DONALD, "Basic Language in a Social Studies Class," *Social Education,* VIII (January, 1944), pp. 17–18.

NIXON, A. F., "Correlation of Biology and the Social Studies," *School and Society,* LXI (May 5, 1945), pp. 297–299.

NYBERG, JOSEPH A., "Geometry, Logic, and Social Studies," *Social Studies,* XXXIV (March, 1943), pp. 104–108.

POOLEY, R. C., "Wisconsin's Program of Integrated Studies," *Journal of General Education,* II (July, 1948), pp. 308–316.

ROGERS, S., "Description of a Teacher's Work with Tenth Grade Pupils in English-Social Science," *Southern Association Quarterly,* VII (August, 1943), pp. 347–365.

RUCHLIS, H., "Correlating Physics with Social Studies," *Science Education,* XXXIII (March, 1949), pp. 115–118.

SHEFTER, H., "English Department Takes Over the Library," *Clearing House,* XVI (May, 1942), pp. 556–557.

SHORT, H. B., and G. GEBERT, "Duplication in the Social Studies and Business Training," *Education Digest,* XII (March, 1947), pp. 37–38.

SIMPSON, R. E., "Study of History, Geography, and Related Subjects in the California Schools," *California Schools,* XVII (September, 1946), pp. 231–239.

STEINER, MARGARET, and ETHEL KING, "A Course in American Life and Culture," *Social Education,* IV (January, 1940), pp. 10–12.

STEWART, BRUCE, "Applying Scientific Methods to Social Problems," *Social Education,* XI (March, 1947), pp. 123–125.

STEWART, DOROTHY H., "Social Studies and Reading," *Social Education,* X (March, 1946), pp. 117–118.

TUCKMAN, WILLIAM, "Music in Junior High School American History," *Social Education,* VI (March, 1942), pp. 128–130.

VAN ALSTYNE, RICHARD W., "Interrelation of Secondary School Subjects," *Social Education,* II (May, 1938), pp. 325–329.

VOGEL, H. L., "Enrichment through Correlation," *High Points,* XXV (June, 1943), pp. 44–47.

WALTHEW, MARGARET, "It Isn't Cheating—It's Integration," *English Journal,* XXX (June, 1941), pp. 463–467.

Chapter 10

INTRODUCTION TO METHODS

Preview. In approaching the topic of methods of teaching the social studies one can profitably give attention to many of the simpler and older techniques that have been used. Among them are project, problem, and socialized recitation. Each has numerous advantages and disadvantages. These should be considered carefully. It is to the interest of the teacher to incorporate the best that can be found in any particular method in procedures that seem adapted to his own classes.

The Project Method Described. Not many years ago a great deal was being written about the project method of teaching. Some of the comments seemed more designed to display a knowledge of definition of terms than to really try to help teachers attain better classroom performance. Even so, it is preferable to have some information about the background of the idea and the characteristics of the method. In some cases the early usage involved work done outside the classroom that was related to study carried on in the class. For instance, this conception was made very popular by agriculture teaching carried on after the passage of the Smith-Hughes Act. Pupils would gain their regular textbook information at school. During the academic year and through the following summer the project would be executed on the farm or ranch and supervised by the classroom teacher by means of periodic visits. Shortly, many teachers were calling such work, executed by pupils outside of class and related to in-class discussions, *projects*. Today the term is used rather broadly and would cover more pupil activities than it once did. Some of the characteristics remain the same. Good's definition of a project is "a significant unit of activity having educational value and aimed at one or more definite goals of understanding; involves investigation and solution of problems, and frequently the use and manipulation of physical materials; planned and carried to completion by the pupils and teacher in a natural life-like manner."[1] The project must grow out of class discussion and be directly related thereto. Its completion should increase the knowledge of and interest in the subject matter. Appeal to the pupil who carries it out is very important. The initiation of it can well come directly from the pupil; otherwise it should be selected from a long list of optional and varied suggestions supplied by the teacher. The project should not be entered upon unless it is likely to have promise of some permanent values to the pupil. These can be in terms of subject-matter mastery or life situations.

One of the basic characteristics of the project is the fact that it ends in a rather basic accomplishment. The pupil or class has something that has been made, something that can be exhibited or some means completed whereby he or they can engage audience interest in a presentation.

In the same manner that individuals execute projects it is possible for group affairs to be undertaken by the entire class. Most of the same factors enter here that are present in the individual project. It is the class as a whole that feels a strong desire to execute the particular task, that does it as part of a normal situation, and that has tangible results to show for its work at the conclusion of the efforts which it expended.

Examples of Projects in Social Studies. While there are unlimited examples of projects that have been used or that are reasonably possible, the first selected for description is that of the social studies field trip. By such a trip a portion of previously studied subject matter can be made more realistic: the trip is under the direction of the classroom teacher and is one that is given official recognition and approval by the school's administrative staff. One of the objectives is to attain realism. It has a chance to succeed because most pupils show keener interest in concrete objects than they do in abstract generalities. We all know the value of illustrating a point with an object in the classroom itself; if a succession of observations of such nature presents itself over a period of from an hour to a full day or more, it can be reasonably assumed that attention and interest will stay at a high level. Next, there are always many pupils taking social studies both by requirement and election who are frank to admit that they do not especially like the courses. This situation obtains more frequently if the method of teaching is along purely traditional lines. Thus an-

[1] From Carter V. Good, ed., *Dictionary of Education,* New York: McGraw-Hill Book Co., Inc., 1945, p. 314. Courtesy McGraw-Hill Book Company, Inc.

other purpose of the field trip can well be that of increasing interest. It will often serve to arouse those who appear to be beyond redemption; it usually increases the interest of those for whom the subject already holds fascination. Much attention is also being given to the development of desirable behavior in social studies situations. That is, in making evaluations of the results of the teaching of social studies it is hoped that the pupils are growing into adults who will respond far better in all social situations than they would if they had not taken the courses. It is quite possible that the additional factual information gained from a field trip will function significantly. Finally, in the planning of the trip there is abundant opportunity for the practice of democratic procedures. There will be few or no members who fail to contribute worthy suggestions designed to make it successful; furthermore, many of them will offer to perform key services during the time thus spent.

Where to go and how much time to spend on the social studies field trip will depend upon the number and variety of points of interest within reach of the local community; likewise it will be necessary to take into account the general enthusiasm for this type of activity. The following are examples of such trips that have been taken by various groups at some time, the grade level being indicated following the identification: city hall, 9; newspaper office, 12; fire station, 9; bank, 12; art gallery, 12; city water plant, 9; broadcasting station, 11 and 12; intensive tour of the nation's capital, 12; all offices in county court house, 9 and 11; voting polls, 11; state legislature in session, 11; and all offices in state capitol building, 11.

It is splendid if the initial suggestion for a social studies field trip comes from the pupils. In any event a discussion in which there is free pupil participation should bring out what the group might conceivably gain from the time thus spent. If it is decided that the trip would be profitable and feasible, opportunity for the appointment of committees follows. Some of the details with which pupils can help are making contacts with individuals at the place or places of the proposed trip, studying possible means of transportation, collecting money in advance for necessary expenses, arranging an itinerary, planning for meals and incidental entertainment, securing information relative to such legal matters as school liability for accident, liability of those who furnish transportation, authority to participate in school field trips, and preparation of an outline of information that the class should learn as a result of the trip. The foregoing statement applies generally to the longer trips: those points that are applicable can be brought into play on the shorter trip. The successful teacher does much directly and indirectly that causes the above-mentioned details to be carried out in the smoothest possible fashion. In addition, it is a specific teacher function to see that the pupils have a complete social studies information background that will enable them to ask searching questions and to gain valuable information.

Let us assume for the moment that a group of pupils enrolled in social studies classes live near a state capital but have not made a detailed study of the practical functioning of state government. Maybe some member of the class observes in reading local current news that the legislature is soon to convene. It is not at all unlikely that another pupil will ask whether or not visitors are permitted to hear debate on bills coming before House and Senate. If encouragement is offered the questions will begin to multiply. Use of the blackboard to note information which pupils would like to learn from such a trip will serve to clarify thinking. The following questions are illustrative of those that may be proposed for first-hand observation:

1. Does any member of either house introduce a bill at any time he desires?
2. How many members are likely to be present when the legislature is in session?
3. Does the governor attend meetings of the legislature?
4. Are the members seated according to any particular plan?
5. Do the groups actually observe perfectly the rules of parliamentary procedure?
6. Where do members of the press sit?
7. How do legislators in our state spend a typical day during sessions?
8. What types of worker are found in attendance in addition to the legislators? How do they secure their jobs?
9. Where are the committee rooms in relation to the legislative rooms?
10. For what are the rooms and offices of the capitol building, other than those serving the legislature, used?

There are several points and guiding principles that must of necessity be given attention before the trip takes place. Some of them have been implied above while others have not.

1. There should be general enthusiasm on the part of the class for the particular trip in question. Pupils who do not share in the spirit of the occasion should not be urged to go.

2. The same generous approval of the principal of the school should be in evidence. Otherwise the trip should not be undertaken.

3. Written permission and waiver of claim against the school for liability should be secured from the parents or guardian of each of the pupils who is to go. Form statements which will require only the insertion of the pupil's name and the signature are easily prepared.

4. All parents and pupils should be supplied with a comprehensive schedule of the trip. This will clarify such routine matters as time and place of departure, where the group will be at a particular hour, time of return to the school, etc.

5. People who regularly work at the places where the group stops and who have consented to guide, answer questions, etc., should be fully informed in advance as to the object of the trip and the length of time that the group can stay.

6. Despite the fact that ordinary classroom procedures do not produce problems of discipline for the capable teacher, the field trip is enough of an innovation to demand the stressing of some fairly obvious points. It should be agreed upon in advance that preferred modes of conduct shall guide behavior, that grateful appreciation for helps of nonschool people shall be demonstrated, and that cooperation shall be evidenced throughout.

In connection with point 6 mentioned above, the following letter is offered as typical of one that might be written in advance requesting help for the class at a place where it is proposed to visit:

University High School
Laramie, Wyoming
Date

Miss ________________
State Superintendent of Schools
Cheyenne, Wyoming
Dear Miss ______________:

We have two classes in our school who are now engaged in a study of Wyoming history and government. In a conference with the junior teachers in this area it was suggested that a social studies field trip to the state capitol while the legislature is in session would be very helpful. When the matter was later discussed with the children it was found that there are thirty-five of them who would like to participate. Accordingly, we have set the afternoon of February 18 as the time that we should like to come.

The request that we have in mind in relation to your office is based on the fact that we feel that we need guidance in and around the capitol building. Therefore, may we inquire as to whether you have someone who would have the time to extend this service to us? We expect to arrive at

1:30 and desire to devote about forty-five minutes to this part of the trip.

Any helps or suggestions that you may offer will be gratefully appreciated.

Cordially yours,
____________________, Head
Department of Social Studies

Point 3 in the above list suggested the necessity of securing written permission and waiver of claim against the school for liability from the parents or guardians of pupils who make such trips. The following form is offered as one that sets forth general information relative to the trip and also secures the desired permission:

University High School
Laramie, Wyoming
Date

Dear Parent:

Some of the pupils of University High School have indicated an interest in taking a social studies field trip to the state capitol at Cheyenne in order to learn from practical observation some things about Wyoming state history and government. The trip is now planned for tomorrow afternoon, [date]. Pupils planning to go will assemble in front of the Education Building at 12 o'clock noon.

A guide from the office of the State Department of Education will help us gain information in and around the capitol building. The State Librarian has agreed to have someone available to assist us in gaining the most possible from our time spent at the State Museum. The Clerk of the United States District Court gives assurance of being willing to help in every way possible. The last observation is planned for the Cheyenne Municipal Building where Police Court will be in session. Our party should leave Cheyenne for Laramie starting at 5:30 P.M.

We feel that the trip will be beneficial to those who participate. We shall exercise our best judgment in matters pertaining to conduct and safety. Naturally, it is impossible for us to assume financial responsibility for accident, illness, or other misfortune that might arise.

It will be helpful to us in planning the trip and keeping proper records pertaining to it if you will indicate by your signature your knowledge of the plans and your approval for ____________________ ____________________ to accompany us.

(Signed) ____________________

Cordially yours,
____________________, Head
Department of Social Studies

As a final step in preparation for the trip it is quite apt to hand each pupil and adult driver or sponsor a mimeographed sheet setting forth final reminders and instructions. The following information is typical of that usually given and pertains to the trip being described:

SOCIAL STUDIES FIELD TRIP TO CHEYENNE, [DATE]

I. Remember
   A. The profit that you derive from this trip and the quality of the judgment that you exercise assures or precludes this type of experience for future classes.
   B. You should have a definite understanding with the driver of the automobile in which you ride in regard to time of departure, expenses involved, etc.

II. To Cheyenne
   A. All automobiles will leave Laramie from the front of the Education Building at 12 o'clock noon.
   B. One stop will be made by all in front of the Summit to determine whether or not the entire group is following properly.

III. Parking: Parking should be in the vicinity of the capitol building and state library.

IV. State Capitol: Assemble at the south entrance of the capitol at 1:30 P.M. Guides from the office of the State Superintendent of Schools will be there to conduct us through the state office buildings and to the two houses of the state legislature in session.

V. State Museum: Meet at the west entrance of the state museum at 2:45 P.M. Register in the guest book at the desk. A member of the regular museum staff will talk briefly about the collections to be seen before we proceed.

VI. Federal District Court: Automobiles should be moved to the vicinity of the post-office building at 4:00 P.M. Unfortunately the court will not be in session but a representative of the clerk will show us the rooms and explain the principal functions.

VII. Eat: At 4:30 P.M. a fifteen-minute period will be set aside to eat a light lunch. There are many suitable places near the post-office building.

VIII. Municipal Court: Meet at the east entrance of the municipal building at 4:45 P.M. Court will be in session. Find seats as quickly and quietly as possible.

IX. Departure: Be in the automobile in which you are to ride promptly at 5:30 P.M. We shall again stop at the Summit as we return in order to make a checkup similar to that made earlier in the day.

Upon return to the regular classroom, opportunity for fruitful discussion presents itself. There will be points of information that various pupils are still seeking. Comparison of textbook presentation and actual observations should be made. Data made possible because of the trip that would otherwise have been passed by completely should be stressed. Finally, the members of the group should be called upon to make suggestions as to how the trip could have been made more profitable. This can be very beneficial should another class in the same subject desire to take a similar trip at a later date.

It is contended that the social studies field trip develops skills in the planning and execution of a rather formidable pupil project. In addition, it fosters such desirable traits as leadership, cooperation, democratic attitudes, correct social behavior, and appreciation for the services of others. No less important is the social studies field trip in its relation to academic consideration. It supplements knowledge that has been partially learned in the classroom, adds important information that would probably fail to come to the pupils' attention otherwise, and arouses wholesome interest in the area of knowledge to which the trip is related.*

The second example is a project involving school-wide participation in election procedures. It has potentialities for bringing benefits to an entire school and even to the community of parents served by the school. There are various places where the idea may have its initiation. These include social studies classes, school-council meetings, allied activities groups, and faculty meetings. Once the idea has been accepted, careful planning must follow if the project is to attain the objective of furthering the cause of good citizenship through the medium of effective instruction. The entire school must participate as a unit. A series of bulletins can well serve as a guide. These are best prepared by students who are intensely interested in social studies under the supervision of the most competent teachers in the department.

The first bulletin should set forth the purpose of the project. The necessity for cooperation, the desire to teach pupils the manner in which an election is conducted, and the importance of voting are items that should be included. The time of the election needs to be

* Clarence D. Samford, "Social Studies Field Trip as an Allied Activity," *School Activities*, XIX (May, 1948), pp. 285–287*ff*., presented the foregoing project as an extracurricular activity.

stated and should coincide with the date of the general election. The exact manner in which the school is to be divided into wards and precincts should be indicated. Home-room organization, grade classification, or departments within the school furnish a point of departure. The names of teachers who are to help with each precinct should be given, without intimating that there shall be faculty domination. The purpose is to ensure orderly procedure and the availability of competent adult help as needed. The manner of selecting precinct officials should be clearly stated, with indications of the number of clerks and judges needed. A plan that distributes these equitably throughout the school is to be desired. Provisions for a group meeting following the selection should be included. Similar considerations apply in relation to a board of elections. A complete cataloguing of the materials and equipment needed is indicated. One of the most vital items in the first bulletin is a statement setting forth plans for the instruction of voters, usually best done in social studies classes on specified days preceding the election. The bulletin should end with a strong concluding statement just as it began with a challenging introduction.

The second bulletin should follow within a few days and might well have the goal of assisting teachers to prepare pupils for voting. Reference should be made to at least the following points: mechanics of voting, offices to be filled, various ballots that will be distributed, special issues to be brought before the voters, biographical sketches of the candidates seeking office, and potential sources of information. A conclusion should stress the necessity for thoroughness of instruction.

The third bulletin is one that would ordinarily have a more restricted circulation than either of the preceding ones. It should be designed to give specific instruction to precinct officials and members of the board of elections. The importance of their role should be stressed. Information should be given on the following points: How to deal with the voter as he presents himself, what to do with the ballots after they have been marked, and the exact procedure to follow after the polls close. In concluding it should be stated that the suggestions given constitute a minimum and that the advisors will be willing to render every needed assistance.

The fourth bulletin should contain last-minute reminders. Recapitulation of many points previously covered is necessary. Careful observation of problems encountered will dictate some items to be included. Announcements should be made concerning the local school program preceding and following the election. Acknowledgement of help given by all whose assistance could be judged vital should conclude the bulletin.

There are many general considerations that will help to make a school election project successful. One has to do with the matter of ballots. These should be printed and be similar in size and appearance to those used in the actual election. School election officials should have opportunity during the day to visit a voting place in the community to observe the precedures in operation and compare them with those used in the school. The fact should be emphasized that the school election project is in no manner merely a straw vote. Careful evaluations of the project should be made following its conclusion. These should be written down carefully, preserved in a folder, and used as a basis of improvement for the project at the time of the next general election.

Individual Projects. Often it becomes desirable and interesting to pupils to have opportunity to pursue individual project work. These projects can be regarded as activities that will add to the comprehension of general units. After giving a few examples of such work to a class, pupil suggestions ordinarily follow in profusion. The following are typical both in ideas and phrasing of those usually evolving from joint teacher-pupil planning:

1. Make a model of an object mentioned in recent reading. (Ivory soap, wood, cardboard, clay, etc., have been used by different pupils for this purpose. Ships, maps, important buildings, and statues of famous persons have been made the subjects of this idea.)

2. Write a theme in which you imagine yourself to have been a character present and participating in an event mentioned in class discussion. (Pupils usually like to consider extremes. For instance, if the study has dealt with France in the days preceding the Revolution of 1789, the tendency is to deal with the poorest group of the third estate or the most favored of royalty.) The use of the project based on imagination can extend to letter writing, entries in diaries, development of dialogues, and production of speeches not historically recorded.

3. Write a play based upon a period of history, attempting to attain historical accuracy of conversation, costuming, and setting. (The tendency of pupils here is also toward exaggeration. Gruesome details appeal to this age group. They usually wish to draft a play in which a murder is com-

mitted on the stage, rather than merely using sound effects off stage or having the murder reported by a messenger.) Credit can be given for writing the play; if it is presented by a group, each member participating can be given additional recognition.

4. Prepare the script for a radio program and present it over an improvised microphone. (Pupils enjoy taking a brief time period from history and giving a newscast summary. More interest is aroused if the commercials are made historical in setting too.)

5. Choose an event of major importance that represents a meeting of numerous delegates and attempt to dramatize its proceedings. (A national nominating convention of a major political party, a meeting of the U.N., or an opening session of Congress are examples of situations that might be considered. An event of outstanding importance that occurs infrequently such as the coronation of a British monarch is used in some instances. Some schools have sponsored one of these more formidable projects and invited delegates from other schools to participate.)

6. Read a book dealing with historical fiction, biography, dramatics, or travel that is related to material recently studied. Give an oral summary for the benefit of those who did not read the selection.

7. Prepare a crossword puzzle using as largely as possible words found in the last unit studied in social studies.

8. Write a song or a poem that might have been inspired by a historical event.

9. Prepare a good notebook dealing with the work covered in social studies during the present grade period.

10. Make an attractive poster for bulletin-board display. (Such posters can assume the form of cartoons, copies of sketches, large map productions, graphs, charts, outlines of content material, chronological arrangement of events, etc.)

11. Present a demonstration showing precisely how an activity described in textbook reading was performed. (Fire making in ancient times, the ceremony of homage in medieval history, and techniques relating to safety and first aid are examples of situations lending themselves to this treatment.)

12. Arrange a debate or select a topic for forum discussion and use a class period for presentation.

13. Prepare a pageant to be presented late in the school year that brings out the most interesting points of the entire year's work.

14. Consider the method used by an interesting radio program or television in conducting a contest and plan one of similar nature over a unit of work in the social studies. ("Dr. I. Q.," "Who Am I?" spelling matches, and numerous other programs are relatively well-known to most pupils.)

15. Visit a museum or other point of historical interest, a community center related to a topic in problems in democracy, or other place designated by the teacher. Report on the trip to the class. (The possibilities of a social studies field trip for the entire class quite readily grow out of individual projects.)

16. Start a collection of stamps from the various countries of the world in order that a knowledge of events and places may be gained from the pictures found.

Advantages of the Project Method. Some of the advantages claimed by those who do a considerable amount of project work in social studies classes are as follows:

1. The study of social studies becomes more interesting. This is based on the idea that day-by-day question-and-answer procedures become monotonous.
2. Individual interests and skills are easily aroused. The examples of projects activities given above indicate that the range is very broad. Scarcely any pupil would fail to find a challenge somewhere.
3. A great deal of incidental learning takes place as the project is pursued. In order to attain fair accuracy in the project the pupil needs the answers to many questions not covered in a textbook.
4. Pupils enjoy the presentation of projects given by their classmates.
5. Qualities of leadership, initiative, cooperation, patience, persistence, etc., are developed as the work is done on the project.
6. Correlation with other subjects being studied by the pupil becomes quite important.

Disadvantages of the Project Method. Many teachers who do not look very kindly upon project work in secondary-school social studies offer the following objections:

1. The method by its nature is more suited to pupils in lower grades.
2. A tremendous amount of time is wasted. Pupils reach decisions slowly as to what they wish to do and have great difficulty in finding materials with which to work.
3. Too little time remains for the effective study necessary to accomplish the objectives of the course if projects are pursued throughout.
4. Many of the basic facts of the course will not be brought into play at all through the work on projects.

On the whole it would seem that most of the disadvantages disappear when modern concepts are accepted. Pupil growth and development are more important than mastering too many obscure facts which are all too soon forgotten. Pupil cooperation in planning and executing classroom work are almost assured in project procedures. Finally, a sense of accomplishment becomes both an individual and group pleasure as projects come to observable conclusions. If the method accords with class desires and teacher personality and aptitude it should surely be looked upon as potentially productive of excellent results.

The Problem Method Described. The problem method of teaching is one that capitalizes on the intellectual needs sensed by the pupil. It is defined by Good [2] as "(1) a method of instruction by which learning is stimulated by the creation of challenging situations that demand solution; (2) a specific procedure by which a major problem is solved through the combined solutions of a number of smaller related problems." These should originate from suggestions by teacher and pupil working cooperatively. Problems vary greatly in nature and complexity. The simplest one is that in which the pupil desires to know the answer to a question involving a small bit of factual information. In all probability he even knows where to look for it in a textbook, reference book, or other source. Once it is found there is little further intellectual ado. Other problems become so involved that they remain as unsolved mysteries throughout the pupil's later life. Conclusions may be arrived at and later discarded for new ones which may in turn be modified or rejected. Teachers who are problem-minded may think of an entire course in terms of one big problem. Units become problems which are subtopics of the one big problem. Chapters become merely smaller subdivisions. An example of a problem large enough to consume an entire year might be an explanation of the rise and growth of American democracy. Unit problems could deal with various chronological phases. A fitting conclusion could be found in attempting to identify and offer solutions for democracy's modern problems. It is readily apparent that each day could be devoted to the discussion of and efforts to solve smaller and related problems.

The steps in problem solving should be clearly conceived. As pointed out above, the pupil must have a definite statement of the problem to be solved. He should advance some possible theories of solution but should keep in mind that they are merely theories and be willing to modify them in the light of facts ascertained in study.

[2] *Ibid.*, p. 310.

Teacher guidance should offer suggestions as to sources of information dealing with the problem at hand. After reasonable study and investigation have taken place, class discussion should follow. This may take the form of reports, forum discussion, general recitation, etc. Throughout, the pupil should be advancing his answer to the problem and supporting it with reliable evidence. A summary of the work of the group should follow. Individual members are always left free to accept or reject majority opinion.

The problem approach in teaching social studies should add materially to the pupil's ability to develop critical thinking. McCutchen [3] stresses this aspect decidedly and indicates the following steps as the intellectual experiences of the pupils:

1. Defines the problem clearly taking cognizance of the social values involved
2. Lists and considers the various feasible courses of action
3. Collects and interprets pertinent data
4. Reaches a tentative decision based on the data
5. Acts in accordance with the decision

In discussing the techniques of teaching that are really quite the opposite of problem solving, Elder [4] observes that ". . . many students, either in high school or college, prefer the lecture method. . . . Although requirements for a diploma or degree can be met in no easier way, educators may well ask themselves what kind of citizens most of the products of such a methodology will become. Will they be thoughtful? Critical? Analytical?" Dealing with this same topic with special adaptation to secondary schools, Elder and Jones [5] commented that "While the problem method and case approach are not convenient panaceas for either teaching ills or grave world problems, used wisely, they may prove to be a worthwhile supplement to more traditional teaching devices."

Suggested Problems. The following examples of problems that might be used for discussion are cited from representative social studies areas:

[3] A. P. McCutchen, "The Problems Approach to the Social Studies," *Journal of Educational Sociology,* XX (May, 1947), pp. 29–36.

[4] Robert E. Elder, "An Experiment with the Problem Method in Social Science," *The Social Studies,* XXXIX (November, 1948), p. 318.

[5] Robert E. Elder and Howard L. Jones, "Lets Get Down to Cases," *Social Education,* XII (April, 1948), p. 162.

American History

1. What factors led European nations to want to come to the New World?

2. Why did England become the most successful colonizer in North America?

3. What steps led to a desire for independence on the part of the colonies?

4. Describe the methods used by the new nation to gain the respect of foreign powers.

5. Explain why the election of Thomas Jefferson can almost be regarded as the "Revolution of 1800."

6. Show similarities and contrasts in Jeffersonian and Jacksonian democracy.

7. Why did sectionalism become an important issue in the history of our country?

8. Explain how the rise of big business in the last half of the nineteenth century became a problem of great importance before efforts to solve it were started.

9. Give the various causes of the Progressive movement that took place in the early part of the twentieth century.

10. What events have changed our nation from the practice of isolationism to that of full participation in world organization activities?

Problems in Democracy

1. In what ways has the Federal Reserve System helped to solve many of the banking problems that faced the country previous to its passage?

2. Would the interests of our country be better advanced at present by a high or a low tariff?

3. Should the Federal Government increase or decrease the amount of its regulation of the sale of stocks and bonds?

4. Suggest some ways in which the differences of opinion that frequently occur between those representing capital and those representing labor could be efficiently handled.

5. In what ways do the workings of the Interstate Commerce Act function for the best interests of all the people?

6. What factors operate at any time to determine the rate of interest that is paid on capital?

7. How is the family budget designed to help make the income serve the best interests of the group?

8. Mention the different items that must be taken into account to determine the amount of rent yielded by a given piece of land.

9. What are the characteristics possessed by a metal which serves society as a good money?

10. What are some of the probable causes of the various phases of the business cycle?

11. Show that the school is more important in a democracy than it is in an autocracy.

12. How would an increasing population give rise to sociological problems?

13. What elements in our civilization can be counted as contributions from immigration?

14. What are the most serious social effects that accompany child labor?

15. Give what you believe to be three of the greatest effects of the employment of women in industry. Justify your conclusions.

16. What are the good and the evil effects that might result from a program of socialized medicine?

17. Show how disease, poverty, and crime are related to each other.

18. What steps might a community take in its efforts to greatly reduce crime?

19. In what ways may morons become especially dangerous if permitted to mingle freely in society?

20. Should our nation adopt a set of uniform laws dealing with marriage and divorce?

Advantages of the Problem Method. There are certain advantages claimed by teachers who are enthusiastic about the problem method. Those most frequently advanced are the following:

1. The method is one that produces good results when used with secondary-school pupils. (As pointed out above, the project method has better claims for excellence when used in the elementary school.)

2. Practically all units of work in social studies lend themselves to problem-solving techniques.

3. Problems as applied to social studies can be stated in larger and more general terms which can be subdivided. Thus an entire course can be stated as a problem; units can be stated in smaller problems that contribute to the solution of the course as a whole. Even if daily assignments are used they can assume the form of discussions which contribute to the solution of unit problems.

4. Problem solving is good preparation for solving personal and community questions that must be faced in later life by the pupils.

5. The interest of parents is often aroused in a wholesome way when social studies pupils work on problem-solving efforts.

Disadvantages of the Problem Method. Since there is no general agreement on methods to be employed in social studies classes, certain disadvantages are usually readily apparent. Some of the most common ones related to the problem method are the following:

1. Too often it is not possible to test the accuracy of the answers that individual pupils or entire class groups get as a result of problem solving.
2. The problems that many pupils work upon are too difficult for the age of the group involved. In fact, capable adults holding responsible positions in our social, economic, and political areas and working with due sincerity fail to solve some of the same problems.
3. It is often difficult to distinguish between the issues that constitute our real problems and those that are merely passing questions of the day.
4. Pupils may develop one of two wrong attitudes. First, it is possible that they will come to think that meeting the problems of society is not difficult at all; in other words, it is easy to find workable solutions. Or, second, attitudes of resignation, futility, and cynicism may develop.
5. Recitations may develop into meaningless discussion and debate that really solve little or nothing.
6. Important factual information that is regularly conceived of as part of a course may never be brought into use through the exclusive use of the problem-solving method.

Again, the disadvantages are rather largely rationalizations on the part of those who do not choose to expend the energy necessary to work out a course with pupils on a problem-solving basis. If the group sincerely enjoys attacking social issues through the media of problems, it is almost certain to make the positive gains given under advantages. Should some isolated facts of a given social study not be brought into use there will probably be little or no harm occasioned.

The Socialized Recitation. The discussion of the methods mentioned above brings attention next to the socialized recitation. In most people's thinking it is a method that is characterized by much pupil participation in regular discussion, in the selection of topics for study and consideration, and in the management of classroom routine.

Since the pupils take an active part in discussion there is a direct contrast in procedure to that involved in, for example, the lecture method. It is presupposed that pupil questions, reactions, and contributions will be advanced freely. In such a situation pupil interest at its highest level may take a discussion in a different direction from that anticipated by the teacher. This is neither commendation nor criticism of the method as such so long as a thirst for knowledge is being quenched and complete sincerity prevails. In general this phase of the method indicates informality. Pupils feel a sense of freedom; no one is repressed.

In the selection of topics it is not always expedient to permit the entire proceedings to rest with the pupils; other times it is more nearly possible to do so. In situations of the first type there are certain traditional courses that embrace fairly standardized content. For instance, pupils taking world history are expected to study Greek and Roman epochs, the period of feudalism, the rise and growth of national states, etc. However, it is entirely possible to socialize the proceedings when studying Greek history. Pupils can express their wishes in respect to how much mythology shall be read, how many projects shall be undertaken, what topics shall be the subjects for special reports, etc. When a sharing of such decisions is extended to the pupils one can reasonably expect increased interest and participation on their part.

Routine management of the classroom can involve varying degrees of socialization. It may extend from such matters as keeping the room orderly in appearance, passing out materials of instruction, and assisting the teacher in record keeping to taking over the full job usually performed by the teacher. This latter conception obviously needs more discussion than does the former. If the pupils manage the class, organization is needed; the situation resulting will, in many ways, resemble the functioning of an adult club. Officers and committees will play an important part. Should the teacher wish to keep a class on such a socialized basis over an extended period of time, a small corps of officers would function continuously, with discussion chairmen being changed frequently.

Example of the Use of Socialized Recitation. For purposes of illustration let us consider that the class is going to use socialized procedures of the formal type for a period of time. The first action might be that of selecting a chairman to serve as leader of discussion. Correct parliamentary procedures should be followed in the making of nominations and conducting the election. If the teacher desires assurance that the leadership shall be of reasonably high quality, it is quite apt to establish a rule that the pupil selected must have a grade standing in the upper one-fourth of the class. (This is justified in that candidates for state and national office must meet specific requirements.) Following the election of a chairman it is quite desirable to choose a secretary in the same manner. The secretary's duty on the days involved shall be that of keeping a record of the meetings, including time, place, and persons taking part; in addition, a very important duty of making summary notes on subject matter is involved. A committee may be appointed by the chairman to supply special features for the discussion day. They may choose to present special reports, to secure and present pictoral materials, or to engage in any of a variety of activities that will generally add to the value of the day's discussion.

Let us assume that the course is World History and that the class is just starting a study of the French Revolution. Teacher and pupils discuss freely what they would like to learn about this period of history. Notations are made either on the blackboard or by an appointed secretary. Some of the topics that such groups usually indicate are included in the following questions:

1. Just what does revolution in government involve?
2. Why did a revolution occur in this particular country and at this time?
3. What are some biographical details about the leaders that offer partial explanations for the events that occurred?
4. Which of the events are regarded as actually momentous? as turning points?
5. What influence did the events in other countries, our own especially, have on this period of French history?
6. What results of this revolution may be regarded as rather permanent?
7. What effect did these have on the history of other countries, our own in particular?

The teacher and discussion leader need numerous conferences. Likewise, the leader and various committees need to work together a great deal. It becomes the leader's duty to constantly keep the objectives before the class during its work periods and to keep any committees or specialized groups working at maximum capacity.

As the time for group discussion arrives the teacher should find a place at the rear of the room. He should attempt to play the role merely of a member of the group; that is, he should consume no more than an equitable share of time in the discussion, refrain from offering authoritative explanations, and advance factual information only when specifically called upon to do so.

The preliminary arrangements described above have been carried out a few days ahead of time. The teacher and leader have had a conference; the latter has been furnished a basic textbook and possibly two supplementary textbooks. The leader thus gains a good grasp of subject matter through extensive reading. In a supervised study period the day before, he takes charge of discussion and announces the objective of the next day's lesson, indicates the pages to be read, and suggests questions which should be answered. The committee on special features may typically announce that two special reports will be given, one on the life of Voltaire and the other on conditions of French peasants in rural France of 1789. On the following day the chairman immediately calls the class to order and does the best teaching job of which he is capable. The regular teacher is available to settle questions of fact, to offer contributions on equal terms with the pupils, and to assure that the class shall proceed on businesslike principles. On the succeeding day the chairman again takes charge and calls upon the secretary to present the report that resulted from careful taking of notes during the previous discussion. A typical report on the situation described above might read as follows:

City, State
Month, year

The fourth-hour World History class met yesterday starting at 11 o'clock. John Smith was the leader of discussion, having been selected for this position in a regular class election two days previously. He conducted the class by asking us questions on the topic we had read. In addition, he told us many interesting facts that he had found in supplementary books and recommended that we too read the same books as part of our help for preparation of notebooks. Two very interesting special reports were presented as had been planned. We profited a great deal from the first one but could not hear most of the second one. (Probably the speaker should have stood at the front of the room when giving it.)

One of the things which we would remember from this period of history is that the causes for the French Revolution had been in existence a long time. Many rulers had spent far too much money for the good of the country. There was a sort of caste system under which people were divided into three groups. The first and second estates (clergy and nobles) had many privileges that weren't fair. The most unfortunate of the third estate had come to have so few rights by 1789 that it is little wonder that they revolted. Their hardships would never have been suspected by us until we read our lesson and had the special report. A second idea that we developed is that revolutions do not succeed unless there are strong leaders of upper groups or classes who have deep sympathy for the lower classes. France had such men in a group that we might call philosophers or thinkers. In their minds the revolution was really pretty well thought out before it began.

After John had summarized the lesson he turned the class meeting back to our teacher, Mr. Nelson, who made brief comments on the topics we discussed. He asked us to vote on whether or not we wanted to carry out our lesson in this same way again sometime using different officers. Twenty-six of us voted yes and two voted no.

Respectfully submitted,
Patricia Joynson, Secretary

The chairman, after asking for corrections or additions to the minutes, ordinarily calls on the regular teacher to again take charge.

Advantages of the Socialized Recitation. This type of teaching does indeed lend itself to an analysis of potential advantages and disadvantages. Some of the former that appear most frequently in comments by those who use it are the following:

1. Pupils who have a democratic voice in determining classroom activities have a greater interest in the class; this results in greater participation and increased learning.
2. Qualities of leadership are developed on the part of those who should be showing growth in this trait.
3. Pupils will sometimes exert renewed efforts to respond in class if that will help their classmate and personal friend to succeed in conducting a recitation.
4. Those who have served as leaders have a keener appreciation of the teacher's problems henceforth; consequently they know better how to cooperate to produce a better class program.
5. Valuable lessons about and practice in correct parliamentary procedure come as incidental results.

Disadvantages of the Socialized Recitation. The disadvantages advanced by opponents of the method contain some pertinent ideas for consideration. The following are among those most often heard:

1. Pupils cannot teach as well as teachers who have adequate preparation and possibly many years of successful experience. There is little logic in substituting poor teaching when it is equally possible to have good teaching.
2. Pupil leaders have little or no way of judging the relative importance

of events or topics, because they have no way of knowing about subject matter that is to follow. Thus they will fail to give correct emphasis as the discussion proceeds.

3. While it is desirable to develop traits of leadership, the same results should be secured in allied activities rather than through classroom teaching efforts.

4. A considerable waste of time is likely to result from procedures which give pupils free rein in determining topics for discussion, setting the pace for daily proceedings through contributions related to their own interests, and conducting the class.

5. A teacher who does not fully appreciate his own role in such a program of teaching may fail to realize the magnitude of his responsibilities.

Summary. The project as a method of teaching social studies was described in this chapter. The definition used recognized the need of activity with educational value leading to definite goals of understanding. It was stressed that projects may be group or individual. The problem method was described next. The creation of challenging situations in need of solution was given as the main essential of the method. It was contended that especially for the upper secondary grades the problem approach often proves superior to the project technique. The third teaching method emphasized was the socialized recitation. It was characterized as involving much pupil participation in regular discussion, in selection of topics to be studied, and in the management of classroom routine.

All these methods, when critically considered, have obvious advantages and disadvantages. Nature of the course content, personality of the teacher, and preferences of the class should determine the procedures to be used.

Questions on the Text

1. Give some historical background related to the project method of teaching.

2. What are the main points that should be stressed in a definition of the project method? Apply these to social studies teaching.

3. Show by example that projects may be either group or individual.

4. State the commonly suggested advantages and disadvantages of the project method.

5. How does the problem differ by definition from the project?

6. Give the steps through which a pupil would normally pass from the conception of the problem to its solution.

7. What are the advantages and disadvantages usually claimed for this method of teaching social studies?

8. How does a socialized recitation differ from one that is nonsocialized?

9. Show clearly every phase of pupil participation that is involved.

10. What are the advantages and disadvantages that could follow from the use of the socialized recitation?

Suggested Activities

1. Compile a list of group projects that you think could be used to advantage in social studies. Mention several activities that might be carried out in relation to each. Indicate the grade level for each one proposed.

2. Make additions to the list given in the chapter of projects to be done on an individual basis.

3. Summarize your personal reactions to the project method of teaching.

4. Follow the same procedures in relation to the problem method of teaching as those given in 1, 2, and 3 for projects.

5. To what degree should a teacher of social studies attempt to attain a socialization of classroom procedures?

6. Visit secondary-school social studies classes to observe the extent to which methods described in this chapter are used.

7. Read and summarize recent magazine articles dealing with teaching techniques mentioned in this chapter.

Selected References

ALDRICH, J. C., "Problems-approach in Secondary-school Social-studies Curriculum," *National Education Association Journal,* XXXVII (October, 1948), pp. 443–444.

BARHAM, T. C., "Our Student Government Interns in Citizenship," *School Activities,* XIX (January, 1948), p. 167.

BECK, ELSIE M., "A Three-level Community Project," *Social Education,* XIV (February, 1950), pp. 69–70.

BOLTZ, JOSEPH K., and SAM M. SNIDERMAN, " 'Scienceville' Was Just a Classroom until Election Time," *Social Education,* XII (October, 1948), pp. 261–262.

BOLZAU, EMMA L., and EMILY D. STEVENSON, "Volunteer Student Social Service Project," *Social Education,* XIII (May, 1949), pp. 237–238.

"Creating a Social Studies Atmosphere; Report on Five Classrooms," *Clearing House,* XXIII (October, 1948), pp. 88–93.

ELDER, ROBERT E., "An Experiment with the Problem Method in Social Science," *The Social Studies,* XXXIX (November, 1948), p. 318.

———, and HOWARD L. JONES, "Let's Get Down to Cases," *Social Education,* XII (April, 1948), pp. 162.

GOETTING, M. L., "Some Teaching Problems in the Social Studies," *Social Studies,* XXXIII (March, 1942), pp. 99–103.

GOOD, CARTER V., *Dictionary of Education,* New York: McGraw-Hill Book Company, Inc., 1945.

HAIMAN, E., "Why High School Projects?" *Secondary Education,* XIII (February, 1948), pp. 1–3.

HARVEY, C. C., "Term Projects in Social Studies Classes," *Social Studies,* XXXIII (April, 1942), pp. 174–175.

———, "Ideas for Social Studies Classes," *Social Studies,* XXXIV (January, 1943), pp. 11–13.

HUNSUCKER, FLORISE, "A Practical Project in Civics," *Social Education,* XI (March, 1947), pp. 120–122.

KILLMER, CLARENCE, "The City Council Comes to Wilbur Wright Junior High School," *Social Education,* XII (November, 1948), pp. 305–306.

LAWRENCE, GRACE, "A Socialized Recitation," *Social Studies,* XXX (February, 1939), p. 75.

LEARSON, J. B., "Ninth Graders Conduct a Public Opinion Poll," *Social Education,* XII (April, 1948), pp. 166–168.

MCCUTCHEN, S. P., "The Problems Approach to the Social Studies," *Journal of Educational Sociology,* XX (May, 1947), pp. 529–536.

MCGLYNN, EDNA M., "Field Trips in Government Courses," *Social Education,* VIII (January, 1944), pp. 19–22.

MORGAN, E. A., "Activity Project in History: The Chronological Chart," *Social Studies,* XXXIV (May, 1943), pp. 214–217.

RAYMER, ROBERT G., "Motivating History with Postage Stamps," *Social Studies,* XXXIII (April, 1942), pp. 151–152.

SPRAGUE, S. H., "Bradford Pupils Are Replanning the City," *Clearing House,* XX (May, 1946), pp. 525–526.

STAPLE, FLORA M., "A Dramatization of the Constitutional Convention of 1787," *Social Studies,* XXXI (November, 1940), pp. 305–310.

TURNER, LAWRENCE E., and CORNELIUS H. SIEMENS, "The Election—A Plan for Citizenship and Education," *Social Education,* VIII (October, 1944), pp. 258–261.

WHITWELL, C. G., "Louisiana Students Hold Constitutional Convention; High School Pupils Draft Basic Document," *National Municipal Review,* XXXVII (April, 1948), pp. 219–220.

"You Can Hold a Model Convention," *Scholastic,* LII (Mar. 22, 1948), p. 12.

Chapter 11

THE UNIT METHOD OF TEACHING

Preview. The proponents of various educational philosophies are almost unanimous in their praise of the unit method of teaching. In many instances the relationship to project and problem approaches is quite apparent. The various divisions of the unit procedure, namely, introduction, work activities, recitation and discussion, testing, and evaluation should be well understood. Practice in the construction of units for teaching purposes should be undertaken early by those teaching in this area.

General Information about the Unit. The extensive use of the unit method of teaching in social studies followed the introduction of problems and projects. In fact the unit method often incorporates the use of both these earlier procedures. The concept of unit teaching becomes more clear if contrast is used. The older idea stressed lesson planning in terms of daily work. Some social studies teachers have been known to make from 150 to 180 plans for a year's work in a single subject. Each of these gave the appearance of being a complete piece of work within itself. Most of them represented such divisions as review and recall, presentation of the lesson, present-day applications, and summary and conclusions. Some indications in margins and spaces at top and bottom of pages often outlined devices and materials to be used. The unit procedure also makes extensive use of plans, but each part of the series indicates work to be done over a period ranging from several days to many weeks. The initial work involved in the construction of units is quite formidable, but possibly the total effort would not exceed that involved in preparing the numerous corresponding daily lesson plans.

Definition of terms is very important today. Recognizing this point, the application will be made to a social studies unit. It is an outline of carefully selected subject matter which has been isolated because of its relationship to pupil needs and interests. Hurd [1] makes the statement, "Carried to a logical conclusion, units should be parts of courses; courses, units in larger curriculum sequences."

The definition of a unit found in a recently published dictionary of terms is as follows: [2] "(1) A major subdivision of a course of study, a textbook, or a subject field, particularly a subdivision in the social studies, practical arts, or sciences. (2) An organization of various activities, experiences, and types of learning around a central theme, problem, or purpose, developed cooperatively by a group of pupils under teacher leadership; involves planning, execution of plan, and evaluation of results."

Appropriate objectives, individual and group activities, means of organizing learning procedures, and final evaluation techniques are provided. The emphasis on the selection of content based upon the needs of the pupil is quite important. It recognizes the idea of a child-centered school, the fact that education is for the pupils, and that the school does not exist for the teachers.

Probably no other one person did more to popularize the unit method of teaching in various subject-matter areas than H. C. Morrison.[3] Early in the process of reading professional literature one becomes acquainted with the steps advocated in his writings, namely, exploration, presentation, assimilation, organization, and recitation. It has been maintained that mastery would result from properly developing and executing these steps. This idea is further based on the Morrison formula of pretest, teach, test, adapt procedures, teach and test again. These steps are substantially the same as those in a Detroit plan described by Barnes: [4] "(*a*) Unit assignment, (*b*) Period of study on material of basic assignment, (*c*) Period of supplementary activities after pupils finish the basic assignment, (*d*) Period of general discussion of the unit—basic material plus supplementary acquisitions, and (*e*) Unit evaluation."

The Unit Method Gains Praise from Many Writers. Typical of the

[1] Archer Willis Hurd, "What Do You Mean by the Unit-Problem-Project Plan of Instruction?" *School and Society,* LXII (Nov. 10, 1945), p. 300.

[2] From Carter V. Good, ed., *Dictionary of Education,* New York: McGraw-Hill Book Co., Inc., 1945, p. 436. Courtesy McGraw-Hill Book Company, Inc.

[3] Henry C. Morrison, *The Practice of Teaching in the Secondary School,* Chicago: The University of Chicago Press, 1926.

[4] C. C. Barnes, "The 'Unit-mastery Method,'" *The Clearing House,* XXI (October, 1946), p. 79.

manner in which enthusiasm has been expressed is a statement from Boldt and Deck [5] prefacing a discussion dealing with a Latin-American unit. "It has been our experience, after careful analysis of existing plans, and after considerable study, that the unit plan of work, following a definite thread in the pattern of the whole, is most adaptable to the students of the secondary school."

Unless certain definite advantages follow from the use of a method of teaching it should not be used. In this case, some advantages that are mentioned most frequently are

1. Pupils feel the urge to take part in activities that are related to the unit procedure. By the very nature of the method much time is devoted to reading, problem solving, project work, personal interviewing, etc. A pupil who does not work becomes uncomfortably conspicuous.
2. Many of the traits that social studies teachers strive to develop in pupils are especially promoted through unit activities. Among these are cooperation, leadership, courtesy, loyalty to a program, and respect for good workmanship.
3. There is a desirable continuity of work from day to day. Pupils return to the classroom ready to resume work where they left it unfinished. Too often when pupils work under traditional patterns they come to class wondering, "What are we going to do today?"
4. The problem of individual differences has caused teachers much concern. With the unit method it is possible to select activities suited to the pupil, both to his capacities and to his interests.
5. Social studies teachers have been regularly concerned about pupils making effective use of supplementary materials. Among these are parallel textbooks, source materials, encyclopedias, world almanac, historical fiction, pamphlets, periodicals, etc. A well-planned unit stimulates the use of these and many others.
6. In teaching procedures that necessitate making frequent assignments, pupils find themselves unable to grasp quickly and easily the jobs that are expected of them. A minimum of time at the introduction of a unit solves this problem for many class periods.
7. Social studies teachers have long recognized the place of summaries and outlines. The conclusion of a unit offers apt opportunity for class and teacher together to work these out to advantage.
8. There is much to be gained in respect to perspective. Concepts are more easily grasped when wholes rather than parts are considered. Interrelationships are more easily sensed.

[5] Albert W. Boldt and Clara M. Deck, "Planning a Latin American Unit," *Social Studies*, XXIV (May, 1943), p. 200.

9. The core curriculum, correlation, fusion, and integration are frequently mentioned in educational circles today. The unit method not only makes ventures in these directions possible; it even encourages these and other progressive measures.

10. Subjective observation and pupil testimony more often than not reveal that pupils in social studies enjoy the unit method of study more than they do traditional methods.

11. Democracy as an ideal can be best exemplified in a classroom through unit procedures. Not only is it taught in spirit but also it can well be made the subject of a unit of study. (Thornton [6] remarked that "Democracy not being an instinct has to be learned. It is worth at least a 'unit' of study.")

No system of teaching can be considered perfect. Some of the disadvantages mentioned occasionally in relation to the unit method in social studies are given below.

1. At present social studies teachers have not had sufficient training in the techniques of writing units and putting them into execution, owing partly to the nature of the directed teaching in teacher-training institutions and to a lack of sufficient textbook and periodical materials.

2. Unless pupils are taught by the unit method in all their secondary-school subjects they become disconcerted when it is used in one subject. There is present a general state of wonder, confusion, and indecision.

3. There is a great loss from the standpoint of economy of time. Pupils arrive at a set of objectives slowly. Materials for general-activity work are often inaccessible or hard to find.

4. Many of the fundamental facts of individual social studies are never learned when the subject is presented by the unit plan. Specific characters, dates, places, and technical vocabulary can easily be overlooked

5. Visitors, particularly parents, who might visit classes at certain stages during the development of a unit would often reach hasty conclusions to the effect that the work was all confusion and without substance. It is difficult for some to understand that noise which attends actual work is justified.

One of the questions that social studies teachers often ask deals with the number of units that they should attempt to teach during a year. Initial consideration often leads to surprises. Even if the teacher is thinking in terms of traditional chapters rather than daily assignments, the number is relatively large. However, since units

[6] E. W. Thornton, "That Unit on Democracy," *Social Studies,* XXXIII (December, 1942), p. 363.

are related to pupil needs, experiences, and preferences and since organization, investigation, and directed activities are involved, the number must of necessity be small. In general, a teacher should not attempt to teach a certain number of units during a year. Rather, it is preferable to develop thoroughly those which are initiated. If one were required to state the approximate number of units that should be attempted annually in representative social studies, grades 7 through 14, it would probably range from eight to fourteen.

Stages in Unit Development. Regardless of the technical names various authors have given to the different stages in teaching a unit of work, the first has to do with introductory activities. It is obviously as important a phase in the whole process as any other one step. "Well begun is half done" was never more true than it is here. We shall assume that the teacher has the course well planned for the year; also that the units to be taught are clearly in mind. Possibly planning has gone so far as to have them fully developed. If the last condition obtains, the teacher must be willing to have pupil interests and desires produce modifications. One of the first questions that must be answered is "What experiences have the pupils already had that are closely related to the subject of the unit and its objectives?" Likewise, the teacher must know pupil knowledges and skills which have already been acquired and which are pertinent. The points must be duly considered and capitalized upon. Pupils must be accepted where they are and directed well toward the goals which they should reach.

Unusual care must be exercised at this stage to ascertain fully the background mentioned above; likewise to arouse interest. The first point may be well met by the administration of a pretest. If this is used, care must be taken to explain that grades will not be computed upon the basis of results obtained. Straightforward questions and answers may be employed. The procedure should not take a great deal of time. Motivation efforts and aspects are more intricate and time-consuming. No two units are likely to be of such nature as to permit the introductions to be identical. Some of the following procedures are frequently employed to good effect: presentation of an overview by the teacher; showing films or using other visual aids; having a speaker from the community give a talk related to the unit; taking a field trip to observe appropriate points.

After the approach is made to a unit the pupils should early grasp the limits and importance of the work at hand. They should perceive the meanings that it can have for them individually and collectively. Objectives should be formulated through the medium of class discussion. The teacher should permit enough flexibility to allow the pupils to state what they personally desire to learn as a result of the impending study. As such ideas are expressed they should be written on the blackboard or recorded by a pupil secretary. Refinement of phrasing, combination of overlapping points, and logical arrangement can properly become teacher functions.

In dealing with the introduction to units of teaching, Farnum [7] makes the following statement: "Much of the success of unit instruction depends on the teacher's plan for introducing the unit. Initial activities orient pupils to the work ahead by developing their interests, by providing them with an overview of the scope of the unit, and by making them aware of the problems to be solved."

After the unit has been duly introduced the work stage logically follows. Any activities that the pupils pursue for the purpose of attaining unit objectives appropriately belong here. By the very nature of social studies it is apparent that a great deal of reading should be done. Possibly more new information is gained and more problems are solved through this medium than any other. Books, pamphlets, newspapers, periodicals, and source materials are pertinent and should be accessible in reasonable proportions. Pupils learn very economically through the use of visual aids. These may be secured from the sources mentioned in Chapter 6. It is granted that these and audio aids can have a place at any stage in unit study, but it is equally true that they are important in the work period. Community resources are more usable in some social studies than in others and in connection with some units than with others. The teacher should make use of them wherever practicable. The radio should be given special consideration because of its usefulness and its availability in most schools and homes. All the aids that can ever be used will find their way into motivated unit-study procedures at one time or another during a year. To trained observers the impression gained upon entering a social studies classroom at this juncture is a delightful one. A committee of five may be meeting in one corner of the room planning a panel discussion. Another group of similar size may be en-

[7] Martha T. Farnum, "How to Prepare for a Social Studies Unit," *California Journal of Secondary Education,* XXIV (January, 1949), p. 31.

gaged in writing a play having a social studies setting. A small group may be leaving the social studies room to go to the art or vocational-trades department to complete a project. Individuals often find secluded spots to investigate sources for specific information. The teacher moves freely from group to group to answer specific questions, offer suggestions, and lend encouragement. Not infrequently, either at the beginning or end of a period the teacher calls the class to attention to discuss work progress briefly, answer questions of a general nature, and state objectives.

It is sometimes difficult to know when to halt the work activities and start recitations, reports, and discussions. Some finish the work much sooner than others. The problem of individual differences will always be present. At the outset an effort should be made to determine whether the group has mastered basic facts. Skillful question-and-answer technique operates here at its best. Special reports, presentation of projects, panel participation, etc., should follow. After each of these, profitable discussion can take place. The teacher's role is that of arranging the program so as to ensure unity, coherence, and balance. Usually, if the teacher entertained misgivings about the success of the unit during the work period, they will be overcome during the developmental stage of recitation, discussion, and presentation of the results of work.

The procedures involved in concluding a unit are closely related to the work described above but are different in that they come last. An effort is made to emphasize the organized pattern of the unit and to determine what conclusions are sound. Most pupils are unable to write concise and clear summaries; likewise few of them are able to produce logically developed outlines. A great deal of time should be spent on this work early in a given year. The successive units should reemphasize these skills and procedures. Since much of the learning during the work period is incidental in nature, this organizing mentally and in writing is quite important. The use of the notebook as an agency of preservation of materials for future reference must not be overlooked. Preparation and distribution of mimeographed sheets is helpful if the class participates in their preparation. Testing is naturally expected and highly recommended. It is necessary only that the objectives of testing and sound procedures of construction be observed (see Chapter 17). The work of the entire unit should be evaluated by the class. Pupils should state freely the manner in which they feel that the study was helpful, ways in which their personal behavior and reaction were changed, and also shortcomings in the method of study. The teacher should not rely on oral statements alone for evaluation. He should actually watch for changes and growth in the pupils; contents of notebooks and statements made in other written work should be evaluated as a reflection of the success of the unit procedures. As a part of the teacher's personal records a written statement of evaluation should be preserved.

Examples of Social Studies Units. A description of the unit method of teaching having been presented, it seems appropriate to give examples from representative social studies. For the first example the subject, "Revolutions That Have Increased Liberty," will be used. (The Puritan, American, and French Revolutions are illustrative.)

I. Objectives
  A. Teacher or general
    1. To present to the class the pattern of causes, events, and results that accompany revolutions resulting in increased liberty
  B. Pupil or specific
    1. To find out the general causes of any revolution and to apply them to the specific ones being studied
    2. To become acquainted with a group of leading characters, both those favoring and those opposing the changes
    3. To study propaganda techniques used by the opposing forces
    4. To find out the part played by armed forces during a revolution
    5. To select a few events that mark the course of individual revolution with emphasis upon dates that have become traditional in the countries involved
    6. To show how the concept of martyrs and martyrdom is related to revolutions
    7. To note how vigorously those who have enjoyed privileges attempt to cling to them
    8. To observe how freely lives and property are sacrificed when the momentum of revolution is established
    9. To find examples of those who enjoyed privileges but who sponsored the cause of change
    10. To establish a workable definition of the word *revolution*
    11. To prepare a list of all the ways in which the countries involved were different at the end of the revolutions
    12. To discover ways in which various revolutions differ

II. General scope of content
 A. General theories of government held by Stuart rulers
  1. Divine right of sovereign not to be questioned
  2. Controls to extend to both state and church
 B. Charles I and parliament
  1. King granted large resources but misappropriated funds
  2. King signed Petition of Right merely to get additional funds
   a. Ruler not to levy taxes without consent of parliament
   b. Soldiers not to be quartered in private homes
   c. Martial law not to be imposed in time of peace
   d. Arbitrary imprisonment to be abandoned.
  3. Parliament not called from 1629 to 1640
   a. Ship tax collected in large amounts
   b. Religious issues caused trouble equal in difficulty to political questions
  4. Long parliaments in session, 1640 to 1660
   a. Led by such men as Hampden, Pym, and Cromwell
   b. Reduced power of ministers and other favorites of the king
   c. Passed law that parliament should meet every three years (Triennial Act)
   d. Saw Cavaliers (king's supporters) and Roundheads (king's opponents) come into being
 C. Puritan Revolution (1642–1646)
  1. Conflict between Cavaliers and Roundheads
  2. Roundheads aided by Scotch Presbyterians
  3. Charles I and Cavaliers defeated at Marston Moor, 1644
  4. Parliament purged of Presbyterian commoners by Colonel Pride, thus leaving the "Rump Parliament"
   a. Beheading of Charles I
   b. Establishment of the Commonwealth
  5. Seizure of power by Oliver Cromwell
   a. Governed by consitution, Instrument of Government
   b. Power dictatorial and based upon support of army
   c. Death of leader the end of the Protectorate
 D. Parliamentary acts pointing toward the American Revolution
  1. Navigation Act
  2. Molasses Act
  3. Royal Proclamation of 1763
  4. Sugar Act
  5. Stamp Act
  6. Quartering Act
  7. Intolerable Acts

E. English leadership of George III, Grenville, Townshend, and North

F. Early events showing colonial opposition
1. Commercial boycotts
2. Resistance to British officials
3. Boston Massacre
4. Boston Tea Party
5. Assembling of First Continental Congress
   a. Chosen by Committees of Correspondence, Committees of Safety, and mass meetings
   b. Great excitement
6. Bloodshed at Lexington and Concord

G. Second Continental Congress guides the colonies to the status of a united nation
1. Meeting in Philadelphia, 1775, to assume charge of matters of general interest to the colonies
2. Washington appointed Commander-in-Chief
3. Did not get full cooperation immediately on idea of independence
4. Assisted by British methods, use of propaganda devices, and enthusiasm over early military successes
5. Acceptance and adoption of Jefferson's draft of a declaration of independence
   a. Preamble
   b. Indictment of British policy
   c. Bill of specific grievances
6. Many obstacles to be met
   a. Loyalty to mother country
   b. Limited finances
   c. Lack of military experience
   d. Need of foreign help
7. Military and naval engagements
8. Diplomatic strategy in European countries
9. Negotiations for peace

H. The Treaty of Paris, 1783

I. Beginnings of the French Revolution in the calling of the Estates General, 1789
1. Three classes represented
2. Original purpose of solving financial difficulties set aside shortly
3. National Assembly formed as new governing body

J. Radical phase starting with the storming of the Bastille, July 14, 1789

K. Role of leading members of royal group, patriots, and philosophers

L. Abolition of older marks of privilege and class distinction
M. Relation of revolutionary activity to foreign affairs
N. Other governing bodies formed as the revolution progressed
O. Realization of the goals of liberty, equality, and fraternity
P. Summary of the gains secured by the peoples living in three countries where revolutions occurred
  1. Increase of personal liberty
  2. Fuller participation of more people in governmental affairs
  3. Extension of real concepts of democracy
  4. More equal distribution of taxes and other sacrifices necessary to operate a government
  5. Less power concentrated in the hands of a favored class
  6. Freedoms essential to full and happy living more generally practiced
  7. Opportunity for progress based upon character and intelligence established

III. Suggested activities

A. All members of the class will read about the various revolutions as presented in one basic textbook. It is recommended that a second parallel textbook be read covering the same content.

B. Each pupil will place in his notebook a list of the most important events associated with each revolution. These will be arranged in the order of their occurrence. Exact dates will be recorded for a few outstanding happenings.

C. Notes will be prepared on the problem of general causes for all revolutions. The findings will be used as part of recitations to follow later.

D. One or more important characters who had a leading part in connection with each revolution will be selected for biographical reports. These will be brief and will constitute a part of the unit notebook. A selected number of these will be read in general class recitation period.

E. An exercise based upon the use of imagination will be worked out by each pupil. The final product should be in the form of a letter, diary, newspaper article, or speech prepared for delivery.

F. If time permits, a reading of one or more historical-fiction books should be completed. Oral reports will be planned.

G. Details of these revolutions will be compared with those of revolutions studied in earlier periods of history.

H. Attempts will be made to find actual or potential revolutions going on in the world today. The general principles learned will be applied.

I. Speculation will be made as to how countries may prevent revolutions. The same data may help to explain the absence of revolutions in our own country over a relatively long period of time.

J. Comparison of the present-day governments of these countries with those established immediately after the revolutions will be made.

K. A call will be made for volunteers to take part in a forum discussion dealing with a selected phase of the topic of revolution.

L. Any films that can be secured having a bearing on these revolutions will be shown to make more vivid the descriptions given in our reading. Possibly some pupils can find pictures in newspapers and magazines dealing with revolutionary subjects.

M. Each pupil will prepare three paragraphs summarizing results of the revolutions in the countries being studied.

N. Be able to discuss well the following questions and exercises:

1. In what ways did Charles I carry on the practices of government started by his father?
2. What are the principal provisions of the Petition of Right?
3. By what means was Charles I able to carry on for eleven years without calling a meeting of parliament?
4. In what manner did John Hampden become famous during the reign of Charles I?
5. What were some of the most famous actions of the Long Parliament?
6. What were Roundheads? Cavaliers? Pride's Purge? the Rump Parliament? the Instrument of Government? the Lord Protector?
7. What are some of the interesting facts that most people who read about Oliver Cromwell remember most easily?
8. What specific event would you say could be associated with the end of the Puritan Revolution?
9. What mistakes in methods of governing the American colonies do you think contributed to their decision to rebel against England?
10. Mention various acts passed by parliament that tended to anger the colonists. Give the general provisions of each.
11. Give the names of three important English political leaders of this period and mention activities of each.
12. Name five or more leaders among the colonists not famous for their military activities and tell what contribution was made by each.

13. Select three military or naval engagements related to the American Revolution and give some interesting facts about each.
14. Summarize briefly the nature and amount of foreign aid which was secured by the colonists during the course of the Revolution.
15. Describe the attitude and activities of those who remained loyal to England during the Revolution.
16. Give the provisions of the peace treaty that ended the American Revolution.
17. One author states that the French Revolution was accomplished in the minds of men before they made it the work of their hands. What does he mean?
18. Describe fully the system of classes of society that existed in France on the eve of the French Revolution.

IV. Reading materials

(The titles given below are typical of those that can aptly be placed on a list of references for the pupils. At the ends of some chapters cited are lists of historical fiction, poems having a historical basis, etc. These would be used in developing problems, projects, and in making provision for individual differences.)

ADAMS, JAMES T., and CHARLES G. VANNEST, *The Record of America,* Chaps. III and IV.

BARKER, EUGENE C., and HENRY S. COMMAGER, *Our Nation,* Chap. IV.

BEARD, CHARLES A., and MARY R. BEARD, *The Making of American Civilization,* Chap. VI.

BOAK, ARTHUR E. R., PRESTON SLOSSON, and HOWARD R. ANDERSON, *World History,* Chaps. XXV and XXVIII.

CANFIELD, LEON H., HOWARD B. WILDER, *et al., The United States in the Making,* Chap. IX.

DUMOND, DWIGHT L., EDWARD E. DALE, and EDGAR B. WESLEY, *History of the United States,* Chap. V.

FAULKNER, HAROLD V., and TYLER KEPNER, *America, Its History and People,* Chap. V.

HARLOW, RALPH V., *Story of America,* Chap. V.

HUGHES, R. O., *The Making of Today's World,* Chaps. X and XII.

MUZZEY, DAVID S., *A History of Our Country,* Chaps. V and VI.

ROGERS, LESTER B., RAY ADAMS, and WALKER BROWN, *Story of Nations,* Parts X and XI.

SOUTHWORTH, JOHN V., *Our Own United States,* Units III and IV.

WIRTH, FREMONT P., *United States History,* Chap. VI.

The second example to be presented is a unit on the U.N.:

I. Possible objectives
  A. To understand the need for international cooperation
  B. To understand the general causes of friction between nations
  C. To understand the problems confronting various peoples in their world relationships
  D. To understand the present organization of the U.N. and to realize the possibility of developmental growth toward more effective organization
  E. To understand the significance of individual people in the striving toward international order
  F. To encourage world-mindedness; to guide pupils into thinking in terms of humanity
  G. To emphasize international concepts in place of competitive nationalistic ideas
  H. To encourage critical reading and thinking about current affairs
  I. To provide opportunity for pupils to develop poise in presenting their ideas before a group
  J. To guide pupils in procedures essential for well-conducted public discussion groups—recognizing opposition, being tactful, waiting for one's turn
  K. To increase pupils' vocabularies by helping them acquire new concepts. Such terms as the following should be included:

partition	technical information	civil liberties
imperialism	facilities	administer
nationalism	stabilizing currencies	Secretariat
independence	rate of exchange	cultural interchange
rehabilitation	economic union	prejudice
fiscal	trusteeship	tensions
commission	aggressor nation	telecommunication
petition	mediation	repatriation

II. Exploring suggested topics and raising questions leading toward areas for investigation:
  A. What is the chief problem in foreign affairs for all nations today?
  B. List reasons why nations engage in war.
  C. What efforts to prevent war have been made in the past?
  D. What nations seem most war-minded today? Why?
  E. What is the foreign policy of the United States? of Great Britain? of China? of the U.S.S.R.? of France?
  F. Is war an inevitable circumstance among nations?
  G. Has the U.N. ever prevented war?

H. How did the U.N. try to stop the war in Korea?

I. Can you see any weakness in the U.N. which might be corrected to make the organization more effective?

J. What kind of help does the U.N. provide for member nations in addition to that of trying to maintain peace?

K. Can you discover any similarity between world peace efforts of the twentieth century and the efforts of the American people to establish an effective national government?

L. What is the attitude of the U.N. toward the control of atomic energy?

M. What are the significant ideas contained within the Atlantic Charter?

Or, a film may serve as an introductory medium providing material for discussion and further investigation. Such a film might be one of the following:

We the People, Young America Film (1945)
The People's Charter, Nu-Ark (1947)
Quest for Tomorrow, Film Forum Foundation (1949)

If not used in the opening of the unit, these films should be shown at some stage of the discussion period and adequate attention given to their potential value.

III. Possible activities

A. Reading—all individuals read

1. For general information on the U.N., its history, purposes, and accomplishments
2. For specific information on some topics for which pupils have assumed responsibility
3. To note location of information in which other pupils are known to be interested
4. To list any questions or problems in which the pupil needs further information and guidance

Foreign Policy Headline Books

Goslin, R. A., *Changing Governments*, 1937, #11
Popper, D. H., *The Puzzle of Palestine*, 1938, #14
Stone, Shepard, *Shadow over Europe*, 1938, #15
Fry, Varian, *Bricks without Mortar*, 1938, #16
Brockway, Thomas, *Battle without Bullets*, 1939, #18
Langsam, W. C., *In Quest of Empire*, 1939, #19
Wolfe, H. C., *Human Dynamite*, 1939, #20
Fry, Varian, *The Peace That Failed*, 1939, #21
Bisson, T. A., *Shadow over Asia*, 1941, #29

Graves, H. N., Jr., *War on the Short Wave*, 1941, #30
Dean, V. M., *The Struggle for World Order*, 1941, #32
Dean, V. M., *Russia at War*, 1942, #34
Kirkland, G. L., and W. R. Sharp, *Uniting Today for Tomorrow*, 1942, #37

We, the Peoples. . . . A Brief History of the United Nations, New York: American Association for the United Nations, Inc., 1947.

Unesco Today, Washington, D.C.: U.S. National Commission for Unesco, 1950.

"The Defense of Peace"—Documents Relating to Unesco, Part I, Washington, D.C.: Department of State Publication 2457, 1946.

Facts and Figures about the United Nations, Washington, D.C.: Department of State Publication 3930, 1950.

Basic Facts about the United Nations, Lake Success, N.Y.: Department of Public Information, 1947.

The World Program of Unesco, Report of the Programme Commission at the First Unesco General Conference.

United Nations Organization, A Handbook of the U.N.O., Columbus, O.: Charles E. Merrill Co., 1946.

Building a New World Economy, Washington, D.C.: Department of State Publication 2618.

Guide to the United States and the United Nations, Washington, D.C.: Department of State Publication 2634.

What We Are Doing in Germany and Why, Washington, D.C.: Department of State Publication 2621, 1946

What We Are Doing in Japan and Why, Washington, D.C.: Department of State Publication 2633, 1946.

War—How Can We Prevent It, Washington, D.C.: Department of State Publication 2300, 1945.

Occupation—Why? What? Where? Washington, D.C.: Department of State Publication 2627, 1945.

Fifty Facts about UNRRA, Lake Success, N.Y.: United Nations Information Office.

The United Nations—Four Years of Achievement, Washington, D.C.: Department of State Publication 3624, 1949.

International Control of Atomic Energy and the Prohibition of Atomic Weapons, Recommendations of the United Nations Atomic Energy Commission, Washington, D.C.: Department of State Publication 3646, 1949.

Action in Korea, First Report of Security Council, Washington, D.C.: Department of State Publication 3935, 1950.

How the Peoples Work Together, New York: U.N. Department of Public Information, Manhattan Publishing Co., 1949.

Textbooks

HOFFMAN, WALTER GAILEY, *Pacific Relations,* New York: McGraw-Hill Book Company, Inc., 1936.

MAGRUDER, FRANK ABBOTT, *National Governments and International Relations,* Boston: Allyn & Bacon, 1947.

STEINER, H. ARTHUR, *Principles and Problems of International Relations,* New York: Harper & Brothers, 1940.

LANSING, MARION, *America in the World,* Boston: D. C. Heath and Company, 1949.

PACKARD, LEONARD O., BRUCE OVERTON, and BEN D. WOOD, *Our Air-age World,* New York: The Macmillan Company, 1944.

B. Group work

1. Dramatization
   - *a.* The Security Council in session
   - *b.* The General Assembly in session
   - *c.* Examples of work done by the Economic and Social Council
   - *d.* A meeting of the International Court of Justice
   - *e.* Examples of work done by Unesco
2. Panel discussions
   - *a.* Topics which explain the work of the specialized agencies of U.N.
     - (1) International Labor Organization
     - (2) International Refugee Organization
     - (3) International Trade Organization
     - (4) World Health Organization
     - (5) International Monetary Fund
     - (6) Universal Postal Union
     - (7) International Civil Aviation Organization
     - (8) Food and Agriculture Organization
     - (9) International Telecommunications Organization
     - (10) International Bank for Reconstruction and Development
   - *b.* The U.N. in Korea
   - *c.* Control of atomic energy by U.N.
   - *d.* The charter of the U.N.
   - *e.* The Atlantic Pact and the U.N.
   - *f.* Possible danger points of international friction
   - *g.* The United States in occupied Japan
   - *h.* Problems in occupied Germany
3. Group projects and reports based on maps, graphs, or charts drawn and constructed by groups investigating a problem relating to U.N. In addition to these suggestions there may be group projects resulting from class discussion.

a. Pupil-drawn flags of members of U.N. mounted on a map of the world
b. A graph showing loans to needy countries
c. A chart of pictures of life in countries where U.N. agencies have given aid
d. A combination of chart, graph, and map showing world movement of displaced persons
e. A map of the trusteeships of the U.N.
f. Maintain a bulletin board of current news about U.N.

C. Individual activities
1. Individual interests may suggest activities growing out of class discussion.
2. A pupil might compose an imaginary diary of a delegate to the U.N. General Assembly recording the events of a series of meetings of that body.
3. A pupil might collect news articles on a given topic over a period of days as it is before the U.N. for discussion. Mount the articles on a poster and prepare a summarizing statement.
4. A pupil might collect pictures showing the U.N. in session. Mount them in some form for efficient showing.

IV. Conclusion and final evaluation
A. Have pupils summarize the class activity and findings in the unit in an article to be published in the school newspaper. Allow the class to select the article to be published or guide the class in combining the outstanding portions of several pupils' work into a final article.
B. Present an assembly program of pupil selections of phases of the unit which seem significant to them.
C. Assign a theme to be written on such a topic as "World Progress and the United Nations" or "Alternatives to World Organization."
D. Construct and administer a test which would seem to measure the achievement of those objectives which were emphasized in the unit.

Self-evaluation Guide for Unit Teaching. After presenting a unit of work the teacher should be concerned about evaluating his own role. One of the most effective means of doing this is to arrange a series of questions to which all answers should be "yes." The following list is proposed:

1. Did the class accomplish the objectives set forth at the beginning of the unit?

2. Did the group as a whole and individually improve in appreciation of things more worth while?

3. Was there an enthusiastic response to proposals for sheer work activity?

4. Could one detect commendable growth in desirable traits of character?

5. Did pupils learn increased respect for others, especially in committee procedures?

6. Were pupils willing to accept new ideas, showing a tendency to become free from prejudice?

7. Did the "we" and "our" spirit increase throughout the study of the unit?

8. Were the pupils interested in improving the quality of their written work and oral expression?

9. Was there a tendency to read widely in order to gain supplementary information?

10. Did the ability to organize material and reach sound conclusions improve?

11. Were pupils increasingly aware of cause-effect relationships?

12. Was there noticeable improvement related to such basic skills as using atlases, dictionaries, and indexes, reading maps, etc.?

13. Were audio and visual aids used in the most advantageous proportions?

14. Was the content of the unit properly related to the past experiences of the pupils?

15. Was unit planning on the basis of teacher-pupil cooperation?

16. Were individual differences taken well into account?

17. Was supervised study successfully employed?

18. Did pupil guidance occupy an important place throughout the developmental period?

19. Was English usage given proper attention, including efforts to gain grammatical perfection?

20. Did the work on the unit correlate with other activities and studies in the school program?

21. Did the teacher strive to use new and experimental means of presenting the particular unit?

Summary. In the foregoing chapter it has been pointed out that the unit method of teaching followed the more general use of problems and projects. The method was presented as being in direct contrast to the older daily-presentation method of teaching, one that attempted to attain an objective fully in a single period. The unit method of teaching in social studies was here defined as an outline of carefully selected subject matter which has been isolated because of its relationship to pupil needs and interests. Henry C. Morrison is given credit for popularizing this method of teaching.

A list of ten advantages of the unit method of teaching was given. Pupil participation, development of desirable social traits, economy of learning efforts, effective use of supplementary materials, use of summaries, and effective evaluations were stressed. Among the five disadvantages presented were insufficient training on the part of present-day social studies teachers, confusion on the part of pupils due to lack of uniformity of teaching methods, failure to learn certain basic facts, and the unsympathetic attitude of parents and others.

Stages in social studies teaching were discussed, including introductory activities, work periods, recitation and discussion, testing, and evaluation. Indications as to what a class should be doing at these times were included.

Two detailed examples of how a unit could be presented were given, one entitled "Revolutions That Have Increased Liberty" and the other, "United Nations."

Questions Based on the Text

1. How does the unit method of teaching differ from traditional daily-lesson procedures?
2. How is the unit idea related to problems and projects?
3. Who was Henry C. Morrison?
4. What are the advantages most commonly claimed for the unit method of teaching? the disadvantages?
5. About how many units of work can a social studies teacher reasonably expect to cover in a year's time?
6. Name the various stages through which the teaching of a unit in social studies would pass. Tell specifically what a class should be doing during each of these.
7. How were the principles of unit teaching illustrated in the examples given?

Suggested Activities

1. Prepare fully the material that you think a social studies teacher should have at hand for the teaching of a unit that you select.

2. Read and summarize one or more current references dealing with the unit method of teaching.

3. Secure for your files outlines of social studies units that you find for distribution or sale at small cost from one or more schools.

4. Arrange to share work with some individual by exchanging units that each of you has prepared.

5. Visit a class in high-school social studies over a period of several consecutive days. Report on the manner in which there is conformity or lack of conformity to the ideas presented in this chapter.

6. Have a conference with someone who uses the unit method of teaching in some field other than social studies. Determine the ways in which underlying principles operate in both areas.

Selected References

BALDWIN, J. W., "Teaching the Social Studies in Units by the Laboratory Method," *The Social Studies,* XL (February, 1949), pp. 58–63.

BARNES, C. C., "The 'Unit-mastery Method,'" *The Clearing House,* XXI (October, 1946), pp. 79–81.

BOLDT, ALBERT W., and CLARA M. DECK, "Planning a Latin American Unit," *Social Studies,* XXXIV (May, 1943), pp. 201–208.

BOODISH, H. M., "A Unit Course Outline in American History," *The Social Studies,* XLI (March, 1950), pp. 102–108.

DEWEY, H. E., "A Pessimistic Unit," *Social Studies,* XXXI (January, 1940), pp. 6–8.

DOUGLASS, HARL R., and HUBERT H. MILLS, *Teaching in High School,* New York: The Ronald Press Company, 1948, Chap. XI.

DYER, J. POPE, "A Unit in Interracial Understanding," *Social Studies,* XXX (February, 1939), pp. 79–80.

FARNUM, MARTHA F., "How to Prepare a Social Studies Unit," *California Journal of Secondary Education,* XXIV (January, 1949), pp. 29–33.

HARDEN, FLORENCE E., and LEE E. TRIEBELS, "A Unit on Pan-American History," *Social Studies,* XXXII (December, 1941), pp. 347–348.

GOETSCH, HELEN B., "Negro Employment: A Curriculum Unit," *Social Education,* VIII (December, 1944), pp. 357–360.

GOOD, CARTER V., ed., *Dictionary of Education,* New York: McGraw-Hill Book Company, Inc., 1945.

HARTWIG, CAROLINE E. E., "Extensive Survey Versus Large Units in High School Economics," *Social Education,* V (October, 1941), pp. 442–446.

HARVEY, C. C., "A Social Unit on the Air Age," *Social Studies,* XLI (February, 1950), pp. 70*ff.*

HAWKINSON, ELLA A., and BETTY ST. PIERRE, "A Unit on Post-war Reconstruction," *Social Education,* VIII (February, 1944), pp. 67–70.

HURD, ARCHER WILLIS, "What Do You Mean by the Unit-Problem-Project Plan of Instruction?" *School and Society,* LXII (Nov. 10, 1945), pp. 300–301.

JACOBSON, PAUL B., "Resource Units for Teachers," *Social Education,* V (November, 1941), pp. 512–515.

MALONEY, M., "A Social Studies Unit in Intercultural Education," *Pittsburgh Schools,* XX (November, 1945), pp. 54–60.

MORRISON, HENRY C., *The Practice of Teaching in the Secondary School,* Chicago: The University of Chicago Press, 1931.

PINGREY, JENNIE L., "Introducing a Unit on Labor," *Social Education,* IX (November, 1945), pp. 305–306.

REHAGE, KENNETH J., "A Unit on the Population of the United States," *Social Education,* VI (November, 1942), pp. 313–314.

RISK, THOMAS M., *Principles and Practices of Teaching in Secondary Schools,* New York: American Book Company, 1947, Chap. XIV.

RIVLIN, HARRY N., *Teaching Adolescents in Secondary Schools,* New York: Appleton-Century-Crofts, Inc., 1948, Chap. V.

SCHUELKE, HERBERT T., "Soviet Russia: A Curriculum Unit," *Social Education,* IX (March, 1945), pp. 113–114.

TABA, HILDA, and WILLIAM VAN TIL, "School Activities, Democratic Human Relations," Washington, D.C.: The National Council for the Social Studies, *Sixteenth Yearbook,* 1945, pp. 161–191.

———, "Study Units, Democratic Human Relations," Washington, D.C.: The National Council for the Social Studies, *Sixteenth Yearbook,* 1945, pp. 127–160.

THORNTON, E. W., "That Unit on Democracy," *Social Studies,* XXXIII (December, 1942), pp. 361–363.

WESTFALL, LETHA M., "Victory Units," *Social Education,* VII (October, 1943), pp. 265–266.

Chapter 12

TECHNIQUES IRRESPECTIVE OF METHODS

Preview. It is impossible within the compass of a few chapters to cover fully everything that might be said about methods of teaching. The previous chapter dealt with a method very generally used, namely, the unit procedure. It is now desired to present some suggestions that can be used within the framework of the unit or in entirely different approaches. The importance of the assignment is stressed. Advance presentation of large blocks of subject matter is advocated. Three detailed examples are given. Means of making shorter daily assignments are described either as part of the unit or as complete procedures within themselves. Since drills are effective in bringing about retention of information learned as a result of any plan of teaching, pertinent information dealing with their conduct is given. Much discussion dealing with the value of notebooks has taken place among social studies teachers. These points are summarized. The close relationship of workbooks to notebooks is recognized, and a summary of basic ideas is included. The special problems related to methods in grades 13 and 14 are presented.

The Social Studies Assignment. The form that assignments take from day to day will depend upon the general method of procedure used by the teacher. The suggestions presented in this chapter are given rather largely for those who do not closely follow the unit method of teaching. In any case the teacher should have in mind and should share with the pupils the general unit objective that is being sought. Examples are found in the following:

1. To determine the motives for exploration and colonization
2. To learn about the causes, main events, and results of the War for Independence
3. To study the causes, steps in, and results of the rise of big business in the late nineteenth century
4. To examine the reasons for, main events in, and results of the overthrow of autocracy

5. To investigate the historical background and present status of labor unions in our country
6. To study the various forms of municipal government that are common in the United States today
7. To trace the historical development of the family

It will be observed that the above statements are quite inclusive. The amount of time that could profitably be spent on any one of them will be limited by such factors as the number of other topics included in the course under consideration, library and other facilities available for use in connection with such study, and teacher and pupil interest in the topic.

The specific objective will change as frequently as the general objective shifts. There may on some occasions be a new one daily. Examples of specific objectives that might be used for one assignment each are given to correspond to the seven general objectives listed above:

1. To learn in detail about Spain's part in exploration and colonization
2. To study the role of George Washington in the War for Independence
3. To study the efforts of Congress to restrain evil practices resulting from the formation of trusts
4. To see the manner in which Louis XIV of France became the symbol of autocracy
5. To learn the names of leading labor unions in United States, who their leaders are, and what their recent activities have been
6. To determine by investigation what type of government our own city has
7. To attempt to find out the causes of the present high divorce rate

No effort is being made to give an all-inclusive list of the assignments pupils in social studies classes have pursued with profit. Neither does a detailed description of each follow, inasmuch as this was the objective for other chapters. The place of projects, problem solving, socialized recitations, field trips, and use of audio and visual aids must be considered from time to time under the heading of assignments. The following are offered as typical of activities:

1. Reading specified pages in a basic textbook
2. Reading indicated pages from reference books
3. Outlining content material in a basic textbook, reference books, or both
4. Writing summaries of topics

5. Preparation of special reports from reference reading
6. Completing specific assignment activities given by the teacher orally, written on the blackboard, or duplicated on sheets passed out to the pupils
7. Compiling of questions on specified materials to hand in or ask fellow pupils
8. Securing information outside the classroom through such means as using the newspaper, listening to the radio, interviewing an informed person, or making a field trip.
9. Initiating and completing a project such as making a poster, map, or carving
10. Arriving at the solution to a stated problem
11. Placing of assigned or optional material in notebooks
12. Pursuing the directions given in a workbook
13. Reviewing the work of several days in preparation for a major test

The making of a good assignment is just as serious an obligation as conducting a good discussion. To meet it, the teacher must give sufficient time and thought to the task. It must have qualities that appeal to the pupil, otherwise he will study reluctantly or not at all. It must be very clearly stated, so simply that the pupils of lowest ability can readily comprehend what is to be done. New words and phrases as well as important dates should be pointed out and given appropriate recognition. Special methods that might prove helpful in the study of the particular lesson should be explained. The teacher may feel that every detail has been well executed and that excellent work will follow. Usually this will be the case. However, if the study reveals that the majority did not comprehend well just what was supposed to be done, the work should be halted and more explanatory suggestions offered. If difficulties are limited to a few individuals, helps can be extended quietly without disturbing the entire group. On the whole, there is far more likelihood of devoting too little rather than too much time to the making of an assignment in a social studies class. Many successful teachers construct and use a check sheet to measure objectively the quality of the assignment given and the success with which it operates. Such procedure should result in teacher improvement on this point.

Introducing New Material. The social studies teacher needs to exercise great caution and skill in making assignments involving the introduction of new content. One has no right to assume that all the pupils are deeply interested in the material; in fact, it may be more in keeping with realities to recognize that some may not have a natural liking for the contemplated proceedings at all. Neither is it likely that any of them will appreciate fully the relationship of the new material to preceding or subsequent content. The foregoing is not designed to contradict the usual procedure of having a class situation in which the pupils share in setting up objectives, selecting units, advocating procedures, etc. Rather, these things are taken for granted and the assumption is that, even so, the teacher still has a positive role in introducing the new material.

The activity in which the teacher engages at this juncture is that of an effective guide in initiatory phases. There is need for a brief summarization of work which pupils have not previously studied but which they are expected to learn during the work and study periods which follow. This is the stage when the social studies teacher probably does more lecturing than in any other situation. The maximum length of time for the teacher's use here in grade 7 should not exceed ten minutes and in grade 12, twenty-five minutes. This is stated on the basis of the ability of various age groups to give sustained attention.

The teacher should consider carefully in advance the purposes to be accomplished. It has been intimated above that the arousing of pupil interest is of paramount importance. In brief, the role of the teacher is that of a successful salesman; it is hoped that the pupils will become more confirmed in their decision as to immediate content and objectives. In some cases the teacher will be greatly in error in his advance judgment as to how much pupils already know about new material. Particular individuals may have failed to attain an average background in previous grades; others may have, through unusual experiences, gained full and ready knowledge before the work is even initiated. The skilled teacher needs to evaluate the class status constantly. It is necessary at this stage to present materials which, if well attended to by the pupils, will be remembered. Such information can function as a foundation for the entire group of lessons to follow; also, many of the better-than-average pupils will remember for purposes of final testing isolated facts that they hear for the first time in the overview. The presentation of the above-mentioned summary has a valuable purpose in providing a variation of routine. Most of the usual classroom procedure represents pupil activity, and rightly it should. However, pupils thoroughly enjoy this small amount of variation. From the point of view of the teacher it might be mentioned that one who has prepared to initiate new work and accomplish reasonable objectives has thus laid a good foundation for several subsequent days of effective work. At least such a teacher will never be accused of being only a day or two ahead of the class. From the pupils' point of view, one observes that they will find satisfaction in knowing in some detail what activities are being planned. Successive class meetings will hold forth something to which they can look forward. Pupil suggestions at the outset in respect to work to be done can be made use of as well as those that might come up later.

It becomes important to analyze teacher qualities that are essential in a good presentation of new teaching content. We do not have in mind the traits that should be possessed by social studies teachers in general; rather, the particular traits for this specific job are those to which reference is made. Public-speaking ability is obviously an asset. This means that a knowledge of and the ability to put into practice the fundamentals of speech will be very helpful. Persuasive oratory is not demanded nor to be desired. The ability to select the details of outstanding importance is a requirement. The time allotment is necessarily brief. The giving of a mass of information would serve only to confuse and bewilder the pupils. The ability to make appropriate use of maps, blackboards, pictures, textbook topics and illustrations, and other visual aids, not only as learning media but as means of maintaining attention and creating interest, is important. The material should be at hand and ready for instant reference in the course of presentation. Willingness to let pupils make contributions is important. The teacher who shows such willingness might be compared to the speaker who announces to his audience that an interruption for questions will not be in the least disturbing.

The above comments may be made more meaningful by including some advance summaries that have actually been used. The following was used in American history, grade 8, preceding the study of the War Between the States:

We are now starting a study of the period in American history when the North and the South drifted so far apart that they finally engaged in war. This difference started as far back as colonial times when the North stressed manufacturing as an important occupation and the South turned toward agriculture with emphasis on cotton. You will recall from our study of the Constitutional Convention that there were some compromises concerning slavery. Will someone review one or more of these? [Various members will make contributions bringing out that the slave trade was to be abolished after 1808, that there was to be a limit on the amount of import tax on slaves, and that slaves would be counted according to the ratio of five to three white people in determining the number of representatives that a state should have in the House of Representatives.]

The slavery question stayed before the people and Congress constantly. You may recall that there was a clause in the ordinance of 1787 that forbade slavery in the Northwest Territory. Soon after that a certain invention made cotton growing more profitable than ever. Who of you know what it was? [Most of the group will be able to answer that it was the cotton gin perfected by Eli Whitney.]

One of the next important steps took place in Congress, one that we have not studied. In 1820, Missouri applied for admission into the Union as a slave state. Should this have been allowed there would have been more slave states than free states. Luckily Maine wanted to enter the Union about the same time. Due in part to the work of Henry Clay, the famous Missouri Compromise was passed. Missouri was admitted the following year as a slave state and Maine as a free state. In addition it was stated that no territory in the Louisiana Purchase north of 36 degrees and 30 minutes except Missouri should ever be formed into a slave state. [This line and the Ohio river will be pointed out on the map.]

A few years later our country acquired a great deal of territory from Mexico. Congress spent much time discussing the question of slavery in this region. [The map will be used to indicate this part of the United States.] Not much actual legislation was passed. Merely the introducing and the discussion of bills kept the question before the people.

One idea that was widely discussed was called popular, or squatter, sovereignty. Stephen A. Douglas was the leader of this idea. It meant that the people who settled in a Territory should decide whether it was to be slave or free. This was tried out in Kansas. What do you suppose the result was? It was civil strife. We shall study about this struggle in Kansas next week.

The next year that saw the division of interests between the North and the South become intense was 1850. The discovery of gold in California two years before caused such an increase in population that she applied for admission into the Union; she naturally wished to come in as a free state. This revived the question of slavery. Leading statesmen became very prominent because of their utterances and attitudes. Henry Clay of Kentucky was known as the great peacemaker. John C. Calhoun of South Carolina upheld the doctrine of states' rights and was the great champion of slavery. He said, "Liberty dearer than union." Daniel Webster of Massachusetts wanted one strong government for the nation. He said, "Liberty and union, one and inseparable, now and forever." Mr. Clay again proved himself to be able to offer a compromise; it goes by the name of the Compromise of 1850. There are five parts or provisions to it. Let us turn to page 96 in our textbook. Will the first five of you to my left, starting with Dorothy, read aloud one of these provisions? Thank you. Some people thought the question of slavery would never cause more serious discussion. Others who were keener in their reasoning saw that it would come up again soon.

While Congress was busy passing laws many people were busy reading *Uncle Tom's Cabin,* written by Harriet Beecher Stowe. Many subscribed to a paper called the *Liberator* that was edited by William Lloyd Garrison. The poet, John G. Whittier, and the orator, Wendell Phillips, attracted the attention of people throughout the North. Of course they were violently opposed to slavery. How many of you have read *Uncle Tom's Cabin?*

In 1857 a very famous case came before the United States Supreme Court. It took its name from its principal character, namely, Dred Scott. Chief Justice Taney ruled that since Scott was a slave he was not a citizen of the United States and therefore could not sue in the courts of the nation. This was clearly a victory for the South. We shall read more about this as a group and shall later assign this topic as a special report.

There were four leading political parties in 1860. All of them had very definite notions concerning slavery. Today, we shall only mention that Abraham Lincoln of Illinois won the election and was on the Republican ticket. Later we shall find the names of the other three candidates and the names of their parties. Mr. Lincoln's election was the signal for secession. The first state to secede was South Carolina, to be followed soon by Mississippi, Florida, Alabama, Louisiana, Georgia, and Texas. Later they were joined by Virginia, Tennessee, North Carolina, and Arkansas. Delaware, Maryland, Kentucky, and Missouri, as you notice on the map, are border states. They remained loyal to the Union. West Virginia separated from Virginia and remained loyal.

We shall read our basic textbook and some reference books, have discussion and special reports, and shall hope to learn a great deal about why the North and the South became so divided in opinion that a War Between the States followed.

World history as usually taught lends itself very nicely to introducing materials by means of advance summaries. The following was recently presented preceding the study of the French Revolution.

Recently we have studied various autocratic governments. We have noticed that many rules had little regard for the needs of those over whom they ruled. We are about ready to study what is called the *French Revolution,* in which the people overthrew their king and queen and set up a different government and system of life in their country.

This movement started in 1789. Who can tell us whether that is after or before our American Revolution? [Answer follows.] Correct. In fact, one man who helped George Washington in America was a leading character in the French Revolution. Who was he? [Answer follows.]

For many years before 1789 many men had been writing about the evils of the French government. Probably no one was more influential than Voltaire. Will you all repeat his name in unison? VOLTAIRE. He is one character whom we shall soon assign for a special report. Other philosophers were Rousseau, Montesquieu, and Diderot. You will notice that I have written their names with the correct pronunciations on the board. These men agreed that government should be based upon the consent of the governed. Of course the people who were victims of the old system read their works and were greatly influenced by them.

You would probably be interested in the things that caused the common people to complain. First, you should understand that France was divided into three social classes, namely, the clergy, nobility, and common people. The first two groups were privileged; that is, they enjoyed the king's protection, paid no taxes, did not have to work on the highways, owned most of the nation's wealth, and did little work. Naturally the Third Estate became more and more jealous as their burdens increased through the expenses of foreign wars, extravagance in the royal household, etc.

Furthermore, the king and queen did little or nothing to prevent growing discontent. The king's name was Louis XVI, a member of the Bourbon family. The queen came to France from the Austrian court while still in her teens to marry the young prince. Her name was Marie Antoinette. Will the first four of you in the front row take turns pronouncing her name?

Let us turn to the third page of the next chapter and look at a picture of the rulers. Louis XVI was a sort of stupid person, at least he was quite weak. He really preferred to work in his little shop as an amateur locksmith rather than to busy himself with affairs of state. The queen enjoyed extravagant parties and entertainments regardless of the costs involved. We are told that one time she was asked by the common people to supply them with bread. Her reply was, "Let them eat cake."

In addition to the points that we have mentioned, the royal treasury became bankrupt. The king tried in many ways to fill it. None worked. At last he performed an act that was the beginning of the French Revolution, namely, the calling together of the Estates General.

This lawmaking body showed much more interest in attempting to get reforms for the nation than in trying to help the king out of his personal difficulties. They talked about how the three groups should vote, how the powers of the government should be distributed, and about grievances that existed throughout the country. Soon they had become in name and fact the National Assembly. Events moved rapidly. Within a short time, July 14, 1789, to be exact, the mob moved to the French national prison (called the Bastille) and proceeded to tear it down; the prisoners were of course allowed to go free. One of the principal sessions of the National Assembly took place on the night of Aug. 4–5 of the same year. The old feudal privileges were abolished. Finally a new constitution was written that provided for a Legislative Assembly. It went into effect in 1791.

During the year that the Assembly was in charge of France many changes took place in the relationship of church and state, in the names and principles of political parties, and in the actual leaders of affairs. We should mention that Marat, Robespierre, and Denton are the characters to whom we shall give more attention in our study.

The next lawmaking body was called the Convention. It was during its period that the king and queen went to the guillotine. Affairs moved rapidly and without logic. Thousands were executed as actual or suspected threats to the progress of the Revolution. One period is called the Reign of Terror because there was so much confusion and so many executions took place. The last governing body in France during the revolutionary period was called the Directory. It was a sort of bridge for the gap between the end of the Revolution and the appearance of Napoleon Bonaparte.

It can never be known whether France could have had the many changes needed by any means other than revolution. Perhaps we should summarize briefly how the country was really different in 1799 from what it was in 1789 when the king called together the Estates General. Let us write these ideas on the blackboard. [The teacher sends one of the better students to the board to do this writing.]

The following points are among the most important. You will find others day by day as we study this unit.

1. Unlimited monarchy was abolished.
2. The privileges of the clergy and nobles were taken away.
3. The will of the people was given expression through their elected representatives.
4. The teachings of the philosophers were reflected in the new constitutions.
5. Titles of nobility were abolished.
6. Land was more evenly distributed.
7. The most unfair taxes and fees were abolished.
8. A new flag was used to symbolize the changes of the times; its colors were red, white, and blue.

9. Those most unfriendly to the changes either left France or were executed.

10. A system of public education was discussed and got partially started, to be more fully developed later.

Not only does this technique function well in history classes; it has equal value in any other social study. The following was used in a twelfth-grade class in a course in problems of democracy:

During the past few days you have all been reading about strikes. Probably you have heard several news commentators discuss the labor situation over the radio. No doubt most of you have talked about this current news item with other members of your family. To many of us, the largest strike now in progress, namely, that of the employees of General Motors, means that we may not get a new automobile as soon as we should like it or that its price may be higher or lower, depending upon the outcome of the strike.

This news item gives us the start for several days of study and discussion. First, we shall be concerned with the brief history of the labor movement on a world basis. Next, we shall want to find out about the history of labor in our own country. Finally, it will be quite important to get as clear a picture as possible of the conditions under which labor and capital work together today in order to produce goods.

In the earliest period man made his living by a sort of *hunting-and-fishing* method. He seized what he needed and wanted if someone stronger than he did not claim it. He did not spend a very long time in any one dwelling place. Cooperation with others and organization for various purposes scarcely existed. Following this came the *pastoral stage.* Man learned to domesticate plants and animals. His dwelling place became slightly more fixed but not permanent. More time for leisure came into existence; likewise, there was more need and capacity for cooperation and group life. The natural period to follow was the *agricultural era.* Groups bound by ties of blood and common interests settled in the same communities. A sound basis for economic, social, and political development was thus arrived at.

We are aware that trade and commerce have existed from the earliest times. With the agricultural development that we have mentioned taking place, it became very desirable for particular regions to exchange surpluses for necessities not readily available.

Somewhere along the way manufacturing started, surely right along with agriculture, trade, and commerce. How many of you know the meaning of the word *manufacture?* [A volunteer is called upon and correctly tells the class that it means to make by hand.] This is exactly what it meant for several centuries. Furthermore, it was commonly carried on in the home, being done in addition to farming. The production of goods that we usually associate with the cities and towns was carried out by the strict regulation of what we knew as the guild system. Maybe someone can tell us the names of each of the three stages that a young man passed through to become completely trained in his trade or industry. [The answer accepted was, "apprentice, journeyman, and master worker."]

The breaking up of these types of manufacturing was brought about by a movement in England starting about 1750. Will someone tell us the name of this change? [A volunteer is called upon who correctly answers by saying, "Industrial Revolution."] We shall surely want to study this topic by reading about it and having a special report on some of the changes that it brought into the lives of the people.

Capital, that is goods and money used to produce more goods, became more important than had ever been known in the world's history. One of the most important changes that came was based upon the fact that few people possessed or had control of enough money to carry on industry under the new system. Therefore those who did have such control could easily dictate the entire set of conditions under which labor worked and lived.

Those who lived by the work of their hands began to protest when conditions became too intolerable. One might say that all grievances of labor from 1750 to the present moment may be classified under one of three demands or a combination of these demands. Will someone who hasn't recited today tell us the three things labor is usually asking for when on strike? [A pupil gave the correct answer of higher wages, shorter hours, and better working conditions.]

It is quite important to know that the principle whereby workers now bargain with the employer through representatives rather than each going in personally for a conference is called *collective bargaining.* [These last two words are immediately written on the blackboard.]

Of course our most personal interest in the way that labor and capital are related to each other has to do with our own country. Labor unions make up an interesting chapter in the history of the United States. How many of you can name the two leading organizations of labor that we have today? [Most pupils are able to name the American Federation of Labor and the Congress of Industrial Organization.] I doubt that all of you know the exact differences between these two groups. We shall study this point very carefully, shall find examples of labor unions in each group, and shall learn the names of leading men in our country today who are leaders of the various groups. Possibly our best way to approach this part of our new unit is to study briefly the history of earlier labor organizations in the United States too, including the Knights of Labor and the Industrial Workers of the World. While we may think that the strike in progress at the present moment is exceedingly important, and it is, we must learn the names, causes, and results of a few other very famous strikes in our nation's history. With the background that we shall get from the study and discussion of the topics already mentioned, we shall be in a position for the still more interesting and important work dealing with precisely what causes the differences in points of view of capital and labor, what methods both use in an attempt to gain their desires, how these differences should be settled, and what the effect of the problem is upon all of us.

After having presented this type of material the teacher should attempt to evaluate results. The following questions are among those that should be answered in the affirmative:

1. Did I feel at ease and thoroughly enjoy this part of the teaching process?
2. Did the pupils appear to be interested throughout the presentation?
3. Were there a reasonable number of pupil questions?
4. Did the pupils suggest any class activities dealing with the new work?
5. Did the pupils demonstrate an eagerness to immediately start reading and other recommended procedures?
6. Did the pupils actually learn several points of new information?

Drill and Review Procedures. Drills and reviews have an appropriate place in both unit procedures and day-to-day teaching techniques. Most people use the word *drill* to describe the rapid covering of a unit or portion of a unit of work recently studied, by means of a relatively large number of short-answer questions. The word *review* ordinarily has reference to a systematic and rather brief restudy of the work covered over a longer period of time, such as that of a grading period of six, nine, or eighteen weeks.

There are several values that can be claimed for the drill lesson. First, it is an aid to complete mastery of subject matter. For many pupils the regular classroom routine ensures fair or better-than-average achievement. Add to this a well-planned and carefully executed drill lesson and the chances are greatly increased that perfect or near-perfect results will be attained.

Second, drill work is very valuable to pupils who do not discriminate readily between the very significant and the relatively unimportant details found in most social studies textbooks. After all, one can scarcely expect younger readers to make careful discrimination and arrive at sound judgments on points dealing with relative importance of facts. The drill lesson that is well-conceived will help materially on this point.

Third, the drill lesson will help the teacher to measure the results of teaching. While this is generally offered as an objective of testing, it is functional here to a slightly less degree. If the pupils respond quite well, it is apparent that learning has taken place. If they do not, it may mean that some of the work should be retaught before testing is applied.

Fourth, as intimated in the preceding paragraph, the drill is directly related to testing that usually follows. It is somewhat like the warming-up procedures carried out by an athletic team just before a game. It is the intellectual-conditioning procedure that will help pupils to make their best scores. Many pupils habitually ask for pretest drills and take notes on the questions asked.

Fifth, drill work affords enjoyment to most members of a social studies class if used judiciously. There is opportunity to demonstrate the possession of knowledge, to compete with others in an intellectual setting, and to learn that which may not have been previously mastered.

In another treatment of this topic one of the authors [1] listed the following values that can come from effective drill work: (1) it aids in achieving complete mastery of subject matter; (2) it helps to isolate the most important points from those of lesser importance; (3) it helps in ascertaining the effectiveness of classroom work; (4) it helps pupils in their preparation for unit tests; and (5) the enjoyment of classroom work is materially increased.

While many teachers very profitably engage in drill work for a few minutes almost daily for the purpose of connecting the previous day's lesson with the new one under consideration, this is not the type of work under discussion at the moment. Rather we are describing a situation where a substantial amount of work has been studied and the drill to be conducted is long enough to involve the major portion of a class period. Best results are obtained when the teacher gives a generous amount of thoughtful preparation to the task. Much of this goes into carefully selecting and phrasing the questions. They must be brief and concise; most of them should require one-word answers and should not be such as to permit optional responses. Ques-

[1] Clarence D. Samford, "Drill Work in Social Studies," *Social Education*, VIII (December, 1944), p. 353.

tions of the "true-false" and "yes-no" types are generally unsuitable. Once they are missed they cannot be passed on to other pupils for a trial.

While many periods have been profitably spent in asking drill questions in a straightforward manner, it should not be overlooked that the contest idea is very appealing to most social studies pupils. People universally enjoy competitive exercises. No doubt this tendency has been accentuated by radio listening habits. Probably younger pupils enjoy contests more than twelfth-grade pupils; however, this does not always obtain. Here again the teacher must plan diligently to offset potential waste of time, undue appearances of lax discipline, disagreements on scorekeeping, etc. After the planning has been done and the preliminaries arranged the teacher will assume a role comparable to that of an official at an athletic contest. The likelihood and the desire are that pupils will enjoy themselves immensely. However, it must not be lost sight of that the primary purpose is pupil mastery of subject matter.

There are innumerable procedures for conducting drill lessons in social studies classes. One fairly constant feature is the division of a class into two rather equal groups in respect to both numbers and abilities. This requirement can be met by having two pupils of about equal rank choose classmates alternately until all have been selected. Often a class can be divided into groups of relatively equal ability by using an alphabetical arrangement. Less frequently the seating plan regularly used by the class will suffice. In some instances it is possible to place the girls on one side and the boys on the other. This is not to be recommended; frequently the contest phase thus becomes overspirited. Should any arrangement result in one side having one more member than the other it is easy to proceed by not giving the last question to the side that received the first question.

Once the division of sides has been made the teacher is ready to ask the questions and to see that an accurate score is kept. It is very important that pupils understand the method employed and that results be visible throughout on the blackboard. A simple procedure is to call on pupils in turn and to allow one point for each correct response. If a pupil fails, the question is simply passed on to the other side and a point scored, assuming that the response is correct. A slightly more complicated procedure is to allow two points for each correct response. If the pupil called on fails to answer correctly, someone on his side may volunteer for one point. If it is still unanswered correctly it may pass to the other side for three points. Some teachers find it desirable and profitable to ask the pupils to prepare questions to be used in the drill. The age and ability of the group will largely predetermine the quality of questions produced. In any event, the teacher can edit the results and make the maximum possible use of them.

If the contest feature is not being stressed, it often works out well to have the pupils ask each other questions that they have prepared. The teacher must feel quite free to rule on the aptness of questions and rephrase them quickly or, if necessary, call for a second question. Should the pupils omit entirely some important questions, these can be advanced by the teacher as supplementary materials.

For variety, it is desirable to conduct some drills that will stress individual rather than group performance. The spelling-bee plan has much to offer in this connection. The pupil seated in a front position can be regarded as being at the head of the class at the outset and a pupil in an opposite position as at the foot. When a question is missed by one or more pupils, the one who answers it correctly moves up as many seats as are occupied by those who failed to respond and they move down one seat each toward the foot of the class. The object of each pupil is to gain the seat at the head of the class. This sort of drill does not offer the competitive aspects that usually follow when two sides are chosen. It is a little easier to conduct in that blackboard scores do not have to be kept and that general quietness is more nearly assured because each member is for himself and not for an entire side. Some teachers use plans whereby members who miss a question drop out by finding seats elsewhere, standing up, or sitting down as the case may be. There is sometimes the possibility of gaining a place in the group again by being able to answer a question missed later, etc.

Much help in devising drill procedures comes from being ordinarily resourceful; further hints can be gained from listening to radio contests and observing athletic sports. Regardless of the methods used the objectives of the drill should be kept in mind throughout.

There are many ways in which the objectives of review may be attained in social studies. The following of some natural division such as chronology is a common procedure. Events, significant facts, and interesting information related to a specified epoch are easily summarized. Information contained in a certain chapter or under the heading of a particular topic is easily recalled for review. Not only is content thus segregated; we also often observe a division of labor in which individual pupils or committees are given responsibility for an equitable share of work. The organizing function is very important during review. Relationships of cause and effect are advantageously introduced. The important must finally be segregated from the unimportant. While teacher guidance is regularly important it is unusually valuable here. The ability to outline well becomes a necessity for pupil progress, as a vehicle to both clear thinking and clear expression.

Notebooks. It seems safe to assume that most teachers of secondary-school social studies devote some time to pupil preparation of notebooks. The word *notebook* has a variety of connotations from the viewpoint of both teacher and pupil. On the part of the former the idea depends entirely upon the purpose that he has in mind. If the notebook is to serve as merely a means of writing down daily assignments it is relatively inconsequential in relation to the total work of the course. Usually the pupil uses such books to record assignments not only in social studies but in all his courses. At the other extreme, a particular teacher may choose to conduct a course largely on a laboratory basis and let individual notebooks be the principal evidence of achievement. Most teachers use notebooks in a fashion that would fall somewhere between these two extremes. To many pupils the mere mention of the word *notebook* seems unpleasant. Reasonable tact needs to be exercised, therefore, in presenting the notebook idea to pupils early in the school year. The teacher need not feel a sense of guilt or apology; many classes have thoroughly enjoyed notebook work and have profited immensely from doing this type of work.

Notebooks will probably serve the best purpose if the teacher regards them as an aid to learning. They are thus not intended to replace classroom discussion, visual aids, drill work, and other regular activities. It is a generally accepted principle that a variety of approaches represents sound pedagogical procedure.

One of the sections found in many excellent social studies notebooks deals with identifications. These are usually one-sentence statements that define or describe the items selected. Names of important characters, places, dates, technical vocabulary, etc., can be well learned by the pupil in his efforts to place them in a notebook in this manner. Pupils should be taught to indent each description as a new paragraph would be started, underline the identification, use expressions that are characteristic of their own speech and expression, and understand a statement well before recording it. The teacher should be judicious in the number of identifications required from a unit of work. It is a well-known fact that pupils will forget much of what they study. For this reason a smaller number of the most important items should be selected and emphasized. In order to assist a class to get well started on this work for the year, the first set of words should be worked out as a group with the help of the teacher. The standards of word usage and physical appearance of the statements on the paper established at this time are likely to prevail throughout the year.

The recording of supplementary reading references is an important part of the notebook activity. As has been pointed out in another chapter, it is recognized that supplementary reading is supremely important in the process of becoming truly a social studies student. In order that the emphasis may be upon the extensive nature of the reading it is usually found advisable to reduce the notebook phase to a minimum. This record might well include author, title of article, book or periodical in which it was found, and a list of the topics read about without detailed statements or summaries of each. Even this amount of recording will usually enable the pupil to recite comprehensively on what he has read or to recall the same for purposes of testing.

Many pupils enjoy reading biographies even more than a well-written textbook in a given area. Often those slightly below average in achievement will welcome the opportunity to prepare a series of brief sketches of the lives of important characters. Including some of these as optional material helps such pupils materially at the time grades are calculated. If the pupil can attain the goals of reading from more than one source, synthesizing material skillfully, and being relatively brief in the process, a worthy accomplishment has been gained.

Other activities that have been used by teachers in connection with notebook work include the following:

1. Time charts. Pupils take the most important events mentioned in a unit of work and list the dates and events in chronological order.

2. Newspaper clippings. During a period of time represented by that between the consecutive dates of the issuing of grade cards pupils collect newspaper clippings dealing with the topics studied. These may either be attached to regular notebook pages or placed in envelopes according to classification and enclosed in the back of the notebook.

3. Classroom discussion. Many pupils have a laudable practice of taking notes on remarks made or placed on the blackboard by the teacher or their classmates. As an optional exercise for the superior pupils this can be very helpful.

4. Outlines or summaries of lessons. Some pupils have a habit of learning content material throughout by the use of the outline or summary technique. This may be helpful as notebook work in limited usage for the class as a whole and for any members who elect it as optional work.

5. Map work. Maps prepared by the pupils help attain the objective of learning specific and relative locations. Since they are ordinarily part of the regular procedure it is quite proper to have a place for them in the notebook. Pupils who have a tendency to produce artistic work welcome this activity.

6. Reports on social studies trips that are designed to study community resources.

7. Original drawings and original cartoons.

8. Reproductions of drawings and cartoons with statement of sources.

9. Comments on selections from literature read as part of correlation ventures between social studies and English.

10. Graphs and charts that have been prepared to portray social studies information. These can take the form presented in mathematics classes being pursued by the same pupils.

It is not claimed at all that the above list exhausts the notebook possibilities. Resourceful teachers and alert pupils will think of many other worth-while things to do. Local circumstances will make many things possible in given instances that are not feasible in others.

For many reasons it is desirable to reduce rules and regulations regarding notebooks to a minimum. Foremost among these is the pupil's desire to feel that the product is his individual creation. Such matters as size of paper, method of dividing the book into sections, amount and type of optional work included, type of cover, etc., should be left to the discretion of the pupil. However, there are a few details that the class should agree upon as requirements. Probably the books should be written in ink or typed. The pages should be numbered. The pupil's name should appear at the top of each page. A table of contents should be found at the beginning of the book. Commonly accepted rules of correct grammar and good form in written work as taught in English classes should be insisted upon.

There are certain cautions to which the successful teacher should be alert. It is possible to substitute notebook work of minor importance for classroom reading and discussion of major importance. This is unpardonable. If pupils engage in notebook work at all, due recognition and appraisal of the results should precede the issuing of report cards. This is time-consuming for the teacher. So are other steps connected with effective teaching. Since the marking of notebooks lends itself so largely to subjective procedures, one might well inspect several notebooks before any efforts to evaluate are expended, then go back through the group placing the superior ones in one pile, those a little less well done in another, etc., until the job has been executed. Promptness is a virtue that should be insisted upon. Throughout the pupil's entire life he must meet obligations on time. The date on which the book is due should be announced well in advance. Books handed in later should be marked lower in proportion to the lateness involved. In many cases it will appear or even be a fact that pupils have copied each other's work. It is impossible to eliminate this completely. At least, by observing some of the above-mentioned suggestions, one can be sure that the pupil wrote his own notes. With even that minimum performance, he will actually profit by some learning.

Workbooks. When one thinks of notebooks as part of social studies activities he is also likely to give attention to workbooks at the same time. The publisher of a workbook would ordinarily contend that it is made available to ensure greater mastery on the part of the pupil, to lighten the burdens of the teacher by furnishing carefully worked-out exercises, and to exemplify the latest and most scientific trends in teaching procedures. Upon examining workbooks it will be noticed that they can be classified in two ways, namely, those that are designed to be used by pupils taking a specified course without regard to textbook or textbooks being used and those prepared to accompany a particular textbook. The former becomes a sort of syllabus for the course. The topics to be studied are shown clearly in outline fashion; basic information to be mastered is indicated; class activities are outlined; and rather extensive bibliographies are placed at the end of units of study. The latter type of workbook can be much briefer. The general outline in the Table of Contents of the text sets the pattern for content. The material to be prepared by the pupil follows closely the reading material in the one textbook. Additional readings and class projects are likely to be included. Both types frequently contain tests covering the material studied, the latter basing the questions exclusively on the one book. The physical make-up of the workbook tends toward paper binding, perforated pages, and every indication that it is to serve one pupil one year. Accordingly it usually retails at a figure between 50 cents and one dollar.

The teacher is obliged to make a decision as to whether or not to use a workbook in each social studies class. One way to arrive at a decision is to think of the probable advantages and disadvantages involved. Some of the advantages offered by enthusiasts for workbooks are as follows:

1. Study activity for the pupil is assured. Sufficient work with full directions accompanies all assignments.

2. Skilled authorship has gone into the production of the workbook, especially if the writer of a reputable textbook prepared the workbook.

3. Stress upon the important concepts that should be mastered comes through the pages of the workbook.

4. Provisions for individual differences are usually found in the optional exercises included.

5. Teacher supervision of pupil activities can be slightly lessened through the use of workbooks.

6. Pupils who have been absent from school or enter late in the semester can more readily catch up by doing workbook assignments than by attempting to proceed with less guidance.

7. For pupils working out a course on a correspondence plan the workbook provides a plan of study.

8. When tests are included they usually represent the work of experts who have scientifically arrived at validity and reliability.

9. Pupils will often accept with more finality the value of learning certain information and doing certain tasks if they are called for in a workbook than if the teacher suggests them.

10. Workbook sheets are neatly and legibly printed. Locally duplicated materials and blackboard directions sometimes fail to meet this criterion.

Some of the disadvantages that are offered by theorists and those who have used workbooks are

1. Pupils tend to read to find workbook answers rather than for the purpose of adding to their general store of information or critical thinking.

2. Conscientious checking of pages completed by pupils in workbooks becomes a tremendous teacher burden.

3. Teacher originality and resourcefulness are virtually crushed. By the time the workbook directions have been executed the time allotment has been consumed.

4. Pupils have a tendency to assist one another in the preparation of assignments, even to use the workbook pages prepared in the same course in a preceding year.

5. Better results are obtained in local situations where the teacher prepares and distributes assignment sheets; also where the teacher prepares a new test for each class in a specific course.

6. Pupil originality is brought into focus less readily through workbooks than through the use of well-planned notebooks.

7. Even though the expense of workbooks is relatively small it is a matter that may sometimes lead to an adverse consideration.

8. Some workbooks appear to have been hastily constructed and poorly organized, just as there is quality and lack of quality in textbooks themselves.

The teacher should be acquainted with the various workbooks available in each social study taught. Even though the workbook is not used it is possible to gain many helpful ideas and suggestions that will function in daily classroom teaching. It is undoubtedly true that many teachers are doing excellent work with the help of workbooks while many others are doing an equally fine job without them.

Methods of Instruction in Grades 13 and 14. In order to make the course in social studies at the level of grades 13 and 14 accord with the philosophy accepted and attain the objectives posed, much attention must be given to methods to be used. Some procedures can be ruled out at the start. No such course can be successful if presented as straight lecture material. This affords too little opportunity for student participation in thought processes or creative expression. Question-and-answer exercises based upon one textbook have even less place here than they do in lower high-school grades. These older people become more bored, if possible, and less tolerant as they suffer resentment. Project work, which is clearly a technique that meets with more success at the elementary level, has few chances for successful application at this stage. The foregoing statements are not construed to mean that the methods mentioned shall never be used.

For instance, in the introduction of new material it is in order to present advance summarizations by the lecture technique. On rare occasions it seems wise to test the mastery of basic material by asking questions to be answered by factual statements. In brief, it is difficult to use the prescription, *never*.

Now that the negative approach has been taken it seems apt to make some positive statements. Probably the most important suggestion that can be made is that the unit method of teaching in these grades ranks second to none. To be most successful the course must be thus organized in advance by the instructor. The steps suggested in Chapter 11 need to be followed diligently. The principal difference here is that much less time in the classroom is devoted to assimilation. Techniques of independent study and investigation have been well developed at least theoretically in lower grades.

Since the unit method permits so many activities and procedures there are some to be especially recommended. Constant efforts toward problem solving should be in evidence. Those arising from natural student curiosity and teacher stimulation ordinarily furnish both quality and number sufficient in amount for the needs involved. A natural outgrowth is extensive reading—not of a type expected by a specialist in any social science area, but rather that resulting from a wholesome thirst to satisfy a natural interest. Such reading should not resemble assigned lists. It should be largely optional. The range of materials pointed out should be so broad as to include not only books but also periodicals, pamphlets, newspapers, and magazines.

In situations where organized forum discussions seem appropriate they should be utilized. Animated participation, which is quite desirable, can scarcely be held in check. Socialization, a goal regularly to be sought, may be found in forum methods, especially if audience contributions following the formal statements by the panel are welcomed.

Working cooperatively with teachers of the same students in other subjects is highly desirable; in actual practice, however, less is being done along this line in these upper grades. There is one hopeful observation, namely, that the trend is to develop these social studies on a fusion basis (see Chapter 9).

Emphasis on contemporary affairs has been practically taken for granted. Stress on the present, with attention to the remote past reduced to a minimum, is a keynote to the whole topic of methodology. Setting aside specific times for the discussion of current events is unnecessary. They are used throughout, and a working knowledge of them is definitely a part of the course.

In comparison with social studies at their best in lower grade levels the difference to be noted here probably grows out of maturity. The amount of reading naturally can be more; the quality of judgments expressed should be higher; the insight exhibited in questions asked is usually deeper; and, the soundness of conclusions reached ordinarily has greater validity.

Summary. The purpose of this chapter has been to present some aspects of methods of teaching social studies that are usable by those who employ the unit method and those who use other techniques. The assignment was held to be of utmost importance. When longer phases of subject matter are to be approached it was recommended that an advance summarization be presented. This is a phase of teaching during which the teacher uses the lecture or semilecture technique. It should be very informal, motivating, and highly instructive. If success in its presentation is attained, excellent results will almost inevitably follow for several days ahead.

The purpose of the drill lesson was set forth as giving an exercise that would help pupils fix well in mind numerous facts that should be remembered over a relatively long period of time. Contrary to generally accepted thought, drill work can be enjoyable. This is especially true if it is reduced to a contest basis. There are many cautions that a teacher must observe. The rules of the contest must be simple and easily understood. Questions must be well phrased and permit of one answer only. Competition must be used as a means to interest the group.

Review lessons are expected to represent the last phases of organizing efforts. Chronological and topical approaches are commonly used. Ability to perfect outlines and summaries needs to be developed.

Notebooks should be used only if in so doing social studies are learned more easily and better. Some teachers use them meagerly whereas others use them generously. Content varies from a mere list of assignments to the inclusion of a full presentation of the course in laboratory fashion. Potential advantages and disadvantages of the use of notebooks should be kept in mind by the teacher who uses them. Precisely the same things that have been said about notebooks can also be said about workbooks.

The extremely important place of the unit method of teaching as it applies to grades 13 and 14 was stressed.

Questions on the Text

1. Mention several cautions that the social studies teacher should have in mind when making an assignment. State this on the basis of a list of "do's and don'ts."
2. What place does advance presentation of content have in social studies teaching?
3. What variations of technique should the teacher employ with different age groups in this phase of teaching?
4. What special traits should the social studies teacher possess in order to carry out well the lecture and semilecture phases of teaching?
5. In the specimen advance summaries presented in this chapter, did you notice efforts to attain any of the objectives called for in question 1 above? Give examples.
6. Suggest several types of activity that teachers have used in making assignments to pupils in social studies classes.
7. Distinguish clearly between general objectives and specific objectives.
8. Contrast the functions of drill and review lessons.
9. Outline the plan by which a successful drill lesson might be presented.
10. Mention some activities that a class would probably be engaged in during a review lesson that would not be in evidence at all during a drill lesson.
11. If notebooks are used by social studies teachers, what should be some of the purposes involved?
12. Give in some detail the typical content of excellent social studies notebooks.
13. Summarize the most common advantages and disadvantages of the use of social studies notebooks.
14. How does a workbook differ from a notebook? Give the advantages and disadvantages that may easily follow the use of a workbook.
15. Make a list of "do's and don'ts" related to methods of instruction in grades 13 and 14.

Suggested Activities

1. Observe the teachers' methods of making assignments in classes in which you are now enrolled. Make a list of the most helpful ones from your point of view as a student.

2. Visit a social studies class in which the teacher is introducing new subject matter. Compare the methods used with those set forth in this chapter.

3. Prepare an advance summarization of social studies content that you would present if you were teaching a selected unit in social studies.

4. Examine some commonly used textbooks in secondary-school social studies to determine how much effort and space are given to introducing new subject matter. Bring examples of the best efforts to class.

5. Assume the role of inquiring reporter. Ask students of different age levels their personal reaction to time spent on review and drill activity. Decide whether or not they think it would be more profitable simply to advance to new subject matter.

6. Confer with a good social studies teacher and ask to examine specimen notebooks and workbooks that have been prepared or used in regular teaching procedures.

7. Suggest some methods of teaching in grades 13 and 14 that are somewhat original with you, giving reasons why you regard them as good ones.

Selected References

Aldrich, J. C., "Do You Teach Safety through the Social Studies?" *Safety Education,* XXV (January, 1946), pp. 21–23.

Atyeo, Henry C., "The Excursion in Social Education," *Audio-visual Materials and Methods in the Social Studies,* Washington, D.C.: The National Council for the Social Studies, *Eighteenth Yearbook,* 1947, pp. 33–52.

Baker, Paul E., "Some Methods of Teaching the Social Studies in Hawaii," *Social Studies,* XXXI (January, 1940), pp. 17–19.

Brown, Ralph Adams, "The Town Meeting Comes to the Classroom," *Social Education,* V (November, 1941), pp. 516–519.

Burdette, F. L., "Integration of the Social Studies: A Discussion Summarized," *Educational Forum,* VIII (March, 1944), pp. 339–347.

Callas, E. E., "We Start with the Community," *Safety Education,* XXV (September, 1945), pp. 20–21.

Chipp, Rodney B., "The National Nominating Conventions in the Classroom," *Social Studies,* XXXI (May, 1940), pp. 203–206.

Chrisman, Richard G., "Panel Discussions in Teaching Controversial Subjects," *Social Education,* X (November, 1946), pp. 314–316.

CLARK, H. F., "Experiments in the Social Sciences," *Science,* CI (Apr. 20, 1945), pp. 393–398.

COULTER, KENNETH C., "The Question Method in Teaching History," *Social Studies,* XXXI (February, 1940), pp. 75–76.

CRYMES, JUDITH, "National Defense—A Project," *Social Studies,* XXXIII (February, 1942), pp. 79–80.

CUNNINGHAM, R., "Needs Approach to Social Studies," *Peabody Journal of Education,* XXIII (May, 1946), pp. 348–352.

DOUGLASS, HARL R., and HUBERT H. MILLS, *Teaching in High School,* New York: The Ronald Press Company, 1948, Chaps. X, XII, XIII, and XVIII.

ELDER, ROBERT E., and HOWARD L. JONES, "Let's Get Down to Cases," *Social Education,* XII (April, 1948), pp. 160–162.

FLINKER, IRVING, "Toward Integrated Teaching: A Step in Transition," *Social Education,* X (January, 1946), pp. 25–26.

FORSYTH, E., "Social Studies: Methods of Learning and Teaching," *Review of Educational Research,* XIV (October, 1944), pp. 339–342.

GERLACH, DOROTHY, "Treating Individual Differences in Texas Schools," *Social Education,* X (November, 1946), pp. 298–300.

GOETZ, D. A., "Integration Instead of Isolation," *Safety Education,* XXV (September, 1945), pp. 4–5.

HARVEY, C. C., "How a High School Used Its Community as a Laboratory for Social Education," *Social Education,* VII (February, 1943), pp. 71–73.

HAWKINS, ELEANOR, "History Drill Can Be Fun," *Social Education,* VI (February, 1942), pp. 74–75.

HEFFERMAN, H., "Methods in the Social Studies," *California Journal of Elementary Education,* XIII (May, 1945), pp. 244–252.

JOHNSON, JANET BASSETT, "Practical Drill and Review Techniques in the Twelfth Grade," *Social Studies,* XXXI (October, 1940), pp. 262–270.

KINDRED, L. W., and O. W. STEPHENSON, "The Technique of the Field Trip," *Social Education,* V (January, 1941), pp. 21–25.

KLEINFELTER, CLAUDE B., and I. HOWELL KANE, "High School Seniors Study Their Social Agencies," *Social Education,* V (January, 1941), pp. 15–17.

KOOS, L. V., "Junior College Teachers: Subjects Taught and Specialized Preparation," *Junior College Journal,* XVIII (December, 1947), pp. 196–209.

"Major Projects in the Social Studies," *Cooperation in General Education,* Washington, D.C.: American Council on Education, 1947, pp. 118–141.

MANNION, LAWRENCE J., "Maps as an Activity in History Teaching," *Social Studies,* XXXI (February, 1940), pp. 78–81.

McGlynn, Edna M., "Field Trips in Government Courses," *Social Education,* VIII (January, 1944), pp. 19–22.

Memler, Henrietta, and Wayne Alvord, "Study Your Town," *Social Education,* X (November, 1946), pp. 311–313.

Moffatt, Maurice P., *Social Studies Instruction,* New York: Prentice-Hall, Inc., 1950, Chaps. IV and V.

Moore, Gladys E., "History Can Be Fun," *Social Education,* X (April, 1946), p. 171.

Musselman, Dayton, "A Semester's Project in Community Citizenship," *Social Education,* VIII (December, 1944), pp. 363–364.

Nelson, Lowry, "Planning and Organizing Cooperative Community Projects," *Social Education,* VII (February, 1943), pp. 68–70.

Parham, Lillian C., "Out-of-school Environments and Activities of Junior High School Pupils," *Social Education,* VI (January, 1942), pp. 27–30.

Perrine, Katherine, "They Play Football in Class," *Social Education,* VIII (December, 1944), pp. 355–356.

Reschke, Alfred, "High School Seniors Study Milwaukee," *Social Education,* V (December, 1941), pp. 590–594.

Rex, Millicent B., "The Use of the Quotation Question in History," *Social Education,* IX (May, 1945), pp. 215–218.

Riley, Noma, "Review and Recall," *Social Education,* V (March, 1941), pp. 199–201.

Samford, Clarence D., "Drill Work in Social Studies Classes," *Social Education,* VIII (December, 1944), pp. 353–354.

Sanders, Jennings B., "Problems-and-interpretations Approaches to College History," *Social Studies,* XLI (April, 1950), pp. 159–161.

Shippard, M., "Fun with Maps and Globes," *Educational Screen,* XXV (May, 1946), pp. 236–238.

Smith, Villa B., "A Field Study from the Terminal Tower in Cleveland," *Audio-visual Materials and Methods in the Social Studies,* Washington, D.C.: The National Council for the Social Studies, *Eighteenth Yearbook,* 1947, pp. 53–60.

Stephenson, O. W., and L. W. Kindred, "The Technique of the Field Trip," *Social Education,* V (January, 1941), pp. 21–25.

Stewart, Dorothy H., "Social Studies and Group Work," *Social Education,* X (October, 1946), pp. 259–260.

Strahan, Marguerite Burbanck, "Global Jaunts in the Classroom," *Social Education,* X (December, 1946), p. 358.

Stuckey, M. M., "Ninth Grade Pupils Dig into Practical Politics," *Clearing House,* XX (March, 1946), pp. 398–400.

Taub, I. S., "Teacher Reports His Problems in Social Studies Method in the 7th, 8th, and 9th Years," *High Points,* XXIX (April, 1947), pp. 43–54.

TURNER, LAWRENCE E., and CORNELIUS H. SIEMENS, "The Election—A Plan for Citizenship Education," *Social Education,* VIII (October, 1944), pp. 258–261.

WAGNER, JEAN, "An Eighth Grade Studies Racial Intolerance," *Social Education,* X (February, 1946), pp. 75–77.

WARREN, GILE J., "Group Study of Social Problems," *Social Education,* V (February, 1941), pp. 104–106.

WEINGAST, DAVID, "Assembly Programs Dramatize Social Studies," *Social Education,* VIII (April, 1944), pp. 161–162.

Chapter 13

SUPERVISED STUDY

Preview. The process of supervised study is explained in this chapter with examples of two kinds of planning for a supervised study period. Study skills of reading, of using reference materials, and of communication are discussed. The values of supervised study, together with the needs for supervised study, are listed. The responsibility of the teacher in conducting the supervised study is explained, and some teacher problems are suggested. Emphasis is given to the establishment of habits of critical thinking as a result of the supervised study experience. Some suggested rules for study in the upper grades conclude the chapter.

Supervised Study Defined. There may be differences of opinion concerning the meaning of supervised study, but the term is used here as defined by Maxwell and Kilzer: [1] ". . . supervised study is the effective direction and oversight of the silent-study and laboratory activities of pupils." From this definition the responsibility of the teacher is immediately evident. "Effective direction" requires more teacher participation in the activity than the mere observing by the teacher that all pupils seem to be busy. The teacher works with each pupil on some phase of the problem confronting the pupil, whether the pupil has a difficulty or not. The teacher may not attend the successful pupil longer than to note that his procedure is correct; on the other hand, the faster pupil may require additional teacher guidance in undertaking more difficult or advanced work related to the unit. "The silent-study and laboratory activities of pupils" indicates the responsibility of pupils in supervised study. There may be several kinds of study activity going on at the same time, depending upon the needs and interests of pupils in following out the

[1] C. R. Maxwell and L. R. Kilzer, *High School Administration*, New York: Doubleday & Company, Inc., 1936, p. 345. Quoted by permission of the Odyssey Press, the latest publisher of this text.

assignment. "Silent study" may consist of reading, analyzing charts or graphs, interpreting maps, or a variety of writing activities. "Laboratory activities" involves the gathering and selection of reference materials, construction of various illustrative devices related to the unit, group practice of dramatization, or possibly a committee's preparation of a panel discussion or debate. From the foregoing description it is apparent that supervised study is an activity period in which teacher and pupils work together to accomplish desirable goals.

The Need for Supervised Study in the Social Studies. The demands upon the time of present-day youth seem extensive, as various worthwhile youth organizations offer attractive programs in addition to the greatly expanded program of the high school. With this increase in activity and its resultant time consumption, it seems that school responsibilities should not be extended into the after-school time. Home study for all courses could present a health hazard. Since the present trend in curriculum plans emphasizes general education and life-adjustment programs centering in the social studies, it seems particularly desirable that supervised study be incorporated into the program.

In addition to these general needs, it appears that for the social studies a directed study procedure by the teacher in the classroom is essential. All materials needed to complete preparation of the work are at hand, and the teacher is present to give helpful suggestions. Certain skills essential to successful use and understanding of social studies materials can be acquired only through practice under the teacher's supervision. As has been pointed out earlier, one important responsibility of the social studies teacher is that he become well acquainted with individual pupils in order to guide them toward the achievement of the objectives of the course. The process of teacher and pupil working together in the supervised study period affords an opportunity for the teacher to be of considerable influence. A study hall in the school program should not be considered as a supervised study for the social studies. The study-hall teacher cannot replace the social studies teacher in the particular teacher-pupil relationship required for effective preparation in the social studies. Remove supervised study from the social studies program and immediately the valuable factor of pupil guidance is lost. For the social studies the process of supervised study must occur in the classroom as an integral part of the teacher-pupil planning and working together. Much preparation of social studies work involves a reading activity which again makes the supervised study period almost mandatory because of the frequent reading difficulties experienced by pupils. When the supervising social studies teacher observes reading failure, he may immediately begin diagnosis of the causes of the difficulty and upon the basis of his investigation bring remedial procedures into action.

Values of Supervised Study in the Social Studies. As indicated in the preceding topic, supervised study meets certain needs of the social studies. After a program of supervised study has started, certain values resulting from its use will become evident. It is the authors' experience that the following desirable values result from supervised study in the social studies class:

1. Pupils benefit from individual attention by the teacher who brings to the situation his knowledge of each pupil, accumulated from observation. The teacher can detect pupil habits of study, efficiency of study skills, and degree of progress. Suggestions to aid individual pupils can be made at the point where guidance is most helpful.

2. Class time is used more efficiently. As pupils proceed into a period of investigation of their problem following the time of teacher-pupil planning, the interest and motivation of the exploratory discussion period continue without an interruption. For some pupils the planning period may thus be extended as they work out further details in conference with the teacher. Pupil time is conserved as the teacher may observe errors in pupil activity which, called to his attention, enable the pupil to redirect his effort.

3. The social studies room is an aid to study. Closely related to the time-saving aspect of supervised study is the ready accessibility of essential materials for pupils in the social studies room. This condition does not exist in a study hall or in the pupil's home.

4. Democratic human relations are encouraged. In supervised study pupils learn to share materials, to wait their turn, to understand their own difficulties and therefore become sympathetic with the difficulties encountered by others. It is evident to the pupils that the teacher is working and learning with them.

5. Pupil differences become guides for the teacher. As the teacher works with each pupil, the individual who proceeds slowly can be guided into effective learning experiences meaningful for him, affording a sense of achievement comparable to the similar type of result sought by the teacher for the individual who works more rapidly and requires a greater challenge to use his ability.

6. The school can become more significant to the pupil. Supervised study which grows out of the planning done by pupils and teacher reflects pupil interests. Frequently such interest is an expression of the pupil's idea of a lifework as well as an interest in a hobby, valuable as the latter may be. When pupils realize that in school they are following their own lines of interest, vocational or avocational, their sense of belonging in school is enhanced. In addition to these interests it is possible for the pupil to experience a sense of achievement as he is guided by teacher questions or suggestions to overcome difficulties. The discontented pupil may thus be given a more satisfying life.

7. More efficient use of materials results. Under the teacher's guidance of individual pupils' selection of material the pupils learn the specific types of information available in various reference books. They learn that one magazine may be devoted to news facts while another is a magazine of opinion. In the field of history it is evident from observation that one historian writes chiefly from an economic point of view while another may be interested in more general culture. Such understanding of sources is more likely to occur in the supervised study period than in some time of independent study by the pupil removed from the social studies class.

8. Knowledge is broadened. In the time of individual pupil study on some phase of the class problem the pupil will probably discover tangent ideas and interesting lines of related knowledge which he will wish to explore. The experience of finding new facts helps him to appreciate greater truths and to see that all knowledge is related, that subject lines are more or less artificial devices.

The Supervised Study Process. As previously pointed out, the supervised study period is a time of cooperative endeavor as teacher and pupils work together to achieve a maximum learning experience. The activities of the period, all of them phases of study, will grow out of preceding periods of teacher-pupil planning or a class discussion which has carried the pupils to a point where it becomes necessary for them to investigate further information. In teacher-pupil planning the pupils' interests are guided by the teacher, who seeks to bring meaningful experiences through the selection of such materials and topics as will seem valuable to the pupils in terms of the social studies objectives. The planning which the teacher must do, together with his guidance of the teacher-pupil planning, becomes a broad outline of the work to be done in the supervised study period. This may be thought of as the assignment portion of a unit, and as such it is a controlling factor in the ensuing study period as indicated by

Kilzer.[2] The teacher who has been unable to guide a teacher-pupil planning experience in which pupils help to set up a problem to be investigated must plan such a variety of activities as will meet the needs of the individual pupils and will be presented to them as a more formal assignment. An example of such an assignment appears later in this chapter. Under the teacher's guidance each pupil will follow chosen lines of investigation, each of which contributes some element of knowledge and experience to the over-all unit. Thus it can be readily seen that the supervised study period is a time of experiencing, of developing new concepts, of forming new associations of ideas, of establishing habits of thinking, and of acquiring right attitudes.

The teacher will have so directed the planning period that a wide range of activities will result, involving various study skills. From these activities pupils will make their selection of a phase of the problem they wish to investigate. Some pupils may become engaged in exploratory reading in order to determine certain facts needed in the solution of their problem. Others may be reading to select material for information from which they will organize a floor talk. A committee may be planning the presentation of a panel discussion and may be busy deciding on the topics to be covered and the probable sources of information best suited to their needs. Another group may be planning a dramatization. Other activities will occur, such as drawing a series of pictures to illustrate a phase of the unit, a graph, a chart, or illustrations to be used on a map; investigating the contents of the resource file to select materials for bulletin-board exhibits on the unit; or planning a field trip to some community resource. In this varied activity the teacher will probably be greatly occupied with individual-pupil concerns. He must seek to guide and direct without helping to the extent that no work remains for the pupil to do.

To conduct the period of study efficiently, the teacher must be well acquainted with the individual pupils, realizing their abilities and weaknesses. He must be thoroughly informed upon the material available for the problem under consideration. His ability to recognize inefficient study skills will enable him to direct the weak pupil into more effective procedures. His general background of informa-

[2] L. R. Kilzer, *A Guide to Effective Supervised Study*, Laramie, Wyo.: College of Education, University of Wyoming, Monograph Series No. 1, p. 20.

tion must be sufficiently extensive to enable him to suggest broader experiences for the pupil who works rapidly and who finishes ahead of others. The amount of time set aside for supervised study is variable according to the needs of the pupils in accomplishing the work which is planned and must be determined by the teacher as he observes pupil activity in his supervision of the study period. From this description of the teacher's responsibility in the supervised study period it is evident that in this phase of the social studies program a challenging opportunity exists for the teacher to be of far-reaching influence and for the pupil to engage in vital and significant learning experiences.

Supervised Study after Teacher-Pupil Planning. In a typical teacher-pupil planning period before a unit of study based upon the early westward movement, some pupils may suggest the desirability of their seeing a moving picture related to the theme of the unit study. When the proper time arrives in the working out of the unit for the film to be used, the pupils will spend a class period in preparing to view the film. The teacher, as part of his preparation for this unit of work, has previewed the film and has selected the chief points of emphasis which this film will contribute as an additional experience in the unit. Seated with the pupils, the teacher may inquire what they think the film will show. Suggested ideas will vary, depending upon pupil background, knowledge, and ability to imagine early Western scenes. The list grows and is written on the blackboard. The following questions and statements are typical of such a procedure:

"What did the clothing look like?"
"How do the people live?"
"Style of houses may be seen."
"The work of the people may be shown."
"There will probably be a scene of the family in their home."
"Indians might be in the picture, too."
"We might see the men hunting wild game."
"There may be scenes along the river as they make their journey."
"What part of the country will this movie show?"

With such a list as a guide, the teacher now asks the pupils how they may know whether this film will present any of these ideas accurately. The pupil response calls for investigation of reading materials of life on the frontier, and the class proceeds to this study activity after deciding upon the materials to be used, which in a typical situation might be history textbooks, a volume from the *Pageant of America,* and a wall map. The teacher moves about among the pupils, observing their activity, questioning a pupil's selection of reading material that reveals failure to use the index properly, inquiring of a pupil as to the meaningfulness of the notes he is taking on his reading, observing whether three pupils at the wall map have chosen a system of rivers significant to the period of history portrayed in the film, discovering that several pupils have found material dealing with difficulties of frontier life, but that less material has been found on descriptions of the people themselves. The teacher reminds a pupil of the purpose of the dictionary when the pupil asks another for a word definition. The pupil then goes to the dictionary and discovers the meaning. Some proportionate time before the end of the study period, the teacher may ask whether any pupil has found any idea, picture, or material which will be helpful to the other pupils, and there will probably be a surprising response, because pupils like to tell what they have done as an expression of their personal achievement, and there is also pleasure in helping someone. The results will consist of pictures in textbooks to illustrate the ideas they imagine will be found in the film, factual ideas relating to general context of material read which seem significant to the pupil, vocabulary items directly related to the period under consideration, and possibly names of characters or events discovered in the materials read.

Such a supervised study period before the viewing of a film establishes a helpful background of knowledge with which to understand the film. Pupils are strongly motivated to concentrate on the film when it is shown, because each is eager to discover whether any of his ideas, questions, and preparation will appear. As pupils view films, they acquire a certain habit of imagination which is a kind of skill to help them in preparing for future observations of films.

Supervised Study after a Teacher-controlled Assignment. The following plan of an assignment might be considered typical of the method a teacher would use to set up a supervised study period when no teacher-pupil planning has worked out the problems to be solved by the class.

The class is ready to begin a study of the early westward movement. At the opening of the class period the assignment is made. The activities planned in the assignment have been listed on the blackboard before the arrival of the class. Steps in the assignment are as follows:

1. The teacher presents the idea of the early westward movement, pointing out various pertinent items on a wall map of the United States.

2. The teacher requests the pupils to open their books to a page where the material for study begins. He then calls their attention to a picture on the page by asking a pupil to compare it with a similar situation today. Following the pupil response the teacher directs the attention of the class to the third page, where a description of life on the frontier is found. The teacher writes the word *frontier* on the board and asks for volunteer definitions. After two or three attempted replies the teacher advises the pupils to consult the dictionary during the study period. Another picture on the next page is remarked upon by the teacher, who turns then to the following page, suggesting that the pupils be able to list the types of people who were found in the westward movement and to describe them.

3. The teacher then directs the class to choose items from the board as things to do after they have read to an indicated page. Of the items on the board the entire class is requested to do the first two items. If they have time after completing these, the individual pupils are to choose from the remaining items. The more activities each pupil completes satisfactorily, the better his understanding of the lesson will be, is the concluding advice from the teacher.

4. The activities listed on the blackboard are read to the class by the teacher:

I. Write answers to the following questions after you have read the lesson:
   A. Contrast life on the frontier with that of the settled areas east of the mountains.
   B. Why did the frontier contribute to the development of democracy?
   C. What contributions did each type of pioneer make to the westward movement?
   D. How did cheap and free land affect the settlement of the early West?
   E. Why was the Indian problem temporarily solved after 1795?

II. Make a list of ten words which you find in your reading that must be known in order to understand this topic.

III. Prepare a floor talk on the early settlements in Ohio.

IV. Prepare a floor talk on the life and influence of "Mad Anthony" Wayne.

V. Draw a map of the Northwest Territory, locating early towns and important Indian battles named in your reading.

VI. Draw a map of the United States in 1810 showing the states, the trails to the West, waterways important in the westward movement, and the mountain barrier.

VII. Construct a graph showing population of the United States in 1790, 1800, and 1810.

VIII. Draw a series of pictures illustrating the material you read in the assignment.

IX. Write an imaginary diary which a pioneer woman might have kept on this journey to the West.

X. Write a short story describing an imaginary incident experienced by a hunter.

XI. With two or three other pupils plan a brief dramatization of the signing of the Treaty of Greenville.

XII. Read an account of the settlement of Marietta from other sources and prepare a floor talk on this important subject.

5. After reading the activities to the class, the teacher asks if anyone has not understood the assignment. If no questions concerning procedure are raised, the teacher tells the pupils that the remainder of the period, or about forty minutes, will be devoted to study. He requests the pupils to ask questions whenever they fail to understand any item as they proceed with their study.

The teacher will then go about among the pupils during the study period, questioning, suggesting, and advising as the study activities proceed.

Study Skills in the Social Studies. Although rules for efficient study may apply generally to study activities in all areas, there are particular skills which seem of significance to the social studies. Pupils in the social studies must become proficient in these skills in order to achieve success in this area of study. The teacher of the social studies must recognize this element of his teaching and provide for it by directing activities which will require the use of these essential skills until pupils show reasonable ability in their practice. Until the pupil has acquired a ready use of these skills, he is unable to proceed independently. These skills may be arranged in three general groups: (1) reading skills; (2) skills in use of reference materials; and (3) communication skills.

Reading skills. For the various approaches to a problem different kinds of reading are needed. Each kind involves the fundamental ability to understand concepts from the printed page. Consequently the pupil in social studies must make a continuous effort to acquire new words and terms, to understand their meaning, and, when more than one meaning exists, to be able to decide when a particular meaning is desired. To gather the meaning from the printed page requires a broad vocabulary. When pupils are attacking new material, the lack of understanding, if any, lies many times in their inadequate vocabulary. The differences which exist in pupil ability in vocabulary command must be considered by teachers in guiding study activities, as some pupils will require greater practice in word study than will others. The social studies teacher must not assume that spelling and definition knowledge can be left to the English class, because new concepts become a part of the pupil's daily preparation. Pupils can be helped in vocabulary study by having them keep a notebook record of new words and terms. Games, in the form of spelling bees involving definition, or spelling, can be used to advantage with junior-high pupils and may be a form of drill on essential terms.

As pupils engage in study they will discover that some study requires that they read a section of material with close attention to detail while another portion during the same study period may require only a general impression to furnish adequate information. At times the pupil must read to compare sources; such reading necessitates the ability to select the important ideas or principles involved. In preparing a floor talk or an essay, the pupil must read from a variety of sources, selecting the ideas which are pertinent to his problem. Reading rate is important, but it is not the chief factor in reading skill in the social studies.

The supervised study period can be a great aid to the pupil who has a reading difficulty. Under the teacher's direction this pupil may be guided in choosing materials to read which offer less difficulty, and as he successfully completes an assignment, he is rewarded by the sense of achievement which it brings and by the pleasure he experiences in being able to read some material. The suggestion that the supervised study period is an opportunity for the retarded reader does not imply that the teacher must devote a disproportionate amount of time to this pupil at the expense of other pupils who also are to be guided in various activities. If a remedial-reading course is being taught in the school, the social studies teacher can often carry out activities in the supervised study period initiated by the remedial-reading teacher. By encouraging all pupils to read more and to select with greater discrimination the materials read, the social studies teacher is contributing effectively to the life of the pupil. The social studies teacher, to be efficient in the reading-program phase of the supervised study period, should be informed on a fairly wide field of reading materials; newspapers, magazines, and a wide range of books, in addition to textbooks, will be used. The supervised study period can occasionally become a period of free reading for the cultivation of a taste for good reading. At such times the teacher can guide pupil choice of reading by discussing very briefly an interesting book he has recently read, or he may bring from the library copies of several books which may appeal to the pupils. By informal talk with the individual pupils about a book the pupil has selected, the teacher obtains information about pupil interests and is also able to guide the pupil to other books.

Skills in the use of reference materials. In using a textbook the pupil must be aware of all the devices in the book intended to be of aid to him. He must understand the difference between the table of contents and the index and how each is to be used. When phonetic pronunciation is included in the index, the pupil must understand how to benefit by it. The need for following the author's suggestions must be understood when reference to related material is cited by the author within a paragraph.

In the social studies an atlas is an important reference, and pupils must know how to use it efficiently. The method of locating a point upon a map by the index key must be mastered and an understanding gained of the types of information indicated on maps such as rainfall, products, population, vegetation, and natural resources.

The interpretation of graphs is an essential skill in the social studies. Pupils will have been aware of numerous examples of graphic representation of ideas from their everyday observation and yet may not be sure of the key to understanding. The pupil must be led to see that a graph is a kind of picture illustrating a comparison. Line, bar, or circle graphs can frequently be used by pupils to illustrate elements of units of study. It has been the authors' experience that a study of graphs affords an excellent correlation between social studies and mathematics. Drill on graphs in a supervised study period thus can establish a study skill of frequent use.

Acquiring a habit of using the dictionary is essential for adequate study procedure. The teacher should provide opportunity in a study period for the various kinds of information in a dictionary to be demonstrated. In addition to spelling, pronunciation, definition, derivation, and currency of use, the dictionary includes a gazeteer, a biographical dictionary, and convenient reference tables.

Communication skills. After he has acquired factual information, the pupil needs to express his learning, either orally or by written communication of ideas. Undoubtedly skill in communication is closely related to skill in thinking. To present a convincing argument the individual must be able to organize his ideas in logical manner, which is the result of orderly thought process.

The ability to outline material is an essential skill for pupils and is needed frequently in the social studies. The basis of an outline is the selection of principal ideas and a recognition of minor, contributing ideas and their degree of importance. Pupils should understand that the outline is the thought framework of the article. The recognized form for an outline is the following:

I. . . . . .
  A. . . . . .
    1. . . . . .
    2. . . . . .
      a. . . . . .
      b. . . . . .
  B. . . . . .

Practice in outlining material will help pupils evaluate ideas within a topic, enabling them to decide upon the amount of detail to be included in an outline. The outline is valuable as an aid to pupils preparing a floor talk as they arrange material gathered from various sources.

In summarizing material the pupil must be able to read and select information in such a way that the significant elements are included in his writing. The summary is frequently helpful to pupils who wish to present accounts of lengthy materials. Both summary and outline skills are valuable to pupils in taking notes from reference materials, as these abilities emphasize coherence and organization in the preparation of a report. The outline of the report will grow as the pupil gathers further ideas. In preparing a news report, pupils will use summarizing skill and be guided by such factors as the social worth of the news article, a comparison of sources, and additional facts they may find in other sources in explanation of the news item.

Acquiring Study Skills. As has been indicated earlier in this chapter, it is the teacher's responsibility to help the pupils learn how to study. Early in the social studies course time should be devoted to a discussion of study problems, and the teacher should provide opportunities for the pupils to observe study techniques. The teacher may use films to demonstrate some study techniques. Time spent viewing and discussing films about study procedures can be of continuing value, as mental pictures of various procedures remain in the pupil's mind long after he has viewed the film. Actual practice of the study technique proposed by the film may be tried out after the class has viewed the film. Evaluation of the individual's method compared with the technique suggested in the film and suggestions for improvement are important elements of a discussion following the film. Some laboratory practice in each technique should occur before the class views the film. The following suggested films are helpful in developing some study techniques:

How to Read a Book (Coronet)
How to Study (Coronet)
Improve Your Reading (Coronet)
Know Your Library (Coronet)
We Discover the Dictionary (Coronet)

In a discussion of how to study outside the classroom pupils can set up a list of helpful suggestions. It has been observed that pupils are aware of distracting conditions which weaken their study efforts, although they have not attempted to change their study habits. Such a list was made by a ninth-grade class under the supervision of one of the authors and included such items as the following:

1. Don't eat candy or chew gum while studying.
2. Don't listen to the radio while studying.
3. Don't put off studying.
4. Don't lounge.
5. Don't have other people around doing other things.
6. Don't telephone a classmate.

With a beginning such as this it is possible to guide a class discussion into the arranging of a list of possible study rules which can be very useful to them when they must prepare materials outside the supervised study hour. After drill exercises in various study skills the teacher must watch for pupil application of the skills. This is a part of the teacher's work in the supervised study period. The inability of the pupil to use any study skill presents a difficulty to that pupil.

Self-evaluation as a Phase of Supervised Study. Pupils become efficient in solving problems to the degree that they are capable of analyzing their own ability. Experience in self-evaluation under the teacher's supervision is the best method by which this desirable habit may be established. To this end, then, it is necessary for the teacher to provide guides for self-analysis and to direct pupils in their use. In the supervised study period an excellent opportunity for such activity is present, since the entire atmosphere is one of evaluation, investigation, and analysis. The following outline for pupil self-evaluation in study skills is an example of such a device:

Self-evaluation in Study Skills

Directions: In the blank before each of the following items write a plus (+) if you think the statement applies to you, write a zero (0) if you know the statement does not apply to you, write a minus (—) if you think the statement applies sometimes.

________ 1. I always have all necessary materials at hand when I start to study (pencils, paper, books to be used).

________ 2. I always have a comfortable table, chair, and light.

________ 3. I always study at approximately the same time each day.

________ 4. I always study in a room by myself.

________ 5. I always work without stopping until the assignment is completed.

________ 6. I always write full directions in class of what is to be done outside of class.

________ 7. I always ask questions to clarify what I do not understand in an assignment before leaving class.

________ 8. I always glance rapidly over the entire assignment before beginning work on it.

________ 9. I always list new vocabulary terms, use the dictionary, and learn to spell each new word.

________ 10. I always think over each topic section after reading it.

________ 11. I always think over the main ideas of chapters or large divisions of reading materials after completing them.

________ 12. I always outline materials I have read.

________ 13. I always use any questions or study helps included with the material.

________ 14. I always try to apply ideas gained from reading to a situation previously known.

________ 15. I always try to apply ideas gained from reading to the general class problem presently being studied.
________ 16. I always study additional material not directly related to the problem when it is interesting to me.
________ 17. I always try to interpret allusions to other knowledge or literature.
________ 18. I frequently delay getting started in study process.
________ 19. I frequently stop during a study hour because of the discovery that some material is missing or because I do not understand a part of the assignment.
________ 20. I frequently eat while studying.
________ 21. I frequently study to radio accompaniment.
________ 22. I frequently study with a school friend.
________ 23. I frequently assume that I already know some material and that therefore I need not study it thoroughly.

The Significance of Supervised Study to Critical Thinking. The supervised study experience will probably be influential in establishing habits of critical thinking, as the entire purpose of the supervised study procedure points toward the realization of good judgment, discrimination in evaluating ideas, and an objective investigation of facts on the part of pupils engaged. Personal problems of pupils, youth interests in the immediate community, world affairs, and the needs of life in a democracy all demand good judgment and clear thinking by pupils. The supervised study period encourages the pupil not only to compare facts but also to evaluate the sources of facts, withholding opinion until enough evidence is at hand to justify a conclusion. As the pupil becomes aware of the importance of primary sources, he will probably be less inclined to depend on a single secondary source but will investigate and compare others. The pupil will become more conscious of words as expressions of thought; shades of meaning of words and correct choice of words will be seen to be important for accurate statement. The very experience of using a variety of materials whose purpose is to furnish authentic information and of acquiring skills in study which emphasize efficiency and reliability will cause the pupil to be alert to situations requiring decisions and opinions. The ability to identify the situation or problem, to remove it from all tangent ideas for accurate analysis, is a phase of critical study. With such experience the pupil increases his ability to apply these values, and in his contact with written or oral expression he becomes sensitive to inefficient thinking by someone else.

The social studies period of supervised study is an excellent place for this sensitivity to be developed.

Teacher Difficulties in Supervised Study. It is obvious that the success of the supervised study period in the social studies will depend largely upon the skill and ability of the teacher. With experience and careful planning for all units of study, the supervised study period should become more effective. There are many things which the teacher must keep in mind in directing the pupil study. To list some of these may suggest others to the teacher who has attempted the direction of a supervised study period. The teacher must not give answers outright in response to pupil requests for information unless that information is available only from the teacher. Help is more valuable for pupils when a teacher's questions are guides in reply to pupil inquiry. Only in rare drill situations will all the pupils do the same thing in a supervised period, although this might be easier for the teacher. The teacher must learn to sense pupil reaction to the work and to know when sympathy, encouragement, or helpful criticism is most needed. The teacher must also develop a sense of timing; he must acquire patience and a willingness to permit what may seem too much time for the performance of given activities in order to secure adequate pupil achievement. The general preparation of the teacher in the social studies field will be a significant factor in the success of his supervised study periods.

Supervised Study, Grades 13 and 14. Even at the advanced level of grades 13 and 14 the problem of teaching students how to study remains important but does not lend itself to supervision of study within the classroom. Consequently the suggestions must become more concrete and specific. Student independence must be attained. Topical or unit procedures are assumed; likewise, suggested bibliographies are a part of the total picture. Thus student identification of central themes, pursuing of pertinent reading, and reaching sound conclusions are objectives of his study habits. All this is quite the opposite of memorization procedures. Without prejudice to the value and place of the many suggestions that are so helpful to social studies pupils at lower-grade levels, the following are offered as especially applicable in these upper grades:

1. Strive to read as widely as possible. This will involve increased speed, greater concentration, and the development of a love for reading in social studies areas.

2. After any considerable amount of reading, put all materials aside and tell yourself the basic ideas gained.

3. Strive to develop a feeling of familiarity with the authors of materials read. Know their background, present professional affiliations, and traditional points of view.

4. Attempt deliberately to read varying points of view on social, political, and economic issues.

5. Gain creativity in the field of social studies by expressing your own ideas either orally or in writing.

6. In written work observe the commonly accepted forms used in the preparation of manuscripts.

7. Attempt to make current applications of social studies materials that represent cultural background information or basic principles.

8. Be a regular reader of one or more of the outstanding weekly periodicals dealing with contemporary affairs.

9. Engage in reflective thinking, which should result in integrating the work learned in social studies with that being pursued in other courses.

10. In order to motivate study, hold fast to the feeling that social studies constitute an area of human knowledge and activity that is second to none in importance.

Summary. The definition of supervised study from Maxwell and Kilzer is the basis for the entire discussion of supervised study presented in this chapter. A discussion of the process of supervised study from the planning period through the study period gives in considerable detail the activities to be carried on by pupils and teacher. The importance of supervised study to the social studies is emphasized, and the significance of this experience in encouraging habits of critical thinking is noted. Study skills especially needed in the social studies are reviewed, and the influence of the teacher in the supervised study period is indicated. A self-evaluation chart on study habits is included as an example of a procedure which a teacher may use to help pupils analyze and improve their study practices outside the supervised study time. It appears that for present-day trends in school programs supervised study is an essential technique.

Questions on the Text

1. What advantages seem to be found in the supervised study method in contrast to home study arrangements?

2. List the values of supervised study which the authors suggest.

3. List study skills essential in the social studies.

4. Suggest some pupil difficulties in study techniques.
5. Describe in detail the process of supervising a study period.
6. Comment on the reading skills essential in the social studies.
7. How does teacher-pupil planning contribute to an effective supervised study period?
8. Why must the pupil show mastery of vocabulary in the social studies?
9. How may the reading program of the social studies be improved through supervised study?
10. Why does the social studies field seem particularly well adapted to training in habits of critical thinking?
11. How does a social studies teacher improve his supervision of a study period?
12. Suggest characteristics which might appear in a poorly directed supervised study period.

Suggested Activities

1. Visit a social studies class to observe a period of supervised study. Summarize your observation as to desirable and undesirable factors in evidence.
2. Write out in detail an assignment providing for a supervised study period.
3. Examine several texts on methods for rules for individual pupil study. Do the activities suggested appear in a supervised study period? Which method seems preferable to you? Why?
4. Set up a list of activities which you think should be present in a well-supervised study period.
5. Demonstrate in detail to the class how you would instruct a high-school class in such study skills as how to use an atlas, a dictionary, an encyclopedia, and other reference materials.
6. Observe a social studies class in the teacher-pupil planning period and the ensuing supervised study activity. Note how each pupil selects his study problem, and note the activity of the teacher with individuals, groups, or the class as a whole.
7. Observe a social studies teacher during the making of an assignment. List as definitely as you can every direction and suggestion given by the teacher. Comment on the assignment. What changes, if any, would you recommend? Why?
8. Plan a vocabulary study for an eleventh-grade class in social studies. List in detail the procedure you would follow.

9. Devise a plan for encouraging pupils to read materials related to a course but not assigned as a part of the study materials.

10. List articles, stories, or books you might use for a retarded reader in a high-school social studies class.

Selected References

Anderson, Howard H., *Teaching Critical Thinking in the Social Studies*, Washington, D.C.: The National Council for the Social Studies, *Thirteenth Yearbook*, 1942.

Badger, W. V., "Suggestions for Supervising the Reading Program in the Social Studies," *Social Studies*, XL (March, 1949), pp. 126–128.

Bond, Guy L., and Eva Bond, *Developmental Reading in High School*, New York: The Macmillan Company, 1941.

Kelly, William A., "How-to-study Problem," *Journal of Education*, CXXVII (March, 1944), pp. 85–86.

Kilzer, Louis R., *Supervised Study*, New York: Professional and Technical Press, 1931.

———, "Some Devices for Checking the Supervision of Study," *American School Board Journal*, XCI (August, 1935), p. 25.

Long, Forrest E., and Helen Halter, *Social-studies Skills*, New York: Inor Publishing Company, Inc., 1942.

Maxwell, C. R., and L. R. Kilzer, *High School Administration*, New York: Doubleday & Company, Inc., 1936.

Quillen, I. James, and Lavone A. Hanna, *Education for Social Competence*, Chicago: Scott, Foresman & Company, 1948.

Traxler, Arthur E., "The Improvement of Study," *School Review*, LIII (May, 1945), pp. 286–293.

Wesley, E. B., *Teaching Social Studies in High Schools*, Boston: D. C. Heath and Company, 1950.

Chapter 14

MEASUREMENT AND EVALUATION

Preview. There are many angles to the problem of measuring results in social studies teaching. The one most commonly thought about has to do with testing. General comments are offered on this subject. Two types of test, the objective and the essay, are presented in some detail. Interpretation of scores is mentioned briefly. The possible uses of standardized tests and sources from which they may be secured are described. The fuller implications of detailed evaluation of the teaching procedures are given. The chapter presentation ends with a discussion of the marking system as applied to the social studies.

General Comments on Testing. One of the most important topics in the realm of social studies teaching is a good testing program. The phase of it that is in many ways most important relates to the tests that the classroom teacher constructs. These range in length from those that the pupils take covering a single day's work to those regarded as finals and dealing with a year's work. They may be objective, essay-type, or a combination of the two.

Regardless of the length and type of tests used the social studies teacher should keep constantly in mind the purposes for giving them. Some of these are identical with those in other secondary-school areas. It is generally felt that testing has a tendency to stimulate pupils to more effective study. During the development of a unit they tend to isolate and learn information on which they feel that they are likely to be tested. Preparation for a test gives opportunity for organization, systematization, and effective review. Next, there are some courses where the assigning of marks might be quite difficult if tests were not used. Tradition has brought about the acceptability of this method. This obtains especially in the case of very large classes. Furthermore, our pupils live in a society where tests are used in the determination of many points relative to an individual. If he joins the armed services, if he wishes to secure a civil-service position or to enter some divisions of industry, he may be obliged to take tests. Should he pursue higher education it is reasonably certain that even his work in the social sciences will be subjected to testing. Finally, in respect to general objectives for testing it must not be overlooked that the results tend to indicate the success or failure of the teaching methods employed. If a test measures up to the criteria of a good one and the results are generally low, a critical appraisal should follow. Needless to say, reteaching should be done before new content is approached. A few words should be said about possible values to be achieved from testing in social studies classes that are not quite as pronounced in other areas. Honesty, fairness, and the exertion of one's best efforts are traits of social behavior. They play a very important role at testing time. The social studies teacher should feel keenly the responsibility for proper stress and development of these traits.

The question of the frequenecy of tests is one that has a proper place. Some teachers find it helpful to administer the short daily quiz. It may consist of one-word answers to a very few questions or a short paragraph written in response to one general question. Usually pupils tire of these if used over a relatively long period. However, the teacher can use them for purposes of making daily preparation uniform and general. They should not be allowed to consume a very large proportion of the period. Small slips of paper should be prepared in advance, passed out quickly, and collected without delay by being passed forward upon completion. Some teachers feel that tests should be given periodically, for instance weekly, monthly, or on the last day of a grading period. This has the advantage of serving a useful purpose in determining marks. It has the disadvantage of not coinciding with times when units of work are being completed, unless as a matter of chance. A systematic scheduling of a semester or final examination probably has more value for the college-preparatory group than for any other.

The Objective Test. The objective test has come into extensive use in the social studies. In general it is identified as one which yields the same score when marked by different individuals; in other words, the opinions or desires of the person grading it do not have an effect upon the results. Many advantages have been claimed for it other than uniformity of scoring. One is that it can be scored quickly. Simply by placing a key beside the answers given and checking items marked incorrectly or omitted, it is possible to score a paper in negligible time. Another is that it is possible to cover very comprehensively all the work that a class has studied, thus being very sure of the extent to which learning has taken place. Finally, it is usually observed that pupils enjoy taking well-constructed objective tests. Many of the fears and dreads that accompany other types disappear. Probably much of the enjoyment is related to the fact that newspapers and radio programs use similar quiz techniques.

The nature of the questions to use on objective tests has to be considered at the outset. The true-false type is subject to much discussion. Many teachers do not use it because the pupil may give correct answers by shrewd guessing. Some teachers try to offset this feature by warning the pupils not to attempt the question unless they are sure of the answer and stating that two points will be deducted for each incorrect response whereas only one point will be deducted for an omitted answer. If the true-false question is used it should be stated in a straightforward manner with no intent to take advantage of the pupil. There should be no effort on the part of the teacher to inject humor into the statements by making them ludicrously false. The following are examples submitted as meeting the requirements of the principles just stated:

Some of the following statements are true and some are false. Place a plus (+) in front of the number of each one that is true and a zero (0) in front of the number of each one that is false.

________ 1. William I was king of Prussia in 1860.
________ 2. Bismarck reasoned that he would have to wage only one war in order to unify Germany around Prussia.
________ 3. Schleswig and Holstein were two provinces that finally became part of Poland.
________ 4. Von Moltke may be said to be the first general to use scientific methods of warfare.
________ 5. The peace of Frankfurt closed the Austro-Prussian War.
________ 6. The upper house in the legislature of the North German Confederation was the Reichstag.

One of the variations of the true-false item as regularly used is to ask pupils to indicate the changes in the item marked false that would be necessary to make them true. The following examples are given to illustrate this procedure:

DIRECTIONS: The following statements are to be read carefully to determine which are true and which are false. Place a plus (+) in front of those which are true and a zero (0) in front of those that are false. For those that you mark false, draw a line through the incorrect part of the statement and place below the 0 the word, date, place, etc., that would be needed to make the statement true.

__+__ 1. Louis XVI and Marie Antoinette were rulers of France at the outbreak of the French Revolution.

__0__ 2. The French Revolution began ~~before~~ the American Revolution.
__after__

__0__ 3. The largest group of French people in 1789 belonged to the ~~First~~ Estate.
__Third__

__+__ 4. Voltaire was a philosopher and writer.

Multiple-choice questions are used extensively. This type ordinarily consists of a statement that is completed correctly by the use of one of the answers given. A few general rules should be observed. There should probably be four or more optional answers. Otherwise the question becomes true-false in nature. The options should be of the same general classification. For instance, characters, places, dates, etc., should be used exclusively and not mixed in the same item. No option should be so obviously incorrect as to be absurd. The following examples are offered to illustrate this type of item:

DIRECTIONS: On the line at the left of each item write the number of the word or group of words that correctly completes the statement.

__1__ 1. Rainfall for any period of time is recorded by our government in (1) inches (2) feet (3) gallons (4) barrels.

__1__ 2. Most of the world's wood is consumed as (1) fuel (2) building material (3) paper (4) furniture.

__1__ 3. The leading coffee-producing country is (1) Brazil (2) Mexico (3) Java (4) El Salvador.

Many teachers develop variations in the use of the multiple-choice item. For instance, they sometimes make all the answers correct except one; it then becomes the pupil's obligation to find the one that is incorrect and identify it. The following are examples of this type of item:

DIRECTIONS: In the following all except one choice is correct. You are to decide which one is incorrect and place its number on the blank provided at the left.

__3__ 1. The following made notable contributions to science: (1) Westinghouse (2) Curie (3) Tolstoy (4) Pasteur.

__2__ 2. Among the states that seceded from the Union at the time of the War Between the States were (1) Georgia (2) West Virginia (3) South Carolina (4) Tennessee.

Still another variation of the multiple-choice item is to include a statement in the directions that if none of the items is correct the answer is to be marked 0. The following examples illustrate this type:

DIRECTIONS: In the following multiple-choice items some do not have a correct answer given. For those particular items place a 0 in the blank spaces at the left. If the correct answer is given place its number on the blank space provided.

__4__ 1. Carthage as an early Phoenician colony was located in (1) Spain (2) Gaul (3) Sicily (4) Northern Africa.

__0__ 2. Piraeus was the harbor used by ancient (1) Troy (2) Rome (3) Memphis (4) Cadiz.

A final variation of the multiple-choice item to be mentioned is similar to the one just described except that all items carry a blank space at the end of the options in which the pupils are asked to write the correct answer should none of those given be correct. The following are examples of this character:

DIRECTIONS: This section deals with definitions of important characters. Some of the problems have the correct answers included while others do not. If the correct answer is included place an X in front of it. If the correct answer has not been included write it on the line below the problem.

Aristotle
__X__ Greek philosopher
_____ Persian military leader
_____ Spartan lawgiver

Phidias
_____ Assyrian military leader
_____ Greek philosopher
_____ Roman emperor
Greek sculptor

The matching type of item is quite generally used. In it a list of words, phrases, or statements from one column are to be paired correctly with those in a second column. Some general principles should be observed in the construction and use of this type of test. First, it should not involve too long a list of items to be matched, otherwise there is a considerable loss of time involved. Second, the items in each group should be of the same general classification, such as characters, vocabulary, places, etc. Third, there should be slightly more items in the column containing the answers than there are in the column containing the test. The following examples are given for this type of test:

DIRECTIONS: Do this section as a matching test. Each part is complete within itself. Do Part A, then Part B.

Part A

________	1. Hebrews	1. Have been called the missionaries of civilization
________	2. Babylonians	2. Popularized the idea of one God
________	3. Egyptians	3. Probably invented coinage
________	4. Prehistoric men	4. Achieved most in the fields of law and government
________	5. Lydians	5. Increased the wealth of Italian cities and introduced Oriental goods into western Europe
________	6. Romans	6. Practiced cuneiform writing
________	7. Greeks	7. Started the Reformation in western Europe in sixteenth century
________	8. Hittites	8. First to light fires, use language, and domesticate plants and animals
________	9. Phoenicians	9. Studied geometry, invented a calendar, and embalmed
________	10. Crusaders	10. Introduced the use of iron
		11. Stressed the beautiful in life and laid the foundations of art and literature

Part B

________	11. Junkers	1. Native soldiers of India
________	12. Kaaba	2. Old Stone Age
________	13. Nihilists	3. Famous prison
________	14. Quadrivium	4. Special sealed letter
________	15. Sepoys	5. Emperor of Japan
________	16. Mikado	6. Russian organization

________ 17. Council of Nicaea	7. Wealthy German landholders
________ 18. Paleolithic	8. Rebirth of learning
________ 19. Vulgate	9. Latin translation of the Bible
________ 20. Bastille	10. Stated the beliefs of the early Christian Church
	11. Group of subjects taught in early universities
	12. Building sacred to Mohammedans

A slight variation of the regular matching test is found in the multiple-matching procedure. The pupil is asked to find a series of answers about an item. The following examples illustrate this type:

DIRECTIONS: You will find below a list of ten historical characters. From GROUP A select the century in which each was most active in his field. From GROUP B select the country of origin of each. From GROUP C select the field of activity in which each character made his greatest contribution. You may use any part of the three groups as many times as you need to. BE SURE to try every problem.

BISMARCK
________ 51. Period
________ 52. Nationality
________ 53. Contribution

CAVOUR
________ 54. Period
________ 55. Nationality
________ 56. Contribution

DAVID LIVINGSTON
________ 57. Period
________ 58. Nationality
________ 59. Contribution

WILLIAM E. GLADSTONE
________ 60. Period
________ 61. Nationality
________ 62. Contribution

METTERNICH
________ 63. Period
________ 64. Nationality
________ 65. Contribution

GROUP A
1. Eighteenth century
2. Nineteenth century
3. Twentieth century

GROUP B
1. Belgium
2. Austria
3. France
4. England
5. United States
6. Russia
7. Spain
8. Germany
9. Italy
10. Scotland

GROUP C
1. Science
2. Military affairs
3. Government
4. Writing
5. Religion

Still other types of matching items that do not depart far from the above are related to map exercises and photos. A map is presented as part of the test which has a series of numbers scattered about on it. Questions having answers related to locations are asked and are answered by the matching procedure. Pictures are often used in the same manner for identification of contemporary characters.

The completion type of question is regarded as excellent in that the pupil must know the exact answer; generally it permits no guessing. It should be so phrased that only one answer can be regarded as correct. Since it is usually the part of the test upon which the lowest scores are made, it should probably be placed at the end, otherwise the pupil becomes discouraged at the outset. For ease of marking, the spaces for answers should be placed at the left of the questions as with true-false, multiple-choice, and matching tests. The following are examples of completion or short-answer questions:

DIRECTIONS: On the line at the left write the word or phrase which best completes the statement.

Example:

Germany 0. Bismarck led in the unification of his native country, _____.

_______ 1. The Federal body which determines the constitutionality of laws passed by Congress is the _____.

_______ 2. European attempts to colonize in the Western Hemisphere caused the United States to formulate the policy called the _____.

_______ 3. The Illinois statesman with whom Abraham Lincoln engaged in a series of debates dealing with slavery was _____.

_______ 4. Voters are given an opportunity to nominate candidates by means of the _____.

_______ 5. The United States purchased Alaska from _____.

_______ 6. The issue involved in the Compromise of 1850 was _____.

_______ 7. The document drawn up by the Pilgrims to pledge allegiance to future laws passed for the general good of the colony was the _____.

_______ 8. Representation for the states in the House of Representatives is apportioned according to the _____.

_______ 9. The Vice-President of the United States is the presiding officer of the _____.

_______ 10. The revolt of the Chinese in 1900 against foreign intervention was called the _____.

_______ 11. The first ten amendments to the U.S. Constitution are called the _____.

_______ 12. The country in which the Fascist party was formed in 1919 is _____.

_______ 13. The country in which the seat of the League of Nations was located is _____.

_______ 14. A colonial court established the right of the press to criticize the acts of public officials in the trial of _____.

_______ 15. A conflict of opinion exists among sociologists as to which is the chief cause of crime, environment or _____.

Frequently teachers feel that memorizing dates in history is not good procedure but that pupils should have a feeling of sequence of events. A frequently used technique of testing in this instance is to list a series of events out of correct sequence and ask the pupils to rearrange them correctly. It would be possible to do such an exercise correctly and not know accurately the date of an individual event, although this would not be likely to occur. Best procedure dictates that the events listed pertain to a given topic and that the number in a group be relatively small, the latter point being governed partly by the age of the pupils. The following examples are given:

DIRECTIONS: The following is a test on time order or sequence of events. In each case select the event that happened most recently and place the number of that event in the blank space. The example is correct. Be sure to try every problem.

Example:

___2___ 0. (1) Treaty of Ryswick (2) Treaty of Utrecht (3) Treaty of Aix-la-Chapelle

_______ 1. (1) Declaration of Independence (2) Magna Carta (3) Bill of Rights

_______ 2. (1) Birth of Christ (2) Council of Claremont (3) Flight of Mohammed

_______ 3. (1) Battle of Tours (2) Battle of Châlons (3) Battle of Marathon

_______ 4. (1) Charlemagne crowned emperor (2) Golden Age of Athens under Pericles (3) Caesar took full charge of Rome

_______ 5. (1) Elaborate irrigation system perfected by the Egyptians (2) Invention of gunpowder (3) Copernicus's theory of the solar system made known

In some classes teachers become concerned about the reading comprehension of pupils. In the absence of a comprehensive-reading-testing program in a school, the plan can be followed of giving a paragraph with the instructions that it be read carefully and that questions pertaining to it be answered. The following single example illustrates the technique:

DIRECTIONS: Read the following paragraph carefully. After finishing it write the answers to the questions in the blank spaces provided. (You may reread the paragraph as many times as you desire.)

The French Revolution is a very interesting period not only for the people of the one nation but for all liberty-loving people of the world. One thing that caused it is that there were three social classes instead of one as there is in America today. These groups were clergy, nobility, and Third Estate. While the first made up only a small per cent of the population they enjoyed the largest number of privileges. Among these were special hunting rights, exemption from many taxes, favors at the king's palace, and special consideration in the courts. Other facts that brought on this revolution in 1789 are the work and writings of French philosophers, the influence of the American Revolution, and a condition of national bankruptcy.

________ 1. What kind of people are interested in the events of the French Revolution?
________ 2. How many social classes were there in France?
________ 3. To which class did most Frenchmen belong?
________ 4. Did the Third Estate enjoy special hunting rights?
________ 5. Did the French Revolution occur before or after the American Revolution?

A similar plan can readily be used if it is desired to see how well pupils can use the dictionary, encyclopedia, atlases, world almanac, etc. Possibly easier adaptations can be made to ascertain ability to interpret tables of figures, graphs, and maps.

An essential type of objective testing, slightly different from any of those described above, is called by Anderson, Forsyth, and Morse [1] *measurement of understanding*. Among the phases that are described for this type of testing are understanding of special vocabulary, chronological relationships, maps, graphs and tables, etc. Naturally many phases of this division of testing involve the presentation in text form of information or data. The pupil is permitted to read the text as many times as he desires and is then asked to answer specific questions or indicate conclusions.

[1] Howard R. Anderson, Elaine Forsyth, and Horace T. Morse, "The Measurement of Understanding in the Social Studies," Chicago: National Society for the Study of Education, *Forty-fifth Yearbook*, 1946, Part I, Chap. V.

No doubt a resourceful teacher can think of other types of objective-test items in social studies teaching. One of his ambitions should be to learn about the finer points of test construction and the interpretation of results. Such skill often leads to useful experimentation and contributes to improved methods of teaching.

It is quite important to measure progress in the development of study skills in social studies. Progressive achievement is impossible unless the attack becomes both more vigorous and more efficient. The techniques of construction of such tests are far different from those used in dealing with subject matter. Morse and McCune [2] discuss ten points to observe in this connection, among them that attention should be paid to formulating directions for making responses to the various sections and that testing should be for possession of a skill rather than for the retention of factual knowledge.

Essay Type of Testing. Some teachers do not sympathize with the use of the tests described and prefer to use the essay type. Some of the advantages that they feel to be associated with it are as follows:

1. The time needed for constructing is much less than that needed for the preparation of a good objective test. In extreme instances only a few minutes have been consumed in making fairly acceptable tests of this type.
2. Pupils have an opportunity to develop and use powers of self-expression. They learn not only to recall facts but also to exercise creative thinking.
3. Organizing ability is brought into play. Information is presented in a proper sequential order for the sake of being convincing.
4. Social studies are correlated well with English. Ability to spell correctly and to express ideas in acceptable grammatical style is placed at a premium.

The following essay test is given as an example of one that might be used following the completion of a unit in early American history:

1. Write a paragraph that explains why England did better than her rivals in colonization. (5 points.)
2. Make an *outline* in which you include the following points about five of the thirteen colonies: name, motive for settlement, important leaders, and interesting facts. (15 points.)
3. List five general reasons for the American Revolution. (5 points.)

[2] Horace T. Morse and George H. McCune, "Testing Study Skills: A Few Considerations," *Social Studies,* XXXIV (February, 1943), pp. 67–69.

4. Give the main provisions of the Treaty of Paris (1763); do the same for the Treaty of Paris (1783). (8 points.)

5. Write *one* identification sentence for each of the following: da Gama, Sir John Hawkins, Spanish Armada, joint-stock company, Tudors, Puritan Revolution, Piedmont, Zenger, mercantilism, Andros, Ohio Company, Pontiac, Proclamation of 1763, Greenville, Declaratory Act, *Common Sense,* Burgoyne, John Jay, and Vergennes. (15 points.)

Only two suggestions dealing with scoring and reading this type of test will be offered. The first is that the questions should be weighted with respect to relative importance; the pupils should have this information when taking the test. (See example above.) The second is that the papers should be arranged in a manner that makes it possible to read all the responses of the pupils to question one before any responses to question two are read, etc. Probably no recording of points should be made until several papers have been read in order that the reader can sense the general quality of the responses of the class as a whole. On the other hand, some teachers follow the practice of having in their own minds a model of the answers expected and marking responses according to the degree of conformity found.

A final word might aptly be offered as to whether a teacher of social studies should use objective or essay tests. Possibly the best answer is that neither should be used to the complete exclusion of the other. In the entire field of education it appears that the former type have the wider usage. If it should be concluded that the absolute advantages favor it, pupils should nevertheless not be denied completely the advantages of the latter. A test on a social studies unit could well contain a generous number of items objective in nature and for its conclusion have at least one well-phrased essay question.

One of the most important points related to testing in the social studies has to do with the use made of the results. If an objective test has been administered, an item analysis should be made. In brief, this means that a check should be made to determine the percentage of correct responses for each item used. The teacher should start with a sheet of paper on which the numbers representing the items are placed vertically at the left side. For each incorrect response found in going through all the papers a check mark should be made. When this has been completed it becomes readily apparent which items were easiest and which were most difficult. For instance, let us assume that there were twenty-five in the class, that item 6 had one check mark, and that item 12 had twenty check marks. It becomes obvious that the former was an easy question and the latter very difficult. Reteaching of the latter item as well as all others of similar difficulty should follow.

Of the many technical terms related to interpretation of test results, it is recommended that the social studies teacher know at least the following: *median, quartile, range,* and *standard deviation.* Most of these can be explained in an elementary fashion to an upper-grade class group; this in turn will help them to understand better their own scores. Furthermore, it is imperative that teachers know well a minimum list of such terms in order to read intelligently the results of research.

Standardized Tests. As in other subjects it is possible for the social-studies teacher to use standardized tests. These have the advantage of having been used rather widely and having a set of established norms. They are available in the specific subjects and in many supplementary areas.

Among the companies that publish these on a large scale are

California Test Bureau
516 Hollywood Blvd.
Los Angeles 28.

Cooperative Achievement Tests
15 Amsterdam Ave.
New York 23.

Educational Testing Service
2207 Shattuck Ave.
Berkeley 4, Calif.

Public School Publishing Company
509–13 North East Street
Bloomington, Ill.

World Book Company
2126 Prairie Ave.
Chicago.

General catalogues are ordinarily available upon request. The social studies section can be consulted in each instance.

A list of tests that are typical of those found in such catalogues, together with grade for which each is recommended and published, follows:

American History—Government—Problems of Democracy: Acorn Achievement Tests. Grades 9 to 16. Acorn Publishing Company.

Cooperative American History Test. Grades 9 to 16. Cooperative Test Service.

Cooperative Community Affairs Test. Grades 9 to 12. Cooperative Test Service.

Cooperative Economics Test. Grades 9 to 16. Cooperative Test Service.

Cooperative Modern European History Test. Grades 9 to 16. Cooperative Test Service.

Cooperative Social Studies Test. Grades 7, 8, and 9. Cooperative Test Service.

Cooperative Test in American Government. Grades 9 to 12. Cooperative Test Service.

Cooperative World History Test. Grades 9 to 12. Cooperative Test Service.

Examination in Civics. Grades 9 to 12. American Council on Education.

Examination in Modern European History. Grades 9 to 16. American Council on Education.

Examination in Problems in Democracy. Grades 11 and 12. American Council on Education.

Geography Test: National Achievement Tests. Grades 6 to 8. Acorn Publishing Company.

Illinois Teachers College Cooperative Social Science Test, 1942 Edition. Grades 10 to 13. McKnight and McKnight.

Kansas American History Test. Grades 9 to 12. Bureau of Educational Measurements, Kansas State Teacher's College, Emporia.

Kansas Modern European History Test. Grades 9 to 12. Bureau of Educational Measurements, Kansas State Teacher's College, Emporia.

Kniss World History Test. Grades 9 to 12. World Book Company.

Mordy-Schrammel Constitution Test. Grades 9 to 16. Bureau of Educational Measurements, Kansas State Teacher's College, Emporia.

Mordy-Schrammel Elementary Civics Test. Grades 7 to 9. Bureau of Educational Measurements, Kansas State Teacher's College, Emporia.

Stanford Achievement Test: Social Studies Test. Grades 4 to 9. World Book Company.

Social Studies Test: National Achievement Test. Grades 7 to 9. Acorn Publishing Company.

Survey Test in United States History. Grades 9 to 12. Turner E. Smith Company.

Tate Economic Geography Test. Grades 9 to 16. Bureau of Educational Measurements, Kansas State Teacher's College, Emporia.

Test of General Proficiency in the Field of Social Studies. Grades 10 to 12. Cooperative Test Service.

There is no certainty that exactly what teachers desire in tests will always be found in those that have been standardized. For instance,

Park examined fourteen such tests in American history and compared the content with the list of dates and persons recommended for various grade levels in the Wesley report, the purpose of which was to set forth "irreducible content." The findings showed that the tests did not emphasize to a very large extent the recommended items! [3]

Evaluation of Social Studies Teaching. After a teaching job has been done it becomes very important to evaluate the results. One should be concerned about such points as whether the maximum good was accomplished, what types of improvement could be introduced on a future occasion, and the extent to which the pupils enjoyed the work.

Possibly the easiest aspect to determine is the amount of learning that took place. In unit teaching the results of pretesting can be compared with the scores on the test at the close of the instruction period. If an entire year is considered, the scores made on form *A* of a test can be compared with those made on form *B*. Assuming that the tests used are valid and reliable, the results are indeed helpful.

When two different groups of pupils have been taught the same social studies content by the same teacher, a comparison of results can be made. Should one group surpass the other noticeably a study of causes should be made. Certainly if the groups represent comparable ability, the methods used should be examined carefully. Sometimes it is possible for social studies teachers of different schools to compare results obtained. This can be done beneficially on a semi-scientific basis or even informally.

Some teachers have an intuitive knack of knowing whether teaching accomplished its objectives. This is certainly based on subjective observations. It is not uncommon to find teachers who record reactions of this nature daily in diary form.

A valuable procedure is to ask pupils to express their feelings freely after a unit of work is completed. If they are told frankly that the purpose is to gain information that will help in their study of subsequent work, they will usually talk sincerely. Such questions as "What activity that we engaged in did you like best?" "Which reading reference appealed most to you?" and "What would you prefer to have studied that we omitted?" will usually arouse helpful discussion.

[3] Joe Park, "An Analysis of Standardized American History Tests," *Social Studies*, XXXV (October, 1944), pp. 267–269.

The essential point is that the pupils share the spirit of the investigation.

Much can be gained by critically examining the written work that pupils prepare. If themes, imaginary speeches, and other written projects are handed in, the type of phrasing used is very revealing of results obtained. It is possible to observe readily whether reactions are those that accompany genuine learning or partial mastery. Likewise, it is equally easy to detect the character of the attitudes that pupils develop. This applies to group relationships, society, and the subject in question. Examination of notebook work will reveal similar information.

Many units in social studies are of such nature that noticeable changes should take place in social behavior. If this manifests itself in good sportsmanship, courtesy, cooperation, effective leadership, and other similar ways, it can be judged that teaching success has been attained. These results can be looked for in the hallways, during assemblies, at games, in the theater, on the streets, and in other diverse places. This may seem to imply that social studies classes are in this manner attempting to fill the functions of home, church, and school, but such is not the case. It takes the combined efforts of all groups to produce the desired development of character.

If the teaching has been concerned with presenting a skill, it is possible to observe and judge whether improvement has been made. Detection of propaganda, selection of the best columnists and commentators, and participation in civic affairs are examples. The teacher will hope and reasonably expect that appropriate and observable growth will take place in these areas.

At the conclusion of a year's teaching it is almost mandatory that the teacher not only find out the gains in factual information but that he also find out class reaction to procedures used. Favorable comments almost invariably mean that learning was effective. Again, it is important that the class sense correctly the reasons for making the inquiry; also, it is essential that they be assured that frank comments will not be related to the grade to be recorded for them personally. The information suggested can readily be ascertained through the use of a check sheet. The entire range of the year's activities should be included. The making of the sheet should be made as objective as possible. The following check list is offered as one that might be used with some degree of success:

Do not sign your name.

The object of this sheet is to find out how you really feel about the various things that we did during the past year in our social studies class. Your carefully considered answers will make it possible to improve the manner of conducting our work in future classes. In front of each type of activity suggested place a 1, 2, 3, 4, or 5. 1 means that you thoroughly enjoyed that phase of the work; 5 means that you very much disliked it. The other numbers show like or dislike ranging between these two extremes. (Your answers will have *no* effect upon the grade that you have earned in this course.)

________ 1. Reading the basic textbook.
________ 2. Reading other textbooks.
________ 3. Reading magazines, current-events papers, pamphlets, etc.
________ 4. Reading encyclopedias and source books.
________ 5. Preparing special reports to present orally.
________ 6. Preparing materials to present as part of forum discussion.
________ 7. Taking part in class discussion of current events.
________ 8. Taking part in class discussion on regular units of work.
________ 9. Presenting an oral report.
________ 10. Taking part in a forum discussion.
________ 11. Listening to the teacher lecture (presenting overviews, supplementary information, and summaries.)
________ 12. Listening to other pupils present reports.
________ 13. Listening to other pupils take part in forum discussions.
________ 14. Taking essay tests.
________ 15. Taking objective tests.
________ 16. Taking part in drills after units of work had been studied.
________ 17. Working out projects of your own selection and presenting them to the class.
________ 18. Setting up questions to find answers to or creating problems and attempting to solve them.
________ 19. Making maps.
________ 20. Turning the class into a socialized recitation period.
________ 21. Acting as leader of a socialized recitation period.
________ 22. Acting as secretary of a socialized recitation period.
________ 23. Preparing notebooks.
________ 24. Doing exercises in the workbook.
________ 25. Having a personal interview with an adult to gain information for the class.
________ 26. Going with the class on a field trip.
________ 27. Learning about how an election is actually conducted by having one at school.

________ 28. Listening to a speaker who has been invited to talk to the class.

Other activities that you recall which are not mentioned above:

________ 29.

________ 30.

________ 31.

________ 32.

Some feel that work representing an individualized type of instruction makes evaluation procedures all the more imperative. In an effort to have something functional in this connection, Simpson [4] published a series of twenty-five questions to which pupils could write answers as their study in history progressed. Among them are "Am I improving in my ability to pick out problems of importance for me to study? Evidence?" "Am I progressing in the matter of my contributions to class discussion? Evidence?" and "Am I learning to check up on what I have done so that I may improve in my future work? Evidence?"

One of the best criteria of evaluation of the results of teaching social studies would come through an examination of the types of adult citizens the pupils become. This procedure has the shortcoming of not being subject to observation and use relatively quickly. However, many excellent social studies teachers maintain a given position long enough to make significant observations and to alter procedures in accordance with them. One of the first points of interest for such scrutiny would deal with how generally and wholeheartedly the group accepted civic responsibilities. If they tended to be well-informed on current affairs, voted regularly at elections, and occupied public office willingly and efficiently, it would seem that they had benefited from their schooling. No doubt such citizens would frequently serve on community committees to help further worthy projects. They would be staunch supporters of the institutions that are basic to the maintenance of the social order. Their attitudes toward home, school, church, and law-enforcing institutions would be sound in every way. They would meet the most rigid tests of social and economic efficiency; that is, they would be making their own way, not hindering others in their progress, and would be actually contributing to the welfare of their fellow men. In many instances this type of effi-

[4] Ray H. Simpson, "Use of a Self-evaluative Test in Individualized History Study," *Social Studies*, XXXV (December, 1944), pp. 363–370.

ciency would entail real sacrifices. Finally, the test of ability in self-entertainment would be applied. The question of whether or not they could find personal adjustment leading to happiness in their social setting would be important. If they could be judged favorably on this point it would seem that their previous training in social studies areas had helped develop a sound philosophy of personal living.

With due respect to all that has been said above, it must be borne in mind that evaluation is difficult. Williams has expressed this as follows: "Thus the teacher who wants to evaluate his students' progress in abilities is left to his own devices. If he works out the problem of objectives and turns to the problem of techniques of measurement, he faces great difficulties if he does not deal with small classes." (See selected references at end of chapter.)

Determining the Grading System. Social studies teachers are no exception in viewing with displeasure the duty of assigning marks to pupils. They have generally felt that grades tend to place a premium on the grades themselves rather than on attaining objectives set for the social studies. There are many possibilities of remedying this situation.

Pupils in social studies classes can have it called to their attention repeatedly that the classroom is a laboratory in the development of democratic living and that growth in this realm should merit a good grade and failure to make such improvement should be cause for a low mark—assuming that marks must be assigned.

It would probably better serve the needs of the social studies teacher to have a progress-report blank to send to parents showing accomplishments dealing with many phases of growth and development. The list decided upon could be placed in a column at the left of the report. To the right of each item would be placed a scale on which a check at the extreme left would mean need for a great amount of improvement while a check at the extreme right would mean unusual proficiency. It would take some time to work out such a scheme to the satisfaction of the department in a particular school. After it was perfected it would not take long to fill in.

The following list is offered as representative of items that might be selected: cooperation, tolerance, leadership, willingness to offer constructive suggestions, use of work periods, attitude toward members of the group, attitude of the group toward the pupil, loyalty, initiative, citizenship, creative ability, and mastery of fundamental facts.

After checking each of the above the teacher could, if required by the school to do so, place a composite letter grade such as A, B, C, D, and F or a per cent grade, etc. The implication is that the highest ideals and best practices of modern progressive social studies teachers show a movement away from emphasis on the composite mark.

The report carrying the traits suggested above should give definitions of each in order that pupil and parent may understand the terminology of the teacher. Those presented herewith are typical of such presentation:

1. *Cooperation.* Willingness to work with the group in the manner in which most individuals desire to proceed.

2. *Tolerance.* Acceptance of the idea that every person is entitled to his own honest and sincere opinions; also, the absence of prejudice against groups, beliefs, and opinions.

3. *Leadership.* Demonstration of skill in directing the time and energy of classmates in activities related to the work of the group.

4. *Willingness to offer constructive suggestions.* The opposite of finding fault and failing to offer ideas for improvement. Continuous criticism that results in a better class program.

5. *Use of work periods.* Efficient management of time schedule; getting much accomplished during work periods set aside as part of units of study.

6. *Attitude toward members of the group.* Proceeding on the basis that one person is entitled to as much consideration as any other; that all are equal in the classroom just as all come from their Creator as equals.

7. *Attitude of group toward pupil.* Manner in which classmates feel toward and work with the pupil.

8. *Loyalty.* Inner feeling of devotion to the work of the group, to the school, and to democracy in our society.

9. *Initiative.* Ability to think out plans for good work activities and to execute them.

10. *Citizenship.* Often called *conduct;* the ability to regulate one's own habits, not to hinder others in their efforts to progress, and to frequently show evidence of helpfulness both to individuals and to the group.

11. *Creative ability.* Doing work that is original; the opposite of only memorizing factual information.

12. *Mastery of fundamental facts.* Gaining basic information that will help in understanding the particular social study being studied—information that gives evidence of a grasp of the field.

One general treatment of this subject [5] indicates that as many as seventy-five different elements have been reported by school administrators and teachers in this connection. It becomes necessary for the social studies teacher to decide which are pertinent and which do not overlap.

Some of the advantages claimed for the procedures described above are

1. Grading as an end in itself is largely eliminated.
2. Emphasis is placed upon traits that are associated with good citizenship in a democracy.
3. A detailed analysis is afforded the pupil as a basis for improvement.
4. Reporting of progress is thus done in terms of the objectives of the social studies.
5. Fewer criticisms and questions come from parents and pupils than when a traditional report card is used.

A still different type of reporting on social studies classroom work is one that has more general usage in elementary grades—the anecdotal-letter method. This system is advantageous in that it is very specific in terms of the pupil about whom it is written. The typical parent expects the teacher to know a great deal about his child, as the teacher must if a good letter is to be written. The one disadvantage is the time involved. If a teacher has from 100 to 200 different pupils, it becomes almost impossible to write that many different letters if they are to be sent out as often as grade cards are usually distributed. Possibly the letter could be substituted for the report card one or more times during the year. The following is an example, offered by a student recently in a methods class, of such a letter:

Dear Mr. and Mrs. Smith:

The object of this letter is to report briefly to you the nature and quality of work done by your son John in Social Studies 9, during the past six weeks. On the whole it has been very good. John has mastered well the textbook and pamphlet materials assigned. He brought to class some mimeographed bulletins that he secured from the Chamber of Commerce that proved helpful to the entire class. He cooperates well with his classmates when committee work is assigned. Mastery of facts and gathering of data seem to be easier for him than summarizing and drawing conclu-

[5] J. B. Edmonson, Joseph Roemer, and Francis L. Bacon, *The Administration of the Modern Secondary School,* New York: The Macmillan Company, 1948, p. 461.

sions. Probably these points will prove easier as John advances in age. His spelling and use of grammar show much need of improvement. I talked with Miss Jones, his teacher of English, about this. We are going to work cooperatively on this point.

Please feel free to get in touch with me if there are questions or suggestions that you wish to offer.

Cordially yours,
Herbert Johnson

Summary. In this chapter the problems of testing, evaluating, and grading have been discussed. Some of the most important reasons for testing include a desire to find out whether the teaching has been effective, to determine relative ranks of pupils for purposes of grading, and to afford the social values that are to be found in such programs. The objective test was described as one in which the personal reactions of the one checking it have little or no influence on the score accorded. Several types of questions or items are popular in this connection. Among them are true-false, multiple-choice, matching, time-sequence, short-answer, and reading-skill questions and numerous variations of each.

The essay examination was presented, and it was pointed out that it has virtues and that many of the shortcomings charged against it can be overcome. A clear statement of questions is essential. Weighting the values of answers is helpful. Reading all the responses written to a particular question by the entire class rather than reading individual papers in entirety is recommended. A combination of a limited amount of essay testing with the regular objective test has possibilities worthy of consideration.

Evaluation is a broad term as applied to social studies teaching. It includes the testing program and much more. Some of the questions that are important are as follows: Did the manner of presentation accomplish the objectives better than any other plan that might have been used? Did the pupils develop attitudes that improved social thinking and social behavior? Did the group enjoy the study of the work at hand? It is only through evaluation that the teacher can be reasonably sure of what has been accomplished and of improvement upon subsequent occasions. Check sheets, pupil testimonials, careful estimates of written work by the class, and subjective opinions are all helpful in evaluative procedures.

Grading is a problem that has perplexed teachers during the preceding generations. Tradition has favored a mark based upon per cent, letter marks starting with A and extending through F, or a similar plan. Many efforts have been made to bring about improvement. In the social studies area it seems especially desirable to give marks on social traits as well as on mastery of content in the individual subject. A procedure that is meeting with increasing acceptance with the lay public is that of writing anecdotal letters. An example was included. At present the matter of time consumed in their production generally precludes their extensive use.

Questions on the Text

1. Mention several purposes that a social studies teacher should have in mind for giving tests.
2. Discuss the topic of frequency of tests in the social studies.
3. Define the word *objective* as applied to testing. Name as many types of objective question as you can, giving examples of each.
4. What are the special advantages claimed for the essay type of testing in the social studies?
5. Give special suggestions as to how the teacher should proceed in grading essay tests.
6. What is the meaning of the word *standardized* as applied to social studies tests? Name three or more such tests.
7. Show the comprehensive nature of evaluation of social studies teaching.
8. Make a list of the factors that should be considered in determining a pupil's grade in social studies.
9. Discuss the nature of the report of progress that should be sent to the parent by the social studies teacher.

Suggested Activities

1. Assemble a collection of tests that have been used by social studies teachers in actual teaching situations.
2. Prepare tests of your own of various length and for different purposes which you indicate in a preface to each.
3. Secure catalogues from leading companies that publish standardized tests. Purchase specimen sets dealing with testing in the social studies. (Be certain that directions for administering and scoring are included.)
4. Prepare a list of selected references containing recent articles dealing with testing in the social studies.

5. Prepare a talk in which you discuss objective, essay, and standardized tests in the social studies.

Selected References

ABRAHAM, HERBERT J., "Testing the Effectiveness of High School Courses in American History," *Social Education*, VIII (May, 1944), pp. 216–219.

ALILUNAS, LEO, "What Do Essay Examinations Show?" *Social Education*, VII (November, 1943), pp. 313–314.

ANDERSON, HOWARD R., ELAINE FORSYTH, and HORACE T. MORSE, *The Measurement of Understanding in the Social Studies*, Chicago: National Society for the Study of Education, *Forty-fifth Yearbook*, 1946, Part I, Chap. V.

ARNOLD, DWIGHT L., "Social Studies Evaluation in the Intermediate Grades," *Social Education*, VII (March, 1943), pp. 117–120.

BALDWIN, JAMES W., "Recent Developments in Social Studies Evaluation," *Social Education*, XI (February, 1947), pp. 74–76.

BARNETT, S. N., "Testing for Objectives in the Social Studies," *High Points*, XXIX (December, 1947), pp. 56–68.

BLANCHARD, W. O., "Geographic Games and Tests," *Social Studies*, XXXIII (January, 1942), pp. 13–17; (February, 1942), pp. 58–62; (March, 1942), pp. 110–114; (April, 1942), pp. 159–162; (May, 1942), pp. 206–211; (October, 1942), pp. 258–260; (November, 1942), pp. 314–316; XXXIV (January, 1943), pp. 16–18; (February, 1943), pp. 60–64; (March, 1943), pp. 116–120; "Answers to Geographic Games and Tests" (May, 1943), pp. 222–225.

BOLTON, FLOYD B., "A Study of Vocabulary Growth in the Social Studies," *Social Education*, VII (January, 1943), pp. 17–18.

BUROS, OSCAR K., ed., *The Third Mental Measurements Yearbook*, New Brunswick: Rutgers University Press, 1949.

CHAUNCEY, HENRY, "The Social Studies Test of the College Entrance Examination Board," *Social Education*, VIII (October, 1944), pp. 253–257.

EDMONSON, J. B., JOSEPH ROEMER, and FRANCIS L. BACON, *The Administration of the Modern Secondary School*, New York: The Macmillan Company, 1948, Chap. XXI.

FINDLEY, WARREN G., "Educational Evaluation: Recent Developments," *Social Education*, XIV (May, 1950), pp. 206–210.

FORSYTH, ELAINE, "Evaluation of Attitudes in American History," *The Study and Teaching of American History*, Washington, D.C.: The National Council for the Social Studies, *Seventeenth Yearbook*, 1946, pp. 384–392.

FRIEDMAN, K. C., "A Word Test in the Social Studies," *Social Studies,* XXXIII (October, 1942), pp. 268–269.

GUINNESS, RALPH B., "A Qualitative Appraisal of American History Teaching," *Social Studies,* XXXVI (January, 1945), pp. 7–10.

———, "Revised Historical Viewpoints," *Social Studies,* XXXVI (January, 1945), pp. 15–17; (February, 1945), pp. 64–66; (March, 1945), pp. 109–111; (April, 1945), pp. 154–155; (May, 1945), pp. 201–203; (October, 1945), pp. 255–258; (November, 1945), pp. 297–300; (December, 1945), pp. 349–352.

HAAS, LEONARD, "Evaluation in the Social Studies," *Social Education,* XII (November, 1948), pp. 314–316.

HUNT, ERLING M., "The *New York Times* Test on American History," *Social Education,* VII (May, 1943), pp. 195–200.

KELLEY, TRUMAN L., and AUGUST C. KREY, *Tests and Measurements in Social Sciences,* New York: Charles Scribner's Sons, 1934.

KIME, HAROLD C., "A Sheaf of Tests on the Western Hemisphere," *Social Studies,* XXXVI (March, 1945), pp. 114–122.

MACNEILL, DORIS E., "In Apologia of an Essay Examination," *Social Studies,* XXXIV (April, 1943), pp. 168–172.

MCCUNE, GEORGE H., and HORACE T. MORSE, "Testing Study Skills: A Few Considerations," *Social Studies,* XXXIV (February, 1943), pp. 67–69.

MOFFATT, MAURICE P., *Social Studies Instruction,* New York: Prentice-Hall, Inc., 1950, Chap. XIV.

MORSE, HORACE T., "The Problem of Evaluation," *The Study and Teaching of American History,* Washington, D.C.: The National Council for the Social Studies, *Seventeenth Yearbook,* 1946, pp. 351–355.

——— and GEORGE H. MCCUNE, "Evaluation of Understanding," *The Study and Teaching of American History,* Washington, D.C.: The National Council for the Social Studies, *Seventeenth Yearbook,* 1946, pp. 356–373.

PARK, JOE, "An Analysis of Standardized American History Tests," *Social Studies,* XXXV (October, 1944), pp. 267–269.

——— and ROBERT SHEED, "Standardized Social Studies Tests," *Social Studies,* XXXIII (November, 1942), pp. 308–312.

QUILLEN, I. JAMES, and LAVONE A. HANNA, *Education for Social Competence,* Chicago: Scott, Foresman & Company, 1948, Chaps. XIII–XV.

RATHS, LOUIS, *Appraising Certain Aspects of Student Achievement,* Chicago: National Society for the Study of Education, *Thirty-seventh Yearbook,* 1931, Part I, pp. 89–118.

RODEHEAVER, NEWTON, and PAUL R. GRIM, "Tests in Civics and Citizenship: Part I," *Social Education,* VI (April, 1942), pp. 175–177; "Part II," *Social Education,* VI (May, 1942), pp. 222–224.

Ross, P. J., Jr., "What Shall We Test?" *Social Studies,* XXXIII (May, 1942), pp. 197–199.

Sachs, G. M., "Evaluation in the Social Studies," *Education,* LXVI (March, 1946), pp. 461–469.

Silver, Doris, "Try This New Testing Program," *Social Studies,* XXXV (November, 1944), pp. 315–316.

Simpson, Ray H., "Use of a Self-evaluative Test in Individualized History Study," *Social Studies,* XXXV (December, 1944), pp. 363–370.

Taba, Hilda, "Influence of Testing on History Teaching," *Education,* LXIV (April, 1944), pp. 492–499.

Volwiler, A. T., "Balance in Examination Questions," *Social Education,* VII (January, 1943), p. 25.

White, Howard, "Types of Examinations: A Compromise," *Social Education,* VIII (March, 1944), pp. 125–126.

Williams, Jay, "The Evaluation of Abilities and Skills," *The Study and Teaching of American History,* Washington, D.C.: The National Council for the Social Studies, *Seventeenth Yearbook,* 1946, pp. 374–383.

Wrinkle, William L., "Reporting Pupil Progress," *Educational Leadership,* II (April, 1945), pp. 293–295.

Chapter 15

RECENT CHANGES IN THE SOCIAL STUDIES

Preview. To those of us engaged in the teaching of social studies there continually comes the challenge of being alert to the latest developments in our field. We are interested in changes in curriculum, methods of presentation, and areas of increasing and decreasing emphasis. During any so-called "normal" times alterations come rapidly; during a period of revolutionary changes in world affairs they naturally appear with accelerated tempo. The implication is quite obvious. The Second World War and the subsequent period have brought into being unprecedented forces not only in international affairs but also in the classrooms of our public schools. One of the subject-matter areas to receive the greatest impact of this change is the social studies.

It will be found that some of the early changes were initiated by forces outside of the teaching profession. Unfortunately some of them were not offered in a spirit that could be regarded as overfriendly. Simultaneously, other and more constructive changes were advanced by those within the profession.

An effort is made herewith to show both the changes that took place while the war was in progress and those that have followed since. Data are presented to describe the situation for the nation as a whole and for certain specific states. Certain aspects of these changes are dealt with rather fully; others are merely mentioned without detailed comments.

It is strongly contended that the changes mentioned have been in the process of development during the period described; however, we are not always certain that the Second World War and the events immediately following caused them. In most cases we can feel reasonably sure, but we are aware that correlation does not necessarily mean causation.

We feel that there has been a lapse of sufficient time since V-E

Day and V-J Day for the making of a fairly critical evaluation. While the emphasis will be placed primarily upon the secondary level, it will be advantageous to make some reference to changes at higher levels, since such alterations have had a very definite influence upon practices and procedures in the secondary school.

Influence of External Forces upon the Teaching of the Social Studies. Most investigators feel that periods such as those of the First World War, the depression following 1929, and the Second World War produce criticism of social studies curricula, methods of teaching in this area, and the entire system of education in general. Shortly after 1919 a wave of feeling swept over our country to the effect that the schools were not teaching enough current events, that pupils in our secondary schools were not well-informed on national and international affairs, and that our country could be saved from future catastrophies only if contemporary affairs were included and were well taught. Thus probably even before Dec. 7, 1941, most social studies classes were giving considerable attention to the teaching of current events. In the decade of the thirties many of us will recall that the Federal Government sponsored numerous agencies that claimed merit not only for affording relief to the needy but also for affording a functional educational program for American youth. No little of this education stressed information and skills that fall within the area of the social studies.

One of the first articles on the teaching of the social studies to appear during the Second World War was so sudden, so comprehensive, and so searching that it had effects in the educational realm similar to those of the attack on Pearl Harbor in the military and political fields. It was produced by Benjamin Fine in the *New York Times,* June 21, 1942, and was a report dealing with requirements in respect to American history as they prevailed in the higher institutions of learning in the United States. Among the things revealed by the survey were the following:

Eighty-two per cent of our higher institutions of learning did not require the study of United States history for the undergraduate degree.

Many completed college courses without taking any history of their own country.

Seventy-two per cent of our colleges and universities did not require that candidates for admission submit high-school credits in United States history.

Many students made their way through high school, college, and professional or graduate school without having explored courses in the history of their own country.

Sixty-nine per cent of the institutions of higher learning thought that American history should be required because it helped develop good citizens, taught the American way of life, built civic responsibility, developed good leadership, and gave members of the armed forces a clearer insight into the democratic institutions which they were defending.

Thirty-one per cent who opposed making the subject compulsory at the college and university levels felt that *no* subject should be forced upon the student, that many college men and women had taken the courses on the secondary level, and that courses in world history were more essential in order to prevent narrow thinking.

The study that revealed the above results was based on a questionnaire sent to virtually every institution of higher learning in the United States—a total of 1,225 schools. Returns were received from 690, or 56 per cent of the total.

Naturally a study of this scope elicited many immediate reactions. Professor Allan Nevins of Columbia University took the stand that there should be a basic amount of instruction at the secondary level in the history and government of our country. He further noted that twenty-six states had legal requirements on this point, and he expected at least a dozen more to fall in line before the beginning of another school year. Professor Max Savelle of Leland Stanford University maintained that since we do not regard it as undemocratic to require pupils to go to school, we should certainly not regard it as undemocratic to require them to gain an appreciation of the history of our country. Dr. John W. Studebaker, U.S. Commissioner of Education, entered the discussion by setting forth a general outline of curricula. He recommended that all students take a social science sequence through high school and university to include American history, economics, geography, and government. During the first two years of high school the course would meet five days per week, while in the last two years of high school and during all four years of college it would meet three days per week. The fact that the sequence was on a continuing basis was stressed. A required course in American history and government was urged for the middle of the college career. At the end of the college years there would be a review covering all the social studies.

In October, 1942, a meeting attended by representatives of the higher institutions of learning in California was held at Stanford University. After discussions lasting over a period of a few days, resolutions were passed advocating the requirement of the study of American history in ten colleges.

Newspapers from coast to coast took up the argument with such titles for editorials as "Ignorance of America, Which the Facts Revealed, Was Appalling," "Something Is Radically Wrong Here," and "Slighting the Study of United States History."

Let us not gather the impression that there were no exceptions to those who received the above-mentioned report as a mandate for action. For instance, Professor Erling M. Hunt, editor of *Social Education,* contended that many of our secondary schools are offering fusion courses not carrying the name of American History but really containing a complete story of social and economic development. Dartmouth College reported that in their graduating class of 1942 only 11 out of 475 men had graduated without having had American history in either secondary school or college. President McClelland of McMurray College, in maintaining that such courses should not be required, asked, "Shall it be factual, or shall it, as Charles W. Warren, President of Harvard Alumni Association, recently said, '. . . be history so taught as to lay more emphasis on its principles of liberty, its democratic traditions, and on the flaming words and heroic efforts of its leaders'?" President Wells of Indiana University felt that our emphasis should be extended to international affairs, since in the postwar era we would live in a world rather than a national economy.

Naturally this study is much less talked about at present than it was for several months following the publication of its results. It may be rather generally forgotten. Even though its inception was undoubtedly prompted by the fact that we were at war, its effect will most likely be to cause the requirement of much more American history at both the college and secondary levels.

It should be mentioned in passing that the *New York Times* did not feel content to let the matter of American history rest with the above-mentioned efforts. In April of 1943 there was a report of a test which one of their correspondents had constructed and administered to 7,000 college and university freshmen. The *New York Times* concluded that these people did not know as much as they should about chronology, identification of characters, and places associated with

American history. In fact, the scores that were reported were very low. By emphasizing the apparently low performance the newspaper caused much discussion of the topic, even getting congressmen interested in studying the results and making recommendations with academic implications. One should examine the questions used before rendering judgment on the results reported. There were fifteen essay-type exercises. The following are illustrative, the question and the per cent of correct responses being given:

1. Name the 13 original states. (6 per cent)

5. Identify at least two contributions of the following famous Americans to the political, economic, or social development of the United States (A) Abraham Lincoln (22 per cent), (B) Thomas Jefferson (16 per cent), (C) Andrew Jackson (12 per cent), (D) Theodore Roosevelt (19 per cent).

9. What were the two principal nationalities to migrate from Europe to the United States between 1845 and 1860? (No report.)

14. Name two prominent figures connected with the growth of trusts and monopolies in the United States. (20 per cent)

Many of the lay public took the results of the test as a mandate to do something quickly to bring about an improvement in the school offerings and the methods of teaching in this area. There was little attention given to the authorship of the test. It was overlooked that the freshmen who took the test were little motivated, since their scores would not influence the mark earned in a particular course. Nevertheless the general influence was that of emphasizing the already popular trend of demanding more American history.

Heroic Work of Social Studies Teachers in Helping Win the War. Before our nation had participated very long in the Second World War certain groups of social studies teachers decided that they should outline a course of procedure. A meeting that was held early in 1942 by the history teachers of Baltimore is illustrative.[1] The following objectives were set up:

1. Creating an understanding of what the war means to youth.
2. Getting the students to appreciate the stakes in this war.
3. Creating an understanding of the causes of the war and the resulting peace.
4. Strengthening the loyalties of our American democracy.

[1] Harry Bard, "Wartime Changes in the History Course," *The School Executive,* LXII (October, 1942), pp. 16–18.

It was decided by the department that best results could be attained by initiating special units, correlating history with other educational media, emotionalizing the meaning of history, integrating, providing an in-service program of education for the teachers, and making a study of long-time educational planning.

While it is evident that most of the activities of this group tended to change immediate practices and procedures in the social studies, the greater interest is in long-time educational planning. As applied to Baltimore it was resolved among other things to keep the following points in the foreground for emphasis:

1. Study of the critical problems in relation to housing, health, transportation, and recreation.
2. Make optimum use of natural and human resources.
3. Be cognizant of the role that the city and surrounding territory face in relation to military effort and civilian defense.
4. To stress that Baltimore youth can contribute to the solution of all problems facing the city and nation.

More than ever before, use was made of pageants, movies, and the radio. The program of in-service training of the teachers, mentioned above, was elaborate and efficiently executed. Such wartime efforts as these that were pursued, not only in Baltimore but throughout the nation, will have an effect on the teaching of the social studies. Some former units will probably be discarded or greatly altered. New courses may be introduced or the content of former ones be much changed. Reference to these points will be made below.

Special Emphasis Placed on Air-age Education. In the discussion of changes in the social studies one would rightfully expect due and proper reference to the new emphasis being given the present and approaching air age. Naturally, much of this comes within the field of the social studies. The teacher may, because of limited training dealing with mechanical devices, feel a certain timidity about including this material. This attitude should not prevail. We teach social issues and implications about many other problems in which we do not have basic occupational skills. The trend is obviously toward the wider use of the airplane; there are relatively fewer accidents by this means of travel; lower rates per mile are imminent. These facts will cause the teaching of the good-neighbor policy to become more vital. Much of the discussion that has previously been devoted to freedom of the seas will henceforth give way to freedom of the airways. Classes will discuss urban decentralization as a means of defense against enemy aerial attacks. Social problems due to shifting of population in response to the new era will furnish the basis for frequent discussion in current events; likewise the economic loss to be suffered by holders of stocks in railway companies and bus lines will be noted.

Pupils will quickly become motivated in this new study. They will enjoy discovering how few hours we are actually removed from any spot on the globe at the rate of 300 miles per hour. The reduction of the size of our own nation, measured in terms of time, will make its appeal. The distances and exact flight routes between the world's leading cities will arouse a never-before-experienced interest in the use of the globe in the classroom.

Special units not previously used will probably have to be worked out. They may take such titles as "History of Aviation," "Air Power as an Aid to Victory in the Second World War," "International Problems Raised by Aviation," etc. Some teachers may prefer to supplement existing units in all the social studies rather than to incorporate new ones.

Teaching aids and materials on this topic are becoming more numerous every year. Most pupils can, over a period of a few weeks, bring an abundance of pertinent newspaper and periodical references to class. The school library can ordinarily maintain subscriptions to pertinent publications to be used in addition to *National Geographic* and other periodicals regularly available. The commercial air lines have good collections of low-cost helps that may be advantageously secured and used over a period of several years. The film libraries of many state universities have splendid collections of films that should be used to make the subject realistic. More publications, such as *Essential Understanding for the Age of Flight,* will become available.

Classroom Materials Furnished to Social Studies Teachers by the Federal Government. One effect of the period under discussion on the teaching of social studies was that the Federal Government became much more active in furnishing materials—materials that could be used as a basis of classroom teaching. The 30 page pamphlet, *What the War Means to Us,* was released in February, 1942. It was published by the Federal Security Agency of the U.S. Office of Education, accompanied by a letter from Mr. John W. Studebaker, Commissioner of Education, and carried brief statements from President Roosevelt and Paul V. McNutt, Federal Security Agency Administrator. Presumably this pamphlet was mailed to all school systems in the nation and made available in quantity upon receipt of requests. From one to two weeks' time could be spent in the study of this pamphlet. Later in the same year the same office distributed another pamphlet, *United Nations Discussion Guide.* Since the group of countries included in the U.N. embrace so much of the globe's space and have so many of the world's social and economic problems within their boundaries, it is readily apparent that a considerable amount of classroom time might be devoted to this study. Still another pamphlet published by the same agency should be mentioned, namely, *High School Victory Corps.* This was the result of the work of the National Policy Committee in cooperation with the War Department, the Navy Department, the Civil Aeronautics Administration of the Department of Commerce, and the U.S. Office of Education Wartime Commission. This was a program embracing the entire secondary school; as such, a large part of it had direct bearing on the social studies.

There are still many helps coming from the U.S. Office of Education of the Federal Security Agency. It is too early to ascertain whether these materials will be more abundant than they were in prewar years. The supposition might be that since teachers have become accustomed to receiving the material and the office has regulated its routine to supplying it, we shall receive more of it and be guided by the points emphasized.

Special Work of the National Council for the Social Studies. One organization to which all of us teaching in this area look for help is *The National Council for the Social Studies.* In November, 1944 a very pertinent pamphlet appeared—*The Social Studies Look beyond the War.* Relative to the needs of high-school youth in the postwar period, the following sentence expresses the viewpoint held throughout: "They will need a high school curriculum that deals with their real concern in a world which they know to be dynamic and fraught with social problems; that never, in a zeal for abstraction and formal learning, loses sight of the problems and tensions of young people who are the central object of education in the school."

Certain factors were recognized as immediate handicaps in the realization of this program. Among them were the shortage of well-qualified teachers, the temporary curtailment of research, the changed nature of home training, and the increased strains on efforts to cultivate domestic, social, and political tolerance. All factors, fortunately, were not negative. More than ordinary emphasis was placed on the democratic way of life throughout the war and postwar period. Our nation as a whole became more cognizant of the history of our freedoms and rights, of the political institutions of democracy, of the duties of citizenship, and of the procedure of diplomacy. In view of these circumstances, it was recommended that three themes—interdependence, expanding democracy, and the need for integrity—should permeate the entire school program of education for citizenship. In pleading for the recognition of the effects of recent events the U.S. Office of Education Wartime Commission expressed itself in the above-mentioned pamphlet as follows:

> Curriculums will vary from section to section, and from urban to rural areas, as well as from grade level to grade level; but great social trends and forces will be reflected in them all. Each school system must plan carefully to insure that its curriculum shall present a coherent sequence of experience, and shall encourage continuous development.

Without prejudice to other topics which are regularly recognized as vital in the social studies curriculum, the following are undoubtedly due to receive increased emphasis: agencies for maintaining peace, methods of protecting minorities, techniques for preventing political disorder, harmonious functioning of industry, government planning and private industry, and consumer education.

Influence of the Veteran on High-school Social Studies Classes. An effect on the teaching of social studies in the present postwar period that cannot be overlooked was occasioned by the fact that veterans were present in high-school classes for some time. While this type of pupil was part of the picture only temporarily, it is not unlikely that the changed techniques demanded of the teacher will be used for several years to come. The subjects pursued most frequently by this group were American history and problems of democracy, the former being ordinarily legally required for graduation and the latter elected because of its challenging title. (Their interest was probably no less in world history, but most of them took this subject in the early years of high school before entering the service.) The social experiences of the group were quite varied; they had learned much more about the world than the average high-school pupil usually knows. One could not and would not ignore that background. It was readily apparent that they knew far more than other classmates and the teacher about specific places and social problems. Their greatest needs seemed to be in matters of organization and interpretation. The goals for the emerging America needed to be clarified for them. Argument needed to give way to discussion and logical thinking. Much wider reading from more varied sources followed when the veteran was properly stimulated than was usually done by the nonveteran secondary-school pupil. The feeling that the teacher finally experienced was that this group represented adult thinking and that they had to be regarded as grownups. With their maturity came impetuosity. They had been taught to remove opposition by the use of force. Every possible effort had to be used to stress the democratic method of solving differences of opinion. This effort to direct sincere and aggressive thinking placed an unprecedented challenge before the teacher. Maybe our pupils of the future will tend to resemble somewhat the veteran in matters of intellectual approach to social problems and issues. If so, appropriate teaching methods will have been developed in advance.

Changes Reported throughout the Nation. After reading the ideas suggested by various thinkers as to what should be done in the area of social studies in the secondary schools, one rightfully raises the question of what has really been done. A member of the faculty of the Laboratory School of the University of Chicago, Dorothy Merideth,[2] reported at considerable length on this subject more than a year after V-J Day. By means of a questionnaire she surveyed the social studies courses offered in American public schools during 1944–1945, replies being received from thirty-four state departments of education and from forty-three city school systems. Care was exercised to secure results dealing with typical school systems within states and representative city schools from the nation as a whole.

A table which presented the results showed central tendencies by grades for social studies offerings. The tabulation gave the following indications: grade 7, United States history and geography; grade 8, United States history and geography; grade 9, civics and geography; grade 10, world history; grade 11, United States history;

[2] Dorothy Merideth, "Secondary School Social Studies in 1945," *Social Education*, IX (December, 1945), pp. 345–350.

and grade 12, modern problems, problems of democracy, etc. It seemed that the usual practice was to require the social studies in grades 7 and 8. The civics course in grade 9 was usually required. World history, although very prominent in grade 10, was usually elective. The United States history course is always required in grade 11 or 12. The majority of the schools that offered the course in problems required it for graduation.

One of the most interesting parts of the survey dealt with courses added or dropped during the last five years. Most of the new ones were listed as elective, one semester in length, and were found in grades 11 and 12. The cities seemed to be experimenting with new courses more generally than were the states. Courses mentioned as new in the states included Community Civics, Consumer Buying, Global Geography, Economic Geography, Air-age Geography, World Geography, Latin-American History, Culture of Canada and Latin America, International Relations, Orientation, Problems of Democracy, and Modern Problems. New courses reported by the cities which are not mentioned among the preceding included American Government, Careers, Current Events, Man and His Environment, Far East, Pacific Area and Far East, Asia and America, Guidance, Psychology, and Salesmanship. In respect to subjects dropped, both the states and the cities seemed to be continuing the trend of eliminating ancient and medieval history and modern European history. (The one-year course in world history is generally taking the place of these two years of history.) Economics appeared to be losing ground as a separate subject, the content previously offered in this subject being taught in the problems course. To only a slightly less extent the same was true of sociology. On the whole it seemed that more courses were being added than dropped.

The report gained added value by taking cognizance of the revision of course materials within current curricular patterns. Many schools found it difficult to add or drop courses; evidently few or none were unable to revise courses to keep pace with changing conditions and demands. The one course that probably was most responsive to revisions was that in modern problems. Topics given most frequently that had received increased emphasis in courses that had retained former names were "The Pacific," "The Far East," "Russia," "Latin America," "International Relations," "Economic and Social

Planning," "Global or Air-age Geography," "Intercultural Relations," and "Community Study."

One of the significant unsolved problems mentioned was that of grade placement. Many of the new courses were mentioned as appearing in two or more grades. Diversity was apparent among the various states and cities. More changes were noted in the senior high school than in the junior high school.

The following quotation [3] is offered to give the author's interpretation of her data:

> The replies indicate that there has been only a slight increase within the last five years in the amount of social studies required in reporting city school systems. State departments of education, however, are definitely requiring more social studies courses in the smaller high schools.
>
> While some schools have made changes by adding courses, a more general trend seems to be that of adding to, subtracting from, and adapting the standard courses already offered.
>
> The resulting social studies program is far from static. Its development, however, is evolutionary rather than revolutionary.

Anderson [4] made a comparative study of the offerings and registrations in social studies using the school years of 1946–1947 and 1933–1934. During the more recent year the seventh- and eighth-grade pupils tended to be taking two years of social studies; one of these was quite universally United States history. In grades 9 to 12 during 1946–1947, pupils tended to take less than three years of social studies; most pupils carried a year of United States history in these grades. During the thirteen-year period considered, increased emphasis in grades 7 and 8 was placed on civics and citizenship, world history, and state history; geography and social science lost in proportion of pupils registered. In grades 9 to 12 the same study revealed that United States along with world history, civics and citizenship, geography, and modern history gained increased emphasis. The subjects which showed declining emphasis were ancient and medieval history. The following quotation aptly summarizes the study: "Considering the entire field of social studies, there was a decrease in emphasis for grades 7 and 8; a slight increase for grades 9 to 12."

[3] *Ibid.*, p. 349.

[4] Howard R. Anderson, "Offerings and Registrations in Social Studies," *Social Education,* XIV (February, 1950), pp. 73–76.

Special Reports on High-school Social Studies in Wisconsin, New Jersey, and Wyoming. After observing what has been taking place in the area of social studies on the secondary level on a national basis, it should be of interest to know what has happened in one or more specific states. Leonard Haas,[5] director of teacher training at the Eau Claire State Teachers College, has given us some of the answers for Wisconsin. A survey of the state's 461 high schools was made by means of a questionnaire sent to the principals and the chairmen of social studies departments. Results were secured from 90 per cent of the schools. (In the introduction to the report it is indicated that the results obtained in Wisconsin were similar to those mentioned in the national survey.)

It was found that Wisconsin schools required from 1 to 5½ units of work in the social studies for graduation, the average requirement being 3 units. Titles of courses tend to follow the traditional pattern even though such courses have in many cases undergone alteration of content. Eighty-one per cent require citizenship; 64 per cent, world history; and 98½ per cent, United States history; 62⁶⁄₁₀ per cent have courses called Problems of Democracy, of which approximately one-third require it for graduation. Geography is offered in 75 per cent of the schools but is required in only 12 per cent of them. Sociology and economics remain significant subjects; some attention, growing in amount, is being given to courses in occupational psychology, Latin-American history, consumer education, orientation, and personality problems. The two years that were formerly given to ancient, medieval, and modern history have, in almost every instance, been abandoned in favor of the one-year course in world history. (Only two Wisconsin high schools were reported as having abolished the traditional curriculum and substituted a "core or integrated" one.) On the whole, the author of the survey felt that Wisconsin schools allot an adequate proportion of the curriculum to the area of the social studies.

Still more recently Edwin M. Barton [6] reported the results of a survey of the teaching of social studies in the state of New Jersey. The data collected covered the school year of 1944–1945. It was stated at the outset that the State Department of Education wished to lead

[5] Leonard Haas, "The Status of Social Studies in Wisconsin Secondary Schools," *Social Education,* X (May, 1946), pp. 213–216.

[6] Edwin M. Barton, "Social Studies in New Jersey Secondary Schools," *Social Studies,* XI (January, 1947), pp. 29–31.

and to stimulate progress rather than to require adherence to detailed courses of study on a mandatory basis. Courses required by law at the beginning of the survey included problems of democracy in senior high school and community civics in the elementary or intermediate grades.

Some of the central tendencies observed showed that in grades 7 and 8 about 66 six per cent of the schools offered two years of geography, 26 per cent offered it during one year, and the remainder devoted only a semester to it. In the same grades United States history was offered during two years by 72 per cent of the schools, during one year by 25 per cent, and during a single semester by the others. In grade 9 the schools generally offered civics, the number giving a full year to it and those devoting a half-year to it being about the same. In grade 10 world history as a one- or two-year course was offered by all the schools as an elective subject. In grade 11 the pattern was uniform throughout: United States history was regularly offered as a full-year subject. As mentioned above, problems in democracy was legally required as a full-year course.

Some courses were designated as those of "marginal social content." These included occupations, sales and guidance, social guidance, orientation, consumer education, and psychology. Subjects mentioned occasionally were Latin-American history, English history, and industrial history.

The median amount of social studies pursued by pupils in four-year high schools was 6½ semesters. Several general tendencies were stressed. The first was that the smaller schools gave a relatively greater time allotment to social studies than did the larger schools. Second, pupils of lower academic ability seemed to be taking more social studies than did the brighter ones. Third, schools offering fusion courses gave less time to social studies than did those following traditional patterns. Fourth, more time was devoted to social studies in the early secondary grades than later. Fifth, schools in which most of the pupils were preparing for college had a smaller enrollment in the field of social studies than other types of schools. Finally, schools having a rich offering in social studies tended to have a smaller relative enrollment in these classes than did schools having a more restricted program.

There are at least two pertinent observations. One is that ancient and medieval history offered as a full-year course was reported more frequently in New Jersey than in other states included in this study. Another is that a state law was passed to take effect in 1945–1946 requiring two years of United States history in the last four years of high school. The interpretation of the law has allowed the problems of democracy course to fill one year of the requirement if it is taught historically. The practice has become that of offering a two-year sequence in grades 11 and 12. This is definitely in line with the point noted earlier, namely, that more and more American history will be taught. It is anticipated that with additional required subjects one can reasonably expect enrollments to decline in social studies that remain elective. The ancient and medieval history mentioned in this paragraph may be the victim of the decrease.

Certain information related to that now being considered was secured for the state of Wyoming by Merril Hatch as part of a graduate course in education taken at the University of Wyoming in 1946. Eighty-three schools were considered; the courses offered during the school year of 1939–1940 were compared with those offered in 1945–1946. The following results were found, the first numeral following the subject being the number of schools that offered the subject at the beginning of the five-year period and the second being the number that offered it at the time of the survey: community civics, 40–39; American history, 67–72; world history, 58–73; government, 22–32; sociology, 30–26; economics, 31–28; American civilization, 1–0; American problems, 7–7; ancient history, 6–1; citizenship, 2–1; current history, 1–0; forum discussion, 1–0; international relations, 2–7; Latin-American history, 0–2; modern history, 4–1; oriental history, 1–1; psychology, 2–2; social problems, 1–2; vocations, 30–8; and world geography, 0–4.

It will be recalled that the author of the Wisconsin survey felt that his state had followed well in the path of the national trend in respect to changes in the social studies area. The findings of Hatch revealed that Wyoming schools too followed the same pattern. For instance, there is an increased emphasis on American history, government, international relations, Latin-American history, and world geography. Ancient history and modern history have definitely lost out as separate courses. Economics and sociology are still significant courses but show loss rather than gain.

Changes Dealing with Methods of Teaching. Since the surveys revealed that many courses were keeping their traditional names but altering their content, it seems reasonable that certain teaching procedures have of necessity been greatly changed. Some of those mentioned most frequently in recent professional literature will be discussed.

The forum discussion as a method of procedure within social studies classes has become immensely popular. Topics selected are those of outstanding importance in contemporary affairs. Entire class groups acquire general information on the topic under consideration. A committee is appointed to secure additional data through reading, listening to the radio newscasts, and personal inquiry. One member serves as chairman. The group assumes a position seated informally around a table or in a semicircle at the front of the class. Factual information and personal opinions are exchanged for a specified length of time, after which members of the class who are not members of the panel ask questions, add information, or express individual opinions. This method of procedure seems to appeal to adolescent fancy far more than the formal debate which was used so extensively before the Second World War. The fact that programs of this nature can be heard regularly on the radio partially accounts for the popularity mentioned. Also, the Junior Town Meeting League has had a very stimulating effect. More than 2,000 high schools are enrolled in this organization. Two specific instances of the use of forum discussion in a campus high school will be mentioned. On one occasion four different classes discussed the pros and cons of a year of compulsory military service for all American youth beginning with the date of their eighteenth birthday. The panel was composed of six members in each class. At the close of each hour class members voted to indicate which two had contributed most to the discussion. The eight people thus selected were placed in a new panel and took part in a forum discussion before the entire school as an assembly program. Audience participation in this instance exceeded that exhibited in any individual classroom. In another instance a forum discussion in which the participants were made up of seniors furnished the major portion of the commencement program.

The use of visual aids has become increasingly prominent. No doubt a great deal of the explanation is in the fact that films were used so extensively in connection with the teaching program of the armed forces. Along with more extensive use seems to come more effective use. Films are used less often for entertainment; adequate class preparation for proper appreciation is the rule. Pupil responsibility for mastering the material covered by films is being demanded through the media of recitation and testing. Teachers are becoming more aware of the necessity of previewing films before showing them to classes. In addition to the large number of films that schools are securing from the libraries of state universities and commercial concerns, it should be mentioned that the *March of Time* series which has been made available to schools has had phenomenal use.

Another area on which increased emphasis is being placed is current events. This phase of classroom activity, as mentioned above, was greatly enlarged following the First World War. In 1943, a personal letter from the editor of one of the publications that has wide usage in secondary schools revealed that their orders were double what they were one year before, and that in the previous year they were the largest they had ever been. In another personal letter a year later, the editor of a different publication, also widely used in high schools, revealed that his subscriptions had reached an all-time high and were continuing to increase. It appears that school administrators are pursuing a policy of having current events taught by social studies teachers, of providing for pupil subscriptions to weekly publications dealing with contemporary affairs, and of having about 20 per cent of the class time devoted to this phase of the work. Varieties of methods of teaching are quite noticeable in the current-events area. Some years ago it was general practice for teachers to merely ask pupils to bring clippings to class on a specified day of the week. Too often pupils forgot to bring them, brought clippings of relatively unimportant items, or did not study well the clippings brought. Now teachers assign reports on topics that have an immediate or continuing interest, ask for dramatization of situations that lend themselves to this type of treatment, make use of a variety of publications prepared for both pupils and the general public, call attention to reputable newscasts, capitalize on the experience of pupils who observe newsreels at local movies, and avail themselves of all media designed for more effective study of contemporary affairs (see Chapter 8).

While progressive social studies teachers have for many years utilized community resources and given attention to special days and weeks that engaged national attention, the professional literature indicates that there is increased attention in these directions. Personal observation and inquiry substantiate the conclusion. Social studies classes are in many instances engaged in compiling brief histories of their respective communities, often in mimeographed form for distribution. Visits are being made to local institutions as a result of topics studied in modern problems. Longer trips that take groups of pupils to the state or national capital are not uncommon. One occasion which gives a biennial opportunity for pupils to study citizenship in a highly motivated setting is the general election. It is one thing for a class to study election laws, mechanics of voting, and biographies of candidates; it is a better plan to provide a participation situation. Many schools quite properly carry out an election, dividing the high school into wards and precincts and providing the regular election officials. Precincts are supplied with regular ballots, poll books, tally sheets, and material comparable in nature to that used at the same hour probably less than a block away where adults are voting. It is reasonable that such a plan when properly conceived and sincerely executed will cause much increase in civic interest. Furthermore, it is also reasonable to suspect that pupils who take an active or even a minor role in such projects will eventually become keenly alert to their responsibilities as voting citizens.

While the evidence is fairly conclusive that the trends in methods of teaching and points of emphasis mentioned above have been stimulated by conditions emanating from the Second World War, there are some trends that could not have originated from any other source. The question of atomic power comes under this category. Social studies classes throughout the entire country are discussing the history of the question, scientific research involved, destruction effected in the Second World War, experiments conducted by our own War Department recently, proposed methods of control, and potential changes likely to affect the civilization of this and succeeding generations as a result of this source of energy. There is little wonder that pupils of all high-school grade levels are interested in this problem, since the manner in which it is handled may mean the difference between destruction and survival. In line with the same reasoning, it is equally evident that a study of the U.N. is an activity that has grown directly out of the Second World War. The idea of world peace and the brotherhood of man is not new; the particular manner of expressing it is unique in many respects. Social studies classes are hoping that through careful study and thorough understanding the people of our own and other countries may accept this organization as the one through which they are willing to travel the way of peace. Consequently there are few social studies classes that have not devoted many full periods to reading and discussion of this topic; furthermore, they continue to keep abreast of the weekly developments coming out of the meetings of this organization.

That the war and postwar periods have had marked effects upon the entire educational program and upon the teaching of social studies is indisputable. In fact, any well-defined period in international and national affairs can be shown to exert such influence. The degree to which such a period varies from what might be considered normal probably measures the amount of the influence. While the changes referred to here are quantitatively great, they are not revolutionary. Enough of the subject matter previously taught and enough course names and formerly used teaching practices are retained to establish this fact.

The effect of the recent periods mentioned above on the teaching of social studies has in many ways been a valuable one. A reexamination of the entire program, including content of curriculum and grade placement, has taken place. Evaluation of techniques has been employed. Significant experimentation has been carried out. If these activities merely confirmed the value of an existing program they would have a place; to the extent that improvement has come, they are indeed valuable.

The high-school classes in social studies and their teachers have, throughout our nation's history, desired to render maximum service to their country. This same spirit was manifested during the days of the war itself; happily, there seems to be an equal desire now to maintain and perpetuate ideals and qualities of American citizenship which will ensure a glorious future that will compare favorably with an illustrious past.

Impending Changes. From the foregoing discussion one is able to observe changes that have to do with names of courses, legal requirements, and methods of teaching. All this causes one to wonder what changes are taking place that can be judged to have value and permanence.

The first conclusion seems to be related to the proportionate emphasis on historical facts and present-day problems. Specifically, there arises the question of how much of the world's array of history we should attempt to teach pupils. One noted authority in the field, lecturing to a group recently, admitted the vast amount of material available dealing with India. He quickly followed by saying that he would devote only fifteen minutes of class time to all this history from the earliest times to 1918. He suggested that he would then give much-deserved time to India's place in world affairs since that date. Russia was mentioned and the same recommendations were advanced. While we do not advocate the extension of this principle to the extent that early American history and the history of all western European countries would be thoroughly sloughed, a basic principle is observed. It is that early historical foundations must be presented in less time in order that contemporary and personal problems may be more adequately studied. This is not a matter of choice; rather, it is a necessity. It is readily observable that so much research is being carried on and so many volumes being written that it becomes impossible to teach a secondary-school pupil more than a minor portion of all that could be attempted. Some older teachers seem to forget that it is impossible to just add more and more to what was already a full schedule of work.

Regardless of how a particular school organizes its work in social studies, there are a number of topics that must be dealt with as adequately as possible. A list of examples with related questions follows:

1. Role of the U.N. in world affairs
   a. What are the previous efforts that have been made to attain world peace without resorting to war?
   b. How is the present organization different from those of the past?
   c. Should one think of himself first as a citizen of the world or of the country in which he lives?
   d. What other topics besides world peace could and does such an organization become interested in?
   e. Why does our nation figure so prominently in the U.N.? How does this change our place in world affairs?
2. Capital and labor
   a. What are the major historical changes that have taken place in the relations between capital and labor?
   b. What function does each have in the process of production?
   c. Are there other factors contributing to production?
   d. How can it best be determined just what share of profits should be returned to each factor involved?
   e. If strikes are permitted, how should they be settled?
3. Marriage and family life

- *a.* In what manner does our success as a nation depend upon a stable family life?
- *b.* What type of training and discussion can secondary-school people plan that will help in the establishment of happy families?
- *c.* What are some significant facts revealed by statistics relating to marriage and divorce?
- *d.* How do local statistics dealing with marriage and divorce compare with those on a national basis?
- *e.* Is the social program provided by the secondary school related to the future family life of its members?
- *f.* To what extent should the general topic of sex education be discussed in the secondary school?

4. Race relations in America today
   - *a.* When did the question of racial discrimination start in America?
   - *b.* What attempts have been made to relieve tensions and frictions in this regard?
   - *c.* In what manner have various races and groups made significant contributions to American progress?
   - *d.* Give examples of individuals of numerous races who have brought honor to themselves and the nation
   - *e.* Why must our country be at least reasonably successful in solving the problem of race relations?
   - *f.* Offer some personal suggestions for improvement of race relations
5. Juvenile delinquency
   - *a.* What is a juvenile delinquent?
   - *b.* Give several causes of juvenile delinquency
   - *c.* Offer suggestions that would help to remedy each
   - *d.* Gather statistics on this subject showing age groups, places of greatest occurrence, and total numbers involved
   - *e.* To what extent have youth centers been helpful in solving the problem?

As intimated above, such topics as those listed have historical origins that should be understood. Likewise their very real existence and gravity make it essential to stress present-day implications. The following topics could and should receive varying degrees of attention at some stage in the secondary-school social studies program: orientation to the school, boy-and-girl relationships, beautifying the community, transportation, communication, early American life, how people in other lands live, Latin-American neighbors, community industry and recreation, making and keeping friends, personal budgeting, community agencies and services, development of the West, living in the air age, intelligent consumers, personal freedom, community citizenship, leaders in American history, technology in relation to living, science and the consumer, conservation of natural resources, education in relation to democracy, propaganda and public opinion, community safety, law enforcement, unemployment, pageant of America, labor unions and management, party politics, taxtion and finance, living in the atomic age, housing, foreign policies, contemporary cultures and religions, choosing a vocation, interpreting and appraising the American way of life, and personal guidance.

The above suggestions are made on the basis of what appear to be actual changes taking place.

Summary. The purpose of this chapter has been to show some of the ways in which the period of the Second World War and subsequent years has brought about changes related to the social studies. Periods of catastrophe have usually caused the school's social studies program to be examined critically. One of the first points of vulnerability in this instance was the amount of American history being taught. The tendency has been to increase it. The sincere motives of social studies teachers have never been questioned. Their efforts in helping to win the war and to bring the nation back to normalcy are illustrated. Because of the strategic importance of the use of air power during the war, it appeared only natural that emphasis upon this phase of social education would follow, and this has come about. The U.S. Office of Education has been most generous in furnishing materials for use in social studies classrooms. The contribution of The National Council for the Social Studies included helpful suggestions for classes during the war and very forward-looking ideas for readjustment in the subsequent period. It has been pointed out that the return of the veteran to the classroom has favorably altered philosophy and methods of teaching.

The trend of changes reported throughout the nation has indicated an increase in amount of social studies being offered. Special reports on changes in Wisconsin, New Jersey, and Wyoming have showed that these states tended to follow the national pattern.

Methods of teaching have generally stressed more pupil participation, greater use of visual aids, a larger proportion of time devoted to current events, and much more extensive use of community resources.

Questions on the Text

1. Do you think that most of the recent changes that have taken place in relation to social studies content and teaching would have occurred in normal times?

2. Give some pertinent facts related to increase in emphasis upon and amount of American history required in the schools.

3. Cite examples of direct helps that social teachers have extended in times of crisis.

4. Mention several topics that can be properly discussed in social studies classes in an effort to emphasize air-age education.

5. From what division of the national government can social studies materials be secured?

6. Mention some predictions made by The National Council for the Social Studies for the period following the Second World War.

7. In what manner has the influence of the veteran been noticeable in social studies classes?

8. Summarize the trend of changes in the social studies area as reported throughout the nation.

9. Give specific statements of changes in this area for a given state.

10. Do you feel that there have been greater changes of recent date in content or in methods of teaching social studies? Explain.

11. Summarize various impending changes that may become positive trends.

Suggested Activities

1. Arrange for an interview with a teacher of many years of experience in the social studies. Try to find out from the conversation the changes that seem most impressive to him related to content and method.

2. Prepare a questionnaire that you think would be suitable to mail to social studies teachers throughout your state to gain a notion of various trends.

3. Write to your state department of education, or state university, or both, asking for a list of recent publications dealing with methods of teaching social studies.

4. Collect clippings from nonprofessional publications that you think might have an influence on content and methods of teaching social studies.

5. Consult the *Education Index* for references to current articles related to this chapter.

6. Arrange a forum discussion in which a topic suggested by this chapter is presented.

Selected References

ALEXANDER, ROBERT J., "New Vistas to World History," *Social Education,* VIII (December, 1944), pp. 351–352.

ANDERSON, HOWARD R., "Offerings and Registrations in Social Studies," *Social Education,* XIV (February, 1950), pp. 73–76.

BARD, HARRY, "Wartime Changes in the History Course," *The School Executive,* LXII (Oct. 4, 1942), pp. 16–18.

BARTLETT, N., "Social Studies Teacher and the Air Age," *Education,* LXIII (October, 1942), pp. 105–110.

BARTLETT, R. J., "Social Studies and Democracy," *Social Education,* VII (April, 1943), pp. 161–164.

BARTON, EDWIN M., "Social Studies in New Jersey Secondary Schools," *Social Education,* XI (January, 1947), pp. 29–31.

BERMAN, E. F., "Social Studies in Post-war World," *Social Studies,* XXXV (December, 1944), pp. 347–348.

CORGELL, V., "New Objectives for the Social Studies," *Social Studies,* XXXIV (May, 1943), pp. 195–201.

CYR, FRANK W., ed., *Rural Schools and the War,* Washington, D.C.: The Department of Rural Education of the National Education Association of the United States, 1944.

DE ZAFRA, CARLOS, JR., "A Post-war Approach to Social Studies Teaching," *Social Studies,* XXXVII (October, 1946), pp. 250–252.

FRASER, H. R., "Neglect of American History," *Education,* LXIII (March, 1943), pp. 432–438.

General Education in a Free Society: Report of the Harvard Committee, Cambridge, Mass.: Harvard University Press, 1945.

HAAS, LEONARD, "The Status of the Social Studies in Wisconsin Secondary Schools," *Social Education,* X (May, 1946), pp. 213–216.

HANKINS, GEORGE C., "The Case for Global Geography," *Social Education,* VIII (September, 1944), p. 209.

HEATHCOTE, CHARLES WILLIAM, "Teaching Current History," *Social Studies,* XXXVI (December, 1945), pp. 357–359.

HEYL, H. W., and W. E. YOUNG, "New York State's Social Studies Program," *School Executive,* LXIII (April, 1944), pp. 31–34.

HENRY, N. B., "War Courses Required of Seniors," *School Review,* LI (September, 1943), p. 391.

HOLTMAN, R. B., "Social Thinking in Wartime," *Social Education,* VII (October, 1943), pp. 262–264.

KNOWLTON, DANIEL C., "History in War-time Britain," *Social Studies,* XXXVI (May, 1945), pp. 196–200.

Levi, A. W., "Social Science and the Post-war World," *Educational Forum,* VIII (November, 1943), pp. 37–42.

McCune, G. H., and H. T. Morse, "War News: Material for Critical Thinking," *Social Education,* VI (February, 1942), pp. 78–79.

Merideth, Dorothy, "Secondary School Social Studies in 1945," *Social Education,* IX (December, 1945), pp. 345–350.

Meyer, Walter E., and Clay Cass, *Education for Democratic Survival,* Washington, D.C.: Civic Education Service, 1942.

Ross, Cameron, "The Impact of the War on the Social Studies," *Social Studies,* XXXV (March, 1944), pp. 116–120.

Ross, Franklin, "Has the War Taught American Teachers Anything?" *Social Studies,* XXXVI (October, 1945), pp. 237–244.

The Social Studies Look beyond the War, Washington, D.C.: The National Council for the Social Studies, 1944.

Sorenson, Frank E., director, *Essential Understandings for the Age of Flight,* Lincoln, Nebr.: Department of Public Instruction, 1944.

Vitcha, Leonard A., "Wartime Social Studies in Junior High School," *Social Education,* VII (November, 1943), pp. 315–318.

"The Waging of Peace: A Program for the Air Age," Washington, D.C.: American Association of School Administrators, 1944.

Chapter 16

IMPROVEMENT OF SOCIAL STUDIES INSTRUCTION

Preview. Supervision of social studies teaching involves a director, a teacher or group of teachers, and pupils in the respective classes. There are many types supervisory position which the regular social studies teacher may hope eventually to attain. For many of them the required traits and specific aspects of training are identical. In fact, all situations involved have in common the point of cooperative effort designed to attain maximally effective results.

Those Who Supervise. One of the first questions that arises in connection with the consideration of the supervisor of social studies is what type of person this individual should be. In brief, he should possess every quality specified for a successful classroom teacher in this field. All the personal traits demanded in the regular classroom teacher should be his. The only difference is that he should have them in even greater degree. For instance, it is one thing to say that the classroom teacher of social studies should possess democratic attitudes and another, even graver, thing to say that the supervisor should be endowed with them. The situation is the same on down the line with fairness, tolerance, sympathy, tact, good judgment, sense of humor, sportsmanship, etc. One of the reasons that some take the lead in supervisory activities is that these very traits are possessed in varying amounts. Some of the readers of a professional magazine recently included the following as qualities and traits the supervisor of instruction should have: sincerity, tactfulness in criticism, sense of humor, kindliness, self-control, tolerance, showing appreciation, giving encouragement, and not having an unapproachable air.[1]

Isaacs and Kolodny [2] in discussing the good supervisor observed

[1] "This Is the Kind of Supervisor We Want," *Educational Leadership,* V (January, 1947), p. 254.

[2] William Isaacs and Jules Kolodny, "Some Notes on Making Supervision Work," *The Education Digest,* XIII (April, 1948), pp. 14–16.

that he lives democracy, inspires confidence, is reasonable, writes fair reports, gives judicious praise, helps fight the teacher's battles, has a healthy skepticism, and is a likable human being.

The supervisor's formal educational training is a matter of concern. Obviously he should have successfully completed as many hours as the average of the rest of the staff, and usually more. Naturally it is better to be able to show superiority in this matter at least for the sake of prestige. The best arrangement in respect to distribution is to have a reasonably attractive array of credit hours in the various social studies. For instance, courses should have been completed in all the fields of history, economics, sociology, political science, and geography. Possibly the greater proportion of the hours should be in history, since more courses are taught in this subject in secondary schools than in any other one of the social studies. Courses in the others are essential in order to be of reasonable service to those teaching in the various fields or in recently devised curricular innovations. Additional courses in professional education should be part of the qualifications of the supervisor, including those designed to increase skill in supervision and administration. Courses usually given such titles as Supervision of Instruction, Secondary-school Administration, etc., are helpful. If the supervision is in a teacher-training institution, courses dealing with supervisory practices and organizations in such schools are invaluable. It cannot be argued indisputably that the possession of more than the usual number of degrees is the best type of educational training for the supervisor. Only if in the securing of the degrees he found opportunity to carry the needed and recommended courses could such argument be well-founded. Quite frequently preparation for supervision has been obtained by carrying surplus hours in both content and professional courses on the undergraduate and the graduate level.

Areas in Which Social Studies Supervisors Should Demonstrate Special Competence. Fundamentally, the best service the supervisor can render the teacher is that of developing to the maximum the special abilities and talents that he already possesses. Any individual teacher can probably execute some phase of teaching better than anyone else. The supervisor should discover this area and both direct and inspire the growth suggested.

The starting point for over-all supervision is the group teachers' meeting. It is here that unity of purpose and teamwork are initiated. By democratic processes a philosophy and definition of education should be evolved; likewise, the objectives of education as stated by national and professional groups and committees should be reviewed. These steps should be followed by intensive study of the objectives of the entire field of social studies and of each individual social study. The latter pursuits should be executed with the idea of articulation being uppermost. Later in the year, and over a period of succeeding years, important topics can be made the subject of study and reports for group teachers' meetings. In discussing the work of the social studies staff under the leadership of the supervisor, Wheeler [3] says, "I recommend to the social studies staff seeking to improve instruction that it: (1) identify objectives in terms of human behavior; (2) select learning experiences to accomplish objectives regardless of how the chips fall on favored academic methods; and (3) evaluate its clientele both in and out of school to determine the effectiveness of its work." Tyler [4] emphasized practically the same points when he paid high tribute to the American high school but felt obligated to point out certain aspects that remain in need of improvement. These are (1) the objectives which are sought, (2) the learning experiences which are used, (3) the organization of these learning experiences, and (4) the evaluation of teaching. While individual teachers will be regularly aware of the numerous problems related to methodology, etc., it is a point of wisdom to judiciously restrict the number discussed annually in group meetings. Without prejudice to all the other interesting and worth-while topics that might at some time be discussed, the following are apt ones: units of work, problems, projects, socialized procedures, testing, evaluation, relation of social studies to general education, syllabi, and trends in secondary-school social studies. Group teachers' meetings can be made interesting and profitable. Aggressive leadership and stimulation on the part of the supervisor coupled with the ability to spur to realization the potentialities of the teachers are the basic essentials. It should not be overlooked that some professional educators have minimized the supervision of

[3] Eldon G. Wheeler, "The Improvement of Instruction in the Social Studies," *Social Education*, XIII (April, 1949), p. 166.

[4] Ralph W. Tyler, "How Can We Improve High School Teaching?" *School Review*, XLVI (September, 1948), p. 387.

the teacher at work and have attempted to remedy all classroom ills by merely improving the curriculum. Bartky [5] was motivated to discuss this point after reading introductory statements by Harold Rugg in the *Twenty-sixth Yearbook* of the National Society for the Study of Education. He concluded that the following duties are essential ones and characterize the efficient supervisor's work:

1. He provides a curriculum or assists the teacher to build her own.
2. He suggests methods or encourages the teacher to develop her own.
3. He encourages the teacher to learn about children.
4. He tells the teacher about parents and public.
5. He cares for the teacher's mental health in order that she may carry on effectively and enthusiastically.

After the groundwork for supervision has been laid in group meetings, the visitation of the teacher in the classroom naturally follows. Too many people holding supervisory titles feel that they can know by intuition what is going on; such is not the case. In any event, too little visitation has taken place. This is probably explained by the fact that social studies teachers are better trained today than they once were; however, this does not imply that they will profit less from supervision. Maybe social studies teachers have not desired supervision. Possibly they have been subjected to the wrong kind. Let us assume that classroom visitation is desirable and that the two parties concerned are both desirous of improving the instruction regardless of its initial quality. The supervisor should observe certain points relative to courteous and efficient visitation. His desire should be to observe as nearly as possible what would take place if he were not present. Of course, his presence will probably cause some alterations; on the other hand, he can obviate many of these. He will do well to observe the following suggestions:

1. Attempt to be present at the beginning of the hour and remain to the end.
2. Refrain from interrupting the class in any manner whatsoever. This precludes adding comments to recitations, asking questions, and calling for summarizations.
3. Make mental notes and observations of what takes place. If written

[5] John A. Bartky, "Helping Teachers Teach," *School and Society*, LXVI (Sept. 27, 1947), p. 242.

notes are desired, formulate them immediately after the visit. Constant writing during the observation is disconcerting to all concerned.

4. Be courteous and cordial upon arriving and departing, just as one would expect others to be who are not supervisors. Twenty-three members of a class at Butler University were reported by Bail [6] to have interviewed 460 persons in the teaching profession. It was found that "teachers desire most frequently supervision which provides constructive criticism, new techniques and methods, demonstration teaching, suggested materials and equipment. Teachers do not receive from supervision the services which they desire."

5. Exhibit an attitude of interest and cordiality which will inspire both teacher and pupils to exert their best efforts.

6. Never yield to an impulse that might result in taking over the class.

7. In brief, try to conduct oneself as a supervisor in such a manner that the things that would normally take place will have an unrestricted chance to happen.

Several years ago supervisors generally felt that it was necessary to travel about well-armed with check sheets in order to show properly the results of classroom observation. This attitude was based partly on the desire to be both comprehensive and objective. Probably both these results were obtained. On the other hand, the practice often brought much distaste for supervision on the part of the teacher. Matters of almost no significance took on the appearance of major deficiencies. The natural abilities of the teachers were not developed. Subsequent conferences were occasions for attention to picayunish details and were consequently quite boresome for all concerned. Nevertheless, if a supervisor today feels that he can function more effectively with a rating scale he can easily construct one with the aid of a pencil and ruler. Appropriate subdivisions would be placed under such general headings as physical conditions of the room, materials and equipment, teacher background and demonstrated skills, pupil response, personal traits of teacher, professional attitudes, etc. However, such check sheets are not used by most supervisors today. Harman,[7] in discussing this point, wrote, "Within recent years the purpose of the visits has tended more and more toward minimizing

[6] B. M. Bail, "Do Teachers Receive the Kind of Supervision They Desire?" *Journal of Educational Research,* XL (May, 1947), p. 716.

[7] Allen C. Harman, "Classroom Visitation as a Phase of Supervision," *American School Board Journal,* CXVIII (June, 1949), p. 40.

the teacher appraisal element and stressing the cooperative study of problems, pupils, teachers, and related activities." Gough,[8] in considering this point, stated, "I dislike having anyone sit in my class and write unless I know the purpose of the observation. It cramps my style; I can't proceed normally."

After the supervisory visit has been made, the logical thing that should happen is a personal conference. Just as there is proper technique in visiting, there are correct procedures associated with the personal conference. It probably should not be held immediately after the visitation. Both supervisor and teacher need some time for reflection. A time and place should be arranged which are convenient for both parties. A state of rapport should exist between the two individuals. The teacher's good points should be stressed in an effort to develop them further. Certainly the criticism extended should be of a sort that can be labeled constructive rather than destructive. The whole atmosphere should be that of two people pooling their resources to solve problems of mutual interest, rather than that of one person telling another specifically what to do. Certainly, more in social studies than in any other area, democratic practices should prevail in conference.

Supervisory Positions to Which the Social Studies Teacher May Look Forward. In the secondary schools a considerable number of supervisors occupy positions in social studies departments with the title of *department head.* Like other administrators, their duties are both administrative and supervisory; likewise, they do varying amounts of classroom teaching. Their importance and potentialities are also variable. For instance, some schools award the position of department head to the member who has longest tenure. In this manner it is possible to recognize long service with a salary at least slightly higher than that enjoyed by coworkers. Usually little is expected in the way of actual additional service over that rendered by regular department teachers. On the other hand, some schools attach real importance to the position. The principal relieves himself of administrative detail by passing on duties to the supervisor. Furthermore, a great deal is expected from year to year in the way of increase in the quality of classroom instruction because of the supervisor's skill. Teachers' meetings, visitations, and personal confer-

[8] Symmie Gough, "Complaints of a Much Supervised Teacher," *Educational Leadership,* VI (December, 1948), p. 157.

ences represent matters in which the department head must have a mastery. Some of the rewards derived from this position are a feeling that the social studies experiences of the group are more effective if coordinated, a sense of satisfaction in seeing teachers improve in their classroom performance, and the observation that social studies can serve as a substantial basis for the curriculum of the entire school.

The person who is successful as a department head may legitimately aspire to become supervisor for an entire city system, assistant principal, or principal. Similar positions will often become available in other systems and will in many cases represent desired promotions.

A type of position that presents itself frequently is that of supervisor of social studies for a city system. This is found more often in the larger-than-average school system. The qualifications include all those suggested above for classroom teachers and heads of departments. In addition, the city supervisor should know the elementary field well. Fortunately, many teacher-training institutions are offering a program which qualifies their graduates for either elementary- or secondary-school teaching. This would be quite an appropriate training background. If the selection of elementary-school training courses is left to the individual, the following are among those that should be included: teaching of social studies in the elementary school, psychology of the preadolescent child, observation and participation in elementary grades, and directed teaching. This work can often be taken as electives; if not, a relatively small amount of additional attendance will suffice.

Duties in this type of work will involve planning, conferences, and meetings such as were described above. More emphasis will be given to coordination and unification. Much of the work involves meetings with groups of department heads, principals, and classroom teachers. The following topics are among those likely to be considered:

1. Relation of the social studies to the objectives of education accepted for the entire school system
2. Objectives for social studies at various grade levels
3. Content of various courses and development of syllabi
4. Use of visual aids
5. Utilization of community resources
6. Development of active participation of pupils in community problems and activities

7. Place of social studies in the education-for-life-adjustment program
8. Development of democratic procedures within the classroom
9. Securing of latest and best supplementary teaching materials
10. Observation and demonstration of good procedures
11. Teacher participation in local groups and in professional organizations

There are many rewards that the social studies supervisor in the city system can reasonably expect. Seeing social studies become functional in the lives of a significant number of pupils is one. Helping teachers reach their maximum abilities is another. Exerting at least an indirect influence on the teaching of other subjects in the secondary school is also a pleasure if in so doing more desirable citizenship practices are established. Finally, the person successful in this position may be chosen for greater responsibilities, as in the positions of curriculum director, assistant superintendent of schools, principal, and similar positions in still larger school systems.

Special Work of the Supervisor Engaged in Teacher Training. Teacher-training institutions have specific needs for supervisors of social studies. The principal job is that of working with those who are shortly to become public-school teachers. Training required for these positions, which carry various titles such as supervising teacher, critic teacher, senior teacher, etc., involves many of the elements pointed out above. Public-school teaching experience is almost mandatory. Intimate familiarity with the public-school system of the state where the training is being done is certainly essential. The ability to both demonstrate excellent teaching and help others develop their own abilities is important. It is quite apt to make a more extensive statement about supervising the student teacher than that which is made about supervising the teacher in the field, based on relative experience. It must be remembered that the student teacher is often quite young, not more than four years older than the pupils whom he is about to teach, also that he is sincerely fearful about the task at hand. This state of affairs calls for gradual induction. During the early periods with a class the student teacher should spend much time in learning about the pupils as individuals. He can well assist those who have been absent and those who are slow in comprehending their work. It will be easy and helpful for him to guide the directed study activities of a class. In anticipation of later work he can be preparing units for teaching purposes. During this stage the supervisor is indeed mindful of his charge and concerned that the basis of desirable teacher-pupil relationships should be laid.

In line with the plan of gradual induction it will be well for the student teacher to assist in some manner with a unit being taught by the regular teacher before taking full and complete charge of a unit of his own. He might be asked to present the overview, to conduct a drill or review exercise, or to administer a test.

Fully responsible student teaching naturally involves the writing of units of work. The supervisor should be assured that this technique has been well learned or, if it has not, devote the necessary time to assure the desired results (see Chapter 11). Some supervisors still make use of daily plans generally; fortunately few adhere to such practices. This is stated advisedly and is an implication that the advantages of the unit method of instruction are understood. However, there are frequently stages within the unit when it is desirable to have a series of daily recitations. If and when such time arrives, the supervisor should be able to make appropriate suggestions.

The plan can be most functional in dealing with the new lesson if it outlines the content involved. Some student teachers have made the mistake of writing out questions they expected to ask. This procedure produces poor results: the transition from one question to the next is rarely good, and the recitation seems to lack the unity and coherence it should have. On the other hand, if the student teacher formulates questions as he proceeds, the lesson will develop naturally. It is advised that a margin of 2½ inches be left on the right-hand side of the page, where devices that are to be used can be indicated. This will have the advantage of stimulating the use of devices and assuring that they will not be forgotten at the appropriate time. (Reference is made to such items as maps, charts, pictures, special reports, blackboard use, etc.)

The things emphasized in a summary of a lesson one day constitute practically the same things that will be brought up again the following day as review and recall. In the summary an effort should be made to have the class participate freely. Each member should feel a responsibility for stating the ideas that seem to him personally to be the most significant. Refinement of phrasing and thought processes can be a teacher function. The discussion should be carefully timed so that the summary will not be neglected.

The assignment for the following day should indicate clearly the specific objective, materials to be used in its accomplishment, plan of attack, and exercises to be performed. Suggested provisions for individual differences should be shown, together with optional work to be executed. As stated in Chapter 12, many lessons are well-planned in so far as discussion and other matters are concerned, but little thought has gone into the making of a good assignment. This is a grave error.

The space on the plan labeled *evaluation* is very important. The student teacher should keep the plan, twenty-four hours if necessary, until he has had time to think through carefully his reactions to the day's work. The entries made here can serve as a basis for the next conferences; likewise, the reasoning necessitated can lead to much improvement in future days of teaching.

The outline which follows shows the divisions of the daily lesson as discussed above:

DAILY LESSON PLAN

Subject ____________________	Teacher ____________________
Unit ____________________	Date ____________________
Discussion objective __________	School ____________________

Review and recall	Teaching aids and devices
Presentation of new material	
Summarization	
Assignment	
Evaluation	(Use reverse side and additional sheets as needed.)

Social studies student teachers are frequently puzzled about the preparation and use of plans. Some supervising teachers have required plans of much greater length and in stricter conformity to certain rigid standards than seem reasonable. This can only occasion worry and wasted energy on the part of the student teacher. It seems that a safe prescription in the matter would be to rule that every word written on the plan should function to the end of a better classroom-teaching performance; otherwise there certainly is no necessity for the writing. Likewise, individual differences between student teachers are a matter of as much concern as is the same problem with pupils. Some will need more elaborate written plans than others. Once the plan has been prepared it should be used to maximum advantage. Some student teachers feel that a plan in evidence involves a loss of prestige, but this is not the case. If such fears persist they can probably be offset by suggesting that the pupils use freely any notes they prepared in working on the lesson.

Most supervisors of social studies in teacher-training institutions are asked to report more than merely a grade at the end of a quarter or semester. This usually takes the form of a check sheet or graph on which values for various areas are indicated plus specific written comments. General information, classroom teaching ability, personal traits, professional attitudes, and supervisor's comments are among the divisions frequently found on such sheet. The one which follows is illustrative.

DEPARTMENT OF SOCIAL STUDIES

Evaluation of Student Teaching

Student Teacher ______________ Supervising Teacher ______________
Subject Taught ______________ Semester and Year ______ Hours Credit ______

Number of periods observed ______ Number of periods tardy ______
Number of periods taught ______ Number of pupils in class ______
Number of periods absent ______

Rating scale: A, excellent; B, good; C, average; D, poor; Inc., incomplete; F, failure

---

Place an x in the appropriate column after each trait or skill.

Classroom Teaching Ability	A	B	C	D	INC	F
General information and culture						
Ability to write and plan units of work						
Daily lesson planning						
Skill in arousing thought						
Use of illustrative materials						
Ability to make good assignments						

Execution of supervised study
Attention to individual differences
Establishment of rapport
Application of methods of teaching social studies
Pupil achievement in relation to objectives

Personal Traits
Originality
Cooperation
Good judgment
Fairness
Appearance
Voice
Tact
Self-control

Professional Disposition
Interest in entire school program
Interest in pupils as individuals
Membership in professional organizations
Dependability
Sincerity

Grade for the Course (Any of the above items may be weighted)
Comments:

The rating sheet should have much more extended use than merely being sent to a registrar's office. It should be placed in the hands of the student teacher early in the teaching period. Full explanations of each point should be given. After a period of teaching representing the time spent in dealing with a complete unit of work the student teacher should fill out the sheet as a self-evaluation exercise. The supervising teacher should do the same independently so that results can be compared. Points of weakness become the basis of a good conference designed for improved teaching. The point of actual grade is really of minor importance, especially in these earlier stages.

Specific Questions Asked by Student Teachers. Good student teachers in social studies, like brilliant pupils in class, ask searching questions. Supervisors must be able to give brief and pointed answers to at least the usual ones. The following list is not intended to be even reasonably comprehensive; rather it is proposed as containing questions comparable to those typically asked. The answers are such as the average or better-than-average supervisor might offer as responses.

If I am attempting to conduct a discussion and the pupils are not responding well, what shall I do?

The discussion under this circumstance should not be continued. The time should be taken for additional supervised study. Neither should the teacher show evidence of anger and displeasure. Rather, there should be a careful analysis of the reason for the failure to secure appropriate response; once the conclusion has been reached it may be possible to prevent the recurrence of the situation. Some of the factors that often lead to poor pupil participation are insufficient study time, failure to understand the assignment clearly, lack of motivation, poor questioning techniques, lack of proper problem-setting situations, insufficient variety in teaching methods, failure to capitalize on opportunity for socialized procedures, and actual difficulty of work for the pupils involved.

What shall I do if the work I have planned does not consume the entire period?

One cannot know in advance how long the work that has been planned will last. The teacher should have in mind various activities in which to engage if there is surplus time. The following are possibilities: reading related and supplementary selections, conducting a short drill, developing a summary outline, using a list of questions that call for an expression of personal opinion, discussing the current events of the past twenty-four hours, and passing illustrative materials around the room.

If a pupil is giving a special report should he stand or sit?

Ordinarily he should come to a position in front of the class and stand. Not only is he heard more easily; he also gains personal help in public-speaking experiences.

Should I stand or sit when teaching?

Much more effective teaching has been done by those who stand than by those who sit. Pupils have more respect for the teacher who thus displays energy and enthusiasm. A small class seated near the teacher's desk might offer an exception. Even then, the teacher should not be seated all the time.

Should I correct errors of grammar and pronunciation made by pupils in classroom discussion?

These errors should be immediately corrected. This will be a valuable service for the pupil, who is learning English as well as social studies. The slogan, "Every teacher is a teacher of English," is a good one. Likewise the old suggestion that we teach children rather than subject matter applies here. A socially acceptable person knows and is able to speak and write good English. We are obligated to extend this help.

Should I continue to write lesson plans when I start teaching on a full-time job of my own?

Planning one's work never stops. The plan should be developed as fully as time permits during the first years of teaching. If the subject is taught in the subsequent year, the plan can be revised even by marginal alterations. As experience is gained, more of the plan can exist in the mind of the teacher and less on paper.

In the event that I am conducting a class and one of the pupils asks a question to which I do not know the answer, what shall I do?

Immediately say that you do not know. Compliment the pupil upon asking a good question if it is really important. Tell him quite specifically where to look for the answer or promise to look for the answer yourself and give the report to the class on the following day. It is not likely that such situations will occur with undue frequency if the teacher is reasonably well prepared in the subject and engaged in a fairly wide reading program.

Should I repeat the answer given by a pupil if most of the pupils failed to hear it?

Usually the pupil who gave the answer should repeat it. He will thus acquire the habit of speaking more distinctly.

Should the pupils be called on alphabetically, as they are seated, or according to some other plan?

It is best to follow a plan of calling on pupils without regard to set procedure, otherwise only those likely to be called upon immediately will give maximum attention. It is desirable to reflect upon the situation occasionally and determine which pupils have suffered neglect. These can become the object of special attention for a while.

What is the best solution to the problem of individual differences?

This is indeed a difficult question. Educators have struggled with it for decades. It is quite proper to ask the brighter pupils to answer the more difficult questions and vice versa. If optional exercises are suggested for unit work activities, it is likely that the superior pupils will undertake them. A few more special reports can be assigned to those in the upper ability level. Interesting supplementary readings can be handed to those who finish their work successfully ahead of the others, not especially for reports but as a matter of recognizing their needs. In no case should superior people be given extra work merely to keep them busy. Their reaction would soon come to be that penalties were being inflicted for being brilliant. The use of praise in a judicious manner will prove stimulating to all ability levels. Every effort should be exerted to ascertain areas in which various individuals are most competent. In most cases the various aptitudes can be used to advantage in the social studies classroom. In no instance should we be tempted to yield to the undemocratic practice of grouping the pupils homogeneously on the basis of intelligence. In all their regular procedures of learning, pupils will work in groups showing evidence of individual differences.

Should the class be permitted to discuss controversial issues?

Definitely, yes. However, it should be remembered that it is possible for a group to state the views held by those on both sides of an issue without stating their own opinions as such. Furthermore, it should be understood that such topics are to be discussed without display of emotion and prejudice. The use of the names of local people, firms, and groups should not be used except to the extent that such illustrations have already appeared in the newspapers. Topics that are of general public interest can even be made the subject of forum discussion or debate.

Shall I tell the class what I think if a controversial issue is being discussed?

In many cases it is quite all right to do so. If it is done, the caution should be extended that this is merely a personal opinion and that members of the class may see the situation differently, which is their privilege. If the question is of such nature that undue prejudice attends it locally, the better judgment is to summarize the opposing views and to refrain from stating a personal opinion.

What should I do if it seems to me that some members of the class are attempting to divert the discussion from the objective of the lesson?

One should show a courteous interest in the trend of thought started by the pupils but at the same time be firm in suggesting that the central thought of the lesson be kept in mind. Perhaps an invitation could be extended to the pupils who wish to discuss the irrelevant topics to come in after school.

When conducting a discussion on the question-and-answer basis should I state the question first or indicate first the name of the pupil who is to answer it?

Stating the question first is always the correct procedure, otherwise the attention of all pupils except the one called upon is likely to fall short of maximum concentration.

Should the same general method of procedure be used as successive units of work are presented?

Ordinarily the method should be varied from time to time. Different units of subject matter do not lend themselves to the same type of treatment. Furthermore, pupils appreciate doing things differently. They regard variety as the "spice of life."

How many pages of work should I cover per day?

Social studies are not taught in terms of pages. Rather, attention is given to units that have meaning to the group. This means reading and investigating books, pamphlets, periodicals, etc., on an extensive scale. The present trend is to read widely on a restricted number of topics rather than to read in a narrow fashion about an extensive list of topics.

Where can the social studies teacher secure free and inexpensive materials to supplement instruction?

Many professional magazines carry a page in each issue devoted to this information. Usually the names and addresses of organizations and firms that have such materials are given, together with the terms upon which the materials may be obtained. The resourceful teacher will be constantly alert and will secure many valuable aids.

Should I assign extra work as a punishment for an individual whose conduct has been irregular?

This practice should never be followed. There should always be enough work that is worth while for regular assignments. Using assignments for punishments will quickly create a distaste for honest, straightforward work.

How familiar should I be with my pupils outside of class?

The teacher can be friendly, courteous, and jovial with pupils outside of class. In fact, these relationships will be favorable to the creation of good teacher-pupil relationships in class. (These statements are not to be construed as condoning courtships and romances between teachers and pupils of approximately the same age at the time the pupil is still enrolled in the school where the teacher is a staff member.)

Should teachers address their pupils by their first names, last names, "Mr." and "Miss," or by still some other title?

Secondary-school pupils should be addressed by their first names. Using the last name breaks with good manners. Girls often feel that their reputations are thus cheapened. "Mr." and "Miss" are too formal and sometimes cause younger pupils to feel too grown-up.

Is it proper to engage the help of pupils in such matters as the filing of materials, arrangement of the room, and checking papers?

Democratic attitudes can be developed through the use of these techniques. The teacher will thus develop an appearance of pupil participation rather than teacher domination. Pupils of lower intellectual ability can be brought to have a much greater interest in a social studies class if they regularly contribute something helpful to the daily proceedings. Pupil help on checking papers should usually not be used except in cases where semester or final examinations are given, and then only if the objective type has been used.

If it is apparent that some pupils are failing to master social studies because of inability to read well, what should the teacher do?

Success in social studies is directly related to reading ability. In cooperation will the English department, tests should be given to determine speed and comprehension ability. Additional tests should be included which reveal special social studies skills and ability to use and apply social studies information secured from special sources. The teacher of social studies should know the fundamentals of developing reading ability. Showing pupils how to read for thought and ideas, for details, and for summarization is essential.

Shall I let the pupils keep their test papers after they have been checked and returned for discussion?

Test papers should be collected and preserved until the grading period has passed. If any question arises that pertains to a particular pupil's grade, the teacher has concrete evidence at hand.

If a pupil has missed a test, should the same test that the rest of the class took be administered for make-up work?

It is better to use an entirely different test. The teacher may quite aptly give an oral test and scale the response value in terms of the grades earned by fellow pupils.

About how many questions should I have prepared for a day's discussion?

There is no specific answer. It is really better to prepare an outline of the lesson than it is to prepare questions. These will take form naturally as the lesson develops. One good thought-provoking question often accounts for more time than a dozen short-answer questions.

Should the advance assignment be written on the board?

This is very good procedure. The objective, pages to be read in various references, and work to be performed to ensure mastery can be listed briefly.

Should pupils be required to make up work that they have missed?

Regardless of the reason for absence, pupils should attempt to master well the work that was missed. The teacher should extend all the assistance that is necessary and within the limits of the time available.

What should be done if a pupil is dissatisfied with the grade he earned?

Evidence should be presented to show him the reason for the grade. Comments should follow in which the methods by which he could improve are outlined.

If the assignment has been made and a supervised study period has been planned but for some reason the group as a whole does not start studying, what is the correct procedure?

Try to determine the reason for the response. Ask the entire group if there is any point about the directions for study that they do not understand. If there are such points they can immediately be clarified. Then it can be emphasized that all will please proceed to work. If isolated individuals fail to conform, the teacher can approach them personally while walking about the room.

Can the teacher plan to work at the desk while the pupils are reading or doing activity exercises?

The pupils must feel keenly both the teacher's presence as part of the working situation and the teacher's willingness to assist when needed. To the extent that other work offers a handicap, it should not be done. It is difficult to read, check papers, write personal letters, etc., and make ideal conditions prevail.

In what ways can the social studies teacher know about books and materials that become available from time to time?

Most of the publishing companies keep school executives supplied with current lists of publications. These can be examined in school offices. Often they are sent directly to the teacher. In addition to depending upon these sources the alert teacher gains many leads by reading advertisements and specific sections in professional magazines.

Is the teaching of social studies easier or more difficult than the teaching of other secondary-school subjects?

There is no positive answer to such a question. A successful teacher of any subject is thoroughly trained for the job, possesses the required personality traits, and works industriously to succeed. One might reasonably conclude that there is no easy job in the realm of teaching. This does not mean that teaching is in the least unenjoyable for those who have conscientiously selected it for a profession.

What can the social studies teacher do to improve his public-speaking techniques and to reduce grammatical errors?

Taking additional courses in these areas is always helpful. Enlisting the help of friends who are competent and sympathetically inclined is good procedure. Listening to the more popular radio announcers and newscasters is time exceedingly well spent. The social studies teacher undoubtedly needs to know current news developments. Thus it is possible to gain two valuable results at one time.

I have heard that a great deal of importance is attached to the matter of getting well started on a new teaching job. How can I be sure of getting such a start?

The beginning social studies teacher should be present on the school premises well before the opening date of school. He should survey comprehensively the materials and equipment already available. To the extent that it is possible to do so he should learn about the pupils to be taught, their names, academic background, out-of-school interests, etc., as revealed in cumulative-record folders. Next, careful plans should be made as to how every minute of the first few periods may be spent profitably and enjoyably.

What are some activities that are valuable and interesting for the opening days of school?

The social studies teacher should attempt to learn quickly a great deal about the pupils as individuals. The first activity might well be that of pass-

ing out slips of paper asking for information on reading habits, radio programs listened to, movies attended, hobbies engaged in, work pursued, etc. A brief statement dealing with the content of the course should be made, followed by an opportunity for the pupils to indicate topics they would especially like to study. Within the first few days, time should be given to examining the basic textbooks to be studied, discussing the objectives for the study of social studies generally and of the specific one at hand, and planning effective methods of study. Likewise, some time should be devoted to defining the particular social study involved. Mention should be made of possible plans for bulletin-board work, treatment of current events, field trips, socialized procedures, audio-visual aids, etc. In short, the first few days should be highly motivating in nature. Actual attack on the first unit of work can properly be slightly delayed until the original desires are accomplished.

If this work has the status to which it is entitled, namely that the teacher is a regular member of the college or university staff, the teacher trainer may well be happy to make the position a permanent one. It should have the attraction of professional rank, good salary schedule, and liberal retirement provisions. If the individual so aspires he may properly think in terms of more responsible executive positions in the teacher-training institution. Director of student teaching, director of curriculum, personnel administrator, etc. are among the positions that could be anticipated if these happened to represent real advancements in the institutions involved.

A supervisory position to which social studies teachers could possibly look forward is sometimes found in state departments of education. On occasion such departments have a person in charge of each subject-matter area, social studies included. In addition to the training and experience described above, this position calls for one who has had extensive public-school administrative experience. Such background enables one to see more fully the place of social studies in the entire educational system, and it ensures ability to work better with school leaders in the effort to alter existing practices. Ability to organize and direct workshop activities, to stimulate the thinking of lay advisory groups, and to develop workable courses of study are quite essential. A very special service can and should be rendered the rural areas inasmuch as they receive less supervision than is characteristic of city systems. One who has held this position could look forward to positions of the type mentioned above and to places of educational leadership of a political character.

Points Common to All Social Studies Teaching Situations. Regardless of the particular type of school organization in which social studies are being taught, there are many points that have equal bearing. Social studies teachers uniformly need dynamic leadership. They work more effectively as a group than as a number of individuals seeking an equal number of different goals. They need to have called to their attention frequently for review and revision such items as a definition of education, the objectives of education, and the objectives of the social studies generally and of each individually. Likewise, in any teaching situation social studies teachers must keep alive the desire for continuous self-improvement, seeking the goal of greater aid to the pupils in the classroom and to society outside the limits of the school. Once a harmonious relationship is established between the supervisor and the group, there are several topics that come up for frank and sincere discussion. Some that rank very high are indicated, with specific questions that are often asked.

A. Curriculum
   1. What are the trends in social studies curriculum throughout the United States today?
   2. What should be included in specific courses in social studies?
   3. Is the core curriculum a good device to use in attaining the objectives of the social studies?
   4. Where do the social studies fit into the pattern of general education? of common learnings? of the experience-centered curriculum?
   5. Is the cycle plan of arranging social studies content desirable?
   6. How can the social studies function in a life-adjustment program?

B. Methods
   1. What should be done about problems, projects, and socialized recitations?
   2. Should class time ever be devoted to drill activities?
   3. How can the forum-discussion method be made interesting?
   4. Should workbooks, notebooks, and commercially prepared drill materials be used?
   5. Do the question-and-answer and textbook methods ever have a place?
   6. How can individual differences be dealt with most effectively?

C. Objectives
   1. Should the instruction be directed chiefly to the interests of the college-preparatory group or of those not planning higher education?
   2. Are objectives fundamentally different today from what they were a decade ago?

3. How should the objectives for our particular community be different from those of other communities?
4. Is it possible to articulate the objectives of social studies with those of education as a whole?
5. What publication contains the latest statements dealing with social studies objectives?

D. Materials of instruction

1. What are the latest reputable textbooks that have been published?
2. What is a good source of pamphlets and materials that will assist materially in teaching current problems?
3. From what firms and corporations may one secure free and inexpensive materials?
4. Should audio-visual materials be used in all the social studies?
5. How much is a reasonable amount to spend per pupil each year in executing successful teaching in the social studies?

This list of examples could be extended indefinitely. It would certainly include topics related to testing and evaluation, formulation of units of instruction, in-service growth of teachers, lesson planning, and many others. Obviously, the number of questions under each topic would greatly exceed that given in the above examples. This leads to the conclusion that the social studies supervisor will be called upon to give information about and answers to numberless questions. First, he should recognize the challenge of the work involved; second, he should not feel embarrassed at not having ready answers for all questions; third, he should feel obligated to work jointly with the teachers concerned in finding the best possible solutions.

In some respects the task of supervising the instruction of social studies teachers should not prove too difficult. Such teachers are conscientious and desire to make progress. Dimond [9] made the following observation: "Better understanding of children, more successful teaching of democracy, and improved methods of teaching have come about because most social studies teachers are inveterate seekers after better ways of doing things."

Summary. In this chapter the first section dealt with the qualifications needed by an efficient supervisor of social studies teaching. Such a person should possess all the qualities demanded of the classroom teacher in this area, but to a greater degree. Successful teaching ex-

[9] S. E. Dimond, "What's Right with the Teaching of Social Studies?" *Social Education,* XIII (January, 1949), p. 11.

perience is an absolute prerequisite. Ability to execute successful demonstration teaching is almost equally important. Social studies teachers have very pronounced notions as to what they want and do not want in their supervisor and his methods. Various types of supervisory positions to which regular social studies teachers may aspire were described. Among these were the department head in a typical high school, supervisor for a city system, senior teacher in a laboratory school, director of social studies in a state department of education, and others of a nature varying widely from one region to another.

There are some divisions of the job of the social studies supervisor that are clearly apparent and in which he should have marked skill. One is the conducting of profitable group teachers' meetings; a second is the visiting of classrooms in such a manner as to permit the normal program to take place; a third is the conducting of personal conferences that really result in stimulating and directing the teacher to do the best work that lies within his capacity.

Those who supervise student teachers need to have methods of gradually inducting the prospective teacher into the work. The profession must be made attractive, interesting, and compelling to candidates at this particular stage. Supervisors must help translate educational theory into practice as students practice guidance, attention to individual differences, writing of units of instruction, directing study, conducting recitations, etc. Ready answers must be at hand for the reasonable questions asked by these beginning teachers.

In many respects supervisors of instruction in social studies have much in common irrespective of the location or the conditions under which the supervising is done. The need for effective supervision exists universally. Most teachers find more pleasure in working cooperatively as a group than in working comparatively alone; furthermore, the results in terms of pupil achievement are infinitely more encouraging.

Questions on the Text

1. Describe the personal characteristics that the successful supervisor of the social studies should possess.
2. Outline in some detail the nature of the training and experience background that you think he should have.
3. After one becomes well qualified to do supervisory work in social

studies, what are some of the types of position available? How does work of this nature in a teacher-training institution differ from that in other settings?

4. Name three areas in which the social studies supervisor should possess special competence. Discuss the elements of success related to each.

5. Do you feel that social studies teachers really desire supervision? that they can profit under a well-organized supervisory program?

6. What are some possible uses and misuses of check sheets in the hands of the supervisor when visiting classes?

7. Discuss the relationship of daily lesson plans to well-written units of instruction.

8. Of what value can a check sheet or graph be in evaluating the work of a student teacher? Give examples of questions that the student teacher in social studies is likely to ask the supervisor.

9. Mention some points common to all social studies teaching situations regardless of the type of school organization.

Suggested Activities

1. Make some inquiry in your own community to find out the nature and extent of supervision being received by secondary-school social studies teachers.

2. Give a brief description of an actual or imaginary secondary school. Outline the type of supervisory program that you would recommend for its social studies teachers.

3. Prepare a forum discussion in which the pros and cons of rating sheets are discussed.

4. Visit a class in secondary-school social studies. Tell what you did that conformed to the recommended techniques of classroom visitation. Mention the points that you would use for discussion with the teacher of the class observed.

5. Make a list of topics in addition to those given in the chapter that you think a social studies teacher might profitably ask the supervisor to use for discussion and investigation.

6. Read one or more recent references from educational periodicals dealing with supervision in the social studies. Write brief summaries of each.

Selected References

Bail, B. M., "Do Teachers Receive the Kind of Supervision They Desire?" *Journal of Educational Research*, XL (May, 1947), pp. 713–716.

Barr, A. S., "The Use of Measurement in the Management of Teacher Personnel," *Education*, LXVI (March, 1946), pp. 431–435.

BARTKY, A. JOHN, "Helping Teachers Teach," *School and Society,* LXVI (Sept. 27, 1947), pp. 241–244.

DIMOND, S. E., "What's Right with the Teaching of the Social Studies?" *Social Education,* XIII (January, 1949), pp. 9–11.

FLINKER, I., "Supervision Can Be Dynamic," *Educational Administration and Supervision,* XXXIV (October, 1948), pp. 337–346.

GILLETT, MYRTLE MANN, "What Teachers Don't Like," *Nation's Schools,* XL (July, 1947), p. 26.

———, "Meaning of Good Supervision," *Journal of Education,* CXXXI (May, 1948), pp. 154–156.

GOUGH, SYMMIE, "Complaints of a Much Supervised Teacher," *Educational Leadership,* VI (December, 1948), pp. 154–158.

HARMAN, ALLEN C., "Classroom Visitation as a Phase of Supervision," *American School Board Journal,* CXVIII (June, 1949), pp. 39–40*ff.*

HART, WILLIAM G., "The Kind of Help a Teacher Wants," *Nation's Schools,* XLIV (July, 1949), pp. 52–54.

ISAACS, WILLIAM, and JULES KOLODNY, "Some Notes on Making Supervision Work," *The Education Digest,* XIII (April, 1948), pp. 14–16.

Leadership Through Supervision, Washington, D.C.: Association for Supervision and Curriculum Development, *1946 Yearbook,* 1946, p. 163.

MOFFATT, MAURICE P., *Social Studies Instruction,* New York: Prentice-Hall, Inc., 1950, Chap. XVII.

PATTINGTON, MEADER G., "Wide-awake Supervisor a Stimulus," *Nation's Schools,* XXXIX (January, 1947), pp. 47–48.

PECKHAM, DOROTHY REED, "Tribulations of a Supervisor," *Educational Leadership,* VI (December, 1948), pp. 158–160.

SAMFORD, CLARENCE D., "A Word to Beginning Student Teachers," *Social Education,* XI (February, 1947), pp. 71–73.

SAYER, ALBERT H., "Horse and Buggy Supervision in the Atomic Age," *High Points,* XXIX (April, 1947), pp. 17–24.

"This Is the Kind of Supervision We Want," *Educational Leadership,* V (January, 1947), pp. 254–261.

TYLER, RALPH W., "How Can We Improve High School Teaching?" *School Review,* XLVI (September, 1948), pp. 387–399.

WHEELER, E. G., "Improvement of Instruction in the Social Studies," *Social Education,* XIII (April, 1949), p. 166.

WHITE, KENNETH B., "The Improvement of Educational Administration and Supervision," *Educational Administration and Supervision,* XXXV (March, 1949), pp. 181–184.

WITHALL, JOHN, "Democratic Leadership: a Function of the Instructional Process," *School Review,* LXVII (May, 1949), pp. 276–281.

LIST OF VISUAL AIDS

The visual materials listed below and on the following pages can be used to supplement the material in this book. It is recommended, however, that each film be reviewed before using in order to determine its suitability for a particular group.

Both motion pictures and filmstrips are included in this list of visual materials, and the character of each one is indicated by the self-explanatory abbreviations "MP" and "FS." Immediately following this identification is the name of the producer; and if the distributor is different from the producer, the name of the distributor follows the name of the producer. Abbreviations are used for names of producers and distributors, and these abbreviations are identified in the list of addresses at the end of the bibliography. In most instances, the films listed can be borrowed or rented from local or state 16-mm. film libraries. Unless otherwise indicated, the motion pictures are 16-mm. sound films and the filmstrips are 35-mm., silent.

Film users who wish a complete bibliography of films dealing with teacher education, including social studies, should obtain *Selected Films for Teacher Education* published by Indiana University, Bloomington. Moreover, teachers and prospective teachers who wish information on specific films available for use in teaching history, geography, and other social studies subjects in the secondary school should examine *Educational Film Guide,* a catalog of some 10,000 films published by the H. W. Wilson Co., New York. The *Guide,* a standard reference book, is available in most college and public libraries.

Broader Concept of Method. Part 1: Developing Pupil Interest (MP, McGraw, 13 min). Contrasts a conventional, teacher-dominated lesson and an informal class with teachers and students planning and working together. (Correlated filmstrip, same title, 33 frames, also available.)

Broader Concept of Method. Part 2: Teachers and Pupils Planning and Working Together (MP, McGraw, 19 min). Students learning to work together in class projects with the help and guidance of the teacher. (Correlated filmstrip, same title, 37 frames, also available.)

Field Trip (MP, Va Ed Dept, 10 min). Basic steps involved in using a field trip as part of the instructional program; values of field trips; and field-trip opportunities in Virginia.

Film Tactics (MP, USN/UWF, 22 min). Right and wrong ways of using instructional films illustrated through imaginative scenes of the mental impressions of students during different types of film utilization.

Giving a Shop Demonstration (MP, USN/UWF, 18 min). How a shop teacher prepares for and demonstrates to a class of Navy trainees the making of a flanged tray. Illustrates elements of a good demonstration and how this method of teaching can be used effectively.

How to Make Handmade Lantern Slides (MP, Ind U, 22 min). Seven types of 3¼- by 4-in. lantern slides, techniques of making them, and possibilities of integrating their use with other instructional materials.

Let's Look at Maps (MP, Va Ed Dept, 10 min). How to understand maps by realizing that they are symbolic representations of reality. While made for student use, the film gives teachers a better understanding of how the ability to read and interpret maps can be developed in their students.

Learning Democracy through School-Community Projects (MP, Mich U/Locke, 22 min). How the public schools of Michigan provide opportunities for students to experience democracy by participating in school and community projects. Curricular innovations, extracurricular activities, and methods of instruction.

Learning to Understand Children. Part 1: A Diagnostic Approach (MP, McGraw, 20 min). Case study of a 15-year-old girl, badly maladjusted in school, and of the teacher's attempts to learn the causes of the girl's maladjustment.

Learning to Understand Children. Part 2: A Remedial Program (MP, McGraw, 22 min). Continuation of Part 1 showing the teacher's program, curricular and instructional, to help the girl become adjusted to herself and to the school environment.

Maintaining Classroom Discipline (MP, McGraw, 15 min). Two methods of discipline and their results in terms of classroom behavior and student learning.

Principles of the Art and Science of Teaching (MP, Iowa U, 55 min). Illustrates through the activities of a high-school class in American history three principles of good teaching: (1) formulation of objectives, (2) selection of content and activities, (3) adaptation of method.

Problem of Pupil Adjustment: The Drop-out (MP, McGraw, 20 min). Characteristics of a high-school program which cause students to leave school as soon as possible.

Problem of Pupil Adjustment: The Stay-in (MP, McGraw, 19 min). How "drop-outs" can be reduced when individual needs are met in a school program that stresses learning in terms of adjustment to everyday living.

Safest Way (MP, AAA, 18 min). Illustrates, through a class project in safety education, basic principles of good teaching, the uses of audio-visual methods, and democracy in the classroom.

School in Centerville (MP, NEA, 20 min). Illustrative example of a rural school with a program geared to the needs of its community.

Teachers for Tomorrow (MP, Wisc U, 22 min). How prospective teachers are chosen and prepared for a teaching career at the University of Wisconsin.

Teaching-materials Center (MP, Va Ed Dept, 12 min). Depicts values to the classroom teacher of a teaching-materials center; materials and resources available from a good center; organization of such a center.

Using the Classroom Film (MP, EBF, 20 min). Techniques of using an educational film in a classroom situation, specifically, in a seventh-grade social studies class.

We Plan Together (MP, TC, 21 min). How an eleventh-grade group plans cooperatively their class work.

Sources of Films Listed

AAA–American Automobile Association, 17th and Pennsylvania Ave., N.W., Washington, D.C.

EBF—Encyclopaedia Britannica Films, Inc., Wilmette, Ill.

Ind U–Indiana University, Audio-Visual Center, Bloomington.

Iowa U–State University of Iowa, Iowa City.

Locke–Locke Films, Inc., 120 W. Lovell St., Kalamazoo, Mich.

McGraw–McGraw-Hill Book Company, Inc., Text-Film Dept., 330 W. 42d St., New York.

Mich U–University of Michigan, School of Education, Ann Arbor. (Films distributed by Locke Films.)

NEA–National Education Association, 1201 16th St., N.W., Washington, D.C.

TC–Teachers College, Columbia University, New York.

Va Ed Dept–Virginia State Department of Education, Richmond.

USN–U.S. Navy Department, Washington 25, D.C. (Films sold under government contract by United World Films.)

UWF–United World Film, Inc., 1445 Park Ave., New York 29.

Wisc U–University of Wisconsin, Bureau of Visual Instruction, Madison.

INDEX

4. The theological usage of *dbq* "to cling to (God)" directly continues the usage treated in 3b. Except for Psa 63:9, "My soul clings to you," all occurrences belong to Dtn-Dtr language: Deut 4:4; 10:20; 11:22; 13:5; 30:20; Josh 22:5; 23:8,(12); 2 Kgs 18:6. Cf. also the different metaphor in Jer 13:11 and *ḥšq* qal "to cling to (in love)" in Psa 91:14. Whether Dtn-Dtr diction connotes the par. expression → *ʾhb* "to love" (cf. Deut 11:22; 30:20; Josh 22:5; 23:11f.; *ʾhb* parallels *dbq* elsewhere in Gen 34:3; 1 Kgs 11:2; Prov 18:24) or obedient faithfulness (cf. 2 Sam 20:2, plus W. L. Moran, *CBQ* 25 (1963): 78; *dbq* beside *ᶜbd* in Deut 10:20; 13:5; Josh 22:5; 23:7f.) can remain undecided (N. Lohfink, *Das Hauptgebot* [1963], 79). At any rate, the verb is usually an optional filler in longer series of verbs of proper relation to God (tables in Lohfink, op. cit. 303f.). In contrast to Dtn → *ʾhb* "to love" and *ḥšq* "to cling to out of love" (Deut 7:7; 10:15), God is never the subj. of *dbq*.

5. The Dtn theological usage is no longer current at Qumran and in the NT (except possibly for 1 Cor 6:17); by contrast, Gen 2:24 plays a greater role (cf. K. L. Schmidt, "κολλάω," *TDNT* 3:822f.).

E. Jenni

דָּבָר *dābār* **word**

S 1697; BDB 182a; *HALOT* 1:211a; *TDOT* 3:84–125; *TWOT* 399a; *NIDOTTE* 1821

I. 1. Lexicographers distinguish between two roots: *dbr* I "to be behind, turn the back" (Arab. *dub[u]r*), and II "word, matter." The rather rare root I includes a series of derivatives (*dᵉbîr* "back room," *dōber* "pasture," *dōbᵉrôt* "raft," *midbār* "steppe"); but root II stands remarkably isolated and is limited primarily to the frequent term *dābār* "word, matter" and to *dbr* pi. "to talk, speak." The much more weakly developed qal, ni., pu., and hitp. stems appear in addition to the pi. form. Also etymologically related to *dbr* II are *dibrâ* "matter" as a secondary development of *dābār, dibbēr* as a rare nom. form based on the verb, and *midbār* (II) "instrument of speech, mouth" as a nomen instrumenti.

M. Dahood (*Bib* 33 [1952]: 47f.) sees a Phoen. construction in the prep. phrase *ᶜal-dibrat* (Eccl 3:18; 7:14; 8:2) on account of the final *-t*.

The hapax legomenon *dabberet* (Deut 33:3) also apparently derives from the verb *dbr* pi.; cf., however, I. L. Seeligmann, *VT* 14 (1964): 80, who argues for a derivation from *dbr* I ("behind you"). *dābār* may also stand behind *deber* "bubonic plague," which could be understood as a euphemism; cf. the Ger. usage of *Ding* as a nebulous designation for "illnesses, esp. if sores and boils are associated with them" (J. and W. Grimm, *Deutsch Wörterbuch* [1860], 2:1164).

HAL 201b and KBL 199b attribute not only Job 19:18; Song Sol 5:6 (2 Chron 22:10 "to eradicate"; cf. *dbr* hi. "to drive off," Psa 18:48; 47:4) to *dbr* pi. I, but also Isa 32:7; Psa 75:6; 127:5. Moreover, *HAL* 202b posits a *dbr* pi. III "to have descendants" for Prov 21:28. Barr (*CPT* 324) catalogs other conjectures.

2. A convincing etymology for *dābār* has not yet been found.

On the etymological connection between *dbr* I and *dbr* II, cf. e.g., W. Leslau, *Language* 25 (1949): 316; J. T. Milik, *Bib* 38 (1957): 252; Barr (*SBL* 129–40) argues against misuse of etymology.

dbr II is normally associated with *d^ebôrâ* "bee," explained as a onomatopoeic "buzz." That *dābār* is used only rarely in legal discourse and *dbr* pi. is not used at all speaks against Buhl's position that the basic meaning of *dābār* is "a matter handled in a legal procedure and in the assembly of the people" (F. Buhl, "Über die Ausdrücke für: Ding, Sache u.ä. im Semitischen," FS Thomsen 33); see III/2.

The rare Akk. *dab/pāru* "to become full" (*CAD* D:104a) belongs in another semantic realm than the Hebr. *dbr* and offers nothing to the etymology of *dbr.*

Meanwhile, in *dabābu* Akk. possesses a richly developed term that corresponds semasiologically—both in the noun and the verb—to the Hebr. root in a remarkable manner. Like Hebr. *dābār,* the subst. *dabābu* represents "speech" and "legal matter"; as a verb it means "to speak" in the broadest sense (*CAD* D:2–14; *AHw* 146f.). Hebr. also knows the root *dbb: dibbâ* "rumor, slander" (9x). The question is, however, whether the semasiological affinity between Akk. *dabābu* and Hebr. *dābār/dbr* is a mere coincidence, or whether it may point to an etymological relationship. The semasiological isolation of NWSem. *dbr* suggests the possibility that *dbr* is only an apparent root and that the words should be understood as analogous formations whereby an original *dbb* was assimilated to the semasiologically related and somewhat synonymous → *ʾmr* "to say." The phonetic kinship between *dbr* and *ʾmr* lies not only in the third, but also in the middle radical (labial). Only a reminder of the well-known phenomenon that groups of roots with two common radicals are often semasiologically identical or related is necessary here (cf. Moscati, *Intro.* 72f.).

3. Beyond Hebr. (cf. also occurrences in the Lachish Letters and in the Siloam inscription, l. 1), the root is restricted to a limited usage in Phoen.-Pun. (pi. "to speak" and subst. "word, matter") and in Imp. Aram. texts (only in the usage *ʿl dbr* "in reference to"; see *DISO* 55). Only the nom. form *dibrâ* "concern" occurs in Bibl. Aram. (Dan 2:30; 4:14; cf. KBL 1063b).

dbr II is unattested in Ug.; the root *rgm* expresses the meanings "to speak" and "word" (cf. *UT* no. 2307; *WUS* no. 2491).

II. The noun *dābār* is attested 1,440x and is the 10th most common subst. With 1,084 occurrences the pi. of the verb is far more frequent than the qal (41x).

Lis. omits 2 Chron 8:14 for *dābār* (1 Chron 17:6; 2 Chron 34:16 in the appendix); Job 16:4 is listed as a qal instead of as a pi. verb. The following table does not count *lōʾ dābār* as a proper name in Amos 6:13 (etc.) and *dbr* pi. III in Prov 21:28 "to have descendants," but does count (against *HP* 231, 282 following *HAL* 201b) Isa 32:7; Psa 75:6; 127:5 (see I/1). The distinction between sg. and pl. consistently follows the Q (sg. in Judg 13:17; 1 Kgs 8:26; 18:36; 22:13; Jer 15:16; Psa 105:28; 119:147; Dan 9:12; Ezra 10:12; pl. in Psa 147:19).

	dābār			*dbr*	
	sg.	pl.	total	pi.	qal
Gen	31	30	61	72	1
Exod	39	23	62	86	1
Lev	7	1	8	66	–
Num	24	5	29	115	3
Deut	49	47	96	69	1
Josh	23	9	32	32	–
Judg	18	7	25	27	–
1 Sam	47	31	78	41	–
2 Sam	55	13	68	37	–
1 Kgs	86	38	124	77	–
2 Kgs	43	65	108	50	–
Isa	33	14	47	46	3
Jer	118	86	204	109	4
Ezek	70	12	82	64	–
Hos	2	2	4	7	–
Joel	2	–	2	1	–
Amos	6	3	9	2	1
Obad	–	–	–	1	–
Jonah	5	–	5	1	1
Mic	2	1	3	2	1
Nah	–	–	–	–	–
Hab	–	–	–	1	–
Zeph	2	–	2	1	–
Hag	6	1	7	–	–
Zech	13	7	20	7	11
Mal	1	2	3	–	–
Psa	48	21	69	46	9
Job	9	11	20	37	1
Prov	17	19	36	7	2
Ruth	3	–	3	3	–
Song Sol	–	–	–	–	–
Eccl	9	15	24	5	–
Lam	–	–	–	–	–
Esth	24	13	37	6	1
Dan	12	9	21	18	1
Ezra	10	4	14	1	–
Neh	16	13	29	4	–
1 Chron	20	10	30	10	–
2 Chron	36	42	78	33	–
Hebr. OT	886	554	1,440	1,084	41

The following also occur: *dbr* ni. 4x (Ezek 33:30; Mal 3:13, 16; Psa 119:23), pu. 2x (Psa 87:3; Song Sol 8:8), hitp. 4x (Num 7:89; 2 Sam 14:13; Ezek 2:2; 43:6), *dibrâ* 5x (Psa 110:4; Job 5:8; Eccl 3:18; 7:14; 8:2), *dibbēr* 2x (Jer 5:13; 9:7), *dabberet* 1x (Deut 33:3); *midbār* 1x (Song Sol 4:3); Bibl. Aram. *dibrâ* 2x (Dan 2:30; 4:14).

III. 1. (a) The basic meaning of *dbr* pi. differs rather sharply from the semasiologically related and somewhat synonymous verb → *ʾmr* "to say, speak." For the latter, attention to the content of the speech is important, but *dbr* pi. indicates primarily the activity of speaking, the production of words and phrases. *ʾmr* requires that the content of the speech (in direct address) be given or sufficiently characterized by the context (accordingly, *ᵓmr* is not used abs.); *dbr* pi. can stand abs. without further reference to that which is communicated (e.g., Gen 24:15; Job 1:16; 16:4, 6; cf. *HP* 165).

In view of the broader significance of *dbr* pi., it is natural that its subjects derive from a much more limited and unified semantic field than is the case for *ᵓmr.* For *ᵓmr* a profusion of speaking subjs. is possible (land, sea, animals, trees, night, fire, work, saying, etc.); the speakers in connection with *dbr* pi. are almost exclusively personal (divine or human) or designations of the organs of speech: mouth, lips, tongue, voice. Even Job 32:7 "the days may speak" has people in mind. In addition, "the spirit of Yahweh" (2 Sam 23:2) and "heart" (Psa 41:7 txt?) stand as subjs. of *dbr* pi.

Meanwhile, *dbr* pi. also often describes the pronunciation of a particular content. Indeed, as a trans., *dbr* pi. has a great capacity for taking objects. The most frequent occurrences are *dābār* (sg. and pl.) and other designations for moral and ideal values that appear as the content of speech: good, evil, truth, lies, faithfulness, apostasy, wisdom, folly, pride, humility, salvation, judgment, justice, perversity, etc.

The manner of speech can also be more nearly qualified with the aid of adverbial additions: "with audacity" (Deut 18:22), "secretly" (1 Sam 18:22; Isa 45:19; 48:16), "uselessly" (Ezek 6:10), "in the heart" (1 Sam 1:13), and "haughtily" (Psa 17:10).

The manner in which the addressee is indicated distinguishes *dbr* pi. markedly from *ᵓmr.* For the latter a simple *l^e* sufficiently expresses the close relationship to the addressee, but *dbr* pi. normally requires the stronger prep. *ᵓel,* approximately ten times more common with this verb than *l^e*.

Occasionally, *dbr* pi. appears in conjunction with complementary temporal expressions illuminating the scope of the verb, e.g., → *šm*ᶜ "to hear" (Isa 66:4; Job 42:4), *ᵓlm* ni. "to be silent" (Ezek 24:27), *ḥšh* "to keep silent" (Eccl 3:7), → *ᶜśh* "to act" (Ezek 12:25, 28).

(b) The connotation of the qal diverges somewhat from the pi. The common act. ptcp. usually indicates someone who customarily functions as speaker, who speaks under commission or because of his/her inner nature: truth (Psa 15:2), lies, falsehood (Jer 40:16; Psa 5:7; 58:4; 63:12; 101:7), right (Isa 33:15; 45:19; Prov 16:13), salvation (Esth 10:3), folly (Isa 9:16), insolence (Psa 31:19); in Zech 11x of the prophet's interpreting angel; Gen 16:13 of *ᵓēl r^{o}ᶜî,* the special god of Hagar who used to speak to her; Num 27:7 and 36:5 of a speech constantly in someone's mouth (Nyberg 221; cf. also the differentiation between *dbr* qal and pi. in *HP* 164–70).

2. (a) Like the Akk. root *dbb,* the Hebr. root *dbr* has a nom. function in addition to the verbal. The basic meaning of the noun *dābār* corresponds, in the first instance, very precisely to that of the verbs: "what is spoken, word."

The difference between *dbr* pi. and *ᵓmr* is reflected in a comparison of *dābār* with *ᵓēmer* (→ *ᵓmr* 3c). As one may infer, not least of all from the frequent expression *ᵓimrê-pî/pîkā/pîw* "the speech of my/your/his mouth," the oral character is essential to *ᵓēmer.* It is primarily a term for communication, a simple means of oral communication and understanding between distant persons. *dābār* is associated with "mouth" by the aid of a cs. phrase only as an exception (Jer 9:19; Psa 36:4; Prov 18:4; Eccl 10:12f.), all the more preferably, however, with terms qualifying the content of the "word," esp. with indications of moral and religious value (see III/1a on the objs. of *dbr* pi.).

(b) *dābār* exhibits an expansion of the verbal meaning that OT persons would hardly have perceived as a shift of meaning: *dābār* stands not only for "word," i.e., for the linguistic carrier of meaning, but also for the content itself. In this regard, however, an important reservation must be made. If one wishes to reckon with a dual meaning for *dābār* (e.g., "word" and "matter"), then one should not refer to the ancient worldview, which knew no sharp distinction between spiritual and concrete, to explain this semasiological duality. The contrast between "word" and "matter" does not primarily concern a contrast between spiritual and concrete. *dābār* does not signify "object" in an empirical sense, i.e., in contrast to "person" or as a designation for someone's property (cf. *k*^e^*lî* "object, device"), but is thoroughly abstract in character. Something of the activity of the verb is always implied in *dābār:* it indicates something that can occasion some discussion or treatment or that can become the object of such a discussion, thus "concern, incident, event" (e.g., 1 Sam 4:16; 10:16; 21:9; 2 Sam 1:4; 1 Kgs 12:30; Ruth 3:18; Esth 1:13; 2:22; 8:5; Ezra 10:9). The formula *dibrê hayyāmîm* "the events of the day" in the sense of "annals" (1 Kgs 14:19 and a further 32x, *sēper dibrê hayyāmîm* in Kgs; likewise in Esth 2:23; 6:1; 10:2; Neh 12:23; cf. 1 Chron 27:24), the frequent association of *dibrê* with a PN, usually that of a king (e.g., 1 Kgs 11:41 "the history of Solomon"), and *hadd*^e^*bārîm hā*ʾ*ēlleh* "these events" (Gen 15:1; 22:1, 20, etc.) are characteristic.

(c) *dābār* is also useful as a replacement when a specific expression is not immediately available or should be avoided (e.g., Gen 19:8; 1 Sam 20:2; 2 Chron 29:36), esp. in conjunction with a negation (e.g., 1 Sam 20:21; 22:15) or with *kōl* "all" (Num 31:23; Judg 18:7; 19:19). In this diminished sense, *dābār* has even assumed the function of an indefinite pron.; a similar generalization and designation has also affected other nouns, e.g., *m*^e^*lā*ʾ*kâ* "word" > "something" (Exod 36:6; Lev 7:24, etc.). *dābār* acquires a more definite meaning by means of attributive or genitival modification or by reference to an event or process.

Thus *dābār* can also indicate the nature and cause for any concern or event (Josh 5:4; 1 Kgs 11:27), esp. following ʿ*al* used as a prep. or a conjunction: "for . . . sake, because"; *dibrâ* appears in the same function in Eccl 3:18; 7:14; 8:2.

(d) It is noteworthy that *dābār* does not find frequent usage in legal language, and it is questionable whether it occurs at all as a technical juristic term. Primary consideration should be given to the unique expression *ba*ʿ*al d*^e^*bārîm* (Exod 24:14): "whoever has a legal case." In other passages it hardly seems possible to conceive of *dābār* as a precise, technical legal term (Exod 18:16; 22:8; Deut 1:17; 16:19; 19:15). *dābār* here apparently stands as an imprecise replacement for the technical term → *rîb.*

*3. In Bibl. Aram., *dābār* and *dbr* pi. are represented by the synonymous *millâ* "word, matter" (24x in Dan) and *mll* pa. "to speak" (5x in Dan). These terms have also entered into Hebr. from Aram. (cf. KBL 1093b, 1094b; *DISO* 152, 154; Wagner nos. 171f.); Hebr. *millâ* "word" occurs 38x (Job 34x, otherwise only in 2 Sam 23:2; Psa 19:5; 139:4; Prov 23:9) and *mll* qal "to give a sign" 1x (Prov 6:13), pi. "to speak, proclaim" 4x (Gen 21:7; Psa 106:2; Job 8:2; 33:3; on 1 Chron 25:4, 26, cf. Rudolph, HAT 21, 166f.).

The Old Pers. loanword *pitgām* "word, message" (KBL 1114b; *DISO* 238) is another synonym in Aram. (Bibl. Aram. 6x: Dan 3:16; 4:14; Ezra 4:17; 5:7, 11; 6:11), which also occurs in Hebr. as an Aramaism (Eccl 8:11; Esth 1:20; cf. Wagner no. 241).

IV. 1. God/Yahweh stands as the subject of *dbr* pi. almost 400x. A fixed theological usage is most likely in passages that use "to speak" absolutely, i.e., without obj. or adv. modifier. "Yahweh/God (or the mouth of Yahweh) has spoken" occurs in about 40 passages, almost without exception in the Prophets, esp. frequently in Ezek (18x) and Isa (12x), rarely in Jer (1x, 13:15); outside the Prophets, Psa 50:1, 7.

The use of preps. accords with the remarks in III/1a, i.e., *ʾel* exhibits a marked predominance in theological language (more than 150x). Far behind are the roughly equal occurrences of the preps. *l^e* and *ʿal*.

2. (a) The noun *dābār*, an important theological term, plays a disproportionately significant role in theological language, esp. in the expression *d^{e}bar yhwh* "word of Yahweh" (besides the OT theologies, cf. O. Grether, *Name und Wort Gottes im AT* [1934]; L. Dürr, *Die Wertung des göttlichen Wortes im AT und im antiken Orient* [1938]; W. Zimmerli, *RGG* 6:1809–12). The expression appears in the sense of "Yahweh's affair" in only 1 Chron 26:32 and 2 Chron 19:11, both times juxtaposed with the par. *d^{e}bar hammelek* "the king's affair." Otherwise *d^{e}bar yhwh* always means "the word of Yahweh" (242x in the OT, incl. 9 passages in which the divine name differs), and the expression appears usually (225x) as a technical term for the prophetic verbal revelation.

The distribution of the 242 passages cited (233x *d^{e}bar yhwh*, excl. 2 Chron 19:11; as well as *d^{e}bar ʾ^{a}dōnāy yhwh* in Ezek 6:3; 25:3; 36:4; *d^{e}bar (hā)ʾ^{e}lōhîm* in Judg 3:20; 1 Sam 9:27; 2 Sam 16:23; 1 Kgs 12:22; 1 Chron 17:3; excl. 1 Chron 26:32; *d^{e}bar ʾ^{e}lōhēnû* in Isa 40:8) exhibits a strong concentration in prophetic literature, incl. the prophetic narratives: Ezek 60x, Jer 52x, 1 Kgs 34x, 2 Kgs 16x, Zech 13x, Isa and 2 Chron 9x, 1 Sam 8x, 1 Chron 6x, Hag 5x, 2 Sam 4x, Jonah 3x, Gen, Exod, Josh, Hos, Amos, Mic, Zeph, Psa 2x each, Num, Deut, Judg, Joel, Mal, Dan, Ezra 1x each, thus 152x in Isa–Mal and 62x in 1 Sam–2 Kgs.

In more than half the cases, *d^{e}bar yhwh* stands as subj., even with *hyh ʾel* "to come to" as predicate 118x (Gen 15:1; 1 Sam 15:10; 2 Sam 7:4; 24:11; 1 Kgs 6:11; 12:22; 13:20; 16:1, 7; 17:2, 8; 18:1, 31; 21:17, 28; 2 Kgs 20:4; Isa 28:13; 38:4; Jer 29x; cf. H. Wildberger, *Jahwewort und prophetische Rede bei Jeremia* [1942], 19–42; Ezek 50x; cf. Zimmerli, *Ezek*, Herm, 1:144f.; Jonah 1:1; 3:1; Hag 1:1, 3; 2:1, 10, 20; Zech 1:1, 7; 4:8; 6:9; 7:1, 4, 8; 8:1, 18; Dan 9:2; 1 Chron 17:3 *d^{e}bar ʾ^{e}lōhîm;* 22:8; 2 Chron 11:2; 12:7; cf. also Gen 15:4 and 1 Kgs 19:9 with *hinnēh* instead of *hyh*). Unique predicates of *d^{e}bar yhwh* are *glh* ni. "to be revealed" (1 Sam 3:7), *yṣʾ* "to go out" (Isa 2:3 = 4:2), and *qûm* "to last" (Isa 40:8).

d^{e}bar yhwh appears as an obj. in 52 passages, 36 times in association with the verb *šmʿ* "to hear" (incl. 1 Sam 9:27 *d^{e}bar ʾ^{e}lōhîm* with *šmʿ* hi.); other predicates are *bzh* "to despise" (Num 15:31; 2 Sam 12:9), *drš* "to seek" (1 Kgs 22:5 = 2 Chron 18:4), *klh* "to be fulfilled" (Ezra 1:1 = 2 Chron 36:22), *mʾs* "to reject" (1 Sam 15:23, 26), *mlʾ* pi. "to fulfill" (1 Kgs 2:27; 2 Chron 36:21); also, with one occurrence each, *bqš* pi. "to seek" (Amos 8:12), *yrʾ* "to fear" (Exod 9:20), *ngd* hi. "to announce" (Deut 5:5), *qûm* hi. "to carry out" (1 Sam 15:13), *rʾh* "to see" (Jer 2:31 txt?), and *šmr* "to pay heed to" (2 Chron 34:21).

Just as *dābār* does not seem to be a legal term native to profane usage, neither can a juristic character be demonstrated for *d^{e}bar yhwh*. The expression unequivocally indicates God's legal word in only seven passages, all of which belong to a late period: Num 15:31; Deut 5:5; 2 Sam 12:9; 1 Chron 15:15; 2 Chron 30:12; 34:21; 35:6.

(b) The pl. cs. phrase *dibrê yhwh* occurs 17x (Exod 4:28; 24:3f.; Num 11:24; Josh 3:9; 1 Sam 8:10; 15:1; Jer 36:4, 6, 8, 11; 37:2; 43:1; Ezek 11:25; Amos 8:11; 2 Chron 11:4; 29:15); to these may be added three passages with *ʾelōhîm* (Jer 23:36; Ezra 9:4; 1 Chron 25:5). The pl. stands as the obj. of verbs of speech much more often than the sg.: *ngd* hi. "to announce" (Exod 4:28) *spr* pi. "to recount" (Exod 24:3), *dbr* pi. "to proclaim" (Num 11:24; Jer 43:1; Ezek 11:25), *ʾmr* "to say" (1 Sam 8:10), *qrʾ* "to cry out" (Jer 36:6, 8). The pl. does apply to prophetic verbal revelation, but not in the almost completely exclusive way in which the sg. does.

(c) Besides the cs. relationship, *dābār/debārîm* occurs more than 300x in reference to God. In approximately 3/4 of these passages, the term indicates prophetic verbal revelation, regarding which the pl. has a much greater frequency than it does in the cs. relationship (the ratio of sg. to pl. is about 4:5). In almost 1/5 of the passages, thus somewhat more frequently than in the cs. relationship, the "word" is an indication of God's legal word. This usage of *dābār* already occurs in pre-Dtn times, although rarely and with some limitations: only in the pl. and only as a characterization of the giving of the covenant law at Sinai. In Deut an expansion to other laws is visible (e.g., Deut 12:28; 15:15; 24:18, 22; 28:14; 30:14). The same loosening of usage is also present in P (Exod 29:1; Lev 8:36, etc.).

In Dtr and post-Dtr texts, furthermore, *dibrê* (cs. pl.) occurs in combination with various terms referring to customs, law, and cult: → *tôrâ* (Deut 17:19; 27:3, 8, 26; 28:58; 29:28; 31:12, 24; 32:46; Josh 8:34; 2 Kgs 23:24; Neh 8:9, 13; 2 Chron 34:19), → *berît* (Deut 28:69; 29:8 [cf. v 18 → *ʾālâ*]; 2 Kgs 23:3; Jer 11:2, 6, 8; 2 Chron 34:31), *sēper* "book (of the law, the covenant)" (2 Kgs 22:11, 13, 16; 23:2; 2 Chron 34:21, 30). The result of this loosening of usage is that the earlier distinction between prophetic and legal *dābār* is greatly effaced in Dtr and post-Dtr texts.

In wisdom literature (Prov and Sir) *dābār,* like the related terms *tôrâ* and *miṣwâ* "commandment," describes the doctrines of wisdom and does not occur in the meaning "word of God" (cf. E. G. Bauckmann, *ZAW* 72 [1960]: 33–63).

(d) As a theological term *dābār* is clearly distinguished in the OT from the related term → *šēm* "name." The two never appear in conjunction as subj. or obj. of a sentence, nor as alternatives or corresponding terms in par. verses. This formal separation of the two terms reflects a conceptual distinction: "As the name of God, the *šēm* describes him as a person, and, therefore, concerns God in his totality. The *dābār* is an expression of the thoughts and will of God" (Grether, op. cit. 169). "The *šēm* mediates God's presence in the world, the *dābār* his activity in it. The former is the representative, the latter the voluntative manifestation of Yahweh" (op. cit. 179). Characteristic of this distinction is the fact that the "holy word" is mentioned only once (Psa 105:42), but *šēm* is regularly associated with the concept of holiness (→ *qdš*).

(e) *dābār* also plays a rather significant role in the discussion of the so-called hypostatization of divine activities and attributes. The autonomy and personification of *dābār,* reaching its highest degree of development only in the postcanonical era, is already present in its initial stages in the OT (Grether, op. cit. 150ff.; Dürr, op. cit. 122ff.; H. Ringgren, *Word and Wisdom: Studies in the Hypostatization of Divine Qualities and Functions in the Ancient Near East* [1947], 157ff.). The following passages are listed as the most unequivocal OT examples: Isa 9:7, "The Lord sends a word against Jacob, and it descends upon Israel"; 55:10f., "For like the rain . . . , so, too, is my word that comes from my mouth: it does not return to me empty, but works what I have decided, and carries out that for which I sent it"; Psa 107:20, "To those to whom he sent his word to heal them"; 147:15, "Who sent his word to earth." The discussion suffers from the almost exclusive perception of hypostatization as a religiohistorical phenomenon, a type of mythologization: a divine attribute is separated from the deity, considered autonomous, and understood as an independent entity or even as a special deity. It is questionable, however, whether one may isolate the "hypostatization" of divine attributes from the general propensity for objectification and personification of the abstract active throughout the OT. Human emotions and activities are objectified and considered autonomous just as often as divine attributes: evil, perversity, anxiety, hope, wrath, goodness, faithfulness, etc. (Psa 85:11f.; 107:42; Job 5:16; 11:14; 19:10, etc.; cf. G. Gerleman, "Bemerkungen zum atl. Sprachstil," FS Vriezen 108–14).

3. The term *millâ* "word," which originated in the Aram.-speaking realm (see III/3), is rare in theological language. It occurs only twice as an indication of the divine word (2 Sam 23:2; Job 23:5; see also the Aram. in Dan 4:30), but never in a cs. relationship with Yahweh or God.

V. In the Qumran texts both the verb and the noun are frequent. Kuhn (*Konk.* 47–49; also *GCDS* 106f.) catalogs over 50 and over 90 occurrences, resp.

The LXX usually renders *dbr* pi. with *lalein* (→ ᵓ*mr* 5). The relatively uniform usage of *dābār* in the Hebr. OT has decayed; two Gk. terms translate it: *logos* and *rhēma,* distributed in the canonical books in a ratio of roughly 2:1 (cf. E. Repo, *Der Begriff "Rhēma" im Biblisch-Griechischen* [1951], 1:188).

NT usage agrees with the OT insofar as "word of God" indicates the self-revelation of God in the spirit and thus appears as a synonym of "gospel." In addition, "the word," the logos, is closely associated and even equated with the person of Jesus. Numerous studies of *logos* also treat, more or less extensively, the backgrounds of the term in the OT and in Palestinian and Hellenistic Judaism. The following may be mentioned: A. Debrunner, H. Kleinknecht, O. Procksch, and G. Kittel, "λέγω," *TDNT* 4:69–143; G. Stählin, "μῦθος," *TDNT* 4:762–95; V. Hamp, *Der Begriff "Wort" in den aram. Bibelübersetzungen* (1938).

G. Gerleman

דּוֹר *dôr* generation

S 1755; BDB 189b; *HALOT* 1:217b; *TDOT* 3:169–81; *TWOT* 418b; *NIDOTTE* 1887

1. *dôr* "generation" belongs to a common Sem. root *dwr,* for which the meaning "duration" dominates in ESem. and the meaning "generation" in WSem. (P. Fronzaroli, *AANLR* 8/20 [1965]: 143, 148). The word group comprises Akk. *dūru* "circular wall" (*AHw* 178); Hebr. *dôr* "(circular) encampment, dwelling" (Isa 38:12) and *dûr* "circle" (Isa 29:3; "ball"? Isa 22:18; cf. also *dûr* "to stack up in circles," Ezek 24:5); Bibl. Aram. *dûr* "to dwell" (7x in Dan; KBL 1064a; in Psa 84:11 as an Aram. loanword; cf. Wagner no. 68), *m^edôr* (Dan 4:22, 29; 5:21), and *m^edār* (Dan 2:11) "dwelling"; Arab. *dawr* "circumference, circle," *dāra* "to circle," and *dār* "dwelling," etc., are apparently not directly related.

Besides the frequent Akk. terms *dāru/dūru* "long duration," *darû* "to last," *dārû* "lasting," *dārītu* "duration, eternity" (*AHw* 164, 178b), *dāru* also occurs once at Mari as a WSem. loanword meaning "lifetime" (*AHw* 164b; *CAD* D:115b).

Ug. *dr dr* corresponds to the Hebr. *dôr dôr* (Exod 3:15); in addition, *dr bn il* (par. *mpḫrt bn il*) "assembly of the sons of God" also occurs (cf. *WUS* nos. 785f.; *UT* no. 697). Phoen.-Pun. *dr* means "family, generation" (*DISO* 60); here too the expression *kl dr bn ʾlm* "the whole generation of the sons of the gods" occurs (Karatepe inscription, *KAI* no. 26A.III.19; cf. *ANET* 654b; F. J. Neuberg, *JNES* 9 [1950]: 215–17; M. Dahood, *Le Antiche Divinità Semitiche* [1958], 66).

Aram. extrabibl. examples are late, e.g., Syr. *dārā* "era, generation" (*LS* 147a).

Opinions regarding etymology are divided, esp. concerning whether *dôr* is associated with the "circle" concept.

If this question is answered affirmatively, then *dôr* would indicate "the circular, self-contained passage of time . . . in which a human generation completes its development" (C. von Orelli, *Die hebr. Synonyma der Zeit und Ewigkeit* [1871], 34; similarly W. A. Ward, *Or* 31 [1962]: 398f., who refers, additionally, to Eg. *tr* "time"). The etymological relationship to "circle" has probably correctly been denied by other scholars (cf. also Fronzaroli, op. cit. 143): Neither Akk. *dāru* nor Hebr. *dôr* concerns the concept "circle"; rather, they belong to the semantic sphere of "duration, continuum" (*CAD* D:108b). A third etymology associates *dôr* with a root *dhr* "wagon race," thus **dahru* > **dāru* > *dôr,* properly, "circuit in a race," then "cycle" (W. F. Albright, *BASOR* 163 [1961]: 50f.).

Bibl. Aram. has *dār* with the same meaning in the dual expression *dār w^edār* (Dan 3:33; 4:31) and a derivative *t^edîr* "duration" (Dan 6:17, 21; KBL 1135f.).

2. *dôr* occurs in the OT 166x (92x alone and 37x in the formula *dôr dôr*), Bibl. Aram. *dār* 4x. The pl. has the masc. form *dôrîm* 3x (Isa 51:8; Psa 72:5; 102:25), otherwise the fem. form *dôrôt* occurs (48x).

The word is esp. frequent in the Psalter (59x with 21 repetition formulae). *dôr* occurs in the Prophets only in Isa (17x, excl. 38:12), Jer (4x), and Joel (5x). In the Pentateuch, the older sources (Gen 7:1; 15:16; Exod 1:6; 3:15; 17:16; Num 32:13) and Deut (11x) use the sg., the priestly layers the pl. (Gen 5x, Exod 4x, Lev 14x, Num 9x).

Regarding the frequency in P and in the Psa, cf. Akk. *dār, dūr,* and *(ana) dūr dār,* limited principally to poetic and juristic language (*CAD* D:108b).

3. In contrast to a series of other collective terms referring to origin and relationship (*zeraᶜ* "descendants," *mišpāḥâ* "tribe," *tôlēdôt* "descendants"), *dôr* is primarily temporal. As the word's etymology indicates, it belongs semantically to the temporal sphere: "duration, continuum." According to the Hebr. concept of time, however, temporal extension is not conceived as a simple abstraction. It must always be perceived in terms of its content (von Rad, *Theol.* 2:100f.). The period of time indicated by *dôr* may be comprehended only as the duration of the people living in it. The past, like the future, is described as a series of many sequential generations.

The referent of the word can vary greatly. The concrete notion of a collective group of people living at a particular time occasionally becomes prominent (Gen 6:9; 7:1; Exod 1:6; Lev 23:43; Num 32:13; Deut 1:35; 2:14; 23:3f., 9; 29:21; 32:5, 20; Judg 2:10; Isa 41:4; Jer 2:31; Joel 1:3; Psa 12:8; 14:5; 24:6; 78:6, 8; Prov 30:11–14; Eccl 1:4). Here *dôr* almost always stands in a very general sense, i.e., "the total group of contemporaries active in public life" (M. Noth, *Deuteronomistic History* [1981], 105n.12). Only rarely does it have an exclusive sense indicating a limited circle within the people (Psa 24:6; 112:2; Prov 30:11–14).

Other passages definitely emphasize the temporal character, i.e., Isa 51:9. *dôr* has the sense of a temporal modifier in particular in a few usually fixed formulae: *dôr wādôr* (30x, 18x in Psa), without *waw:* Exod 3:15; 17:16; Prov 27:24 K; cf. Ug. *drdr* and Akk. *dūr dār* "forever." Other double forms, which do not serve as temporal advs., are *dôr lᵉdôr* (Psa 145:4), *dôr dôrîm* (Psa 72:5; with prefixed *lᵉ* Isa 51:8; with *bᵉ* Psa 102:25). The pl. with suf. and prefixed *lᵉ* characterizes P and is almost exclusively employed by it (39x); *lᵉdōrōtēkem/lᵉdōrōtām/lᵉdōrōtāyw* "according to your/their/his generations" functions as a temporal adv. pointing to the future and is roughly synonymous with *lᵉᶜôlām* (→ *ᶜôlām*).

Regarding Isa 53:8, where G. R. Driver (*JTS* 36 [1935]: 403) and others translate *dôr* with "destiny" (e.g., D. W. Thomas, *ETL* 44 [1968]: 84), cf. Westermann, *Isa 40–66,* OTL, 265.

4. *dôr* has no specifically theological usage. As a temporal adv. *dôr* is noneschatological. The infrequency of the word in the prophets and in their statements concerning the future are noteworthy. As a designation for a group of people, too, *dôr* exhibits no specifically theological references. The "generation" is rather rarely the topic of religious and ethical assessment (Deut 1:35; 32:5, 20; Psa 12:8; 14:5; 24:6; 78:8; 112:2; Prov 30:11–14).

5. Kuhn (*Konk.* 49) catalogs roughly 30 occurrences in Qumran texts (see also *GCDS* 108). OT usage continues for the most part. The expressions *dôrôt neṣaḥ* (1QH 1:16) and *dôrôt ᶜôlām* (1QH 1:18; 6:11; 4QPBless 4) "eternal generation" (cf. Isa 51:9) are noteworthy.

The LXX translates *dôr* almost exclusively by *genea,* which indicates origin and descent. On the NT, cf. F. Büchsel, "γενεά," *TDNT* 1:662–65.

G. Gerleman

דִּין *dîn* to judge

S 1777; BDB 192a; *HALOT* 1:220a; *TDOT* 3:187–94; *TWOT* 426; *NIDOTTE* 1906

---

1. The root *dîn* is common Sem. (cf. *HAL* 211).

The word group occurs among Israel's neighbors frequently, in Akk. (*AHw* 150f., 167f., 171f., 571f.), Ug. (*WUS* no 766; *UT* no. 657), and Aram. (*DISO,* 56f., 143), but is absent from Phoen.-Pun. (→ *špṭ*).

In the OT, the verb *dîn* occurs in the qal and ni.; the following substs. derive from it: *dîn* "legal case" (substantivized inf., BL 452), *dayyān* "judge" (nomen agentis, BL 478), *mādôn* and *midyān* "conflict" (verbal nouns with *m-* prefix, BL 491; on *midyān* cf. I. L. Seeligmann, FS Baumgartner 256), and *m*ᵉ*dînâ* "jurisdiction, province" (*m-* locale, BL 492; cf. Wagner no. 152).

dîn also occurs in the PNs *dînâ* (see 3), *ʾᵃbîdān,* and *dānîyēʾl* (*HAL* 219a), in the personal, place, and tribal name *dān,* and in the place name *mādôn* (Noth, HAT 7, 67f.; M. Weippert, *Settlement of the Israelite Tribes in Palestine* [1971], 34n.100); for extrabibl. proper names, cf. Stamm, *AN* 355b; Huffmon 182f.; Gröndahl 123).

2. The verb *dîn* occurs in the Hebr. OT 22x in the qal (Psa 8x, Jer 4x) and 1x in the ni. (2 Sam 19:10 "to quarrel"); also in Bibl. Aram. 1x in the pe. (Ezra 7:25). The subst. *dîn* appears 20x (incl. Job 19:29 K; 35:14; Prov 5x, Job and Jer 4x each), in addition to 5x in Bibl. Aram.; *dayyān* 2x (1 Sam 24:16; Psa 68:6), Aram. 1x (Ezra 7:25); *mādôn/midyān* 23x (incl. 2 Sam 21:20; in Prov 19x); *m*ᵉ*dînâ* 53x (39x in Esth, often in a distributive reduplication), Aram. 11x.

3. Contrary to the judgment of J. van der Ploeg (*CBQ* 12 [1950]: 248) and B. Gemser (*SVT* 3 [1955]: 124n.4), who attribute a broad, fluctuating meaning to *dîn,* it may be established that the root originally designated precisely authoritative, binding judgment in a legal procedure. The usage in the Code of Hammurabi (Driver-Miles 1:73), in Ug. (*WUS* no. 766), and in the OT and the fact that the subjs. of *dîn* are almost always authorities—indeed, primarily the king (king: Jer 21:12; 22:16; Psa 72:2; Prov 20:8; 31:5, 8f.; high priest in a royal function: Zech 3:7, cf. Horst, HAT 14, 228; the leaders of the tribe of Dan: Gen 49:16)—support this viewpoint; on the basic forensic meaning of *dîn* cf. also H. J. Boecker, *Redeformen des Rechtslebens im AT* (1964), 85n.7; Seeligmann, op. cit. 256. Deut 17:8 may also be easily explained if *dîn* together with *dām* "bloodguilt" and *negaᶜ* "misdeed" had the precise meaning "contested authoritative-judicial decision."

The basic meaning of *dîn* is thereby distinguished from → *špṭ,* which originally referred to decisions reached in nonbinding arbitration. Both roots expand in meaning to full synonymity. Consequently *špṭ* can play the dominant role in the OT that *dîn* has in Akk. (B. Landsberger, "Die bab. Termini für Gesetz und Recht," FS Koschaker 223), while *dîn* plays only a secondary role in the OT. In 1 Sam 24:16; Isa 3:13; 10:2; Jer 5:28; 21:12; 22:16; Psa 7:9; 9:5, 9; 72:2; 76:9; 140:13; Prov 31:9; 1QH 9:9, *dîn* occurs alongside *špṭ* (cf. Ug. *KTU* 1.17.V.7f.). In addition to *ʿam* "people" (Gen 49:16; Psa 72:2), the poor, suffering, orphans, and widows are objs. of *dîn* (Jer 5:28; 21:12; 22:16; Prov 31:5, 8f.; on the extra-Israelite parallels of this *justitia adiutrix miseri*, see Wildberger, *Isa 1–12*, CC, 50f.). Here *dîn* takes the meaning "to create justice" or "legal claim."

In *mᵉdînâ* the root tends toward "to govern" (→ *špṭ*); *mᵉdînâ* designates the "judicial and administrative region" of the kingdom of Israel (1 Kgs 20:14–19), Judah (Lam 1:1), the Neo-Bab. Empire (Dan 3:2, etc.), the satrapy of the Pers. Empire (Esth, Ezra, Neh); cf. C. C. Torrey, "Medina and Polis," *HTR* 17 (1924): 83ff.

The (partially synonymous) parallelism of *dîn* and *rîb* (Isa 3:13; with *dayyān* 1 Sam 24:16; with *mādôn* Jer 15:10; Hab 1:3; Prov 15:18; 17:14; cf. 1QH 5:23, 35) points to another extension of *dîn*'s meaning. *rîb* develops from the basic meaning "conflict" to "procedure" (→ *rîb*). In Job 35:14; 36:17; Esth 1:13, *dîn* means "procedure, legal struggle" (*HAL* 211b; cf. *AHw* 172a; *PRU* 3:223f.; *DISO* 56f.). Similarly, in *mādôn*/*midyān* "conflict, quarrel," *dîn* assumes, in assimilation to *rîb*, the latter's basic meaning (thus, insightfully, Seeligmann, op. cit. 256f.). The expressions *ʾēšet midyānîm*, etc., "quarrelsome wife" (Prov 19:13; 21:9, 19; 25:24; 27:15; cf. Gemser, HAT 16, 81) are characteristic.

dîn "to judge, hold proceedings" in Eccl 6:10 belongs here (cf. 2 Sam 19:10 *dîn* ni. "to squabble"), as does the fem. name *dînâ* "legal struggle," which was probably artificially formed for Gen 34 (J. J. Stamm, FS Baumgartner 331).

4. Passages in which Yahweh is the subj. of *dîn* exhibit the meanings "to judge = pronounce judgment" and "to judge = create justice" (subst. "legal claim"): Gen 15:14; 30:6; Deut 32:36 = Psa 135:14; 1 Sam 2:10; 24:16; Isa 3:13; Psa 7:9; 9:5, 9; 50:4; 54:3; 68:6; 76:9; 96:10; 110:6(?); 140:13; Job 19:29; 36:7. Yahweh "judges" the nations (Gen 15:14; Psa 7:9; 9:9; 96:10; Job 36:31[?]) and his people Israel (Deut 32:36 = Psa 135:14; Isa 3:13; Psa 50:4). These two statements may fuse Jerusalem's pre-Israelite cultic tradition (God as creator-king-world judge) with specifically Israelite tradition (Kraus, *Psa*, CC, 1:84f., 492). Yahweh creates justice for the suffering, etc. (Psa 9:5; 54:3; 68:6; 76:9; 140:13; 1 Sam 24:16; for Rachel, Gen 30:6). The laudatory names *dānîyēʾl*, "El is judge" (*IP* 35, 92, 187; cf. further the bibliog. in *HAL* 219a and in the comms. on Dan and Ezek 14), the abbreviation *dān* (*HAL* 218b with bibliog.; *BHH* 1:317f.), and the likewise theophoric name *ʾᵃbîdān* (*HAL* 4b) "(my) father has judged" reflect the usage of *dîn* in lament (Psa 7:9; 54:3; 140:13) and praise (Deut 32:36 = Psa 135:14; 1 Sam 2:10; Psa 9:5, 9; 76:9; 1QH 5:13).

5. Qumran texts (esp. 1QH 5:13) use *dîn* similarly to the OT; on *dîn* in the Talmud, cf. Z. W. Falk, *JSS* 5 (1960): 352; on the LXX, Judaism, and the NT, cf. F. Büchsel and V. Herntrich, "κρίνω," *TDNT* 3:921–54.

G. Liedke

דַּל *dal* **poor** → ענה *ʿnh* II

דָּם *dām* **blood**

S 1818; BDB 196a; *HALOT* 1:224a; *TDOT* 3:234–50; *TWOT* 436; *NIDOTTE* 1947

1. The biradical root *dm "blood" is common Sem. (*GVG* 1:344; Ug.: *WUS* no. 754).

In addition to Hebr. *dām*, a form *ʾᵃdāmâ* with prosthetic *aleph* occurs in Deut 32:43, just as Akk. *adam(m)u* occurs alongside the more customary *dāmu; HAL* 15b and *AHw* 10a explain them as by-forms of the root *ʾdm* "to be red." On the uncertain Phoen.-Pun. examples (*KAI* no. 43.11; no. 103.2) and Augustine's "nam et Punice edom sanguis dicitur" (*Enarratio in Psalmos* 136:18), cf. *DISO* 58; *KAI* 2:61, 114; according to J. Hoftijzer (*VT* 8 [1958]: 289) *ʾedom* should be understood as the form with the art. prefixed. Aram. *ʾedmāʾ* in addition to *dᵉmāʾ* can be explained as the result of a purely phonetic process (*GVG* 1:217; *NB* 118).

2. The OT attests *dām* 360x (sg. 288x, pl. 72x).

The word is most frequent in Lev (88x) and Ezek (55x), followed by Exod (29x; Lis. does not list Exod 12:22a), Deut (23x, as well as *ʾᵃdāmâ* in Deut 32:43), Psa (21x), Num and Isa (15x each).

3. As the only OT term for "blood," *dām* has a broad range of usage: it designates human and animal blood, esp. blood spilled in sacrifice, war, or some other violence. The phrase "to spill blood" is the semasiological background of a natural transferral of meaning, also encountered in other languages, which uses *dām* (sg. and pl. *dāmîm*) in an abstract sense: "the shedding of blood, war." *deber* "plague" appears a few times as a par. (Ezek 5:17; 28:23; 38:22). In this abstract sense, *dām* has become an ethically qualified concept: "bloody deed" and (in accordance with Hebr. thought almost synonymously) "bloodguilt" (Num 35:33; Deut 17:18; 19:10; 21:8; 22:8; Judg 9:24; 1 Sam 25:26, 33; Hos 1:4; 4:2; 12:15; Prov 28:17). "To spill blood" is often, esp. in Ezek, synonymous with "to commit murder" (Gen 9:6; 37:22; Num 35:33; Deut 21:7; 1 Sam 25:31; Psa 79:3; Prov 1:16; Ezek 16:38; 18:10; 22:3f., 6, 9, 12, 27; 23:45; 33:25; 36:18).

Not only murder is considered to be bloodshed, but also nonritual slaughter in which the blood of the animal is not brought to the altar (Lev 17:4).

The expression *bên dām lᵉdām* "between blood and blood" (Deut 17:8; 2 Chron 19:10) involves a distinction between acts of bloodshed to be assessed variously (murder, manslaughter).

A genuine metaphor occurs only in the expression "blood of the grape(s)" (Gen 49:11; Deut 32:14; Sir 39:26).

The OT very rarely uses *dām* to designate colors. The only clear passage is 2 Kgs 3:22 (cf. Isa 63:1–6 with the word *nēṣaḥ* "stream of blood" in vv 3, 6).

The Akk. (*AHw* 158b; *CAD* D:79b) and perhaps Phoen. (*DISO* 58) use of *dām* to designate descent and relationship is entirely absent (Dhorme 11). Hebr. associates this semantic function with → *bāśār* "flesh."

4. (a) The language of sacral law employs a manifold usage of the word *dām*, esp. in P and Ezek. The peculiar formula *ᶜmd ᶜal-dām* "to stand against someone's life" refers to appearance before a legal body in session, whether as plaintiff, witness, or judge (cf. 1 Kgs 21; Elliger, HAT 4, 258f.).

The apparently ancient taboo declaration of the blood of purification with the formula *mᵉqōr dāmeyhā* "source of her blood" (Lev 12:7; 20:18; cf. 15:19) is priestly.

The formula of bloodguilt, "his blood be on him (or on his head)," also belongs to the legal sphere and establishes the guilt of one condemned to death and thereby the innocence of the executor of the sentence (H. Reventlow, *VT* 10 [1960]: 311–27; K. Koch, *VT* 12 [1962]: 396–416). The formula occurs in its pure form (always *dāmîm* in pl. with suf. and *bᵉ* with suf.) only in P (Lev 20:9, 11–13, 16, 27), but also in a somewhat altered form elsewhere (Josh 2:19; 1 Kgs 2:37; Ezek 18:13; 33:4f.).

(b) Some religiohistorical concepts associated with blood may be mentioned briefly at this point in order to call attention to terms that stand in a special relationship to *dām* in the OT, esp. in P.

Blood is considered the locus of life (Lev 17:11, "The soul of the flesh is in the blood"; → *nepeš*) or is identified with it (Gen 9:4; Lev 17:14; Deut 12:23). For this reason, blood may not be consumed (Lev 3:17; 7:26f.; 17:10, 12, 14; Deut 12:16, 23; 15:23), nor flesh "that has its blood" (Gen 9:4; cf. Lev 19:26; 1 Sam 14:32–34; Ezek 33:25). Probably originally understood animistically (on religiohistorical aspects cf. W. E. Mühlmann, *RGG* 1:1327f.; J. H. Waszink, *RAC* 2:459–73), the statements are stripped of this character through attribution to the revelation of God's will and foundation upon it (Elliger, HAT 4, 228).

A similar phenomenon is also true of the significance of blood as a means of atonement (Lev 4:5–34; 16:14–19; 17:11, etc.; → *kpr*) and as a community-building factor in making covenant (Exod 24:6, 8; → *bᵉrît*). Blood does not act by means of inherent expiative power, but because Yahweh designated it as a means of atonement (Lev 17:11, "I gave it to you for the altar so that it may work atonement for you"; cf. Vriezen, *Theol.* 266).

Human blood enjoys God's special protection (Gen 9:5f.). It is regarded as the property of the tribe; consequently, the tribe is obligated, in the event of a murder, "to redeem" (→ *gᵓl*) the blood by the death of the murderer, to reacquire it for the family (*gōᵓēl haddām* "blood avenger," Num 35:19–27; Deut 19:6, 12; Josh 20:3, 5, 9; 2 Sam 14:11; cf. Koch, op. cit. 409–14).

5. Kuhn (*Konk.* 50) catalogs 16 occurrences of the word in the Qumran texts (3x pl.; see also *GCDS* 110). The usage conforms to that of the OT: spilling of blood, bloody deed, blood of the sacrifice, menstrual blood.

Expressions such as "blood arrow" (1QM 6:3) and "to hear of bloody deeds" (*dāmîm,* 1QH 7:3) go beyond OT usage.

On Judaism and the NT, cf. E. Bischoff, *Das Blut im jüdischen Schrifttum und Brauch* (1929); J. Behm, "αἷμα," *TDNT* 1:172–77; L. Morris, "Biblical Use of the Term 'Blood,' " *JTS* 3 (1952): 216–27; 6 (1955): 77–82.

G. Gerleman

דמה *dmh* to be like

S 1819; BDB 197b; *HALOT* 1:225a; *TDOT* 3:250–60; *TWOT* 437; *NIDOTTE* 1948

כְּ *k^e^* **like**

BDB 453a; *HALOT* 2:453b; *TDOT* 7:1–7; *TWOT* 937; *NIDOTTE* 3869

---

1. *dmh* "to resemble" is extant beyond Hebr. in Aram. (*DISO* 58; KBL 1066b; *LS* 156f. with reference to Fraenkel 272: Arab. *dumyat* "picture" is an Aram. loanword). The demarcation between one of more homonymous roots with the meaning "to be silent," "to destroy," etc. (*HAL* 216b; J. Blau, *VT* 6 [1956]: 242f.; cf. N. Lohfink, *VT* 12 [1962]: 275–77; A. Baumann, "דָּמָה *dāmāh* II," *TDOT* 3:260–65) is disputed in individual cases.

The verb occurs in the qal "to be like," ni. "to become like," pi. "to equate, compare" and estimatively "to consider appropriate, plan, imagine," and hitp. "to equate oneself." Derived noms. are *d^e^mî* "half," *dimyôn* "resemblance," and *d^e^mût* "figure, representation."

The last subst. occurs once in Imp. Aram.: *BMAP* 3:21 *byt ldmwt bytk,* "a house like yours."

2. According to Lis. 366, *dmh* occurs in qal 13x (excl. Jer 6:2 [cf., however, Rudolph, HAT 12, 42] and Hos 4:5 [cf. Rudolph, KAT 13/1, 97]), pi. 14x (incl. Hos 12:11), hitp. 1x (Isa 14:14); additionally, ni. 1x in Ezek 32:2 according to Zimmerli, *Ezek,* Herm, 2:154, and *HAL* 216a. The substs. *d^e^mî* (Isa 38:10) and *dimyôn* (Psa 17:12) are hapax legomena: *d^e^mût* occurs 25x.

Bibl. Aram. has two occurrences of *dmh* pe. (Dan 3:25; 7:5).

3. (a) *dmh* qal "to be like" introduces comparisons in laments (Isa 1:9 "like Gomorrah"; Psa 102:7, "I am like the bittern in the wilderness"; 144:4, "The human being is like a breath"; cf. Lam 2:13 pi.), in prophetic metaphorical language (Ezek 31:2, 8[bis], 18, concerning the pharaoh), in love songs (Song Sol 2:9, 17; 7:8; 8:14; cf. 1:9 pi.), and in hymnic language (Isa 46:5; Psa 89:7; pi. in Isa 40:18, 25; 46:5; see 4a).

The following verbs that parallel *dmh* qal/pi. have similar meanings: (1) *hyh k^e^* "to be like" (Isa 1:9; Ezek 31:8; Psa 102:7; cf. Psa 50:21); (2) *šwh* qal "to be like" (Isa 40:25 pi.), hi. "to compare" (Isa 46:5 pi.; Lam 2:13 pi.); *šwh* qal occurs a total of 8x, ni. 1x "to be alike" (Prov 27:15), pi. "to make alike, equal, appease" 5x, and hi. "to equate, compare" 2x; cf. *HP* 35, 111; Bibl. Aram. *šwh* pe. "to be like," Dan 5:21 K (Q pa.); hitpa. "to be made like" Dan 3:29; (3) *mšl* hi. "to compare" (Isa 46:5); otherwise *mšl* qal "to speak a metaphor, a proverb" 10x, pi. "to recite metaphors" 1x, hi. "to become like" 5x, hitp.

"to become similar" 1x; also *māšāl* "proverb"; cf. O. Eissfeldt, *Der Maschal im AT* [1913]; A. R. Johnson, *SVT* 3 (1955): 162–69; for further bibliog. see Sellin-Fohrer 311; (4) *ᶜmm* "to equal" (Ezek 31:8; otherwise only in Ezek 28:3); (5) *ᶜrk* qal in the meaning "to juxtapose, compare" (Psa 89:7; Isa 40:18 pi.; without par. to *dmh:* Psa 40:6; Job 28:17, 19; otherwise in the meaning "to arrange").

(b) The question as to whether the abstract form *dᵉmût* "semblance, resemblance," best translated in many passages with "something like" (L. Köhler, *TZ* 4 [1948]: 20f.), refers to equivalence or only to some diminished similarity (Köhler, op. cit.; W. H. Schmidt, *Die Schöpfungsgeschichte der Priesterschrift* [1964], 143; Westermann, *Gen*, CC, 1:146f.) may be answered by observing that the word in and of itself refers to total comparability and not to a perceptibly lesser degree of mere similarity, but that the need to refer to comparability exists only if similarity is not self-evident.

In a few passages (Isa 13:4 and Psa 58:5, the text is questionable), *dᵉmût* refers to pictorial or fig. representations (2 Kgs 16:10, model or plan of an altar; Ezek 23:15, mural painting; 2 Chron 4:3, cattle figures under the bronze sea) underscoring their correspondence to the original ("imitation, copy"). *dᵉmût* occurs most frequently in descriptions of visions in Ezek (as nomen regens: Ezek 1:5bis, 10, 13 [txt?], 16, 26bis, 28; 10:1, 10, 21f.; distanced from the related word: 1:22; followed by *kᵉmarᵓēh* "like the appearance of": 1:26; 8:2) and Dan (Dan 10:16), where the identification of that which is seen with divine reality is only suggested.

On the *imago* passages (Gen 1:26; 5:1, 3) and on Isa 40:18, where *dᵉmût* also means "copy, likeness," see 4a and → *ṣelem*.

The closest semantically related word is *tabnît* "image, model" (20x, derived from the root *bnh* "to build"). On the words for "figure" *(tᵉmûnâ, tōᵓar, qeṣeb)* and "picture" (*maśkît*, etc.) → *ṣelem*.

(c) The semantic field of equality and similarity is not dominated in Hebr. by verbs and nouns, but by the comparative particle *kᵉ* "like" (on form and usage, cf. GKC §118s-x; Joüon §§103b, c, g, 133g, 166l, m, 174d, i; BrSynt 96, 104f., 126).

Of the more than 3,000 occurrences of the particle *kᵉ* in the Hebr. OT (57x *kᵉmô;* in Bibl. Aram. *kᵉ* is attested around 80x, incl. 22x *kol-qᵒbēl* "correspondingly," *kᵉᶜan/kᵉᶜenet/kᵉᶜe t* "now" 17x, *kᵉdî* "like, as" 5x), over 500 fall to the conjunction *kaᵓᵃšer* "like, as," and about 250 to the combination *kᵉ* + inf., which should be primarily rendered in Eng. with a temporal clause (most often with *šmᶜ* "to hear" 46x, *bôᵓ* "to come" 26x, *klh* pi. "to finish" 25x, *rᵓh* "to see" 25x). Most frequently *kᵉ* *(or kᵉmô)* precedes substs. of general and abstract meaning: *kōl/kol-* "totality, all" (127x, 75x *kᵉkōl ᵓᵃšer* "according to all, that which"), *dābār* "word" (94x), *yôm* "day" (78x), *mišpāṭ* "prescription, custom" (42x), *marᵓeh* "looks, appearance" (25x), *maᶜᵃśeh* "deed" and *ᶜēt* "time" (22x each); comparisons to concrete elements and living beings are more rare: *ᵓîš* "man" and *mayim* "water" (23x), *ṣōᵓn* "sheep" (20x), *ᵓēš* "fire" (19x), *ḥôl* "sand" (14x).

Although passages with *kᵉ* comprise only a small fraction of the occurrences of most of the nouns associated with *kᵉ* (of around 600 different Hebr. terms with *kᵉ* something more than half occur only once in this combination), some words, e.g., *môṣ* "chaff," apparently specialize in usage in the simile. The proportion of designations for animals is also somewhat above average. Statistically, following *ṣōʾn* in animal similes are: → *ʾarî/ʾaryēh* "lion" (16x, incl. 1x Aram.; also other designations for lions, e.g., *kᵉpîr* 9x, *lābîʾ* 6x, *šaḥal* 3x, *gôr* 1x), *nešer* "eagle, vulture" (12x), *ṣippôr* "bird" (10x), *sûs* "horse" and *yônâ* "dove" (9x), and *ʾayyāl(â)* "deer" (8x). Of course, these figures are true only for the similes with *kᵉ;* indirect similes and metaphorical comparisons cannot be included here.

The most frequent forms with suf. per. prons. (*kā-, kᵉmô-, kāmô-*, something over 100x) are *kāmôkā* "like you" (31x), *kāmôhû* "like him" (24x), and *kāmônî* "like me" (17x). Finally, *kᵉ* with proper names occurs about 60x. Comparison is most often made to David (9x), the Anakim and Daniel (3x each), all other PNs (even Moses and Job), only once each. The place-names Lebanon and Sodom (4x each), Gomorrah and Shiloh (2x each) are worthy of mention (all others, even Jerusalem, e.g., only once). On the divine designations, see 4b.

4. (a) In theological contexts, *dmh (dᵉmût)* and synonyms function in hymnic statements concerning Yahweh's incomparability (cf. C. J. Labuschagne, *Incomparability of Yahweh in the OT* [1966], 28–30). In addition to Psa 89:7, "For who in the clouds compares to Yahweh *(ʿrk lᵉ)*, is like Yahweh [*dmh* qal] among the divine beings?" (cf. Psa 40:6, "Nothing is to be compared to you *[ʿrk ʾel]*"), a few passages from Deutero-Isa may be cited here: Isa 40:18, "To whom will you compare God (*dmh* pi.) and what will you set beside him *(ʿrk)* as a likeness *(dᵉmût)*?"; 40:25, "To whom will you liken me (*dmh* pi.), that I should be like him (*šwh* qal)?"; 46:5, "To whom will you liken me (*dmh* pi.), to whom compare me (*šwh* hi.)? To whom will you equate me (*mšl* hi.), that we should be alike (*dmh* qal)?" In each case, the context indicates that Yahweh's incomparability with respect to the impotent gods is intended, his claim to uniqueness, in contrast perhaps to frequent similar statements in Bab. texts (with *maḫāru* and *šanānu* "to equal"; cf. Labuschagne, op. cit. 31–57) that hyperbolically praise first one, then another, god (cf. J. Hehn, *Die biblische und die babylonische Gottesidee* [1913], 99). Consequently, any other power's claim to equality with Yahweh is harshly contested; cf. Isa 14:14, where the hubris of the king of Babel is characterized in mythical terms: "I will ascend above the clouds, I will become like (*dmh* hitp.) the Most High."

Concerning humanity's resemblance to God, manifest in dominion over the animal world (Gen 1:26f.; cf. 5:1, 3; Psa 8:6–9), but which goes back to unique concepts, comparison should be made to → *ṣelem*, with which *dᵉmût*, which interprets this term (combined with *bᵉ* or *kᵉ*), seems to be rather interchangeable.

(b) Statements concerning God's incomparability composed with the particle of comparison *kᵉ* (Labuschagne, op. cit. 8–29) divide essentially into two groups, both with formal pars. in daily language: negated nom. clauses of the form *ʾên . . . kᵉ . . .* "there is none . . . like . . . " (Exod 8:6; 9:14; Deut 33:26; 1 Sam 2:2bis; 2 Sam 7:22 = 1 Chron 17:20; 1 Kgs 8:23 = 2 Chron 6:14; Jer 10:6f.; Psa 86:8; cf. Isa 46:9, with the negation *ʾepes*) and rhetorical questions with an implied negation *mî kᵉ . . .* "who is like . . . ?" (Exod

15:11bis; Isa 44:7; 49:19 = 50:44; Mic 7:18; Psa 35:10; 71:19; 77:14; 89:9; 113:5; cf. Deut 4:7). The sentence names *mîkāyâ(hû), mîkāy*ᵉ*hû, mîkâ(hû), mîkāʾēl* ("Who is like Yahweh/God") also belong in the latter category (cf. *IP* 144; Labuschagne, op. cit. 21f., 126–29; contra B. Hartmann, *ZDMG* 110 [1961]: 234).

Designations used for God in this context are: *yhwh* (Exod 8:6; Deut 4:7; 1 Sam 2:2; Psa 113:5; associated with *k*ᵉ only 4x), *ʾ*ᵉ*lōhîm* (1 Sam 2:2; Psa 77:14; *kēʾlōhîm* otherwise only in Gen 3:5 on the lips of the serpent: "That you will become like God"; Zech 12:8 in a hyperbolic promise: "The one who stumbles will be like David, and the house of David like a deity"; 2 Chron 32:17 of the gods of other peoples), *ʾēl* (Deut 33:26; otherwise only in Job 40:9, "Is your arm like the arm of God?"; with *k*ᵉ*mô,* Job 19:22, "Why do you persecute me like God?"), also *kāmônî* "like me" (Exod 9:14; Isa 44:7; 46:9; Jer 49:19 = 50:44), *kāmôkā* "like you" (Exod 15:11bis; 2 Sam 7:22 = 1 Chron 17:20; 1 Kgs 8:23 = 2 Chron 6:14; Jer 10:6f.; Mic 7:18; Psa 35:10; 71:19; 86:8; 89:9), and *kāmôhû* "like him" (Job 36:22; cf. Job 40:9, "Do you have the voice of the thunder like him?").

The statement of incomparability, which is hymnic in the broader sense, is always established, whether by the context, by a direct formulation, or, indeed chiefly, by the mighty intervention of Yahweh in history as a just deliverer (not accidentally also in the plague and exodus tradition; in the individual lament Psa 35; 71; 77; 86 as a motivation for the individual sufferer's cry for help), but also by his creative power (in Deutero-Isa closely associated with deliverance). The following are special formulations: in the Song of Hannah, 1 Sam 2:2, "No one is holy *(qādôš)* like Yahweh," and in the speech of Elihu, Job 36:22, "Who is a teacher *(môreh)* like him?" (on the content and origin of these statements, cf. the extensive treatment of Labuschagne, op. cit. 64–153).

5. Formulae that state God's incomparability in an OT manner also occur at Qumran (1QH 7:28; 1QM 10:8; 13:13).

The LXX primarily uses *homoios* and its derivatives, less frequently *isos* (only in 2 Macc 9:12 *isotheos* of Antiochus, in a negated usage); usually *homoiōma* stands for *d*ᵉ*mût,* less frequently *homoiōsis,* once each *homoios* (Isa 13:4), *idea* (Gen 5:3), and *eikōn* (Gen 5:1).

On the LXX and the NT, where 1 John 3:2 constitutes the eschatological counterpart to Gen 3:5 and where Jesus' equality with God (Phil 2:6) appears as a new theme, cf. G. Stählin, "ἴσος," *TDNT* 3:343–355; J. Schneider, "ὅμοιος," *TDNT* 5:186–199.

E. Jenni

דַּעַת *daᶜat* **knowledge** → ידע *ydᶜ*

דֶּרֶךְ *derek* **way**

S 1870; BDB 202b; *HALOT* 1:231b; *TDOT* 3:270–93; *TWOT* 453a; *NIDOTTE* 2006

אֹרַח *ʾōraḥ* **way**

S 734; BDB 73a; *HALOT* 1:86b; *TWOT* 161a; *NIDOTTE* 784

1. The root *drk* "to tread (with the feet)" is common Sem.; it exhibits numerous, sometimes phonetically or semantically divergent, manifestations (*HAL* 221f.; P. Nober, *Bib* 40 [1959]: 196*f.).

Akk. *daraggu* "path/trail" (*AHw* 163a; *CAD* D:108b) is a rare synonym for the more common *urḫu* or *ḫarrānu;* cf. also *darāku* "to follow after(?)" and *darku* "following" (*AHw* 163a, 164a).

The Ug. fem. subst. *drkt* "dominion, might" (*WUS* no. 792; *UT* no. 703; *CML*[1] 154; *CML*[2] 145) parallels *mlk* "kingdom" (*KTU* 1.108.6f.: *bʿlt mlk* par. *bʿlt drkt* of Anat, *Ugaritica* 5:551); see 3c.

The root seems to occur in Phoen.-Pun. and in Old Aram. only verbally: "to tread upon, enter, draw (a bow)" (*DISO* 60).

The Hebr. noun *derek* "way" (*qitl* formation? cf. Brønno 134) can be construed as both masc. and fem. (K. Albrecht, *ZAW* 16 [1896]: 54f.). In addition to the noun and the verb (qal and hi.), the derived subst. *midrāk* "footprint, foot breadth" (only Deut 2:5) also occurs.

2. The noun *derek* is attested in the OT 706x, predominantly in the sg. (543x; counting Prov 21:29 Q as sg., Jer 17:10 Q as pl.). It may be that the two duals in Prov 28:6, 18 should be read as pl. (cf. e.g., F. Nötscher, *Gotteswege und Menschenwege in der Bibel und in Qumran* [1958], 56).

	qal	hi.	sg.	pl.	dual	subst.
Gen	–	–	31	–	–	31
Exod	–	–	12	1	–	13
Lev	–	–	–	1	–	1
Num	1	–	23	–	–	23
Deut	4	–	37	11	–	48
Josh	2	–	15	2	–	17
Judg	2	1	15	–	–	15
1 Sam	1	–	24	3	–	27
2 Sam	–	–	11	1	–	12
1 Kgs	–	–	40	6	–	46
2 Kgs	–	–	21	1	–	22
Isa	8	3	33	14	–	47
Jer	7	2	41	16	–	57
Ezek	–	–	85	22	–	107
Hos	–	–	4	4	–	8
Joel	–	–	–	1	–	1
Amos	2	–	3	–	–	3
Jonah	–	–	2	–	–	2
Mic	4	–	–	1	–	1
Nah	–	–	2	–	–	2

	qal	hi.	sg.	pl.	dual	subst.
Hab	1	1	–	–	–	–
Hag	–	–	–	2	–	2
Zech	1	–	–	3	–	3
Mal	–	–	2	1	–	3
Psa	6	4	47	19	–	66
Job	3	1	20	12	–	32
Prov	–	1	52	21	2	75
Ruth	–	–	1	–	–	1
Eccl	–	–	3	1	–	4
Lam	3	–	2	4	–	6
Ezra	–	–	3	–	–	3
Neh	1	–	3	–	–	3
1 Chron	2	–	–	–	–	–
2 Chron	1	–	11	14	–	25
OT	49	13	543	161	2	706

3. (a) The meaning of *derek* developed in many ways in both spatial-geographical as well as metaphorical-figurative senses from the basic meaning "(traveled and thus established) way." Only the most important of the numerous uses of the word will be treated here (in addition to the lexicons, see the extensive presentation of Nötscher, op. cit. 17–69).

Among the numerous spatial-geographical "ways," the OT knows those specifically designated because they are highly traveled highways: the "king's highway" in the Transjordan, leading from Damascus to Aqaba (Num 20:17; 21:22; cf. *HAL* 222b; Y. Aharoni, *Land of the Bible* [1968²], 49–52), the "highway of the tent dwellers" (Judg 8:11), and the "highway of the sea," leading to the sea or running in the region of the sea (Isa 8:23; cf. Aharoni, op. cit. 41–49).

The concrete meaning "way" evolves imperceptibly into the meaning "movement on the way": A person who travels on a street goes "his way," in order to reach a goal (e.g., Gen 24:27, 48; 32:2, etc., frequently combined with → *hlk* "to go"; *badderek* = "underway").

The action of travel is even more strongly emphasized when *derek* means "journey," "undertaking," or even "military campaign" (Gen 42:25; 45:21, 23; 1 Sam 21:6 *derek ḥōl* "profane undertaking"; cf. also Akk. *ḫarrānu* "way, journey, caravan, campaign," *AHw* 326f.; *CAD* H:106–13).

From the vantage point of the goal, "way" acquires the meaning "way that has been traveled, stretch of the way (between two points)" (cf. e.g., Gen 31:23 "seven days' journey long").

A similar idea lies behind the use of *derek* to indicate the direction of a movement, whether it is undertaken or only described. Direction can be indicated by the four points of the compass (Deut 11:30, etc., esp. in the description of the new temple in Ezek 40:6ff.) or by regions and locales (Gen 16:7, etc.).

(b) In a fig. meaning, the life of a person can be described as the "way" on which one finds oneself (cf. A. Gros, *Le thème de la route dans la Bible* [1957], 17–30); often, then, one may translate "conduct, behavior" (e.g., Gen 6:12). This terminology acquired special significance in wisdom literature (Prov 1:15, etc.) and for the religious realm (see 4). If the goal of all human lives is in view, the "way" of all people, which leads to death, can be indicated (Josh 23:14; 1 Kgs 2:2; on Prov 14:12, cf. *HAL* 223a). In a rather general manner, *derek* indicates particular givens in human life or in nature, in the sense of "behavior, condition, practice, manner" (e.g., Prov 30:19f.; Gen 19:31, of the ways of the sexes toward one another; Gen 31:35, of the condition of the woman in the monthly cycle; cf. Gen 18:11 with *ʾōraḥ;* see 3d).

(c) Whether one can use Ug. *drkt* "dominion, might" to elucidate some passages in the OT must remain questionable. The passages adduced for this purpose (with *drk* qal: Num 24:17; with *derek:* Jer 3:13; Hos 10:13; Amos 8:14; Psa 67:3; 110:7; 119:37; 138:5; Job 26:14; 36:23; 40:19; Prov 8:22; 19:16; 31:3) are largely comprehensible even without this assumption or could be explained in some other manner.

The series of suggestions begins with Albright's remark on Num 24:17; further passages were cited now and again by various authors; cf. W. F. Albright, *JBL* 63 (1944): 219; id., *SVT* 3 (1955): 7; id., FS Robert 23f.; P. Nober, *VD* 26 (1948): 351–53; S. Bartina, *VD* 34 (1956): 202–10; J. B. Bauer, *VT* 8 (1958): 91f.; M. Dahood, *TS* 13 (1952): 593f.; 15 (1954): 627–31; id., *Bib* 33 (1952): 33; 38 (1957): 320; id., *PNSP* 40; id., *UHP* 55, etc.

The following authors have criticized this opinion: H. Zirker, *BZ* 2 (1958): 291–94; Nötscher, op. cit. 17f., 25f.; cf. further Rudolph, KAT 13/1, 206, on Hos 10:13; Fohrer, KAT 16, 522, on Job 40:19.

*(d) Nötscher (op. cit. 12–17) treats semantically related substs. The following merit mention:

(1) *ʾōraḥ* "way" (57x, except for Gen 18:11 only in poetical texts, in 1/4 of the cases par. to *derek;* most frequent in Prov, 19x; also Psa 14x, Job 10x, Isa 8x, Gen and Judg 2x each, Joel and Mic 1x each; additionally *ʾrḥ* "to wander, travel" 6x and *ʾōrᵉḥâ* "caravan" 3x) and Bibl. Aram. *ʾᵃraḥ* "way" (Dan 4:34; 5:23) with a range of meaning similar to *derek;* cf. Akk. *urḫu* and Aram. *ʾrḥ/ʾorḥāʾ* (*DISO* 24; KBL 1053b);

(2) *hᵃlîkâ* "way, lane; caravan, procession; activity" (6x; → *hlk*);

(3) *mᵉsillâ* (27x) and *maslûl* (Isa 35:8) "(piled up) street" (*sll* qal "to pile up");

(4) *maʿgāl* "rut, track" (13x, in Prov 7x; from *ʿᵃgālâ* "wagon");

(5) *nātîb* (5x) and *nᵉtîbâ* (21x; almost always par. to *derek* or *ʾōraḥ* "path"; cf. Ug. *ntb* and *ntbt* "path," *WUS* no. 1870; *UT* no. 1715);

(6) *šᵉbîl* "path" (Jer 18:15; Psa 77:20; in each case par. to *derek*).

All these terms may also be used fig. or picturesquely.

(e) The verb *drk* qal always maintained the basic meaning "to tread" (obj.: land, Deut 1:36; way, Isa 59:8; waves, 1 Sam 5:5; etc.). The verb was occasionally specialized in two ways: the warrior "treads" his bow with his feet in order to bend it (Isa 5:28; 21:15, etc.; cf. *BHH* 1:264, 267), and the farmer "treads" the winepress in order to press grapes (e.g., Judg 9:27; cf. Dalman, *AuS* 4:364f.; on Mic 6:15, cf. Dalman, op. cit. 207).

drk hi. renders the causative meaning "to cause to tread, cause to travel" (Isa 11:15, etc.; with an elliptical obj., "feet" = "to tread down, step on" in Jer 51:33; Job 28:8; on Judg 20:43 cf. *HAL* 222a). "To cause to walk in a way" then becomes "to lead" (Prov 4:11, etc.).

4. (a) Religious language can also, at first, refer concretely to the way or journey of a god (1 Kgs 18:27), divine being (Gen 19:2), or Yahweh (Deut 1:33; Nah 1:3; cf. A. Kuschke, "Die Menschenwege und der Weg Gottes im AT," *ST* 5 [1952]: 106–18; F. Nötscher, *Gotteswege und Menschenwege in der Bibel und in Qumran* [1958], 23ff.). Here, however, the primary intention is a metaphorical reference to the behavior and volition of God (cf. Gros, op. cit. 30–40), who turns attention to the people but nevertheless transcends them (Isa 55:8f.; Job 34:27, etc.). The people and its members should walk in God's way, i.e., lead their lives in obedience to God (Exod 32:8, etc.), to which end God's commandments serve as guideposts (e.g., Deut 5:33). To diverge from them (Deut 11:28, etc.) is to pervert God's ways (Num 22:32) and to go in other ways (one's own, Isa 53:6; the sinner's, Psa 1:1; strange gods', Jer 10:2). This behavior by Israel's kings, who do not walk in David's, and thus Yahweh's, way (thus in 1 Kgs 3:14), but in that of Jeroboam (1 Kgs 15:26, etc.), is esp. condemned.

(b) The verb *drk* qal can describe God's movement: on the heights of the earth (Amos 4:13; Mic 1:3; cf. U. Devescovi, *RivB* 9 [1961]: 235–37), on the heights of the sea (Job 9:8; cf. Hab 3:15). The bending of the bow is mentioned in Zech 9:13; Lam 2:4; 3:12 (cf. Psa 58:8); the treading of the winepress in Isa 63:3(bis) and Lam 1:15.

The hi. describes Yahweh's guidance of the pious, etc. (Isa 48:17; Psa 25:5; etc.; Devescovi, op. cit. 237–42).

5. In the community of Qumran the nuance of meaning indicated in 4a is particularly represented, a phenomenon that reflects the character of the texts. In essence no new viewpoints are added; cf. Nötscher, op. cit. 72–96.

Although not explicit in the formulation of the NT (Matt 7:13f.), the dualism of the two ways is already present and prefigured in essence; cf. B. Couroyer, "Le chemin de vie en Egypte et en Israël," *RB* 56 (1949): 412–32; Nötscher, op. cit. 64–69; Michaelis, "ὁδός," *TDNT* 5:53–55.

On "way" in the NT and in early Christianity, cf. W. Michaelis, op. cit. 42–118; Nötscher, op. cit. 97–122; A. Gros, *Je suis la route* (1961); E. Repo, *Der "Weg" als Selbstbezeichnung des Urchristentums* (1964).

G. Sauer

דרשׁ *drš* to inquire after

S 1875; BDB 205b; *HALOT* 1:233a; *TDOT* 3:293–307; *TWOT* 455; *NIDOTTE* 2011

---

1. *drš* is a WSem. verb, also attested outside Hebr. in Ug., Aram., Eth., and Arab.

Syr. *drš* "to dispute," or the like, apparently a Hebr. loanword, has assimilated to a word for "to tread" (cf. Hebr. and Aram. *drk;* Mid. Hebr., Jew. Aram. *drs*, Arab. *drs* "to thresh," Akk. *darāsu* "to force out," *AHw* 163b), but is nevertheless to be distinguished from it (cf. *NB* 38n.4). Concerning a questionable occurrence of Akk. *darāšu* "to attempt(?)" in hymnic-epic language, cf. W. von Soden, *ZA* 49 (1949): 175f.; *AHw* 163b.

2. The OT has *drš* only in the Hebr. portions: qal 155x (Chron 40x), ni. 9x. The late verbal abstract *midrāš* "exposition" (Aram. pe. inf., GKC §85h) occurs only twice (2 Chron 13:22; 24:27; cf. Sir 51:23).

3. (a) The range of profane usage is rather limited, esp. in comparison to the semantically related → *bqš* pi., and makes up only about 1/4 of the total occurrences. But even the profane usage of *drš* is clearly distinguished from that of *bqš* pi. There are only isolated examples of *drš* meaning "to search for someone or something" (Deut 22:2; Job 10:6 with *bqš* as a preceding par.; 39:8 with *ʾaḥar*). The usage in Psa 109:10 "to seek (futilely), beg," paralleling → *šʾl* pi., is semantically related (cf., nevertheless, *BHS*).

(b) In contrast to *bqš* pi., *drš* belongs primarily to the cognitive sphere: "to inquire after something, ask about something, investigate." One examines not the location of a thing or event but its nature. In this sense, the verb can be grammatically constructed in a variety of ways: abs. (Deut 13:15; 17:4; 19:18; Judg 6:29; Isa 34:16; Eccl 1:13), with a direct obj. (Lev 10:16; Ezra 10:16 txt em), or with the preps. *ʾel, bᵉ, lᵉ,* and *ʿal.*

The verbal abstract *midrāš* "exposition" is also rooted in this sphere of meaning (cf. Rudolph, HAT 21, 238; G. Rinaldi, *Bib* 40 [1959]: 277).

(c) A shift of meaning toward the emotive occurs in an even greater degree for *drš* in the meaning "to strive after something, aspire" than for *bqš* pi. Objects of the verb are mostly qualitative-ideal values, primarily of a positive nature: "justice" (Isa 1:17; 16:5), "good" (Amos 5:14; Esth 10:3), "Yahweh's works" (Psa 111:2), but also "evil" (Prov 11:27). *drš* occurs in the expression "to strive for someone's hurt *(rāʿâ)*" only in Psa 38:13 (*drš* here parallels *bqš* pi., which precedes it and apparently determines its meaning) and Prov 11:27 (cf. Jer 38:4). The contrasting "to seek someone's well-being *(šālôm)*" is attested 4x (Deut 23:7; Jer 29:7; 38:4; Ezra 9:12; cf. Esth 10:3).

In contrast to *bqš* pi., *drš* never governs a subsequent inf.

Emotional coloration is even more pronounced when *drš* means "to take care of something, take charge of," a meaning that belongs first to theological language, but that also has nontheological application (Jer 30:14; Psa 142:5; Prov 31:13; 1 Chron 13:3).

(d) *drš* in the sense of "to demand, require" belongs to theological language. The only exception is 2 Chron 24:6 *(drš ʿal),* the only passage where a human being makes demands (C. Westermann, "Die Begriffe für Fragen und Suchen im AT," *KerD* 6 [1960]: 16).

4. (a) Most occurrences of *drš* are by far theological and cultic. In the sense of "to demand, require," the verb almost exclusively has Yahweh as subj. Objects are "blood" (Gen 9:5a; Ezek 33:6; Psa 9:13; ni. Gen 42:22), "soul" (Gen 9:5b), "a vow" (Deut 23:22), "my sheep" (Ezek 34:10), and "sacrifice" (Ezek 20:40); also Mic 6:8 "what Yahweh requires of you." In the remaining pertinent passages, the obj. is godless behavior so that the verb assumes the sense "to punish" (Deut 18:19; Psa 10:4, 15,; 2 Chron 24:22).

(b) A series of narratives use *drš yhwh* as a fixed expression for the prophetic inquiry of Yahweh (according to 1 Sam 9:9, originally through a seer or man of God) in a crisis situation, temporally limited to the monarchic period. Here, too, the inquiry does not primarily seek information, but is intended to bring about the removal of the inquirer's distress. Only crises of a political order are related (even when personal distress is at issue): (1) the endangerment of the dynasty by the illness of the king (2 Kgs 8:7–15) or of the crown prince (1 Kgs 14:1–6, 12–13a, 17, 18); cf. 2 Kgs 1:2ff.; 2 Chron 16:12; Gen 25:22; further, without *drš*, Isa 38 and 2 Kgs 5); (2) endangerment of the totality in the perils of war (1 Kgs 22 = 2 Chron 18; 2 Kgs 3; cf. Jer 21:1–10; 37:3–21) and in a threat from Yahweh's wrath (2 Kgs 22 = 2 Chron 34). The narratives treated here belong to a broader group with the pattern: announcement through the word of the prophet—arrival of this word; i.e., the focal point is not the inquiry but the functioning of the prophetic word, which intervenes in history and, e.g., rejects and deposes kings (1 Kgs 14; 2 Kgs 1; 8). Ezek 14:1–11; 20:1–3 bring this possibility for inquiry to an end, because it is in principle rejected by the prophet.

The process is always as follows: In a crisis situation, the king sends a messenger (always a high-ranking personality from those very near to the king) with a present to the prophet at home in order to inquire of him concerning the outcome of the crisis. The prophet answers with a word of God. The whole process transpires *outside* the cultic sphere (Westermann, op. cit. 18).

The inquirer is an individual, in the transmitted narratives usually the king, with the only exceptions being the matriarch Rebekah (Gen 25:22), the elders (Ezek 14; 20), and "someone" in 1 Sam 9:9. Yahweh is always the acc. obj. *(drš ʾet-yhwh)*, in 1 Kgs 22:5 = 2 Chron 18:4 it is modified *drš ʾet-dᵉbar yhwh*. *mēʾittô* "from him," referring to the prophetic mediator, usually follows. The use of the prep. *min* indicates that the prophet is seen only as the mediator of the word that proceeds from God, never as the instrument of the inquirer. The question concerning the outcome of the crisis follows. But this question "implies supplication . . . to God" (Westermann, op. cit. 18) that he might transform the crisis. In Jer 37:3, 7 the prophet is expressly requested to intercede (cf. Ezek 36:37, "I will allow myself to be entreated for *[lᵉ]* Israel"). The institution of inquiry may have been related to the intercessory office of the prophet (Westermann, op. cit. 21). Presumably, inquiry of God through a man of God originally occurred because of personal crises of individuals and was only later expanded to include community crises (Westermann, op. cit. 28). The gloss in 1 Sam 9:9 supports this supposition, even if it is a late reminiscence.

1 Kgs 22 associates inquiry by means of a prophet with elements of the → *šʾl* inquiry via the lot, known esp. in the context of holy war. The narrative in 2 Kgs 3 is similar, apparently composed in literary dependence upon 1 Kgs 22 (Westermann, op. cit. 19); it associates the threat posed by enemy superiority with a natural crisis (the troops' lack of water). Accordingly, there is a two-part question and a two-part prophetic answer. The *šʾl* inquiry occurs through the priestly lot. It is attested only for the premonarchial period. Its gradual dissolution, which led to its disappearance after the establishment of the Davidic monarchy, may be clearly followed in Sam (Westermann, op. cit. 10–13).

Otherwise, the institution of prophetic inquiry of Yahweh is presumably referred to in the accusation in Isa 31:1 (cf. 30:2 with *šʾl*) and in the warning in Amos 5:4; i.e., "Here institution stood against institution: Amos opposed the appeal to Yahweh at the cultic site with the appeal to Yahweh that is possible only through a prophet" (Westermann, op. cit. 22); see further Isa 9:12; Jer 10:21; Hos 10:12.

Exod 18:15 refers presumably to the same process as Deut 17:9, namely the procurement of a divine decision in a difficult legal case.

(c) *drš* is used with *bᵉ* in reference to the interrogation of a strange god, Baal-zebub, in 2 Kgs 1:2f., 6, 16, perhaps in order to direct attention to the frequent practice in polytheism of calling upon a lesser deity in prayer in order that this deity may intercede for the supplicant with a higher deity or even with the high god. The usage in 1 Sam 28:7, "I will inquire through *(bᵉ)* her (i.e., the spiritual medium)," also supports this interpretation. Two apparent exceptions are qualified by the polemical antithesis to the inquiry of strange gods: in the gloss 2 Kgs 1:16 "to inquire by the word of Yahweh," and Ezek 14:7, where an idolatrous Israelite has the gall to approach the prophet in order to inquire of Yahweh in the same manner as one of his idols.

(d) If a ghost is the obj. of *drš*, the construction *drš ᵓel* is used in the sense of "to turn to" (Deut 18:11; Isa 8:19; 19:3; cf. 1 Chron 10:13), as *drš ᵓel* with a person (Isa 11:10, the shoot of Jesse) or a place (Deut 12:5, the cultic site chosen by Yahweh) as obj. indicates. It is revealing in both passages that the approach involves the journey to the place on a pilgrimage. This observation suggests a conclusion concerning the original sense of *drš ᵓel hāᵓôb:* one must travel to the ancestral cultic site or the ancestral burial place in order to interrogate the dead.

(e) The last two attempts to inquire of Yahweh (Ezek 14; 20; certainly rejected by the prophet) belong in the early exilic period. With the cessation of the pre-exilic institution of inquiry, a far-reaching evolution of meaning transpired. *drš yhwh* acquired the general meaning "to have recourse to Yahweh" and soon no longer indicated a concrete action but the habit of the pious.

One may explain this evolution of meaning primarily on two bases. First, in ancient times prophetic inquiry of Yahweh belonged directly to the lament of the supplicant in distress (see 4b). After one component, inquiry via a prophet, dropped out of the process as a whole, the term for the whole became the designation for the remainder, namely the lament. *drš yhwh* as "turning to Yahweh in distress" was now only possible through the lament. Second, the lament climaxed in the questions directed to God: "Why have you . . . ?" and "Yet how long will you . . . ?" The commonality here is not only the interrogation of Yahweh but also the question once addressed to God by the prophet. "Will I recover from this illness?" (2 Kgs 8:8) is very near in intention to the lamenter's question "Yet how long . . . ?"

Now, in a few passages, *drš* indicates the process in which an individual turns to God in lament (Psa 22:27; 34:5; 69:33; 77:3; Job 5:8; cf. Lam 3:25; Psa 9:11; 34:11). These passages all stem from the late period when this pre-exilic institution was hardly still in existence; but the designation had survived. In a late, diminished usage, *drš* twice means only "to call to God" (1 Chron 21:30, by David; Psa 105:4 = 1 Chron 16:11, in the call to praise).

In other passages *drš* also indicates the process of communal lament. Isa 58:2 paraphrases the individual elements of the communal lament that v 3a quotes directly: v 2a "they desire knowledge of my ways" = "How long will you yet be angry?"; v 2b "like a nation that practices justice . . . " = confession of innocence; v 2c "they ask me for righteous judgments" = "Why have you brought this evil upon us?"; v 2c "they desire God's nearness" = "Why do you hide your countenance?" The whole process is called *drš yhwh* in v 2a. Psa 78:34 "When he slaughtered them, they asked *(drš)* after him" is explicated in v 35 through the citation of the confession of confidence from the communal lament. 2 Chron 20:3 is a royal call to communal lament. Cf. also Jer 29:12f.; Isa 55:6; 2 Chron 15:2, 4 *(drš = bqš).*

Lament rituals dominated worship in the exilic and post-exilic eras, at least until the rebuilding of the temple (cf. Lam; Zech 7:3; 8:19; Isa 58:2), where a confession of guilt such as Psa 79:8 (cf. Psa 106; Isa 63:10, 17) could even respond to pre-exilic prophecy of judgment (cf. the tendency of the Dtr history; see H. W. Wolff, "Kerygma of the Deuteronomic Historical Work," in W. Brueggemann and Wolff, *Vitality of Old Testament Traditions* [1982^2], 83–100). Thus, "to abide by the community and its worship" could become synonymous with "to abide by Yahweh and his regulations." This evolution is completed in Dtr theology, where repentance and new observance of the commandments on the part of people are prerequisites for God's attention to laments (cf. e.g., 1 Sam 7:3–4 before vv 5ff.; furthermore, Deut 4:29; Isa 55:6f.; 58; Jer 29:13; 2 Chron 15:2, 4). "Here, the one-time procedure occasioned by a particular circumstance has become an attitude, a habit . . . 'to turn to God' has become 'to abide by God' " (Westermann, op. cit. 24). "This abiding by God is an important, characteristic designation of relationship to God from the Deuteronomic era on to the time of the Chronicler. It has roughly the same meaning in the OT as the NT and then Christian 'believing in God' " (ibid. 28).

drš yhwh became such a comprehensive designation for Yahweh worship that it often stands as the antithesis of idolatry (Isa 65:1, 10; Jer 8:2; Zeph 1:6; Ezra 6:21; 2 Chron 15:12f.; 17:3f.; 34:3; cf. Psa 24:6; Ezra 4:2; 2 Chron 25:15, 20). Consequently, it occurs regularly in the evaluations of kings in Chron (2 Chron 12:14; 14:3; 17:4; 19:3; 22:9; 26:5; 30:19). But, at the same time, *drš yhwh* became synonymous with "to fulfill God's will" or "to keep the commandments" (1 Chron 22:19; 2 Chron 14:6a; 31:21; likewise Psa 14:2 = 53:5; 119:2, 10); the lament no longer stands in the background here—only the conditional promise of blessing.

Because the proclamation of the commandments and the conditional promise of blessing was increasingly individualized, it became possible in Psa 34 for not only the concrete warning in v 6 to follow the report of deliverance in the individual thanksgiving song (v 5), but also a general promise of salvation for the individual who abides by God (vv 9b–11) and an admonition to keep the commandments (vv 12ff.). As with the communal lament above, here too the possibility of being heard and delivered depends upon the supplicant's fulfillment of the commandments.

In a few late passages even the commandments could be the obj. of *drš* (Psa 119:45, 155; 1 Chron 28:8), in the late gloss Isa 34:16 even "the scriptures." Cf. here also *midrāš* "exposition, edifying paraphrase" (see 2, 3b).

The use of preps. varies without pattern in late texts. Thus *drš yhwh* (2 Chron 34:21) stands alongside *drš byhwh* (2 Chron 34:26; 1 Chron 10:14) and *drš lēʾlōhîm* (2 Chron 34:3; *lyhwh*, 2 Chron 20:3) or Job 5:8 *drš ʾel-ʾēl*.

5. In the available Qumran texts *drš* appears about 40x (according to Kuhn, *Konk.* 52f.). As in the OT, "to seek God" is a general designation of reverence for God in many passages.

Above all, however, the cognitive sense of *drš* is richly attested and expanded to new realms of meaning, esp. in theological language: "to study the commandments," "to study the law." Esp. noteworthy are a few usually fixed expressions: *dwrš htwrh* "student of the law" (CD 6:7; 7:18; 4QFlor 1:11); also *dwršy ḥlqwt* "producers of smooth interpretations" (1QH 2:32, etc.), a formula with which the Qumran community described the Pharisees. The opposing position is represented by the Talmudic phrase *dôr^e^šê ḥ^a^mûrôt* "producers of strict interpretations," the pharisaic designation for the Qumran sectarians (cf. C. Roth, *RQ* 2 [1960]: 261–65). Concerning the usage of *drš* in Talmud and Midrash, cf. further L. Margoulies, *Leshonenu* 20 (1956): 50ff. (Hebr.).

On "to seek" in the NT, cf. H. Greeven, "ζητέω," *TDNT* 2:892–96.

G. Gerleman (1–4a, 5)/E. Ruprecht (4b–e)

הֶבֶל *hebel* **breath**

S 1892; BDB 210b; *HALOT* 1:236a; *TDOT* 3:313–20; *TWOT* 463a; *NIDOTTE* 2039

---

1. Words related to *hebel* "breath" occur in Aram. and in SSem. (cf. *HAL* 227a). The verb *hbl* qal "to become/be involved with nothing" and hi. "to make nothing, delude" are denominative.

This word is apparently related to the name *hebel* (= Abel; cf. the pausal form in Gen 4:2a), which may be an appellative.

2. The noun occurs 73x, the verb 5x (qal 4x, hi. 1x). The noun appears 41x in Eccl alone; a concentration is also evident in the langauge of the Psa (9x; also Isa 49:4; Jer 10:3, 8, 15; 14:22; 16:19; 51:18; Job 7:16). A group of 6 passages belong to texts influenced by Dtr (see 4a).

hebel usually occurs in the abs. st. When used like a genuine noun it usually has the meaning "idol" (see 3c). In the cs. relationship it serves as governing noun (on the form *h^a^bēl* see Wagner 134) mostly to intensify the concept (*h^a^bēl h^a^bālîm*, Eccl 1:2bis; 12:8); as the governed noun it should be translated adj. In addition there is an adv. use (e.g., Job 9:29 "uselessly"). The frequent construction with a bipartite nom. clause (about 30x) is noteworthy.

3. (a) The basic meaning of *hebel* is "wind, breath" (only Isa 57:13 par. *rûaḥ* "wind"); this is adduced in comparisons for useless and transitory things (Psa 62:12; 144:4; Prov 21:6; cf. Akk. *šāru;* J. Hehn, *ZAW* 43 [1925]: 222f.; O. Loretz, *Qohelet und der Alte Orient* [1964], 127f.).

(b) The basic meaning totally disappears in the largest category of occurrences (nom. clauses); here *hebel* is simply a negative term characterizing human experiences and basic qualities. The common translation "nothingness, nothing" is often too general. The precise negative connotation intended results only from the context: the scale reaches from "unstable" (par. *kāzāb* "deceit," Psa 62:10), "transitory" (par. *ṣēl* "shadow" in Psa 144:4; cf. 39:7), and "useless, vain" (par. *ᵓên yitrôn* "no gain," Eccl 2:11; *rîq* "empty, nothing," Isa 30:7; 49:4) to "senseless, nonsense, bad" (par. *ḥᵒlî rāᶜ* "evil plague," Eccl 6:2; *rāᶜâ rabbâ* "great evil," Eccl 2:21).

(c) The notion of uselessness gained separate status as a designation for other gods. Here *hebel* means idols (→ *ᵓᵉlîl* 4); cf. the formulaic usages "to provoke Yahweh with idols" (Deut 32:31; 1 Kgs 16:13, 26; Jer 8:19) and "to follow after the idols" (2 Kgs 17:15; Jer 2:5).

4. *hebel* occurs predominantly in three areas:

(a) As a designation for other gods in the Dtr accusation against Israel's apostasy (Deut 32:31; 1 Kgs 16:13, 26; 2 Kgs 17:15; Jer 2:5; 8:19) and as a contrasting motif in the confession of confidence: the worshiper relies upon Yahweh, not upon the idols (Psa 31:7; Jer 14:22; 16:19; Jonah 2:9; see also the late idol polemic in Jer 10:3, 8, 15).

(b) *hebel* occurs as a disqualifying term in the individual lament. The supplicant laments the uselessness of his effort (Isa 49:4) and the transience of his life (Job 7:16); both refer to human fate per se in a generalization typical for the lament (Psa 39:6f., 12). This limited humanity is occasionally juxtaposed with the unlimited goodness and power of God (Psa 62:10; 94:11; 144:4).

(c) The actual focus of the exceedingly concentrated use of *hebel* in Eccl is judgment (nom. clause). On the basis of trial, observation, and reflection, Qohelet repeatedly comes to an annihilating judgment, mostly concerning very concrete things (*[gam-] zeh hebel* "[even] this is nothing," Eccl 2:15, 19, 21, 23, 26; 4:4, 8, 16; 5:9; 6:2, 9; 7:6; 8:10, 14; cf. 2:1; 11:10); it more or less broadens only rarely (*hakkōl hebel* "all is nothing," 2:11, 17; 3:19; cf. 11:8). The summary motto of 1:2 and 12:8 is to be attributed to a redactor (F. Ellermeier, *Qohelet* [1967], 1/1:94ff.). For Qohelet, *hebel* refers not simply to everything, but to three specific complexes: (1) his efforts, indeed, human work in general, are unproductive, useless, and vain (2:1, 11, 19, 21, 23; 4:4, 8; 5:9; 6:2); here *hebel* is an exact antonym for *yitrôn* "use" (cf. 2:11; so also Ellermeier, op. cit. 38). Work is senseless, because God capriciously allows one to enjoy the fruits of one's work but denies them to another (2:24–26); finally, however, because humans are mortal and must leave their possessions to another (2:18–21; 6:1f.). (2) The wisdom mastery of life, which seeks to order human behavior and actions, is senseless, for, as it happens, the righteous have the fate of the godless (8:10–14); in the final analysis, the wise die like the foolish (2:15; 6:7–9). (3) Behind these judgments stands Qohelet's insight into human transience (6:12; 11:8, 10; cf. 7:15; 9:9), which makes humanity equal to all creation (3:19). In the light of the impending fate of death, all the future (11:8), all events whatsoever, are incomprehensible and senseless (1:14; 2:17). God is certainly not subject to the *hebel* verdict, but neither is he a savior from that verdict (thus Hertzberg, KAT 17/4, 222ff.; Loretz, op. cit. 234ff.); rather, in his incomprehensible actions he is the final cause for human finitude.

5. The LXX translates *hebel* primarily with *mataiotēs, mataios.* Thus a moral element comes into play; the fallibility intended is no longer so much creaturely as ethical (cf. G. Bertram, *ZAW* 64 [1952]: 30–34). Qumran identifies transience with sinfulness even more directly (1QS 5:19; 1QM 4:12; 6:6; 9:9; 11:9; 14:12). On the NT, see O. Bauernfeind, "μάταιος," *TDNT* 4:519–24.

R. Albertz

הָדָר *hādār* **splendor**

S 1926; BDB 214a; *HALOT* 1:240a; *TDOT* 3:335–41; *TWOT* 477b; *NIDOTTE* 2077

---

1. Extra-Hebr. words related to *hādār* "ornament, splendor, majesty" may be identified with certainty only in Aram.

On Ug. *hdrt* see 3b; on Old SArab. *hdr* "ornament(?)" cf. Conti Rossini 131b; on Eg. *hʾdrt* cf. H. Donner, *ZAW* 79 (1967): 331n.57.

A relationship to Hebr. *ʾdr (LS* 172a; → *ʾaddîr)* or Arab. *hdr* "to effervesce" (GB 175a), which is sometimes posited, is rather doubtful.

The verbal forms are apparently denominatives from the subst. *hādār* (W. J. Gerber, *Die hebr. Verba denominativa* [1896], 163f.; BLA 273). In addition to *hādār* (in Dan 11:20 with a segholate cs. form *heder* instead of the more common *hᵃdar,* cf. BL 552; *HAL* 230a), a fem. *hᵃdārâ* "finery, grandeur" occurs (see 3b); Bibl. Aram. has *hᵃdar* "majesty" amd *hdr* pa. "to glorify."

Imp. Aram. has *hdr* "majesty" (Aḥ. 108) and *hdyr* "majestic" (Aḥ. 207; cf. *DISO* 63).

2. The root occurs 42x in the Hebr. OT (excl. *hᵃdûrîm* in Isa 45:2, where *hᵃrārîm* should be read according to 1QIsaᵃ; cf. *HAL* 229b; contra e.g., Zorell 185a); it is represented 6x in Aram.

The verb appears 6x in Hebr., 4x in the qal and 1x each in the ni. and the hitp. (see 3c). The subst. *hādār* occurs 31x (incl. *heder* in Dan 11:20; pl. only in Psa 110:3), *hᵃdārâ* 5x. The word group occurs most often in the Psa (15x; Isa 8x; Prov 4x; Lev 3x); it is entirely absent from narrative texts.

Aram. occurrences are limited to Dan (noun and pa. 3x each).

3. (a) The subst. *hādār* characterizes nature's grandeur (Lev 23:40; Isa 35:2a) and human beauty (Isa 53:2; Psa 8:6; Prov 20:29; 31:25). In reference to God, the declaration of beauty acquires the meaning "glory, grandeur, majesty" (cf. Isa 35:2b with v 2a; see 4). In the sense of "majesty," *hādār* is also an attribute of the earthly king (Psa 21:6; 45:4, 5 [txt?]; Aram. Dan 4:27, 33; 5:18; cf. *hᵃdārâ* Prov 14:28). The pl. in Psa 110:3 may more likely refer to the royal finery (consisting of various ornamental pieces; cf. G. Widengren, *Sakrales Königtum im AT und im Judentum* [1955], 103n.22). *hādār* also pertains, however, to cities (Isa 5:14; Ezek 27:10; Lam 1:6) or a tribe (Deut 33:17). According to Dan 11:20, Israel is *heder malkût* "an ornament of the kingdom."

Several passages describe God or a person as "clothed" with *hādār* (Yahweh, Psa 104:1; Job 40:10; housewife, Prov 31:25; Jerusalem, Ezek 16:14; qal ptcp. Isa 63:1).

Par. terms for *hādār* are → *hôd* "loftiness" (Psa 21:6; 45:4; 96:6; 104:1; 111:3; Job 40:10; 1 Chron 16:27), *kābôd* "glory" (→ *kbd;* Isa 35:2; Psa 8:6; 21:6; cf. Psa 145:5, 12), *paḥad* "terror" (Isa 2:10, 19, 21), → *kōaḥ* "might" (Psa 29:4), *ᶜōz* "strength" (→ *ᶜzz;* Psa 96:6; Prov 31:25), *tipʾeret* "ornament" (→ *pʾr;* Psa 96:6; Prov 20:29), and *tōʾar* "stateliness" (Isa 53:2). Other synonyms for *hādār* include *ʾeder* (→ *ʾaddîr* 1), *gāʾôn* (→ *gʾh*), *ḥemed* (5x, → *ḥmd*), and *sᵉbî* "splendor" (18x, used in Dan 8:9; 11:16, 41, 45 for Jerusalem or Israel; cf. v 20).

In Aram. *ḥᵉsēn* "might" (Dan 4:27), *zîw* "splendor" (Dan 4:33), *malkû* "dominion," *gᵉbûrâ* "strength," and *yᵉqār* "honor" (Dan 5:18) accompany *hᵃdar.*

(b) *hᵃdārâ* occurs only in the cs. state, 4x in the phrase *hadrat-qōdeš* (Psa 29:2; 96:9 = 1 Chron 16:29; 2 Chron 20:21), once in *hadrat-melek* (Prov 14:28). In the last passage, like *hādār* in corresponding contexts, *hᵃdārâ* means "majesty, splendor, loftiness" in contrast to *mᵉḥittâ* "ruin, fall." The other passages have been traditionally understood as "fall down before Yahweh in holy ornaments," or the like. This interpretation should be maintained with H. Donner, *ZAW* 79 (1967): 331–33 (cf. too, however, A. Caquot, *Syria* 33 [1956]: 37–41; E. Vogt, *Bib* 41 [1960]: 24; W. H. Schmidt, *Königtum Gottes in Ugarit und Israel* [1966²], 56) over against the translation "revelation, appearance" (F. M. Cross, *BASOR* 117 [1950]: 19–21; Kraus, *Psa*, CC, 1:344f.; *UT* no. 752; P. R. Ackroyd, *JTS* 17 [1966]: 393–96) on the basis of Ug. *hdrt* in *KTU* 1.14.III.51, which parallels *ḥlm* "dream" and could mean something like "vision, face"; the derivations in *UT* no. 752 and *WUS* no. 817 remain uncertain in any case.

(c) The qal verb means "to adorn someone's appearance, honor someone" (Lev 19:32 "you should stand up in the presence of a gray head and honor the aged"). In juridical terminology it acquires the nuance "to give preference (in judgment)." Lev 19:15 demands impartial judgment: "You should not regard the person of the poor *(nśʾ pᵉnê-dāl),* nor favor the mighty *(hdr pᵉnê gādôl).*" The apodictic saying in Exod 23:3 is also usually emended as an apodosis (*BH*³; *HAL* 230a; Exod 23:6 represents the protasis).

The Aram. pa. always means "to honor (God)" (par. *brk* pa. Dan 4:31; par. *rûm* po. 4:34; par. *šbḥ* pa. 4:31, 34; 5:23).

The hitp. refers to self-attributed honor ("before the king" Prov 25:6, par. to "to assume the place of the mighty.") The ni. should be rendered "to come to be honored" or the like (Lam 5:12).

4. *hādār* plays a special role in Israel's praise (Psa 96:6; 104:1; 111:3; 145:5, 12; 1 Chron 16:27) as an expression of God's royalty (cf. H. Gross, FS Junker 96; H. Wildberger, *TZ* 21 [1965]: 481f.). Hymnic praise of Yahweh's "beauty" (von Rad, *Theol.* 1:364–67) grows out of the experience of his historical deeds (Psa 111:3; 145:5, 12). The communal prayer (Psa 90:16) is based on it. The association of God's splendor with his activity in history is broadened to include Yahweh's glory revealed in his creation (Psa 104:1). Even when Israel speaks of God's majesty as unwavering (Psa 96:6; 1 Chron 16:27), it means that which takes place at God's impulse (Isa 35:2b; cf. 63:1). The "splendor of

his majesty" is experienced even in Yahweh's judgment (*hᵃdar gᵉʾōnô*, Isa 2:10, 19, 21; the combination of two synonymous words has superlative force, Joüon §141m).

Yahweh's chosen, Israel's king (Psa 21:6; 45:4f.; Prov 14:28), the pious (Psa 149:9; cf. Mic 2:9), Jerusalem (Ezek 16:14), and Zion (Lam 1:6), participate in his majesty. Israel also recognizes God's grandeur in creation and consequently praises the creator (Psa 8:6). But Israel knows that it cannot obtain divine glory for itself (Job 40:10). Perfect beauty exists only insofar as God grants *hādār* (Ezek 16:14).

5. The LXX renders the root *hdr* by some 20 different terms, most frequently by *doxa, megaloprepeia, euprepeia,* and *timē*. The influence of *hādār* is active in NT statements concerning the beauty of God (and of Jesus; cf. the use of Psa 8:6 in Heb 2:5–10); cf. G. Kittel and G. von Rad, "δοκέω," *TDNT* 2:232–55; J. Schneider, "τιμή," *TDNT* 8:169–80.

G. Wehmeier (1–3)/D. Vetter (4–5)

הוֹד *hôd* **highness, majesty**

S 1935; BDB 217a; *HALOT* 1:241a; *TDOT* 3:352–56; *TWOT* 482a; *NIDOTTE* 2086

---

1. *hôd* "highness, majesty" occurs only in Hebr.

The etymological relationship to Arab. *ʾawada* "to be heavy," WSem. *ydh* hi. "to praise," or Arab. *nahuda* "to be beautiful, strong" is uncertain (GB 176b; KBL 227b, 364a; *HAL* 231a; Zorell 186a).

2. The subst. occurs 24x in the OT (Psa 8x, Job and 1 Chron 3x each, Zech and Dan 2x each, Num, Isa, Jer, Hos, Hab, and Prov 1x each).

3. The declaration "highness, majesty" obviously derives from the usage of the term as a royal predication (Jer 22:18; cf. Rudolph, HAT 12, 141f.; Psa 21:6; 45:4; Dan 11:21; 1 Chron 29:25; in Zech 6:13 of the priest-king). This derivation also stands in the foreground when *hôd* expresses God's majesty (Hab 3:3; Psa 8:2; 148:13; Job 37:22). The expression also applies in isolated cases—in somewhat the sense of "splendor"—to people (individuals: Num 27:20; Prov 5:9; Dan 10:8; a nation: Hos 14:7), animals (Zech 10:3; Job 39:20), and plants (Hos 14:7). In Dan 10:8 *hôd* (like Aram. *zîw*, Dan 5:6, 9f.; 7:28) means the radiance of the face, "complexion"; by contrast, in Prov 5:9 the term does not refer to the external appearance but indicates "the product of the best years of life" (Gemser, HAT 16, 34). To a greater or lesser degree, the expression implies the experience of astonishment and joy in all passages.

On par. terms, see 4. In Dan 10:8 *mašḥît* "ruin" is the opposite of *hôd*.

The weight of the term lies in theological usage. God's *hôd* has been revealed to Israel in the deeds of the Lord of history and of creation. Israel magnifies Yahweh and acknowledges his majesty with the expression of his *hôd*.

The confessional names (*hôdᵉyâ, hôdîyâ,* short form *hôd*) formed with *hôd* (or *hûd*) also express this position (*IP* 146; on *ʾᵃbîhûd, ʾᵃḥîhûd, ʾammîhûd,* and *ʾēhûd* cf., however, Stamm, *HEN* 416a, 418a).

The word occurs in the description of God's immanence (Isa 30:30; Hab 3:3; cf. Job 37:22). It also reflects Israel's experience of God's majesty in the descriptive psalm of praise (Psa 111:3; 145:5), as well as its astonished perception of God's majesty in his creation (Psa 8:2; 104:1; 148:13). The same psalm motif (praise of the creator—praise of the Lord of history) determines the structure of Job 38–41; here praise takes the form of divine speech (cf. C. Westermann, *Structure of the Book of Job* [1981], 105–23; id., *Isa 40–66*, OTL, 154f., on Isa 44:24–28). *hôd* recurs in the development of both parts: in the praise of the creator (under the description of the frightful might of the horse, 39:20) and the praise of the judge (40:10). Israel can speak of Yahweh's dominion over the world only in praise of his majesty (Psa 96:6; 1 Chron 16:27; 29:11).

A king's *hôd* is a gift of Yahweh's own dignity (Isa 22:18; Zech 6:13; Psa 21:6; 45:4; Dan 11:21; 1 Chron 29:25; cf. Sir 10:5). According to P, Moses and Joshua also possess *hôd* (Num 27:20). The notion that Moses is to grant something of his *hôd* to Joshua with his commission, as previously a portion of Yahweh's *hôd* was granted to him, seems to underlie this statement. Moreover, the predicate applies in two metaphorical sayings to the people to whom God has devoted himself. Once, the Israel restored by Yahweh is compared with the "glory" of the fruitful olive tree (Hos 14:7); again, in the saving activity of Yahweh Judah assumes the role of the "glorious" war steed (Zech 10:3).

Combinations with similar terms illuminate the connotation of the term in reference to God's grandeur and majesty: *hôd* parallels *tᵉhillâ* "glory," *nōgah* "radiance," and *ʿōz* "strength" in Hab 3:3f.; *zāhāb* "gold(en brilliance)" in Job 37:22 (perhaps to be read *zōhar* "brilliance" according to BH^3). In a series of five divine predications, *hôd* parallels *gᵉdūllâ* "greatness," *gᵉbûrâ* "might," *tipʾeret* "majesty," and *nēṣaḥ* "brilliance" in 1 Chron 29:11. The pair *hôd wᵉhādār* (→ *hādār*) describes Yahweh's royal radiance in Psa 96:6; 104:1; 111:3; 145:5 (*hᵃdar kᵉbôd hôdekā,* → *kbd);* 1 Chron 16:27; Job 40:10 (par. *gāʾôn wāgōbah,* → *gʾh,* → *gbh),* but also the dignity granted the king (Psa 21:6; 45:4).

5. The LXX renders *hôd* by almost a dozen different terms, most frequently by *doxa* (9x) and *exomologēsis* (4x).

The animated diction and meanings associated wtih *hôd* are found in its most important NT equivalent: *doxa* refers to the king/kingdom (e.g., Matt 4:8; 6:29), to the creation (e.g., 1 Cor 11:7; 15:40f.), and to God, in particular (cf. G. Kittel and G. von Rad, "δοκέω," *TDNT* 2:232–55.

D. Vetter

הוֹי *hôy* **woe**

S 1945; BDB 222b; *HALOT* 1:242a; *TDOT* 3:359–64; *TWOT* 485; *NIDOTTE* 2098

1. Among the interjections that cannot be traced to verbal roots, *hôy* "woe" and other exclamations included here (e.g., → *ʾᵃhāh* "ah") may be classified as pure exclamations, while → *hinnēh* "behold" and *has* "hush!" (→ *ḥrš*), together with impvs. that have devolved into interjections (→ *hlk*, → *qûm*, → *rʾh*), have the character of a demand.

In respect to phonetics and, to a degree, to usage, *ʾôy*, *ʾôyâ*, *ʾî*, and *hô* could be grouped with *hôy*. *heʾāḥ* (*ʾāḥ*), which expresses a more joyous excitement, stands alone.

2. Ch. Hardmeier (cited in Wolff, *Joel*, Herm, 242f.) offers precise statistics for *hôy* in its various constructions. *hôy* occurs 51x, almost exclusively in prophetic literature (Isa 21x, Jer 11x, Hab 5x, Zech 4x, Ezek 3x, Amos and Zeph 2x, once each in 1 Kgs 13:30; Mic 2:1; Nah 3:1), in 3/4 of all cases it introduces a prophetic woe oracle.

ʾôy has a significantly broader distribution; it occurs 24x (twice in Ezek 16:23), most frequently in Jer (8x; Isa and Ezek 4x, Num, 1 Sam, Hos 2x each, Prov and Lam 1x each). *hô-hô* occurs in Amos 5:16, the lengthened form *ʾôyâ* in Psa 120:5, the form *ʾî*, common in Mid. Hebr., in Eccl 4:10 and 10:16 (cf. *HAL* 37b).

heʾāḥ occurs 12x (Psa 7x, repeated in three passages; Ezek 3x; Isa 44:6; Job 39:25). Passages with *ʾāḥ* (Ezek 6:11; 18:10; 21:20) are textually uncertain (cf. Zimmerli, *Ezek*, Herm, 1:180f., 371, 430).

3. *hôy* "ah! woe!" may be first identified as the introductory cry of a lament for the dead (1 Kgs 13:30 "woe, my brother!"; Jer 22:18 "ah, my brother, ah, sister!" and "ah, lord, ah, your majesty!"; cf. Rudolph, HAT 12, 142; 34:5 "woe, lord!" in each instance with *spd* "to lament the dead"; cf. Jahnow 83–87, and others), like *hô-hô* in Amos 5:16 (alongside *mispēd* and *nᵉhî* "lament for the dead"), and perhaps *hôy* in Jer 48:1 ("concerning Nebo," with *ʾel*) and 50:27 (Babel, with *ʿal*) in a prophetic funeral song (G. Wanke, *ZAW* 78 [1966]: 217).

In eight or nine passages, *hôy* serves in other contexts as an introductory declaration of excitement: "ha!" (Isa 1:24; 17:12; 18:1; Jer 30:7 txt?; 47:6) or as an agitated demand: "up!" (Isa 55:1; Zech 2:10[doubled]; 2:11).

The remaining passages contain *hôy* with a subsequent noun as an introduction to a woe oracle (often in series: Isa 5:8, 11, 18, 20–22; 10:1; cf. Wildberger, *Isa 1–12*, CC, 188–217; Hab 2:6, 9, 12, 15, 19; otherwise: Isa 1:4; 10:5; 28:1; 29:1, 15; 30:1; 31:1; 33:1; 45:9f.; Jer 22:13; 23:1; Ezek 34:2; Amos 5:18; 6:1; Mic 2:1; Nah 3:1; Zeph 2:5; 3:1; Zech 11:17; followed by the prep. *ʿal* or *lᵉ*, Ezek 13:3, 18; cf. above, Jer 48:1; 50:27); see 4.

ʾôy is sharply distinguished from *hôy* in grammatical and semantic usage (G. Wanke, *ZAW* 78 [1966]: 215–18). With the exception of Num 24:23 and Ezek 24:6, 9, *ʾôy* (*ʾôy-nāʾ* Jer 4:31; 45:3; Lam 5:16; *ʾôyâ* Psa 120:5; *ʾî* Eccl 4:10; 10:16) is always followed by a particular person or group of persons introduced by *lᵉ* (without further qualification by ptcps., adjs., and substs.) and a causal clause.

The most original usage is in the 1st per. "woe is me" (Isa 6:5; 24:16; Jer 4:31; 10:19; 15:10; 45:3; cf. Psa 120:5) or "woe is us" (1 Sam 4:7f.; Jer 4:13; 6:4; Lam 5:16) in the context of the sudden arrival of a threat in the so-called cry of anxiety (1 Sam 4:7f.; Isa 6:5; 24:16; Jer 4:13, 31; 6:4; cf. Num 24:23), which metamorphoses ambiguously into a complaint in the context of an already present crisis (Jer 10:19; 15:10; 45:3; Lam 5:16; Psa 120:5).

In the address "woe to you" (Num 21:29 = Jer 48:46; Jer 13:27; Ezek 16:23; with *ʾî*, Eccl 10:16), *ʾôy* acquires the character of a secondary threat (or reprimand), as is also true for usages of the 3d per. (Isa 3:9, 11; Ezek 24:6, 9; Hos 7:13; 9:12; with *ʾî* Eccl 4:10; cf. Prov 23:29 with a substantivized *ʾôy* "woe" par. to a synonymous *ʾᵃbôy* "ah").

4. Exhaustive examinations of the form-critical derivation of the woes have been offered (cf. the detailed study by Wolff, *Joel*, Herm, 242–45; W. Schottroff, *Der altisraelitische Fluchspruch* [1969], 112–20). Despite some analogies of a formal (series and appended ptcps.; cf. Deut 27:15–26) and semantic nature (opposition to antisocial behavior), one cannot very well view *hôy* as a weakened *ʾārûr* (→ *ʾrr*) or the woe as a mutation of the cultic curse (so S. Mowinckel, *Psalmenstudien* [1924], 5:2, 119–21; P. Humbert, *Problèmes du livre d'Habacuc* [1944], 18–23; Westermann, *BFPS* 189–94; J. L. Crenshaw, *ZAW* 79 [1967]: 47f.; cf. too H.-J. Hermisson, *Studien zur isr. Spruchweisheit* [1968], 89f.; Wildberger, *Isa 1–12*, CC, 196), because the curse formulae, "in contrast to the *hôy* sayings, do not simply emphatically specify dangerous consequences of a particular deed that are immanent and result from the deed itself; rather, they attribute such consequences to the deed, in the first place, through the express pronouncement of curse and thus actually first establish them" (Schottroff, op. cit. 117; cf. Wolff, op. cit. 242). The explanation of the prophetic woe as an adaptation of the funeral lament seems more illuminating: "The *hôy*, which probably originally belonged to the lament for the dead, should make it clear that the seed of death is already inherent in a particular human behavior" (so G. Wanke, "אוֹי und הוֹי," *ZAW* 78 [1966]: 218; cf. R. J. Clifford, *CBQ* 28 [1966]: 458–64; J. G. Williams, *HUCA* 38 [1967]: 75–91; Schottroff, op. cit. 113–17, who treats ancient Near Eastern pars. for secondary usage of the woe cry of the lament for the dead in the sense of a threat or warning). It is possible, in this respect, that the prophets adopted a form of speech in this use of the woe cry already developed in pedagogical tribal wisdom (E. Gerstenberger, *JBL* 81 [1962]: 249–63; H. W. Wolff, *Amos the Prophet* [1973], 17–34; id., *Joel*, Herm, 242–45; Schottroff, op. cit. 117–20).

hôy does not occur in pairings with → *ʾašrê* "blessed be the one who . . . " (cf. W. Janzen, *HTR* 58 [1965]: 215–26), but, at most, with *ʾôy* or *ʾî* and in parallelisms clearly influenced by wisdom: Isa 3:10ff. (read *ʾašrê* for *ʾimrû;* Wildberger, *Isa 1–12*, CC, 125, 134f.; contra W. L. Holladay, *VT* 18 [1968]: 481–87) and Eccl 10:16f. (cf. Schottroff, op. cit. 118).

5. The LXX renders the interjections mostly with *ouai*. On early Judaism (Qumran has no available examples) and on the NT, cf. StrB 1:778f. and the comms. on Luke 6:24–26; C. H. Dodd, FS Robert 406f.

E. Jenni

היה *hyh* to be

S 1961; BDB 224a; *HALOT* 1:243a; *TDOT* 3:369–81; *TWOT* 491; *NIDOTTE* 2118

1. Aram. *hwh* (KBL 1068f. and suppl. 200; *DISO* 63f.) corresponds to the verb *hyh* "to become, be" in the OT (rarely *hwh* as an Aramaism; cf. Wagner no. 72) and in the Siloam Inscription (*KAI* no. 189).

Akk. *ewû* "to become" (*AHw* 266f.; cf. P. Fronzaroli, *AANLR* 8/19 [1964]: 164, however, with regard to the initial sound of the root) and the Amor. PNs derived from the root **hwy* (Huffmon 72f., 159f.) must also be taken into consideration; comparison with the Hebr. *hwh* II "to fall" (only in Job 37:6) and Arab. *hawā* "to fall" contributes little.

Semantic counterparts to *hyh* "to be" are formed in Akk. with *bašû*, in Ug., Phoen.-Pun., Arab., and Eth. with verbs of the root → *kûn*.

The ni. "to take place" occurs in addition to the qal; Hebr. has no other derivatives of the root; cf., however, → *yhwh*.

*2. With 3,540 occurrences of the qal (excl. Hos 13:14 *ʾehî*, → *ʾayyēh* 4; Lis. omits Gen 42:36; 1 Kgs 22:33; 2 Kgs 1:17) and 21 occurrences of the ni., *hyh* is the second most frequent verb in the OT. Hebr. *hwh* "to be, become" appears 5x (Gen 27:29; Isa 16:4; Eccl 2:22; 11:3; Neh 6:6), Bibl. Aram. *hwh* 71x (plus read with MSS *hᵃwāh* instead of *hûʾ* in Dan 6:11).

	qal	*wayᵉhî*	ni.
Gen	316	122	–
Exod	234	41	1
Lev	147	1	–
Num	180	16	–
Deut	169	7	2
Josh	145	63	–
Judg	118	49	3
1 Sam	168	56	–
2 Sam	153	42	–
1 Kgs	195	78	2
2 Kgs	120	55	–
Isa	211	11	–
Jer	262	43	2
Ezek	335	62	2
Hos	27	1	–
Joel	10	–	1
Amos	10	–	–
Obad	7	–	–
Jonah	10	5	–
Mic	18	–	1
Nah	3	–	–
Hab	3	1	–
Zeph	11	–	–
Hag	9	2	–
Zech	66	9	1
Mal	11	–	–

	qal	*wayᵉhî*	ni.
Psa	104	4	–
Job	50	10	–
Prov	27	–	1
Ruth	21	5	–
Song Sol	4	–	–
Eccl	47	–	–
Lam	23	–	–
Esth	17	6	–
Dan	20	5	3
Ezra	5	1	–
Neh	47	14	1
1 Chron	105	27	–
2 Chron	132	46	1
OT	3,540	782	21

The proportion of the form *wayᵉhî* in the total is, therefore, a good measure of the narrative character of a book; cf. the sequence of frequency for the totals (Ezek, Gen, Jer, Exod, Isa, 1 Kgs, etc.) with that for *wayᵉhî* (Gen, 1 Kgs, Josh, Ezek, 1 Sam, 2 Kgs, etc.).

3. The verb *hyh* is not necessary to indicate the simple existence or identity of a person or thing. A nom. clause is employed, i.e., *ʾānōkî yhwh ʾᵉlōheykā* "I (am) Yahweh, your God" (Exod 20:2); *šemeš ûmāgēn yhwh* "Yahweh (is) sun and shield" (Psa 84:12). The use of *hyh* generally gives rise to a more fully packed and dynamic statement concerning the being of a person or thing, a being expressed in the entity's actions or deeds, fate, and behavior toward others.

hyh qal signifies not only "to be" but also "to become, act, happen, behave"; the verb combines with various preps. that modify its meaning; thus e.g., *hyh bᵉ* "to be located, happen in," *hyh lᵉ* "to serve as, become, belong to" (as in several languages, it serves the functions of the absent verb "to have"; cf. G. Benveniste, *Problèmes de linguistique générale* [1966], 187–207), *hyh ʿim* "to stand beside"; *hyh ʾaḥᵃrê* "to abide with (someone)"; *hyh ʾel* is esp. typical in the narrative introductions of prophetic oracles: *wayᵉhî dᵉbar yhwh ʾel* (→ *dābār* IV/2a), where *hyh* describes the intrusion of the word in the life of the prophet (cf. *HAL* 233f. and, exhaustively, C. H. Ratschow, *Werden und Wirken: Eine Untersuchung des Wortes hajah als Beitrag zur Wirklichkeitserfassung des AT* [1941], 7–30; independently, T. Boman, *Hebrew Thought Compared with Greek* [1970], 38–49, whose conclusions, however, should be restricted; cf. *SBL* 58–72).

These meanings are approximated in poetic parallelism, e.g., *ʿmd* "to stand (there)" (Psa 33:9), *kûn* ni. "to exist" (Psa 89:37f.; cf. 90:17 po.), *qûm* "to come about" (Isa 7:7; 14:24); further synonymous and antithetical pars. in Ratschow, op. cit. 5f.

In conjunction with a predicate adj., *hyh* expresses the behavior or the characteristics of a thing or a person: "But the serpent was more cunning than all the animals" (Gen 3:1); "It is not good that the man should be alone" (Gen 2:18). Combined with the inf. abs., it indicates the duration of a movement: "But the water sunk even further" (Gen 8:5; cf. v 3). In a highly attenuated meaning, *hyh* serves only to temporally establish the statement:

"It should be a male and a female" (Gen 6:19), and can be viewed as a simple copula (BrSynt 28; BM 2:96). But even then *hyh* often maintains the function of describing a behavior or a status: "and both the man and his wife were naked" (Gen 2:25). Preceding a narrative verb, *wayᵉhî* "and it happened" becomes a mere stylistic figure, which L. Köhler (*VT* 3 [1953]: 304) designates a "hypertrope," although the *hyh* treated under 4b(1) still resonates through it.

The ni. occurs primarily in late texts (and in Qumran) in the meaning "to come to pass, happen" (e.g., Deut 4:32; Jer 5:30; Zech 8:10), perhaps also "to be away" (Dan 8:27).

4. Three theological usages of *hyh* may be distinguished: (a) the implicit, (b) the explicit (in reference to miracle accounts, in prophetic oracles, in legal prescriptions, and in the covenant formula), and (c) the abs. theological use in Exod 3:14a (on which cf. Ratschow, op. cit. 31–86).

(a) In curse and blessing texts, *hyh* indicates the destiny of the cursed or blessed person; this fate takes effect in accordance with the evil or good power in its bearer: "So I will make you a great nation and bless you and make your name famous, and you will be a blessing" (Gen 12:2); Abraham is already blessed, and this blessing, which is inherent in his being, will manifest itself in results. "And your descendants shall be like the dust of the earth" (Gen 28:14): this promise of descendants is not yet realized, but it "is" due to the blessing that presses toward its realization. Similarly, "that man shall be like the cities that Yahweh has destroyed" (Jer 20:16). These formulae mention Yahweh not as the actual agent; they place the blessing or curse in direct relationship to its actualization in history. Here *hyh*, usually in the pf., expresses the inner dynamics of the blessing or the curse, a force released by the word that will unavoidably take effect.

Yahweh worship critiqued this dynamistic-realistic concept of blessing and curse. It tied the effects of the word to the personal intervention of God. Through the use of *hyh* in the impf., blessing becomes promise and curse becomes threat that Yahweh himself will actualize in the future. Here *hyh* indicates the historical fulfillment of the word of Yahweh, events that will transpire as a result of his intervention: "Count the stars, if you can count them . . . so shall your descendants be" (Gen 15:5); "Your land shall become a wilderness and your cities rubbish heaps" (Lev 26:33). *hyh* emphasizes the reality of that which Yahweh has foretold and which shall be actualized in historical events.

Blessing and curse appear in weakened forms as wish and prayer; a person speaks the word, but the actualization is implicitly left to the decision of Yahweh: "They should become like the grass on the roofs that withers even before it grows" (Psa 129:6); "Their wives shall be robbed of children, shall become widows" (Jer 18:21). Even in the wish form, the verb *hyh* remains dynamic; it indicates the tension between that which is already present, hidden or incognito, and that which will be actualized according to Yahweh's decision.

(b) *hyh* occurs in explicit relation to Yahweh in four literary contexts:

(1) Miracle accounts use numerous verbs of action, but *hyh* appears at the climax of the narrative to describe the wondrous event: "Then Moses and

Aaron went to Pharaoh and did what Yahweh had commanded: Aaron cast his staff before Pharaoh and his people and it became a serpent" (Exod 7:10); "But Lot's wife behind him looked back, and she became a pillar of salt" (Gen 19:26); "And Gideon said . . . : The wool alone should remain dry, while dew falls upon the ground all around. And God did so that night" (Judg 6:39f.). In each case, the report uses *hyh* to describe not a simple historical process but the reality of the event that intervenes in earthly affairs and manifests the absolute power of Yahweh. The *hyh* of the event is the evidence of the → *ᶜśh* ("deed") of God; cf. Amos 3:6b, "Does a mishap take place in a city and Yahweh has not done it?" The same meaning occurs in the creation accounts (Gen 1:3; 2:7). Elsewhere God's personal intervention is not always so carefully expressed. But as in the miracle narratives, in reports concerning banal historical events *hyh* can still indicate the dynamics of occurrences through Yahweh's action—even if the individual cannot always recognize God's hand therein (Eccl 1:9).

(2) In addition to more banal usages, the prophets employ *hyh* in prophetic oracles to describe events embodying Yahweh's personal intervention in judgment and grace: "For Gaza will be desolate" (Zeph 2:4); "Therefore your way will become a slippery path for you" (Jer 23:12); "And a pure street will be there" (Isa 35:8), etc. This usage concerns that which Ratschow calls the "proper prophetic usage" (op. cit. 67). One finds it frequently in Hos (6x), Mic (3x), Isa (28x), relatively less frequently in Jer (12x) and Ezek (29x); see the summary in Ratschow, op. cit. 67–74. The emphasis of the prophetic statements lies on the unexpected, incredible, and yet certain and real nature of the announced events. By multiplying par. statements with a plethora of images, but without thoroughly describing the process, the prophets indicate that their *hyh* is not meant to express the precise course of events, but essentially the sovereign intervention of Yahweh in its various manifestations: "and it will come to pass in the coming days . . . " (Isa 2:2); "in that day it will come to pass . . . " (Isa 7:18, 21, 23, cf. v 22). This intervention, both in judgment and in salvation, remains a wonder transcending the normal course of events and demonstrating the effectiveness of divine decision: "Truly, as I purposed, so did it come to pass *(hyh)*, and what I decided comes to be *(qûm)*" (Isa 14:24).

(3) In legal prescriptions, *hyh* dictates the relationship of the covenant people vis-à-vis God, people, and the environment: "On the first day you shall hold (lit. 'there shall be for you') a holy assembly" (Exod 12:16); "Everything banned in Israel shall fall to you" (Num 18:14); "Anything, however, which does not have scales and fins . . . shall be to you an abomination. Indeed, they shall be an abomination to you" (Lev 11:10f.). Noteworthy in the final example is the coincidence of a simple nom. clause and a clause with *hyh*, in which the verb makes it clear that the concern is not a determination of fact but a legally prescribed behavior. This legal circumstance reflects the situation as God sees it and as he has established it for the well-being of the people. But it is also concerned that the people recognize the situation and give it place in their daily life. "You shall have no other god beside me *(lōᵓ yihyeh lᵉkā)*" (Exod 20:3); here the verb appears in the sg., for the commandment does not seek to deny the existence of other gods but to demand that

Israel acknowledge no other gods. In all of these Torah texts, the dynamic meaning of *hyh* describes the movement of God's will impinging repeatedly upon the daily life of his people and bringing Israel truly to become that which it should be according to God's will: "You shall become holy, for I (am) holy, Yahweh, your God" (Lev 19:2).

(4) The final literary context of the theological usage of *hyh* to be treated is that of the covenant formula (cf. R. Smend, *Die Bundesformel* [1963]). Both covenant partners are obligated thereby to a particular behavior toward one another. The short form reads: "I will be your God and you shall be my people" (Jer 7:23; cf. 11:4; 24:7; 31:33; Ezek 36:28, etc.); Deut 26:17f. offers a longer, bipartite formula: "Yahweh has declared to you today that he wishes to be your God . . . and you have declared to Yahweh today that you wish to be his own people . . . " (cf. Smend, op. cit. 7f.). One may also compare the covenant formula with David: "I will be his father, and he will be my son" (2 Sam 7:14). Here *hyh* indicates the mutual behavior of the covenant partners in the present and in the future in its active and dynamic character: What they are for one another owing to the covenant is renewed by each act of one toward the other so that they become ever more and ever better what they already are. Thus the characteristic exhortation of Deut parenesis to Israel is to become the people it already is by "walking" *(hlk)* and "obeying" *(šmr)*.

The texts do not direct such a call to the other covenant partner, Yahweh himself. Deut 26:17f. ties the two clauses of the covenant formula to Israel's obedience. This conjunction does not mean, however, that the validity of the covenant depends exclusively on Israel's obedience. To the contrary, the covenant exists only because Yahweh established it (the formula is mostly transmitted as God's 1st-per. speech), and God's *hyh*, in itself, implies the measures that Yahweh will use in the future on Israel's behalf. But Israel's *hyh* is threatened by the disobedience, the forgetfulness, the inaction of those who fancy themselves to have reached the goal and must consequently be activated by the call to obedience.

(c) Exod 3:14a uses *hyh* abs., without prep. or predicate noun, as Yahweh's 1st-per. speech in a formula: *ʾehyeh ʾašer ʾehyeh* (ZB, GNB mg. "I will be who I will be"; see Noth, *Exod*, OTL, 45).

(1) The passage is problematic in four ways:

(a) A literary-critical problem: vv 14f. give a dual answer to v 13 "what is your name?" Is the original answer contained in v 14 where the tetragrammaton appears in its usual form? In this case v 14a would be a theological amplification seeking to clarify the sense of the tetragrammaton, and v 14b would be a redactional transition (so B. D. Eerdmans, *Atl. Studien* 3 [1910], 12–14; Noth, *Exod*, OTL, 43f.). But v 14 could also be regarded as original; its more difficult content would have then led to an expansion in v 15 in more traditional forms (so G. J. Thierry, *OTS* 5 [1948]: 37).

(b) An etymological problem: The formula very probably contains an allusion to the tetragrammaton. Is it a philologically tenable eytmology or a merely theological paronomasia? What is the original meaning of the tetragrammaton?

(c) A historical problem: When did the name Yahweh come into use? Are E and P correct when they attribute the first usage in Israel to Moses? What are the origins of the name? With respect to these two groups of questions, cf. the article → *yhwh*.

(d) An exegetical problem: Do the two *ʾehyeh*s in v 14a have the same significance? There is no decisive reason to contest this point (E. Schild, *VT* 4 [1954]: 296–302, wants to differentiate the notion of identity in the first verb from the notion of existence in the second: "I am he who is"). The repetition of the verb is not tautological but emphatic (cf. Exod 33:19). Moreover, is the syntax of *ʾᵃšer* correct? Yes, for if the subj. of the clause introduced by *ʾᵃšer*, in the form of a pron., is already the subj. or attribute of the main clause, the verb remains in the same person (GKC §138d; Schild, op. cit. 298; cf. Exod 20:2; 1 Kgs 8:22f.; 1 Chron 21:17).

(2) The formula is understood in three different ways:

(a) As a statement concerning God's being: cf. LXX *egō eimi ho ēn* "I am the one who is"; Luther: "I alone have being, whoever clings to other things errs" (*Weimarer Ausgabe* 16:49); Schild, op. cit. 301: "It is a positive answer in which God defines himself as the One who is, who exists, who is real." Cf. too O. Eissfeldt, *FF* 39 (1965): 298–300 = *KS* [1968], 4:193–98. Other usages of *hyh*, however, call this interpretation into question and show that the sense of the passage exceeds the simple statement of God's being (aseity).

(b) As an attempt to avoid revealing the name: so Köhler, *Theol.* 242n.38: "God does not reveal to Moses the secret of His nature (= His name). Moses will see who God is from His works. . . . *Deus absconditus* in the strictest sense"; cf. Gen 32:30; Judg 13:18. The context (a positive answer parallel to v 12, repetition of the expression in v 14b) requires a word that gives a positive answer to v 13 without violating God's secret.

(c) As a statement concerning the activity of God. The majority of exegetes (with slight nuances of opinion) understand the passage as a proclamation of the ever-new activity of God in history; thus Eichrodt 1:190: "I am really and truly present, ready to help and to act, as I have always been" (cf. among others, Th. C. Vriezen, FS Bertholet 498–512; id., *Theol.* 179f.; von Rad, *Theol.* 1:180f.; Noth, *Exod*, OTL, 44f.). The active and dynamic meaning of *hyh* speaks for an interpretation along these lines.

(3) Three elements of the formula are esp. noteworthy: (a) It does not go beyond 1st-per. forms, not merely for syntactical reasons. God remains a sovereign "I" and cannot become an "it" at the disposal of human curiosity. (b) The verb is in the impf., the tense of action open to new acts. God offers himself to be known as a result of his historical deeds for his people. (c) The usage of *hyh* here stands in the lineage of the three chief theological usages in the miracle reports, the prophets, and the covenant formula: it treats the ever-renewed activity with which Yahweh intervenes in history in order to prove himself to be the true Lord.

Apart from Exod 3:14, this abs. use of *hyh* occurs only in Hos 1:9, "I (am) *lōʾ-ʾehyeh* (I am not present) for you," i.e., I decline to continue playing the role that I assumed in response to Moses in Exod 3:14.

Several authors have suggested a textual correction along the lines of the covenant formula ("I am not your God"). Nevertheless, the lectio difficilior is preferable (cf. Wolff, *Hos*, Herm, 9).

Moreover, the absence of an echo of Exod 3:14 is not remarkable. Even in its context, the formula stands to the side; the weight lies on the commission of Moses in v 15. In order to describe Yahweh's faithful assistance, the texts prefer the frequent expression *hyh ʿim* over the abs. *hyh*: "I am with you" (Exod 3:12; cf. Josh 1:5; Judg 2:18; 1 Sam 18:12), where the prep. does not complement the verb but underscores its active and purpose-oriented significance.

5. In its modifications of the formula of Exod 3:14, early Judaism primarily emphasizes God's eternity; so Tg. Ps.-J. Exod 3:14b, "It is I, who was and will be"; similarly, Midr. Exod 3:14. The formula is also interpreted, however, in terms of God's creative activity in accordance with Psa 33:9; thus Tg. Ps.-J. 3:14a, "He who spoke and the world came into being, who spoke and the universe existed," or in the sense of Deutero-Isaiah's polemic against the impotence of the idols (Isa 43:10f.; 44:6), thus Tg. Ps.-J. Deut 34:39, "I am he who is and was, and I am he who will be, and there is no other god beside me." Even when eternity is emphasized, the concept of existence inherent in the verb *hyh* retains an active character.

In the NT *einai* very often appears where the Hebr. uses a simple nom. clause (e.g., Matt 26:26 par. "this is my body") or a verb of being (Matt 26:38 "my soul is troubled," an allusion to Psa 42:6 with *šîaḥ* hitpo.). Elsewhere it assumes the function of the narrative *wayᵉhî* "and it came to pass" (e.g., Luke 6:6) or of the prophetic *wᵉhāyâ* "and it will come to pass" (e.g., Matt 13:42); cf. M. Johannessohn, "Das biblische καὶ ἐγένετο und seine Geschichte," *Zeitschrift für vergleichende Sprachforschung* 53 (1926): 161–212; id., "Die biblische Einführungsformel καὶ ἔσται," *ZAW* 59 (1942/43): 129–84; K. Beyer, *Semitische Syntax im NT* (1962), 1:29–65. But *einai* still preserves the active force of the theological *hyh* in a few significant christological texts: "Behold, I am with you always" Matt 28:18, along the lines of the Hebr. *hyh ʿim;* the Johannine usage should esp. be mentioned here, in the prologue "in the beginning was the Logos," and in the words by which Jesus assumes the divine title of Exod 3:14: *egō eimi* "I am" (John 8:4, 28, 58; 13:19). The tripartite formula in Acts 1:4, 8, "he is and he was and he comes," refers to God (cf. 4:8; 11:17; 16:5); E. Stauffer, "ἐγώ," *TDNT* 2:349–51; F. Büchsel, "εἰμί," *TDNT* 2:398–400; E. Schweizer, *Ego eimi* (1939).

S. Amsler

הֵיכָל *hêkāl* **temple** → בַּיִת *bayit*

הלך *hlk* **to go**

S 1980; BDB 229b; *HALOT* 1:246a; *TDOT* 3:388–403; *TWOT* 498; *NIDOTTE* 2143

1. The verb *hlk* "to go" occurs in most Sem. languages (with dissimilar meanings in Old SArab., "to behave" [*HAL* 236a], and Arab., "to perish" [Wehr 1031]).

Cf. Akk. *alāku* (*AHw* 31–34; *CAD* A/1:300–328); Ug. *hlk* (*WUS* no. 830; *UT* no. 766); Can. *yilaku* (impf. in an Amarna Letter, *AO* 7098, rev. 27; F. Thureau-Dangin, *RA* 19

[1922]: 98); Phoen.: Friedrich 70; Old Hebr. and Moab.: *DISO* 65; Aram.: KBL 1069; *DISO* 65; *LS* 176f.; Drower-Macuch 148b.

Hebr. exhibits the qal, pi., hitp., ni., and hi. conjugations.

As with expressions for "to go" in many Indo-European languages (F. Rosenthal, *Or* 11 [1942]: 182f.), the inflection of *hlk* is rather irregular. Impf., impv., qal inf. cs., and all forms of the hi. are formed like the verbs with initial *y/w*. This phenomenon is usually explained (GKC §69x; Berg. *HG* 2:131; BL 384f.) as a result of the apparent initial *y/w* form in the hi. pf. (*hahlaka* > *hālaka* > *hōlaka* > *hôlîk*, BL 214; Meyer 2:142); somewhat differently Z. S. Harris, *Development of the Canaanite Dialects* (1939), 33; J. M. Allegro, *WO* 2/3 (1956): 264–66.

Some Aram. formations appear to be based upon a root **hwk* (Bibl. Aram. pe. impf. *y*ᵉ*hāk*, inf. *m*ᵉ*hāk*; cf. BLA 144; *DISO* 65; F. Degen, *Altaram. Grammatik* [1969], 79; contra F. Rundgren, *AcOr* 21/4 [1953]: 304–16). In addition, the impv. *lēk* in the Can. languages allows for the inference of a biradical base **lk* (Meyer 2:142). On this basis, Gordon suspects that the triconsonantal *hlk* may have arisen through the combination of **hk* and **lk* (*UT* no. 766).

Nevertheless, the form occasionally occurs with three consonants in Hebr., as in Moab. (*w*ʾ*hlk* "so I went," *KAI* no. 181.14f. alongside *lk*, "go" l. 14; *ANET* 320b) and in Old Phoen. (*hlk*, *KAI* no. 27.21, along with *lkt*, *KAI* no. 26.II.4; *wylk*, II.19; cf. Friedrich 70): *yah*ᵃ*lōk* "he goes," Jer 9:3, etc.; ʾ*eh*ᵉ*lōk*, Job 16:22, etc.; *tih*ᵃ*lak*, Exod 9:23; Psa 73:9; inf. *h*ᵃ*lōk*, Exod 3:19; cf. Berg. *HG* 2:131.

Bibl. Aram. consistently substitutes forms of ʾ*zl* for *hlk* in the pe. pf. and impf. (KBL 1069a). Instead of the ha. it may be better to read the pa. in Dan 3:25; 4:34 (BLA 274).

Derived substs. include:

(a) *hālîk* "step," better "foot" according to Vg.; cf. M. Dahood, *Bib* 45 (1964): 404;

(b) *h*ᵃ*lîkâ* "way, road; caravan, procession; one's entire behavior" (*HAL* 236a);

(c) *hēlek* "(going >) flow; (visit >) visitor" (nomen actionis, BL 460; *HAL* 238a);

(d) *mah*ᵃ*lāk* "path, stretch of the way" (BL 490);

(e) *tah*ᵃ*lūkôt* "procession" (BL 497; yet cf. *BHS* on Neh 12:31; KBL 1020a);

(f) Bibl. Aram. *h*ᵃ*lāk* "tax" (KBL 1069; cf. Akk. *ilku*, a type of tax that vassals were obligated to pay; *AHw* 371f.; *CAD* I/J:73–81; H. W. Bailey, *Asia Major* 7 [1959]: 18f.).

The fem. PN *hammōleket* (1 Chron 7:18, perhaps also in v 15; cf., however, J. Morgenstern, *ZAW* 49 [1931]: 58) is also a derivative.

2. The verb *hlk* occurs 1,547x in the Hebr. OT: 1,412x in the qal, 64x in the hitp., 45x in the hi., 25x in the pi., and 1x in the ni. In addition, it occurs 7x in Bibl. Aram. (pe. 4x, pa. 1x, ha. 2x, but see 1).

Mandl. does not list Isa 55:1b *l*ᵉ*kû* (1 Chron 18:13 is listed in the addendum); Zech 3:7 *mahl*ᵉ*kîm* is attributed to *mah*ᵃ*lāk* according to Lis.; Num 17:11 *w*ᵉ*hôlēk* to the hi. (Lis.: qal).

	qal	ni.	pi.	hi.	hitp.	total
Gen	113	–	–	–	8	121
Exod	70	–	–	2	1	73
Lev	18	–	–	1	1	20
Num	44	–	–	1	–	45

Deut	48	–	–	4	1	53
Josh	48	–	–	1	2	51
Judg	110	–	–	–	1	111
1 Sam	128	–	–	–	9	137
2 Sam	94	–	–	1	3	98
1 Kgs	120	–	1	1	–	122
2 Kgs	93	–	–	5	1	99
Isa	56	–	1	4	1	62
Jer	111	–	–	5	–	116
Ezek	58	–	1	5	3	67
Hos	21	–	–	1	–	22
Joel	4	–	–	–	–	4
Amos	8	–	–	1	–	9
Obad	–	–	–	–	–	–
Jonah	6	–	–	–	–	6
Mic	12	–	–	–	–	12
Nah	2	–	–	–	–	2
Hab	2	–	1	–	–	3
Zeph	1	–	–	–	–	1
Hag	–	–	–	–	–	–
Zech	10	–	–	1	6	17
Mal	2	–	–	–	–	2
Psa	38	1	12	3	14	68
Job	20	–	2	2	5	29
Prov	30	–	3	1	4	38
Ruth	18	–	–	–	–	18
Song Sol	7	–	–	–	–	7
Eccl	25	–	3	2	–	30
Lam	4	–	1	1	–	6
Esth	3	–	–	–	1	4
Dan	3	–	–	–	–	3
Ezra	3	–	–	–	–	3
Neh	13	–	–	–	–	13
1 Chron	20	–	–	–	3	23
2 Chron	49	–	–	3	–	52
OT	1,412	1	25	45	64	1,547

Of the substs., *hālîk* occurs 1x (Job 29:6), *h*ᵃ*lîkâ* 6x (Nah 2:6; Psa 68:25bis; Job 6:19; Prov 31:27), *hēlek* 2x (1 Sam 14:26; 2 Sam 12:4); *mah*ᵃ*lāk* 5x (Ezek 42:4; Jonah 3:3f.; Zech 3:7; Neh 2:6), *tah*ᵃ*lūkôt* 1x (Neh 12:31), Aram. *h*ᵃ*lāk* 3x (Ezra 4:13, 20; 7:24).

3. (a) The meaning of the verb is firmly established with "to go" and varies only little according to the context, i.e., when not used of people to express the capacity for self-locomotion (Gen 9:23, etc.), but of some animals or things: serpents crawl (Gen 3:14), foxes dash about (Lam 5:18 pi.), ships sail (Gen 7:18; Psa 104:26 pi.), a limb drags along (Gen 32:31), etc. Even water "goes," i.e., "flows" (Gen 2:14; 8:3; etc.; cf. also l. 4 of the Siloam Inscription, *ANET* 321b), and the tone of the trombone "sounds" (Exod 19:19).

In a few cases, the inf. abs. *hālôk* joins other verbal forms to strengthen the notion of enduring action (e.g., Gen 8:3, 5; 12:9; Judg 14:9; 2 Kgs 2:11; cf. GKC §113u; BrSynt

82–84). The finite verb form of *hlk* can also serve similarly to clarify, i.e., in combination with *lqḥ*, Gen 27:14; *npl*, Gen 50:18; *šlḥ*, 2 Kgs 3:7; *ᵓmr* Isa 2:3 (*HAL* 236b).

In addition to the usage expressing the simple commandment, the impv. forms *lēk*, *lᵉkâ*, and *lᵉkû* are also frequently used in combination with another verb to strengthen a demand and can then be best translated "up! now then!" (Gen 37:13, 20; Exod 4:19, etc.). In this respect, *lᵉkâ* has often "become a fixed interjection and, as such, may also be directed to a fem., Gen 19:32, or to several persons, Gen 31:44" (BL 385).

The verb acquires a special nuance when it describes the way leading to an end or goal; e.g., of the end of the rain (Song Sol 2:11), of the dew (Hos 6:4), of the wind (Psa 78:39), of the clouds (Job 7:9), and of pain (Job 16:6). Applied to human life, the meaning "to go to death, die" results (Gen 15:2; Josh 23:14; 1 Kgs 2:2; Psa 39:14; 58:9; Job 10:21; 14:20; 16:22; 19:10; 27:21; Eccl 1:4; 3:20; 6:4, 6; 9:10; 1 Chron 17:11).

The hi. in Psa 125:5, the pi. in Hab 3:11 (sun and moon), and the only ni. (Psa 109:23) also belong here.

In conjunction with *ᵓaḥar* and *ᵓaḥᵃrê* "behind," it comes to mean "to follow, follow after" (Gen 24:5, 8; 32:20, etc.), which is frequent in religious usage (see 4b).

The meanings of *hlk* hi. are all more or less clearly causative ("to cause to go, lead, bring," etc.). On *hlk* pi. "to go around, go back and forth," cf. *HP* 151–53. The hitp. "to stroll, go back and forth," the qal, and the pi. also have the fig. meaning "to live" in the general sense of personal conduct (see 4b).

Semantically related motion verbs all have a somewhat more specialized meaning; cf. *rûṣ* "to run," → *bôᵓ* "to come, enter," → *yṣᵓ* "to exit," → *ᶜlh* "to go up," → *šûb* "to return," etc.; → *yšb* "to remain" and → *ᶜmd* "to stand" have the opposite meaning.

(b) The substs. of the root *hlk* with their manifold meanings (see 1) may all be derived from the basic meaning "to go." In regard to Hab 3:6 (paths of the stars), cf. the Akk. and Ug. (*KTU* 1.19.II.3, 7, IV.38) pars. cited in *HAL* 236a. The fig. meaning "life-style" (*hᵃlîkôt* Prov 31:27) is also present in Akk. *alaktu*, pl. *alkakātu* (*AHw* 31, 36b; *CAD* A/1:297–300).

4. (a) It is of minor importance in the religious sphere that even Yahweh, like the gods, can be envisioned as "going" (Psa 115:7 pi.). Here one remembers Yahweh's walking in the Garden of Eden (Gen 3:8 hitp.) or his departure following the visit to Abraham (Gen 18:33). Yahweh can also go on the clouds (Psa 104:3 hi.) or walk in heaven (Job 22:14 hitp.). Righteousness precedes him (Psa 85:14 pi.).

More important than these anthropomorphic concepts, however, are references in which Yahweh's going has the specific dimension of coming to aid his people or to punish them. He goes to redeem a people for himself (2 Sam 7:23 = 1 Chron 17:21), and is experienced as aid (Psa 80:3; Zech 9:14; also Hos 5:14f.). In the vast majority of cases, Yahweh's accompaniment is experienced as the exercise of a leadership role in the period of the wilderness wandering (Exod 33:14–16; 34:9; cf. Lev 26:12 hitp.; Deut 20:4; 23:15 hitp.; 31:6, 8; 2 Sam 7:6f. hitp. = 1 Chron 17:6; in the new exodus: Isa 45:2; 52:12), and it found picturesque representation in the discussion of the pillars of cloud and fire in which Yahweh precedes the people (Exod 13:21; Num 14:14; Deut 1:30, 33).

The function of the ark of Yahweh may also be understood in this context as a visible symbol of Yahweh's presence leading the people and behind which later participants in cultic acts assembled in procession, even if this use of *hlk* is not very sophisticated (Josh 3:6; 6:9; 1 Sam 6:12; cf. Num 10:33–36; Judg 4:14; 2 Sam 5:24; 6:5). The people's manufacture of gods that were meant to assume the same function signifies apostasy (Exod 32:1, 23; cf. 1 Kgs 12:28–30). If the people prove disobedient, Yahweh can only move against them (Lev 26:24, 28, 41; Num 12:9).

(b) From the human standpoint, obedient following after Yahweh corresponds to God's movement toward his people to accompany them and guide them (cf. F. J. Helfmeyer, *Die Nachfolge Gottes im AT* [1967]). The expression *hlk ʾaḥ^{a}rê* "to follow after" is immediately and fully comprehensible to Israelites conversant with nomadic life and can consequently be used to describe the totality of the communal and individual life-style. But only a few passages, chiefly in Dtr texts, refer to following after Yahweh (Deut 13:5; 1 Kgs 14:8; 2 Kgs 23:3 = 2 Chron 34:31; also Jer 2:2 in the picture of bridal courtship; Hos 11:10; cf. also 1 Kgs 19:20f. "to follow after a prophet"; on synonymous expressions, cf. Helfmeyer, op. cit. 93–122). More often, this behavior refers to apostasy, and thereby to following after strange gods (Baal, etc.: Deut 4:3; 6:14; 8:19; 11:28; 13:3; 28:14; Judg 2:12, 19; 1 Kgs 11:5, 10; 18:18; 21:26; 2 Kgs 13:2; 17:15 = Jer 2:5; Jer 2:8, 23, 25; 7:6, 9; 8:2; 9:13; 11:10; 13:10; 16:11; 25:6; 35:15; Ezek 20:16; cf. N. Lohfink, *Das Hauptgebot* [1963], 76f.) and some illusions and delusions (Jer 3:17; 16:12; 18:12; Ezek 13:3; 33:31). The act of following after other gods always includes apostasy from Yahweh too, as 1 Kgs 9:6; 18:21; and Jer 5:23 clearly express. For synonyms for following after strange gods, cf. Helfmeyer, op. cit. 152–79.

In addition to public apostasy, expressed by following after strange gods, living without God is described by various expressions that always emphasize the self-sufficient human action: to follow deceit, etc. (Jer 6:28; 23:14; Job 31:5), to walk according to one's own or evil counsel (Jer 7:24; Psa 1:1; Job 34:8), to walk after one's own heart (Jer 11:8; 23:17) or in darkness (Isa 59:9 pi.; Eccl 2:14).

The fact that following after strange gods is explicitly discussed much more often than following after Yahweh may be explained by the origin of the theme of "following after" in the pagan cultic procession (thus *HAL* 237a; *BWL* 38f.). Israel, therefore, avoided this means of expression (P. Volz, *Der Prophet Jeremia* [1928^{2}], 17; G. Kittel, *TDNT* 1:211; on the whole question, see E. G. Gulin, "Die Nachfolge Gottes," *StudOr* 1 [1925]: 34–50). On the one hand, the argument that it applied not at all to behavior toward Yahweh but only to behavior toward strange gods, because the pious Israelite led his/her life "before" and not "behind" Yahweh (thus H. Kosmala, "Nachfolge und Nachahmung Gottes, II: Im jüdischen Denken," *ASTI* 3 [1964]: 65–69), is untenable in the light of the texts cited above. On the other hand, Helfmeyer (op. cit.) affords the expression "to walk after Yahweh" too much significance when he does not even try to explain the different frequencies of usage. In his view (e.g., op. cit. 202), the concept arises from the events associated with holy war and has been transformed by Dtn-Dtr circles into theological language.

At any rate, it is noteworthy that the pious Israelite's attitude toward Yahweh is primarily oriented to keeping Yahweh's commandments. A multitude of expressions are available to the OT for describing this posture, expressions that also sometimes speak of going in the ways (→ *derek*), in the commandments and instructions of Yahweh, etc. (so too Helfmeyer, op. cit.). One should remember that apostasy and walking in the ways of strange gods can be discussed together because, at least for the Israelites, Yahweh's ways were clearly prescribed by the revealed commandments, while apostasy is characterized by the negation of these very commandments. Now, although during the wilderness wanderings and the conquest the notion of following after the divine Lord was more prominent, this idea was replaced in the period of settlement by the knowledge that Yahweh dwells in the midst of his people. Any apostasy was, then, estrangement from Yahweh and synonymous with following after strange gods. Thus life *with* Yahweh can be described with *hlk* alone (without *ʾaḥᵃrê*) in conjunction with words like *ṣᵉdāqôt* (Isa 33:15 "in righteousness"), *haṣnēaʿ* (Mic 6:8 "humbly"), or *tāmîm* (Psa 15:2 "blamelessly"). The hitp. particularly expresses this relationship. The pious walks "with God" (thus P: Gen 5:22, 24; 6:9) or "before" him, i.e., face-to-face with him and in responsibility to him (Gen 17:1; 24:40; 48:15; 1 Sam 2:30; 2 Kgs 20:3 = Isa 38:3; Psa 26:3; 56:14; 101:2; 116:9; Prov 6:22; 20:7; in the qal also 1 Kgs 2:4; 3:6; 8:23, 25[bis]; 9:4).

(c) In most cases Yahweh is the subj. of hi. forms of the verbs (24 of 45x). He can "cause" the water of the sea "to go away" (cf. Luther, Exod 14:21) or lead the blind (Isa 42:16, etc.); for the most part, however, Israel is the obj. of divine leadership and guidance (Lev 26:13; Deut 8:2, 15; 28:36 into exile; 29:4; Josh 24:3; Isa 48:21; 63:13; Jer 2:6, 17 txt?; 31:9; Hos 2:16; Amos 2:10; Psa 106:9; 136:16).

5. Concerning the usage of the Qumran community, one can determine that *hlk* was also used as the verb of motion in general (e.g., of the sallying forth of the army, 1QM 7:3f.). Nevertheless, the usage in the sense of ethicoreligious behavior is by far the more frequent, in accordance with the nature of the texts (e.g., CD 2:15, 17; 3:2, 5; 7:7; 1QS 1:6; 4:5f.; 5:4; 8:2; 1QSᵃ 1:1; 1QH 15:18).

In early Judaism and in the NT, the verb "to go" was used as widely as *hlk* in the OT; cf. F. Hauck and S. Schulz, "πορεύομαι," *TDNT* 6:566–79; G. Kittel, "ἀκολουθέω," *TDNT* 1:210–16. On the theme of discipleship and imitation, H. Kosmala produces material that exceeds the information in *TDNT* ("Nachfolge und Nachahmung Gottes, I. Im griechischen Denken," *ASTI* 2 [1963]: 38–85; "II. Im jüdischen Denken," *ASTI* 3 [1964]: 65–110). M. Hengel (*Nachfolge und Charisma* [1968], with bibliog.) demonstrates the degree to which the NT notion of following advances its OT model. Jewish-Hellenistic concepts are also treated here. The root *hlk* is the basis for the subst. Halakah, which designates the entire early Jewish-rabbinical doctrine of proper conduct (cf. *WTM* 1:471f.; Jastrow 353; *UJE* 5:172–75; *JE* 6:163; *BHH* 2:626f.).

G. Sauer

הלל *hll* pi. **to praise**

S 1984; BDB 237b; *HALOT* 1:248b; *TDOT* 3:404–10; *TWOT* 500; *NIDOTTE* 2146

1. *hll* pi. "to extol, praise," probably an onomatopoeic formation, has counterparts in most Sem. languages (e.g., Akk. *alālu* Gt, "to sing a joyous song," Š "to rejoice," *AHw* 34; Ug. *hll* "to rejoice"? *UT* no. 769; but *WUS* no. 832 "crescent moon," cf. *hēlēl* Isa 14:12; further citations in *HAL* 238b).

The verb occurs only in the pi. (*HP* 246), pu., and hitp. Derivatives are *hillûlîm* "rejoicing" (Lev 19:24, at the feast of the harvest; Judg 9:27, at the vintage festival of the Shechemites), *mah^{a}lāl* "praise, acknowledgment, cry" (Prov 27:21), and above all *t^{e}hillâ* "glory, praise." The PNs *hillēl, y^{e}hallelʾēl,* and *mah^{a}lalʾēl* also occur (contra *IP* 169, 184, 205: from *hll* I "to light up").

2. *hll* pi. occurs 113x (Psa 75x, 2 Chron 12x, 1 Chron 7x, Prov 4x), pu. 10x (Psa 6x), hitp. 23x (Psa 8x, Jer 7x, Prov 4x), *hillûlîm* 2x (see above), *mah^{a}lāl* 1x (see above), and *t^{e}hillâ* 57x (Psa 30x, Isa 11x, Jer 6x).

Of the total of 206 passages (146 verbal, 60 nominal) almost 2/3 occur in the Psa or in Psa motifs and 1/7 in the Chr material. In addition, a small group occurs in Prov (10x) and in prophetic texts, mostly in the context of the announcement of salvation. This preliminary overview already shows that *hll* has its proper place in worship; worship is the execution of that which the call to praise invokes; all passages in the Chr material treat cultic praise of God.

3. Both verb and noun can indicate an interpersonal exchange that should usually be rendered "praise." A person's beauty (pi. Gen 12:15; 2 Sam 14:25; Song Sol 6:9; pu. Psa 78:63) or an insight (Prov 12:8 pu.) are praised. Nom. usages refer esp. to a city's fame (in the oracles against the nations, Jer 48:2; 49:25; 51:41; Ezek 26:17 pu. speaks of Tyre, the famous city on the sea). Wisdom mentions praise or self-praise (hitp.): the able housewife is praised (pi. Prov 31:28, 31; hitp. 31:30); "The one who binds on the sword may not boast like one who lays it aside" (1 Kgs 20:11); similarly, Jer 9:22f.; Prov 20:14; 25:14; 27:1; pi. 27:2. One praises the king (2 Chron 23:12f.) or boasts of him (Psa 63:12).

4. Most passages by far praise God (Judg 16:24, the Philistine god): in the Psa (4a-c), in the Chr (4d), and in prophetic discourse (4e); cf. Westermann, *PLP* 15–162; F. Crüsemann, *Studien zur Formgeschichte von Hymnus und Danklied in Israel* (1969).

(a) The use of the verb and of the noun *t^{e}hillâ* in the Psa is concentrated in two groups; the main group is in the call to praise. The majority of the Psa passages involve this one form of the impv. call to praise: "Praise, you servants of the Lord, praise the name of the Lord!" (Psa 113:1bis; also Psa 22:24; 117:1; 135:1bis; 148:1bis, 2bis, 3bis, 4, 7; 150:1bis, 2bis, 3 [bis], 4bis, 5bis, 6; Jer 20:13; 31:7; further *hal^{e}lû(-)yāh* 24x [→ *yhwh* 2]; with *t^{e}hillâ,* Psa 100:4; 149:1; cf. Psa 66:2, 8; Isa 42:10; in addition the version in the hitp. in Psa 105:3 = 1 Chron 16:10).

That this is by far the most widely represented use of the word is only clear, however, if one considers the multitude of par. verbs that constitute the totality of impv. calls to praise (most significant → *ydh* hi.; further → *rnn,* → *šîr,* → *brk* pi. "to praise," → *gdl* pi. "to exalt," → *rûm* po. "to exalt"); *zmr* pi. "to sing, play, praise" occurs 45x (Psa 41x, additionally Judg 5:3; 2 Sam 22:50; Isa 12:5; 1 Chron 16:9), 19x in impv. pl., 20x sg. and 1x pl. in the voluntative, 4x in the juss., 1x in the inf. (Psa 92:2). Cf. also Bibl. Aram. *šbḥ* pa. "to praise" (5x in Dan) and Hebr. *šbḥ* pi. (6x: Psa 63:4; 117:1; 145:4; 147:12; Eccl 4:2; 8:15; hitp. "to boast" Psa 106:47 = 1 Chron 16:35), an Aramaism (Wagner nos. 299–302).

What is the significance of this call to praise? It is necessary because it calls for something that is not taking place or is not taking place sufficiently; indeed, the call issues forth unrelentingly, untiringly, ever anew, because that for which it calls is recognized as absolutely necessary, sustaining, supportive of the community and because a very strong impulse to give praise is present in the community. This compulsion, the conviction that *hll* pi. must take place, is the first element determining the call to praise. It must occur so that God may be recognized, affirmed, confirmed in his deity, indeed, in the fullness of his deity. But that is only one aspect; the many par. verbs of celebration and rejoicing (→ *gîl,* → *rnn,* → *śmḥ*) demonstrate that this praise of God can take place only in joy, that it is an expression of joy addressed to God. One cannot, therefore, hear the call to praise God in the OT without hearing the encompassed call to joy. The elements that the NT differentiates in the invitation to faith and the call to joy are still one in the OT call to praise.

As a second feature, the use of the verb demonstrates a marked predominance of pl. forms. The impv. call to praise virtually exists only in the pl. (sg. only Psa 146:1 "Praise Yahweh, O my soul"; 147:12 "Praise your God, O Zion" addresses a collective entity). The fact that, almost without exception, a congregation is called to praise shows that the act of praising God has its proper setting in the congregational gathering; the choir, the plurality of voices, is inherent in it (cf. Isa 64:10 in retrospect: "your holy house, where our fathers praised you"). Through God's praise, the congregation expresses its self-understanding, its being vis-à-vis God. Correspondingly, accompanying instruments are mentioned explicitly in the impv. call to praise; they, too, belong to a communal act. Thus *hll* pi. is established as an essential element of worship.

A third element is closely related: This call to praise is not issued in the OT solely to people. This phenomenon is often not sufficiently noted. Praise is an act directed to God that can involve the whole creation; in it, the human being stands as one creature amid others. This observation implies that the human being as a rational being, with the faculties of judgment and conviction, is not properly intended as the subj. of the process described by *hll* pi., but as a creaturely being, with characteristics shared by the other creatures. In short, the intellect cannot praise God—only the breathing, rejoicing, singing person. An existence relative to God is intended that absolutely cannot come about through reason. Thus the exuberant phrase concluding Psa 150 and the whole Psalter precisely captures the proper sense of God's praise: "All that has breath, praise the Lord!" (v 6).

The impv. call to praise is appropriate to a particular psalm genre, the descriptive praise of God or hymn. The elements set forth above are characteristic of this genre. The necessity of the ever-new call to praise presupposes the continuation of ever-recurring worship. The recognition of the life-sustaining significance of this praise of God standing behind this call to praise is exhibited in the structure of the descriptive psalm of praise: it seeks to present God in the fullness of his being and action (cf. *PLP* 116ff.). In the affirmation of God's deity in the joy, which is intended by *hll* pi., the community at worship recognizes itself over against the God who is not only Israel's Lord but also the creator and Lord of history; therefore, nations and kings, all of creation can be called to praise (Psa 148; 150).

hll pi. cannot, however, be limited to this one psalm genre where it originated because, given the tendency to concentrate verbs of praise and joy, the boundaries between the individual verbs of praise were no longer strictly maintained and they more or less assimilated to one another. At any rate, the texts still show that *hll* pi. is the dominant verb of the impv. call to praise as an element of the descriptive praise of God.

The impv. call to praise can be expanded through the juss.: "they should praise" (most clearly in Psa 148:5, 13; also Psa 22:27; 69:35; 107:32; 149:3; grammatically sg. in 150:6). The juss. occurs otherwise in anticipation of praise in the conclusion of the individual lament (Psa 74:21; 102:19; *t^ehillâ*, Psa 102:22; 149:1).

(b) In addition to the impv. call to praise, only one other form of the term's use has great significance: the voluntative, in which an individual announces or expresses, in the presence of another, his intention to praise God. This announcement occurs in the vow of praise at the end of the individual lament and in the introit of the descriptive praise (psalm of thanksgiving) of the individual. But the term specific to this form is not *hll* pi. but → *ydh* hi.; thus *hll* pi. occurs in this form only as a variant or supplementary term: at the conclusion of individual laments, Psa 22:23; 35:18; 69:31; 109:30; at the beginning of the psalms of praise, only 145:2 and 146:2; additionally, in the middle of Psa 56:5, 11(bis). Psa 119:171 can also be classified here. Characteristically, however, the special significance of *hll* pi. appears here too: even individual praise occurs in community (expressly emphasized in Psa 22:23, "In the midst of the congregation I will praise you"; 35:18; 109:30). The "I will praise" is frequently expressed nominatively: Psa 119:171, "My lips shall overflow with praise"; 145:21, "My mouth shall proclaim Yahweh's praise"; elsewhere Psa 9:15; 22:26; 35:28; 71:6, 8, 14; 109:1; Jer 17:14.

The relationship of this form "I will praise" (which can only be insufficiently characterized as "vow of praise" or "announcement of praise") to the form "praise!" is clear: the *hll* pi. is affirmed, accepted by an individual. One can also recognize the vital significance of praise in this form; it is so important that the decision for it and the joy in it must be expressed: "His praise shall ever be in my mouth!" (Psa 34:2). As the call to praise must be issued, so also must it be expressed in the presence of others: I want to be present! One senses in this group of texts that the speakers saw the affirmation of God's praise and the affirmation of life as a participation in the stream of events. This form particularly manifests the distinction from the Chr's use (see 4d): The institutionalization of God's praise makes such an affirmation, such a decision to praise God, unnecessary; it was, after all, decreed, established, and proceeding according to official decree. But that which the Psa refer to by *hll* pi. requires personal impulse; the spontaneous character is necessarily inherent in it; it is only authentic praise of God if it arises from this spontaneous impulse.

The special character of *hll* pi. becomes even clearer in a small group of passages that belong to neither of these two forms but that fosters reflection concerning God's praise and thus reflectively highlights the uniqueness of this praise. In this reflective usage, God's praise and God are closely identified with one another, on the one hand: "You are due praise" (Psa 65:2; cf. 147:1). Jeremiah can confess: "For you are my praise" (Jer 17:14). Psa 109:1 addresses God: "God my praise," and Deut 10:21 states: "He is your praise and your God." Psa 22:4 is unique: "You who are enthroned upon the praise of Israel." On the other hand, human existence and praise of God are closely identified with one another: "let my soul live, that it may praise you!" (Psa 119:175). The statement "the dead do not praise Yahweh" (Psa 115:17; Isa 38:18) negatively articulates the same sentiment: Praise of God is essential to existence; it is itself a manner of existence. If it has ceased, authentic life has also ceased. Thus the one who participates in the fullness of existence is praised as fortunate, as is the one who praises God (Psa 84:5). *hll* pi. is existential joy directed to God, singing to God.

(c) The word has another only slightly different meaning, although it should still be classed separately, in which the profane meaning "renown (noun), to laud" (see 3) refers to God. This difference is esp. true for *hll* hitp. and *tᵉhillâ*. Everyday or gnomic self-praise is applied to descriptions of God so that one can say: "Glorify his holy name!" (Psa 105:3 = 1 Chron 16:10) or "Glorify the Lord, O my soul" (Psa 34:3). As the form shows (Psa 105:3 belongs to the impv. call to praise, Psa 34:3 to the announcement of praise), *hll* hitp. with God as obj. approximates here an alternative term for "to praise." Thus it can parallel *śmḥ* "to be happy" in the conclusion of a psalm (Psa 64:11).

Accordingly, God's glory can be discussed: "The earth is full of his renown" (Hab 3:3). Thus *tᵉhillâ* can parallel *kābôd* "glory" (Isa 42:8) or *šēm* "name" (Psa 48:11; cf. Isa 48:9). God's renown is proclaimed (Isa 42:12; 60:6), reported (Psa 78:4; 79:13), and amplified (71:14).

A few of these passages have the pl. *tᵉhillōt* (Exod 15:11; Psa 78:4; Isa 60:6; 63:7), which can be rendered "famous deeds." It is typical of Hebr. that this pl. does not mean to express, e.g., the variety of statements of praise (cf. Psa 22:4), but the variety of occasions to praise, i.e., God's deeds that awaken praise or exaltation. Exaltation and that to be exalted are understood as a unity. This linguistic peculiarity also has a theological component: Passages in which *hll* pi. with God as obj. means "to extol" and *tᵉhillâ* means "famous deed" presuppose that the deity of God cannot be understood in the OT as being per se, as a transcendental Being; God is not God other than in his action, and, in turn, nothing other than human experience reacts in praise.

(d) The second group of occurrences in addition to the Psa is found in the Chr. A remarkable difference in usage consists in the fact that here almost all passages report or express something concerning God's praise; but the Psa employ the word only to set the praise of God in motion (in the impv. call to praise), to ignite it (voluntative), to state that it should take place (juss.), while narrative and declarative forms are almost totally absent. Moreover, not only the frequent occurrence in the Chr but also the accentuated meaning of *hll* pi. is noteworthy; it occurs frequently at high points in the narrative of the sequence of events, and it is particularly emphasized (e.g., 2 Chron 5:13; 7:6; 29:30; Ezra 3:10f.). This emphasis is often specifically articulated: "with a loud voice" (2 Chron 20:19), "with all might" (30:21 txt em), "with joy" (29:30), and esp. informative, 2 Chron 5:13: "And as they blew and sang together, they sounded as one voice to the glory and praise of Yahweh." It is evident that God's praise was something decisively important, something supremely central, not only for the concept of worship but also for the concept of relationship to God. At the same time, however, it must be an expression of the core of the speaker's existence; personal engagement is involved in all these phrases. God's praise must have expressed the fulfillment of existence for these people in a special way. It must be born in mind, in this respect, that the clergy speaks here.

Consequently, the second, even more marked component is the institutional character of this praise of God. (1) It is explained as an institution, i.e., God is praised in a service arranged for this purpose (2 Chron 8:14), and this arrangement goes back to David (2 Chron 7:6; 8:14; Neh 12:46), it occurs "according to David's direction" (Ezra 3:10). (2) Praise of God is conducted according to a fixed order of service (Neh 12:24) that regulates even the details; singers are "appointed" and wear vestments (2 Chron 8:14; 20:21; Ezra 3:10); it is commissioned (1 Chron 16:4). The order of service also regulates the time: "Moreover, they are to appear morning by morning and in the evenings for the glory and praise of Yahweh" (1 Chron 23:30); this is an inherent obligation of their service (2 Chron 8:14; 31:2). (3) Thus the decisive change with respect to the pre-exilic era is apparent: the praise of God has become a matter for the temple singers. The congregation can certainly join in praise (Ezra 3:11) or it can respond with the Amen (1 Chron 16:36; Neh 5:13); but the priests and Levites are expressly named as subjs. in the vast majority of passages that mention the praise of God.

There can be no question that the cultivation of this cultic music, which is at once vocal and instrumental, brought it to a high state, and that we must recognize a high cultural achievement in the Jerusalemite temple music of the Pers. and Gk. eras. There can also be no question that the temple music performed by the priests and Levites was a concern of the whole nation and an essential element of the community's worship in which the community participated, body and soul. But, at the same time, one must recognize the deep change that resulted from the institutionalization of God's praise. An objectivization and technologization of God's praise is almost necessarily linked to this institutionalization; it resounds unmistakably in some of the expressions cited above; it is evident in the fact that many passages consistently give the content of God's praise in the refrain "thank the Lord, for he is good" (2 Chron 5:13; 7:6; 20:21; Ezra 3:10, 11), which is now formulaically fixed. It is also evident in the fact that various Psa are mechanically combined in the psalm excerpts cited in Chron; the original structure of the psalms no longer seems to have meaning. One phrase is highly informative for the understanding of *hll* pi. in the Chr: ". . . who is exalted above all praise and fame" (Neh 9:5). To be sure, this phrase intends to pronounce a very special praise; in reality, it can lead to the severance of the mainspring of praise. In the early period, God is seen as exalted above all praise, but the majesty of God is present in Israel's praise rising to him (Psa 22:4).

(e) Another usage occurs in a relatively small group of texts in the context of prophetic speech. Although both the Psa and Chr deal exclusively with the ongoing praise of God, prophetic passages, esp. in the context of the announcement of salvation, speak of God's future praise or future glory. This language is best understood on the basis of the nom. usages. The intended obj. of the *tᵉhillâ* here is Israel. Interestingly, the present or past of famed Babylon, Tyre, etc., are discussed, but not the *tᵉhillâ* of Israel or Jerusalem. The discussion of Israel's glory is possible only in the dismay of the deep shame signified by the collapse of Judah, as mirrored in Lam. Only now does prophecy announce that Israel or Zion will again come to glory, *tᵉhillâ*. This glory will, however, be entirely the work of God: "Until he makes it (Zion) the glory of earth" (Isa 62:7); "You will call your walls salvation and your gates glory" (60:18; cf. 61:11; Jer 13:11; 33:9; Zeph 3:19, 20; also Deut 26:19).

But the verbal use also undergoes a turn to the future in prophetic speech: in the very brief songs of praise with which Deutero-Isaiah occasionally concludes a section, the impv. call to praise appears in a new sense: already in the present, the prophet calls for praise and jubilation over God's newly announced saving act to restore Israel's homeland. Here, however, mostly terms of joy and jubilation appear (*tᵉhillâ* only Isa 42:12); this form of song, praising God's saving act in the future, is imitated in Jer 20:13; 31:7 (pi.). In Isa 62:9 and Joel 2:26, the praise of God responds to God's new act of blessing announced for the era of salvation.

5. The LXX translates *hll* pi. mostly with *ainein*, etc., also with *hymnein* and *exomologeisthai*, *hll* hitp. with *enkauchasthai*, *epainein*, and *endoxazesthai*, etc. The noun is rendered mostly with *ainesis*, as well as with *hymnos*. The translation covers the semantic range of the Hebr. word rather extensively. The call to praise *halᵉlû-yāh* is already so liturgically established that it is transliterated by LXX: *allēlouia*. Verb and noun are also attested in Qumran (Kuhn, *Konk.* 60, 230; also *GCDS* 516). The few NT occurrences stand entirely in the OT tradition; cf. H. Schlier, "αἰνέω," *TDNT* 1:177f.; id., "ἀλληλουϊά," *TDNT* 1:264; G. Delling, "ὕμνος," *TDNT* 8:489–503.

C. Westermann

המם *hmm* to confuse

S 2000; BDB 243a; *HALOT* 1:251a; *TDOT* 3:419–22; *TWOT* 507; *NIDOTTE* 2169

1. The verb *hmm* and its by-form *hûm* in the meaning "to bring into confusion" are limited to Hebr. and, with only a few examples, Aram.

Together with *hmh* "to make noise" and *nhm* "to growl, snarl," they may belong to a biradical root *hm* "to make noise, be restless, startle," etc., widespread in SSem. with an intrans. meaning and in reduplicated formations.

hmm occurs in Tg. Aram. and *hûm* in Old Aram. in the etpe. "to be beside oneself, be confused, lament" (*KAI* no. 226.6: *hwm ʾthmw; ANET* 661b "being distraught"; *DISO* 64). Cf. also Ug. *nhmmt* "confusion, concern" (so *WUS* no. 846; *CML*[1] 156a; contra *UT* nos. 778, 1621; *CML*[2] 152).

A root *hmm* II is apparently present in Jer 51:34, which, following an Arab. counterpart, should be rendered "to suck dry" in accord with the par. expression *ʾkl* "to devour" (cf. *HAL* 241a).

The ni. forms may derive from *hmm* or *hûm*. The hi. forms of *hûm* are textually very problematic. The subst. *m^ehûmâ* "confusion, panic" derives from *hûm*.

2. *hmm* qal occurs 12x (excl. Jer 51:34; see 1), *hûm* qal 1x (Deut 7:23), ni. 3x (1 Sam 4:5; 1 Kgs 1:45; Ruth 1:19), and hi. 2x (Mic 2:12 and Psa 55:3, emended by *HAL* 232b as a form of *hmh* or *hûm* ni.). *m^ehûmâ* occurs 12x.

3. The basic meaning of *hmm* is "to bring into unrest, confuse." The subj. is Yahweh 10x (or the "hand of Yahweh" in Deut 2:15); thus the word has an almost exclusively religious usage (as does *hûm* qal and, with the exception of Amos 3:9 "tumult" and Prov 15:16 "unrest," *m^ehûmâ;* see 4b).

Exceptions are Esth 9:24, with Haman as subj. (*hmm* "to confuse," par. *ʾbd* pi. "to destroy"; cf. Bardtke, KAT 17/5, 394), and Isa 28:28, with "the ploughman" as subj. (obj. "wagon wheel and steed"; "to bring into confusion, drive along" may be considered as a possible meaning).

Ni. passages (see 2) may all be rendered "to fall into unrest, agitation."

4. (a) The religious usage of the verb has its original setting in the narratives of holy war (Exod 14:24, exodus from Egypt; Josh 10:10, battle in Gibeon; Judg 4:15, Deborah's battle; 1 Sam 7:10, victory at Ebenezer; cf. G. von Rad, *Holy War in Ancient Israel* [1991], 48f.). The concept suggests that at the beginning of the battle Yahweh sends confusion among the enemy troops. Yahweh, not the Israelite army, is the expressed author of the confusion; the process occurs "before the eyes of the Israelites" (Josh 10:10) or "before Barak" (Judg 4:15). According to 1 Sam 7:10, Yahweh sends the confusion in the midst of a thunderstorm. Deut 7:23 characterizes the whole event in its ideal course and in reference to the conquest (cf. Exod 23:27).

In Deut 2:15, conceptual horizons and vocabulary resemble those of the passages just treated, yet the obj. of the confusion is Israel itself, placed under the "terror of God" as punishment for its disobedience. This use is an original variation of the motif by the author of the first Dtn introductory discourse; cf. also 2 Chron 15:6.

2 Sam 22:15 = Psa 18:15 (in the theophany, Yahweh brings confusion among the powers of chaos) and Psa 144:6 (a theophany of Yahweh in battle against the nations) stand within the specifically Jerusalemite tradition of battle with chaos and the nations. One should probably attribute the use of the verb *hmm* to the influence of the holy war tradition; both streams of tradition apparently began to have influence in Jerusalem very early.

(b) The subst. *mᵉhûmâ* "confusion" is also at home in the ideology of the holy war (Deut 7:23; see 4a; 28:20 in the curse threat; cf. Deut 2:15 and 2 Chron 15:5; 1 Sam 5:9, 11: the ark taken away to Philistia causes a divine terror; in the Prophets: Isa 22:5 par. *mᵉbûkâ* "confusion"; Ezek 7:7; 22:5; Zech 14:13; → *yôm*), as well as in its eschatological form in the prophetic concept of the "day of Yahweh" (cf. von Rad, *Theol.* 2:119–25).

The OT knows of the following additional terms for the phenomenon of "divine terror":

(1) *ḥᵃrādâ* or *ḥerdat* ᵓᵉ*lōhîm:* 1 Sam 14:15(bis) with an earthquake as an accompanying manifestation;

(2) ᵓ*ēmâ:* Exod 15:16; 23:27; Josh 2:9 (in each case in reference to the conquest); Deut 32:25 as a curse threat; in another usage in Gen 15:12 (terror falls upon Abraham);

(3) *paḥad:* Exod 15:16; Deut 2:25; 11:25 (in each case in reference to the conquest); Isa 2:10, 19, 21 (in conjunction with the day of Yahweh); according to 1 Sam 11:7 after Saul's call to arms, the terror of Yahweh fell on the people;

(4) *ḥittat* ᵓᵉ*lōhîm:* Gen 35:5 (in conjunction with Jacob's pilgrimage from Shechem to Bethel, the surrounding cities are overcome by divine terror).

What may one conclude on this basis concerning the phenomenon of divine terror? It consists of a primarily neutral "being beside oneself," an ecstasy called forth by God that paralyzes any capability for action. It can have a positive character (Gen 15:12; 1 Sam 11:7); in the holy war, however, it affects the enemies, who then fall defenselessly victim to Israel. Like the holy war in general, the concept is linked with the ark (1 Sam 5:9, 11) and goes back to the nomadic existence of Israelite tribes (similar concepts among Bedouin tribes, for whom the clan god, represented by a mobile sanctuary and identified with Allah, is warlord in decisive battles and fights the enemy; cf. A. Musil, *Manners and Customs of the Rwala Beduins* [1928], 571ff.).

In the Dtn ideology of the holy war, the motif characterizes Israel's victory over the enemy as the work of Yahweh alone (cf. von Rad, *Holy War,* 115–27). Its basic connotation is thus the "soli deo gloria."

5. In the NT the motifs indicated here are no longer active.

F. Stolz

הִנֵּה *hinnēh* **behold**

S 2009; BDB 243b; *HALOT* 1:252a; *TWOT* 510a; *NIDOTTE* 2180

1. Interjections and particles comparable to *hēn* or (the expanded form) *hinnēh* "behold" are attested in almost all Sem. languages (cf. *HAL* 242a).

In the OT environment, cf. Ug *hn* (*UT* §12.7 and no. 782), Akk. *annû* in EA (*AHw* 53b; *CAD* A/2:138; cf. too A. Salonen, *AfO* 19 [1959/60]: 157b), Phoen.-Pun. *hn* (Friedrich 120; Sznycer 77f., 89, 106f.).

Aram. *hn* means "if" (*DISO* 66; Bibl. Aram. *hēn*, 15x; KBL 1069f.), but *h*ʾ (*DISO* 62; Bibl. Aram. *hāʾ*, Dan 3:25) or *hlw* (*DISO* 65; Bibl. Aram. *ʾălû*, Dan 2:31; 4:7, 10; 7:8bis; KBL 1050b; along with *ʾărû*, Dan 7:2, 5–7, 13; KBL 1053b) are used as the interjection "behold" (Leander 128; BLA 266).

hēʾ "behold" appears twice in the Hebr. OT (Gen 47:23; Ezek 16:43 txt?), cf. Aram. *h*ʾ. Some authors view *hēmmâ* in a series of passages not as the per. pron. "they" (3d masc. pl.) but as an equivalent to *hinnēh* (see T. F. McDaniel, *Bib* 49 [1968]: 33f. on Lam 1:19; following the Ug. *hm*, *WUS* no. 837).

2. *hinnēh* occurs (according to Mandl.) a total of 1,057x in the OT *(hinnēh* 446x; *wᵉhinnēh* 360x, incl. Jer 18:3 Q; *wᵉhinᵉnî* 181x, in Isa 65:1 twice; with other sufs. 70x, 37x *wᵉhinnām);* it is distributed over all portions, numerous in Jer (138x), Gen (125x), Ezek (114x), 1 Sam (84x), Isa (77x), Min. Pr. (63x), Kgs (55x each), 2 Sam (46x), Judg (44x), Exod (41x), 2 Chron (40x), thus primarily in the Prophets and in the narrative literature.

hēn (100x) is frequent in only a few books (Job 32x, Isa 27x, Gen 12x, Exod and Psa 5x each, Num and Deut 4x each, Lev 3x, Jer, Prov, and 2 Chron 2x, Ezek and Hag 1x each).

3. *hinnēh (hēn, hēʾ)* can still be recognized as a component of a primitive command, presenting the substance of the command (e.g., Gen 47:23b; cf. BrSynt 3). In the dual function of an address or exclamation as well as the temporal characterization of an event or circumstance, the interjections refer to a person or thing. Followed by a noun they form a clause (e.g., Gen 12:19; 15:17), they precede a complete nom. clause (e.g., Gen 28:15), or they replace a clause (e.g., Gen 22:1, 7; 30:34; Job 9:19). Rarely, they introduce a verbal clause and accent the predicate (e.g., Gen 12:11). On the syntax and style of *hēn/hinnēh*, cf. GKC §§116p, q, 147b; BrSynt 3, 52, 56; K. Oberhuber, *VT* 3 (1953): 5, 10; L. Alonso-Schökel, *Bib* 37 (1956): 74–80; J. Blau, *VT* 9 (1959): 132f.

The (asyndetic) impv. of *rʾh* "to see" can assume a similar function as a call for attention and a demonstrative in that it loses its proper verbal significance (in approximately 1/3 of all cases, e.g., Gen 27:27; 31:50; 41:41; Exod 7:1; 31:2; 33:12; Deut 1:8, 21, etc.; fem. 1 Sam 25:35; pl. Gen 39:14; Exod 35:30; Josh 8:4, 8; 23:4; 2 Sam 15:28; recognizable e.g., in Gen 37:14; 1 Sam 24:12; 26:16; 1 Kgs 12:16; Ezek 40:4, etc.); cf. 2 Sam 7:2 *rᵉʾēh nāʾ* with the par. passage 1 Chron 17:1 *hinnēh;* see Lande 15f., 53.

In a few passages (not clearly distinguishable owing to the fluid transition) *hēn* has assumed the meaning "if" under Aram. influence (e.g., Exod 8:22; Isa 54:15; Jer 3:1; Hag 2:12; 2 Chron 7:13; cf. Wagner no. 74).

4. From a theological perspective, the frequent use of *hinnēh* as an introduction to the prophetic announcement of judgment indicating God's intervention should be emphasized. In this position, the attention getter combines readily with 1st-per. divine speech as *hin*ᵉ*nî* with ptcp. (cf. P. Humbert, "La formule hébraïque en *hineni* suivi d'un participe," *REJ* 97 [1934]: 58–64 = *Opuscules d'un hébraïsant* [1958], 54–59; K. Koch, *Growth of the Biblical Tradition* [1969], 211f.); cf. also the so-called challenge formula *hin*ᵉ*nî* ᵓ*ēleykā* "behold, I want at you" (P. Humbert, *ZAW* 51 [1933]: 101–8 = *Opuscules* 44–53). As a rule, the formula precedes the causal clause (cf. H. W. Wolff, *ZAW* 52 [1934]: 2–6); it frequently stands in the immediate context of the messenger formula (e.g., Jer 6:21; 9:6; 10:18); cf. *BFPS* 149; R. Rendtorff, *ZAW* 74 [1962]: 176f.). Usually a pf. cons. follows. Less frequently the formula is formed with *hinnēh* ᵓ*ānōkî*/ᵓᵃ*nî* instead of with *hin*ᵉ*nî* (e.g., Amos 2:13; on this and the use of *hinnēh* in Amos, cf. Wolff, *Amos*, Herm, 142). A simple *(w*ᵉ*)hinnēh* also introduces the announcement of intervention for judgment (rarely in the divine 1st per. with a finite verb, e.g., Jer 7:20; Ezek 22:13; more often in the 3d per. of God, e.g., Amos 9:8; Isa 3:1; most frequently in the description of God's activity, e.g., Amos 4:2; Jer 7:32) and in isolated cases the consequences of intervention (e.g., Ezek 30:21); a few times it underscores the cause (e.g., Jer 6:10; Ezek 22:6).

hinnēh probably comes to prophetic judgment speech from the prophetic vision report (e.g., Amos 7:1, 4, 7; Jer 4:23–26; Ezek 1:4; 2:9; cf. H. W. Wolff, *Frieden ohne Ende* [1962], 38ff.). Here it assumes the same positions as in the seer's oracle and in the dream account, both of which belong to the background of the prophetic vision report. In the seer's oracle, the deictic particle is connected to a verb meaning "to see" and signals the narration of the vision perceived by the seer alone (e.g., Num 23:9). In the dream account, *w*ᵉ*hinnēh* follows the introductory verb *ḥlm* "to dream" (Gen 28:12; 37:6f., 9; 41:1, 5; Judg 7:13) or the subst. *ḥ*ᵃ*lôm* "dream" (Gen 40:9, 16; 41:22; *hin*ᵉ*nî* with ptcp. in Gen 41:17). It opens the description of the vision and simultaneously marks its importance for the hearer.

By contrast, the indicative function of the particle in prophetic announcements of salvation (e.g., Isa 38:5) as in symbolic announcements (which derive from them; e.g., 1 Kgs 11:31; 13:3; Isa 38:8; cf. Josh 3:11) may be explained in terms of a divine decision pronounced in response to an inquiry (e.g., in holy war: Judg 1:2; 1 Sam 24:5; cf. G. von Rad, *Holy War in Ancient Israel* [1991], 42f.; cf. also the designation formula, e.g., 1 Sam 9:17 with Isa 42:1; 52:13).

5. In the LXX in by far the majority of cases, *idou* corresponds to the Hebr. interjections, in vision reports (esp. in Ezek) also *eidon kai idou.*

The later history of this command for attention, "behold," reaches into apocalyptic literature (e.g., Dan 8:3, 5; 10:5), visionary presentations (e.g., Matt 17:3; Acts 4:1), and announcements of God's activity in the NT (e.g., Luke 1:31; 2:10; cf. W. Michaelis, "ὁράω," *TDNT* 5:315–82; P. Fiedler, *Die Formel "Und siehe" im* NT [1969]).

D. Vetter

הַר *har* **mountain** → צִיּוֹן *ṣiyyôn*

זכר *zkr* **to remember**

S 2142; BDB 269b; *HALOT* 1:269b; *TDOT* 4:64–82; *TWOT* 551; *NIDOTTE* 2349

1. (a) *zkr* is the form of the common Sem. root *ḏkr* shared by Hebr., Akk., most NWSem. dialects, and Eth.

ḏkr occurs in Ug. (in PNs: *UT* no. 724; Gröndahl 71, 196), Old SArab. and Arab., *dkr* in dialectical variants of old WSem. PNs (W. L. Moran, FS Albright 68n.34; cf. Huffmon 187) and in later Aram. dialects (esp. Bibl. Aram.). On Phoen.-Pun. *skr* (not yet *zkr* in the hypocoristic PNs on 11th/10th cent. BCE arrowheads, *KAI* no. 22), cf. *GVG* 1:164; Friedrich 20.

Of the root's two meanings in Old SArab. and Arab., "to remember" and "to mention," the former, "to remember," is the basic meaning of *zkr* in Hebr. and the NWSem. inscriptions (*DISO* 76f.). In contrast, Akk. *zakāru* "to say, speak, mention, swear" (*CAD* Z:16–22) is purely a verb of speaking (a thorough treatment of *zkr* in the Sem. languages is in W. Schottroff, *"Gedenken" im Alten Orient und im AT* [1967²], 1–106).

In Akk. and Ug., where, however, the meaning of *ḏkr* is not yet discernible, *ḫasāsu* (*CAD* H:122–25; *AHw* 329f.) and *ḫss* (*UT* no. 986; *WUS* no. 1060) mean "to remember."

Contrary to the equation of the meanings of Hebr. *zkr* and Akk. *zakāru* proposed by P. A. H. de Boer (*Gedenken und Gedächtnis in der Welt des AT* [1962], esp. 44, 63f.), the Can. gloss in EA 228:19 from Hazor (*li-iḫ-šu-uš-mi/ia-az-ku-ur-mi* "may the king, my lord, remember everything that has been done against Hazura") already supports the identification of *zkr* with Akk. *ḫasāsu* "to remember" that took place in pre-Hebr. SCan. (Meyer 1:24f.).

There is no evidence for an etymological relationship to the homonymous word *zākār* "male" (yet Ug. diverges with *dkr: WUS* no. 740, or *da-ka-rum:* C. F. A. Schaeffer, *AfO* 19 [1959/60]: 194; cf. Schottroff, op. cit. 4–8, 372; P. Fronzaroli, *AANLR* 8/19 [1964]: 244).

(b) Besides the qal of *zkr,* "to remember," Hebr. attests the hi. counterpart to Akk. *zakāru,* "to mention, name," and the ni. pass. of the qal and hi. "to be remembered" (cf., however, J. Blau, "Reste des i-Imperfekts von *zkr,* qal," *VT* 11 [1961]: 81–86). Nom. formations of the root occurring in the OT are:

(1) the segholate *zēker* "memory, mention, name," also attested as an nomen actionis in the nom. form *qitl* in Akk. (*zikru* "statement, command, name," *CAD* Z:112–16), Phoen.-Pun., Aram. (*zkr, DISO* 77), Old SArab. (*ḏkr, RES* 2693.7), and Arab.;

(2) the abstract noun with (*-ān* >) *-ōn, zikkārôn* "memorial" (Eccl 1:11; 2:16, Aramaizing *zikrôn;* Bibl. Aram. **dokrān,* **dikrôn;* cf. BLA 195; J. Cantineau, *Le*

Nabatéen [1930]: 1:47f.) occurring also in Phoen. *(skrn)*, Aram. (*zkrn, dkrn, dkrwn, DISO* 78), and Old SArab. (*dkrn;* G. Ryckmans, *Muséon* 71 [1958]: 127 no. 4);

(3) the sacrificial term *ᵓazkārâ* (cf. R. Rendtorff, *Studien zur Geschichte des Opfers im Alten Israel* [1967], 185–87), probably related to the technical usage of the hi. for sacrifice (Isa 66:3; Psa 38:1; 70:1) and perhaps to be translated with "appeal (to a name)" (R. Dussaud, *Les origines cananéennes du sacrifice israélite* [1941²], 93–95; D. Schötz, *Schuld- und Sündopfer im AT* [1930], 55) in analogy to the appeal to the deity during sacrifice in Akk. (cf. Schottroff, op. cit. 27f., 328–38) and Aram. (a statue of Hadad from Zinjirli, *KAI* no. 214.16: *yzbḥ hdd wyzkr ᵓšm hdd* "undertakes sacrifices for Hadad and calls on the name of Hadad");

(4) the substantival hi. ptcp. *mazkîr* "speaker, herald," translating the Eg. official title *whm.w* as a term for an office in the Jerusalemite royal court (J. Begrich, *ZAW* 58 [1940/41]: 1–29 = *GS* [1964], 67–98; R. de Vaux, *RB* 48 [1939]: 394–405; differently, H. Reventlow, *TZ* 15 [1959]: 161–75; contra H. J. Boecker, *TZ* 17 [1961]: 212–16);

(5) the verbal adj. *zākûr* "mindful" (GKC §50f; Meyer 2:28).

It is disputed whether *zēker* should be understood as a denominative from the hi. (B. Jacob, *ZAW* 17 [1897]: 48f.; J. Begrich, *Studien zu Deuterojesaja* [1963²], 33n.94; id., *GS* [1964], 79n.29; B. S. Childs, *Memory and Tradition in Israel* [1962], 12) or as a causative of the qal (J. J. Stamm, *TZ* 1 [1945]: 306; de Boer, op. cit. 15f., 63) and whether *ᵓazkārâ* should be treated as a subst. with an ᵓ as an element of the stem and a concrete meaning like *ᵓalmānâ* "widow" (G. R. Driver, *JSS* 1 [1956]: 99f.) or as an abstract formation in the form of an Aramaizing ha. inf. (Meyer 2:33) or ap. inf. (GKC §85b; Wagner 133).

The two Bibl. Aram. examples of the root, *dokrān* (Ezra 4:15) and *dikrôn* (Ezra 6:2), have the meaning "record," which occurs frequently in Imp. Aram. papyri from Egypt (*DISO* 78); under Aram. influence, Hebr. *zikkārôn* in Exod 17:14; Mal 3:16; Esth 6:1 also adapts to this meaning (Wagner no. 76a; on *zikkārôn* in Isa 57:8, cf. Schottroff, op. cit. 319–21).

On the PNs formed with *zkr,* see 4a.

2. Forms of the root *zkr* occur in the MT a total of 288x: qal 171x (Psa 44x, Deut 15x, Jer 14x, Ezek 10x, Neh 9x, Job 8x, Deutero-Isa 7x), hi. 31x (Psa 6x), ni. 20x (Ezek 8x), *zēker* 23x (Psa 11x), *zikkārôn* 24x (only exilic and post-exilic, P in Exod–Num 14x), *ᵓazkārâ* 7x (P in Lev–Num), *mazkîr* 9x, *zākûr* 1x (Psa 103:14); in addition, Bibl. Aram. *dikrôn* and *dokrān* 1x each. The root does not occur in Joel, Obad, Zeph, Hag, Ruth, Dan.

Textual criticism: Exod 34:19 read with Vers. *hazzākār;* Isa 63:11 read *wayyizkᵉrû;* Jer 23:36 read with LXX *tazkîrû;* Ezek 16:22, 43 read with Q *zākart;* Nah 1:14 read probably *yizzākēr* (cf. *BHS*); Nah 2:6 read probably *yizzākᵉrû* (cf. LXX; see *BHS* and E. Sellin, *Das Zwölfprophetenbuch,* KAT, 365, 368); Psa 77:12a read with Q, Vers. *ᵓezkôr;* Psa 89:48 read *zᵉkor-ᵓᵃdōnāy;* 1 Chron 16:15 read *zākar* (cf. Psa 105:8).

3. (a) *zkr* may hardly be understood as a primarily cultic (F. Schwally, *ZAW* 11 [1891]: 176–80; H. Gross, *BZ* NS 4 [1960]: 227–37; contra B. Jacob, *ZAW* 17 [1897]: 48–80), legal (H. Reventlow, *TZ* 15 [1959]: 161–75; contra H. J. Boecker, *TZ* 17 [1961]: 212–16; id., *Redeformen des Rechtslebens im AT* [1964], 106–11),

or ancient magical term (*ILC* 1–2:106f., 256f.; de Boer, op. cit. 64; contra Childs, op. cit. 17–30). The various usages of the root in the OT oppose derivation from a single origin. The basic meaning of the qal (and, correspondingly, of the related ni. pass.) is "to remember." Evidence of this basic meaning can be seen in the use of the verb in contrast to *škḥ* "to forget" (13x) and *mḥh* "to wipe away, blot out" (Isa 43:25; Psa 109:14; Neh 13:14) and parallel to verbs and expressions for acts of thought, e.g., *bîn* "to pay attention to, understand, perceive" (Deut 32:7; Isa 43:18), *hgh* "to consider (begrudgingly)" (Psa 63:7; 77:7 txt em; 143:5), *ḥšb* "to take into account, consider" (2 Sam 19:20; cf. Psa 77:6f.), *śîaḥ* "to meditate" (Psa 77:7; 143:5), *ᶜlh ᶜal lēb* "to come to mind," etc. (2 Sam 19:20; Isa 46:8; 47:7; 57:11; 65:17; Jer 3:16; 44:21; 51:50), as well as the occasional purposive focusing of memory on recognition (Mic 6:5; Ezek 6:7–10).

But that *zkr* connotes an active relationship to the obj. of memory that exceeds a simple thought process (*ILC* 1–2:106f., 256f.; cf. Childs, op. cit. 17–30; Schottroff, op. cit. passim) is already indicated somewhat by these contrasts and pars., and even more clearly by others, e.g., *gzr* ni. "to be cut off" (Psa 88:6), *brk* pi. "to bless" (Psa 115:12), which also parallels *zkr* in the Sem. languages (esp. in the Nab. Sinai graffiti; cf. Schottroff, op. cit. 71f.), *ᶜśh ḥesed* "to demonstrate covenant loyalty" (Gen 40:14; Judg 8:34f.), *pqd* "to be concerned about" (Jer 3:16; 14:10; 15:15; Hos 8:13 = 9:9; Psa 8:5 106:4; cf. Isa 23:17), the opposition with *šmr* "to observe, keep" (cf. Exod 20:8 with Deut 5:12; also Psa 103:18; 119:55), moreover, the purposive focusing of memory on a particular deed (*zkr lᵉ* plus inf. cs., similar to *ʾmr lᵉ* plus inf. cs., "to remember to do something," Exod 20:8; Psa 103:18; 109:16; or *zkr kî* plus obj. clause, Job 36:24; cf. Num 15:39).

(b) No semantic evolution may be traced. Yet terms in the semantic field and special constructions occasionally demonstrate nuances of meaning.

Thus in passages that have lament expressions in the semantic field of *zkr* (Num 11:4f.; Psa 42:5, 7; 137:1; Lam 3:20), memory participates in the lament emphasis. In other passages, e.g., Neh 4:8, where *yrʾ* "to fear" is an antonym for *zkr*, the verb expresses an attitude of trust or, as in Ezek 23:27, where *nśʾ ᶜênayim ʾel* "to raise the eyes toward" parallels it, a longing need.

Inclusion among terms for hymnic praise of God (Psa 105:1–5 = 1 Chron 16:8–12; cf. Psa 63:6f.) or use as an expression for the call to prayer (Job 2:8; cf. Psa 119:55) indicates that the basic stem can also signify an announcement (B. Jacob, *ZAW* 17 [1897]: 63; cf. too de Boer, op. cit. 14f.).

In passages that use *zkr* with the dativus commodi (incommodi) of person and the acc. of object construction (e.g., Jer 2:2; Psa 79:8; 98:3; Neh 13:22), that append a prep. expression with *kᵉ* "according to" (Neh 6:14; cf. Psa 25:7) or *ᶜal* "on account of (particular deeds)" (Neh 13:14, 29), or that state the obj. of memory with *lᵉṭôbâ* "for good" (Neh 5:19; 13:31; cf. *bṭb* in the Nab. Sinai graffiti and *lṭb* in the Aram. inscriptions from Hatra; Schottroff, op. cit. 68–78, 83–85) instead of the objective acc., *zkr* conveys a saving or harmful intention: "to remember to someone's benefit/harm."

(c) Nevertheless, the most frequent construction is the acc. of object or of person (indicated in late texts by an Aramaism with *lᵉ*: Exod 32:13; Deut 9:27; Psa 25:7; 136:23; BrSynt 87) or the obj. clause introduced by *kî*, *ʾēt ʾᵃšer*, *mâ*. Memory pertains to past events that the memory awakens to realization because of their present significance (Gen 42:9; Num 11:5; 2 Kgs 9:25), to places and objects to which the one remembering clings (Jer 3:16; 17:2; Psa

42:5, 7; 137:1, 6), but also to present realities that have a formative character for existence (Isa 54:4; Job 11:16; Prov 31:6f.; Eccl 5:18f.; Lam 1:7; 3:19f.) or demand observation as an obligation (Num 15:38–40; Josh 1:13–15; Mal 3:22; Amos 1:9 too; cf. the usage of *zkrn* with a view to the content of an international treaty: *KAI* no. 222C.2f.; Fitzmyer, *Sef.* 18f., 73).

Fixed usages are:

(1) the application of *zkr* in the experience of amenable circumstances, which in the wisdom realm will be given imperative, examined reflection, with regard to their consequences and in the service of certain admonitions (Job 4:7; 40:32–41:1; Eccl 11:8; Sir 7:11, 16; 8:5, 7; 9:12; 14:11f.; 31:12f.; 41:3; cf. also Judg 9:2; Job 21:6f. and Isa 47:7; Lam 1:9); Job 13:12 seems to call such admonishing reminders *zikkārôn;*

(2) the courtly use of *zkr,* also attested extrabiblically (Lachish Letter II = *KAI* no. 192.4; cf. *ANET* 322a; Aḥ. 53, Cowley 213, 221; cf. *ANET* 428a), to indicate the relationship in which a superior approaches an inferior (Gen 40:14, 23; 1 Sam 25:31; cf. Eccl 9:15). Discussion of a ruler's remembering (EA 228:18–25; Esth 2:1; cf. too Esth 6:1–11) or not remembering (2 Sam 19:20; 2 Chron 24:22) an act of loyalty or disloyalty done him belongs in the context of this courtly use (Schottroff, op. cit. 43f., 116f., 164, 384f.), which is still not a specifically juristic use of *zkr* (thus Boecker, *Redeformen* 106–11). Such remembering finds expression in demonstrations of mercy or vengeful interventions as acts of dominion.

(d) In the derived stems and the nom. formations of the root the following peculiarities are noteworthy: parallelism with various verbs of speaking (cf. Exod 23:13; Isa 43:26; 49:1; Jer 4:16; 23:35f.) and contrast with words for "keeping silent" (Isa 62:6; Amos 6:10) are characteristic for the meaning of *zkr* hi. "to mention, name" (and the corresponding ni. pass.), which competes primarily with *qr*ʾ "to call"; for the meaning of *zēker,* competition with *šēm* "name" (Exod 3:15; Isa 26:8; Psa 135:13; Job 18:17; Prov 10:7; see also Hos 12:6; Psa 30:5; 97:12; and cf. B. Jacob, *ZAW* 17 [1897]: 70; contra de Boer, op. cit. 17f.), which may also be observed in Akk. and Phoen. (cf. *CIS* 1:7 = *KAI* no. 18.6–8 *lkny ly lskr wšm n*ʿ*m tḥt p*ʿ*m* ʾ*dny b*ʿ*l šmm l*ʿ*lm* "that it may be a memorial and a good name for me at the feet of Ba'al-shamem forever"); for the meaning of *zikkārôn,* the parallelism with ʾ*ôt* "sign" (Exod 13:9; Josh 4:6f.).

Fixed usages are:

(1) the use of the hi., ni. (mostly with the obj. or grammatical subj. *šēm* "name"), and the noms. *zēker* and *zikkārôn* (so too Phoen. *skr, skrn,* Aram. *zkr, dkr[w]n,* and Old SArab. *ḏkrn* in burial inscriptions) for the living's remembrance of the dead in the form continuing laudatory mention of the name (for the Akk. see F. R. Kraus, *JNES* 19 [1960]: 127–31; *za-kar šu-me* also occurs in this context in a more specialized sense as the invocation of the ghost to a sacrifice for the dead; cf. A. L. Oppenheim, *BASOR* 91 [1943]: 36–39). The name of the dead may be preserved through the son (2 Sam 18:18) or (as a substitution) through the memorial stele (cf. Isa 56:5 and Phoen. *mṣbt skr bḥym* "memorial stele among the living," *CIS* 1:116 = *KAI* no. 153.1, etc.; cf. W. F. Albright, *SVT* 4 [1956]: 242–58; K. Galling, *ZDPV* 75 [1959]:

1–13). A lasting good memory is expected for the righteous (Psa 112:6; Prov 10:7); the cessation of memory, equivalent to total annihilation, is expected for evildoers and enemies (Isa 26:14; Psa 9:7; 34:17; Job 24:20) or conferred upon them in curse and judgment sayings (Exod 17:14; Deut 25:19; 32:26; Jer 11:19; Ezek 21:37; 25:10; Hos 2:19; Zech 13:2; Psa 83:5; 109:15). Qohelet denies any lasting memory for the dead whatsoever (Eccl 1:11; 2:15f.; 9:4f.).

(2) the juristic use of the hi. with a per. obj. as a technical term for the charge in a legal proceeding (Isa 43:26; cf. J. Begrich, *Studien zu Deuterojesaja* [1963], 33; but not Gen 40:14) and with the obj. *ʿāwôn* "guilt" (Num 5:15; 1 Kgs 17:18; Ezek 21:28f.; 29:16; but not Gen 41:9 with the obj. *ḥ^{a}ṭāʾay*, "I must mention my failures"); as a designation for the demonstration of guilt in investigations involving subjective evidence (Num 5: ordeal oath; Ezek 21: arrow oracle) or through encounter with the numinous quality surrounding the man of God (1 Kgs 17; cf. Schottroff, op. cit. 264–70; contra H. Reventlow, *TZ* 15 [1959]: 161–75; H. J. Boecker, *TZ* 17 [1961]: 212–16; id., *Redeformen*, 106–8, who understand *zkr* hi. *ʿāwôn* as the activity of the plaintiff in court and see the hi. ptcp. *mazkîr* as describing the function of bringing charges).

(3) the cultically shaped use of *zēker* (Psa 6:6; 111:4; 145:7) and of the hi. of *zkr*, which, like the qal, occurs in hymnic calls to praise in series with synonyms (Isa 12:4–6; Psa 71:16; cf. 1 Chron 16:4), to designate the hymnic praise of God. As a human act of confession (in Josh 23:7; Isa 48:1 alongside other acts of confession), *zkr* hi. *(b^{e})šēm ʾ^{e}lōhîm* "to call on the name of God (in the cult)" (Exod 23:13; Isa 26:13; Amos 6:10; Psa 20:8; cf. H. A. Brongers, *ZAW* 77 [1965]: 17f., and the analogous use of the Akk. *šuma zakāru* "to call on the name [of a deity]," *CAD* Z:17f.) corresponds to God's self-declaration legitimizing a particular cultic site (Exod 20:24; cf. J. J. Stamm, *TZ* 1 [1945]: 304–6; H. Cazelles, *Etudes sur le Code de l'Alliance* [1946], 40–43). In the unique passage Neh 2:20, *zikkārôn* refers to participation in the (Jerusalem temple-) cult in general (cf. F. Horst, *RGG* 2:1405).

4. In the theological realm, *zkr* describes the reciprocal relationship between Yahweh and Israel or individual Israelites.

(a) As already indicated by NW and SWSem. equivalents to the OT theophoric thanksgiving name *z^{e}karyâ(hû)* "Yahweh remembered," its variants and abbreviations (cf. *IP* 186f.; Schottroff, op. cit. 96–106, 382–84), as well as statements such as that of a benefactor in Lapethos on Cypress (*KAI* no. 43.16: "May salvation and goodness become my lot and the lot of my seed, and may Melqart remember mine"), the OT's discussion of God's memory for his worshipers involves a religious conception already preexistent in its environment. Such divine remembrance refers to the deity's beneficial and sufficient attention to the individual (cf. Num 10:9: *zkr* ni. par. to *yšʿ* ni. "to receive help"), as experienced e.g., by the barren in the gift of the child (Gen 30:22; 1 Sam 1:11, 19, as the background of the thanksgiving name mentioned), but also in other situations of distress and generally in participation in the divine blessing (Psa 115:12). The dead are excepted from such remembrance (Psa 88:6; cf. C. Barth, *Die Errettung vom Tode* [1947], 67–76); yet, as an exception, Job 14:13–15 envisions the possibility that God's remembrance, in the sense of the resumption of concern for life and salvation (cf. Gen 8:1; cf. for the contrary Lam 2:1), could also apply to one hidden in Sheol.

(1) Impv. *zkr* occurs as a fixed religious term since antiquity in exclamations of petition (Judg 16:28; cf. 1 Sam 1:11), and then primarily in individual supplications (Jer 15:15; Psa 25:7) and collective laments (Psa 74:2; 106:4); the corresponding indicative describes Yahweh's reversal of need retrospectively in the song of thanksgiving (Psa 136:23; cf. 115:12) and in the descriptive praise of the hymn (Psa 8:5; 9:13). Even more frequent than this usage of *zkr* with a per. obj. is the use of the verb in exclamations of request that call Yahweh to remember the frailty of human life (Psa 89:48; Job 7:7; 10:9), the shame of the supplicant (Psa 89:51; Lam 5:1), the slander attributed to Yahweh by his opponents (Psa 74:18, 22), as well as his promise (Exod 32:13; Deut 9:27; Psa 119:49; Neh 1:8), the covenant maintained by him (Jer 14:21), and his gracious mercy (Hab 3:2; Psa 25:6f.), as motivations for his beneficial intervention on behalf of the supplicant. The laudatory discussion of Yahweh's remembrance of human frailty (78:39; 103:14) and his promises (Psa 105:8 = 1 Chron 16:15; Psa 106:45; 111:4) in the thanksgiving song and hymn correspond to these requests. A third group of requests challenge Yahweh to decide for a saving relationship by remembering the good deeds of his worshipers (2 Kgs 20:3 = Isa 38:3; Jer 18:20; cf. also Psa 20:4; 132:1; 2 Chron 6:42) or by forgetting their shortcomings (Isa 64:8; Psa 25:7; 79:8), but a malevolent memory of the deeds of the enemy should pertain (Psa 137:7; cf. Psa 109:14 ni.).

(2) This usage of *zkr* can be observed primarily at the end of various sections of Neh in Nehemiah's pleas for Yahweh to remember his deeds in a benevolent sense (Neh 5:19; 13:14, 22, 31) and the deeds of his enemy in a malevolent sense (Neh 6:14; 13:29).

(3) The specifically prophetic usage of the verb always has, from God's perspective, the deeds of people as the obj. (Isa 43:25; Jer 2:2; 14:10; 31:34; 44:21; Hos 7:2; 8:13; 9:9; ni. Ezek 3:20; 18:22, 24; 33:13, 16), apart from Jer 31:20 and Ezek 16:60, where the objs. are, resp., Israel and the covenant maintained by Yahweh for Israel. In this respect, *zkr* has a benevolent sense only in Jer 2:2f., where Yahweh mentions, as the motive for his former disposition to benevolent relations with his people, Israel's youthful faithfulness in response to Israel's objection that he had not sufficiently cared for it (cf. Jer 2:5). Otherwise, Hosea (14:10) and Jeremiah (44:21) characteristically threaten that Yahweh will remember in a way that makes Israel's transgression the standard for his punitive intervention. In Ezek *zkr* ni. (cf. Psa 109:14 and perhaps also the qal in Psa 20:4; but on this passage cf. E. Kutsch, *Salbung als Rechtsakt* [1963], 11–13) has close contact with *ḥšb*, the term for the cultic-declarative accounting of righteousness for life or of unrighteousness for death (cf. von Rad, *PHOE* 125–35, 243–66; Zimmerli, *GO* 178–91; H. Reventlow, *Wächter über Israel* [1962], 95–134). Ezekiel uses this cultic concept in order to sharpen the contrast between the judgment fatalism of the exilic generation and individual responsibility for one's actions. Looking forward to the coming salvation, Deutero-Isaiah (43:25) and Jeremiah (31:34) an-

nounce nonrecollection of guilt as Yahweh's forgiveness (cf. S. Herrmann, *Die prophetischen Heilserwartungen im AT* [1965], 179–85, 195–204).

(4) Although K. Koch (*ZTK* 52 [1955]: 20f.) relates this usage of *zkr* to the association of human deeds with God's initiation of the cause-effect relationship (cf. H. Reventlow, *TZ* 15 [1959]: 161–75; E. Pax, *Liber Annuus* 11 [1960/61]: 74–77; cf. also F. Horst, *Gottes Recht* [1961], 286–91; id., *RGG* 6:1343–46), H. J. Boecker (op. cit. 106–11; cf. Childs, op. cit. 31–33, and for the Neh passages, U. Kellermann, *Nehemia: Quellen, Überlieferung und Geschichte* [1967], 6–8, 76–88) traces this usage of *zkr* with the acc. of obj. and the dative of person only to the legal sphere: "to remember to the benefit of (in defense)/to the detriment of (an accusation)." Still, the usage in dedicatory inscriptions seems more likely to have been adopted here (K. Galling, *ZDPV* 68 [1950]: 134–42; Schottroff, op. cit. 217–38, 392–95).

(5) As attested extrabiblically, e.g., in the dedicatory inscription no. 14 in M. Dunand and R. Duru, *Oumm el-ᶜAmed, Texte* (1962), 193 (ll. 1f.: "[this is what] your servant Abdosir, the son of Ariš, praised as a memorial *[skrn]*"; cf. also Aram. *dkr[w]n ṭb l* . . . "good memory for PN," e.g., Nab.: J. Cantineau, *Le Nabatéen* [1932]: 2:11–13; Dura-Europos: A. Caquot, *Syria* 30 [1953]: 245f.), the use in the dedicatory inscriptions is reflected by *zikkārôn* in Zech 6:14 and esp. in P (Exod 28:12, 29; 30:16; 39:7; Num 10:10; 31:54; cf. K. Koch, *ZTK* 55 [1958]: 44; Childs, op. cit. 67f.), which also characteristically uses the verb *zkr* as a term for the divine covenant giver's keeping of the covenant (Gen 9:15f.; Exod 2:24; 6:5; Lev 26:42, 45; cf. W. Elliger, *Kleine Schriften zum AT* [1966], 174–98; Zimmerli, *GO* 205–16; Childs, op. cit. 42–44).

(b) Israel's remembrance of Yahweh and his saving acts corresponds to Yahweh's remembrance of Israel.

(1) *zkr* occurs in the Psa as a term for confident appeal to Yahweh, as those who voice songs of lament and thanksgiving confess (Psa 42:7; 63:7; 77:4; 119:55; cf. also Isa 64:4; Jonah 2:8; Jer 20:9), esp. for actualizing remembrance of Yahweh's saving acts (Psa 77:6f., 12.; 119:52; 143:5; in the call to actualizing praise: Deut 32:7; Psa 105:5 = 1 Chron 16:12; in the historical psalm as an act Israel sometimes undertakes but usually neglects: Psa 78:34f., 42; 106:7; Isa 63:11; Neh 9:17; cf. also Judg 8:34). Such remembrance can, indeed, hardly be understood as a reflection of an actualization of the past in cultic drama (S. Mowinckel, *Psalmenstudien* 2 [1920]; A. Weiser, *Glaube und Geschichte im AT* [1961], 280–90, 303–21); rather, it is a reminiscent and laudatory reprise of the past in authentic recognition of the temporal interval, but for the sake of its present significance (cf. H. Zirker, *Die kultische Vergegenwärtigung der Vergangenheit in den Psalmen* [1964]; Westermann, *PLP* 214–49; W. Beyerlin, *ZAW* 79 [1967]: 208–24).

(2) In Deuteronomic parenesis, the representation of particular individual motifs from the salvation-history tradition serves to inculcate Yahweh's commandments (Deut 5:15; 7:18; 8:2, 18; 9:7; 15:15; 16:3, 12; 24:9, 18, 22; 25:17). The fixed schema of this parenesis (cf. N. Lohfink, *Das Hauptgebot* [1963], 125–36; Schottroff, op. cit. 117–25, 385–88), which binds together commandment, exhortation to remembrance, and renewed admonition, may be explained on the basis of Levitical preaching, usually seen against the background of the covenant formula, esp. with respect to the derivation of the obligation from the

benevolent deeds of the covenant giver (K. Baltzer, *Covenant Formulary* [1971], 31–38; N. Lohfink, op. cit.; D. J. McCarthy, *Treaty and Covenant* [1963], 109–40; von Rad, *Deut*, OTL, 19–23; W. Beyerlin, FS Hertzberg 9–29; but cf. Schottroff, op. cit. 385–88). In addition, Deut (16:3), Dtr (Exod 13:3, 9; Josh 4:7), and the other exilic and post-exilic documents (P: Exod 12:14; Lev 23:24; Num 17:5; moreover: Neh 2:20; Esth 9:28) use *zkr* and *zikkārôn* for feast days and cultic events, which are thereby historicized and made to serve the representation of some salvation-history traditions. Here, too, *zkr* is not participation in dramatic cult representations but reminiscent involvement in the matrix of events by representing past phenomena through proclamation or symbol (cf. M. Noth, *EvT* 2 [1952/53]: 6–17; Childs, op. cit. 45–65, 74–89; N. W. Porteous, FS Weiser 93–105; von Rad, *Theol.* 2:99–112; S. Herrmann, FS Rost 95–105; J. M. Schmidt, *EvT* 30 [1970]: 169–200).

(3) Prophecy since the 8th cent. BCE employs *zkr* in a comparable usage. The condemnation in Mic 6:3–5 demands that the people remember Yahweh's saving acts in order to recognize the untenable nature of their objections against Yahweh. Isa 17:10 bases the threatened judgment on the fact that Israel had not considered Yahweh. *zkr* also occurs in this sense later on in the invectives (Isa 57:11; Ezek 16:22, 43; 23:19; cf. also Isa 47:7). Nevertheless, in exilic and post-exilic prophecy, *zkr* appears primarily in salvation oracles (Isa 44:21f.; 46:8; Jer 51:50; Ezek 6:9; 16:61, 63; 20:43; 36:31; Zech 10:9) in close association with the call to repentance (see Wolff, *GS* [1964], 130–50), esp. in conjunction with the announcement of a new saving act of Yahweh surpassing all previous ones (Isa 43:18; 46:9; 54:4; 65:17; cf. C. R. North, FS Robinson 111–26; von Rad, *Theol.* 2:243–50; Zimmerli, *GO* 192–204; S. Herrmann, *Die prophetischen Heilserwartungen im AT* [1965], 298–304).

5. On Judaism and the NT, cf. J. Behm, "ἀνάμνησις," *TDNT* 1:348f.; O. Michel, "μιμνήσκομαι," *TDNT* 4:675–83; G. Schmidt, FS Meiser 259–64; K.-H. Bartels, "Dies tut zu meinem Gedächtnis" (diss., Mainz, 1959); M. Thurian, *Eucharistie: Eihneit am Tisch des Herrn?* (1963); de Boer, op. cit. 44–62.

W. Schottroff

זנה *znh* to commit harlotry

S 2181; BDB 275b; *HALOT* 1:275a; *TDOT* 4:99–104; *TWOT* 563; *NIDOTTE* 2388

---

1. The root *znh* also occurs outside Hebr. in (postbibl.) Aram., Arab., and Eth.

For Judg 19:2 one may assume a root *znh* II "to become angry," corresponding to Akk. *zenû* "to be angry" (*CAD* Z:85f.; G. R. Driver, *WO* 1/1 [1947]: 29f.; *HAL* 264; *CPT* 286, 326).

Nom. derivatives are *zᵉnûnîm* (cf. D. Leibel, *Lešonenu* 20 [1956]: 45f.), *zᵉnût*, and *taznût*. The verb occurs in the qal (with a substantivized fem. ptcp. *zōnâ* "whore"), the pu. (only Ezek 16:34), and the hi. (causative, on Hos 4:10, 18; 5:3 cf. Rudolph, KAT 13/1, 105, 116).

2. The verb occurs in the qal 83x (excl. Judg 19:2; see 1; 33 are substantivized *zōnâ;* Ezek 21x, Hos 10x), in the pu. 1x, and in the hi. 9x (Hos 4x, 2 Chron 3x). *z^enûnîm* occurs 12x (Hos 6x), *z^enût* 9x (Jer and Ezek 3x each), and *taznût* 20x (only in Ezek 16 and 23).

Of the total 134 occurrences of the root, 47 fall to Ezek (42 in Ezek 16 and 23), 22 to Hos, 9 each to Lev and Jer, 5 each to Judg and Isa, and 4 each to Gen, Josh, and Prov.

3. (a) The basic meaning of the qal should be translated "to whore, commit harlotry" (of the woman; Num 25:1 of the man). The verb is either used abs. (Gen 38:24, etc., in about half the cases) or constructed with: *ʾaḥ^arê* "after" (Exod 34:15f., etc.; frequent), a simple acc. (Jer 3:1), *ʾel* (Num 25:1; Ezek 16:26, 28), *ʾet* (Isa 23:17), *b^e* (Ezek 16:17); in the meaning "to be unfaithful to" it is used with *taḥat* (Ezek 23:5) or *mittaḥat* (Hos 4:12), *mēʿal* (Hos 9:1) or *min* (Psa 73:27).

The pu. form attested in Ezek 16:34 represents qal pass. ("to be solicited for prostitution"). The hi. in Hos 4:10, 18 is usually translated as an inner-causative like the qal (e.g., Wolff, *Hos*, Herm, 72f.), otherwise causatively "to lure into lewdness" (see 1).

znh has no direct synonym.

(b) *znh* referred originally to unregulated, illicit sexual behavior between man and woman. Par. terms include *ḥll* pi. "to profane" (Lev 19:29; 21:9), *bgd* "to behave treacherously" (Jer 3:8), *mʿl* "to behave treacherously" (1 Chron 5:25), *ṭmʾ* ni. "to make oneself unclean" (Ezek 20:30; 23:30; Hos 5:3; Psa 106:39), or *nʾp* pi. "to commit adultery" (Hos 4:13f.).

Whoever commits harlotry commits an abomination in Israel (Lev 19:29 *zimmâ;* Deut 22:21 *n^ebālâ*). Accordingly, harlotry is punished: whoever commits harlotry is burned (*śrp* ni. Gen 38:24; Lev 21:9), annihilated (*krt* hi. Lev 20:6; *bʿr* pi. Deut 22:21; *ṣmt* hi. Psa 73:27).

4. Theological language uses *znh* in a fig. sense to describe apostasy from Yahweh and conversion to other gods. This usage has four focal points:

(a) In Hosea's prophecy: Here the subj. is not just any woman but the northern kingdom of Israel (9:1), the land (1:2), presented fig. as Yahweh's wife; it is unfaithful to Yahweh and "whores away from Yahweh" (4:12; 9:1). With the aid of this concept adapted from the Canaanite Baal cult and its cultic prostitution, Israel's pro-Canaanite inclination is sharply attacked. "To whore away from Yahweh" is synonymous with adultery (4:13f.), with worshiping Baal as husband, and therefore calls forth prophetic judgment (cf. Wolff, *Hos*, Herm, 13f.).

(b) This fig. usage is employed again by Jeremiah. Here, too, it is not the individual but Judah/Israel who is accused of harlotry (2:20; 3:1, 6, 8). The high hills, mountains, and green trees (2:20; 3:6) are named as the sites of the harlotry (as already in Hos 4:13), apparently specific Baalistic cultic sites.

(c) The use of *znh* is markedly concentrated in Ezek 16 and 23, which reprise the images of Hos 1–3 and Jer 3 (the term *taznût* occurs only in Ezek 16 and 23). Here, too, Israel exercises its idolatry at specific cultic sites (heights 16:16) or with cultic objects (masc. images, 16:17). The strange gods are described as idols (*gillûlîm* 6:9; 23:30) or horrors (*šiqqûṣîm* 23:30). Israel pursues them although they are totally unconcerned for Israel (16:34).

The following must also be emphasized: (1) The charge of harlotry with strange gods is expanded in 16:26, 28; 23:5 through the idea of harlotry with foreign nations, thus through the charge of political bondage. (2) According to 23:3, 19 whorish apostasy did not begin with the conquest and contact with the Can. Baal religion, but already in Israel's early era, in Egypt. (3) 6:9 speaks fig. of "prurient hearts."

(d) Following Hosea, the term then found acceptance primarily in Dtr theology, namely in the stereotypical form "to play the harlot after (strange) gods (of the land)" (Exod 34:15f.; Deut 31:16; Judg 2:17; 8:27, 33; cf. Num 25:1; Psa 106:39; 1 Chron 5:25).

5. On NT usage in the context of the environment of the NT, cf. F. Hauck and S. Schulz, "πορνή," *TDNT* 6:579–95.

J. Kühlewein

זעם *zᶜm* **to curse** → קלל *qll*

זעק *zᶜq* **to cry out** → צעק *ṣᶜq*

זָר *zār* **strange**

S 2114; BDB 266a; *HALOT* 1:279a; *TDOT* 4:52–58; *TWOT* 541; *NIDOTTE* 2319

---

1. *zār* "strange, different" is the (often substantivized) verbal adj. of the root *zûr* II "to turn away" (Hebr. qal, ni., ho.; with counterparts in SSem. and Aram.; cf. L. A. Snijders, *OTS* 10 [1954]: 1–21).

The root should be distinguished from *zûr* I "to press" (Judg 6:38; Isa 59:5; Job 39:15) and *zûr* III "to stink, be repugnant" (Job 19:17; *HAL* 256b). Akk. *zêru* "to hate" also belongs to the latter (**ḏir;* cf. Arab. *ḏāra;* cf. Akk. *zāʾiru* "hostile, enemy," *CAD* Z:14f., 97–99; cf., nevertheless, P. Wernberg-Møller, *VT* 4 [1954]: 322–25).

Counterparts to *zār* occur outside NWSem. (*DISO* 80) in SSem.; cf. *HAL* 268a on the meanings that have developed somewhat further (Mid. Hebr. "layman"; Arab. "pilgrim").

2. *zār* occurs 70x in the OT (excl. Prov 21:8 *wāzār;* cf. *HAL* 249b), most frequently in Prov (14x), Isa (9x), Num (8x), Jer and Ezek (7x each). Concentrations lie in the Prophets (29x), wisdom (17x), and the priestly literature (Exod–Num 15x).

3. In both adj. and subst. usages *zār* assumes rather varied meanings (cf. the more detailed investigation by L. A. Snijders, "Meaning of *zār* in the OT," *OTS* 10 [1954]: 1–154); it often appears in proximity to → *nēkār* "foreign land" or *nokrî* "strange, foreign" (cf. P. Humbert, "Les adjectifs *zār* et *nôkrī* et la femme étrangère des Proverbes bibliques," FS Dussaud 1:259–66 = *Opuscules d'un hébraïsant* [1958], 111–18), but should be distinguished from *gēr* "sojourner" (→ *gûr*).

(a) The most common meaning, esp. in the Prophets, is "stranger" in the ethnic or political sense, thus usually "non-Israelite." *zārîm* indicates the foreign peoples with whom Israel had contact, esp. its political enemies: the Assyrians or Egyptians (Hos 7:9; 8:7; Isa 1:7), Judah's immediate neighbors (Lam 5:2), and the Babylonians (Jer 51:51; Ezek 28:7, 10; 30:12; 31:12, etc.). Thus *zār* occurs in proximity to → *ṣar* "enemy"; the stranger is simultaneously the enemy.

Designations for "foreign" gods, i.e., of the deities of foreign nations, belong in this category too (Deut 32:16; Isa 17:10; Jer 2:25; 3:13; Psa 44:21; 81:10; cf. Jer 5:19).

(b) *zār* occurs chiefly in wisdom literature, at first in the rather neutral meaning "belonging to another" (Prov 6:1; 11:15; 14:10; 20:16, etc.), but this expression can also convey overtones of animosity (Job 19:15; cf. v 17; cf. G. R. Driver, *Bib* 35 [1954]: 148f.; contrast *CPT* 256f., 326), illegitimacy (Hos 5:7 "strange children"), etc. The other is the outsider whose behavior endangers the existence of the group because he/she stands outside the laws of the community. The *ʾiššâ zārâ* "strange woman" in Prov 1–9 (2:16; 5:3, 20; 7:5) should be mentioned here, a woman who seems to be less the ethnic stranger or the devotee of an Astarte cult (cf. G. Boström, *Proverbiastudien* [1935]) than the (Israelite) wife of another, a lascivious wife against whom the wise warns students (cf. Humbert, op. cit.; id., *Revue des Etudes Sémitiques* [1937], 49–64; Snijders, op. cit. 88–104; Gemser, HAT 16, 25f.). Thus *zār* "other" can acquire a rather negative meaning ("dangerous, hostile").

(c) Esp. in the post-exilic priestly tradition, *zār* indicates that which is contrary to something holy or to a cultic prescription (Elliger, HAT 4, 137), thus e.g., someone who does not belong to the Aaronide priesthood (Exod 29:33; Lev 22:10, 12f.; Num 3:10, 38; 17:5; 18:4, 7), to the Levites (Num 1:51), or to the cultic community (Exod 30:33). In many cases, then, *zār* virtually means "layman, unauthorized" ("profane" in the cultic sense). The fire (Lev 10:1; Num 3:4; 26:61) or the incense stand (Exod 30:9) can also be termed *zār* "illegitimate, forbidden" in reference to the incense offering, because it does not accord with cultic prescriptions (Snijders, op. cit. 111–23).

d) Finally, the meaning "unusual, unheard-of" in the description of Yahweh's behavior in Isa 28:21 (similarly Prov 23:33 "rare") should be mentioned; only this text uses *zār* predicatively.

4. For the most part, Israel relates very reservedly to that described as *zār*. The foreigner almost always signifies a threat, something that calls existence into question, esp. from the Dtr-P viewpoint. The *zārîm* thus become the "pagans," with whom no covenant can be made (Deut, Ezra, Neh; cf. A. Bertholet, *Die Stellung der Israeliten und der Juden zu den Fremden* [1896]). The *zār* is somehow irreconcilable with Yahweh; cf., nevertheless, the position of Deutero-Isa, Jonah, and Hellenistic Judaism, as well as the attitude toward the *gēr* (→ *gûr*).

5. On *zār* "strange" in early Judaism and in the NT, cf. F. Büchsel, "ἄλλος," *TDNT* 1:264–67; G. Stählin, "ξένος," *TDNT* 5:1–36.

R. Martin-Achard

זְרוֹעַ *zᵉrôaᶜ* arm

S 2220; BDB 283b; *HALOT* 1:280b; *TDOT* 4:131–40; *TWOT* 583a; *NIDOTTE* 2432

---

1. Counterparts to Hebr. *zᵉrôaᶜ* "arm" formed from the same root occur only in the NW and SWSem. languages (*HAL* 269a).

According to P. Fronzaroli (*AANLR* 8/19 [1964]: 259, 279) **ḏirāᶜ* is common Sem., although replaced in ESem. by **yad-* > *idu* "arm," which, in turn, is replaced by *qātu* in the meaning "hand"; in WSem. **ḏirāᶜ* limited **yad-* to the meaning "hand" from the original meaning "hand plus arm" (→ *yād*). Arab. *ḏirāᶜ* is restricted to the meaning "forearm" and has replaced the common Sem. word *ʾ*ammat-* (Hebr. ʾ*ammâ*, Akk. *ammatu*) "cubit, forearm" as a designation for the body part as well as the unit of length.*

On a possible relationship to **ḏrᶜ* "to sow" (Hebr. *zrᶜ*), cf. Fronzaroli, op. cit. 259; *UT* §5.4).

If the Neo-Assyr. *durāʾu* is related to the same root (*CAD* D:190f.; see, however, *AHw* 177b), it is probably a WSem. loanword. The glosses of EA 287:27 and 288:34 attest the Old Can. *zuruḫ*.

Ug. *ḏrᶜ* (*WUS* no. 2723; *UT* no. 733) retains the original *ḏ* instead of the normal *d* (cf. *UT* §5.3).

Bibl. Aram. ʾ*edrāᶜ* (Ezra 4:23; on the vocalization, cf. BLA 215) with a prosthetic *aleph* occurs in addition to *derāᶜ* (Dan 2:32; cf. *DISO* 61). As a result, Hebr. ʾ*ezrôaᶜ* (Jer 32:21; Job 31:22) may also be explained as an Aramaism (*HAL* 28a).

2. Of 93 occurrences in the OT (2x ʾ*ezrôaᶜ*; and 2x in Aram.), 39 appear in the prophetic literature (17 alone in Isa, 13 in Ezek), 14 in Psa, 9 in Deut, 7 in Job, and 6 in Dan.

The pl. is formed 19x with a fem. and 4x with a masc. ending.

3. In the proper sense, *zᵉrôaᶜ* indicates one's "arm," esp. the "forearm" (e.g., Isa 17:5; 44:12; Ezek 4:7). The masc. pl. occasionally means the

"shoulders" (2 Kgs 9:24); in the cultic sphere, the sg. may also mean the shoulder portion of the sacrificial animal (Num 6:19; Deut 18:3).

Like → *yād*, in the fig. sense (Dhorme 140) the word represents the powerful (Job 38:15; cf. 22:8), strong (Jer 48:25), and helpful (Psa 83:9) "power, might" of its owner. Just as *z^erōa^c g^edôlâ* "strong arm" corresponds to a "populous nation" in Ezek 17:9 and Akk. *emūqē* "armed forces" can also alternate with *idā(n)*, in Dan 11:15, 22 *z^erō^côt* indicates an army (*z^erō^cîm* 11:31; sg. 11:6, on the text, cf. Plöger, KAT 18, 155, and P. Wernberg-Møller, *JSS* 3 [1957]: 324f.; cf. also Ezek 22:6, where many exegetes, e.g., A. M. Honeyman, *VT* 1 [1951]: 222, nevertheless prefer the reading *zar^cô* "his seed").

z^erō^cōt ^côlām "everlasting arms" parallels the "ancient gods(?)" in the hymn in Deut 33:27; cf. I. L. Seeligmann, *VT* 14 (1964): 78, 87f.

Both → *yād* "hand" and *yāmîn* "right hand" often parallel *z^erôa^c*, and terms like → *kōaḥ* "might" and *g^ebûrâ* "strength" (→ *gbr*) are fig. pars.

4. Corresponding to the profane usage, various literary genres employ *z^erôa^c* anthropomorphically to describe the strong (predominantly in the hymns: Psa 89:14; 98:1; Exod 15:16; in vows to praise, Psa 71:19), helpful (Psa 44:4; 77:16; 79:11; 89:22; Isa 33:2; 40:11; Hos 11:3), and punitive (Isa 30:30) might of God (P. Biard, *La puissance de Dieu* [1960]). The benevolent aspect is often emphasized through the stereotypical expression "with strong hand and outstretched arm." This usage, however, is limited to Deut (4:34; 5:15; 7:19; 11:2; 26:8) and literature influenced by Deut (Isa 32:21; Psa 136:12), and always refers to the divine act of redemption in the exodus from Egypt (without explicit reference in Solomon's prayer dedicating the temple, 1 Kgs 8:42 = 2 Chron 6:32). It is related to the new exodus from the Diaspora in Ezek 20:33f. The notion of judgment upon Israel, which is also involved in this text, is absent from Deutero-Isa, where God's saving might is esp. accentuated and eschatologically interpreted by the expression "arm of Yahweh" (Isa 51:5, 9; 52:10; 53:1; cf. H. L. Ginsberg, "The Arm of YHWH in Isaiah 51–63 and the Text of Isaiah 53:10–11," *JBL* 77 [1958]: 152–56). In Trito-Isa Yahweh's arm even appears as a type of hypostasis (in reference to the exodus from Egypt in Isa 63:12; more generally, 59:16; 63:5; cf. also 62:8, which discusses Yahweh's oath by his arm; cf. G. Pfeifer, *Ursprung und Wesen der Hypostasenvorstellungen im Judentum* [1967], 17). The expression "with great strength and outstretched arm" in Deut 9:29 and 2 Kgs 17:36 (Dtr) refers to the exodus from Egypt, but in Jer 27:5 and 32:17 it indicates God's creation (portrayed as a battle).

The OT contains little or no celebration of human arms (Gen 49:24, but in the context of the "strength of Jacob"). Rather, the "arm of flesh" as a description of feeble human strength is contrasted with God's might (2 Chron 32:8; cf. Jer 17:5; Psa 44:4), which breaks (Ezek 30:21f., 24b; cf. Psa 10:15) and cuts off (1 Sam 2:31; Mal 2:3 txt em) human arms, but which can also strengthen them (Ezek 30:24a, 25).

5. The NT discusses God's arm only in the sense of its saving demonstrations of power; cf. H. Schlier, "βραχίων," *TDNT* 1:639f.

A. S. van der Woude

חָדָשׁ *ḥādāš* new

S 2319; BDB 294a; *HALOT* 1:294a; *TDOT* 4:225–44; *TWOT* 613a; *NIDOTTE* 2543

1. The root **ḥdṯ* occurs in all Sem. languages with the same meaning (Berg., *Intro.* 220).

Hebr. has *ḥdš* pi. "to renew," hitp. "to renew oneself," and the noms. *ḥādāš* "new" (in the place-names *ḥ^a^dāšâ* Josh 15:37; and Aram. *ḥāṣôr ḥ^a^dattâ* Josh 15:25; cf. Wagner no. 88) and *ḥōdeš* "new moon, month" (on the fem. PN *ḥōdeš* in 1 Chron 8:9, see J. J. Stamm, FS Baumgartner 322).

Hebr. *ḥādāš* corresponds to Akk. *eššu* (cf. *eddēšû* "being ever renewed"), Ug. *ḥdṯ* (*WUS* no. 908; *UT* no. 843), Phoen.-Pun. *ḥdš* (in the name of the city Carthage, *qrtḥdšt* = "new city"), and Aram. *ḥ^a^dat* (*DISO* 83; KBL 1074a), which occurs once in Ezra 6:4 as a textual error.

The place-name *ḥodšî* in 2 Sam 24:6 should be disregarded in favor of an emendation.

2. *ḥdš* pi. occurs 9x, hitp. 1x (Psa 103:5), *ḥādāš* 53x (Isa 40–66 10x, Psa 6x, Ezek 5x), and *ḥōdeš* 283x (Num 38x, Ezek 27x, Esth 24x).

ḥādāš appears 20x in narrative texts (also Deut 32:17 and Judg 5:8 txt?), 19x in prophetic texts, 6x in Psa, 2x in Job and Eccl, 1x in Song Sol and Lam.

3. (a) Like *ḥādāš* "new," the verb *ḥdš* pi. "to renew" has no genuine synonyms and is usually contrasted to "old, former": the temple (2 Chron 24:4, 12, par. *ḥzq* pi. "to renovate"), an altar (2 Chron 15:8), and cities (Isa 61:4, par. *bnh* "to rebuild") are renewed, i.e., reestablished; the monarchy is renewed (1 Sam 11:14). God is called upon once again to maintain the former good fortune or salvation (Lam 5:21 "renew our days as of old"), to renew life (Psa 51:12, beside *br᾿* "to create"; cf. L. Kopf, *VT* 9 [1959]: 254f.); he is praised because he renews the face of the earth (Psa 104:30, beside *br᾿*) and sees to it that youthfulness is renewed (Psa 103:5 hitp.). Only Job 10:17 ("to renew witnesses" = "repeatedly to produce new witnesses") contrasts "new" with "already at hand."

(b) The everday usage of *ḥādāš* "new" occurs primarily in the narrative texts, both in contrast to "old" and in the meaning "not yet existent." In the realm of production there is mention of new grain (Lev 26:10, in contrast to *yāšān* "old, last year's"), of the offering of firstfruits (Lev 23:16; Num 28:26), of new (fresh) fruits (Song Sol 7:14, in contrast to *yāšān*); in the realm of craftsmanship of new houses (Deut 20:5; 22:8), new wineskins (Josh 9:13; cf. *bāleh* "old, used" in vv 4f.; Job 32:19), new ropes (Job 15:13; 16:11f.), new wagons (1 Sam 6:7 = 1 Chron 13:7; 2 Sam 6:3[bis]), a new sword (2 Sam 21:16), a new coat (1 Kgs 11:29f.), a new vessel (2 Kgs 2:20), and the new forecourt (2 Chron 20:5). Prophetic texts mention a new threshing sled (Isa 41:15) and the new temple gate (Jer 26:10; 36:10; cf. the "old gate" in Neh 3:6; 12:39). With respect to persons, *ḥādāš* decribes the newly married woman (Deut 24:5; on Akk. and Ug. pars. see *HAL* 282b), the new king over Egypt (Exod 1:8), and new gods, i.e., those which Israel has only come to know in Canaan (Deut 32:17 "newcomers, who have only recently appeared").

The adjs. *ṭārî* "fresh, moist" (Judg 15:15, bones; Isa 1:6, wounds) and *laḥ* "still moist, fresh" (Gen 30:37; Num 6:3; Judg 16:7f.; Ezek 17:24; 21:3; subst. *lēaḥ* "fresh ones" in Deut 34:7; on the root *lḥḥ* cf. A. van Selms, FS Vriezen 318–26) are somewhat related to *ḥādāš* in meaning.

Reviewing these texts, one notices that the term occurs with extraordinary rarity. It has only one large category of usage: the discussion of the newly crafted. If one compares the frequency of occurrence of the term "new" in modern European languages, as well as in Gk. and Lat., the limited usage in the OT is all the more remarkable. The same conclusion is also indicated by the slight number of derivatives from the root. One may compare in Eng.: renew, renovation, newness, novelty, news, newcomer, newly, New Year, etc. Ancient Israelites apparently perceived relationships between occurrences so strongly that they did not consider "new" what moderns would, or at least they did not describe them as "new." This question deserves further investigation. It is certain, at any rate, that the experience of the new is limited for the Israelite to very few areas of experience; the Israelite only rarely speaks of the new.

4. (a) *ḥādāš* occurs in prophetic texts only during the exile or very near to it (Deutero-Isa 5x, Trito-Isa 5x in three passages, Jer 4x, Ezek 5x in three passages; the date of Jer 31:22, 31 is disputed; cf. e.g., Sellin-Fohrer 396 with bibliog.). This fact is significant in itself: only the exilic period—no other period in the whole history of Israel!—discussed an innovation in the history of God's relationship with Israel. This circumstance becomes even more suggestive when one examines the passages more closely: Apart from those passages that belong to everyday usage (Isa 41:14; Jer 26:10; 36:10), exilic or immediately post-exilic prophets speak of a novelty in three contexts: (1) Isa 42:9f.; 43:19; 48:6 (Deutero-Isa): the former and the new; (2) Jer 31:31 and Ezek 11:19; 18:31; 36:26 (cf. Jer 31:22): new covenant and new heart; (3) Isa 65:17; 66:22 (Trito-Isa; cf. 62:2): new heaven and new earth.

(1) The group of texts in Deutero-Isa is the most significant theologically because this series of texts consciously and reflectively contrasts the new with the former; here "the new" becomes an explicit theme of theological reflection (cf. also, without the contrast, Jer 31:22 "for Yahweh creates a novelty in the land"; Isa 62:2 "you will be called by a new name"). Of four passages, three (42:9; 43:19; 48:6) belong in the context of salvation preaching, the fourth (42:10) is a response of praise: the new song corresponds to the new act of God.

The newly announced innovation is contrasted with the former that has already appeared (*rīšōnôt*, Isa 42:9; 43:18), a reference both to God's prior saving activity (esp. in 43:18) and to the announcement of judgment (42:9). It must be said of the innovation now announced: "From now on I will let you hear something new that you did not know" (48:6).

This is not clear solely from the three passages in which the term "new" occurs. Rather, in order to understand the intention of these passages, one must also consider the condemnation speeches that refer to this innovation as the "future" (*habbāʾôt*, → *bôʾ*; 41:21–29, esp. v 22: "the former . . . the future"; cf. 46:9–13), in addition to Deutero-Isaiah's salvation preaching as a whole, which makes it clear why the announced saving act of God is really an innovation. The entirety of Israel's prior history is seen as "the former" in comparison to this innovation. The "new" consists in the fact that the deliverance from exile now proclaimed will no longer be carried out by Israel's armies and by an Israelite leader inspired by Yahweh, but by the Pers. king Cyrus (44:24–45:7), thus dissociating Israel's deliverance from Israel's might, and that this deliverance is based upon forgiveness (43:22–28), so that the nations too can be invited to this new salvation of Yahweh (45:20–25). It may be emphasized once again that this explanation of the "innovation" in the three passages (42:9; 43:19; 48:6) is possible only on the basis of the total proclamation of Deutero-Isa. Only in this manner does it become clear that here, for the first time in the entire history of salvation preaching, a "new" thing is proclaimed.

(2) The saying concerning the new covenant in Jer 31:31–34 contrasts this covenant with the former things, as does the group of "new" passages in Deutero-Isa: "Not like the covenant that I made with your fathers." As in Deutero-Isa, this new covenant in Jer is based on forgiveness (v 34b). That this new covenant concerns the behavior of an individual (v 33) is distinctive and unique to Jer 31:31–34. The Ezek passages that speak of the "new" make the same statement (11:19; 18:31; 36:26). They discuss the new heart and the new spirit that God creates for people and that he will place within them (Psa 51:12 could be influenced by this discussion).

The Jer saying (cf. also Jer 31:22) and the three Ezek sayings are close to one another topically and temporally; Jer 31:31–34 also belongs in the exilic period. These passages are distinct from the Deutero-Isa passages primarily in that they shift the emphasis to individual behavior, while for Deutero-Isa the "new" is to be experienced.

(3) The promise of a new heaven and a new earth in Isa 65:17 (echoed in a later addition, 66:22) deals with an expansion of Deutero-Isa's promise of an innovation into a cosmic promise. Although one cannot say whether Jer 31:31 and Ezek 11:19; 18:31; 36:26 are influenced by Deutero-Isa, this influence is certain for Isa 65:17. This text assumes that Yahweh will bring about an act of deliverance for Israel that will be new in comparison to the totality of prior history. Already in Deutero-Isa this promise to creation had influenced the description of the return from exile, for which the desert is transformed into a garden; nevertheless, the promise of salvation in Deutero-Isa remains within the bounds of historical phenomena. Isa 66:22, a promise of the creation of a new heaven and a new earth, completes the transition to apocalyptic speech that transcends history. Whether 65:17 is already so intended is uncertain; if it should be translated: "I create anew the heavens and the earth" (Westermann, *Isa 40–66*, OTL, 408), then it refers only to a wondrous renewal of everything that does not necessarily include a prior annihilation. As 66:22 demonstrates, however, the phrase was later understood apocalyptically; for the first time here the new thing that God creates no longer stands in historical continuity with the current reality, but transcends it.

(b) In the Psa, *ḥādāš* occurs only in a single context: the discussion of the "new song." The impv. demand "sing to Yahweh a new song!" is issued in Psa 33:3; 96:1; 98:1; 149:1, the same call in the cohortative in 144:9, and, also in the 1st per. but transposed into narrative praise, in 40:4 "Put a new song in my mouth, praise our God."

Because the impv. demand in Isa 42:10 calls to praise in response to Yahweh's new act of deliverance using the same diction as these Psa texts, and Psa 96 and 98 also demonstrate the influence of Deutero-Isa in other ways (Kraus, *Psa*, CC, 2:251f., 263f.; Westermann, *PLP* 138–42), it is possible that the "singing of the new song" in this whole group of texts derives from Deutero-Isa. But even if one cannot prove dependence upon Deutero-Isa, the "new song" is in any case meant as it is in Isa 42:10, i.e., as a response to Yahweh's new act.

The song called for here is not "new" because a new text is to replace the old, or a new melody the old; this notion is thoroughly foreign to these psalms. The song is "new" because God has brought about something new, and the song is to respond to this new act of God; this new act of God is to resound in the new song.

(c) A few passages in the third portion of the canon remain to be treated. Lam 3:23, "His mercy is new every morning," uniquely describes the persistence of God's mercy in analogy to the new harvest or the new garment. This idiom accords with modern thought; hence it is not accidental that this very phrase became the inspiration for a hymn: "Great is thy faithfulness, morning by morning new mercies I see." (A well-known Eng. hymn has been substituted for the Ger. here; they parallel rather closely.) But this phraseology is not typical for the OT; it occurs only in this one passage. "New" also refers to people in the sense of "not exhausted": Job 29:20, "My honor remains new with me."

Taking all occurrences of the term into account, one can understand Qohelet's skeptical wisdom at the close of the OT period: "There is nothing new under the sun" (Eccl 1:9f.). Yet this phrase seems already to assume a higher assessment of the new in daily experience itself than is otherwise attributed to it in the OT.

5. In conclusion, one can identify a precise use of the word "new" in the OT that, in the concentration of prophetic passages, points to one moment in history and, in the response to this novelty in the "new song" of the Psa, to a particular act of God in Israel's history: the innovation proclaimed after the political collapse of Israel/Judah, the end of the monarchy, and the destruction of the temple in Jerusalem. The OT no longer unequivocally treats this innovation based on God's forgiveness, the dissociation of Israel's deliverance from Israel's might, and the prospect of a call to salvation for the nations as an already present historical reality (it never reports the new covenant, the new salvation, or the new form of the people of God); thus the NT discussion of the innovation that has appeared in Christ is thoroughly consistent with OT usage.

On the NT, cf. J. Behm, "καινός," *TDNT* 3:447–54; id., "νέος," *TDNT* 4:896–901.

C. Westermann

חוה *ḥwh* hišt. **to bow down**

HALOT 1:295b; *TDOT* 4:248–56; *TWOT* 619; *NIDOTTE* 2556

1. Although *hištaḥ*ᵃ*wāh* has been traditionally understood as a hitpaᶜlel of the root *šḥh* (as a by-form of *šûaḥ* and *šḥḥ;* cf. e.g., GKC §75kk; BL 420; Joüon §79t; KBL 959), derivation from the root *ḥwh* is now established by the Ug. root *ḥwy,* and the form is explained as a *t*-reflexive of the old *šap*ᶜ*el* (*WUS* no. 912; *UT* 83 and no. 847; Moscati, *Intro.* 128; *HAL* 283b with bibliog.; Meyer 2:126, 162f.). In addition to Hebr. and Ug., the root is attested in Arab.: *ḥawā* "to gather, collect, unite," V "to curl (up), coil (up)" (Wehr 219).

One should distinguish *ḥwh* I pi. "to announce" (Aram. loanword in Hebr.; cf. Wagner nos. 91f.; J. A. Soggin, *AION* 17 [1967]: 9–14) from *ḥwh* II.

2. The 170 occurrences of *ḥwh* hišt. are esp. well represented in the narrative books (Gen 23x, Psa 17x, 2 Sam and Isa 13x, 1 Sam and 2 Kgs 12x, Exod, 1 Kgs, and 2 Chron 11x, Deut and Jer 8x, Judg and Ezek 4x, Josh, Zeph, Esth, Neh, and 1 Chron 3x, Num and Zech 2x, Lev, Mic, Job, and Ruth 1x; Lis., 1421b overlooks Zech 14:17).

3. The evidence suggests the meaning "to bow (deeply)" for *ḥwh* hišt. (cf. Ug., Arab.). The Aram. portions of Dan use the synonymous *sgd* (Dan 2:46; 3:5–28 11x), which also appears in Isa 44:15, 17, 19; 46:6 alongside *ḥwh* hišt. (Aram. *sgd* is a loanword in Hebr., Arab., and Eth.; cf. Wagner no. 195).

ḥwh hišt. can be combined with ᵓ*arṣâ* "to the ground" (Gen 18:2; 24:52; etc.; ᵓ*ereṣ* Isa 49:23) or ᵓ*appayim* ᵓ*arṣâ* "with the face to the ground" (Gen 19:1; 42:6, etc.; with *l*ᵉ Gen 48:12; with ᶜ*al* 2 Sam 14:33), with the resulting meaning "to bow down to the ground, fall prostrate" or "to bow with one's face to the ground, fall on one's face" (before someone or something: with *l*ᵉ of the person or the thing, rarely ᶜ*al,* Lev 26:1, or ᵓ*el,* Psa 5:8).

The verbs *qdd* (only in conjunction with *ḥwh* hišt. as an act preparatory to the latter) "to bow (in homage), kneel down" (Gen 24:26; Exod 34:8; 1 Sam 24:9, etc.; cf. KBL 821b), *npl* "to fall down" (2 Sam 1:2; 9:6, 8, etc.), and *kr*ᶜ "to kneel down, genuflect" (Esth 3:2, 5; in Psa 95:6 with *brk* qal "to kneel down") also occur in the semantic field of *ḥwh* hišt.; other related verbs are *kpp* qal "to bend," ni. "to bow" (Isa 58:5; Psa 57:7; 145:14; 146:8; ni. Mic 6:6), *šḥḥ* qal/ni., "to stoop" (Isa 2:9, 11, 17, etc.; hi. "to stoop to someone" Isa 25:12; 26:5), and *šḥh* qal "to bow one's head" (Isa 51:23; hi. "to bow down" Prov 12:25); also likely, *hbr* qal in Isa 47:13 (cf. J. Blau, *VT* 7 [1957]: 183f.; E. Ullendorff, *JSS* 7 [1962]: 339f.; *HAL* 227b).

According to W. von Soden, forms such as *uš*ḫ*e*ḫ*in,* which occur in the Akk. of the Amarna Letters and the Ug. texts and which are associated with Hebr. *šḥḥ*/*šḥh* (KBL 959f.), derive via Hurrite from Akk. *šukênu* "to fall prostrate" (*GAG* §109m).

The same stereotypical expression is almost always encountered in Ug.: *lp*ᶜ*n il thbr wtql tšt*ḥ*wy wtkbdnh* "she (Anat) bowed down at El's feet and fell prostrate, did homage and honored him" (*KTU* 1.6.I.35–38, etc.; cf. J. Aistleitner, *Die mythologischen und kultischen Texte aus Ras Schamra* [1959], 18).

The gesture indicated by *ḥwh* hišt. approximates the Islamic *sujūd* described by E. W. Lane: "He next drops gently upon his knees . . . places his hands upon the ground, a little before his knees, and puts his nose and forehead also to the ground (the former first) between his two hands" (as cited by D. R. Ap-Thomas, *VT* 6 [1956]: 229; cf. the illustrations in *ANEP* no. 355, as well as nos. 45f.). On the bowing down "from afar" in Exod 24:1, cf. S. E. Loewenstamm, "Prostration from Afar in Ugaritic, Accadian and Hebrew," *BASOR* 188 (1967): 41–43.

One falls down before a superior and to express extreme honor and homage, e.g., before strange guests (Gen 18:12), as a supplicant before the powerful (Gen 33:7; 2 Sam 16:4), Moses before Jethro (Exod 18:7, with *nšq* "to kiss"), Abigail before David (1 Sam 25:23, 41), before the priest (1 Sam 2:36), the prophet (2 Kgs 2:15; 4:37), the king (2 Sam 14:4, 33; 24:20; 1 Kgs 1:16, 23; 2 Chron 24:17; Psa 45:12, etc.), and figuratively, nations or kings before Israel (Gen 27:29; Isa 45:14; 49:23; 60:14).

4. Similarly, in the cultic realm *ḥwh* hišt. also describes homage and worship (proskynesis) before stars (Deut 4:19; Jer 8:2), before the holy mountain (Psa 99:9), in the temple (2 Kgs 5:18), before the angel of Yahweh (Num 22:31), before Yahweh (Gen 24:26, 48, 52, etc.), before strange gods (see below; among other things, the verb *ᶜbd* "to serve," which often accompanies *ḥwh* indicating the close association of cultic act and proskynesis). *ḥwh* hišt. here describes the attitude of prayer frequently assumed (with a following *pll* hitp. "to pray," Isa 44:17; 1 Sam 1:28; the prayer is mentioned in Gen 24:26, 48; Exod 34:8; on other prayer gestures, cf. *BHH* 1:521; de Vaux 2:458f.) or the prayer itself (a verbum proprium for "to pray" beside *ḥwh* hišt. occurs rarely; see J. Herrmann, *TDNT* 2:789). Yet *ḥwh* hišt. does not merely describe the external gesture of "bowing down," but "very quickly came to be used for the inward religious attitude" (Herrmann, ibid.) and can itself, therefore, often be rendered by "to pray, plead."

One should not view *ḥwh* hišt. as a specifically Yahwistic term. Indeed, a great number of occurrences are in texts that denounce Israel's apostasy and the cults of the foreign gods and idols (cf. Isa 2:8, 20; Jer 1:16; 8:2). In the Dtn-Dtr literature, *ḥwh* hišt., together with *ᶜbd* "to bow down and serve," becomes a fixed expression, otherwise unattested, which describes the worship of strange gods (according to Zimmerli, "Das zweite Gebot," FS Bertholet 553 = Zimmerli, *GO* 237, a total of 27 passages; cf., among others, Deut 4:19; 5:9 = Exod 20:5; Deut 8:19; 11:16; Judg 2:19; 2 Kgs 17:16; 2 Chron 7:19, 22; Jer 13:10; see also N. Lohfink, *Das Hauptgebot* [1963], 74f., 99f., 178). Only Deut 26:10 (without *ᶜbd*!) offers *ḥwh* hišt. in a positive sense as prostration before Yahweh, and it belongs to an older, adapted cultic tradition (cf. von Rad, *Deut*, OTL, 157f.). The Psalms differ (with the exception of Psa 81:10; 106:19); they exhibit *ḥwh* hišt. as the act of homage paid to Yahweh, the God(-king) enthroned on Zion, and go back to old Jerusalemite (originally Can.) cult tradition (Psa 22:28; 29:2; 86:9; 95:6; 96:9; cf. 1 Chron 16:29; Psa 97:7; 99:5, 9; 132:7; cf. also Zech 14:16f.; Isa 27:13).

5. The LXX almost always renders the root with *proskynein.* On the NT, cf. J. Herrmann and H. Greeven, "εὔχομαι," *TDNT* 2:775–808; H. Greeven, "προσκυνέω," *TDNT* 6:758–66.

H.-P. Stähli

חזה *ḥzh* to see

S 2372; BDB 302a; *HALOT* 1:301a; *TDOT* 4:280–90; *TWOT* 633; *NIDOTTE* 2600

---

1. Hebr. *ḥzh* "to see" is apparently a loanword from Old Aram. (Wagner nos. 93–98; otherwise e.g., Ginsberg and Dahood, see below), where *ḥzh* is the usual word for "to see" (Hebr. → *r'h;* KBL 1074b, suppl. 201a; *DISO* 84f.; > Arab. *ḥāzin* "seer"; cf. Ug. *ḥdy, CML*[1] 138n.18; *CML*[2] 146).

Cf. also Phoen. *ḥzh* "to see" in the 9th-cent. Kilamuwa inscription, *KAI* no. 24.11f., and in Lidzbarski, *KI* no. 38 from the 4th cent. (*DISO* 84f.).

On Old Aram. *ḥzh* pa., cf. Fitzmyer, *Sef.* 40; R. Degen, *Altaram. Grammatik* (1969), 78.

H. L. Ginsberg (FS Baumgartner 71f.) associates Hebr.-Phoen.-Aram. **ḥzw* "to see" with Arab. *ḥḏw* "to be facing"; cf., however, the rejection of the verb *hdh* II "to see" postulated by M. Dahood (*Bib* 45 [1964]: 407f.; *HAL* 280 too) on the basis of the equation of Ug. *ḥdy* with *ḥzh* (contra *WUS* no. 905; tentatively *UT* no. 839).

ḥzh occurs in Hebr. and Bibl. Aram. only in the qal and pe., resp.; derived noms. are *ḥōzeh* I "seer," *ḥōzeh* II "covenant" (see 3b and → *b*ᵉ*rît* I/2d), *meḥ*ᵉ*zâ* "window," and the numerous expressions for "seeing," incl.: *ḥāzôn, ḥāzût, ḥ*ᵃ*zôt, ḥizzāyôn, maḥ*ᵃ*zeh,* Aram. *ḥ*ᵉ*zû/ḥezwā'* and *ḥ*ᵃ*zôt* (BL 185). PNs formed from *ḥzh,* e.g., *ḥ*ᵃ*zā'ēl, yaḥ*ᵃ*zî'ēl,* etc. (*HAL* 289a; see 4c) are also numerous.

2. *ḥzh* and its derivatives are attested 175x in the OT (Hebr. 130x, Aram. 45x, excl. proper names); specifically, the verb occurs in Hebr. 55x (Isa 12x, Ezek, Psa, and Job 9x each, Prov 3x, Exod, Num, Mic, Song Sol, and Lam 2x each, Amos, Hab, and Zech 1x each), in Aram. 31x (Dan 30x, 1x the pass. ptcp. *ḥ*ᵃ*zēh* in the meaning "appropriate, customary"; Ezra 1x), the substs. *ḥōzeh* 17x (2 Chron 7x, Isa [incl. 28:15] and 1 Chron 3x each, 2 Sam, 2 Kgs, Amos, and Mic 1x each), *ḥāzôn* 35x (Dan 12x, Ezek 7x, Isa, Jer, and Hab 2x each), *ḥ*ᵃ*zôt* 1x (2 Chron 9:29), *ḥāzût* 5x (Isa 3x, Dan 2x), *ḥizzāyôn* 9x (Job 4x, Isa 2x, 2 Sam, Joel, and Zech 1x each), *maḥ*ᵃ*zeh* 4x (Num 2x, Gen and Ezek 1x each), *meḥ*ᵉ*zâ* 4x (1 Kgs 7:4f.), Aram. *ḥ*ᵉ*zû/ḥezwā'* 12x, and *ḥ*ᵃ*zôt* 2x in Dan. Forms of the root are concentrated, then, primarily in Dan (58 = 1/3 of the total), Isa and Ezek (22 and 17x, resp., 17x in the other prophets together), and Job (13x).

3. (a) The meaning "to see (in a vision)" is the basis of 23 Hebr. verb forms (see 4a); 32 verbs in the meaning "to see" (incl. even Exod 18:21 and Mic 4:11) are dispersed in later literary traditions (Psa, Job, Prov, Song Sol, post-exilic passages in Isa). Of 32 passages, about 21 fall to a theological usage (see 4b-d) and 11 to a profane usage (see 3b). With the exception of the substs. treated

in 3b, all derived substs. may be accounted for by the meaning "to look." About 3/4 of all occurrences of the root, then, develop this meaning (cf. A. Jepsen, *Nabi* [1934]: 43ff.). In a modification of this chief meaning, *ḥzh* is used when Israel or an individual "sees" Yahweh and his activity in history and creation (16x; see 4b), less often, when Yahweh "sees" (see 4c). The verb appears as a "poetic synonym" (GB 220b) for → *rʾh* "to see" only in its final phase of development.

(b) Profane diction distinguishes between "to see" (on Job 8:17, cf. *BH*[3]; Horst, BK 16/1, 125f., 134) in the sense of "to experience" (Psa 58:9; cf. Eccl 7:1), "to look upon with joy" (Song Sol 7:1[bis]; cf. Prov 23:31) or with connotations of malicious glee (Mic 4:11; cf. Obad 12f.; BrSynt 96), "to perceive (with understanding)" (Prov 22:29; 29:20; cf. 1 Sam 25:17), "to experience, acquire for oneself" (Job 15:17; 27:12; Prov 24:32; cf. Eccl 1:16), and "to observe, watch carefully" (Isa 47:13; cf. Exod 1:16).

The profane substs. *meḥᵉzâ* "window" (1 Kgs 7:4f.), *ḥōzeh* and *ḥāzût* = *bᵉrît* (Isa 28:15, 18; cf. bibliog. in A. R. Johnson, *Cultic Prophet in Ancient Israel* [1962²], 13f.n.3; → *bᵉrît* I/2d: "to perceive" > "to prescribe"), and *ḥāzût* "appearance" also belong to the meaning "to see."

(c) The Aram. root seems to exhibit a similar semantic development. The primary usage in the context of visions gives rise to the common use of *ḥzh* in the sense of "to look (on with)" (Ezra 4:14; Dan 3:25, 27; 5:5, 23), "to examine, experience" (Dan 2:8), and "to be appropriate" (pass. ptcp. Dan 3:19), and of *ḥᵉzû*/*ḥezwāʾ* in the meaning "figure" (Dan 7:20). In contrast, *ḥᵃzôt* "sight" is used only in a profane sense (Dan 4:8, 17).

4. (a) *ḥzh* and its derivatives indicate, first of all, visionary experience. Num 24:4, 16 transmit an ancient example of this usage (W. F. Albright, "Oracles of Balaam," *JBL* 63 [1944]: 207–33). *ḥzh* and *maḥᵃzeh* occur in every instance of this usage in the introduction to a visionary oracle containing the self-introductory and legitimation formula, *nᵉʾūm bilʿām.* Balaam sees visions from God and renders them in his own words. As the history of the gen. construction → *neʾūm* with a human PN indicates, the prophets used visionary genres. Nonetheless, they never use *ḥzh* to report a vision, but → *rʾh* directly introduces (as in the seer's oracle in Num 23:9, 21; 24:17) the prophetic vision report (e.g., Amos 7:1, 4, 7; Isa 6:1; Jer 4:23ff.; Ezek 1:4; 2:9). *ḥzh* refers generally to the reception of revelation (cf. Wildberger, *Isa 1–12*, CC, 5f.; Wolff, *Amos*, Herm, 124). It occurs in the foundation of the announcement of judgment that Israel cites (Isa 30:10[bis]; Ezek 12:27), in the condemnation of false prophets who cause Yahweh to act through "deceptive visions" (Ezek 13:6–9, 16 [citing the people], 23; 21:34; 22:28; Zech 10:2), and in the archaic tradition in Exod 24:9–11 (v 11b), which relates the finalization of the covenant in the form of a third-party vision narrative.

The equation of seer and prophet (Amos 7:12, 14; Mic 3:7; cf. v 5; Isa 29:10; 2 Kgs 17:13; cf. 2 Chron 9:29; 12:15 with 13:22; cf. S. Mowinckel, *Psalmenstudien* [1923], 3:9ff.; H. Junker, *Prophet und Seher in Israel* [1927], 77ff.; esp. Jepsen, *Nabi* [1934], 43ff.; R. Hentschke, *Die Stellung der vorexilischen Schriftpropheten zum Kultus* [1957], 150; S. Lehming, *ZTK* 55 [1958]: 163n.3; A.

Gunneweg, *ZTK* 57 [1960]: 6) mirrors a historical process (1 Sam 9:9; cf. O. Plöger, *ZAW* 63 [1951]: 157–92; J. Lindblom, *Prophecy in Ancient Israel* [1962], 87ff.). The prophets applied the old designations of the seers to themselves, as well as their specific forms of experience and expression. The term *ḥōzeh* in specialized usage signifies a charismatic office (perhaps the "seer") for which not every *nābîʾ* was qualified (Amos 7:12, 14 [cf. Wolff, *Amos*, Herm, 312f.]; Isa 28:7; 30:10: *rōʾîm* and *ḥōzîm* are par.; cf. Wildberger, *Isa 1–12*, CC, 5f.).

The uses of *ḥzh* and *rʾh* are explained in terms of the contrast of "true" and "false" prophets (F. E. König, *Der Offenbarungsbegriff des AT* [1882], 2:29ff., 72f.; contra J. Hänel, *Das Erkennen Gottes bei den Schriftpropheten* [1923], 7ff.) or in terms of varied functions of the *nᵉbîʾîm* and the writing prophets (Jepsen, op. cit. 53ff.; contra Johnson, op. cit. 12n.2), or they are regarded as synonymous (Lindblom, op. cit. 90). The usage of the verb and its derivatives almost contradicts the depiction of *ḥzh* as probably a reference to auditions rather than to visions (cf. Johnson, op. cit. 11ff.; similarly Jepsen, op. cit. 48f.). Thus Balaam's self-introduction mentions *ḥzh* and *maḥᵃzeh* (Num 24:4, 16 testifies to the origins of both in the visionary oracle) together with the "hearing of divine words"; consequently, forms of the root were related from the earliest period onward to experiences that incorporated vision and audition. In Dan 8–11 1st-per. accounts preserve the meaning of *ḥāzôn* as a vision (frequently associated with *rʾh* qal/ni.); it may also be present in Isa 29:7; Ezek 7:26; 12:22–24, 27; 13:16 (contra Johnson, op. cit. 7, 14, 37f.). All other passages give evidence of the subst. as a synonymous expression for → *dābār* "word" (e.g., 1 Sam 3:1; Hos 12:11; Mic 3:6f.; Psa 89:20). The early usage of the root in Num 24:4, 16 already demonstrates a line of development further strengthened in the prophetic tradition; cf. the combination of *ḥzh* qal with *ḥāzôn* (Johnson, op. cit. 14n.1: "to make an observation" Isa 1:1; Ezek 12:27; 13:16), with *dābār* (Isa 2:1; Amos 1:1; Mic 1:1), *maśśāʾ* (→ *nśʾ*; Isa 13:1; Hab 1:1; Lam 2:14bis). It is equally possible that *ḥāzût* (Isa 29:11 and sg. *ḥᵃzôt* 2 Chron 9:29) = *dābār*; but Isa 21:2 likely refers to a vision. *ḥizzāyôn* (Joel 3:1; Job 7:14; 20:8; 33:15; cf. Job 4:13; in a place-name in Isa 22:1, 5) emphasizes the proximity of dream and visionary experiences (in addition to *ḥāzôn*, Isa 29:7; Dan 1:17; cf. 1 Sam 3:1; Mic 3:6); it occurs in the sense of *dābār* in 2 Sam 7:17.

(b) "To see" Yahweh or his act means: to experience God's intervention either in the history of the people or of the nations (Zion hymn, Psa 46:9; salvation oracle for the eschaton, Isa 33:17, 20; in the Isa apocalypse, Isa 26:11[bis]; on Isa 48:6, see Westermann, *Isa 40–66*, OTL, 194) or in individual existence (all occurrences appear in the context of the individual lament: in Psa 17:15 it modifies, in 58:11 it replaces, a vow of praise; cf. *PLP* 74f.nn.23f.; in Job 23:9 it follows God's accusation as a prayer; 24:1 is an indirect accusation of God; cf. C. Westermann, *Structure of the Book of Job* [1981], 57f.; Job 19:26f. is a confession of confidence, ibid. 102f.; Psa 11:7; 27:4; 63:3 are portions of individual psalms of confidence). *ḥzh* occurs once in the descriptive praise of the creator (Job 36:25, alongside *nbṭ* hi. "to look").

(c) Conversely, "God sees" means: God intervenes on someone's behalf, thus in Psa 17:2 (introductory request of an individual lament) and Psa 11:4 (psalm of confidence).

PNs formed with *ḥzh* also mirror the doubled usage of "to see." In this regard, they correspond either to the request for God's attention in the psalm of lament ("May God/Yahweh see") or to narrative praise ("Yahweh has seen"); cf. *IP* 186, 198.

(d) Finally, a few varied meanings may be mentioned: *ḥzh* "to see" = "to gain insight" (Job 34:32, a confession of sin), "to feast one's eyes" (Isa 57:8, the justification for an announcement of judgment; contra G. R. Driver, FS Eilers 54), "to recognize" = "to choose for an office" (Exod 18:21).

(e) The Aram. verb is used in connection with visions like *ḥzh* (e.g., Dan 2:26) and *r*ʾ*h* (e.g., 4:7, 10). The derivative *ḥezwā*ʾ (emphatic st.) occurs only in a dream context (e.g., 2:28) and resembles in this respect Hebr. *ḥāzôn* and *ḥizzāyôn*.

5. On the rendering of the Hebr. and Aram. terms in the LXX, cf. W. Michaelis, *TDNT* 5:324–28.

The various meanings of *ḥzh* and its derivatives are echoed in the NT: *blepō* (e.g., Acts 1:11), *eidon* (e.g., Acts 9:12; Rev 1:2), *horama* (e.g., Acts 9:10, 12), and *horasis* (e.g., Acts 2:17; Rev 9:17) refer formally to a vision; *blepō* appears in the sense of historical experience of God's action (e.g., Matt 13:16); *eidon* (e.g., Matt 5:16), *blepō* (e.g., Rom 7:23), and *theōreō* (e.g., Acts 4:13) occur in the fig. meaning "to perceive"; *theōreō* in the sense of "to live" (e.g., John 8:51); cf. W. Michaelis, "ὁράω," *TDNT* 5:315–82.

D. Vetter

חזק *ḥzq* to be firm

S 2388; BDB 304a; *HALOT* 1:302b; *TDOT* 4:301–8; *TWOT* 636; *NIDOTTE* 2616

---

1. The verbal root *ḥzq* is also attested in Aram. and Arab., in addition to Hebr. (Jew. Aram., Mand., and Arab. also *hrzq*).

Isa 22:21 and Nah 2:2 (pi.) together with the Arab. *ḥazaqa* (cf. Syr. *ḥ*ᵉ*zaq*) "to bind firmly" (Lane 2:560) support the thesis of J. L. Palache (*SNHL* 29) that the basic meaning of *ḥzq* is "to tie up, gird up firmly."

Wagner no. 99 is correct not to consider *ḥzq* pi. in the meaning "to gird" an Aramaism (contra G. R. Driver, *SVT* 1 [1953]: 30).

Whether Akk. *ešqu* "massive" should be attributed to the same root (cf. *AHw* 257) is questionable. *iz/šqātu* "fetter" is an Aram. loanword in Akk. (*AHw* 408b; W. von Soden, *AfO* 20 [1963]: 155). The same may be true of Akk. *ḥazīqatu* "headband," which Palache cites in support of his thesis (op. cit.), but which is attested only in Neo-Bab. and Neo-Assyr. (*AHw* 339a).

The adjs. *ḥāzāq* and *ḥāzēq* and the substs. *ḥēzeq*, *ḥōzeq*, *ḥezqâ*, and *ḥozqâ* with the meanings "strong" or "strength" derive from the root (*ḥezqâ* "to become strong" and *ḥozqâ* in 2 Kgs 12:13 "restoration" function as infs.).

On the PNs *ḥizqî*, *ḥizqîyâ(hû)*, *yeḥizqîyâ(hû)*, and *yeḥezqēl*, cf. *IP* nos. 474f., 659f.

2. Of the 290 occurrences of the verb (qal 81x, pi. 64x, hi. 118x, hitp. 27x), 98 passages fall to the Chr literature alone (1 Chron 12x, 2 Chron 39x, Ezra 5x, Neh 42x). The remaining examples occur primarily in the Dtn-Dtr books (Deut 9x, Josh 8x, Judg 12x, 1 Sam 6x, 2 Sam 18x, 1 Kgs 9x, 2 Kgs 15x), in the major writing prophets (Isa 21x, of these 13x in Deutero-Isa, Jer 15x, Ezek 12x), and in Dan (13x). The use of the verbal root in the three post-exilic prophets (Hag 3x), Zech (5x), and Mal (1x) stands out markedly from that of the other Minor Prophets (Hos 1x, Mic 2x, Nah 3x). The remaining figures are: Gen 6x, Exod 15x, Lev and Num 1x each, Psa 5x, Job 7x, Prov 4x. Thus *ḥzq* is chiefly attested in the Dtr-Chr literature and esp. in the late books of the OT.

The use of the adj. *ḥāzāq* (total 56x, Deut and Ezek 10x, Exod 7x, 1 Kgs and Jer 4x each) paints the same picture. *ḥāzēq* occurs only 2x (Exod 19:19; 2 Sam 3:1), *ḥēzeq* 1x (Psa 18:2), *ḥōzeq* 5x (3x *beḥōzeq yād* "mightily" in Exod 13:3, 14, 16), *hezqâ* 4x, and *ḥozqâ* 6x (5x *beḥozqâ* "with force," as well as 2 Kgs 12:13, where a pi. inf. may be read; cf. *HAL* 292b).

3. The chief meaning "to be/become strong, firm" in the qal produces the most important meanings in the derived stems: pi. "to strengthen," hi. "to grasp, hold firm," and hitp. "to prove to be strong/courageous" (*HAL* 290–92; cf. *HP* 283), with no basic distinction between physical and mental/emotional strength.

→ *ᶜmṣ* "to be strong," → *ᶜzz* "to be powerful," and the substs. *ᶜōz* "power" and → *kōaḥ* "strength" function as synonyms; cf. also → *yād* "hand" and → *zerôaᵓ* "arm."

The qal is used esp. of the dominant strength of a people (Judg 1:28; Josh 17:13; 2 Sam 10:11; 1 Kgs 20:23), a king's might (2 Chron 26:15), a battle's intensity (2 Kgs 3:26) and, above all, of a famine (Gen 41:56f.; 47:20; 2 Kgs 25:3; Jer 52:6). In conjunction with *yād* "hand" the qal means "to be courageous, take courage" (2 Sam 2:7; Ezek 22:14), the pi. "to encourage, urge on," either of another person (1 Sam 23:16; Judg 9:24; Isa 35:3; Jer 23:14; Job 4:3) or of oneself (Neh 6:9 inf. abs. instead of 1st per.). This usage of *ḥzq* also occurs without the addition of *yād* (qal 2 Sam 16:21; pi. 2 Sam 11:25). *ḥzq* pi. is attested in conjunction with *beyād* in the sense of "to help" in Ezra 1:6, in the same meaning without *be* but with *yād* in Ezra 6:22, without *beyād* in 2 Chron 29:34 (also as hi. Ezek 16:49; Lev 25:35). In a military-defensive sense, the pi. means the fortification of cities (2 Chron 11:12), towers (2 Chron 26:9), or kingdoms (2 Chron 11:17), the hi. the strengthening of a guard (Jer 51:12). While 2 Kgs 12:6–15; 22:5f.; 1 Chron 26:27; 2 Chron 24:5, 12; 29:3; 34:8, 10 employ the pi. of *ḥzq* for the repair of buildings, Neh 3:4–32 (34x) uses the hi. for the repair of city walls (with one exception: 3:19 pi.; cf. *HP* 103f.). The subjs. of a hi. form in the meaning "to grasp" are often terms such as "terror" (Jer 49:24), "horror" (Jer 8:21), "distress" (Jer 6:24; 50:43), and "woes" (Mic 4:9). The hi. too can be combined with *yād* (with *beyād* "to take by the hand" Gen 19:16; Judg 16:26, etc.; with *yād* "to help" Ezek 16:49; Job 8:20; cf. Gen 21:18 with *yād* and *be* "to hold one's hand over another protectively").

Other usages of *ḥzq* include: with *dābār* "word" (as the subj. of *ḥzq qal*) and *ʿal* of the person (2 Sam 24:4 = 1 Chron 21:4 "the commandment of the king remained firm with respect to X"; Mal 3:13 "you spoke impudently against me"), as well as the formula for reporting visions, "the hand of Yahweh lay hard (adj.) on me," Ezek 3:14 (→ *yād*).

4. In the theological sphere the pi. (Ezek 30:25 hi. following v 24 pi.; cf. *HP* 89) means Yahweh's strengthening. It refers primarily to military-defensive strength (Judg 3:12; Ezek 30:24; Hos 7:15; Psa 147:13). Yet Samson too prays for divine power in his final stand (Judg 16:28), and once God "heals" the sheep neglected by the bad shepherds (Ezek 34:16; cf. v 4).

J uses forms of → *kbd* to describe "intransigence"; E and P use *ḥzq* qal for willful intransigence and *ḥzq* pi. for hardening of the heart through God's agency (F. Hesse, *Das Verstockungsproblem im AT* [1955], 18f.). In Exod the obj. is always → *lēb* "heart" (cf. also Ezek 2:4, with adj.). Phrases with *pānîm* "face" (Jer 5:3 pi.) and *mēṣaḥ* "forehead" (Ezek 3:7–9, adj.) also occur in Jer and Ezek. This intransigence can more likely be explained from a salvation history perspective, as a "process in the universal, eschatologically oriented judgment of God" (J. Moltmann, *RGG* 6:1385), than as a theological aporia (the OT could not charge delusion to demonic powers) or as a religiopsychological principle (cf. von Rad, *Theol.* 2:151–55; E. Jenni, *TZ* 15 [1959]: 337–39).

The impf. of *ḥzq* (sg. and pl. qal) and the expanded usages (*ḥzq* alongside *ʾmṣ* "be firm and steadfast," Deut 31:7, 23; Josh 1:6f., 9, 18; 1 Chron 22:13; pl.: Deut 31:6; Josh 10:25; 2 Chron 32:7; together with *ʿśh* "and do it" in various combinations, Ezra 10:4; 1 Chron 28:10, 20; 2 Chron 19:11; 25:8; qal alongside hitp., 2 Sam 10:12 = 1 Chron 19:3; qal impf. repeatedly, Dan 10:19) have their place in salvation oracles as a formula of encouragement (probably originally before battle: Deut 31:6f., 23; Josh 1:6, 9; 10:25; 2 Sam 10:12; 2 Chron 32:7) and, more generally, in the promise of divine guidance as attested by the frequent addition "do not fear" (Deut 31:7; Josh 1:9; 10:25; etc.) and the support formula "I will be with you" (Deut 31:8, 23; 1 Chron 28:20; 2 Chron 19:11; cf. H. D. Preuss, " . . . ich will mit dir sein!" *ZAW* 80 [1968]: 139–73). In the Dtr-Chr literature, the formula (in various forms) also refers to keeping the law (Josh 1:7; 1 Chron 22:13; 2 Chron 15:7; cf. Ezra 10:4; 2 Chron 19:11; Deut 12:23), and in Hag 2:4 and 1 Chron 28:10, 20 to the construction of the temple. The usage supplemented by *ʿśh* (see above; cf. Hag 2:4) remains limited, meanwhile, to Hag and Chron (W. A. M. Beuken, *Haggai-Sacharja 1–8* [1967], 53–60, who, like N. Lohfink, "Die deuteronomistisch Darstellung des Übergangs der Führung Israels von Moses auf Josua," *Scholastik* 37 [1962]: 32–44, views the encouragement formula as an element of the genre for induction into office). *ḥᵃzaq waḥᵃzāq* occurs only once in a vision report (Dan 10:19). Cf. also → *ʾmṣ* 4.

The formula *bᵉyād ḥᵃzāqâ* "with a strong hand" in Num 20:20 (J) refers to Edom, but otherwise (esp. in Deut, where the expression is usually expanded to "with a strong hand and an outstretched arm") to the divine saving act of redemption from Egypt (on which see, however, → *yād* and → *zᵉrôaʿ*; B. S. Childs, "Deuteronomic Formulae of the Exodus Tradition," FS Baumgartner 30–39).

5. The usage of *ḥzq* in the Qumran literature resembles that of the OT, except that the pi. in the sense of "to harden" does not occur and the usage "with a strong hand" in reference to the exodus is lacking. On the NT, cf. W. Michaelis, "κράτος," *TDNT* 3:905–15; W. Grundmann, *Der Begriff der Kraft in the neutestamentlichen Gedankenwelt* (1928).

A. S. van der Woude

חטא *ḥṭʾ* to miss

S 2398; BDB 306b; *HALOT* 1:305a; *TDOT* 4:309–19; *TWOT* 638; *NIDOTTE* 2627

---

1. The root **ḫṭʾ* "to miss" is common Sem. (Berg., *Intro.* 220; P. Fronzaroli, *AANLR* 8/20 [1965]: 252f., 263, 268); Akk. *ḫaṭû* "to miss, sin" (*AHw* 337f., 350; also e.g., *ḫīṭu*/*ḫiṭītu* "lack, sin"), Ug. *ḫṭʾ* "to sin" (*WUS* no. 1019; *UT* no. 952), Aram. *ḥṭʾ* "to sin" (*DISO* 85; KBL 1075a; the verb does not occur in Bibl. Aram.; the oldest occurrence is Aḥ. 50 *ḥṭʾyk* "your failures" with the 3d radical ʾ, later > y), Arab. *ḫaṭiʾa* "to commit an error" (Wehr 245), Eth. *ḫaṭʾa* "to not find" (Dillmann 619f.).

In the OT the verb occurs in the qal "to miss (a mark), fall short," in the hi. either the normal causative "to occasion to sin" or the inner-causative "to let oneself err, fail" (*HP* 267), in the pi. either the estimative-declarative "to have to recognize something as failed" (Gen 31:39), the denominative "to remove sin" (privative with *ḥēṭʾ*), or "to bring as a sin offering" (resultative-productive with *ḥaṭṭaʾt*), in the hitp. the reflexive-privative "to remove one's sin" (on Job 41:17, "to withdraw," cf. Hölscher, HAT 17, 96).

There are four fem. substs. for "sin," etc., in addition to the masc. segholate formation *ḥēṭʾ* (< **ḥiṭʾ-;* cf. Akk. *ḫīṭu*): *ḥeṭʾâ* (only Num 15:28 txt?), *ḥᵃṭāʾâ* (BL 463), *ḥaṭṭāʾâ* (only Exod 34:7; Isa 5:18; BL 477), and *ḥaṭṭāʾt* (BL 611, 613). There is also the nomen agentis *ḥaṭṭāʾ* "sinful, sinner" (BL 479).

Bibl. Aram. has the subst. *ḥᵃṭāy* "sin" (Dan 4:24) and (as a loanword from Hebr.) *ḥaṭṭāyāʾ* "sin offering" (Ezra 6:17 K, Q *ḥaṭṭāʾâ*).

2. An overview of the 595 occurrences of the root in the OT (verb 237x, noun 356x Hebr., 2x Aram.; Lis. does not list Num 29:25 *ḥaṭṭāʾt*) produces the following table (*ḥeṭʾâ* [1x Num], *ḥaṭṭāʾâ* [1x each in Exod and Isa], and *ḥᵃṭāʾâ* are included under "other"):

	qal	pi.	hi.	hitp.	*ḥēṭʾ*	*ḥaṭṭāʾ*	others	*ḥaṭṭāʾt*	total
Gen	7	1	–	–	1	1	1	4	15
Exod	8	1	1	–	–	–	4	8	22
Lev	25	5	–	–	4	–	–	82	116
Num	8	1	–	8	4	2	1	43	67
Deut	5	–	1	–	8	–	–	4	18
Josh	2	–	–	–	–	–	–	1	3
Judg	3	–	1	–	–	–	–	–	4

1 Sam	14	–	–	–	–	1	–	6	21
2 Sam	4	–	–	–	–	–	–	1	5
1 Kgs	13	–	10	–	–	1	–	18	42
2 Kgs	3	–	15	–	2	–	1	15	36
Isa	5	–	1	–	4	3	1	12	26
Jer	13	–	1	–	–	–	–	13	27
Ezek	11	5	–	–	1	–	–	24	41
Hos	5	–	–	–	1	–	–	5	11
Amos	–	–	–	–	–	2	–	1	3
Mic	1	–	–	–	–	–	–	6	7
Hab	1	–	–	–	–	–	–	–	1
Zeph	1	–	–	–	–	–	–	–	1
Zech	–	–	–	–	–	–	–	3	3
Psa	8	1	–	–	3	6	3	13	34
Job	11	–	–	1	–	–	–	6	18
Prov	6	–	–	–	–	3	–	7	16
Eccl	6	–	1	–	1	–	–	–	8
Lam	3	–	–	–	2	–	–	3	8
Dan	4	–	–	–	1	–	–	3	8
Ezra	–	–	–	–	–	–	–	1	1
Neh	5	–	1	–	–	–	–	5	11
1 Chr	2	–	–	–	–	–	–	–	2
2 Chr	7	1	–	–	1	–	–	9	18
OT	181	15	32	9	33	19	11	293	593

More than one-fourth of the occurrences of the verb belong to the language of the priestly traditions (Lev, Num, Ezek). A further one-fourth occur in the historical books (esp. 1 Sam–2 Kgs); a great segment of these occurrences, esp. the hi. forms, is shaped by Dtn-Dtr linguistic traditions, incl. also Hos and Jer. The prophets (somewhat) independent of these two groups do not use the word or use it only minimally.

The oldest examples are to be found in J (11x) and E (10x), in older layers of the books of Sam, in Isa, Hos, and in Deut and Josh. They constitute about one-fourth of the occurrences.

Almost one-third of the various nouns belong to priestly language (P, Ezek; cf. also Psa, Deutero-Isa, and Trito-Isa). Dtn-Dtr diction is also represented with about 50 occurrences. In two-fifths of all passages *ḥaṭṭāʾt* means "sin offering" (cf. the statistics in R. Knierim, *Die Hauptbegriffe für Sünde im AT* [1965], 19f.).

3. (a) The basic meaning "to miss (a mark)" is lit. apparent in Judg 20:16 (hi.) "they all hurled stones and hit precisely, without missing," while in Prov 19:2 "whoever rushes about missteps," the transition from the lit. to the fig. usage in the sense of a perverted life-style is clear. More important is the observation that the root—apart from a few exceptions (cf. also Prov 8:36, with the antonym *mṣʾ* "to find" in v 35; Job 5:24 "so you will miss nothing")—is used almost exclusively to describe religious circumstances. This area uses the term fig. only to disqualify particular procedures. That the term objectively disqualifies an act, left otherwise unspecified, as a crime, an error,

makes it a comprehensive term for "sin." In this respect, both the basic meaning itself and the usage of all derivatives in whatever context indicate the factuality of the error (cf. e.g., qal, Gen 39:9; 40:1; 42:22; 1 Sam 2:25; *hattā*ʾ Gen 13:13; *ḥēṭ*ʾ, Lev 19:17, etc.).

For these reasons the OT prefers the root *ḥṭ*ʾ above all other terms for "sin." The verb outstrips all verbs for "to sin" (Knierim, op. cit. 13, 19). The substs., taken together, also lead, although they are closely followed by → *ʿāwōn*. Only the adj. *rāšāʿ* (→ *ršʿ*) decisively outweighs *ḥaṭṭā*ʾ.

(b) The term is used formulaically to a noteworthy degree. The formulaic usages and phrases and their life settings point to a great range of distribution of realms of experience that exposed Israel to the experience of error (cf. Knierim, op. cit. 20–55, 257f.). Error was expressed in institutionalized procedures like Yahweh's convicting sentence in the cultic-judicial act, the priestly Torah, the sermon, the (political or legal) act of submission, and the (cultic or politicolegal) individual or communal confession of sin. This distribution and the thoroughly legal implications of the usage of the term express the fact that "sin" is demonstrated and condemned officially (institutionally) and objectively with the aid of unilateral and universally binding categories and is accordingly to be acknowledged by the one found guilty.

The following usages of the verb merit attention: (1) the old, official individual confession of sin, for which *ḥāṭāʾtî* "I have sinned" is the OT's primary formulation (30x); it occurs primarily in the confession after (sacral or profane) legal sentencing (Josh 7:20; 1 Sam 15:24; 2 Sam 19:21; 24:10; Psa 41:5; 51:6) and in the affirmation of innocence following an indictment (Judg 11:27; 1 Sam 24:12); (2) the communal confession of sin, *ḥāṭāʾnû* "we have sinned" (24x), in rites of penance or prayers of repentance; it forms the prerequisite for the reversal of a crisis situation and stands in close connection with the removal of strange gods and the communal lament (cf. Num 14:40; 21:7; Judg 10:10, 15; 1 Sam 7:6; 12:10; Jer 3:25; 8:14; 14:7, 20; Dan 9:5ff.; Neh 1:6); (3) the indictment or verdict formulae (qal pf. 3d per. sg. or pl.) with a setting in profane (Gen 40:1; 1 Sam 19:4) or sacral procedures or diction (Exod 32:31; Hos 4:7; Psa 78:32; Zeph 1:17); it discloses an error or justifies the sentence; (4) this same genre occurs in the 2d per. sg. or pl. in the direct, indicting address of the prophetic or Dtn preacher (e.g., Exod 32:30; Num 23:23; Deut 9:16, 18; Jer 40:3; Hos 10:9).

One may identify about 15 usages for the noms. (Knierim, op. cit. 43–54), which generally refer, in various settings, to all types of errors (legal, cultic, social, etc.); cf. one example each in 2 Sam 12:13; Jer 16:10; Hos 8:13; Gen 41:9; Lev 16:16; Mic 3:8; Psa 59:4; 32:5; Lam 4:22; Psa 51:4; Jer 36:3; Psa 85:3; Isa 44:22. Worthy of specific attention are: (1) *nś*ʾ *ḥēṭ*ʾ "to bear an error" (17x), often translated "to forgive"; the usage refers, however, to the basic procedure whereby an error must be borne; the question as to whether it signifies the forgiveness or the punishment of the sinner depends upon the context, which speaks of burdening either the sinner or a representative (cf. Lev 19:17; 22:9; 20:20 beside Exod 34:7 and Gen 50:17; Exod 32:32; 1 Sam 15:25); (2) the combination of the root *ḥṭ*ʾ with *mût* "to die" (11x); cf. e.g.,

Deut 22:26 (mortal sin) and Amos 9:10; Deut 21:22; 24:16; 2 Kgs 14:6; Ezek 18:4, 20.

(c) The etymology of the term ("to miss a mark") and the contexts indicate that the criterion for "error" is not particular commandments but injury to a communal relationship: a person sins against a person or against God (cf. the programmatic statements in 1 Sam 2:25; Jer 16:10–12; 1 Kgs 8:46). Nevertheless, to the extent that a particular communal relationship implies norms of relation, violation of the norms results in injury to the relationship. In this sense, then, norms appear in the context of the discussion of "error," i.e., in reference to crimes against the ban (1 Sam 14:33ff.), adultery (2 Sam 12:13) or sexual folly (Lev 20:20), theft (Gen 31:36), crimes against innocent blood (2 Kgs 21:17), against Yahweh's anointed (1 Sam 24:12), idolatry (Deut 12:29f.), social misdeeds (Mic 3:8; 6:6–8, etc.). Hosea encompasses legal, ethicosocial, and cultic errors without distinction (Hos 4:1, 6–8).

The use of the word in the so-called profane-legal sphere is also significant, e.g., in Hezekiah's confession of rebellion (2 Kgs 18:14) or in reference to the failure to discharge professional duties by Pharaoh's baker and butler (Gen 40:1); cf. also Gen 42:22; 43:9. Beside the known impossibility of strictly distinguishing between the profane and the sacral realms, these usages of the term indicate that the discussion of "sin" applies to all areas of life and was in no way limited only to the religious sector.

For the rejection of a behavior as "error," it is basically inconsequential whether a deed occurs consciously or unconsciously. In a great many passages, such a distinction plays no role whatsoever. Neither the motive nor the attitude is characterized, but the fact as such. Unconscious errors are named in Gen 20:9; Num 22:34; Lev 4–5; Psa 38:4, 19; 41:5 (cf. Knierim, op. cit. 68). Thus the person is also responsible for unconscious error. On the one hand, this objective, unpsychologized evaluative criterion demonstrates the dependence of the sinner on external judgment. On the other hand, passages like Gen 4:7; Deut 15:9; 22:26, which emphasize subjective attitudes, and those like Gen 20:7, 17; 1 Sam 14:45; Num 22; Exod 21:13f., etc., which regulate unintentional misdeeds, indicate a growing tendency to consider subjective responsibility and esp. to bring about a clearer understanding of the failure of human conscience.

The term is clearly used in the context of the dynamistic understanding of existence ("destiny determining spheres of action"), namely with reference to the unity of error and judgment, as well as the relationship between community and individual. "The sinner must die in his *ḥēṭ*ʾ" is a phrase valid for centuries (cf. Num 27:3; Deut 19:15; 24:16; 2 Kgs 14:16; Psa 51:7; Dan 9:16). Here, as elsewhere, an interaction of legal and phenomenal spheres of thought is apparent, the sense of which is to express the legal unity of error and judgment (by legal notions) as well as the unity of the two legal categories (by phenomenal spheres of thought).

Totality or corporate thought is also original to the discussion of "sin" (cf. Gen 9:22; 20:9; 26:10; Josh 7:11; 8:5; 10:5, 7; 14:1). But it was modified under the influence of diverse experience and breached at several points. Types of such modification are found (1) in Exod 20:5f.; Jer 32:18: emphasis on the superabundance of grace over judgment with a view in each case to a community (cf. Exod 34:6f.; Num 14:18); (2) in Gen 18:17ff.: a question as to whether the fate of a society is determined by the minority of the righteous or the majority of the guilty; (3) in Josh 7: the relief of the national unit to the burden of the family unit (cf. 2 Sam 24:17); (4) Num 16:22: "God of the spirits of all flesh, a (one) person sins, and you will be angry with the whole community?" Here the differentiation between the sinners and the righteous reveals the individual. Cf. the transition to the legal statement in Ezek 18; Deut 24:16; Jer 31:20. As far as may be determined, this discovery of the individual has its setting in the distinction between the righteous and the sinners practiced in the priestly handling of the Torah.

(d) The root *ḥṭ*ᵓ is the major term in the highly differentiated OT terminology for "sin" (cf. Knierim, op. cit. 13nn.1, 19). Although almost all terms originally had a specific significance with respect to content, *ḥṭ*ᵓ, *rāᶜâ* (→ *r*ᶜᶜ), → *ᶜāwōn*, and *pešaᶜ* (→ *pš*ᶜ) are formal terms, preferred as generic terms for "sin." Of these *rāᶜâ* "bad, evil" stands alone; the other three are used complementarily, a phenomenon evident in that they are combined 4x in an immediate or an extended context: Exod 34:7; Lev 16:21; Num 14:18; Ezek 21:29; Psa 32:1, 5; 59:4; Dan 9:24, as well as Isa 59:12; Jer 33:8; Mic 7:18f.; Psa 51:3–7; Job 7:20f.; 13:23 (cf. Isa 1:2, 4; Ezek 33:10, 12). Even though this triad is formulaic and systematically expresses the mass of all possible errors, one may not simply view the three terms in the triad as synonyms. Each disqualifies "sin" in its own way. Nevertheless, where they are used together as a formula, they are intended to represent all other terms for "sin."

4. (a) The term *ḥṭ*ᵓ is used in all of its derivatives, apart from a few exceptions, in the context of theological statements. It is moreover the most frequently used theological term for "sin" in the OT, second only to *rāᶜâ* in the general semantic field of terms related to "evil" (on this general theme cf. the OT theologies and Th. C. Vriezen, *RGG* 6:478–82 with bibliog.; further Knierim, op. cit.; and Š. Porúbčan, *Sin in the OT* [1963]). As such, it characterizes some deeds or behaviors theologically; it disqualifies an act or behavior as condemned by Yahweh. The disqualification comes to expression in a great many forms and settings, which nevertheless all presuppose Yahweh's condemnatory actions and thereby imply a specific theological motif. The theological character of the understanding of "error" is therefore not only grounded in the meaning of the word, formally and psychologically only minimally developed, but in terms of whether and how Yahweh views a misdeed. In this sense "error" has the same weight as all other types of "sin." The statistical assessment of the terminology preferred to different degrees in the individual sources of the OT supports this observation (cf. Knierim, op. cit. 245ff.).

(b) The following may be mentioned as the chief contexts in which disqualification is expressed as Yahweh's judgment: (1) the realm of Yahweh's judgment in the oracle or sermon of Yahweh, and the resultant confession of sin (cf. the formulaic usages in 3b). These settings make it most clearly apparent that the confession of "sin" corresponds to a revelatory (disclosing) process (cf. also Lam 2:14; 4:22b; Mic 3:8; Isa 58:1); (2) where *ḥṭ*ᵓ implies acts against Yahweh or Yahweh's regulations or against people under Yahweh's protection; (3) where the violation of norms affects Yahweh's privileges and a communal relationship protected by him; (4) where in the objective apprehension of guilt Yahweh approaches people as the judge beyond human control, and where the person becomes aware of the inevitability of the confrontation with God in the demonstration of subjective responsibility; (5) where legal and phenomenal spheres of thought are means by which Yahweh punishes "error" (cf. Knierim, op. cit. 82ff.; cf. e.g., Hos 5:12, 14; Amos 3:6b); (6) where Yahweh sovereignly determines, modifies, or graciously breaks through the unified, fatal relationship between "sin" and judgment in history, the life of the individual, and of the community.

5. In the Qumran texts the verb occurs (4x), as well as the nom. forms *ḥēṭʾ* (1x) and *ḥaṭṭāʾt* (15x, according to Kuhn, *Konk.* 70; see also *GCDS* 253). The almost consistent formulaic usage in conformity with OT usage is noteworthy.

The situation in the LXX is enlightening in that about 26 Hebr. expressions for "sin" are rendered by only 6 Gk. terms, a circumstance that doubtless points to a strong thematization and theoretization of the OT concept of sin in the Gk.-speaking world; cf. G. Quell, *TDNT* 1:268f. Correspondingly, the LXX regularly renders all derivatives of *ḥṭʾ* by *hamartanō*, *hamartia*, etc., only occasionally by *adikeō*, *adikia*, and only the derived stems of the verb are rendered otherwise. Thus for the NT *ḥṭʾ* would be represented primarily by *hamartia*, but *hamartia* would by no means have had ḥṭ' as its only Hebr. equivalent—without taking into account the entirely new ontological and hamartiological understanding in the NT (cf. G. Quell, G. Bertram, G. Stählin, and W. Grundmann, "ἁμαρτάνω," *TDNT* 1:267–316). Nevertheless, in one passage an OT mode of thought seems to recur in the NT discussion of "bearing the burden of guilt" *(nśʾ ʿāwōn/ḥēṭʾ):* John 1:29; cf. 1 Pet 5:7; Gal 6:2.

R. Knierim

חיה *ḥyh* to live

S 2421; BDB 310b; *HALOT* 1:309a; *TDOT* 4:324–44; *TWOT* 644; *NIDOTTE* 2649

1. (a) The root *ḥyy/ḥwy* "to live" is richly developed in the WSem. realm, but is absent from Akk., which has the equivalent *balāṭu* (P. Fronzaroli, *AANLR* 8/19 [1964]: 248f., 263; 8/23 [1968]: 280, 291, 300; → *plṭ*). Several examples occur already in old Sem. inscriptions (Can.: EA 245:6; cf. *CAD* H:32b; Ug.: *WUS* nos. 911, 916; *UT* no. 856; Gröndahl 137; Phoen.-Pun., Hebr., and Aram.: *DISO* 86f.; *HAL* 295f.).

In Ug. and Phoen.-Pun., *w* is also encountered as the 2d radical (cf. also the Amor. names in Huffmon 71f., 191f.); on the orthography in Pun., and on the form borrowed in Lat. as a salutation using the impv. *ave*, cf. Friedrich 17, 78, 120.

No satisfying etymology may be demonstrated. Neither "to breathe" (Gesenius, *Thesaurus* 1:467f.) nor "to draw together" (H. J. Fleischer, *Kleinere Schriften* [1885], 1:86) is illuminating.

The following OT forms derive from a second root *ḥwh: ḥawwâ* "tent village," *ḥay* "kin" (1 Sam 18:18; according to L. Delekat, *VT* 14 [1964]: 27f., also Psa 42:9) and *ḥayyâ* "troop" (2 Sam 23:11, 13; Psa 68:11); cf. *HAL* 284a, 296b, 297b.

(b) The verb appears in Hebr. in qal, pi., and hi. The qal pf. 3d masc. sg. sometimes, esp. in the Pentateuch, resembles a geminate (BL 423).

Among the noms. derived from the verb one finds, first of all, the subst. and adj. *ḥay* "life," "alive," as well as its fem. *ḥayyâ*, which as an abstract occasionally signifies "life" but more often, as a collective, "living beings." The plurale tantum *ḥayyîm* in the sense of "life" is usually understood as an abstract pl. (pl. of duration).

According to Brockelmann, it involves an abstract variant of the adj. *ḥay: bᵉḥayyîm* "among the living" > "in life" (BrSynt 16; *bḥym* in a late 6th-cent. Phoen. inscription [*KAI* no. 13.7] can mean "among the living" [so *ANET* 662a] or "in life"). *ḥayyîm* has also been understood as an artificial analogous formation, a secondary back-formation of an abs. st. of the cs. st. sg. *ḥê* falsely understood as a pl. (J. Barth, *ZDMG* 42 [1888]: 344; Nyberg 202).

The *ma*-noun *miḥyâ* "sustenance," "animation," and the hapax legomenon *ḥayyût* "lifetime" formed with the abstract suf. *-ût* (2 Sam 20:3; cf. BL 505) occur as verbal abstracts. The fem. pl. adj. *ḥāyôt* "lively" is also a hapax legomenon (Exod 1:19; cf. BL 465; contra G. R. Driver, *ZAW* 67 [1955]: 246–48).

The root is sparsely attested as part of a PN, in fact only in the two theophoric sentence names *yᵉḥîʾēl* and *yᵉḥîyâ* "God/Yahweh lives" (juss. with an indicative meaning).

Pe. and ha. occur in Bibl. Aram., as well as the noms. *ḥay* "living," *ḥayyîn* "life," and *ḥêwâ* "animal."

2. An overview of the occurrences of the root (in the arrangement of Mandl., which differs from that of Lis., but Psa 18:47 treated as adj., like 2 Sam 22:47) results in the following table (II = *ḥayyâ* "life"):

	qal	pi.	hi.	*ḥay*	*ḥayyâ*	II	*ḥayyîm*	total
Gen	49	4	6	26	20	–	20	125
Exod	3	4	–	3	2	–	4	16
Lev	3	–	–	23	9	–	1	36
Num	5	1	2	6	1	–	–	15
Deut	15	3	–	8	1	–	12	39
Josh	3	1	4	2	–	–	2	12
Judg	1	1	1	1	–	–	1	5
1 Sam	2	3	–	22	1	–	2	30
2 Sam	4	1	1	15	1	–	4	26
1 Kgs	6	2	–	22	–	–	4	34
2 Kgs	16	1	5	18	1	–	2	43
Isa	7	1	3	8	6	1	4	30
Jer	9	1	–	16	3	–	4	33

Ezek	43	4	1	24	31	2	2	107
Hos	1	2	–	2	4	–	–	9
Amos	3	–	–	2	–	–	–	5
Jonah	–	–	–	–	–	–	3	3
Hab	1	1	–	–	–	–	–	2
Zeph	–	–	–	1	2	–	–	3
Zech	3	–	–	1	–	–	–	4
Mal	–	–	–	–	–	–	1	1
Psa	11	20	–	13	8	3	26	81
Job	5	2	–	5	5	6	7	30
Prov	4	–	–	1	–	–	33	38
Ruth	–	–	–	2	–	–	–	2
Song Sol	–	–	–	1	–	–	–	1
Eccl	3	1	–	8	–	–	13	25
Lam	1	–	–	1	–	–	2	4
Esth	1	–	–	–	–	–	–	1
Dan	–	–	–	1	1	–	1	3
Neh	4	2	–	–	–	–	–	6
1 Chron	–	1	–	–	–	–	–	1
2 Chron	2	–	–	4	1	–	–	7
OT	205	56	23	236	97	12	148	777

In addition, *miḥyâ* occurs 8x (for texts see 3f), *ḥāyeh* and *ḥayyût* 1x each; the place-name *b^e^ʾēr laḥay rōʾî* is not counted (Lis. erroneously lists Gen 16:14 under *ḥay*).

Pe. occurs in Bibl. Aram. 5x, ha. 1x, *ḥay* 5x, *ḥayyîn* 2x, *ḥêwâ* 20x.

Of the approximately 800 occurrences of the root, Gen (126x), Ezek (107x), and Psa (81x) are the most involved. The absence of *ḥayyîm* in Chron/Ezra/Neh and the sparse usage in the Prophets (14x) are noteworthy.

3. All instances of the root may be grouped rather closely around the concept "life." A good approach is to proceed from the verb and to consider the various nom. abstract and collective forms on the basis of the verb.

(a) The basic and most frequently attested meaning of the qal is "to be/remain alive"; the contrary, "to be dead, to die" (→ *mût*) is always involved somehow, even if it is not explicitly expressed. An accentuated contrast occurs often, e.g., in the expression "live and not die" (Gen 42:2; 43:8; 47:19; Deut 33:6; 2 Kgs 18:32; Ezek 18:21, 28; 33:15; Psa 89:49; 118:17) or "die and not live" (2 Kgs 20:1 = Isa 38:1).

A weakened sense results when *ḥyh* is more precisely modified by the addition of the place or the time ("to stop for a time at a place": Gen 47:28; Lev 25:35f.; Lam 4:20; time: esp. in the genealogies of P in Gen 5 and 11, also Gen 47:28; 2 Kgs 14:17 = 2 Chron 25:25; Jer 35:7; Job 42:16; Eccl 6:3, 6; 11:8).

The verb acquires a somewhat altered meaning in those passages in which it describes not an enduring situation but a momentary process: "to become alive again" (1 Kgs 17:22; 2 Kgs 13:21; Isa 26:14, 19; Ezek 37:3, 5f., 9f., 14; Job 14:14). Closely related, and for the ancient Israelites hardly distinct, are the passages in which *ḥyh* means becoming well, recovery from an illness (Gen 45:27; Num 21:8f.; Josh 5:8; Judg 15:19; 2 Kgs 1:2; 8:8–10, 14; 20:7; Isa 38:9,

21). The depiction of recovery as becoming alive or coming to life bespeaks the fact that sickness diminishes life, that genuine life is health. Here it can be clearly seen that "life" in the OT does not mean simply being alive, but having complete, fulfilled life.

The meaning is modified along other lines when the limited duration of corporal life is emphasized (Gen 27:40; Deut 8:3; 2 Kgs 4:7).

In addition to persons, subjs. of the verb are *lēbāb* "heart" (Psa 22:27; 69:33), *nepeš* "soul" (Gen 12:13; 19:20; 1 Kgs 20:32; Isa 55:3; Jer 38:17, 20; Ezek 13:19 pl.; 47:9; Psa 119:175), *rûaḥ* "spirit" (Gen 45:27), and *ᶜaṣāmôt* "bones" (Ezek 37:3, 5).

Plants and, remarkably, animals are never the subj. of *ḥyh*.

In the acclamation *yeḥî hammelek* (1 Sam 10:24; 2 Sam 16:16; 1 Kgs 1:25, 31, 34, 39; 2 Kgs 11:12 = 2 Chron 23:11; cf. Neh 2:3), the verb is apparently a juss. with an indicative meaning: "the king lives, he possesses royal power" (P. A. H. de Boer, *VT* 5 [1955]: 225–31; cf., however, Dan 2:4; 3:9; 5:10; 6:7, 22 with impv.).

(b) Pi. and hi., both with the meaning "to keep alive, let live," are distinct in that the pi. places greater emphasis upon the contrast to "to die, be dead," while the hi. expresses the weakened concept of "duration" (*HP* 37, 58, 61–64).

An expanded use of the pi. as vigorous technical language occurs in a few passages: 2 Sam 12:3; Isa 7:21 "to rear (young animals)," Hos 14:8 "to raise (grain)," 1 Chron 11:8 "to rebuild (a city)"; the last meaning also occurs in Phoen. (*KAI* no. 4.2; *ANET* 653a "restored").

(c) *ḥay* means both "lively" and "alive," vivus and vivens, and has adj. and subst. functions. It can refer to people and animals as well as to God, but not to plants, which are never considered living things in the OT (E. Schmitt, *Leben in den Weisheitsbüchern Job, Sprüche und Jesus Sirach* [1954], 116). The designation *ḥay* can also be attributed to *nepeš* "soul" (Gen 1:20f., 24, 30; 2:7, 19; 9:10, 12, 15f.; Lev 11:10, 46; Ezek 47:9) and *bāśār* "flesh" (Lev 13:10, 14–16 of the excresence of a wound; 1 Sam 2:15 of raw animal flesh). The expression "living (i.e., flowing) water" is an expanded usage (Gen 26:19; Lev 14:5f., 50–52; 15:13; Num 19:17; Jer 2:13; 17:13; Zech 14:8; Song Sol 4:15).

On the expression *kāᶜēt ḥayyâ* "at this time next year" (Gen 18:10, 14; 2 Kgs 4:16f.) cf. Akk. *ana balāṭ* "in the coming year" (*AHw* 99a; R. Yaron, *VT* 12 [1962]: 500f.; O. Loretz, *Bib* 43 [1962]: 75–78: *ḥayyâ* does not mean "life" but "next year").

The superlative formula *ḥy ḥym* "living of the living" occurs as a royal title on a Neo-Pun. burial inscription (*KAI* no. 161.1).

ḥay occurs as a subst. only in the oath formula: *ḥê* X "by the life of X" (M. Greenberg, *JBL* 76 [1957]: 34–39). The nomen rectum of the cs. relation is almost always God/Yahweh; the nomen regens is then *ḥay*. In rare cases in which a human being takes an oath, the formula is normally *ḥê-napšekā*, and it usually appears in conjunction with a simultaneous oath by God: "as surely as God lives and as surely as your soul lives"; only *ḥê-ᵓadōnî* (2 Sam 15:21) and *ḥê parᶜōh* (Gen 42:15f.) occur without *nepeš*. *ḥay* is adj. in *ḥay-ᵓānî* "as surely as I live" (texts in *HAL* 295).

(d) The fem. adj. *ḥayyâ* "living" in the sg. as well as the pl. designates the "living being" in general, i.e., esp. "animals" (cf. Gk. *zōon*). The word usually means free-living, untamed animals in distinction from domesticated animals (*b^ehēmâ;* Gen 8:1; Ezek 14:15; 33:27; Zeph 2:15; Psa 148:10: Job 37:8). A further limitation is occasionally made: land animals in contrast to birds and fishes (Gen 1:28; 8:19; Lev 11:2). In exceptional cases, *ḥayyâ* can also indicate domesticated animals (Num 35:3) or beasts of burden (Isa 46:1).

ḥayyâ also has the abstract meaning "life," chiefly in Psa and Job (5x in the speeches of Elihu), where it is a synonym for → *nepeš.*

(e) The pl. *ḥayyîm* serves as a comprehensive term for "life." Like the verb, its semantic field is determined primarily in contrast to "dying/death." This contrast comes to explicit expression esp. in Dtn, also e.g., in 2 Sam 1:23; 15:21; Jer 8:3; Jonah 4:3, 8; Prov 18:21.

A reduction of the meaning to "lifetime" results when *ḥayyîm* is used in temporal designations, esp. in the expressions *y^emê ḥayyîm* "days of life" (Gen 3:14, 17, etc., about 30x), *(y^emê) š^enê ḥayyîm* "years of life" (Gen 23:1; 25:7, 17, etc., about 15x). *ḥayyîm* may also be almost a temporal term apart from these expressions, e.g., Gen 7:11; Lev 18:18; Judg 16:30; Eccl 3:12; 6:12.

Without accentuating duration, *ḥayyîm* can have a generalized sense and almost mean mere "existence," e.g., Gen 27:46; Exod 1:14; Eccl 2:17; 9:9; 10:19.

In some passages, *ḥayyîm* and → *nepeš* appear almost as interchangeable terms. "Everything alive" can be *kōl-hannepeš* as easily as *kōl-ḥay,* e.g., Josh 10:28, 30, 32, 35, 37; cf. also Psa 21:5; 64:2 *(ḥayyîm)* with Job 31:39; Esth 7:7 *(nepeš).* Nevertheless, the difference is usually clear; it seems to lie primarily in the higher degree of objectivization that seems inherent in the term *ḥayyîm:* in contrast to *nepeš, ḥayyîm* is not considered an inherent, life-related principle, but a possession or, more properly, a good gift (see 4b).

(f) The verbal abstract *miḥyâ* has a rather specific sphere of usage and mirrors variously the action or the process of the verb, either of the qal: "becoming alive" (Lev 13:10, 24 as a sacro-medicinal term for the growth of the flesh of a wound; 2 Chron 14:12; Ezra 9:8f. of the revival, resuscitation of the enslaved), or of the causative: "sustenance of life" (Gen 45:5; cf. Sir 38:14). *miḥyâ* can also have a concrete reference: "provisions" (Judg 6:4; 17:10). Prov 27:27 has *ḥayyîm* in the same meaning.

4. (a) OT references to the "living God" belong, primarily and predominantly, to the oath formula "by the life of Yahweh/God" (cf. M. R. Lehmann, *ZAW* 81 [1969]: 83–86, with ancient Near Eastern pars.). The most frequent form is *ḥay yhwh* (41x, 30x in Judg–2 Kgs; also *ḥay ᵓ^adōnāy yhwh* Jer 44:26; *ḥay hāᵓ^elōhîm* 2 Sam 2:27; *ḥay-ᵓēl* Job 27:2). The formula also appears in Lachish Letters III, VI ("as Yahweh liveth" *ANET* 322; *KAI* no. 193.9 *ḥyhwh;* no. 196.12 *ḥy yhwh*). The oath *ḥay-ᵓānî* (*ḥay ᵓānōkî* Deut 32:40) "as surely as I live" occurs 23x as a divine self-declaration (Num 14:21, 28; Deut 32:40; Isa 49:18; Jer 22:24; 46:18; Zeph 2:9; and 16x in Ezek).

Aside from the oath formula, only 14 passages describe God as *ḥay: ᵓ^elōhîm ḥayyîm* Deut 5:26; 1 Sam 17:26, 36; Jer 10:10; 23:36; *ᵓēl ḥay* Josh 3:10; Hos 2:1; Psa 42:3; *ᵓ^elōhîm ḥay* 2 Kgs 19:4, 16 = Isa 37:4, 17; *ḥay yhwh* "Yahweh lives" 2 Sam 22:47 = Psa 18:47. Remarkably, several of these passages are related in content, esp. texts from 1 Sam and 2 Kgs, which contain invectives against a foreign opponent who has slandered Israel's God. Jer 10:10, too, is reminiscent of these passages because it expresses a polemic against foreign gods. The contrast to foreign gods governs Josh 3:10: the living God of Israel will expel the Canaanites, Hittites, etc. These passages evidently involve conventional diction. Polemical statements against foreign nations and foreign gods prefer to mention the "living God."

L. Delekat (*VT* 14 [1964]: 27f.) has suggested that *ḥay* in the phrase *ʾēl ḥay* may have originally meant "kin" (cf. 1 Sam 18:18) and that from the very beginning the *ʾēl ḥay* stood in opposition to foreign gods.

The impression that the "living God" is discussed only with reservation is strengthened if one also considers the *ḥayyîm* passages. The OT never mentions life or vitality as a divine attribute, but often as a result of God's saving activity. With God as the subj., "life" serves as the obj. of the following verbs: *ntn* "to give" (Deut 30:15, 19: Mal 2:5; Job 3:20), *gʾl* "to redeem" (Psa 103:4; Lam 3:58), *nṣr* "to preserve" (Psa 64:2), *ṣwh* pi. "to order" (Psa 133:3), *ʿśh* "to make" (Job 10:12). God is the "source of life" (Psa 36:10); the fear of God brings life (Prov 19:23). One can ask him to grant life (Psa 21:5) and not to take away the life of the supplicant (Psa 26:9). Quite consistently, the factitive and causative verbal stems are used in statements about God. Of the 56 pi. passages, 26 have God as subj. (19x in Psa). Of the 23 hi. passages, God stands as subj. in 9 (never in Psa).

The lexical evidence suggests that the OT lays no great weight on a presentation of the living God. Life and vitality are almost never viewed as Yahweh's attributes. Every emphasis lies on the fact that Yahweh gives life and has power over life, but not that he himself participates in it. OT diction is distinguished from that of the other nations of the ancient Near East, which quite unabashedly speak of the life and vitality of their deities (Chr. Barth, *Die Errettung vom Tode in den individuellen Klage- und Dankliedern des AT* [1947], 36–41; cf. also L. Dürr, *Die Wertung des Lebens im AT und im antiken Orient* [1926]). The various idioms express the various notions of god: on the one hand, the deification of the vital force, which actually signifies the identity of God and life; on the other hand, a clear distance between the creator and creaturely vital forces.

(b) In contrast to *nepeš*, *ḥayyîm* "life" is not an obvious human characteristic, but a gift of God.

This point is expressed with particular clarity in the "Psalm of Hezekiah," Isa 38:9–20, which describes the newly granted life of the convalescent as life in relation to God, as life in praise: v 19, "Life, life, which praises you, as I do today." This statement, in contrast to v 18, "death does not praise you," shows that *ḥayyîm* is understood as healthy life, as life bestowed by God (cf. Westermann, *PLP* 155, 158–61; Chr. Barth, op. cit. 151 comments here: "One should note, however, that the praise of Yahweh functions at the same time as a characteristic of vitality.")

Life is God's gift because the human being is created for life, i.e., as *nepeš ḥayyâ* (Gen 2:7). One's life is identical with one's creatureliness; one recognizes oneself as God's creature through one's existence. Because life is continually threatened, however, it can be promised anew, esp. in the concluding speech of Deut 30:15–20, in the face of these dangers and threats, in the face of every diminishment of life. In this context, the promise of life is closely related to the proclamation of commandment. The commandments promise Israel life. This promise takes place primarily in the cult (Lev 18:5; Deut 30:15, 19). G. von Rad (" 'Righteousness' and 'Life' in the Cultic Language of the Psalms," *PHOE* 243–66) sees this coupling of proclamation of commandment and promise of life as a constitutive element of Yahwistic faith (p. 254). Obedience to God's commandments is linked to life in Deut, in particular, but elsewhere as well (Deut 4:1; 5:33; 8:1; 11:8f.; 16:20; 22:7; 25:15; cf. Exod 20:12; Job 36:11; on Ezek 20 and 33, cf. W. Zimmerli, *TZ* 13 [1957]: 494–508 = *GO* 178–91).

In wisdom, too, life is offered as a gift of salvation, and, indeed, is linked to attention to the exhortations of the wisdom teacher or to the call to follow personifed wisdom (Prov 3:1f.; 4:10, 13, 22f.; 7:2; 8:35; 9:6; cf. Ch. Kayatz, *Studien zu Proverbien 1–9* [1966], 102–7, on the Eg. pars.). The offer of life has been detached here from the cult and is not directed to Israel as a whole but to individuals (von Rad, *Theol.* 1:441ff.).

(c) The question as to whether the OT knows of a life after death receives highly varied responses. The answer depends, above all, upon the understanding of a few Psa that speak of a preservation from death and a redemption from Sheol, esp. Psa 27; 49; 73. According to Barth (op. cit. 165f.), "to redeem from death" means "to redeem from hostile, threatening, and condemning death" and does not refer to a continuation of life after death. In contrast, von Rad (*Theol.* 1:406f.) finds, esp. in Psa 49 and 73, "a strong striving after a principle which does not stop short at a single calamity," but makes a fundamental reference to a life beyond death. Nevertheless, these hymnic statements do not deal with a widely held hope in the afterlife, but with the believer's personal conviction that the living relationship with Yahweh must be indestructible, even beyond death.

The expectation of a general resurrection of the dead occurs first in the apocalyptic literature. The Isa apocalypse mentions a resurrection of the pious (Isa 26:19); Dan 12:1–3 expects a general resurrection, some "to eternal contempt" and others "to eternal life."

5. Both the verbal and the nom. forms are attested in the Qumran texts. The subst. *ḥayyîm* appears frequently as the governing noun in some rather bold metaphorical cs. phrases, e.g., "insight, light, source, trees, stylus of life."

On the LXX and the continuation of the tradition in the NT, cf. G. von Rad, G. Bertram, and R. Bultmann, "ζάω," *TDNT* 2:832–75; H.-J. Kraus, "Der lebendige Gott," *EvT* 27 (1967): 169–200.

G. Gerleman

חַיִל *ḥayil* **power** → כֹּחַ *kōaḥ*

חכם *ḥkm* to be wise

S 2449; BDB 314a; *HALOT* 1:314a; *TDOT* 4:364–85; *TWOT* 647; *NIDOTTE* 2681

1. The root *ḥkm* is attested in most Sem. languages (in addition to GB 229b, see esp. *HAL* 301a; Ug.: *WUS* no. 924; *UT* no. 859; H.-P. Müller, *UF* 1 [1969]: 89n.81; Phoen.: *KAI* no. 26A.I.13; Aram.: *DISO* 87f.; KBL 1075b), although the originality of Akk. *ḫakāmu* "to understand, comprehend" has long been discussed (*HAL* 301a with bibliog.; *CAD* H:32f.; *AHw* 309a; cf. also A. Finet, *AIPHOS* 14 [1954/57]: 132; *CAD* A/2:345a).

In addition to the verb *ḥkm* "to be/become wise" (qal, pi., pu., hi., hitp.), Hebr. also has the noun *ḥākām* "clever, cunning; wise" and the abstracts *ḥokmâ* "wisdom" (only sg., but see below) and *ḥokmôt* "wisdom," which is understood either as an abstract pl. of *ḥokmâ* (*GVG* 2:59; Joüon §§88Mk, 96Ab, 136d; G. Fohrer, *TDNT* 7:476n.85) or as a late sg. formation (GKC §86l; BL 506; W. F. Albright, *SVT* 3 [1955]: 8; cf. *HAL* 302a).

Bibl. Aram. has the person designation *ḥakkîm* "wise ones" (only pl.) and the abstract *ḥokmâ* "wisdom."

2. The concentration of occurrences in wisdom literature is apparent in the following table:

	verb	*ḥākām*	*ḥokmâ*	*ḥokmôt*	total
Gen	–	3	–	–	3
Exod	1	9	8	–	18
Deut	1	5	2	–	8
Judg	–	1	–	–	1
2 Sam	–	4	2	–	6
1 Kgs	1	3	17	–	21
Isa	–	9	5	–	14
Jer	–	11	6	–	17
Ezek	–	3	5	–	8
Hos	–	2	–	–	2
Obad	–	1	–	–	1
Zech	1	–	–	–	1
Psa	4	2	6	1	13
Job	2	8	18	–	28
Prov	13	47	39	3	102
Eccl	4	21	28	–	53
Esth	–	2	–	–	2
Dan	–	–	3	–	3
1 Chron	–	1	1	–	2
2 Chron	–	6	9	–	15
OT	27	138	149	4	318

The verb appears 19x in the qal (Prov 12x), 3x in the pi., 2x in the pu., 2x in the hitp., and 1x in the hi.

The examples in Exod all belong to P, those in Ezek are in Ezek 27f., those in Dan concentrated in Dan 1.

Aram. *ḥakkîm* occurs 14x (in Dan), *ḥokmâ* 8x (Ezra 7:25 and 7x in Dan). Thus the root is represented in the entire OT 340x.

3. The chief meaning of *ḥkm*, depending upon the grammatical form, is traditionally "to be wise; wise one; wisdom." This understanding expresses the special character shared by terms in the word field (cf. H.-J. Hermisson, *Studien zur israelitischen Spruchweisheit* [1968], 11f., 187–192, contra G. Fohrer, *TDNT* 7:476; see also H. H. Schmid, *Wesen und Geschichte der Weisheit* [1966], 196–201, and esp. G. von Rad, *Wisdom in Israel* [1972], 7ff.); nevertheless, semasiological analysis must first examine differences in word usage and the semantic range of the words categorized by grammatical form.

(a) The verb in the basic stem refers, first of all, to the state of "being wise," indeed, as something objectively determinable, whose effectual (even if only imagined; cf. Deut 32:29; Prov 9:12[bis]) presence makes other activities possible, and whose absence prohibits other actions (cf. *HP* 27ff.): in addition to the passages already mentioned, Zech 9:2 (ironic-concessive); Prov 23:15; Eccl 2:15, 19 (all in the pf.), as well as 1 Kgs 5:11 (impf. cons., resumptive); cf. Job 32:9 (with an impf. in the so-called compounded nom. clause). By contrast, the remaining 9 Prov passages (see *HAL* 301a, where all Prov passages are incorrectly listed in one category) use an impf. (9:9; 13:20 Q; 19:20; 20:1; 21:11) or an impv. (6:6; 8:33; 23:19; 27:11) as the predicate (cf. also Eccl 7:23 with a cohortative), and the verb acquires an ingressive meaning: "to become wise," a reference to "being wise" as a future, resultant event, often as the result of another phenomenon; this "other phenomenon" refers to the various means of becoming wise, through either experience (Prov 6:6; 13:20) or instruction (cf. 9:9; 21:11), but esp. through an obedient "listening" that leads to behavior (8:33; 23:19; esp. 19:20: "give heed to counsel [*ᶜēṣâ*] and receive instruction [*mûsār*, → *ysr*]"). "Becoming wise" means training; the impvs. are pleading warning cries to that end.

The production of wisdom is expressed by the factitive reduplicated pi. stem: "to make wise" (Psa 105:22; 119:98; Job 35:11; the subjs. are, resp., Joseph, the commandments of God, God). The related pu. ptcp. gives the result ("to be made wise"), particularly in some technical sense: to be (in some way) "skilled" (Psa 58:6; Prov 30:24; cf. *HAL* 301a; *HP* 162f.). The self-actualization of wisdom comes to expression in the hitp. (Exod 1:10; Eccl 7:16) and once the cause in the hi. ptcp. (Psa 19:8; cf. *HP* 73f., 85).

The following may be mentioned as synonymous or, at least, par. verbs: → *bîn* "to understand" (Job 32:9), yet *bîn* in Deut 32:29 (par. *śkl* "to understand") is more the result of (admittedly lacking) "wisdom"; also *lqḥ daᶜat* "to receive insight" (Prov 21:11), *ysp* hi. *leqaḥ* "to increase in learning" (Prov 9:9; cf. 1:5); *ᶜml* "to toil" is characteristic of Eccl (Eccl 2:19); *ʾlp* pi. "to teach" parallels *ḥkm* pi. (Job 35:11). The par. in the hitp. in Eccl 7:16 to the vetitive "be not too righteous" is remarkable. Antonyms include: *lîṣ* "to mock" (Prov 9:12; cf. 20:1; 21:11) and *rᶜᶜ* ni. "to go badly (for someone)" (Prov 13:20).

(b) Being wise is expressed nom. by *ḥākām* (masc. sg. 78x, fem. sg. 3x, masc. pl. 54x, fem. pl. 3x), often used adj. (cf. *ʾîš ḥākām* "wise man," e.g., 2 Sam

13:3; 1 Kgs 2:9; Prov 16:14; *bēn ḥākām* "wise son," Prov 10:1; 13:1; 15:20; *melek ḥākām* "wise king" Prov 20:26), as well as 15x predicatively (*HP* 26 lists passages), but most often functioning as a subst. ("wise one"). Apart from Prov 30:24, where it is predicated to animals, and Isa 31:2, where it is used of God (cf. Job 9:4; as well as Jer 10:7 and 2 Sam 14:20), the noun describes people in various ways.

Human "cunning and skill" is realized in a broad range of ways; in general, *ḥākām* means "someone who has a masterful understanding of something" (Fohrer, *TDNT* 7:483ff.). This mastery sometimes concerns some technical capability like the artisanship of women (Exod 35:25), but esp. of men (Jer 10:9; cf. BH^3 on Isa 3:3; associated in later texts esp. with the construction of the temple, Exod 28:3; 31:6; chs. 35–36; 1 Chron 22:15; 2 Chron 2:6, 12f.; in Isa 40:20 *ḥārāš ḥākām* "skilled master" of the production of idol images). An abstract subject can also be a skilled activity, then, e.g., the mourning of women (Jer 9:16f.), the many forms of magic (Isa 3:3; cf. Psa 58:6, pu. ptcp.), esp. associated with foreigners (esp. in the pl.; see e.g., Exod 7:11; Isa 44:25; Esth 1:13; as well as most passages in the Aram. of Dan; cf. KBL 1075b; see also Fohrer, op. cit. 483f.; also extensive, with a treatment of the Ug. material: H.-P. Müller, "Magisch-mantische Weisheit und die Gestalt Daniels," *UF* 1 [1969]: 79–94), as well as the political advising of the king in the courtly sphere (→ *yᶜṣ;* cf. P. A. H. de Boer, *SVT* 3 [1955]: 42–71; W. McKane, *Prophets and Wise Men* [1965], 15ff.; in reference to the neighboring nations, see e.g., Gen 41:8; Isa 19:11f.; Jer 50:35; 51:57; Ezek 27:8f.; Esth 6:13; Dan 2:27), where a woman's crafty cunning can also be used (2 Sam 14:2; 20:16ff.). Royal counsel is an element of wise and just government, incumbent esp. upon the king himself (cf. Prov 20:26; Eccl 4:13), in respect to which Solomon, in particular, as *ʾîš ḥākām* (1 Kgs 2:9) and David's "wise son" (1 Kgs 5:21; 2 Chron 2:11), became the prototype of the wise king, whose gift of wisdom was beyond all measure (1 Kgs 3:12; 5:11ff.; cf. also Prov 1:1; 10:1; Eccl 1:1, 16; 2:3ff.; Alt, *KS* [1964³], 2:90–99; Noth, *GS* [1969], 2:99–112; R. B. Y. Scott, *SVT* 3 [1955]: 262–79; and N. W. Porteous, *SVT* 3:247ff.). All of these cases deal with individuals and groups who are knowledgeable in a special, professional manner; this characterization is also true of Joseph (Gen 41:33, 39; cf. G. von Rad, "Joseph Narrative and Ancient Wisdom," *PHOE* 281–91) and of the mythically portrayed "prince of Tyre" who is "wiser than Daniel" (Ezek 28:3; cf. Zimmerli, *Ezek*, Herm, 2:72ff., and Dan 1:4, 17, 20; see 3c).

At the same time, the texts—esp. those in wisdom books—describe an independent type of *ḥākām/ḥᵃkāmîm* who is not related directly to any other profession, but who as a "wise one" executes his own office alongside priests and prophets (Jer 18:18, where, however, a political and courtly aspect may not be overlooked; cf. McKane, op. cit. 42, 128n.1). The "wise one" is primarily a man of the word who gives counsel (Jer 18:18) and crafts and assembles sayings (Prov 22:17; 24:23; Eccl 12:9–11; cf. Prov 1:6; Eccl 9:17), whose words win favor (Eccl 10:12), but who can also reprimand and discipline (Eccl 7:5; cf. Prov 15:12, 31), whose tongue (Prov 15:2) and lips bring insight (Prov 15:7) and healing (Prov 12:18), and whose speech issues from a "wise heart" (Prov 16:21, 23; cf. 1 Kgs 3:12). In addition to the authority of his own "wise heart," in addition to his own experience—for he is an "investigator" who seeks to "find out" and "to understand the significance of things" (cf. Eccl 8:1, 5, 17; 12:9; see Hertzberg, KAT 17/4, 215ff., and Job 15:7ff.)—he draws upon the received traditions of his predecessors (cf. Job 8:8–10; 15:18; see Fohrer, op. cit. 492f.); he receives instruction (Prov 9:9; 12:15; 21:11) and administers his own instruction (*tôrâ*), which is a "source of life" (Prov 13:14). Thus the "wise one" is not just a counselor but equally a teacher and instructor (see e.g., Prov 11:30; 15:31; 18:15; 22:17; Eccl 12:9; W. Zimmerli, "Concerning the Structure of OT Wisdom," *Studies in Ancient Israelite Wisdom* [1976], 177ff.; W. Richter, *Recht und Ethos* [1966], 147ff.; Hermisson, op. cit. 113ff.).

If this usage, which signifies *the* "wise one" in the proper (and somehow status-bound) sense, may be described as the more limited usage, there is also a broader usage that—as already demonstrated above—could characterize other circles as "wise," although the boundaries are fluid. Above all, one is "wise" who heeds "counsel" (Prov 12:15) and loves "instruction" (Prov 13:1 [cf. comms.]; 19:20; 29:15). He pleases his father (10:1; 15:20; 23:24). He is a strong (cf. Prov 21:22; Eccl 7:19) and even-tempered person who quiets anger (Prov 29:8, 11); he is humble and not wise in his own eyes (Prov 3:7; 26:12; Isa 5:21; Jer 9:22). With a wise heart he heeds commandments (Prov 10:8), and so fears and avoids evil (14:16).

A religioethical component is perceptible in Prov 14:16 (see 4); such is also the case where *ṣaddîq* "righteous" appears in Prov as a synonym for *ḥākām* (Prov 9:9; 11:30; 23:24; cf. Eccl 9:1). The more frequent synonym, however, is *nābôn* "insightful" (→ *bîn;* Gen 41:33, 39; Deut 4:6; 1 Kgs 3:12; Isa 3:3; 5:21; 29:14; Hos 14:10; Prov 1:5; 18:15; 16:21, definitively: "one who is wise of heart is called insightful"; cf. 28:11b). Other synonyms are: *ʾîš daʿat* "man of understanding" (Prov 24:5), *ʾanšê lēbāb* "men of understanding" (Job 34:34), *yōdᵉʿîm* "insightful ones" (Job 34:2; cf. Eccl 8:1), *niptālîm* "crafty ones" (Job 5:13). The picture of the "wise" is completed, finally, by the special dialectic of opposition: his opposite is, above all, the "fool" (thus esp. → *kᵉsîl*, 21x, predominantly in Prov and Eccl; otherwise → *ʾᵉwîl*, 7x; → *nābāl* Deut 32:6; *sākāl* Eccl 2:19), but also the "mocker" (*lēṣ*, Prov 9:8; 13:1; 15:12; 21:11; *ʾanšê lāṣôn* Prov 29:8) and the "lazy" (*ʿāṣēl* Prov 26:16).

The line of demarcation expressed by the antonyms refers not only to the "wise" in the limited sense, but equally to the "wise" in the broader sense. In accord with the expanded usage, the people are described as foolish (Deut 32:6), or Ephraim is scoldingly called an "unwise son" by Hosea (Hos 13:13).

The question of the setting of the "wise" in the more limited sense has not yet been sufficiently explained; but one should apparently think of both the court and the school in some form (cf. e.g., L. Dürr, *Das Erziehungswesen im AT und im antiken Orient* [1932], 104ff.; McKane, op. cit. 36ff.; Hermisson, op. cit. 97ff.; von Rad, *Wisdom* 15ff.; in contrast, E. Gerstenberger, *Wesen und Herkunft des "apodiktischen Rechts"* [1965], 128–30; and H. W. Wolff, *Amos the Prophet* [1973], 85–89, emphasize clan instruction and wisdom). See 4 on the rising critique of the thought and doctrine of the wise.

(c) The usage of the abstracts *ḥokmâ* and *ḥokmôt* corresponds largely to that of the personal terms *ḥākām*/*ḥᵃkāmîm*. Thus *ḥokmâ* can mean technical expertise and other professional capabilities of various types (of temple construction: Exod 28–36, see 3b; 1 Kgs 7:14; cf. 1 Chron 28:21; in war: Isa

10:13; nautical skill: Psa 107:27), particularly of the courtly skill of political advising (among the neighboring peoples: Isa 47:10; Jer 49:7; Dan 1:4, 20; in Israel: cf. 2 Sam 20:22; Isa 29:14; also Jer 8:9), and the special gifts of the regent. The historical works occasionally discuss the wisdom of Joshua and David (Deut 34:9; 2 Sam 14:20), although most passages refer to Solomon (1 Kgs 2:6; 3:28; 5:9f., 14, 26; 10:4ff.; 11:41; 2 Chron 1:10–12; 9:3ff., 22f.). Ezek 28:4f., 7, 12, 17 deal with the great wisdom of the Tyrian kings.

With the concentration of occurrences in Prov and Eccl, as well as in Job (see 2), however, *ḥokmâ*/*ḥokmôt* means esp. the "wisdom" of the "wise" in the more limited sense, whereby—as in the courtly sphere—it may concern first of all an educational wisdom (cf. Fohrer, op. cit. 485; also von Rad, *Wisdom* 155n.12), although a broadened usage is also found here; "wisdom" aims at education, among other things. Thus on the one hand "wisdom," which is "too high" for the foolish (Prov 24:7) and is sought to no avail by the mocker (14:6), is often praised: it is better than corals and finery (Prov 8:11; Job 28:18), the pursuit of it better than gold (Prov 16:16); it is better than might and weapons of war (Eccl 9:15f., 18), it is as good as an inheritance (Prov 7:11); through it a house is built (Prov 24:3); it illuminates a person's countenance (Eccl 8:1); through it the wise recognizes their way (Prov 14:8), have a future and hope (24:14), and will obtain life (Eccl 7:12; see 4). On the other hand, because wisdom is such a precious thing, a "pleasure" for the "man of understanding" (Prov 10:23), various exhortations are issued to pursue it, to purchase it (Prov 4:5, 7; 23:23), to pay it attention (5:1), to lend it one's ear (2:2; 5:1), to love and "embrace" it (4:7f.; cf. comms.), to consider it a sister (7:4); it is to be acknowledged (Eccl 1:17; 8:16; cf. Prov 24:14) and sought (Eccl 7:25). It is to be obtained through "rod and reproof" (Prov 29:15), i.e., through education, and to be found with those "who receive counsel" (Prov 13:10). It is an "ability to navigate" (LXX *kybernēsis* for *taḥbūlôt*, Prov 1:5) for the practical conduct of life; it is valuable "to apply (it) properly" (Eccl 10:10b; cf. Zimmerli, ATD 16/1, 235). Wisdom "rests in the heart of one with understanding" (Prov 14:33; also 2:10; Psa 51:8; 90:12), in the center of the person, which can only mean total control over the person, so that he proves to be a *ḥākām* in all of his life and thought; this does not occur in a religiously neutral manner, but in the company of religioethical elements (see 4).

Although the practical orientation of the word dominates, esp. in the older wisdom sayings (cf. e.g., von Rad, *Theol.* 1:418–41), an interest in organizing perception is also unmistakable in the abstract (cf. von Rad, ibid. and 441ff., and esp. id., *Wisdom* passim), which is of the greatest theological consequence (see 4). The abstract *ḥokmâ* seems to have formed a chief and central concept of wisdom thought, in contrast to the rich wisdom literature of Israel's neighbors, with which OT wisdom literature is associated in many ways (reference may be made e.g., to the Eg. *maʿat;* cf., among others, H. Brunner, *HO* 1/2 [1952]: 93–95; H. Gese, *Lehre und Wirklichkeit in der alten Weisheit* [1958], 11ff.; this background cannot be further investigated here; cf., however, Fohrer, op. cit. 477ff.; Schmid, op. cit.; H. D. Preuss, *EvT* 30 [1970], 393–417, with comprehensive references to text editions and secondary literature).

Yet one may not overlook at this point that *ḥokmâ* is often supported by or can be interchanged with synonyms (cf. von Rad, *Wisdom* 12ff.), esp. the "perception root" → *bîn: bînâ* "insight" (16x, 7x in Prov, 5x in Job, also Deut 4:6; Isa 11:2; 29:14; Dan 1:20 *[ḥokmat bînâ]*, but not in Eccl), *tᵉbûnâ* "insight" (11x, 7x in Prov, also Job 12:12f.; Jer 10:12; Ezek 28:4), as well as *tᵉbûnôt* "cleverness" (Psa 49:4 par. *ḥokmôt*); then *daᶜat* "knowledge, perception" (→ *ydᶜ*, 14x: 6x in Eccl, 4x in Prov, also Isa 11:2; 33:6; 47:10; Dan 1:4; not in Job), *maddāᶜ* "understanding" (2 Chron 1:10–12; Dan 1:4; cf. 1:17, as well as Aram. *mandaᶜ* "understanding" Dan 2:21); *śēkel* "insight" (Psa 111:10). The following may also be mentioned: *ᶜēṣâ* "counsel" (Isa 11:2; Jer 49:7; Job 12:13; Prov 21:30); *mûsār* "instruction" (Prov 1:2, 7; 23:23) *ᵓᵉmet* "truth" (Psa 51:8) *mišpāṭ* "justice" (Psa 37:30); *tôrat-ḥesed* "loving instruction" (Prov 31:26; cf. Gemser, HAT 16, 110). Notably, the usage of synonyms or pars. occurs least in the Dtr history (only Deut 4:6) and most in the latest portion of Prov (chs. 1–9); cf. also the series in Aram., Dan 5:11, 14. Antonyms are few and occur most frequently in Eccl: *hôlēlôt* "folly, delusion" (1:17; 2:12; 7:25), *siklût* "folly" (2:12f.; 7:25; = *śiklût* 1:17); *kesel* "folly" (7:25); finally, *ᵓiwwelet* "folly" (Prov 14:8, 33 txt em).

4. (a) Religioethical implications of the root *ḥkm* find expression in the older portions of Prov (chs. 10ff.), esp. in the pars. of *ḥākām* and *ṣaddîq* "righteous" as well as in the contrast "wise-fool," regularly parallel to "righteous-evildoer." These usages are not accidental polarizations, but recognize behaviors in accordance with or contrary to established order (cf. U. Skladny, *Die ältesten Spruchsammlungen in Israel* [1962], 7ff., etc.; H. H. Schmid, *Gerechtigkeit als Weltordnung* [1968], 157ff.; as well as Hermisson, op. cit. 73ff.). Folly results in evil and ruin for fools (→ *ᵓᵉwîl* 4; cf. von Rad, *Theol.* 1:428f.), but wisdom leads one in "right paths" (Prov 4:11); it is a "source of life" (cf. 13:14; 16:22; also 14:27), and it serves to manage and assure human life (16:17; 28:26); through it one avoids "the evil" (14:16) and "the snares of death" (13:14). Thus one with wisdom benefits from the relationship between deed and consequence (cf. K. Koch, *ZTK* 52 [1955]: 1–42; also Schmid, *Gerechtigkeit* 175ff.; von Rad, *Wisdom* 124ff.).

Wisdom derives its beneficial power and function, however, from God; the religioethical significance of the root *ḥkm* lies primarily in relationship to Yahweh, the God of Israel. He himself is "wise" (Isa 31:2; Job 9:4) and has wisdom "with him" (Job 12:13); only he—not people—knows "its place" and "the way to it" (Job 28:23, cf. vv 7, 12, 20). It is associated primarily with his creative acts (Jer 10:12 = 51:15; Psa 104:24; Job 28 and 38; Prov 3:19; see below on 8:22ff.). He can, however, declare the "secret of wisdom" to people (Job 11:6), a reference to the "hidden wise action of God" (Fohrer, KAT 16, 226). He can also "give" wisdom (to Solomon: 1 Kgs 5:9, 26; 2 Chron 9:23; also Exod 31:6; 36:1f. P; Prov 2:6; Eccl 2:26; Aram. Dan 2:21), "fill with the spirit of wisdom" (Exod 28:3; cf. 31:3 P; also Deut 34:9 of Joshua's charisma), or "teach" it (*ydᶜ* hi., Psa 51:8; cf. 90:12).

(b) The relationship of wisdom to God has further, first of all, positive consequences: As the "fear of Yahweh" *(yirᵓat yhwh,* → *yrᵓ)* is a "source of life" (Prov 14:27; see above), so is it the "beginning" (or "sum," *rēᵓšît*) of wisdom (cf. 1:7; 9:10; 15:33; Psa 111:10). In addition, wisdom experienced a salvation-historical (cf. Psa 107:43; Deut 32:6, 29) and a prophetic application, even in the proclamation of judgment (Hos 13:13; Isa 5:21; 29:14; Jer 8:8f.; 18:18; also Isa 10:13; 19:11f.; 47:10; Jer 49:7; 50:35; 51:57; Ezek 28:4ff.;

Obad 8; Zech 9:2; cf. Hos 14:10; Jer 9:11, 22), as well as salvation-eschatological (Isa 33:6) and messianic (Isa 11:2; cf. Deut 34:9; 1 Kgs 3:28; 5:26) applications. Then, too, one may recognize a negative-critical manifestation: when Isaiah and Jeremiah inveigh against the hybrid wisdom of both Israelite (cf. Isa 29:14; Jer 18:18) and foreign wisemen or rulers in order to contrast the wondrous action of Yahweh (Isa 29:14), his wisdom (Isa 31:2), or his word (Jer 8:9), the reference may primarily be to wisdom as the art of governing or as the art of political counsel that is unsuccessful if directed against Yahweh (cf. also Prov 21:30f.).

Otherwise, the disputations in the book of Job and the critique of Qohelet undertake an inner-wisdom corrective; in this manner, the principle of order is guarded from the danger of a "dogmatization" in the sense of an "independent law of the created orders," while the boundaries between wisdom and the sovereign freedom of God can be simultaneously preserved (see with extensive references, Zimmerli, "Place and Limit of the Wisdom in the Framework of the OT Theology," *Studies in Ancient Israelite Wisdom* [1976], 314–26; Schmid, *Wesen* 173ff.; Fohrer, *TDNT* 7:495f.; and esp. von Rad, *Wisdom* 97ff.).

(c) Finally, two manifestations of the religioethical affinities of wisdom, pertinent primarily to the latest phase of the OT, are noteworthy. On the one hand, wisdom gradually comes to be related to Yahweh's commandments and law (cf. already Deut 4:6; see J. Malfroy, *VT* 15 [1965]: 49–65; also perhaps Psa 19:8; 119:98; cf. J. Fichtner, *Die altorientalische Weisheit in ihrer israelitisch-jüdischen Ausprägung* [1933], 81ff., with references to pertinent passages). On the other hand, it achieves independence in relation to God and is personified to a degree (the extent to which one must reckon with a hypostasis here continues to be disputed; cf. H. Ringgren, *Word and Wisdom* [1947], 89ff.; R. Marcus, *HUCA* 23/1 [1950/51]: 157–71; Fohrer, op. cit. 490f.), thus esp. in Prov 1–9 (cf. also Job 28; see C. Kayatz, *Studien zu Proverbien 1–9* [1966]; also R. N. Whybray, *Wisdom in Proverbs* [1965]; otherwise, von Rad, *Wisdom* 144ff., with bibliog.). Thus the figurative personified *ḥokmâ* appears here as "the mediator of revelation in the sense that in her proclamation she is like a prophet and can claim supreme authority, revealing God's will to man, offering man life, and understanding acceptance as that of the divine will" (Fohrer, op. cit. 494).

5. Both the nomistic and the personifying tendencies are continued in post-OT literature (above all in Sir; cf. E. G. Bauckmann, *ZAW* 72 [1960]: 33–63; J. C. H. Lebram, "Nachbiblische Weisheitstraditionen," *VT* 15 [1965]: 167–237; von Rad, *Wisdom* 240ff.).

On Qumran literature (according to Kuhn, *Konk.* 72, *ḥākām* 5x and *ḥokmâ* 13x), which otherwise readily uses → *śkl* (cf. J. A. Sanders, *ZAW* 76 [1964]: 66), as well as on the LXX, where the rendition of *ḥkm* is dominated by *sophos*/*sophia*, as well as for the wealth of early Jewish, Gnostic, and NT materials, see U. Wilckens and G. Fohrer, "σοφία," *TDNT* 7:465–528; cf. further, e.g, U. Wilckens, *Weisheit und Torheit* (1959); F. Christ, *Jesus Sophia: Die Sophia-Christologie bei den Synoptikern* (1970).

M. Sæbø

חלה *ḥlh* to be sick

S 2470; BDB 317b; *HALOT* 1:316b; *TDOT* 4:399–409; *TWOT* 648; *NIDOTTE* 2703

1. Hebr. *ḥlh* "to be weak, sick" (by-form *ḥlʾ*) has no direct counterparts in the other Sem. languages (SSem. etymologies have been suggested by *HAL* 302a, 303b, among others; cf. also D. R. Ap-Thomas, *VT* 6 [1956]: 239f.).

Akk. *ḫalû* occurs at Mari as a Can. loanword (*CAD* H:54a; *AHw* 314b).

G. R. Driver (*JTS* 29 [1928]: 392; id., FS Kahle 98–101; cf. *CPT* 326) finds a new root *ḥlh* in 1 Sam 22:8 in the sense of "to be concerned" (cf. Eth. *ḫly* "to ponder, to be agitated in spirit," etc.; Dillmann 577f.). This root may also be postulated for Jer 5:3 ("to take to heart," par. *lqḥ mûsār* "to receive instruction") and in the ni. in Amos 6:6 ("to be concerned for").

Zorell 242b attributes the expression *ḥlh* pi. *pānîm* "to appease" not to *ḥlh* I but to *ḥlh* II "to be sweet, pleasant" ("to make someone's countenance pleasant"); Ap-Thomas (op. cit.) discusses other possibilities.

ḥlh is the only intrans. that occurs in the OT in all seven stems (cf. → *glh* 1). Nom. derivatives with the meaning "illness" are *ḥ^{o}lî, maḥ^{a}leh, maḥ^{a}lâ, maḥ^{a}lūyîm,* and, from the root *ḥlʾ*, *taḥ^{a}lūʾîm.* Regarding the (artificial?) PN *maḥlôn* (alongside *kilyôn*) in Ruth 1:2, 5; 4:9f.; cf. *IP* 10 (contrast, however, Rudolph, KAT 17/1, 38).

2. Incl. *ḥlʾ* (2 Chron 16:12 qal; Isa 53:10 hi.) and the passages discussed above that may not contain forms of *ḥlh* I, the verb occurs 74x, 36x in the qal (contrary to Mandl., one should attribute 1 Sam 31:3; Jer 5:3; 1 Chron 10:3 with Lis. to *ḥîl* I "to quake"), 10x in the ni., 17x in the pi. (according to Lis., Psa 77:11 belongs to *ḥll* II qal "to pierce"), 1x in the pu., 4x in the hi., and 3x each in the ho. and the hitp.

The statistics for the subst. are: *ḥ^{o}lî* 24x (2 Chron 6x, 2 Kgs and Isa 4x each), *maḥ^{a}leh* 2x, *maḥ^{a}lâ* 4x, *maḥ^{a}lūyîm* 1x, *taḥ^{a}lūʾîm* 5x.

Of the total of 110 instances of the root, 16 occur in 2 Chron (qal, pi., ho., and all 5 noms.), 12 in Isa, 11 in 2 Kgs, 9 each in 1 Kgs and Jer. The distribution exhibits no peculiarities; the root is—probably by accident—only rarely attested in the Pentateuch.

3. (a) Apart from the expression *ḥlh* pi. *pānîm* (see b), the root always describes a situation of bodily weakness (cf. J. Scharbert, *Der Schmerz im AT* [1955], 36–40; J. Hempel, "Heilung als Symbol und Wirklichkeit im biblischen Schrifttum," *NAWG* 3 [1958]: 237–314, esp. 238n.1).

Synonyms include esp. the roots **dwy* "to be weak, sick" and **mrḍ* "to be sick, feel pain" (P. Fronzaroli, *AANLR* 8/19 [1964]: 250, 263f.), which unlike *ḥlh* are common Sem.; derivatives of the former are the adjs. *dāweh* and *dawwāy* "sick" (Lam 1:13; 5:17; and Isa 1:5; Jer 8:18; Lam 1:22, resp.) and the substs. *d^{e}way* "illness" (Psa 41:4; Job 6:7) and *madweh* "illness, pestilence" (Deut 7:15; 28:60); *dwh* qal "to be ill" (just like *dāwâ* "ill" in Lev 15:33; 20:18; Isa 30:22) is used euphemistically for menstruation in Lev 12:2; derivatives of **mrḍ* are *mrṣ* ni. "to be in pain" (1 Kgs 2:8; Mic 2:10; Job 6:25) and hi. "to vex" (Job 16:3).

The qal of the verb signifies, first of all, "to be/become weak" (Gen 48:1 probably means the weakness of age; Judg 16:7, 11, 17, weakness as the normal human state in comparison to the strength of the charismatic Samson; Isa 57:10 txt?, sexual weakness). But usually the verb means weakness in the sense of "to be ill" (1 Sam 19:14; 30:13; 1 Kgs 14:1, 5; 17:17; 2 Kgs 8:7; 20:12 = Isa 39:1; Isa 38:9; Psa 35:13, without further characterization of the illness). Illness can also consist of an injury (2 Kgs 1:2; injury in battle, 2 Kgs 8:29 = 2 Chron 22:6; blows, Prov 23:35). Sometimes the illness is described more precisely: it can involve a foot condition (1 Kgs 15:23) or a mortal illness (2 Kgs 13:14; 20:1 = Isa 38:1 = 2 Chron 32:24). The verb can also be used of animals (Mal 1:8 par. *pissēaḥ* "lame"; such sick animals—external blemishes must be intended—are cultically unacceptable; cf. also Mal 1:13). The fig. language of Ezek 34 (cf. esp. vv 4, 16) shows that the responsibilities of the shepherd include special care for the "weak and ill" in the herd. This image illustrates Israel's guidance by its leaders or by Yahweh.

The verb is also used of emotional suffering, as of "love sickness" (Song Sol 2:5; 5:8) and to translate into the expression *rāᶜâ ḥôlâ* "a terrible evil" (Eccl 5:12, 15; 6:1 txt em).

The ni. has approximately the same meaning as the qal: "to be/become weak" (Jer 12:13 par. *bôš* "to be/become ashamed," opposite *yᶜl* hi. "to have success") and "to become sick" (Dan 8:27). The substantivized ptcp. indicates "the sick" (Ezek 34:4, 21; see above); the expression *yôm naḥªlâ* "day of illness" (Isa 17:11 par. *keʾēb ʾānûš* "unrelievable pain") probably takes up curse terminology and uses it to describe the coming judgment of Yahweh. *makkâ naḥlâ* "ruinous blow" (Jer 10:19; 14:17; 30:12; Nah 3:19) is a fixed formulation; it apparently belongs to the vocabulary of the lament in the description of distress (formal elements can be recognized in Jer 10:19; 14:17; cf. also Psa 41:4) and was then transferred by prophecy into other contexts.

In Deut 29:21 the pi. signifies "to allow to become sick" (with *taḥªlūʾîm*, in conjunction with curse threats; the usage of *ḥºlî* in Deut 28:59, 61 is similar). The pu. means "to be made weak" (Isa 14:10 of the transition into the realm of the dead), the hitp. "to feel sick" (2 Sam 13:2, the cares of love; 13:5f. "to feign illness").

The hi. has the meaning "to make sick" (Prov 13:12; with the obj. "heart" it can also describe emotional suffering; the text is uncertain in Isa 53:10; Hos 7:5; Mic 6:13), the ho., "to be drained of strength" (1 Kgs 22:34 = 2 Chron 18:33; 2 Chron 35:23, always of injuries).

Thus it is apparent that *ḥlh* in the various stems describes conditions of bodily as well as emotional weakness; the same conclusion results from a review of the derivatives (*ḥºlî* is used in reference to an emotional condition in e.g., Eccl 5:16; 6:2; and probably also Isa 1:5). Religious practices (which often seem to have manifested a struggle between Israelite and Can. religion; cf. 2 Kgs 1:1ff.) and medicinal means (cf. P. Humbert, "Maladie et médecine dans l'AT," *RHPR* 44 [1964]: 1–29; J. Hempel, " 'Ich bin der Herr, dein Arzt,' " *TLZ* 82 [1967]: 809–26) were used to treat illnesses.

(b) In the pi. the root *ḥlh* acquired another possible meaning in a fixed expression (see 1): *ḥlh* pi. *pānîm* means "to appease"; the obj. can be either a person (Psa 45:13; Job 11:19; Prov 19:6 "to flatter") or God (this usage is a technical cultic term). It can refer to sacrifice (1 Sam 13:12; Mal 1:9), prayer (Exod 32:11; 1 Kgs 13:6; 2 Kgs 13:4; Jer 26:19; Zech 7:2; 8:21f. par. *bqš* pi. *yhwh* "to seek Yahweh"; Psa 119:58; 2 Chron 33:12), or reform of conduct (Dan 9:13).

4. In summary, illness has special significance for the OT in that it is either experienced as distress that leads to lament (cf. in various contexts, e.g., Isa 38:9; 1 Kgs 8:37 = 2 Chron 6:28; 2 Chron 16:12) or is understood as the effect of God's curse (cf. Deut 28:59, 61; 29:11; Isa 1:5; Jer 10:19; 12:13; 2 Chron 21:15, 18f.; pity: Exod 15:26; 23:25; Deut 7:15; *ḥ^{o}lî* is a key term, then, in Isa 53:3f., 10). In later times, OT voices hope for a future without illness established by Yahweh (Isa 33:24; cf. 1 QH 11:22).

5. In the NT, the aspect of illness just mentioned is particularly essential in that Jesus actualizes that future without illness (cf. esp. Matt 11:2ff.); on the whole NT, cf. G. Stählin, "ἀσθενής," *TDNT* 1:490–93; A. Oepke, "νόσος (μαλακία)," *TDNT* 4:1091–98.

F. Stolz

חלל *ḥll* pi. **to desecrate**

S 2490; BDB 320a; *HALOT* 1:319b; *TDOT* 4:409–17; *TWOT* 661; *NIDOTTE* 2725

---

1. Hebr. *ḥll* pi. "to desecrate," the other stems with corresponding meanings (hi. "to desecrate" only in Num 30:3 and Ezek 39:7; ni. and pu. "to be profaned"; on the forms, cf. BL 436), and the noms. (*ḥôl* "profane" and, in the event that it should not be considered, following *HAL* 307b, with *ḥll* II "to pierce through," *ḥālāl* "profane, desecrated" in Lev 21:7, 14; Ezek 21:30; also *ḥalîlâ* "may it not be so") belong to a root represented in the whole Sem. linguistic realm with the original meaning "to loose, set free" (cf. *SNHL* 31f.); the meaning dominant later is "to desecrate, profane" (in late and postbibl. Hebr. an unambiguously definable term, a characteristic notion for the thought of the era; cf. *WTM* 2:58f.; Ben-Yehuda 2:1580–83). In the hi. the meaning "to begin" dominates alongside "to desecrate" (in addition to ho. "to be begun" and *t^{e}ḥillâ* "beginning"); the connection between the two groups is clarified by the use of *ḥll* pi. in the sense of "to place in profane use" (Deut 20:6bis; 28:30; Jer 31:5, of the beginning of the use of a vineyard at the end of a period of consecration in which the harvest was forbidden for one's own use; cf. Lev 19:23–25; see *ILC* 3–4:271).

The Akk. *elēlu* in the basic (G) stem means "to be clear" or "to be cultically pure" (persons, lips, incantations) and "to be free" (of promises), in the reduplicated (D) stem "to purify" (oneself, mouth and hands, the bodies of the gods), "to consecrate through cleansing" (the daughter), and "to set free" (slaves); cf. *AHw* 197f. Arab. also attests the broadly distributed root *ḥll* in the meaning "to free, be permitted" (Lane 1/2:619ff.).

An original relationship to *ḥll* (**ḫll*) "to pierce (through), wound" may not be assumed despite a few points of contact (esp. in Arab.). The older NWSem. texts do not attest the verb with certainty (cf. *WUS* no. 928; *DISO* 89). In the later Sem. languages and dialects the post-exilic OT usage became dominant under the influence of Judaism and also gained even broader formal influence (cf. further *LS* 231; Dillmann 66; Littmann-Höfner 52f.; Drower-Macuch 148b).

2. The verb occurs 134x in the OT, 66x in the pi. (Ezek 22x, Lev 14x, Isa and Psa 5x each), and 56x in the hi. ("to desecrate" only 2x, otherwise "to begin": 2 Chron 11x, Judg 8x, Deut 7x, Gen 6x, Num and 1 Sam 4x each); in addition, the ni. is attested 10x (Ezek 7x) and the pu. and ho. 1x each. Only 2 of the 75 passages that use the verb in the sense of "to desecrate" (pi. 62x, hi. 2x, ni., and pu.) are unobjectionably pre-exilic: Gen 49:4 and Exod 20:25 (on Amos 2:7, cf. Wolff, *Amos*, Herm, 133f.; on Zeph 3:4 cf. Sellin-Fohrer 457). Almost 2/3 of all occurrences of "to desecrate" are contained in Ezek (31x) and in H (16x). Otherwise, the term occurs in isolated passages in P, Deutero-Isa (and Isa 23:9; 56:2, 6), Jer, Mal, Psa, Lam, Dan, and Chron.

ḥôl occurs 7x (1 Sam 21:5f. and—always in explicit opposition to *qōdeš*—Lev 10:10; Ezek 22:26; 42:20; 44:23; correspondingly 48:15 "profane residential area"), *ḥālāl* 3x (see 1), *hālîlâ* 21x (1 Sam 8x, Gen 4x, 2 Sam 3x, Josh and Job 2x, 1 Kgs and 1 Chron 1x, twice in 2 Sam 20:20), and *tᵉḥillâ* 22x (Gen 4x, Judg, 2 Sam, and Dan 3x each).

3./4. (a) In H, concepts connected to the term *ḥll* pi. "to desecrate" may be adduced with greatest assurance. The holiness (→ *qdš*) of Yahweh and of that which pertains to him, esp. the priesthood, should be ensured against desecration. Commandments to this end almost always have the form *lōʾ* + impf. and represent professional priestly knowledge (J. Begrich, "Die priesterliche Tora," BZAW 66 [1936], 85–87 = *GS* [1964], 256–58; R. Kilian, *Literarkritische und formgeschichtliche Untersuchung des Heiligkeitsgesetzes* [1963], 84–103 on Lev 21f., attributes the *ḥll* regulations to his layer II of the Ur-Holiness Code). The priest becomes desecrated through engagement in particular mourning rites (Lev 21:20), through the harlotry of his daughter (21:9; cf. 18:29), through contact with the corpse of a married sister (21:4); he becomes merely unclean through contact with the corpse of an *un*married sister and other near relations (→ *ṭmʾ*; Elliger, HAT 4, 288f.). The high priest may not approach any corpse whatsoever, lest he desecrate the sanctuary (21:12); such would also be the case if one afflicted with deformities were to exercise the priestly office (21:23). The descendants of the high priest would be desecrated by his marriage to a widow, divorcée, rape victim, or prostitute (21:15). The pericope Lev 22:1–16 commands the priests to handle the sacrificial offerings with greatest reverence so that Yahweh's name or the offering itself may not be desecrated (22:2, 9, 15; cf. H. Reventlow, *Das Heiligkeitsgesetz formgeschichtlich untersucht* [1961], 92–103; C. Feucht, *Untersuchungen zum Heiligkeitsgesetz* [1964], 44f.); P has a corresponding instruction (Num 18:32). All other Israelites are also warned against the desecration of Yahweh's name; it would result from child sacrifice (Lev 18:21; 20:3), the enjoyment of the flesh of the sacrifice as late as the third day after the sacrifice (19:8), false oaths (19:12), and general inattention and disobedience of the commandments (22:32).

Concepts associated with the fear of desecrating Yahweh's name may not be deduced with confidence. Noteworthy is the general explanation that this fear referred to a desanctification and thereby a debilitation of the name (H. A. Brongers, *ZAW* 77 [1965]: 11). Yet such a consequence is hardly a real possibility for Yahwism. The facts of the case of a severely punishable and fatal offense are presented for the witness in every instance.

(b) In contrast to the self-contained conceptual world of H, the term spans a broader area in Ezek. The discussion here most often concerns the (mostly already transpired) desecration of God or of his name (11x), of the Sabbath (7x), and of the temple (7x). The guilty parties are always the Israelites, but the essence of the guilt and desecration is not always discernible. It is explicitly stated that Yahweh is desecrated by magical rites among the deportees in Babylon (13:19; Zimmerli, *Ezek*, Herm, 1:297). Five times Ezek 36:20–23 denounces the desecration of God's name. The profanation of the name results from the fact that—in view of the separation of Israel from the promised land—he is slandered among the heathen as powerless. Even if one may distinguish this desecration by the situation from that resulting from Israel's behavior, the guilt lies with Israel because it must finally be punished with rejection on account of its apostasy (Fohrer, HAT 13, 109f.; Zimmerli, *Ezek*, Herm, 1:409, 416; 2:246–48), although formerly Yahweh had foregone the deserved punishment in order to avoid a desecration of his name (20:9, 14). Yet he will take care that in the future his name is not desecrated again (20:39; 39:7). The "history of sin" of the exodus esp. emphasizes the desecration of the Sabbath, in addition to charges of idol worship and transgression of the commandments (Ezek 20:13, 16, 21, 24; cf. 22:8; 23:38). Exod 31:14 P; Isa 56:2, 6; and Neh 13:17f. agree with this characterization. The desecration by Israel and its priests of the temple and of that which is holy to Yahweh (Ezek 22:26, by blurring the distinction between holy and profane; 23:39, by child sacrifice; 44:7, by allowing foreigners access to the temple) means the desecration of the holy God himself (22:26) and is requited through the destruction of the temple and the sanctuaries; thus the catastrophe of 587 is also a desecration (7:21f., 24; 25:3), and one can say that God himself has desecrated his sanctuary (24:21). This usage supports a more general understanding of the word, as indicated in the Tyre section: the punishment of Tyre by violent enemies is also desecration (28:7), as is the fall to hell of its hybrid king (28:16; cf. Isa 23:9), who had desecrated his sanctuaries (Fohrer, HAT 13, 163: "my sanctuary"; 28:18).

(c) Isa 43:28; 47:6; Psa 74:7; and Lam 2:2 also depict the collapse of 587 as desecration, but in contrast to Psa 74:7, Deutero-Isa attributes the event to God alone. Psa 89:40 likewise acknowledges the desecration of Judah's king as God's act. A new occurrence of *ḥll* is conjectured for Deutero-Isa in Isa 52:5 (*y*ᵉ*ḥull*ᵉ*lû* instead of *y*ᵉ*hêlîlû*; cf. S. H. Blank, "Is 52,5 and the Profanation of the Name," *HUCA* 25 [1954]: 1–8). Later, the author of Dan regarded the ravaging of the temple by Antiochus Epiphanes as desecration (Dan 11:31).

(d) The word does not occur in the 8th-cent. prophets, if Amos 2:7 is to be regarded as an addition (Wolff, *Amos*, Herm, 133f.); here the name of Yahweh is seen as desecrated by the fact that son and father go (together) to a prostitute. For Jeremiah, the land is desecrated by idol worship (Jer 16:18) and the name of Yahweh by the return of debt slaves to slavery (34:16); Zephaniah brands the egoistic usage of holy things by the priests as desecration (Zeph 3:4); Malachi finds it in cultic as well as in moral transgressions (Mal 1:12, sacrifices of poor quality; 2:10, infidelity with one another as desecration of the covenant of the fathers; 2:11, marriage with foreigners). Twice the breech of word or covenant is called "desecration" (Psa 55:21; Num 30:3 P); and God does not want to desecrate his → *b^e^rît* through the breech of his promises (Psa 89:35).

(e) Only the two occurrences of *ḥll* pi. in the blessing of Jacob and the Covenant Code are transmitted from the first five hundred years of Israelite literary history: Reuben desecrated his father's couch through intercourse with Bilhah (Gen 49:4, cited in 1 Chron 5:1), and the altar stones are desecrated by being dressed with an iron implement (Exod 20:25). Reuben's deed is a matter of forbidden involvement in the father's intimate sphere and an endangerment of the peace of the extended family (de Vaux 1:117; W. Elliger, *ZAW* 67 [1955]: 8–12 = *KS* [1966], 239–44; id., HAT 4, 238–40). The prohibition against dressing the altar stones used to be frequently explained in terms of avoiding the displacement of the numen dwelling in the stone (K. Marti, *Geschichte der israelitischen Religion* [1903^4], 100; Baentsch, *Exodus–Leviticus–Numeri*, HKAT, 188; Beer, *Exodus*, HAT, 106). Nomadic traditions and norms averse to everything civilized—specifically regarding cultic arrangements—offer a more likely explanation (de Vaux 2:408).

(f) *ḥôl* and *ḥālāl* occur only in Lev and Ezek except for the 2x *ḥôl* appears in the old narrative 1 Sam 21: the priest Ahimelek has no bread designated for profane consumption *(leḥem ḥôl)*, only bread for holy use; David certifies that his people's "vessels" were holy even on ordinary journeys *(derek ḥôl)* and that they are certainly holy today (1 Sam 21:5f.). Already in this early witness, then, *ḥôl* is the opposite of *qādôš* (→ *qdš*), "holy," as in Lev 10:10 and in Ezek. The Sam texts, as well as the occurrence in old texts of the interjection *ḥālîlâ* "may it not be so," lit. "for the profane," show that the word group must be understood in relationship to the OT → *qdš* concept (BL 654; see also M. Held, *JCS* 15 [1961]: 21; M. R. Lehmann, *ZAW* 81 [1969]: 82f.; cf. *BHH* 1:415; *BLex*^{2} 398f.).

5. The paramount significance of the term in Mid. Hebr. is illuminated by the numerous examples in *WTM* and Ben-Yehuda (see 1). The elaborate delineation of the "profane" is the urgent concern of rabbinic literature; the mishnaic and talmudic tractate V/3 bears the name *Ḥullin*.

At Qumran and in the related literature, *ḥll* occurs in the Damascus document in connection to the Sabbath commandment (CD 11:15; 12:4; cf. Kuhn, *Konk.* 72).

The NT surmounts the customary understanding of the profane and revokes the boundaries drawn in contemporary Judaism between holy and profane (F. Hauck, "βέβηλος," *TDNT* 1:604f.; id., "κοινός," *TDNT* 3:789–809; id., "μιαίνω," *TDNT* 4:644–47.

F. Maass

חלק *ḥlq* to divide

S 2505; BDB 323b; *HALOT* 1:322b; *TDOT* 4:447–51; *TWOT* 669; *NIDOTTE* 2745

1. The root *ḥlq* occurs in the meaning "to divide, distribute" only in Hebr. and Aram. (*DISO* 89f.; KBL 1076a). Linguists generally associate it with Arab. *ḫalaqa* "to measure off, form" and other SSem. verbs (*HAL* 309b under *ḥlq* II). It is unclear whether and how, on the one hand, the group incl. Ug. *ḫlq* "to be destroyed," Akk. *ḫalāqu* "to go forth, be destroyed," and Eth. *ḫalqa* "to disappear" (*HAL* 310 under *ḥlq* III; → *ʾbd* 3), and, on the other hand, the group comprising Hebr. *ḥlq* "to be smooth" (*ḥālāq* "smooth"), Arab. *ḫalaqa* "to smooth" etc. (*HAL* 309b under *ḥlq* I) belongs with *ḥlq* "to divide."

The Hebr. verb occurs in all verbal stems except the ho.; there are also the nom. derivatives *ḥēleq* "portion," *ḥelqâ* "parcel of land," *ḥ*ᵃ*luqqâ* "division," and *maḥ*ᵃ*lōqet* "portion, division." *ḥ*ᵃ*lāq* "portion" and *maḥl*ᵉ*qâ* "division" are attested in Bibl. Aram.

2. The OT attests the word group (excl. proper names) 188x in Hebr. and 4x in Aram.: verb 56x (Josh 7x, Isa and 1 Chron 5x each), specifically, qal 17x, ni. 8x (1 Chron 23:6 and 24:3 should apparently be understood as qals; cf. Rudolph, HAT 21, 154; *HAL* 309b), pi. 26x, pu. 3x, hitp. 1x, and hi. 1x; *ḥēleq* 66x (Josh 9x, Deut and Eccl 8x each, Psa 6x, Job 5x); *ḥelqâ* 23x (2 Kgs 6x, 2 Sam 5x, excl. the place designation in 2 Sam 2:16; cf. *HAL* 311b), *ḥ*ᵃ*luqqâ* 1x (2 Chron 35:5), and *maḥ*ᵃ*lōqet* 42x (1 Chron 26x, 2 Chron 11x, Josh 3x, Ezek and Neh 1x); Aram. *ḥ*ᵃ*lāq* 3x and *maḥl*ᵉ*qâ* 1x.

3. (a) The qal means "to divide, distribute," whereby the weight often lies less on the dividing procedure as such and more on the distribution. It can thus refer to the division/distribution of plunder (Josh 22:8; 1 Sam 30:24), a field (2 Sam 19:30), silver (Job 27:17), inheritance (Prov 17:2), supplies (Neh 13:13), division with the thief (Prov 29:24), division of people into different groups (1 Chron 24:4f.; 2 Chron 23:18; this specifically Chr usage includes the usage of *maḥ*ᵃ*lōqet* and *ḥ*ᵃ*luqqâ* as "division," similarly attested only in the Chr history), and, in the context of the conquest narrative, the division and distribution of the land or the inheritance (Josh 14:5; 18:2; cf. Neh 9:22 with God as subj.; corresponding to the the pass. ni. in Num 26:53, 55f.).

2 Chron 28:21, where the verb must be translated "to plunder," etc. (cf. LXX and 2 Kgs 16:8), should probably be read *ḥillēṣ* instead of *ḥālaq* (cf. Rudolph, HAT 21, 292).

On Deut 4:19; 29:25; Job 39:17, see 4.

(b) The ni. (except in the passages already discussed, Num 26:53, 55f.) is reflexive: "to divide/distribute among themselves" (Gen 14:15, Abraham and his colleagues; 1 Kgs 16:21, the people Israel; Job 38:24 txt?, the light or the wind; cf. Fohrer, KAT 16, 492).

The pi. can be rendered almost exclusively "to divide/distribute" (on the distinction from the qal, cf. *HP* 126–30). Objs. of the division/distribution are things (plunder, Gen 49:27; Exod 15:9; Judg 5:30; Isa 9:2; 53:12b; Psa 68:13; Prov 16:19; pu. pass., Zech 14:1 = 1 Chron 16:3; clothing, Psa 22:19; cf. Mark 15:24 par.) or land (Josh 13:7; 18:10; 19:51; 1 Kgs 18:6; Ezek 47:21; Joel 4:2; Mic 2:4 txt?; Psa 60:8 = 108:8; Dan 11:39; hitp. "to divide among themselves," Josh 18:5), with a divine subj., objs. also include fate, etc. (Isa 34:17; 53:12a; Job 21:17). Gen 49:7 and Lam 4:16 should be translated "to scatter."

The hi. in Jer 37:12 means "to divide an estate" (cf. Rudolph, HAT 12, 238).

(c) The usage of the noun *ḥēleq* "portion" (of plunder: Num 31:36; 1 Sam 30:24; cf. Gen 14:24; of sacrifice: Lev 6:10; cf. Deut 18:8) corresponds to the usage of the verb.

Semantically related terms are *mānâ* (12x) and *m^enāt* (9x, Aram. loanword; cf. Wagner no. 175) from the root *mnh* "to count," and *mišḥâ* (Lev 7:35) and *mošḥâ* (Num 18:8) from the root *mšḥ* II "to measure."

As a par. term for → *naḥ^alâ*, → *gôrāl*, *ḥebel* "line (for measuring) > (allotted) parcel of ground," etc., *ḥēleq* often stands for the "portion of the land" (Josh 15:13; 19:9; Ezek 45:7; 48:8, 21, etc.; cf. Zech 2:16; see J. Dreyfus, RSPT 42 [1958]: 3–49; F. Horst, FS Rudolph 135–56). In a narrower sense, *ḥēleq* is the land or field coming to the individual (Amos 7:4; Hos 5:7); the term *ḥelqâ* also has the same meaning (2 Sam 23:11f.; Ruth 2:3; 4:4, etc.) and finally comes to mean simply "tract of land" (Gen 33:19; Josh 24:32, etc.).

BL 567, etc., assume that *ḥēleq* "portion" has been fused here with a word **ḥeleq* (or **ḥeqel*) "field" (cf. Akk. *eqlu*, Aram. *ḥaqlāʾ*, Arab. and Eth. *ḥaql*); cf., to the contrary, *GVG* 1:277.

Discussion of the fact that Aaron or the Levites should receive no portion of the land, but that Yahweh will be their "portion" (Num 18:20; Deut 10:9; 12:12; 14:27, 29; 18:1; Josh 14:4; 18:7; see 4), prepares the way for the fig. use of *ḥēleq* (par. *naḥ^alâ*). This fig. meaning of *ḥēleq* in the sense of that which comes to one, where one belongs, is rather frequent in various forms. The noun occasionally depicts "fate" (Isa 17:14 par. *gôrāl*, a play on words with the double entendre "portion of the plunder/fate"; cf. Isa 57:6; Job 20:29; 27:13; 31:2, etc.), otherwise e.g., participation in the paternal estate (Gen 31:14), with Yahweh (Josh 22:25, 27), with David (2 Sam 20:1; 1 Kgs 12:16 = 2 Chron 10:16).

The usage of *ḥēleq* in Eccl requires special mention here. Qohelet's thoughts revolve repeatedly around the question concerning what his "part," his "reward," will be, what will be left *(yitrôn)* for him (*ḥēleq:* Eccl 2:10, 21; 3:22; 5:17f.; 9:6, 9; cf. 11:2). He is less concerned here with the complaint that a person can have only a part, never the whole (W. Zimmerli, *Die Weisheit des Predigers Salomo* [1936], 37; id., ATD 16/1, 138, etc.), than with the question of the "portion," the place of the person in the world (H. H. Schmid, *Wesen und Geschichte der Weisheit* [1966], 187f.).

4. The concept behind Deut 32:8, that Israel was allotted to Yahweh by *(ʾēl) ʿelyôn* (v 9, *ḥēleq*), is very ancient. Analogously, Deut 29:25 discusses the gods to whom Yahweh did not allot Israel, and Deut 4:19, according to which

Yahweh alloted the stars to all nations, probably belongs in the same arena (cf. further Job 39:17, the apportionment of insight).

The word group acquires a specifically theological meaning where Yahweh appears as the "portion" of a group or of an individual. Passages that depict Yahweh as the "portion" of Aaron or the Levites have already been mentioned (3c). In Jer 10:16 = 51:19 Yahweh is "Jacob's portion," and laments acknowledge in context of the terms → *gôrāl*, → *naḥ*^{a}*lâ*, *ḥebel*, etc.: "Yahweh is my portion," etc. (Psa 16:5; 73:26; 142:6; Lam 3:24; cf. H.-J. Hermisson, *Sprache und Ritus im altisraelitischen Kult* [1965], 107–13). In addition, cf. the PNs *ḥilqîyâ(hû)* "Yahweh is my portion" and its abbreviated forms *ḥēleq* and *ḥelqāy* (*IP* 163f.).

Finally, that the poet's "portion" in Psa 119:57 is keeping the commandments is as self-evident as the viewpoint represented in the poetry of Job that "the portion" of the wicked will come from God (Job 20:29; 27:13; cf. 31:2).

5. No particularly significant postbibl. role can be traced for this word group. The pair of occurrences at Qumran conform to OT usage. Gk. knows no precise equivalent; the LXX prefers to render *ḥlq* with *merizein* and composites or *klēronomia* or *klēros*. On the NT usage of *klēros*, see W. Foerster and J. Herrmann, "κλῆρος," *TDNT* 3:758–85.

H. H. Schmid

חמד *ḥmd* to desire

S 2530; BDB 326a; *HALOT* 1:325a; *TDOT* 4:452–61; *TWOT* 673; *NIDOTTE* 2773

---

1. The root **ḥmd* "to desire" is widely distributed in the WSem. languages (SSem. in the meaning "to praise"; cf. Muḥammad, "the praised").

Older examples stem from Ug. (cf. *WUS* no. 936; *UT* no. 872), Can. (EA 138:126, pass. ptcp. *ḫa-mu-du* "desirable"; cf. *CAD* H:73b), Phoen. (*KAI* no. 26A.III.14f. *yḥmd ʾyt hqrt z* "he would like to have this city" [cf. *ANET* 654b "even if he has good intentions toward this city"]; l. 17 *bḥmdt* "with covetousness" [cf. *ANET* 654b "with good intentions"]) and Eg. Aram. (*BMAP* no. 7.19, *ḥmdyh*, perhaps *ḥ*^{a}*mīdîn* "valuables"); cf. also Huffmon 196.

In addition to qal "to desire" and pi. "to consider desirable" (*HP* 220f.), Hebr. has the qal pass. ptcp. and the ni. ptcp., as well as various nom. forms (segholate forms: *ḥemed* and *ḥemdâ;* with *m*-preformative: *maḥmād* and *maḥmōd;* abstract pl. *ḥ*^{a}*mūdôt*), predominantly to indicate the desired obj. *ḥemdān* occurs as a PN (Gen 36:26).

2. The verb occurs rather rarely in the OT, perhaps because Hebr. has many options to express emotion and volition (modes, tenses, particles, etc.). In its three stems, *ḥmd* is represented a total of only 21x (qal 16x, ni. 4x, pi. 1x). The narrative literature is represented by Gen 2:9; 3:6; Josh 7:21; otherwise, wisdom, legal, liturgical, and prophetic texts exhibit the verb *ḥmd.* The nom. forms (*ḥemed* 5x, *ḥemdâ* 16x, *ḥ*^{a}*mūdôt* 9x, *maḥmād* 13x, *maḥmōd* 1x) seem to

have come into prominence only in exilic and post-exilic literature; for *maḥmād,* see Lam 1:10f.; 2:4; Ezek 24:16, 21, 25; for *ḥ^{a}mūdôt,* see Dan 9:23; 10:3, 11, 19; 11:38, 43.

3. One may distinguish between two functions for *ḥmd:* (a) a usage describing the act., acting subj., and (b) a usage describing the pass., sought-after obj.; the nom. meanings fall into the latter category.

(a) As an active behavior, *ḥmd* (qal and pi.; causative hi., only Sir 40:22) is the goal-oriented intention toward something, the pressing desire for possession (cf. J. Herrmann, FS Sellin 69–82; J. J. Stamm, *TRu* 27 [1961]: 301–3). Just as this desire can vary with respect to motivation and intensity ("to desire," "to be eager," "to long for"), so, in each case, is the actor's need and an external stimulus presupposed; sexual desire is also present in the word field, as is true also for → *ʾwh.* Enemies want to take possession of the land (cf. Exod 34:24); Yahweh wanted to have the mountain of God and now occupies it (Psa 68:17); the fool desires the seductive, married woman (Prov 6:25). Legitimate desire can and may be fulfilled (cf. Song Sol 2:3 pi.), illicit desire is banned by commandment (Exod 20:17; 34:24; Deut 5:21; 7:25; Prov 6:25) because it results in destruction (Job 20:20) and injures neighbors as well as the entire society (cf. Josh 7:21; Mic 2:2).

(b) Unattractiveness is undesirable (Isa 53:2); the ni. ptcp. can describe that which elicits desire or covetousness (Gen 2:9; 3:6; Psa 19:11; Prov 21:20). Such objs. are naturally valuable for the participant (Isa 44:9: the implement of the sculptor, qal pass. ptcp.; cf. Job 20:20 and the adj. and then also subjectival usage of *ḥ^{a}mūdôt* "costly," "treasure"). The stimulating effect of the obj. is expressed clearly in the phrase *maḥmad ʿênayim* "desire of the eyes" (1 Kgs 20:6; Ezek 24:16, 21, 25; Lam 2:4; cf. Eng. "feast for the eyes," "welcome sight"); the lover sings: *kullô maḥ^{a}maddîm* "everything about him is delight" (Song Sol 5:16; cf. further Isa 64:10; Hos 9:6, 16; Joel 4:5; Lam 1:10f.; 2 Chron 36:19). *ḥemed,* always in a cs. relationship, describes the beauty of a field (Isa 32:12; cf. Amos 5:11), and the stateliness of human figures (Ezek 23:6, 12, 23). In the same way *ḥemdâ* is a collective term for "beauty, worth, charm, significance" (cf. 1 Sam 9:20, Israel's greatness; Hag 2:7, the treasures of all nations; Dan 11:37, the idol of the woman, apparently Tammuz; 2 Chron 21:20, Jehoram died worthlessly = without being mourned?); *ḥemdâ* is also predominantly used as a governing noun: Isa 2:16; Jer 3:19; 12:10; 25:34; Ezek 26:12; Hos 13:15; Nah 2:10; Zech 7:14; Psa 106:24; Dan 11:8; 2 Chron 32:27; 36:10.

4./5. A specifically theological meaning cannot yet be identified for the OT. As with → *ʾwh* and in contrast to expressions with clearly fixed ethical significance (cf. e.g., → *śnʾ* "to hate," *gnb* "to steal"), *ḥmd* embraces the entire complex concept of "desire"; no single aspect had yet achieved status as an independent theological technical expression. Only in early Judaism is desire, esp. of sexual desire, denigrated and made taboo. Pursuant to the prohibitions of the Decalogue (the prohibition of theft in Exod 20:15 suggested the false conclusion that v 17 must intend a "thought crime"), every material, externally stimulated desire is marked a temptation and a rebellion against God (cf. *epithymia,* concupiscentia; Matt 5:28; Rom 7:7; further, StrB 3:234ff.;

4/1:466ff.; J. J. Stamm, *Der Dekalog im Lichte der neueren Forschung* [1962[2]], 55–59, translated and expanded in M. E. Andrew, *Ten Commandments in Recent Research* [1967], 101–7); → ᵓ*wh.*

E. Gerstenberger

חֵמָה *ḥēmâ* excitement

S 2534; BDB 404a; *HALOT* 1:326a; *TDOT* 4:462–65; *TWOT* 860a; *NIDOTTE* 2779

1. The subst. *ḥēmâ* (**ḥim-at-*, BL 450) derives from the root *yḥm* (**wḥm;* Barth 94), which, in turn, is associated with *ḥmm* (Arab. also *ḥmw/y*) "to be hot." The subst. is common Sem. in the meaning "venom, poison" (Berg., *Intro.* 216; P. Fronzaroli, *AANLR* 8/19 [1964]: 250, 264, 276): Akk. *imtu* "venom, poison" (*AHw* 379b; *CAD* I/J:139–41), Ug. *ḥmt* "poison" (now frequently attested in *KTU* 1.100, 107; cf. *Ugaritica* 5:599a), Hebr. *ḥēmâ* (Deut 32:24, 33; Psa 58:5bis; 140:4; Job 6:4), Aram. *ḥimtāᵓ/ḥēmtāᵓ* (attested only in the later dialects), Arab. *ḥumat* "(insect) poison" (*i* > *u* preceding a labial, *GVG* 1:199), Eth. *ḥamōt* "gall" (Dillmann 77f.). The meaning "excitement, wrath" (< "venom, foam" or derived directly from the root "to be hot, excited") is attested outside Hebr. esp. in Aram. (Hadad inscription, *KAI* no. 214.33 *ḥmᵓ;* Aḥ. 140 *ḥmt[ᵓ];* Bibl. Aram. *ḥ*^{a}*mâ,* Dan 3:13, 19; Syr., etc.).

2. Although the verb *yḥm* qal/pi., "to be in heat" occurs only 6x in the OT (qal: Gen 30:38f.; pi.: Gen 30:41bis; 31:10; Psa 51:7), the subst. *ḥēmâ* is represented 125x (incl. passages mentioned with the meaning "poison"; in the meaning "excitement, wrath" 119x, 2x in the pl. *ḥēmôt,* Psa 76:11 [txt?] and Prov 22:24, as an abstract formation, "wrath," *GVG* 2:59), most frequently in Ezek (33x), Jer (17x), Psa (15x), and Isa (13x).

Like → ᵓ*ap, ḥēmâ* is less often used of human wrath (28x) than of divine wrath (89x, excl. Psa 76:11b txt em and Job 19:29 txt em): of human emotions, Prov 9x, Esth 6x, Psa, Isa, and Dan 2x each, Gen, 2 Sam, 2 Kgs, Ezek, Hos, Hab, and Job 1x each; of divine wrath, Ezek 32x, Jer 17x, Isa 11x, Psa 9x, 2 Chron 5x, Deut 3x, 2 Kgs, Nah, and Lam 2x, Lev, Num, Mic, Zech, Job, and Dan 1x each.

3. In view of the meaning of the root, the basic meaning of *ḥēmâ* may indicate "being hot (from excitement)," thus e.g., "boiling," then "wrath"; cf. Hos 7:5, which mentions the effect of wine. The distinction from → ᵓ*ap* would then be seen in the fact that ᵓ*ap* describes more the physically visible state of excitement of an individual breathing heavily as a consequence of anger, while *ḥēmâ* emphasizes more the inner emotion, the inner fire of anger. Nevertheless, one may hardly recognize an essential distinction in meaning or in usage between ᵓ*ap* and *ḥēmâ,* as demonstrated by the fact that *ḥēmâ* appears in conjunction with ᵓ*ap* about 40x (in series: Deut 9:19; 29:22, 27; Isa 42:25; 66:15; Jer 7:20; 21:5; 32:31, 37; 33:5; 36:7; 42:18; 44:6; Ezek 5:15; 22:20; 25:14; 38:18; Mic 5:14; Dan 9:16; in par.

expressions: Gen 27:44f.; Isa 63:3, 6; Ezek 5:13; 7:8; 13:13; 20:8, 21; Nah 1:6; Hab 2:15 [cf. *HAL* 313a]; Psa 6:2; 37:8; 78:38; 90:7; Prov 15:1; 21:14; 22:24; 27:4; 29:22; Lam 4:11).

Other phrases are: with derivatives from the stem → *qṣp*, Deut 9:19; 29:27; Isa 34:2; Jer 21:5; 32:37; Psa 38:2; with *gᵉʿārâ* "scolding," Isa 51:20; 66:15; with *tôkaḥat* "reprimand," Ezek 5:15; 25:17; with the root → *qnʾ*, Ezek 16:38, 42; 36:6; Nah 1:2; Zech 8:2; Prov 6:34; with → *nqm*, Nah 1:2; with *zaʿam* "cursing," Nah 1:6.

Wrath can burn out (*yṣt* ni., 2 Kgs 22:13, 17) or intensify (*ʿlh*, 2 Sam 11:20; Ezek 38:18; 2 Chron 36:16); it can abate (*škk*, Esth 7:10); one can forsake it (*ʿzb*, Psa 37:8) or turn it aside (*šûb* hi., Num 25:11; Isa 66:15; Jer 18:20; Psa 106:23; Prov 15:1).

ḥēmâ "excitement, agitation" overcomes the king on hearing bad news (2 Sam 11:20; Esth 1:12; 2:1; 7:7); a person can feel it against his brother (Gen 27:44) or against a rival (Esth 3:5; 5:9). Proverbial wisdom expresses in many images how detrimental this excitement can be (Prov 6:34; 15:1; 19:19; 22:24; 27:4; 29:22). Patience (Prov 15:18) and wisdom (Prov 16:14) protect against it, as well as a timely gift (Prov 21:14). Other examples of human *ḥēmâ* are 2 Kgs 5:12; Isa 51:13(bis); Hos 7:5; Psa 37:8; 76:11(bis); Esth 7:10; Dan 8:6; 11:44. A (holy) excitement can also overcome a prophet enraptured by Yahweh's spirit.

On the text and translation of Isa 27:4; Hab 2:15; Job 36:18 (and Jer 25:15), cf., in addition to *HAL* 313, G. R. Driver, "On *ḥēmāh* 'hot anger, fury' and also 'fiery wine,' " *TZ* 14 (1958): 133–35.

4. God's *ḥēmâ* "wrath" is directed at individuals (Psa 6:2 = 38:2; 88:8; 90:7; Job 21:20), but esp. against his own people in conjunction with punitive judgment (Jer 4:4, etc.; Ezek 5:15, etc.; Lev 26:28; Deut 9:19; 29:27; 2 Kgs 22:13, 17; Psa 78:38; 89:47; 106:23; Lam 2:4; 4:11; Dan 9:16). The other nations also stand under divine wrath, thus e.g., Sodom and Gomorrah (Deut 29:22), Edom (Isa 63:3, 5f.; Ezek 25:14), the Philistines (Ezek 25:17), Egypt (Ezek 30:15), and all foreign nations (Isa 34:2) and enemies of Yahweh (Psa 59:14; 79:6).

A distinctive concept underlies the picture of the cup of wrath that Yahweh gives his enemies to drink (Isa 51:17, 22; Jer 25:15; cf. Rudolph, KAT 17/3, 255, on Lam 4:21).

5. *ḥēmâ* occurs occasionally in the Qumran literature (cf. Kuhn, *Konk.* 73), once in conjunction with *rgz* "excitement" (1Q20 1:2) and once in the phrase "to pour out wrath" (*špk*, 6Q10 2:4, cf. Ezek 20:8, etc.).

On the NT, cf. G. Stählin, "ὀργή," *TDNT* 5:419–47; R. Hentschke, *BHH* 3:2246–48 (bibliog.); H. Reinelt, *BLex*² 1934–36 (bibliog.).

G. Sauer

חמל *ḥml* **to have compassion** → רחם *rḥm*

חָמָס *ḥāmās* violence

S 2554; BDB 329a; *HALOT* 1:329a; *TDOT* 4:478–87; *TWOT* 678; *NIDOTTE* 2803

1. The word group *ḥms* qal "to act violently," ni. "to suffer violence," and *ḥāmās* "violence" seems to have few direct counterparts outside texts dependent upon the OT; worthy of mention are Yaudi *ḥms* "abominable act" (*KAI* no. 214.26 in a fragmentary context) and Imp. Aram. *śhd ḥms* "witness who exercises injustice" (Aḥ. 140 [*ANET* 429b "false witness"] = Hebr. *ᶜēd ḥāmās*). In the event that *ḥms* should be associated with the root *ḥmṣ* II (Hebr. *ḥmṣ* qal "to oppress," Psa 71:4; subst. *ḥāmôṣ* "oppressor," Isa 1:17 txt?, read *ḥāmûṣ* "oppressed"; cf. Wildberger, *Isa 1–12*, CC, 36), then Aram., Akk., and Eth. equivalents may be included.

HAL 316a distinguishes the verb in Job 21:27 as *ḥms* II "to devise."

2. The qal occurs 6x (Jer 22:3; Ezek 22:26; Zeph 3:4; Prov 8:36; Lam 2:6; in Job 15:33 of dropping fruits; excl. Job 21:27), the ni. 1x (Jer 13:22). The noun is more frequent: 60x (excl. Ezek 9:9, where some MSS have *ḥāmās* instead of *dāmîm;* Psa 14x, Prov 7x, Ezek and Hab 6x each, Gen and Jer 4x each).

3. (a) *ḥamas* is usually sg.; the pl. forms in 2 Sam 22:49 (Psa 18:49 sg.!), Psa 140:2, 5 (v 12 sg.), and Prov 4:17 form attributive descriptions ("*ḥāmās*-full" man or wine) as an extension of the sg. form (*ʾîš ḥāmās*, etc.; cf. Prov 3:31; 16:29). As a rule, gens. accompanying nouns indicate the obj. of the violence (Judg 9:24; Joel 4:19; Obad 10; Hab 2:8, 17; with pron. suf., Gen 16:5; Jer 51:35), rarely the actor (Ezek 12:19; with pron. suf., Psa 7:17).

Prophetic diction often uses *šōd* "misdeed, destruction" as a synonym for *ḥāmās* (Isa 60:18; Jer 6:7; 20:8; Ezek 45:9; Amos 3:10; Hab 1:3; 2:17; *šōd* occurs a total of 25x in the OT, with the exceptions of Psa 12:6; Job 5:21f.; Prov 21:7; and 24:2 only in prophetic books; in addition, *šdd* qal "to destroy, rape" occurs 32x, ni. 1x, pi. 2x, pu. 20x, po. 1x, and ho. 2x, likewise almost exclusively in the Prophets, rarely in Psa, Job, and Prov, elsewhere only in Judg 5:27). The difference may lie in the fact that *šōd* emphasizes the active doing, *ḥāmās* the nature or consequence of the deed.

(b) Religious and a profane usage may not be strictly distinguished because *ḥāmās*, even if interpersonal, violates an order established or guaranteed by God (von Rad, *Theol.* 1:157n.34). Nevertheless, various aspects of the concept may be noted.

The word is anchored first in the legal sphere (R. Knierim, "*Cht* und *Chms.* Zwei Begriffe für Sünde in Israel und ihr Sitz im Leben" [diss., Heidelberg, 1957], 125ff.), but already had various usages there.

In the independent *ḥāmās* cry (Hab 1:2; Job 19:7; on Jer 20:8, see 4), von Rad (*Theol.* 1:157n.34), Knierim (op. cit. 129ff.), and H. J. Boecker (*Redeformen des Rechtslebens im AT* [1964], 60f.) see a cry of the legal community for legal protection (the opening of a hearing). Because Yahweh is addressed in both cases, however, these passages more likely deal with a direct cry for help (similarly, *šmᶜ* ni. in Isa 60:18 and Jer 6:7 should also be understood as "to be heard by" [contra Knierim, op. cit. 131], because *ḥāmās* in Jer 6:7 is combined with *šōd* and Isa 60:18 speaks of foreign oppression).

The expression *ʿēd ḥāmās* (Exod 23:1; Deut 19:16) probably indicated originally the plaintiff in a case of *ḥāmās* (not the witness who perverts justice; Deut 19:18 indicates explicitly after subsequent investigation that the accusation is false by *šeqer* "deceit"), but then in a shift of meaning generally the "violent, law-breaking witness." *ḥāmās* may indeed have originally meant the misdeed that objectively burdens the land and disturbs its relationship and its inhabitants' relationship to God, so that anyone who knows of it must appear as plaintiff before the legal community in order to divert the consequences (cf. H. J. Stoebe, *WD* 3 [1952]: 121ff.; on → *ʿēd* as "plaintiff" see also B. Gemser, *SVT* 3 [1955]: 130; contra Knierim, op. cit. 127f., although he emphasizes correctly the term's connotation of a concept of an independent sphere of action, op. cit. 135). The law in Deut 19:15–19 also lies on the level of regulations concerning murder committed by an unknown hand (Deut 21:1–9), and the series of curses (Deut 27:15–26; cf. Lev 5:1) gives evidence of an advanced legal praxis concerned for legal certainty (Deut 19:15).

This element is also active where *ḥāmās* is combined with *mlʾ* "to be full" (land, city, and secondarily the temple; Gen 6:11, 13; Ezek 7:23; 8:17; 28:16; Mic 6:12; Zeph 1:9). If the land is full of *ḥāmās,* then the consequence for its inhabitants is punishment and destruction. This understanding is esp. clear in Gen 6:13; despite later testimony (P), it is not a late theologoumenon (contra Knierim, op. cit. 134), but the direct consequence of the original meaning.

A similar situation pertains where the *ḥāmās* procedure itself overtakes the perpetrator (Judg 9:24 with *bôʾ* "to come"; Psa 7:17 with *yrd* "to descend"), or *ḥāmās* is otherwise bound to *ʿal* "on" (Gen 16:5 J; Jer 51:35; Mal 2:16; Gen 16:5 seems ancient: the consequence of the *ḥāmās* that lies upon Sarai is barrenness; she lays it on Abram as cosufferer and thus characterizes the gravity of Hagar's deed; cf. Knierim, op. cit. 134; von Rad, *Gen,* OTL [1972²], 192).

4. The substance of such a *ḥāmās,* even in the Prophets, is the spilling of blood (Gen 49:5f.; Judg 9:24; Isa 59:6; Jer 51:35; Ezek 7:23; Joel 4:19; in Jer 22:3 *ḥms* qal) and presumably moral crimes (reference to this only in Jer 13:22 ni.) that pollute the land in the same way (Lev 18:28; 20:22) and also stand under the verdict of capital punishment in the law (e.g., Lev 20:11–18).

According to a promising suggestion by J. Berridge, *Prophet, People, and the Word of Yahweh* (1970), 152–54 (cf. also S. Marrow, *VD* 43 [1965]: 241–55), Jer 20:8 could be influenced by the preceding rape metaphor; *ḥāmās* would be the maiden's cry for help (cf. Deut 22:24), not the cry for legal protection. Whether Prov 26:6 also belongs in this context (cf. Gemser, HAT 16, 94) may not be decided given the uncertainty of the text.

Now, independent spheres of action in the OT are to be delineated theoretically and not precisely, because the concept behind them is a borrowed form that does not itself demonstrate the essence of OT thought but is given new content (cf. N. H. Ridderbos, *GTT* 64 [1964]: 226ff.). The revelation unique to the OT focuses attention upon human responsibility in the relationship between Yahweh and his people. Thus the emphasis of the word lies on the perpetrator and his individual guilt. This analysis results less from the formulations (Isa 59:6; Ezek 12:19; Jonah 3:8; Mic 6:12; Mal 2:16; Job 16:17; 1 Chron 12:18, often with *yād/kap* "hand" in which there is *ḥāmās;* these texts could—even if with reservations—be included with the passages discussed earlier) than from the sphere of the acts so categorized. Combined with *bgd* "to act deceitfully" (Zeph 3:4; Mal 2:16; Prov 13:2; similarly 16:29 with *pth* pi. "to delude") *ḥāmās* characterizes the diminution of another's rights and living space as violation of duty to the neighbor and encompasses the entire range of antisocial behavior (Amos 3:10) in opposition to justice and righteousness (Jer 22:3; Ezek 45:9). Arrogance (Psa 73:6), deceit (Zeph 1:9) in speech (Mic 6:12; cf. Prov 10:6, 11 and, conversely, the description of the servant's virtue in Isa 53:9), and, finally, improper legal proceedings (Psa 55:10; Hab 1:3 txt?) are named.

Ezek 22:26 and Zeph 3:4 mention attacks on Yahweh's Torah (*ḥms* qal, subj., the priests). Yahweh himself turns against the *ḥāmās* that he hates (Psa 11:5), from which he delivers (2 Sam 22:3, 49 = Psa 18:3, 49; Psa 140:2, 5; cf. Psa 72:14, the king under Yahweh's commission), because of which one calls to him (Hab 1:2; Psa 25:19), and which he avenges (Ezek 7:23; 8:17f.; 12:19; 28:16; Zeph 1:9). If, paradoxically, *ḥāmās* comes from Yahweh himself (Job 19:7), there is no remedy for it.

Thus *ḥāmās* becomes an encompassing term for sin per se (Ezek 7:11; Jonah 3:8; cf. also the phrase *ʾîš ḥāmās/ḥ^{a}māsîm;* see 3a). Characteristically, too, *ḥāmās* is practiced not only in Israel but also by foreign nations against Israel (Joel 4:19; Obad 10; Hab 1:9; 2:8, 17). This development is the context in which psalmic diction equates *ʿēd šeqer* "lying witness" and *ʿēd ḥāmās* (Psa 35:11; cf. 27:12, → *kzb* 3a), an equation that was not original (see 3b).

5. In the Qumran texts *ḥāmās* finds little usage (Kuhn, *Konk.* 73c; also *GCDS* 256). On the LXX and the NT, cf. G. Schrenk, "ἄδικος," *TDNT* 1:149–63; W. Gutbrod, "ἀνομία," *TDNT* 4:1085–87.

H. J. Stoebe

חנן *ḥnn* to be gracious

S 2603; BDB 335b; *HALOT* 1:334b; *TDOT* 5:22–36; *TWOT* 694; *NIDOTTE* 2838

---

1. The root *ḥnn* "to be gracious (to someone), demonstrate goodwill," etc., is common Sem. (lacking in Eth.); it occurs verbally and in various nom. derivatives with meanings similar to the Hebr., e.g., in Akk. (*enēnu*, *AHw* 217, 219; *CAD* E:162–64), Amor. in PNs (Buccellati 134; Huffmon 200), Ug. (*WUS* no. 947; *UT* no. 882; Gröndahl 135f.), as a WSemitism in the Amarna Letters (EA 137:81; 253:24; cf. *CAD* E:164f.), in Phoen.-Pun. (*DISO* 91f.; PNs like Hanno, Hannibal, etc.: Harris 102f.), in Aram. (*DISO* 91f.; KBL 1076b), and in Arab. (Wehr 209).

Etymologically, *ḥnn* may be related to *ḥnh* "to bow oneself, lie down" (e.g., GB 243b; on *ḥannôt* in Psa 77:10 cf. GKC §67r and Nyberg 142: qal inf. from *ḥnn;* contra *HAL*

319b: pi. inf. from *ḥnh* II) or to an older biradical root *ḥn* (D. R. Ap-Thomas, *JSS* 2 [1957]: 128).

The hapax legomenon *ḥnn* II "to stink" (Job 19:17) goes back to a root attested in Syr. and Arab. with an original *ḫ* as the first radical.

Apart from cases in which *ḥnn* is a name component (e.g., *ʾelḥānān, ḥannîʾēl, ḥananyâ[hû], ḥannâ*, etc., cf. *IP* 187), the root occurs verbally in the OT in the qal, pi., hitp., and po. stems, as a nom. in the substs. *ḥēn* "goodwill, grace" and *ḥanînâ* "mercy" (only Jer 16:13), as well as in the abstracts *teḥinnâ* and *taḥanûnîm/ôt* "pleading" derived from the reflexive stem (BL 495, 497), as an adj. in *ḥannûn* "gracious, friendly," and as an adv. in *ḥinnām* "undeservedly, without reason, uselessly."

The apparent ni. form *nēḥantî* in Jer 22:23 is a miswritten form of *ʾnḥ* "to sigh"; cf. BL 351; the apparent ho. forms *yūḥan* in Isa 26:10 and Prov 21:10 should be viewed as qal pass.; cf. BL 286 and the PN *ḥānûn*.

The ending *-ām* in *ḥinnām* should not be explained as mimation of an adv. acc. (as *GVG* 1:474; Meyer 2:39; cf. *UT* §11.4), but represents a fossilized 3d masc. pl. suf. (BL 529; cf. also H. J. Stoebe, *VT* 2 [1952]: 245).

2. The verb *ḥnn* occurs 78x in the Hebr. OT, specifically, 55x in qal (30x alone in Psa, incl. 77:10; Isa 5x, Gen, Job, and Prov 3x each), in the hitp. 17x, po. and ho. 2x, ni. and pi. 1x. The most frequent subst. is *ḥēn*, 69x (Gen 14x, Prov 13x, Exod 9x, 1 Sam and Esth 6x each; the concentration is in the narrative books [47x] and in wisdom [15x]; the word is rare in the Psa [2x] and the Prophets [5x]); then follow *teḥinnâ* (25x, 9x in 1 Kgs and 5x each in Jer and 2 Chron), *taḥanûnîm/ôt* (18x, 8x in Psa), and *ḥanînâ* (1x). *ḥannûn* occurs 13x (6x in Psa), *ḥinnām* 32x (Psa and Prov 6x each, Job 4x).

Bibl. Aram. pe. and hitp. occur once each (Dan 4:24 and 6:12, resp.).

3. Nontheological usages will be classified according to parts of speech: *ḥēn* (a-c), *ḥannûn* (d), verb (e-f), *teḥinnâ* and *taḥanûnîm* (g). For the whole group, see W. F. Lofthouse, "Ḥen and Ḥesed in the OT," *ZAW* 51 (1933): 29–35; W. L. Reed, "Some Implications of Ḥen for OT Religion," *JBL* 73 (1954): 36–41; D. R. Ap-Thomas, "Some Aspects of the Root ḤNN in the OT," *JSS* 2 (1957): 128–48; K. W. Neubauer, "Der Stamm CHNN im Sprachgebrauch des AT" (diss., Berlin, 1964).

(a) The noun *ḥēn* occurs exclusively in the sg. An esp. frequent formula in narrative texts is *mṣʾ ḥēn beʿênê* . . . "to find favor in the eyes of . . ." This phrase makes it clear that the prerequisite for such favor is not discrete acts but an attitude.

The noun therefore is also only rarely definite (determined): in Prov 31:30 by the article (there, however, *ḥēn* signifies "graciousness"), in Gen 39:21 by a pron. suf., in Exod 3:21; 11:3; 12:36 by a governing noun (here the formula is *ntn ḥēn beʿênê* . . . "to create goodwill in the eyes of . . . ," in which Yahweh is the subj. of the verb, but the "*ḥēn*-attitude" is taken with the people, the prison guard, and the Egyptians). The expression *nśʾ ḥēn beʿênê* (Esth 2:15, 17; 5:2) represents a confusion of original linguistic boundaries (see also "before him" in Esth 2:17).

The formula under discussion (cf. Lande 95–97) expresses chiefly an interpersonal relationship, even in Gen 18:3; 19:19; Judg 6:17, where a conversation takes place with God or an angel, but which does not abandon the style of legendary narrative. More rarely, Yahweh is explicitly the subj. of *ḥēn;* these passages are for the most part limited to a characterization of Moses' relationship with Yahweh (Exod 33–34; Num 11).

The one in whose eyes one finds *ḥēn* is always the superior, never vice versa (the king: 1 Sam 16:22; 27:5; 2 Sam 14:22; 16:4; 1 Kgs 11:19; Esth 5:2, 8; 7:3; the crown prince: 1 Sam 20:3, 29; the royal vizier: Gen 47:25). The formula presumably has roots in the style of court speech, but can then be applied in the course of a process of democratization to anyone who faces a weaker party as the superior (officer: Gen 39:4, 21; the stronger brother: Gen 32:6; the rich landowner: Ruth 2:2, 10, 13). Finally, the word merely signifies that the addressee can grant something that the supplicant desires quite independently (Gen 34:11; Num 32:5; 1 Sam 25:8). Even though, owing to the nature of the concept, boundaries are fluid here too, the formula still never becomes attenuated to a mere polite expression.

In Gen 50:4 Joseph could request the mediation of the court officials because he himself, unclean because of his father's death, cannot go to Pharaoh (thus H. Holzinger, HSAT 1, 96). In Gen 47:29 the formulation of Jacob's request in formal style is required by the high status of the son.

The origins of the expression in the sphere of courtly speech shine through the attestations of loyalty in address and self-presentation associated with it (cf. *ʾādôn* "lord," Gen 18:3; 32:6; 33:8, 15; 47:25; 2 Sam 14:22; 16:4; *ʿebed* "servant," Gen 19:19; Num 32:5; *šipḥâ* "maiden," 1 Sam 1:18; Ruth 2:13). To have found *ḥēn* is the prerequisite for stating a request (Gen 18:3; 47:29; 50:4; Exod 33:13; Judg 6:17; 1 Sam 20:29; 27:5), just as, conversely, a fulfilled request or an unexpected gift evidences the giver's *ḥēn* (2 Sam 14:22; 16:4; Ruth 2:13).

As the behavior of a superior, *ḥēn* doubtlessly implies an element of condescension or partiality (N. H. Snaith, *Distinctive Ideas of the OT* [1964] 127–30). Still, it should be noted the phrase *mṣʾ ḥēn bᵉênāyw* accents "in his eyes" and not "find" (contra Lofthouse, op. cit., who sees the chief characteristic of the phrase in the finding). This emphasis makes clear that the demonstration of *ḥēn* includes an evaluation of the other so that both, subj. and obj., are considered and both participate, even if in different roles, in the event (cf. H. J. Stoebe, *VT* 2 [1952]: 245). This participation is underscored when the formula is supplemented, admittedly in loose association, by an expression of perception (Ruth 2:10 *nkr* hi.; Esth 2:15 *rʾh;* Zech 12:10 *nbṭ* hi.).

This assessment can determine one suited for a given task. It becomes clear to Potiphar that the blessing that rests upon Joseph makes him suited for service (Gen 39:4); Saul keeps David at court because he recognizes his capabilities (1 Sam 16:22; the spontaneous attraction is expressed in v 21 by *ʾhb* "to love"; cf. also 18:1); Nabal should recognize the helpful kindness of David's people (1 Sam 25:8). This aspect becomes most clear in the marriage law in Deut 24:1: the marriage can be dissolved if the husband discovers "something undesirable" in his wife, i.e., he becomes aware of something that makes it impossible for her to find *ḥēn* with him and that is, in his judgment, a hindrance to marriage.

Nevertheless, weakness and pitifulness should be considered (care of the helpless is also a royal duty); the appearance of Jacob's wives and children should change Esau's mind (Gen 33:8). Zech 12:10 should also be seen in this context. The passage is difficult because the presupposed events are unknown. Juxtaposition with *taḥ*ᵃ*nûnîm* does not signify that it is the human counterpart to God's *ḥēn*. *ḥēn* is the emotion, the shock, at the sight of a martyr that leads one to *taḥ*ᵃ*nûnîm* "pleading."

In the original semantic range of the word, *ḥēn* is exercised by a king, whose obligations also included the protection of the unfortunate but whose interest in the qualifications of a subordinate can be quite varied. Thus there are always overtones of gracious condescension, although precise distinctions are impossible. One can no more say that *ḥēn* signifies a spontaneous demonstration of grace (Lofthouse, op. cit., with a one-sided emphasis on the relationship of superiority and subordination; contra, rightly, Reed, op. cit. 39) than one can speak of a socially appropriate behavior in the sense of a legal right, arising from the good conduct of the partner (Neubauer, op. cit.). From the outset, "socially appropriate" is too imprecise, because everything that takes place between persons involves community in some way; the phrase is extremely nonspecific.

In the usage discussed to this point, *ḥēn* could be rendered "favor," or even better, "consideration," as well as "partiality." These three terms encompass the semantic range of the word, the idea of a subordinate, who, whether by the recognition of an accomplishment or by an unmotivated act of goodwill on the part of the lord, is elevated from the faceless masses and taken into consideration personally by the lord (cf. "I know you" Exod 33:12, → *yd*ᶜ).

(b) In the course of a development encountered esp. in wisdom diction, the association with the *b*ᵉᶜ*ênê* "in the eyes of" a concrete other is lost; thus the expression's focal point is shifted one-sidedly to the recipient, who becomes the possessor. The term acquires a more general meaning and simultaneously becomes static.

Even when, as in Prov 3:4, the formula still occurs, it loses concrete reference because of the breadth of the qualifier "before God and the people"; the softening of the form is also demonstrated by the coordination of the expression *śēkel ṭôb* with *ḥēn*, which should be understood, both here and elsewhere, as "success-bringing prudence" and not ad hoc as "approval." More clearly, *ḥēn* without further qualification in Prov 13:15 is the result of such *śēkel ṭôb;* in 22:1 *ḥēn ṭôb* is a desirable good alongside a good name; in Psa 84:12 the par. is *kābôd* "honor." Thus *ḥēn* becomes the objective reputation that one no longer "finds" but enjoys. This development is already apparent in Exod 3:21; 11:3; 12:36. The significance of ᵓ*eben ḥēn*, the talisman in Prov 17:8 which is otherwise difficult to categorize, seems also to lie in the direction of something readily available. The verbal form *yūḥan* in Isa 26:10 probably also belongs here; the context should be understood (without textual emendation) as an abbreviated conditional clause (GKC §159c). It cannot mean that the godless find grace with Yahweh (that would be blasphemy); rather, it envisions the reputation that a godless individual enjoys and because of which one could doubt God's righteousness.

(c) This shift of accent reaches a logical conclusion when *ḥēn* assumes the meaning "attractiveness, loveliness" as a visually perceptible personal or objective characteristic that can also involve the notions of success and fortune. Even if not exclusively (cf. Prov 11:16), this understanding occurs predominantly in the later collection, Prov 1–9 (1:9; 3:22; 4:9).

ḥēn śᵉpātāyw "attractiveness of his lips," Prov 22:11, should be understood as the eloquence of the wise. Nah 3:4 and Zech 4:7 are related. Here the translations "lovely, lovely" (W. Nowack, *Die kleinen Propheten* [1897[1]], 330) or "bravo, bravo" (E. Sellin, *Das Zwölfprophetenbuch* [1930], 501) seem appropriate (cf. also Stoebe, op. cit. 245), although "*Heil, Heil*" (Elliger, ATD 25, 117) seems too objective, and "grace, grace" (Sellin, op. cit. 504) too formal. In the event that *ḥyn (ḥîn)* in Job 41:4 is *ḥēn* with a *plene* spelling (König 107a), it also belongs here; but it is probably an unknown word.

(d) The adj. *ḥannûn* "gracious" refers to people only in Psa 112:4, and even there not unequivocally (cf. Kraus, *Psa*, CC, 2:362); in any case, it should be understood against the background of sacral usage (see 4b).

(e) The verb *ḥnn* qal "to show someone *ḥēn*" is not very common in everyday usage. Although the traditional translation "to be gracious" better fits cases with God as the subj. of the demonstration of *ḥēn* (see 4c), the entire semantic range of *ḥēn* "goodwill, consideration, partiality" may be observed in profane diction, although the weak and suffering are generally the recipients of *ḥēn* (Lam 4:16, the aged, par. *nśʾ pānîm* "to regard someone"; Deut 28:50, a boy; Psa 109:12, orphans).

In Job 19:21, Job does not expect grace or mercy from his friends, for they cannot alter his ill-fortune, but they could at least show consideration for it and cease their talk.

Deut 7:2 involves a more positive assessment. Here *ḥnn* does not indicate the consequence and content of the previously forbidden covenant making (as argued by Neubauer, op. cit., who finds confirmation here of his understanding of *ḥnn* as socially appropriate behavior); rather, one should neither make a covenant with the inhabitants of the land nor pay them any recognition whatsoever because they are great and mighty (v 1).

On the difficult passage Judg 21:22, cf. W. Rudolph, FS Eissfeldt (1947), 212 (read *ḥannônû ʾôtām* "we are sorry for them"); G. R. Driver, *ALUOS* 4 (1962/63): 22.

In Psa 37:21, 26 and 112:5, the qal ptcp. *ḥônēn* (par. *ntn* "to give" and *lwh* hi. "to lend," resp.) was already correctly rendered by older scholarship as "to give." One should not think here of mercifulness in the strict sense (as does e.g., Tholuck), but of generosity as a virtue (cf. Psa 112:4).

Prov 14:31 and 19:17 (indirectly also 28:8) bases the behavior required toward the neighbor on obligation to God. Thus the concept approaches the sacral use of *ḥēn*. The poor are named here as the objs. (*ʾebyôn* 14:31; *dal* 19:17; 28:8; cf. *ʿānî* 14:21 po.).

(f) Among the derived verb stems, *ḥnn* pi. "to make pleasant" and the po., similar to the qal in meaning, have only profane usages; in contrast, *ḥnn* hitp. "to request consideration, grace" occurs mostly in theological contexts.

Prov 26:25 pi. "to make (his voice) pleasant," is reminiscent of the usage of *ḥēn* "attractiveness, loveliness" in Prov 1:9; 3:22; 4:9; 22:11. Thus the verb also participates in the noun's full range of meaning (*HP* 269 understands the passage somewhat differently).

The po. in Psa 102:15 concerns not people but the ruins of Jerusalem that the servants of Yahweh mourn (par. *rṣh* "to love"). As already in passages with the qal ptcp., the development of the term through which *ḥnn* becomes a moral good and an ideal for life may also be ascertained in Prov 14:21, "Blessed be he who has mercy on those who suffer."

That *ḥēn*/*ḥnn* is not unilaterally oriented toward the one who demonstrates goodwill is underscored by the fact that the reflexive stem never means "to demonstrate oneself to be gracious" (cf. *ḥsd* hitp.). It expresses, first very generally, a request for attention, consideration, and then, in a broader sense, for grace. The specific content is determined by the specific situation, the position and the capacities of the one called upon.

In Esth 4:8 and 8:3, a demonstration of goodwill—i.e., grace—in opposition to the attacks of an anti-Jewish vizier is sought from the king. Gen 42:21 expects liberation from fear. In 2 Kgs 1:13, Obadiah pleads for consideration for his life and the lives of his people. In Job 19:16, the choice of the expression characterizes the reversal of the relationships; the lord accustomed to commanding must now plead. Job 9:15 complains about the same reversal, now in a legal procedure; the note of grace can already be heard quite loudly here, particularly because the opponent in the proceeding is God himself.

(g) Accordingly, noms. derived from the reflexive stem, *t*^{e}*ḥinnâ* and *taḥ*^{a}*nûnîm*, have the basic meaning "petition"; they occur mostly in the sacral area, rarely for interpersonal relationships.

In Prov 18:23 *taḥ*^{a}*nûnîm* acquires meaning in opposition to *ʿazzôt* (→ *ʿzz*): the poor person pleads modestly. The same circumstance applies in Job 40:27 (synonymous parallelism). The precise understanding of *t*^{e}*ḥinnâ* in Josh 11:20 is difficult. By consensus it is translated "mercifulness," explained by Neubauer (op. cit. 53) against the background of covenant obligation. This understanding would actually be a departure from the norm (cf. Ap-Thomas, op. cit. 130, who consequently suggests an emendation to *ḥ*^{a}*nînâ* "mercy"). One must ask whether the connotation "petition" may not be heard here too. The contrast is battle/attack–petition. Yahweh has arranged it such that they must immediately go forth to battle with no room for negotiations (petitions). The theological background of the concept strongly underscores grace in the word's conceptual scope; but the context of Ezra 9:8, to which reference is frequently made, has another effect. In Jer 37:20; 38:26; and 42:9 *t*^{e}*ḥinnâ* is an urgent petition to someone who can grant it.

4. Because the difference between God and people is immeasurable, the nuance of free grace assumes prominence when God is the counterpart. The believer's concept of God is not determined by what one thinks about *ḥēn;* to the contrary, what one believes about and hopes and expects from God determines the content of (a) *ḥēn*, (b) *ḥannûn*, (c) *ḥnn* qal, (d) *ḥnn* hitp., and (e) *t*^{e}*ḥinnâ* and *taḥ*^{a}*nûnîm*.

(a) *ḥēn* does not occur very frequently in theological speech. With the exception of Jer, it is entirely absent from the Prophets (on Nah 3:4 and Zech 4:7, see 3c; on Zech 12:10, see 3a). Perhaps the term did not appear to have a sufficiently theological profile.

From the outset, Gen 6:8 emphasizes the giver by stating no reason for the grace Noah finds (v 9 P is not a basis for v 8 J). Gen 19:19 accentuates the → *ḥesed*, the magnitude of which Lot experiences in undeserved deliverance and in which he recognizes that he has found the *ḥēn* that allows him to voice an additional request. 2 Sam 15:25 further underscores the freedom of the decision to grant grace by the contrary statement, "I am not pleased with you" (v 26). Exod 33:12ff. acquires its characteristic feature as a consequence of the fact that God himself, his presence on the journey, is requested, so that *ḥēn* signifies the full communication of his grace. The oscillation in the meaning of *ḥēn* in Exod 3:21; 11:3; 12:36 (see 3a) may also be understood on this basis. Jer 31:2 is textually difficult, but *ḥēn* is too profiled to be altered (Rudolph, HAT 12, 193). Most exegetes identify a conceptual relationship to Exod 33; assuming the correctness of this view, it still does not mean that *ḥēn* may be understood as a behavior within an established community (thus Neubauer, op. cit. 69). It is, rather, a promise of grace without prerequisite or limit. In addition to differences with respect to Exod 33, there are also points of contact, at least conceptually, with Gen 19:19 (cf. *ḥesed* in v 3). Correspondingly, the word *ḥ^anînâ*, which occurs only once in the OT (Jer 16:13), approaches → *ḥesed*, or at least *raḥ^amîm* "mercy," in content.

(b) Isolated *ḥannûn* "gracious" (Exod 22:26) is a constitutive characteristic of the king, who must have an ear open to the complaints of his subjects. This concept also echoes when *ḥannûn* is complemented by *ṣaddîq* "righteous" (Psa 116:5); Psa 112:4 is uncertain with reference both to text and content, but it belongs, if only very generally, to this category. Otherwise, the combination with *raḥûm* "merciful" is stereotypical; it is an established liturgical formula first encountered in the predication in Exod 34:6 (prepositive *ḥannûn:* Joel 2:13; Jonah 4:2; Psa 111:4; 112:4 txt?; 145:8; Neh 9:17, 31; 2 Chron 30:9; cf. Psa 116:5; postpositive: Psa 86:15; 103:8). It represents God's presence for people in analogy to the actions of a lord (kings) as well as of a father (→ *rḥm*), both from the standpoint of its polarity and from that of the promise inherent in it.

Reference should also be made to Mal 1:9 for this concept; the statement made here differs from the predication in that it more strongly accents the requirement under which it places people (cf. also Psa 103:12).

(c) The same notion occurs in Exod 33:19, where, in finite qal verbs, the name Yahweh is interpreted both with respect to content and to the sovereignty of divine action. The concept is also active in 2 Kgs 13:23 and Isa 30:18 (v 19 *ḥnn* alone in response to a cry of lament) and occurs, finally, in a reduced form in Isa 27:11, where the subjs. "his creation" and "who formed it" shatter the original bounds of the concept (cf. also Psa 102:14).

The impv. with suf. finds frequent usage in the liturgical diction of the Psa as a cry of petition. Understandably, the meaning becomes more general here and loses its marked profile, yet here too the context is often informative. If a specific request follows *ḥonnēnî* "be gracious unto me" (Psa 4:2; 6:3; 9:14; 27:7; 30:11; 41:5, 11; 51:3f.; 86:16), the notion of inclination as a prerequisite for the petition can be heard more strongly. In addition, overlapping constructions in which the impv. follows such a specific request often occur so that *ḥnn* is understood more abs. (25:16; 26:11; 27:7; 30:11; 86:16). In the same way one must understand passages in which the cry for *ḥēn* stands alone (31:10; 56:2; 57:2; 86:3; cf. 123:2f. pl.). The development present here is marked in Psa 119:29.

The expression *w^etôrāt^ekā ḥonnēnî* may hardly be understood as presentation of the Torah (so A. Deissler, *Psalm 119 und seine Theologie* [1955], 124f.; 123: "favor me"); this would be wisdom language, which should not be so understood with respect to God. Here the Torah is the substance of self-communication and favor. Vv 58 and 132 are also to be understood from this viewpoint.

In summary, the blessing formula in Num 6:25, "may he be gracious to you," exemplifies the wish for Yahweh's favor (Psa 67:2 is dependent). Characteristically, a justification for the request, a reference to the character of the supplicant, is frequently stated, either introduced with *kî* "for" (Psa 25:16; 31:10; 41:5; 57:2; 86:3; 123:3) or asyndetically (Psa 4:2; 9:14; 26:11; 27:7; 56:2; cf. Isa 33:2). A reference to the distress (Psa 4:2; 6:3; 9:14; 25:16; 56:2; probably also 102:14, "it is time"), less often to the personal piety, of the supplicant (Psa 26:11; 27:7?; 57:2; 86:3; 119:58; cf. Isa 33:2 and Mal 1:9) constitutes the content of this justification. Psa 41:5 "I have sinned against you" should be emphasized; the ultimate conclusion is drawn here: God is inclined to forgive.

Emendations (see *BH*³, omitted in *BHS*) are unnecessary because the same notion occurs in Psa 51:6 (cf. also Psa 103:3). Here the compass of the formula *ḥannûn wᵉraḥûm* (see 4b) receives clearest expression.

Outside this liturgical usage, the contexts become somewhat clearer.

In 2 Sam 12:22 the hope for the preservation of the child stands in relationship to David's penitence (contra Hertzberg, *Sam*, OTL, 316). The same cautious "perhaps" occurs in Amos 5:15, where the "being gracious" of v 14 corresponds to "Yahweh will be with you"; in any case the sovereignty of the divine decision is preserved. In Gen 33:11 *ḥnn* is not merely "to give"; here too unexpected riches characterize the special attention of Yahweh. Job 33:24 diverges only formally, not substantively. Because of the guiding intervention of a mediator (*malʾāk mēlîṣ* v 23), the divine judge reaches a positive decision; the translation "has mercy" is not entirely correct.

The verb occurs in Gen 43:29, diminished to a greeting corresponding to Eng. "God be with you!" (cf. *ḥesed weʾᵉmet,* 2 Sam 15:20).

(d) As in the profane realm, the content of the request is determined by the power of the one to whom it is addressed when *ḥnn* is used (cf. Deut 3:23, the reference to the prior demonstrations of Yahweh's might). Often *ḥnn* hitp., together with *pll* hitp. "to pray" (cf. also Psa 30:9 with *qrʾ* "to call"; 142:2 with *zʿq* "to cry"), becomes a general term for requests addressed to God ("to you" 1 Kgs 8:33; "before you" 9:3), while the accent lies here on the forgiveness sought. Occasionally, the possibility for such petition seems tied to particular prerequisites (1 Kgs 8:33, 47; 2 Chron 6:24, 37, repentance, return).

This requirement also stands in the background of Bildad's orthodox reprimand in Job 8:5, where sincere seeking and petitioning go together and uprightness and integrity are requirements for being heard. Hos 12:5 remains unclear to some degree. Regardless of the question whether Hosea gives evidence here of a tradition other than Gen 32 (cf. Th. C. Vriezen, *OTS* 1 [1942]: 64–78), *ḥnn* hitp. is qualified, at least in the usual translation "he prevailed, he cried and pled" (contra Wolff, *Hos*, Herm, 212f.), by the contrast. Crying and pleading are the actions not of the victor but of the vanquished.

(e) Only once does *tᵉḥinnâ* characterize an answered prayer (Ezra 9:8; cf. Ap-Thomas, op. cit. 131; see 3g). Otherwise it is generally the request that God hears (1 Kgs 8:30, 45, etc.; 2 Chron 6:35, 39; Psa 6:10), to which he turns (1 Kgs 8:28; 9:3), which he does not shut out (Psa 55:2), or which comes before him (Psa 119:170). Phrases involving the root → *pll* are common here too (1 Kgs 8:28, 30; Psa 6:10; 55:2, etc.).

Baruch's diction in Jer 36:7; 37:20; 38:26; 42:2, 9 (see 3g) is characteristic; cf. also Dan 9:20 (v 18 *taḥ^a^nûnîm*). Phrases with *npl* hi. "to let fall" are meant to characterize particularly urgent pleading; one may ask whether an external association with *t^e^pillâ* may be involved here.

The same is true of *taḥ^a^nûnîm;* it also occasionally parallels *t^e^pillâ* (Psa 86:6; 143:1; Dan 9:3, 17; 2 Chron 6:21). In the Psa, it accompanies *qôl* "voice," usually with suf., as a gen. and is dependent upon a term for hearing (Psa 28:2, 6; 31:23; 86:6; 116:1; 130:2; 140:7; 143:1). This combination probably expresses the urgency and bitterness of this pleading, as Jer 3:21 does through combination with *b^e^kî* "crying."

Nonetheless, one should probably read Jer 31:9 with LXX *b^e^tanḥûmîm* (cf. Rudolph, HAT 12, 195); on Zech 12:10, see 3a.

5. The LXX usually, although not exclusively, translates *ḥēn* by *charis, ḥnn* by *eleein* and rarely by *oiktirein.* This is not a strictly precise translation; it indicates the manner in which the content of the individual pronouncements of grace have assimilated to one another. Using these terms, NT proclamation unfolds the fullness of God's grace in Jesus Christ (see esp. R. Bultmann, "ἔλεος," *TDNT* 2:477–87).

H. J. Stoebe

חנף *ḥnp* to be perverted

S 2610; BDB 337b; *HALOT* 1:335b; *TDOT* 5:36–44; *TWOT* 696; *NIDOTTE* 2856

---

1. The root is common in WSem. languages (Ug. *ḥnp* "impious," *WUS* no. 1053; *UT* no. 981; subst. and verb as Canaanisms in EA 288:8 "the villainy that they did," and 162:74 "who knows villainy"; cf. *AHw* 320a, 321a; *CAD* H:76b, 80f.; on later languages, see 3; cf. *HAL* 322).

The Hebr. root occurs in the intrans. qal and in causative hi., as a verbal adj. *ḥānēp,* and in two nom. abstract forms, the segholate noun *ḥōnep* and the fem. form *ḥ^a^nuppâ* (BL 467).

2. All 26 occurrences appear exclusively in poetic or elevated language: qal 7x (Isa 24:5; Jer 3:1bis, 9; 23:11; Mic 4:11; Psa 106:38), hi. 4x (Num 35:33bis; Jer 3:2; Dan 11:32), *ḥānēp* 13x (8x in Job, 3x in Isa, as well as Psa 35:16; Prov 11:9), *ḥōnep* 1x (Isa 32:6), and *ḥ^a^nuppâ* 1x (Jer 23:15).

3. A specific basic meaning "to be twisted, crooked" can be inferred from the Arab. *ḥanifa* "to have a twisted foot" and *ḥanafa* "to turn to the side" (conjectured by G. R. Driver, *TZ* 9 [1953]: 468f. for Psa 35:16 *b^e^ḥanpî* "at my limp"; cf. *HAL* 322b and *BHS;* perhaps still evident in Mic 4:11 "[Zion] wil be turned [profaned]"); nevertheless, the fig. meaning, qal "to be perverted," hi. "to pervert," dominates otherwise (cf. Mid. Hebr. and Jew. Aram. "to dissemble," Syr. *ḥanpā* "godless person, heathen," Eth. *ḫōnāfī* "heathen, heretic," etc.).

The meaning "to be perverted" (hi. "to pervert") is recognizable in all occurrences of the verb (Dan 11:32, seduction to apostasy; Jer 23:11, prophet and priest; Mic 4:11, Zion; in the remaining cases the land is either the subj. or the obj. in typical expressions of priestly theology). Perversion is either legal in nature (bloodguilt, Psa 106:38; Num 35:33; violation of the commandments, Isa 24:5; cf. the context vv 3f., according to which the dissolution of the world order is a consequence of the perversion of the land), or it is complex (legal-social-moral-cultic), as in Jer 3:1f., 9, where *ḥnp* refers to the perversion of a—legally definable—social relationship:the land belongs to strange gods instead of to Yahweh, as the wife belongs to another husband instead of to her original husband. Num 35:33 similarly describes the way in which the land is perverted if bloodguilt remains unatoned.

The substs. also give evidence of the basic meaning "perversion": Jer 23:15b cites *ḥōnep* as the reason for judgment reflecting the character of the announcement; Isa 32:6 parallels "to do *ḥ^anuppâ*" with "to speak perversion *(tôʿâ).*"

Adjs. in Isa imply the meaning "perverted" (Isa 9:16; 10:6; 33:14; cf. also Prov 11:9), while Psa 35:16 txt? and esp. Job (8:13; 13:16; 15:34; 17:8; 20:5; 27:8; 34:30; 36:13) use the word in the parameters of poetic language in contexts broadened beyond the original situation (cf., nevertheless, 15:34 *ḥānēp* together with "tent of corruption"). The adj. in particular, then, merely presupposes the root's backgrounds and uses it as a general repudiation. Of the usual translations, "wicked, wickedness" (hardly "godless, evildoer") commends itself to the degree that the basic meaning "perverted, to be perverted" no longer corresponds to the semantic referent.

4. In all occurrences, the word more or less signifies a theological judgment. Whether perversion occurs in the legal (see 3), social (Prov 11:9), cultic (Isa 24:5), moral, or political (Job 34:30) realms, whether it consists of deeds (Isa 9:16; 32:6) or words (Psa 35:16; Prov 11:9), it always distorts given orders of existence. This ontological dimension of the straight, healthy, and true that perversion implies lends it the heavy weight of the basic distortion of the world order. The formula of the "perversion of the land," which takes place in individual deeds, may also be understood against this background. But because God is understood in ancient and biblical thought in relation to the maintenance of the world order, any "perversion" signifies the dissolution of the world order in the ultimate sense, i.e., God's significant presence in it. This notion explains the fact that God himself turns the world around in judgment after it has been thoroughly perverted by people (Isa 24:5). The designation of such a phenomenon by the root *ḥnp* is, in every case, the condemnation of a profound transgression against God.

5. The usage of *ḥōnep* in 1QS 4:10 in the list of the characteristics of the "spirit of evil" is more reminiscent of psychological "perversion" than of "godlessness."

The LXX did not know how to handle the Hebr. concept. This confusion is shown not only by the thoroughly inadequate translation, but in particular also by the multitude of substitute terms.

R. Knierim